Advances in Econometrics and Quantitative Economics

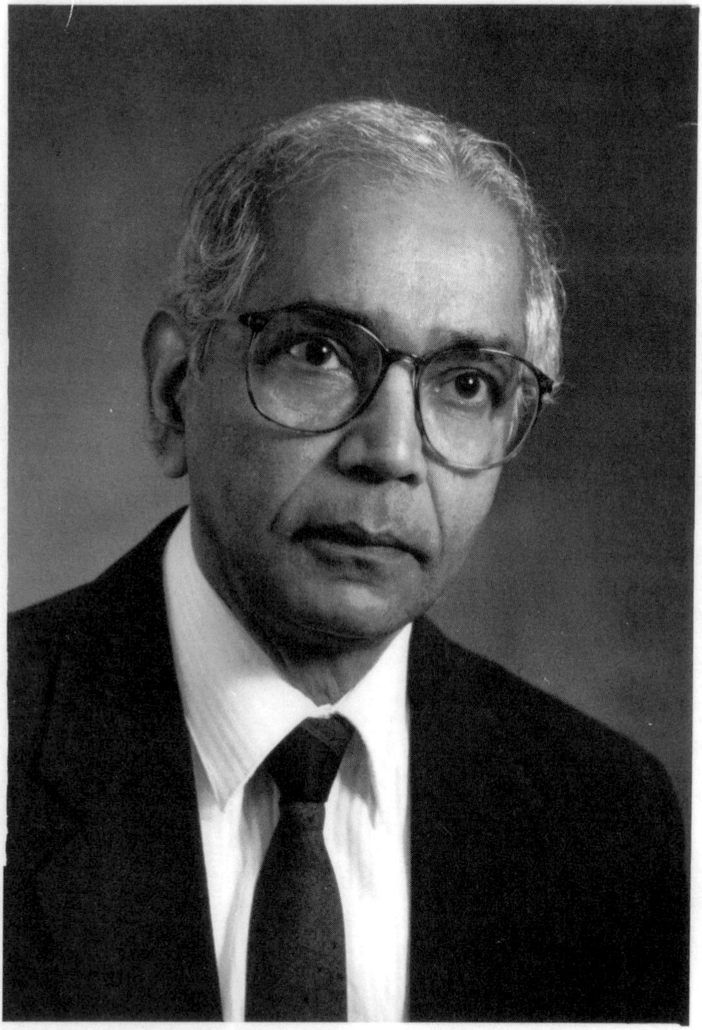

C. R. Rao

Advances in Econometrics and Quantitative Economics

Essays in honor of Professor C. R. Rao

Edited by

G. S. Maddala,
Peter C. B. Phillips,
and
T. N. Srinivasan

BLACKWELL
Oxford UK & Cambridge USA

First published 1995

Blackwell Publishers Inc.
238 Main Street
Cambridge, Massachusetts 02142, USA

Blackwell Publishers Ltd
108 Cowley Road
Oxford OX4 1JF
UK

Library of Congress Cataloging in Publication Data

Advances in econometrics and quantitative economics: essays in honor of C. R. Rao / edited by G. S. Maddala, Peter C. B. Phillips and T. N. Srinivasan.
p. cm.
Includes bibliographical references and index.
ISBN 1-55786-382-2 (acid-free paper)
1. Econometrics. 2. Economics, Mathematical. I. Rao, C. Radhakrishna (Calyampudi Radhakrishna), 1920– . II. Maddala, G. S. III. Phillips, P. C. B. IV. Srinivasan, T. N., 1933– .
HB139.S688 1995 94-48513
330′.01′5195—dc20 CIP

British Library Cataloguing in Publication Data

A CIP catalogue record for this book is available from the British Library.

Typeset in 10 on 12 pt Times
by Best-set Typesetter Ltd., Hong Kong
Printed in Great Britain by Hartnolls Limited, Bodmin, Cornwall

This book is printed on acid-free paper.

Contents

Contributors

T. W. Anderson	Stanford University, USA
R. N. Bhattacharya	Indiana University, USA
C. L. Cavanagh	Columbia University, USA
J. G. Cragg	University of British Columbia, Canada
S. G. Donald	Boston University, USA
L. Gardiol	University of Lausanne, Switzerland
C. Gourieroux	CREST – CEPREMAP, Paris, France
A. Holly	University of Lausanne, Switzerland
U. Jensen	University of Kiel, Germany
O. Linton	Oxford University, UK
M. Loretan	Federal Reserve Board, Washington DC, USA
G. S. Maddala	The Ohio State University, USA
A. Monfort	CREST – Paris, France
M. Nerlove	University of Maryland, USA
W. K. Newey	Massachusetts Institute of Technology, USA
P. C. B. Phillips	Yale University, USA
C. A. P. Pinske	University of British Columbia, Canada
M. L. Puri	Indiana University, USA
E. Renault	GREMAQ – University of Toulouse, France
P. M. Robinson	London School of Economics, UK
T. J. Rotherberg	University of California, Berkeley, USA
T. Schuermann	AT&T Bell Labs, USA
K. Tanaka	Hitotsubashi University, Japan
P. K. Trivedi	Indiana University, USA
J. M. Wooldridge	Michigan State University, USA

Preface

Professor C. R. (Calyampudi Radhakrishna) Rao will be seventy-five on September 10, 1995. This collection of essays celebrates both Professor Rao's many fundamental contributions to statistical foundations of econometrics and his seventy-fifth birthday.

An interesting account of how Professor Rao started to work in statistics can be found in his autobiographical essay (Rao, 1991). He joined the Indian Statistical Institute in 1941, after receiving an MA with a first class and first rank in mathematics from the Andhra University in 1940. He obtained an MA degree in statistics from Calcutta University in 1943 with a first class, first rank and a gold medal. Subsequently he went to Cambridge England to work under R. A. Fisher and was awarded his doctorate in 1948.

A steady stream of original contributions from him began in the early 1940s and continues to flow in good measure to this day. A very early contribution, later to become famous as the Cramér–Rao inequality, was derived by him in 1943 (in a hard night's work in response to the question of a student, V. M. Dandekar, who later became one of India's leading economists). Because of the suspension of the publication of journals in India during the Second World War, this paper (Rao, 1945) was published only in 1945. It contains many other results, including what was later known as the Rao–Blackwell theorem. This paper is also notable for its introduction of differential geometric methods in statistical inference for the first time. It is also perhaps the first attempt to discuss the theme of estimation in small samples in terms of actual variance and methods of obtaining best unbiased estimates.

Econometricians extensively use what they call the LM (Lagrangean Multiplier) test following the terminology introduced by Silvey. In fact, this test is none other than the "score" test introduced in 1947 by Professor Rao ten years before Silvey. Besides the score test, many other tests and techniques in econometrics can be traced to Professor Rao's pioneering work. For example, a very popular test in econometrics that is known as the Hausman test follows from a result (on page 317) of Professor Rao's book *Linear Statistical Inference* (1973). This book has been translated into six major languages of the world. It is the one most likely to be on the bookshelf of almost every econometrician because it contains an extraordinarily valuable compendium of results in matrix algebra as well as statistical theory. According to the Social Science Citation Index, it is the most cited book in statistics in econometric work.

As Director of the Research and Training School at the Indian Statistical Institute (ISI), Professor C. R. Rao developed a variety of educational programs in the theory and applications of statistics at various levels. Under his leadership, the ISI won international recognition as an outstanding center for theoretical disciplines. His colleagues, students and others who have worked with him at the ISI and elsewhere over the years have experienced his wonderful hospitality and charm and his characteristic modesty. *The Times of India* (December 31, 1988) chose Professor C. R. Rao to be among the top ten greatest contributors of all time to Indian science.

Professor Rao's many contributions to theoretical statistics in general and multivariate analysis in particular arose from his involvement in the analysis of large data sets at the ISI, such as the Anthropometric Survey in 1941 in the United Provinces of India. He believed with R. A. Fisher that the development of statistical methodology must be firmly rooted in the problems of inference thrown up by actual data. His interest in careful collection and analysis of socio-economic data led to his founding the Indian Econometric Society to encourage econometric work in India. With his enthusiastic support, the Indian Econometric Society has held seven conferences since 1972 on the data base of the Indian economy and has so far published five volumes of conference papers.

We believe that econometricians would find many contributions of Professor Rao useful in their work, and have therefore appended his complete bibliography to this volume. It is hard to do full justice to the many facets of Professor Rao's work in a single volume. The present volume is just a modest contribution by some econometricians in tribute to his work.

G. S. Maddala
P. C. B. Phillips
T. N. Srinivasan

References

Rao, C. R. (1945) Information and accuracy attainable in the estimation of statistical parameters. *Bulletin of the Calcutta Mathematical Society*, 37, 81–91 (also published in *Breakthroughs in Statistics, volume 1: Foundations and Basic Theory*. New York: Springer-Verlag, pp. 235–48).

Rao, C. R. (1947) Large sample tests of statistical hypotheses concerning several parameters with applications to problems of estimation. *Proceedings of the Cambridge Philosophical Society*, 44, 50–7.

Rao, C. R. (1973) *Linear Statistical Inference and Its Applications*, 2nd edn. New York: Wiley.

Rao, C. R. (1991) *Statistics as a Last Resort: an Autobiographical Account of Research Work*. Published by T.D. Dwivedi, Concordia University, Montreal.

A Conversation with C. R. Rao

Morris H. DeGroot

Calyampudi Radhakrishna Rao was born on September 10, 1920, in Hadagali, Karnataka State, India. He received an MA in mathematics from Andhra University in 1940; an MA in statistics from Calcutta University in 1943; a PhD from Cambridge University in 1948, with a thesis entitled "Statistical problems of biological classification"; and an ScD from Cambridge in 1965 on the basis of his published work in statistics as a whole. He joined the Indian Statistical Institute as a statistician in 1944 and became a professor in 1949, the director of the Research and Training School in 1964, the secretary and director of the Institute in 1972, and the Jawaharlal Nehru Professor in 1976. In 1979 he was appointed a University Professor in the Department of Mathematics and Statistics at the University of Pittsburgh. He has been the President of the International Statistical Institute, the Institute of Mathematical Statistics, the International Biometric Society, and the Indian Econometric Society; and since 1964, an editor of *Sankhyā*. He is a Fellow of the Royal Society (FRS) of the United Kingdom; a Foreign Honorary Member of the American Academy of Arts and Science; an Honorary Member of the International Statistical Institute; an Honorary Fellow of the Royal Statistical Society; an Honorary Life Member of the Biometric Society; a Fellow of the Indian National Science Academy and Indian Academy of Sciences; an Honorary Fellow of King's College, Cambridge; and a Founder Fellow of the Third World Academy of Sciences, Trieste. He has received honorary degrees from Andhra University, India, 1967; Leningrad University, USSR, 1970; Delhi University, India, 1973; Athens University, Greece, 1976; Osmania University, India, 1977; Ohio State University, USA, 1979; Universidad Nacional de San Marcos,

Peru, 1982; University of the Philippines, 1983; and University of Tampere, Finland, 1985.

The following conversation took place in his office at the University of Pittsburgh one morning in November 1985.

DeGroot: To start at the beginning, tell me a little about your childhood in India, what your home life was like, and how you came to get interested in statistics.

Rao: Well, I come from a family of a kind of landed aristocracy. They had a lot of property and never cared to go and study and try to make a living on the knowledge that they acquired in their studies. However, at one stage they were interested in the legal profession and they all became lawyers and judges and so on.

DeGroot: Who do you mean by "all"?

Rao: My ancestors, my relations. I was, so to say, the first one to get interested in science. I started off with mathematics, but then the war broke out when I was just finishing my master's degree in mathematics and there were not many opportunities for those with a degree in mathematics to get a job. So I tried to get a job in the military service. I applied to the Department of Survey, which is sort of a party to any military expedition. I was disqualified because I was too young and they didn't want me, but that took me to a place called Calcutta. I belonged to the South but I had gone to Calcutta for the interview to get into the military service. At that time I came to know of the Indian Statistical Institute which had been established by Mahalanobis, so I just casually visited the place and talked to people there. They said that statistics was a new subject and if there are no opportunities for a job with a mathematics background, why not come and study statistics.

So I applied for a course of studies at the Indian Statistical Institute and I was admitted. At that time there were no courses in statistics in the universities. Some universities used to teach statistics as a part of the undergraduate program but not at the postgraduate level. The Indian Statistical Institute was the first place to have what they called a one-year training course in statistics. I took that course, but by the time the course ended Calcutta University had started a master's program in statistics. Mahalanobis said to me, "You join the university and get a formal degree." Since a formal degree is always useful in India as a passport to get jobs, I joined Calcutta University and got a master's degree in statistics. I am one of five first batch students to be awarded an MS degree in statistics by an Indian University. So that's how it all began.

DeGroot: When did you then go to Cambridge and how did that come about?

Rao: After I finished my master's degree, Mahalanobis asked me to work on anthropometric data which had been collected by Dr. D. N. Mazumdar, a well-known anthropologist, in the state of Uttar Pradesh during the 1941 Indian population census. The data were sent to the Indian Statistical Institute for analysis; at that time Mahalanobis had already invented the Mahalanobis distance for studies in anthropology. He assigned the project to me. So my first experience was analyzing data collected on some five thousand individuals, with twenty characters measured on each individual. I produced a report using the Mahalanobis D^2 (distance) in the analysis, and Mahalanobis was very happy with that.

Right at the time when I finished that report, he got a telegram from the anthropological museum in Cambridge saying that a British expedition from Africa had brought a large number of bones and stones and so on. Would he please send one of his students to analyze the data. Mahalanobis replied, "Of course. I have one who is very good in statistics, but he does not know anthropology. So I'll send an anthropologist along with Rao to help you with this project." So we went there and we found a very interesting collection of bones. They had dug out ancient graves, about 1,000 years old, from a place called Jebel Moya in North Africa, and brought the skeletal material to the museum in Cambridge. I was actually employed in the Cambridge museum for a couple of years to work on the skeletal material. Incidentally I joined King's College, where Mahalanobis used to be when he was a student, and I also registered for a PhD degree under R. A. Fisher. But Fisher said I must work on his mice, whether it leads to a thesis or not. So I was doing some experiments on mice for R. A. Fisher which involved the mapping of chromosomes, in addition to my work at the Anthropological Museum.

DeGroot: He actually was treating live mice in his experiments?

Rao: Oh, yes. He had a laboratory where he was breeding mice because he was mapping their chromosomes. Lots of mice, maybe thousands. I think we were some ten people working there at that time. He asked me to study the linkage of four genes on a chromosome and find the distances between them. So I was doing that project for R. A. Fisher in the evenings, and in the daytime I was working in the anthropological museum. After two years we wrote the report on this skeletal material which is published as a book by the Cambridge University Press, *Ancient Inhabitants of Jebel Moya* [with R. K. Mukherji and J. C. Trevor, 1955]. The Cambridge anthropologist and my Indian colleague who was an anthropologist also got their PhD theses out of that same project. I think my Indian colleague wrote on the anthropological technique and interpretation of results. The Cambridge anthropologist was also a sociologist, so he looked at the artifacts along with the bones. He made his own conclusions and we put everything together.

DeGroot: And your PhD dissertation?

Rao: My PhD dissertation was based on the theoretical work I did in connection with this project, which is partly in the book. But I had some additional results in my thesis. Fisher's discriminant function was used for classification within two categories, and I developed a method for many categories. I also developed another test. We had to do all the multivariate computations by hand at that time. If I had fifty characters it would be impossible to use all of them, so selection of characters was a major problem. I invented a test of whether it is really necessary to take so many characters. I said, "All right, given a set of measurements, is there further information in an additional set of measurements?" So this is the kind of test which I developed and which went into the thesis. R. A. Fisher was my supervisor. Wishart was an examiner.

DeGroot: Was Fisher much involved in your work?

Rao: Well, he thought my test for additional information was very good because it was an extension of a test he developed in discriminant analysis. That is, if somebody specified the discriminant function, he could examine whether that was the true discriminant function or not. This really involved the idea that the given discriminant function carries all the information; given that function, nothing else is needed. So when I extended that test to a given set of measurements, not necessarily one discriminant function, Fisher was happy. I also mentioned to Fisher that I was working on the problem of classification into more than two categories. I used the Bayesian approach to the problem. He asked me to work along a different line, but I used essentially Bayesian techniques. [Laughs] That's the appropriate thing to do in problems of that kind. Later on I described what you should do when you could not know the prior probabilities. I also created a kind of doubtful region where you can take the position that you are unable to say whether an observation belongs to this group or that group, and described how to operate with that region. That is an abstract of what I did for my thesis.

DeGroot: With both Fisher and Wishart at Cambridge at that time, there must have been a lot of statistical activity around the university.

Rao: That is true, but Fisher was mostly interested in mathematical genetics. So I took various courses in mathematical genetics. I had enough knowledge when I came back to India to direct research work by my students in mathematical genetics. I actually produced three PhD's in mathematical genetics at that time, very valuable people, but unfortunately they are all working in this country. And Wishart of course was in the school of agriculture. Bartlett was there for a while; then he went to Manchester and Daniels came. About that time the statistical laboratory in Cambridge was established for training statisticians. We had students like Durbin and Bailey and some others. Most of the statisticians at that time were being trained in the statistical laboratory at Cambridge, but it just started in '47 or '48.

DeGroot: Was it unusual for an Indian to be studying at Cambridge at that time?

Rao: No, lots of Indians used to go to Cambridge. It was the place that Indians went for their higher education. But I didn't study in Cambridge in that sense. I was working in Cambridge at the museum, but formally attached to King's College as a research scholar. Later on, King's College honored me by electing me a life fellow. When I was formally enrolled as a research student there, I was not allowed to walk on the lawns in King's College.

DeGroot: I've seen those signs: "Only fellows are allowed to walk on the grass."

Rao: Right. But now I have the privilege of walking on the lawns, and whenever I go there I can stay in the college, have a free dinner, and probably drink as much wine as I want. [Laughs] There are only eleven life fellows at any time. Only if somebody dies do they elect another one.

DeGroot: Some of the most famous results in statistics have your name on them. One example is the Cramér–Rao inequality, as it is commonly known. I know that Cramér and you did not work on this together. Could you tell me how it came about that your names are paired on this result in this way?

Rao: After I completed my master's degree in 1943, I was asked to teach my juniors in the master's course. There was a shortage of teachers. I think R. C. Bose and S. N. Roy were the two main teachers, and there were a few others.

DeGroot: This was at the Indian Statistical Institute?

Rao: At both the Institute and Calcutta University. You see, when Calcutta University started the master's program they had no teachers, so they borrowed all the teachers from the Indian Statistical Institute.

Actually, the lectures were held in the Indian Statistical Institute. Many of our teachers did not know much statistics. They were trying to learn and teach the students. So when I had my formal education, they thought I would be a good teacher and I was asked to teach. I was giving a course on estimation covering all the large-sample properties of maximum likelihood. I proved the asymptotic inequality of R. A. Fisher that the asymptotic variance is not smaller than one divided by the information. Then one student asked, "Why don't you prove it for finite samples?" So I went back home and worked all night. The next day I came up with this inequality, using unbiasedness and the Schwarz inequality. I proved this result in the class in January 1944. Once I started all this, I looked at sufficient statistics. Of course the maximum likelihood estimate is a function of sufficient statistics. Is there an independent small sample justification for sufficient statistics? I thought I must be able to prove some exact properties, and that's how the Rao–Blackwell theorem came up. Which I did two years before Blackwell.

DeGroot: So your work on that type of improvement of an estimator really grew out of your work on inequalities.

Rao: Yes, they are all in the same paper. ["Information and accuracy attainable in the estimation of statistical parameters," *Bull. Calcutta Math. Soc.*, 37 (1945) 81–91.] That's in 1945. Blackwell's work was in 1947. I saw Cramér's work on the information inequality when his book on *Mathematical Methods of Statistics* came out in 1946. That is sort of a basic paper mostly arising out of my teaching that course on estimation. I also developed the differential geometric method. I tried to connect Fisher information with a metric in a Riemann space. So my differential geometric approach to estimation is also in the same paper.

DeGroot: That's quite a paper. This differential geometry approach to estimation is now becoming of interest to many statisticians.

Rao: Yes. It's so difficult, nobody liked to work on problems of that kind. I am gratified to see that the geodesic distance I defined using the Fisher information metric is now referred to as Rao distance. Now to complete the story, Fisher came out with second-order properties of a maximum likelihood estimator. That's a very difficult concept and Fisher's investigation lacked some details. Since very difficult computations were involved I tried to modify his definition of second-order efficiency and came out with a quantity which characterizes maximum likelihood estimators in a sense if you go to second-order terms by expanding the asymptotic variance. In the second-order terms, the maximum likelihood estimator has the smallest coefficient. Now that coefficient has been termed the Fisher–Rao inequality by Efron.

DeGroot: That notion of second-order efficiency is very closely associated with you.

Rao: It really started with Fisher. What I did was try to correct Fisher's computations and also modify his criterion of the minimum loss of information because it is very difficult to work with. That's an exact property which does not really hold, but asymptotically to the second order that idea works.

DeGroot: Who do you feel have been the major influences both on your life and on your career?

Rao: I would say Professor Mahalanobis in India. His whole idea was that statistics must have a purpose. So he said, don't try to solve problems in mathematical statistics. First look at the data and see what the problems are, and then try to develop the appropriate methodology for that kind of data. The next is, of course, R. A. Fisher. When I went to work with him, I first told him, "I have studied mathematical statistics; I have also done some research. Would you give me a problem that I could work for my thesis?" – as students do in this country. Fisher said, "No, the problem must be yours. I can help you to solve the problem." [Laughs]

Also, I wrote a paper in mathematical genetics and said that the method I developed was superior to one that somebody else gave, but Fisher said, "I won't read your paper unless you do some computations. Gather the data and compare what your method gives with what the other method gives, and then come with a paper and I shall read it." This is the kind of advice which I think was very useful later in my consultation work and also in my own research in mathematical statistics. I always develop methodology from the data given to me for analysis rather than look at others' work and try to extend it in terms of mathematics.

I used to meet Wishart frequently when I was in Cambridge because we used to discuss lots of problems. That was also useful, but the two people who provided inspiration for me are R. A. Fisher and Mahalanobis. Of course, at that time Neyman's work was becoming popular and everybody had to read that. So I read a lot of work that Neyman did and I think he was also responsible for my getting into the current research at that time in testing of hypotheses.

DeGroot: Did Fisher ever discuss Neyman's work with you?

Rao: Yes. He was critical about Neyman. Whenever I had discussions and wanted to use Neyman's ideas in solving some of the problems, Fisher always discouraged me from doing that. Actually, I now feel that I could have done some work which is currently popular if I had used Neyman's ideas in those days. I was not reluctant to use Neyman's ideas, but I did not probably because of Fisher's influence.

DeGroot: Was Fisher generally pretty good about reading things that you would give him?

Rao: Oh, yes. He would take great interest. And then he would read and comment on it. He was also a very exciting teacher. Not many could follow what he was teaching; but if one tried to see what he was saying, he was an inspiring teacher. I also used to attend his seminars and they were very good. But most of the time when I was at Cambridge I used to help him in his genetic experiments.

DeGroot: You've published, according to my count, nine books and about 230 papers. Your book *Linear Statistical Inference and Its Applications* is of course widely known [second edition, John Wiley, New York, 1973]. I've always felt that the title was something of a misnomer because that book really covers much more than linear statistical inference. In fact, it covers much of what is in a standard graduate course in statistical theory.

Rao: Actually, I had a different title but the referees suggested this title because it would compete better with other books with similar titles at that time. So I said, "OK. From the commercial point of view, if that title will sell very well then you may choose that title." [Laughs] It had a different title to begin with.

DeGroot: What was your original title?

Rao: Advanced Statistics or something like that. Actually, when I wrote my first book and called it *Advanced Statistical Methods in Biometric Research* [first edition, John Wiley, New York, 1952; reprint, Haffner, New York, 1974], I really summarized what I did in Cambridge on the anthropological material. Most of the examples there are all from anthropometric data. People wondered how I suddenly introduced data on head length and head breadth and so on in between theoretical discussions. But the major emphasis in that book is the applications of statistical methodology to univariate and multivariate data. It's slightly more theoretical than R. A. Fisher's book, but because the title said biometric methods the statisticians were not attracted to it.

DeGroot: Yes, that's another book whose title is much narrower than the content of the book – where you cover much more material.

Rao: Well, I thought I was discussing some biological problems and so the title was appropriate.

DeGroot: I remember using that book when I was a student just for learning about statistical theory generally.

Rao: My *Linear Statistical Inference* is really only a mathematical version of that book, I think.

DeGroot: I see. Well, have you been giving any thought to a new edition of *Linear Statistical Inference*?

Rao: When I try to review the book. I find that much has happened since the second edition came out, so I was thinking of working on a third edition not as a single volume but maybe as a couple of volumes. It depends on how much time I have because in this country there is a lot of pressure for writing papers, getting grants, writing more papers for the grants, and so on. [Laughs] So I don't have much time to think of revising the book. But I have given a variety of courses in this country and made some notes which would be useful in making a third edition of the book.

DeGroot: I'm also curious about your book with Kagan and Linnik, *Characterization Problems of Mathematical Statistics* [John Wiley, New York, 1973]. That book was published first in Russia and I first saw it in the Russian language edition when Kagan sent me a copy. Then subsequently it was translated into English. How did that collaboration with the Russians come about?

Rao: I think I was interested in characterization problems right from my student days. There was a paper by Ragnar Frisch in which the following problem was proposed. If there are two random variables X and Y where $X = \psi + \eta$ and $Y = \psi + \upsilon$, so there is a common variable ψ, under what condition is the regression of X on Y linear? X and Y have only one common variable ψ; the other variables η and υ are independent. I gave a general solution to this problem in my thesis as a partial requirement for the MS degree. This was ultimately published in *Econometrica* in 1947 [15, 245–9; correction, 17, 212].

Then when I had my research students, I gave them problems on characterization for their thesis work. I was doing some work on characterization right before Linnik's first visit to India in 1955. I told him what I was doing, and being a mathematician he liked the idea. When he went back he started working on very complicated characterization problems using ideas of number theory and so on. It was very surprising. I was visiting the Soviet Union frequently at that time and we used to meet. I attended the first mathematics conference held in the Soviet Union after the war in 1956. At that time I met other acquaintances of Linnik. Linnik introduced me to his student Kagan subsequently. As I said, at that time Linnik used number theory ideas and he was trying to characterize the normal distribution by the identical distribution of two linear statistics. Then I took Linnik's ideas and tried to extend his methods to problems involving linear statistics but under different conditions and so on. During a subsequent meeting with Linnik, he suggested that we all write a book together on characterization problems in mathematical statistics. We decided how many chapters I would write and what Kagan and Linnik would write. I think within a year or so, we put our material together. I wrote in English and they translated it into Russian. They kept me informed of what they were doing.

DeGroot: So you would communicate with each other in English.

Rao: Yes. Linnik knew English and Kagan knows English. We formed a good team and were able to complete the work within a year or so.

DeGroot: Linnik must have died just about the time that the book came out.

Rao: Yes, he died in June '72. Linnik and Kagan also translated my *Linear Statistical Inference*.

DeGroot: That's very interesting. They were also influential in translating my decision theory book into Russian.

Rao: There's one interesting thing I must tell you about the translation of my *Linear Statistical Inference*. I had made the comment that in the Fisher–Behrens problem, there is no similar-region test when σ_1 and σ_2 are different. Linnik had proved that in a certain class a similar-region test actually exists. So Linnik said my statement was wrong and they just modified it in the Russian translation. In this connection, when Wilks was alive I discovered that he had an abstract in *The Annals of Mathematical Statistics* where he claimed that no similar-region test exists. So I wrote to Wilks in the 50s or so, asking him to please send me the proof or tell me how he had done it. Wilks replied that this was done during the wartime, that his office was moved after the war and the whole folder containing the proof of this proposition was lost in the process, and that he does not recall how he did it. You can look at the abstract by Wilks [11, 475–6, 1940].

DeGroot: Wow!

Rao: There was another incident recently in which somebody claimed priority because he had mentioned a result slightly less general than mine in an abstract in the *Annals*. You can say anything in an abstract. If it is right, you can claim credit and priority.

DeGroot: Yes. Take a chance; maybe it will be right. There is no serious screening of abstracts. I think that's OK, as long as everyone realizes that the results are not necessarily correct or original.

Rao: Actually when that person wrote the full paper on the basis of the abstract, I was a referee and it turned out that this result was also not correct as stated.

DeGroot: Do you still visit the Soviet Union?

Rao: I was there last year for the conference at Vilnius. As Director of the Indian Statistical Institute, I was very much involved in the exchange of scientists between the Soviet Academy and the Indian Statistical Institute. In fact, we had a separate agreement between us for the exchange of up to eight scientists every year on either side. So we send our people and they still come to the Institute.

DeGroot: What is your impression of the political situation in the Soviet Union? Have you seen any changes through the years?

Rao: Well, there was some change since the fifties. I think that in matters of science they now just do the same thing as the rest of the world.

DeGroot: Do you see Kagan when you are there? I know he has been trying to emigrate for several years.

Rao: Not this time. He was not at the conference that I attended. The last I saw him was in 1976. But I am in correspondence with him. We still try to collaborate a bit. I used to like the Leningrad group because whenever I was there I would give seminars and they would tell me what they were doing. I used to give them some problems and they would solve them immediately. [Laughs] So there were some papers on problems posed by Rao. It was quite a good group. Ibragimov and others were there. I am an honorary professor of Leningrad University. That came along with the honorary doctorate I got from there. So I always visit the university when I go there.

DeGroot: Do you have royalties in the Soviet Union?

Rao: Yes, I have royalties for the translation of *Linear Statistical Inference* and for *Characterization Problems*.

DeGroot: I found it difficult to spend my royalties when I was there. How do you spend yours?

Rao: Generally when I go there I just call my friends and give them a party. [Laughs] I still have unspent money there because when I go as a vistor the Soviet Academy pays all my expenses. So this money is in the bank. By the way, they give interest on money. I put the money in the bank and the second time I went to find out how much money I had, I found some amount of money added in red ink. They said that was my interest.

DeGroot: What are your favorite publications among your many books and papers? Do you have any particular favorites that you enjoyed doing, and which ones do you think have been the most influential?

Rao: I enjoyed doing my applied work, especially the applications in anthropology, but that work gave rise to the development of methodology in multivariate analysis. I think the papers where the work I have done was followed up by many others are my early papers on estimation. Then there are papers on second-order efficiency, and now the papers on differential geometry that are coming up. So I am happy because somebody is following up the work I initiated. A second set of papers I like are mostly in the analysis of repeated measurements and in singular linear models, i.e. when the design and covariance matrices are deficient in rank. I developed generalized inverses of matrices for dealing with such problems. My work on orthogonal arrays is widely used in industrial experimentation, and has led to important inequalities in coding theory. I found that special courses on orthogonal arrays are given in this country. In 1947 (*Proc. Cambridge Philos. Soc.*, 44, 50–7) I introduced two general asymptotic test criteria called score tests for simple and composite hypotheses as alternatives to Wald's tests. I find that my score test for composite hypotheses has become entrenched in the econometrics literature under a fancier name, the Langrangian Multiplier Test. So those are a few papers which I like and which have received some attention.

DeGroot: What are your current research interests?

Rao: I am working on two types of problems. One is prediction, not in time series but in repeated measurements like growth models. I think I have done some fairly useful work for applications in practice. And now I am working on what is really discrimination but what electrical engineers call signal detection. Problems like when one can recognize that a real signal is coming and not just pure noise.

DeGroot: That's a classical problem.

Rao: Yes, that's right. But there are some new problems that arise in this connection which we are currently solving. There is also another problem. For instance, in a discrimination problem we essentially estimate a discriminant function on the basis of data, and then we use this for discriminating the future observations. So the real performance of the estimated discriminant function has not been properly studied in the past, because when they studied the properties of the discriminant function they always studied them on the average; that is, the properties if you would go on estimating the discriminant function each time with fresh data, and then apply these estimates. But in a real problem you get stuck with a particular estimate of the discriminant function for use in discriminating future observations.

DeGroot: You really want the properties conditionally on the given estimate.

Rao: Yes, and to know how it's going to perform in the future – how we can estimate its performance from the available data itself.

DeGroot: Sounds Bayesian to me.

Rao: Yes. So that's the new type of problem which we are trying to work on, and already we have written some papers on that subject.

DeGroot: Who are the "we"?

Rao: Visitors who come here who are assigned to the project on signal detection that we have. So I am doing this work in collaboration with visitors because that way we can work faster. Of course, the problems are conceived and some groundwork is done before the visitors come. To write, say, two papers in a month or two months is not unusual although it is strenuous. Probably one writes a paper once in four months or six months in the normal course. But if we have good visitors who are good in mathematics and have similar interests, then one can work faster.

DeGroot: How did you get to know Nehru and Indira Gandhi?

Rao: Well, statistics was originally with the Prime Minister's office; that is, all decisions about the Indian Statistical Institute and the development of statistics were taken directly by the Prime Minister for a long time. It was not under any particular ministry. Probably no ministry wanted statistics. So whenever we wanted to discuss problems or ask for fresh grants or make proposals for the development of statistics in India, we used to go to the Prime Minister. Jawaharlal Nehru was the Prime Minister at that time. So we met him very often to discuss problems of statistics and he was very helpful. Actually, Jawaharlal Nehru was responsible for recognizing the Indian Statistical Institute as an institute of national importance. He moved a bill in the parliament declaring the Indian Statistical Institute an institute of national importance and giving it a charter to award degrees. Formerly we had been training statisticians, giving them courses both in the theory and the applications of statistics, but we were not allowed to give degrees. We used to give a diploma, but after this bill was passed in the parliament we started giving BS, MS, and PhD degrees in statistics.

DeGroot: When was that?

Rao: Oh, this was in '60 or '61. Before that, when we did not have the charter to give degrees, all of our students who were doing research with us had to submit their theses to some university in India, either Calcutta University or Bombay University. We were recognized as supervisors for theses, but the Institute could not give them degrees. The Prime Minister used to like us, and he gave us a lot of support by giving us as much money as we wanted for educational, research, and consulting purposes. And then after Nehru died, Indira Gandhi took his position and we continued our association with her. She knew Mahalanobis and the Indian Statistical Institute he founded because of her father's relationship with the Institute and the help he had given to the Institute.

DeGroot: Have you had other relationships with the Indian government?

Rao: Actually, the Indian Statistical Institute was responsible for drafting one of the five-year plans.

DeGroot: The economic plans?

Rao: Yes. Much of the second plan was drafted by the Indian Statistical Institute under the guidance of Mahalanobis.

DeGroot: When was that?

Rao: 1954 or so. So we continued our association with the planning commission, and the Prime Minister is the chairman of the planning commission. There are a large number of projects which we did for the planning commission. As a matter of fact, the Indian Statistical Institute branch at Delhi was located in the planning commission for a long time. It's only recently, when we built a new campus for the Indian Statistical Institute which was opened by Indira Gandhi, that we moved from the planning commission to our own premises. So we were very much attached to the government because of our involvement in working on projects for the planning commission. And I used to work on some committees on statistics formed by the Prime Minister.

DeGroot: Do you know the present Prime Minister?

Rao: I don't know him because he was not in politics when we were in contact with the Prime Minister's office. Occasionally we saw his brother, Sanjay, but not Rajiv.

DeGroot: I'm sure you've had many interesting and fascinating experiences during your time at the Indian Statistical Institute. I remember hearing about some of the problems that you had when you took over as director in Calcutta. Could you tell me a little bit about your experiences during that period?

Rao: The Indian Statistical Institute is a very large organization. It employs 3,000 people. There are lots of divisions engaged in working on different kinds of problems. Our idea was that everybody must use statistical ideas in their investigations although they are working on their own scientific problems. So that was a difficult job, to keep in touch with the various scientists working on different kinds of problems, to see to what extent they were using statistical methods in their investigations and to give them proper advice. There was also the problem of bringing scientists working in different disciplines together to work on some kind of common projects. For instance, when I sent a team for a demographic survey, I included some physical anthropologists who would go and do the measurements, sociologists to do studies on families and relationships, and seriologists to take blood samples and do the blood grouping and so on. So this was the most difficult problem and I succeeded in most cases and failed in other cases.

We had some trouble when we brought in the computers. The Indian Statistical Institute was the first organization in India to acquire digital computers. We had one computer brought from the Soviet Union in '55 and another digital computer brought from Great Britain. But the workers in India did not like our introduction of computers in a big way. They had wrong ideas about computers. They thought it would affect their employment opportunities.

DeGroot: Are the workers unionized?

Rao: Oh yes, we have very strong unions in every organization in India. Let me continue. I had developed an interest in computers when I was working in Urbana-Champaign at the University of Illinois in 1953–1954. I think that university had the first digital computer, called Illiac, and I used to work on that computer. I took a course on programming. So I was probably the first programmer of India. I was one of the few who could do programming using machine language. The University of Illinois gave me two students to develop computer programs for statistical methods at that time. So I made them work, and in order to understand those programs I learned computer programming myself. Nowadays it's easy, but at that time to use sixteen instructions to write the whole formula was a difficult problem. So I had a lot of interest in computers and I really wanted to develop computers in India, which was not possible under the conditions prevailing in India. That was a big disappointment for me. We lost the opportunity to do certain kinds of research or develop methodology based on complex computations.

DeGroot: I seem to remember that at about that time you moved from Calcutta to Delhi.

Rao: No, I moved from Calcutta to Delhi much later.

ReGroot: It was unrelated?

Rao: It was unrelated. Because I was not finding much time for doing research in Calcutta, I moved over to Delhi and asked somebody to share the administrative responsibilities in Calcutta. It was purely to get time to do research that I moved to Delhi.

DeGroot: What are some of your more pleasant recollections of your tenure there?

Rao: The Indian Statistical Institute is really a fantastic place. It used to attract famous scientists from all over the world. For instance, Norbert Wiener worked at the Institute for six months in, I think, '52 or '53. And J. B. S. Haldane was a regular employee of the Indian Statistical Institute. He was there for five years, and I was formally head of the department where Haldane was working. Mrs Haldane also used to work there. A number of famous economists visited the Indian Statistical Institute: Ragnar Frisch, Simon Kuznets, Richard Stone, who got the Nobel Prize in Economics last year; and some of the presidential advisors in economics from the USA. That tall economist, John Kenneth Galbraith, spent three months at the Indian Statistical Institute. On occasions I used to go for a walk with him. He is so tall I had to look up in order to carry on a conversation with him. Oscar Lange from Poland also visited the Indian Statistical Institute. And the Indian Statistical Institute was declared a show piece which every visitor to Calcutta must visit. So Kissinger came to the Indian Statistical Institute. I have nice photos shaking hands with Kissinger and Mrs Kissinger, and taking him around the Institute and explaining to him what we are doing. Premiers of all countries would come – Ho Chi Minh, Chou En-lai. It was quite an interesting place. And lots of scientists; at any point of time there would be ten or twelve foreign scientists visiting the Institute.

DeGroot: I remember your telling me that it's the only statistical institute in the world that has a dinosaur in it.

Rao: Oh yes, there is a geological department, and dinosaurs were discovered for the first time in India by the Indian Statistical Institute. We have a geological museum. By the way, Jawaharlal Nehru was a geologist. He studied geology when he was a student at Cambridge, so he had a lot of interest in geology. He was very much excited when we found the dinosaur. And so when the first bone, the dinosaur's thigh bone, was discovered somewhere in South

India we took the dinosaur bone all the way to Delhi to show it to Nehru.

DeGroot: There seems to be a tradition in India of mathematically talented young people going into statistics rather than into other branches of mathematics proper. Is that a correct impression, and if so, how do you think that came about?

Rao: I think that was true only for some time when there were no jobs for those who studied mathematics. They used to study mathematics just for the love of mathematics. Generally, Indians are more abstract minded; they are not practical-oriented people. That's the reason why Indians did not contribute much to science in the past. But physics, metaphysics, philosophy, mathematics, they just love, because they think that anything can be proved by argument. [Laughs] Of course, in mathematics there are axioms, and therefore argument is relevant. But not in areas where there are no fundamental axioms. But when they found that there were no good jobs in mathematics and that statistics was a developing field, many mathematicians thought it logical to study statistics! And that's the reason why a lot of good statisticians developed in the late '40s and '50s in India.

DeGroot: Is the situation still the same?

Rao: No, nowadays we are not getting such good students for statistics as we used to get in the past. Probably there are areas of applied physics and chemistry which are more attractive now. Some students still go for mathematics. So it was only a temporary phenomenon that all good mathematicians came to statistics. That was true in this country, too.

DeGroot: What prompted you to accept a faculty position in the United States here at the University of Pittsburgh in 1979? You had, of course, visited the United States often.

Rao: Yes, several times. And I also worked briefly at various universities in the United States. Actually, I had retired from the Indian Statistical Institute, but they gave me another position – a special chair called the Jawaharlal Nehru Professorship.

DeGroot: That chair was awarded upon your retirement as director?

Rao: Yes. It was approved by the Prime Minister, Indira Gandhi. But after retirement I thought I should visit the States for just one year. So I took a visiting professorship at the Ohio State University, Columbus. At that time my son, who was studying engineering in India, came to the United States to visit me. I was briefly in Pittsburgh, and I think he met the Dean and the Dean said that he could continue his engineering courses here. He already had done three years in

India. So he met the engineering faculty; they gave him credit for what he had done and told him that if he studied for another two years here, he would get the same kind of degree, a Bachelor's in Engineering, that he would get in India. So he accepted admission here and did not go back. A few days later the Dean sent word through the chairman of the Math Department here asking whether I would take a job here. One of the attractions was that I wouldn't have to pay tuition for my son if I took the job. So I said maybe, temporarily for two years, I will accept, because I have my job in India; I have to get back. He said, "You take the job. I'll give it to you on a permanent basis. You can go back whenever you like, or you can work part of the time here and part of the time in India."

DeGroot: That sounds like an offer you couldn't refuse. Have you been dividing your time going back and forth?

Rao: Not much. I have been spending most of my time in Pittsburgh because this department itself needed some development. I think that when I joined they didn't have many graduate students in statistics. I even heard that they were going to close down their graduate studies in statistics. But over the course of the past five years we tried to develop advanced courses in statistics, and to increase the number of graduate students, and also to write some papers. I think the department is now very well rated.

DeGroot: During the years that you have been in Pittsburgh, I've come to learn of your many talents outside of statistics, such as gardening, photography, and cooking. Let's take these one at a time. Would you tell me about your interest in gardening?

Rao: Well, I've always loved gardening. I used to work in my garden in India. The Indian Statistical Institute has a big campus and there's a lot of area for gardening. I think they have about 50 gardeners working there. So I used to go around early in the morning to watch what they are doing and to direct their work. I used to advise them on the type of flower plants they should grow, give them a design for planting trees, and indicate where they should grow vegetables. So I always took an interest in gardening. But I never allowed anybody to cut the flowers from the plants, so everybody had a grudge against me. [Laughs] They used to come stealthily and cut some flowers in the evenings. But I used to go down to the garden several times a day – in the morning, at lunch time, and in the evening. So when I came here I found a small space, but it is too small a place for doing gardening compared to what I had at the Indian Statistical Institute.

DeGroot: A small space in your backyard here?

Rao: Yes. I tried to grow some exotic vegetables from India, oriental vegetables. It was very successful, and I think I had better crops here than I had in India. That is because I used fertilizers here. We don't have good fertilizers in India; I used farmyard manure there.

DeGroot: Do you perform statistical experiments in your garden and analyze the data?

Rao: Yes, I used to. Here also I tried one experiment, but in India I generally experimented. For instance, one of the experiments which I was doing in collaboration with my colleague T. A. Davis at the time of my retirement was the following: The cowpea is a creeper. It is a plant which twines on the right when it grows. That is, it grows up around a pole in a right-spiral. At the Indian Statistical Institute, Davis had already done some work on the right-handed and left-handed palms. Some palms grow in a right-spiral and some grow the other way, i.e. the positions of successive leaves as a palm grows form a right-handed or a left-handed spiral. It's a very nice phenomenon. You know how a flower unfolds. For some flowers the petal to the right will be below the petal to its left, but in some flowers it's the other way, the petal to the right is above the petal to the left. That shows that some flowers unfold in a clockwise direction and some flowers unfold the other way. So there are left flowers and right flowers. We were very much interested in knowing what causes this difference among flowers. So we used to count. We had a team of students who used to go and count how many flowers on a plant are of the left and right kinds.

DeGroot: On the same plant?

Rao: On the same plant; even on the same branch. So there is some random mechanism going on which causes this. Davis made these observations on thousands and thousands of flowers and also on palm trees for left–right spirality. We also studied the yields of these palm trees, and we found that the left-handed palms gave greater yield than the right-handed palms.

So we said kill all the rightists. By selective plantation, choosing only the left-handed palms from the nursery and growing them, you can possibly increase the yield by 5 to 10 percent. This creeper, the cowpea, gave us a lot of trouble. It always used to grow on the right side. We grew a large number of plants and found that all of them were growing in the right-spiral. And I was told there are some creepers which always grow in the left-spiral. So we used to go early in the morning and pull the growing tips from the right to the left direction and tie them with ropes to the poles to force the plants to change their habit. Sometimes we used to stretch the growing top straight and tie it up and see the next morning where it had grown. But it always used to have a right tendency. We tried to measure the yields of the cowpeas that were forced to go left but unfortunately some damage might have been caused to the plants because we were handling them. So we did not think that the data we collected gave any evidence that forcibly making a plant grow on the left increased the yield. [Laughs] I had a garden where we used to do experiments of this kind right in front of the place where I was staying. It is quite exciting to do things like this and to get students interested in this phenomenon.

DeGroot: What about your interest in photography?

Rao: Oh, I have some interest in photography. Some of my pictures are very good; I used to win some prizes by submitting them in competitions.

DeGroot: Do you just take pictures where you find them?

Rao: Yes, wherever. I don't really have time to especially go on photographic expeditions. When I just go out and feel like taking my camera, I take pictures. But not on any planned basis. If I had done that, maybe I would have made a lot more pictures; but I never did.

DeGroot: Do you usually take your camera with you when you travel?

Rao: Not generally, but sometimes I take it. It depends on my mood. I also took a lot of movies when I was young. But it's a very expensive hobby. I could do that only when I came to this country and gave a lecture and earned $50 or $100. [Laughs] Of course in India I could never take pictures because we don't have the proper film; and developing and printing costs are very high. And I didn't have a good camera. Well, I took all my good pictures with very cheap cameras costing five to ten dollars. We really don't have opportunities for this kind of hobby back in India.

DeGroot: So this is more of an American development with you?

Rao: I don't know the current statistics; an average American takes a thousand pictures a year or something like that. [Laughs] That's how Kodak flourishes. But I am also interested in cultural activities like dance and music. We put our daughter in dance school very early because of our own interest in dancing.

DeGroot: I've seen her dance and she's an excellent dancer.

Rao: Yes, she's a very good dancer. She runs a dance school in Buffalo.

DeGroot: Does she do any Western dancing?

Rao: She does a little bit of Western dancing but mainly she does Indian classical dancing. I developed a new dance academy in

Delhi and was its president. We covered some neglected areas of dancing.

DeGroot: So you are quite knowledgable about Indian classical dance and Indian classical music.

Rao: More dance than music, because dance also has the visual effect.

DeGroot: What about Indian classical cooking?

Rao: Well, traditionally I used to like cooking because I used to help my mother cook. My mother also had other interests and she used to visit other places. At that time there were only boys and my father in the house, and we used to do all the cooking for days and days. My wife comes from a family where there was only one girl and five brothers, so she was very much pampered and did not know cooking. So all the cooking she now knows, she learnt from me. [Laughs] My son is a very good cook. So it seems to me that there's some gene in the family for this culinary art. I think basically that cooking is an art, so I think that it's an interest in art.

DeGroot: Are any of your brothers or sisters interested in statistics or other mathematical things?

Rao: My brothers and sisters were all basically very intelligent people. I had an elder brother who was a doctor who was phenomenal. He had a wonderful memory. If you gave him 150 names, he could just read them once and then repeat all those names. One brother was an engineer, quite a good one. You see, we are a family of ten, so many of them died. Another was in commerce. One of my sisters was a poet; she wrote poetry in Telugu. And one was really a business woman; she did a lot of business and made a lot of property along with her husband. They didn't have any formal education because girls did not study years ago in India. So it was all an innate thing. My sister who was a poet just studied by herself and started writing poetry. But they were not mathematicians, except for the engineer who had to study some mathematics.

DeGroot: Are there other things that you like to do when you are not doing statistics?

Rao: Well, as I grow old I find that there's not much time to do many things. But in the next two or three years I may be visiting the Third World countries and helping them in developing research in statistics. This is an assignment that the Third World Academy of Science, of which I am founder fellow, is trying to give me. I have not replied to their letter yet because I am not sure how my health will be in the coming years. But this is something which I would like to do because I know the Third World countries are not developing basic research. They are dependent on foreign countries for all technological improvements, which is not good in the long run. That's the reason why we founded the Third World Academy. In addition, I may have some assignments in India which would keep me busy and occupied for a long time to come.

DeGroot: What do you think are the important trends in contemporary statistics? Where do you see the field going? Where do you think it should be going?

Rao: Those are questions about which I am constantly thinking. I believe the two great methodologies in statistics are sample surveys, which is essentially collecting existing information, and design of experiments, where you generate observations to provide information on some given questions. Different types of data analyses are, of course, then applied depending upon what the statistician thinks is the right thing to do. They are not as fundamental as the data which are collected through principles of design and sample surveys. If data are good, results should be obvious; the analysis is only to convince somebody that there is a real difference and so on.

DeGroot: So you are saying that with a good design or a good survey, the answer should be obvious without doing any complicated analysis.

Rao: The analysis is only to make sure that we are not deceived by what we are seeing. Much of it should be obvious by looking at the data or by simple analysis. Even graphics is very important. That's the reason why R. A. Fisher emphasized graphical representation of data as part of statistical analysis. Although many people are not aware of this, the very first chapter of his book, *Statistical Methods for Research Workers*, is graphics. Nobody reads that although it is a very nice chapter. So I think we should be doing more graphical analysis, especially with the help of the computers we have. We can do things now, which we could not previously do, with transformations of variables and graphics. Further research in sample surveys and design of experiments to refine the already refined methods in these two areas would be helpful.

Then we should be developing some routine methods of statistics for applications, like the quality control methods and what Shewhart did in industry: a simple and efficient way of presenting data which enables them to see whether everything is OK or something is going wrong, or whether there is scope for improvement. There is a great need for developing simple techniques for routine applications in other areas to improve the overall efficiency of goods we produce and services we offer.

DeGroot: The medical area is one example.

Rao: Yes, there are many challenging problems in applications of statistics to medicine. We don't seem to have done much in that area. So this is where we should be working, along with the medical doctors, to try to see how statistics can be applied to improve diagnosis, treatment, monitoring the effect of drugs on the patients, and so on. Statistics is used in a slightly different way in problems of bioassays and the screening of drugs. But I think a lot remains to be done in medical diagnosis. I don't know whether I told you this story or not. When I was working at Johns Hopkins – that's the place where many famous doctors are – I went to a doctor because I felt some uneasiness in my stomach. He made a large number of tests and asked me what was wrong with me. I said that the Indian doctors told me that the food I take does not stay in the stomach long enough. It gets into the intestines within half an hour but normally, in other cases, it takes one-and-a-half hours or so.

So he said, "The fact that the food stays only for half an hour doesn't mean there is something wrong with you. You know, if you take a set of normal individuals and find how long the food stays in the stomach for each individual, that's a variable and it is normally distributed." He tells *me*. [Laughs] So the fact that you are a member of that normal group having a small value doesn't mean there is something wrong with you. If a person is five feet tall, that's not pathological; some healthy individuals are five feet high and some are six feet high, and so on. So if it's not by looking at the battery of tests, how does the doctor decide whether there is something pathological or not? Suppose that with all those abnormal values, the patient looks all right. Does that mean there is something wrong with him? So it's probably a combination of the tests and the doctor's evaluation of the patient's general condition.

As soon as you go to the doctor he asks what is wrong with you, and he takes a case history. Are you all right? Are you able to think? Are you able to write papers? Are you able to walk? Are you able to drink? You see, if you do all this with your bad cholesterol, then it's OK, that's normal with you. So diagnostic tests like measurements on the blood chemistry are not by themselves enough to make a diagnosis. The patient's condition must also be an input into it. The question is how to put them together and come up with a diagnosis. It's an art for the doctor. Probably in the past nobody made any tests. If you went and told the doctor that you had a fever and other things, he felt your pulse and prescribed a medicine. So the general condition of the individual is probably far more important to the diagnosis than what the diagnostic tests reveal. So I am working on this kind of problem: how to put together the results of tests and the doctor's judgment of the patient's case history, and other prior evidence, which may be personal and subjective, and come to the right diagnosis.

DeGroot: That's great.

Rao: So there should be more routine applications of statistics wherever they are needed, and we should be getting into new areas where the classical approaches really do not work.

DeGroot: I think many statistical techniques have become standard simply because they were easy to apply, just the reason you are talking about, regardless of whether they were always relevant.

Rao: They all arose from applications in biology, but now that stage is past. I don't think we are very successful with statistical methods in psychology or even in economics. Possibly what is wrong with the economists is that they are not trying to refine their measurements or trying to measure new variables which cause economic changes. That is far more important than dabbling with whatever data are available and trying to make predictions based on them. So there's a lot of work that needs to be done in the soft sciences such as psychology and economics.

DeGroot: What does the future hold for C. R. Rao? You mentioned the possibility of travelling in Third World countries.

Rao: Well, I will try to continue research to the extent possible with the facilities available wherever I am. And I like teaching and talking to students, trying to inspire them, giving them new problems – so probably I'll continue to do that. And if the Third World Academy forces me to go out and give lectures, I guess I could do that. But I do not know. I would like to continue the type of work I have been doing before, but probably at a slower pace than before.

DeGroot: I'm sure that in whatever you do, you will be as highly successful as you always have been. Thank you, C. R.

Acknowledgments

The editors and publishers are grateful to the Institute of Mathematical Statistics for permission to reproduce "A conversation with C. R. Rao," from *Statistical Science*, vol. 2, no. 1, pp. 53–67, in the introductory pages of this volume.

C. R. Rao receiving Bhatnagar cash award for outstanding contributions to science from Pandit Jawaharlal Nehru, the then Prime Minister of India (1963)

1 Specification Tests in Limited Dependent Variable Models

G. S. Maddala

To know the truth one must imagine myriads of falsehoods
Oscar Wilde, quoted by Orme, 1992

1 Introduction

One of the major developments in econometrics during the past two decades has been the emphasis on specification tests (or diagnostic checks). Most of these tests are score tests, first suggested by Rao (1947). In the econometric literature these tests are often referred to as LM tests or Lagrangian multiplier tests, following the terminology of Silvey (1959), whose paper appeared ten years after Rao's paper. Though the use of specification tests is very common (several are now built into most computer programs) their use in limited dependent variable models is not very common, except for tests of sample selection bias. However, as the following survey indicates, there are many specification tests that have been suggested in the literature, and illustrated with examples. Most of these are score tests but some are Hausman (1978) type tests and some are conditional moment tests following the work of Newey (1985) and Tauchen (1985). Pagan and Vella (1989) argue that the use of specification tests in limited dependent variables is not common because they are difficult to compute. They suggest a number of specification tests based on conditional moments that they argue are easier to use. We shall comment on these tests as well. In the following sections we shall consider the following types of models:

1 Binary choice models (probit and logit).
2 Multinomial logit models.
3 Tobit models.
4 Self-selection models, or sample selection models.
5 Disequilibrium models.

The conserve on space, we shall not discuss duration models and count-data models. The chapter is organized according to the types of tests rather than by the type of the model. The following tests will be considered:

1 Tests for heteroskedasticity (section 3).
2 Tests for nonnormality (section 4).
3 Tests for autocorrelation (section 5).
4 Tests for sample selection bias (section 6).
5 Tests for exogeneity (section 7).
6 Tests for omitted variables (section 8).
7 Tests for stability (section 9).
8 Multinomial logit specification tests (section 10).

Before we proceed to these tests it would be helpful to review the different categories of tests.

2 The Different Categories of Specification Tests

The specification tests in use in econometrics are:

1 The Rao (1947) score test.
2 Hausman's (1978) specification test, which dates back to a relatively neglected paper by Durbin (1954) and hence is also known as the Durbin–Hausman test, or the Durbin–Wu–Hausman test due to another earlier paper Wu (1973).
3 White's (1982) information matrix (IM) test.
4 The conditional moment (CM) tests suggested by Newey (1985) and Tauchen (1985).

In addition to these four general categories, we shall discuss, in the context of tests of selection bias and exogeneity, another category of tests: the CML (conditional maximum likelihood) tests.

The score test

Suppose there are n independent observations $y_1, y_2, \ldots, y_n$ with identical density functions $f(y, \theta)$ where θ is a $p \times 1$ vector of p

parameters. Then the log-likelihood function $L(\theta)$, the score vector $d(\theta)$ and the information matrix $I(\theta)$ are defined by

$$L(\theta) = \sum_{i=1}^{n} \ln f(y_i, \theta) = \sum_{i=1}^{n} L_i(\theta)$$

$$d(\theta) = \frac{\partial L(\theta)}{\partial \theta}, \quad \text{for given } \theta,\ E[d(\theta)] = 0.$$

$$I(\theta) = \operatorname{cov}(d(\theta)) = E[d(\theta)d(\theta)'] = E\left[-\frac{\partial^2 L}{\partial\theta\partial\theta'}\right].$$

The ML estimator $\hat{\theta}$ is given by the equation $d(\hat{\theta}) = 0$.

For testing the hypothesis H_0: $h(\theta) = 0$, where $h(\theta)$ is an r-dimensional vector function of θ ($r \leqslant p$) and c is a given constant, Rao (1948) proposed the statistic

$$d'(\tilde{\theta})[I(\tilde{\theta})]^{-1}d(\tilde{\theta})$$

where $\tilde{\theta}$ is the (restricted) ML estimate of θ under H_0. If H_0 is true, then $d(\tilde{\theta})$ is expected to be close to $d(\hat{\theta})$ and hence close to zero. Rao (1948, 1973) shows that the score test statistic has a χ^2 distribution with d.f. r under H_0. He also conjectured that the score test is likely to be locally more powerful than the Wald (W) and likelihood ratio (LR) tests. A general review of the score test in econometrics can be found in Godfrey (1988) and Bera and Ullah (1991). Mukerjee (1993) gives a brief history of the score test and recent developments in its asymptotic theory. Rao and Mukerjee (1993) present further results on the power properties of score tests.

About ten years after Rao's paper, Silvey (1959) proposed the same test and called it the Lagrangian multiplier (LM) test. In the econometric literature this terminology was popularized by Breusch and Pagan (1980), who suggested its use as a specification test. As will be seen in the following sections, a general approach to specification testing based on the score test is to consider a more general model $f(y, \theta, \phi)$ for which $f(y, \theta)$ is a special case and test the hypothesis $\phi = 0$ using the score test. The advantage of the score test is that it depends on only the ML estimates from the restricted model, although the score vector and the information matrix have to be based on the full model. Sometimes this complicates the score test statistic. An extension of the score test, based on general $\sqrt{n}$ consistent estimates rather than the restricted ML estimates, is the Neyman–Rao test discussed in Hall and Mathiason (1990).

Different forms of the score test are in use in the econometric literature. These depend on the different estimates used for $I(\tilde{\theta})$. Note that

$$I(\theta) = E[d(\theta)d'(\theta)] = E\left[-\frac{\partial^2 L}{\partial\theta\partial\theta'}\right].$$

Evaluating the expectations is often cumbersome and hence the sample analogous of these expressions are used. Consider the $n \times p$ matrix $G(\theta)$ whose (i, j)th element is $G_{ij}(\theta) = \partial L_i/\partial\theta_j$, $i = 1, 2, \ldots, n$, $j = 1, 2, \ldots, p$. Since $E[d(\theta)d'(\theta)] = E[G'(\theta)G(\theta)]$, $I(\theta)$ can be consistently estimated by $G'(\theta)G(\theta)$. This estimator of $I(\theta)$ is called the *outer product gradient* (OPG) version of $I(\theta)$. It has been popular in the econometrics literature because it simplifies the computation of the score test statistics. An alternative estimator of $I(\theta)$ is the Hessian

$$H = \left(-\frac{\partial^2 L}{\partial\theta\partial\theta'}\right).$$

Whereas the OPG version involves computation of only the first derivatives of L, the Hessian involves computation of the second derivatives. The score test based on the information matrix is often known as the "efficient" score test. Bera and McKenzie (1986) discuss the merits and demerits of the different forms of the score test statistic.

Note that $d'(\theta) = i'G(\theta)$ where i is an $n \times 1$ vector of ones. Hence the score test statistic, using the OPG version of $I(\theta)$, can be written as:

$$d'(\tilde{\theta})[I(\tilde{\theta})]^{-1}d(\tilde{\theta}) = i'G(\tilde{\theta})[G'(\tilde{\theta})G(\tilde{\theta})]^{-1}G'(\tilde{\theta})i$$

This is nothing but the regression sum of squares in an artificial regression of i on $G(\tilde{\theta})$ with no constant term, where i is a vector of all ones. Since the total sum of squares is $i'i = n$, what one does to compute the score test statistic is to regress i on $G(\theta)$ and take nR^2 as the test statistic, where R^2 is the (uncentered) squared multiple correlation coefficient. The OPG version of the score test, though easy to compute, has been found to have bad small sample properties (see Davidson and MacKinnon, 1989; Orme, 1990; and the references in these papers). An alternative version is the score test based on the Hessian, and this has been found to perform only slightly better than the OPG version (see Taylor, 1991). In the case of the binary choice models (logit and probit), Davidson and MacKinnon (1989) show that the score test statistic based on the information matrix $I(\tilde{\beta})$ can be computed easily using a different artificial regression. In the case of the normal truncated regression model and censored regression model (tobit model), Orme (1992) shows that the score test statistic based on the information matrix can be computed by a double-length artificial regression. Thus, in the case of these models, there is no need to use the OPG version of the score test. We shall elaborate on this when we discuss tests for heteroskedasticity (section 3).

Lee and Chesher (1986) discuss a generalization of the score test when the latter breaks down because the score test statistic is identically zero. They give examples in limited dependent variable models where this happens. In such cases, they suggest an alternative which they call the "extremum test" or a "generalized score test". This test is based on the argument that the score test is exploiting the first derivative of the log-likelihood for a maximum and, if this breaks down, one should consider "extremum" tests based on higher order derivatives.

Durbin–Hausman tests

The specification test suggested by Hausman is based on a comparison of two sets of parameter estimates (Davidson and MacKinnon, 1989, refer to this test as the Durbin–Wu–Hausman test or the DWH test). Let $\tilde{\theta}$ be an estimator of θ which is efficient under H_0 but usually inconsistent under H_1, and $\bar{\theta}$ be an estimator of θ which is consistent under both H_0 and H_1, but not efficient under H_0. Let $d = \bar{\theta} - \tilde{\theta}$ and $\text{var}(\sqrt{n}\bar{\theta}) = V_1$ and $\text{var}(\sqrt{n}\tilde{\theta}) = V_0$. Then the Hausman test is based on the result that $\text{var}(\sqrt{n}d) = V_1 - V_0$ under H_0 (this is based on a theorem in Rao, 1973, p. 317). The test statistic is $(\sqrt{n}d)'(V_1 - V_0)^{-1}(\sqrt{n}d)$ which has a χ^2 distribution with d.f. p, the dimensionality of θ. In case $(V_1 - V_0)^{-1}$ does not exist, one can use the generalized inverse (see Rao and Mitra, 1971) but the χ^2 distribution has smaller degrees of freedom in this case. Generalized inverses are not unique but Holly and Monfort (1986) show that all generalized inverses give the same test statistic.

There is also another class of "Hausman type" tests where *both* estimators are inconsistent under H_1, but generally $p\lim\tilde{\theta} \neq p\lim\bar{\theta}$ under H_1. These are suggested in Ruud (1984), but the discussion following his paper raises some questions about the interpretation of these tests. We shall discuss the Hausman-type tests suggested by Ruud in the following sections.

Very often the Hausman test reduces to the score test. White

(1982), Ruud (1984) and Newey (1985) show that tests asymptotically equivalent to the Hausman test can be computed as score tests. Ruud and Newey suggested the use of artificial regressions to coumpute these tests but the artificial regression suggested is for the OPG variant of the score test. Unfortunately, as mentioned earlier this variant of the score test has bad finite-sample properties.

White's information matrix (IM) test

White's (1982) information matrix test is based on the fact that for a correctly specified model we have

$$E[d(\theta)d(\theta)'] = E\left[-\frac{\partial^2 L}{\partial\theta\partial\theta'}\right].$$

Hence if we consider the statistic

$$\left(d(\theta)d(\theta)' + \frac{\partial^2 L}{\partial\theta\partial\theta'}\right),$$

it should have mean zero for a correctly specified model. The major problem here is obtaining the variance of this test statistic, which involves higher order derivatives of L. However, Lancaster (1984) has shown that this can be avoided and that the IM test statistic can be obtained from the artificial regression:

$$r = Gc_1 + Zc_2 + \text{residual}$$

where

r is a vector of ones

G is the matrix defined earlier whose i, jth element is $\partial L_i/\partial\theta_j$ and

Z is a matrix whose typical element is

$$\frac{\partial^2 L_i(\theta)}{\partial\theta_j\partial\theta_k} + \left(\frac{\partial L_i(\theta)}{\partial\theta_j}\right)\left(\frac{\partial L_i(\theta)}{\partial\theta_k}\right) \quad \text{for } j = 1, 2, \ldots, p, \quad k = 1, 2, \ldots j.$$

Both G and Z are evaluated at the restricted ML estimate. The number of columns in Z is $\frac{1}{2}(k^2 + k)$ although in practice some columns have to be dropped if $[G, Z]$ does not have full rank.

However, the Lancaster version of the IM test is the OPG version and it has been found to perform dismally for even moderately large sample sizes (see Davidson and MacKinnon, 1989, p. 382 and the references therein). White's original test statistic depended on using the Hessian and the third derivatives of the log-likelihood. Orme

(1990) finds its performance to be only marginally better than that of the OPG version. He argues that White did not evaluate the expectations of the third (or even second) derivatives of the log-likelihood. Orme suggests an improved version of the IM test based on these expectations and shows that its performance is much better than Lancaster's OPG variant or White's original test statistic. Newey (1985) proposes the OPG version of the IM test for the probit model. Orme (1990) and Davidson and MacKinnon (1989) suggest an improved version of the IM test for the probit model. These tests will be discussed when we come to tests for heteroskedasticity (section 3). Finally, Cox (1983) and Chesher (1984) demonstrate that the IM test statistic may be interpreted as a score test for neglected heterogeneity or random parameter variation in θ.

Conditional moments (CM) tests

The CM tests suggested by Newey (1985) and Tauchen (1985) are based on the premise that, under correct specification, we have not only the condition based on the scores

$$E[d(\theta)] = 0$$

but also several other over-identifying conditions which can be stated as

$$E[m(y, \theta)] = 0.$$

The CM tests have been very popular in the area of specification testing and in fact White (1987) argues that essentially all specification tests should be regarded as conditional moment tests. However, although many score tests can be regarded as CM tests, as noted by Pagan and Vella (1989), the predictive score test (see section 8) does not have an interpretation as a CM test.

To see the relationship between score tests and CM tests, consider the case where the vector θ is partitioned into (θ_1, θ_2) of dimensions $(p - r)$ and r, and the null hypothesis tested is $\theta_2 = 0$. This implies that the last r elements of the score vector $d(\theta)$ have expectation zero under the null; that is,

$$E[d_i(\theta_1, 0)] = 0 \quad \text{for } i = p - r + 1, \ldots, p.$$

Thus, the CM test in this case is the score test. This correspondence is, however, not always so obvious. For instance, in tests for normality, we can just base the tests on the third and fourth moments of the errors: $E[u^3] = 0$ and $E[u^4 - 3u^2] = 0$. These are CM tests although it will be seen later that the score tests also reduce to these tests (see Bera et al., 1984; Lee and Maddala, 1985). In this case, the score test is implemented by starting with a general distribution of which the normal distribution is a special case and testing the restrictions on this general distribution (see section 4).

To test a moment condition

$$E[m(y, \theta)] = 0$$

we consider the test statistic

$$\hat{\tau} = \frac{1}{n}\sum m(y_i, \hat{\theta}) = \frac{1}{n}\sum \hat{m}_i$$

where $\hat{\theta}$ is the ML estimator of θ (or any other $\sqrt{n}$ consistent estimator of θ). Pagan and Vella (1989) consider the generalized method of moments (GMM) estimator. To obtain the distribution of $\hat{\tau}$ we expand $m_i(\hat{\theta})$ around θ_0. We have, retaining only the first order term,

$$\sqrt{n}\left[\frac{1}{n}\sum m_i(\hat{\theta})\right] = \sqrt{n}\left[\frac{1}{n}\sum m_i(\theta_0) + p\lim_{n\to\infty}\left(\frac{1}{n}\sum\frac{\partial m_i(\theta_0)}{\partial\theta}\right)(\hat{\theta} - \theta_0)\right].$$

The exact distribution of $\sqrt{n}(\hat{\theta} - \theta_0)$ is unknown. If $\hat{\theta}$ is the MLE then $\sqrt{n}(\hat{\theta} - \theta_0)$ is asymptotically normal with variance $[I(\theta)]^{-1}$. Newey shows that

$$p\lim_{n\to\infty}\left[\frac{1}{n}\sum\frac{\partial m_i(\theta_0)}{\partial\theta}\right]$$

can be consistently estimated using just m_i and the scores. This result is based on what is known as the *generalized information equality*, which is derived as follows:

Under correct specification $E[m(y_i, \theta)] = 0$. But

$$E[m(y_i, \theta)] = \int m(y_i, \theta)f(y_i, \theta)dy_i.$$

Differentiating this with respect to θ we get

$$\int\frac{\partial m(y_i, \theta)}{\partial\theta}f(y_i, \theta)dy_i + \int m(y_i, \theta)\left(\frac{1}{f}\cdot\frac{\partial f}{\partial\theta}\right)fdy_i = 0$$

or

$$E\left[\frac{\partial m(y_i, \theta)}{\partial\theta}\right] = -E[m(y_i, \theta)d(y_i, \theta)].$$

This means that

$$p \lim_{n\to\infty} \frac{1}{n}\sum \frac{\partial m_i}{\partial \theta}$$

can be consistently estimated by $-\frac{1}{n}\sum \hat{m}_i \hat{d}_i$. Using the OPG version of the information matrix, it can be shown that the CM test reduces to the artificial regression

$$i = \hat{G}c + b\hat{m} + \text{residual}$$

where G is the matrix defined earlier ($G_{ij} = \partial L_i / \partial \theta_j$) in connection with the score test, and i is the vector of ones. $\hat{G}$ is always orthogonal to i because $i'\hat{G} = 0$ are the equations solved for the MLE $\hat{\theta}$. $\hat{m}$ is orthogonal to i if the moment condition is satisfied. Hence a test for the moment condition is a test for the hypothesis $b = 0$. In the case where there are r moment conditions, we define the $n \times r$ matrix $\hat{M} = M(\hat{\theta})$ and test the hypothesis $b = 0$ in the artificial regression

$$i = \hat{G}c + \hat{M}b + \text{residual}$$

Note that even if $i'\hat{G} = 0$, it is important to include $\hat{G}$ in this artificial regression (see MacKinnon, 1992, p. 132).

This artificial regression is based on the information equality

$$E[dd'] = E\left[-\frac{\partial^2 L}{\partial\theta\partial\theta'}\right]$$

which is valid only when the complete density of the observations is correctly specified. Wooldridge (1990) suggests more robust specification tests that are not based on this assumption. However, these tests are not easy to apply in limited dependent variable models.

As with the score tests and IM tests, in the CM tests one can use the Hessian or the information matrix to estimate $\text{cov}(\hat{\theta} - \theta_0)$. Also,

$$E\left[\frac{\partial m_i(y_i, \theta)}{\partial \theta}\right]$$

can be estimated directly. This was done by Skeels and Vella (1993a) for the probit and tobit models. They use the Hessian and call this the "direct (DR) test". However, they find, in their Monte Carlo studies, that the DR test's performance was not much better than that of the OPG version. This finding is similar to that of Orme (1990), in the case of the IM test, that the use of the Hessian instead of the OPG version did not improve the performance of the IM test. It is after taking expectations that the performance improved. Except for their OPG versions, the CM tests are not any easier to implement than the score tests.

3 Tests for Heteroskedasticity

One of the early papers to discuss specification errors in limited dependent variable models is the paper by Maddala and Nelson (1975). The paper argues that whereas in the case of the usual regression model, under heteroskedasticity of the errors, the OLS estimator is consistent, though inefficient, in the case of the tobit model, the usual ML estimator is inconsistent in the presence of heteroskedastic errors. Thus, it is very important to test for heteroskedasticity in limited dependent variable models. Since then, many papers have reviewed the effects of heteroskedasticity in the tobit model. A more recent paper is by Brannas and Laitila (1989), who review the work on the effect of heteroskedasticity in the tobit model and present some Monte Carlo evidence on the performance of the Buckley–James semiparametric estimator and the tobit ML estimator.

In the usual regression model, tests for heteroskedasticity are based on the OLS residuals. Pagan and Vella (1989) suggest CM tests by analogy with this. Pagan and Pak (1993, p. 499) start their paper with the argument that all existing tests for heteroskedasticity can be regarded as CM tests, with the differences between them revolving around the moments used and how nuisance parameters are dealt with. The moment condition for CM tests is

$$\frac{1}{n}\sum E(z_i(u_i^2 - \sigma^2)) = 0,$$

where u_i is the error with variance σ^2 (under homoskedasticity) and z_i is a misspecification indicator, as, for instance, if we assume

$$\text{var}(u_i) = \sigma^2(1 + z_i\gamma)^2.$$

We shall show that this condition follows from the score test in the case of the tobit model. But first we discuss binary choice models. In this case the moment condition involves u_i only.

Probit and logit models

In the case of binary choice models we have a latent variable y_i^* defined as

$$y_i^* = \beta' x_i + u_i, \quad u_i \sim IID(0, \sigma^2) \tag{3.1}$$

and the observed y_i is defined by

$$\begin{aligned} y_i &= 1 \quad \text{if } y_i^* > 0 \\ &= 0 \quad \text{otherwise} \end{aligned}$$

Since y_i^* is observed only as a dichotomous variable, only β/σ is estimable. Hence we assume that $\sigma = 1$. We have

$$\Pr[y_i = 1] = F(\beta' x_i)$$

where $F(.)$ is the cumulative distribution function of u_i and the distribution of u_i is symmetric, which is the case for the logit and probit models. For the probit model we have

$$F(\beta' x_i) = \Phi(\beta' x_i)$$

where Φ is the cumulative distribution function of the standard normal.

For the logit model we have

$$F(\beta' x_i) = \frac{\exp(\beta' x_i)}{1 + \exp(\beta' x_i)}.$$

For compactness of notation, let us denote $F(\beta' x_i)$ by F_i. Then the log-likelihood L can be written as

$$L = \sum_{i=1}^{n} [y_i F_i + (1 - y_i)(1 - F_i)] = \sum L_i.$$

Then

$$\begin{aligned} G_{ij}(\beta) &= \frac{\partial L_i}{\partial \beta_j} = \left[\frac{y_i}{F_i} - \frac{1 - y_i}{1 - F_i}\right] f_i x_{ij} \\ &= [(y_i - F_i)/F_i(1 - F_i)] f_i x_{ij} \end{aligned} \tag{3.2}$$

where $f(z)$ is the first derivative of $F(z)$ with respect to z. For the probit model $f(z) = \phi(z)$, the standard normal density, and for the logit model we have

$$f(z) = \frac{\exp(z)}{[1 + \exp(z)]^2} = \frac{1}{4} Sech^2\left(\frac{z}{2}\right)$$

the density function of the $Sech^2$ distribution.

The jth element $d_j(\beta)$ of the score vector $d(\beta)$ is equal to

$$\sum_{i=1}^{n} G_{ij}(\beta).$$

If we use the OPG version of the score test for the hypothesis $\beta = 0$, we get the score test statistic as nR^2 in an artificial regression of $\mathbf{i}$ on $G(\beta)$ where $\mathbf{i}$ is a vector of ones. Davidson and MacKinnon (1984) denote this as the LM_1 test.

Consider now the test statistic based on the information matrix. Differentiating L_i twice with respect to β we get

$$\begin{aligned}\frac{\partial^2 L_i}{\partial\beta\partial\beta'} &= \frac{\partial}{\partial\beta'}\left[y_i\frac{f_i}{F_i} - (1 - y_i)\frac{f_i}{1 - F_i}\right]x_i \\ &= \left[y_i\frac{F_i f_i' - f_i^2}{F_i^2} - (1 - y_i)\frac{(1 - F_i)f_i' + f_i^2}{(1 - F_i)^2}\right]x_i x_i' \qquad (3.3)\end{aligned}$$

where $f_i' = \partial f_i/\partial\beta$. Since $E(y_i) = F_i$, taking expectations and noting that f_i' cancels out, we get

$$I(\beta) = E\left[-\sum_{i=1}^{n}\frac{\partial^2 L}{\partial\beta\partial\beta'}\right] = \sum_{i=1}^{n}\frac{f_i^2}{F_i(1 - F_i)}x_i x_i'.$$

Based on this simplification of $I(\beta)$, Davidson and MacKinnon (1984) suggest the following score test. Define the $n \times p$ matrix $R(\beta)$ whose typical element is

$$R_{ij}(\beta) = [F_i(1 - F_i)]^{-1/2} f_i x_{ij} \qquad (3.4)$$

and the n-vector $r(\beta)$ with the typical element

$$r_i(\beta) = y_i\left(\frac{1 - F_i}{F_i}\right)^{1/2} - (1 - y_i)\left(\frac{F_i}{1 - F_i}\right)^{1/2} \qquad (3.5)$$

Then it can be verified that the information matrix $I(\beta) = R'(\beta)R(\beta)$ and the score vector $d(\beta) = R'(\beta)r(\beta)$. Hence the score test statistic is

$$LM_2 = d'Id = r'R(R'R)^{-1}R'r$$

which is nothing but nR^2 from the artificial regression $r = Rc +$ error.

In this case the score test statistic based on the information matrix is not much more complicated than the OPG version. Davidson and MacKinnon argue (on the basis of a sampling study) that whereas LM_1 is badly behaved, rejecting the null too often, LM_2 has a small sample distribution close to its asymptotic one.

To test for heteroskedasticity, we specify $\text{var}(u_i) = (1 + \gamma' z_i)^2$ and test H_0: $\gamma = 0$. Davidson and MacKinnon specify $\text{var}(u_i) = \exp(2\gamma' z_i)$ but the algebra is the same. Now, $\beta' x_i$ in (3.1) is replaced by $\beta' x_i/(1 + \gamma' z_i)$. Let $\tilde{\beta}$ be the ML estimator of β under H_0: $\gamma = 0$. The expressions for the two score test statistics LM_1 and LM_2 are as described earlier with β replaced by $\tilde{\beta}$ and the following changes.

The matrix G will now be an $n \times (p + m)$ matrix where m is the dimensionality of γ. Its ith row is defined by (corresponding to (3.2))

$$\left.\frac{\partial L_i}{\partial \beta}\right|_{\beta=\tilde{\beta},\gamma=0} = \left[y_i \frac{f_i}{F_i} - (1 - y_i)\frac{f_i}{1 - F_i}\right] x_i$$

$$\left.\frac{\partial L_i}{\partial \gamma}\right|_{\beta=\tilde{\beta},\gamma=0} = \left[y_i \frac{f_i}{F_i} - (1 - y_i)\frac{f_i}{1 - F_i}\right] (\tilde{\beta}' x_i)(-z_i) \tag{3.6}$$

with f_i and F_i being evaluated at $\beta = \tilde{\beta}$, $\gamma = 0$. The vector r given by (3.5) is the same with $\tilde{\beta}$ substituted for β. However, the matrix R given by (3.4) is now an $n \times (p + m)$ matrix. Its ith row is given by

$$[R_i(\beta), R_i(\gamma)] = [F_i(1 - F_i)]^{-1/2} f_i [x_i, (\beta' x_i)(-z_i)]. \tag{3.7}$$

The score vector $d(\tilde{\beta}, 0)$ is $R'r$ which is a $(p + m)$ vector.

Equations (3.6) imply that

$$f_i(y_i - F_i)[F_i(1 - F_i)]^{-1} x_i = 0$$

$$f_i(y_i - F_i)[F_i(1 - F_i)]^{-1}(\tilde{\beta}' x_i) z_i = 0.$$

Since $E(u_i | y_i) = f_i(y_i - F_i)[F_i(1 - F_i)]^{-1}$ (see Gourieroux et al., 1987), we can call this the *generalized residual* and denote it by η_i. Then equations (3.6) can be written as

$$\frac{1}{n}\sum \tilde{\eta}_i x_i = 0 \quad \text{and} \quad \frac{1}{n}\sum \tilde{\eta}_i(\tilde{\beta}' x_i) z_i = 0 \tag{3.8}$$

Thus, the score test for heteroskedasticity involves only $\tilde{\eta}_i$ and not $\tilde{\eta}_i^2$. The first condition is the one required to obtain the (restricted) ML estimates. The second is the "moment condition" arising from the specification test. The CM test is based on the second condition. Newey (1985, p. 1062) gives the moment condition for the CM test for heteroskedasticity in the probit model. It is the second condition given here.

Coming to the IM test, which is a very general test and not specifically for testing heteroskedasticity, there is a very special interesting case where it reduces to the score test. In the case of the probit model, Davidson and MacKinnon (1989, p. 381; and Orme in an unpublished paper quoted there) show that if the heteroskedasticity is of the form

$$V(u_i) = \exp\left[2\sum_{k=1}^{m}\sum_{j=1}^{k} x_{ij}x_{ik}r_{jk}\right]$$

then the score test for heteroskedasticity is equivalent to the IM test. The condition is intuitively appealing because it says that the heteroskedasticity depends on the cross products of the explanatory variables.

Censored regression (tobit) model

The censored regression model in its simplest form is given by

$$\begin{aligned} y_i^* &= \beta' x_i + u_i \\ y_i &= y_i^* \quad \text{if } y_i^* > 0 \\ &= 0 \quad \text{otherwise.} \end{aligned}$$

u_i can have any distribution but here we shall consider the case where $u_i \sim IN(0, \sigma^2)$ or what is known as the tobit model. To test for heteroskedasticity, Lee and Maddala (1985) proceed with a general functional form $\text{var}(u_i) = \sigma_i^2 = G(\alpha + \delta' z_i)$ and suggest testing $\delta = 0$. Given that the score test is for local alternatives, we can assume $\sigma_i = \sigma + \delta z_i$ without any loss of generality. Hence we shall proceed with this assumption.

Define the indicator function

$$\begin{aligned} I_i &= 1 \quad \text{if } y_i^* > 0 \\ &= 0 \quad \text{otherwise.} \end{aligned}$$

Then the log-likelihood function L is given by

$$\begin{aligned} L = \sum_{i=1}^{n} I_i\left[-\frac{1}{2}\ln\sigma_i^2 - \frac{1}{2\sigma_i^2}(y_i - \beta' x_i)^2\right] \\ + \sum_{i=1}^{n}(1 - I_i)\ln\left[1 - \Phi\left(\frac{\beta' x_i}{\sigma i}\right)\right]. \end{aligned}$$

The score vector is given on p. 180 of Maddala (1983). Under H_0: $\delta = 0$ we get, after some arrangement, that $\partial L/\partial\delta$ is proportional to

$$\sum\left[I_i\left(\frac{(y_i - \beta' x_i)^2}{\sigma^2} - 1\right) + (1 - I_i)\left(\lambda_i \frac{\beta' x_i}{\sigma}\right)\right] z_i$$

where λ_i is the Mills ratio

$$\frac{\phi(\beta' x_i/\sigma)}{1 - \Phi(\beta' x_i/\sigma)}.$$

The interpretation of the first term is obvious. It compares $\hat{u}_i^2/\hat{\sigma}^2$ to 1. To interpret the second term we note that

$$E[u_i^2 | y_i = 0] = \sigma^2 + \sigma^2 \lambda_i (\beta' x_i / \sigma).$$

(This follows from the recurrence relation for moments given in Lee and Maddala, 1985, p. 4. This is also presented in equation (4.1) in the next section). Hence

$$\lambda_i \frac{\beta' x_i}{\sigma} = E\left[\frac{u_i^2}{\sigma^2}\middle| y_i = 0\right] - 1.$$

Thus, this term also compares $\hat{u}_i^2/\hat{\sigma}^2$ to 1. Thus the score vector is proportional to

$$\sum [\hat{u}_i^2 - \sigma^2] z_i.$$

The moment condition for testing heteroskedasticity in CM tests is

$$\frac{1}{n} \sum [\hat{u}_i^2 - \sigma^2] z_i = 0.$$

Thus, the score test for heteroskedasticity in the tobit model reduces to a CM test.

One can simplify the other derivatives on p. 180 of Maddala (1983) under H_0: $\delta = 0$ to derive the OPG version of the score statistic. However, to get the efficient score statistic we need to evaluate the information matrix under H_0. Orme (1992, 1993a) derives a double length artificial regression for easy computation of the efficient score test statistic in truncated and censored regression models.

An informal Hausman-type test

Hurd (1979) studied the effect of heteroskedasticity on the estimates of the tobit model, but he used only the truncated sample (i.e. zeroes excluded). Brown and Moffitt (1983) investigated the effect of using the full sample. Since the biases found by Hurd were much larger than those they found, Brown and Moffitt replicated their results with the truncated samples and indeed found larger biases. In ratio terms, they found the biases in the truncated estimator to be around ten times larger than the bias in the complete sample. Based on this they suggest obtaining estimates with and without the limit observations. If the underlying distributional assumptions (normality and heteroskedasticity) are correct, the estimates should be close. But if either assumption fails, the difference in the estimates would be large. Hence, one can derive a Hausman type test statistic comparing these two estimators. As discussed in section 4, Ruud (1984) makes a similar suggestion.

4 Tests for Normality and Other Distributional Assumptions

CM tests

As shown by Arabmazar and Schmidt (1982) and Goldberger (1983), nonnormality can produce serious biases in the estimators for the censored and truncated regression models. Thus, testing for normality is very important.

Pagan and Vella (1989) suggest CM tests for normality based on the third and fourth moments of the residuals. With censored regression models and binary choice models, the main problem is evaluating the moments $E[u_i^p | y_i = 0]$. Lee and Maddala (1985, p. 4) give a recursion for the moments of $u_i = (y_i - \beta' x_i)/\sigma$ which is as follows:

$$E[u_i^{p+1} | y_i = 0] = p\sigma^2 [E(u_i^{p-1} | y_i = 0)] - \sigma\lambda_i (-\beta' x_i)^p \qquad (4.1)$$

for $p \geqslant 1$ and $E(u_i | y_i = 0) = -\sigma\lambda_i$ where

$$\lambda_i = \frac{\phi(\beta' x_i/\sigma)}{1 - \Phi(\beta' x_i/\sigma)}$$

and $\phi(.)$ and $\Phi(.)$ are the density function and distribution function for the standard normal. Again, define the indicator:

$$\begin{aligned} I_i &= 1 \quad \text{if } y_i > 0 \\ &= 0 \quad \text{otherwise.} \end{aligned}$$

Then using (4.1) we get

$$\theta_{1i} = E(u_i^3 | y_i) = I_i u_i^3 - (1 - I_i)\sigma\lambda_i (2\sigma^2 + (\beta' x_i)^2)$$

and

$$\begin{aligned} \theta_{2i} &= E(u_i^4 - 3\sigma^4 | y_i) \\ &= I_i (u_i^4 - 3\sigma^4) + (1 - I_i)\sigma\lambda_i (\beta' x_i)(3\sigma^2 + (\beta' x_i)^2). \end{aligned}$$

The test for normality would be based on θ_{1i} and θ_{2i}. This is the method used by Pagan and Vella (1989) and Skeels and Vella (1993a).

To implement these tests we need the residuals. For the residuals, one cannot use $(y_i - \hat{\beta}' x_i)$ because these do not have zero mean.

Correcting it so that they have zero mean, we get the *generalized residuals*

$$\hat{\eta}_i = -\hat{\sigma}(1 - I_i)\hat{\lambda}_i + I_i\hat{u}_i. \tag{4.2}$$

These are the residuals used in diagnostic tests by Chesher and Irish (1987) and Gourieroux et al. (1987). For the probit model, the expected value of the error term is given by

$$E(u_i|y_i) = \phi_i(y_i - \Phi_i)\Phi_i^{-1}(1 - \Phi_i)^{-1}. \tag{4.3}$$

By analogy to this, the generalized residual $\hat{\eta}_i$ for any discrete choice model is defined as

$$\hat{\eta}_i = \hat{f}_i(y_i - \hat{F}_i)\hat{F}_i^{-1}(1 - \hat{F}_i)^{-1} \tag{4.4}$$

Pagan and Vella (1989) suggest using other types of residuals such as Powell's symmetrically censored residuals in specification testing. Powell (1986) developed the symmetrically censored least squares (SCLS) estimator for the tobit model. First he deletes the observations for which $\hat{\beta}'x_i < 0$, and second he sets $y_i = 2\hat{\beta}'x_i$ for all y_i that exceed $2\hat{\beta}'x_i$. The resulting y_i are then symmetrically distributed over $(0, 2\hat{\beta}'x_i)$ and hence the errors $(y_i - \hat{\beta}'x_i)$ are symmetrically distributed over $-\hat{\beta}'x_i$ and $\hat{\beta}'x_i$, and hence have mean zero.

CM tests for normality in the probit model can also be found in Newey (1985, p. 1062). Following Ruud's suggestion, he formulated the distribution function F_i under the alternative as $F_i = \Phi(\mu_i + \gamma_1\mu_i^2 + \gamma_2\mu_i^3)$ where $\mu_i = \beta'x_i/\sigma$. This gives the moment conditions:

$$\frac{1}{n}\sum\hat{\mu}_i^2\hat{u}_i = 0$$

$$\frac{1}{n}\sum\hat{\mu}_i^3\hat{u}_i = 0$$

where $\hat{u}_i$ is given by (4.3).

Score tests based on generalized distributions

The alternative method, followed by Bera et al. (1984), is to construct a score test by nesting the normal distribution in the Pearsonian family, for which the density function $g(u)$ satisfies the differential equation

$$\frac{\mathrm{d}\ln g(u)}{\mathrm{d}u} = \frac{a + u}{b_0 + b_1u + b_2u^2}$$

If u is specified to have a zero expectation, it implies $a = -b_1$. After reparameterization we get

$$\frac{d \ln g(u)}{du} = \frac{c_1 - u}{c_0 - c_1 u + c_2 u^2}$$

$c_1 = 0$, $c_2 = 0$ and $c_0 = \sigma^2$ gives the density of $N(0, \sigma^2)$. Thus, a test for normality is a test for $c_1 = 0$, $c_2 = 0$. As noted by Bera et al. (1984, p. 572), these score tests use estimated third- and fourth-order sample moments of the residuals. Thus, the tests reduce to CM tests, considered by Pagan and Vella (1989).

Lee has extended this approach of embedding the normal distribution in the Pearsonian family to other more complicated models. In Lee (1983), score tests are derived for testing the distributional assumptions (half-normal and truncated normal) used in the estimation of stochastic frontier production functions. The tests are based on the Pearsonian family of *truncated* distributions. The computation of the score test statistics depends on moments of the truncated normal and half-normal. The recurrence relations for this are given on p. 257 of Lee's paper. The tests are based on the third and fourth estimated moments of a certain conditional distribution and comparison of them with the moments of the truncated normal (for the standard normal, the third and fourth moments are 0 and 3 respectively but this is not the case for the truncated normal). In this sense, the tests can again be considered as CM tests. Lee also applies his score tests to data on the Colombian food products industry and Indonesian weaving industry, for which he had previously estimated frontier production functions. The assumption of half-normal distribution was overwhelmingly rejected for the Colombian data but was not rejected for the Indonesian data.

In Lee (1984a), score tests are derived for testing distributional assumptions for the accelerated failure time models. In these models, the hypothesized distribution is not normal. He suggests that for testing any specified distribution, one can transform the distribution to a normal distribution and then test this transformed variable for normality, nesting it in the Pearsonian family using the methods in Bera et al. (1984). Let $\Phi(.)$ be the distribution function of the standard normal and $G(.)$ the distribution function of the error ε_i in the given equation. Then Lee defines $J = \Phi^{-1}G$ as the normalized transform and $u_i = J(\varepsilon_i)$ has a standard $N(0, 1)$ distribution. Next Lee develops score tests for the normality of u_i. For the distributions of ε_i he considers exponential, log normal and two types of gamma distributions. He presents some

Monte Carlo evidence that indicates that the distributions of the score test statistics have longer tails than the corresponding asymptotic distributions and thus tend to overreject the null. But the tests have good power after a size correction in moderate sized samples. The over-rejection problem might be rather pervasive in all these tests considered here, although the evidence is scattered.

The same method of embedding the given distribution in a more general distribution and deriving the score test statistics has been used by Lee (1986) in specification tests for Poisson regression models. He considers the negative binomial, a general family of discrete distributions based on Pearson's difference equations, and series expansions of distributions, and derives the score tests with these distributions as the alternative. He concludes that the score test statistics amount basically to a formal analysis of the residuals from the Poisson distribution. Hence he describes some informal procedures of residual analysis that would provide guidance as to which of these generalizations would be fruitful to pursue.

Smith (1989) suggests the use of orthogonal polynomials (rather than the Pearsonian family) and then construction of a score test for the distributional assumptions. Under very general conditions we can write a given density $h(z, \theta, \psi)$ of z as the product of another density $f(z, \theta)$ with finite moments of all orders and a series of orthogonal polynomials $p_k(z, \theta)$. Specifically,

$$h(z, \theta, \psi) = f(z, \theta) \sum_{k=0}^{\infty} a_k(\theta, \psi) p_k(z, \theta)$$

where $a_o(\theta, \psi) = 1$ and $p_o(z, \theta) = 1$. Smith then constructs score tests for the hypothesis

$$H_0\colon a_k(\theta, \psi) = 0 \quad \text{for } k > 1.$$

Distributional tests for the logit model

A generalization of the logit model is the Burrit model based on the Burr II(k) distribution

$$f(u) = \frac{k \exp(-u)}{[1 + \exp(-u)]^{k+1}}, \quad -\infty < u < \infty.$$

For $k = 1$ we have the $Sech^2$ distribution and the logit model. The density function for the Burr distribution is skewed, unlike the $Sech^2$, which is symmetric. Smith (1989, p. 188) describes a score test for the hypothesis $k = 1$. This is a test for the distributional assumptions of the logit model. Poirier (1980) derived earlier a similar score test.

Hausman-type tests

Newey (1987) considers Hausman-type tests for normality. He considers the model

$$y_t^* = Z_t\delta + \varepsilon_t \quad \text{with } y_t = y_t^* \quad \text{if } y_t^* > 0$$
$$= 0 \quad \text{otherwise,}$$

where Z_t includes possibly some endogenous variables. He considers Powell's (1986) symmetrically censored least squares (SCLS) estimator (this estimator was extended by Newey for the case of endogenous explanatory variables). The test is based on the difference between the tobit MLE, say $\hat{\delta}$, and the SCLS estimator, say $\hat{\delta}_s$. The Hausman test statistic is

$$H = n(\hat{\delta}_s - \hat{\delta})'[V(\hat{\delta}_s - \hat{\delta})]^{-1}(\hat{\delta}_s - \hat{\delta}).$$

One could take $\hat{V}(\hat{\delta}_s) - \hat{V}(\hat{\delta})$ as an estimate of $V(\hat{\delta}_s - \hat{\delta})$ but this may not be positive semi-definite. Newey suggests some alternative estimators, one of which is an OPG version. The tests are also extended to the case of exogeneity.

Newey illustrates his Hausman tests with an example of the determinants of female labor supply taken from Smith and Blundell (1986). The latent variable is y_t^*, the desired weekly hours of work. Details of the data can be found in Blundell and Meghir (1986). The specification tests Newey uses overwhelmingly reject the hypothesis of normality. Adjusting for endogeneity, the test statistics are lower but they still reject normality. It is not clear whether these tests exhibit substantial size distortions like the IM test and hence overreject the null hypothesis. Also, as remarked by Newey, tests for distributional assumptions can be affected by misspecification in the equation of interest (see Blundell and Meghir, 1986).

One question that arises is what we should do if we reject the hypothesis of normality. In this case one would use the SCLS estimator, which is anyway computed by Newey in the process of the Hausman test. Thus, the test statistic in his paper suggests that we should make inferences from the SCLS estimates and not from the tobit estimates. In the case of models with selectivity, one can use semiparametric methods suggested in Cosslett (1991), Newey (1988) and Ahn and Powell (1993). For the tobit model, an alternative to

Powell's SCLS is the Buckley–James estimator. Deaton and Irish (1984) use this in a tobit-type model. This has been also suggested by Horowitz (1986).

The alternative method of testing for normality followed by Bera et al. (1984) is to construct a score test by nesting the normal distribution within the Pearsonian family and applying a score test. This type of test is for a specific alternative, whereas the Newey type test is for an unspecified alternative. Newey argues that it would be interesting to compare the power of these two tests. The score tests for a specific alternative should, of course, be asymptotically more powerful than the general test for that alternative. For other alternatives, there are no explicit score test statistics. But Newey suggests calculating their local power numerically using the results in Newey (1985). Alternatively, one could also ask the question: "For which distribution does the score test coincide with the test based on the distribution robust estimator?" Newey (1987, p. 143) suggests an alternative distribution $g(\varepsilon|Z, \delta, \sigma, \eta)$ for which the score vector for the tobit model at $\eta = 0$ is equal to the first order condition for SCLS.

Ruud (1984) also has Hausman-type tests for specification. For the tobit model, two related estimators are the probit and truncated regression estimators. The probit estimator uses just the sign of y^* and hence estimates only $\gamma = \beta/\sigma$. The truncated regression model is based on strictly positive values of y^*. It gives the ML estimator of β and σ. None of these estimators are robust to departures from normality. However, Ruud argues that the estimators from the three models converge to different values under misspecification and hence one can construct Hausman type test statistics. Let (b, s, c) denote ML estimates of (β, σ, γ), and the subscripts 0, 1, 2 refer respectively to estimates from the tobit, probit and truncated models. Ruud considers the following contrasts:

$$d_0 = (b_0', s_0) - (b_2', s_2)$$

$$d_1 = c_0 - c_1$$

$$d_2 = c_2 - c_1.$$

(Note that for the probit we have estimates of γ only.)

Ruud (1984, pp. 214–15) discusses several problems that might arise in the estimation of the variances of these contrasts. The usual procedure of using $\hat{V}(\hat{\theta}_1 - \hat{\theta}_0) = \hat{V}(\hat{\theta}_1) - \hat{V}(\hat{\theta}_0)$ might not work. Some of these problems have been discussed earlier (in section 2) and hence will not be pursued here.

Score versions of Hausman tests

Ruud (1984, p. 215) discusses several suggestions that have been made in the econometric literature for the computation of score tests analogous to the Hausman tests. For example, we can test whether the first derivatives of the probit likelihood function evaluated at the tobit MLE $\partial L(c_0)/\partial \gamma$ are significantly different from zero. In fact this line of investigation has been pursued in Peters and Smith (1991) who suggest score versions of the Hausman type test considered by Newey. Whereas the test suggested by Newey (1987) involves a comparison of Powell's SCLS estimator and the tobit ML estimator, the test of Peters and Smith depends on computing the tobit ML estimator only and testing whether the first order condition of the SCLS estimator evaluated at the tobit estimates is zero.

Peters and Smith suggest different versions of the Hausman score test statistic (one of which is the OPG version). However, they recommend only the efficient version based on the information matrix, which they simplify (p. 181) using the invariance properties of generalized inverses in Rao and Mitra (1971, p. 21). Peters and Smith argue, on the basis of their Monte Carlo studies, that the score version of the Hausman test performed well and had the correct size predicted by asymptotic theory and in fact, in some cases, had better power properties than the test that Newey considered, which depended on both the tobit and SCLS estimators.

One of the earliest specification tests in the category of Durbin–Hausman tests is the test proposed by Nelson (1981). Nelson's test is based on the random variable

$$\frac{1}{\sqrt{n}}(p - \hat{\Phi})$$

where p is the sample proportion of the nonzero observations, and $\hat{\Phi}$ is the tobit MLE estimate of the probability $I_i = 1$. Lee and Maddala (1985, pp. 10–12) show that Nelson's test is asymptotically equivalent to a score test of the tobit model against the more general Cragg model. Ruud (1984, pp. 237–8) criticizes Nelson's test, arguing that it is a Hausman test that compares the tobit MLE with an unusual, inefficient binary data estimator, not probit. This criticism is also repeated in Pagan and Vella (1989, pp. 5–39). The analysis given in Lee and Maddala clarifies the score interpretation of Nelson's test.

Tests of normality in multivariate models

In Lee (1984b), score tests are derived for bivariate normality in econometric models with selectivity. The model consists of two equations

$$y_{1i} = \beta' x_i + \sigma u_i$$
$$I_i^* = \gamma' z_i - \varepsilon_i.$$

I_i^* is observed only as a dichotomous indicator I_i. $\mathrm{I_i} = 1$ if $I_i^* > 0$ in which case y_{1i} is observed. $I_i = 0$ if $I_i^* \leqslant 0$ in which case y_{1i} is not observed. x_i and z_i are observed for all i. u_i and ε_i have a bivariate normal distribution $\phi(u, \varepsilon)$. Estimation under the assumption of bivariate normality has proceeded by a two-step procedure applied to the equation

$$y_i = \beta' x_i + \rho E(\varepsilon_i | I_i = 1) + w_i.$$

See Maddala (1983, chapter 8).

Lee derives score tests by considering a bivariate density which is the product of a normal density and a series of Hermite polynomials, i.e.

$$f_{u\delta} = \phi_{u\sigma}\left[\sum_{r+\delta \geqslant 3} \sum \alpha_{rs} H_{rs}(u, \varepsilon)\right].$$

Lee derives a score test for $\alpha_{rs} = 0$.

Pagan and Vella (1989, pp. 50–1) argue that a better procedure for testing normality would be to consider the following density, suggested by Gallant and Nychka (1987):

$$f_{u\delta} = \phi\left(\sum_{k=0}^{K} \sum_{j=0}^{J} \alpha_{kj} u^k \varepsilon^j\right)$$

with $\alpha_{00} = 1$. They show, after some simplification, that a test for normality simplifies to adding $(\gamma' z_i)^j \hat{\phi}_i / \hat{\Phi}_i$, $j = 1, 2, 3$ to the two-step estimator and tests whether the coefficients of these variables are jointly zero. This test is much simpler than the one derived by Lee (1984a), which appears to have not been used anywhere. However, Lee (1982b) also suggests adding extra terms like those used by Pagan and Vella in the selectivity model. The motivation is different but the final result is the same.

Smith (1985) also considers the Edgeworth distribution in terms of Hermite polynomials considered by Lee, to test bivariate normality.

Though he presents the score test statistics in a form that can be generalized to multivariate models, his approach is more complicated than the regression approach suggested in Pagan and Vella. Like Chesher et al. (1985), Smith also considers the omnibus test, the IM test, and derives diagnostics not only for bivariate nonnormality but also for bivariate heteroskedasticity and bivariate exogeneity. In a subsequent paper, Smith (1987) extends these results to the case of multivariate simultaneous limited dependent variable models. In this paper he uses the multivariate Edgeworth distribution truncated at the fourth order.

Graphical methods

Chesher et al. (1985) discuss graphical methods for detection of the failure of distributional assumptions. Although less formal than the test statistics, graphical plots can often be very informative. Their procedure consists of taking the residuals $\hat{u}_i$ and computing their empirical distribution function *EDF* using the Kaplan–Meier (1958) method. The visual comparison of this *EDF* with the hypothesized distribution function F is made easier by plotting $F^{-1}[EDF(\hat{u}_i)]$ against $\hat{u}_i$ (in the case of the normal distribution $F = \Phi$). If the model is correct, the resulting plot will be a straight line. Horowitz and Neumann (1989) also illustrate this graphical method.

Goodness of fit tests

In addition to the preceding tests for normality, some more comprehensive tests based on the shape of the entire distribution have appeared in the literature. An example of this is the paper by Heckman (1984), who advocated the chi-square test comparing the actual and predicted fractiles of empirical distribution functions. A more detailed discussion of these tests is in Andrews (1988). For sample selection models one can test for normality but one must use the distribution of residuals after selection.

Data transformations

The tests in the preceding section and this section are for homoskedasticity and normality. If either one or both of these hypotheses are rejected, the question is what to do next. One possibility is to use semiparametric methods like Powell's SCLS method, which is robust to both heteroskedasticity and normality. Another alternative is to try data transformations. One such transformation is the inverse hyperbolic sine (ihs) transformation suggested in Burbidge et al. (1988). It is given by

$$I(y_i) = \gamma^{-1}\log[\gamma y_i + (\gamma^2 y_i^2 + 1)^{1/2}].$$

$I(y_i) \rightarrow y_i$ as $\gamma \rightarrow 0$, and for large values of γ, $I(y_i)$ behaves like $\log y_i$ (see Reynolds and Shonkwiler, 1991). They report how the IM test suggested that there was misspecification with the tobit model, as well as the tobit model with heteroskedasticity, but that it showed no misspecification when the estimation was repeated with the ihs transformation.

5 Tests for Serial Correlation

The estimation of limited dependent variable models gets very complicated if we assume serial correlation in the errors (see Maddala, 1983, p. 185). For instance, for the tobit model, with T observations, the likelihood function involves T-dimensional integrals. There are some special forms of serial correlation where this problem does not arise. For instance, in panel data models with random effects (the equicorrelated case) the likelihood function involves only bivariate integrals. Also, recent advances in simulation-based inference have made estimation of limited dependent variable models with more general serial correlation possible. However, these methods are also complicated to use and hence it is very important to have tests for serial correlation in these models.

Lee and Maddala (1985, pp. 13–17) present a score test for the null hypothesis of no serial correlation against the alternative of first-order autoregressive errors in the tobit model. They show that the test simplifies to a test of the first-order serial correlation r_1 of the generalized residuals (defined in equation 4.2). Since the asymptotic variance of the serial correlation is $1/T$ where T is the sample size, we have the result that Tr_1^2 has an asymptotic χ^2 distribution with 1d.f.

Robinson et al. (1985) consider a more general pth order autoregressive process as the alternative and derive a score test for the hypothesis of no serial correlation. Their test statistic is again based on serial correlations of lag k ($k = 1, 2, \ldots, p$) of the generalized residuals. Their test statistic is:

$$LM(p) = T\sum_{k=1}^{p} r_k^2$$

which has a χ^2 distribution with d.f. p.

Lee (1984c) considers the problem of serial correlation in the disequilibrium model.

$$D_t = \beta_1' x_{1t} + u_{1t}$$

$$S_t = \beta_2' x_{2t} + u_{2t}$$

$$Q_t = \min(D_t, S_t).$$

u_{1t} and u_{2t} have a covariance matrix

$$\begin{bmatrix} \sigma_1^2 & \sigma_{12} \\ \sigma_{12} & \sigma_2^2 \end{bmatrix}$$

and are first-order autoregressive. Lee derives the score test for the null hypothesis of no serial correlation and shows that it depends on estimated residuals $\hat{u}_{1t}$ and $\hat{u}_{2t}$ and their sample autocovariances. Specifically, the score test depends on:

$$c_{1t} = E\left[\left(u_{1t} - \frac{\sigma_{12}}{\sigma_2^2} u_{2t}\right) u_{1,t-1} | Q_t, Q_{t-1}\right]$$

$$c_{2t} = E\left[\left(u_{2t} - \frac{\sigma_{12}}{\sigma_1^2} u_{1t}\right) u_{2,t-1} | Q_t, Q_{t-1}\right].$$

Thus, the errors have to be corrected for the contemporaneous correlation between u_{1t} and u_{2t}. Bera and Robinson (1989) also discuss tests for serial correlation in the disequilibrium model. They consider general autoregressive $AR(p_i)$ and moving average $MA(p_i)$ processes, $(i = 1, 2)$. Subscript 1 stands for u_{1t} and 2 stands for u_{2t}. However, they make the assumption that u_{1t} and u_{2t} are not contemporaneously correlated. They show that the score test simplifies to the same form that was derived in Robinson et al. (1985), namely

$$LM(p_1, p_2) = T\sum_{i=1}^{2}\sum_{k=1}^{p_i} r_{ik}^2$$

which has a χ^2 distribution with d.f. $(p_1 + p_2)$. Here r_{ik} is the serial correlation of order k in the residuals $\hat{u}_{it}$. Note that what we need to compute for $\hat{u}_{it}$ are the generalized residuals for the disequilibrium models. These are presented in Quandt (1988, chapter 4). Bera and Robinson apply their tests to the example of housing starts considered by Fair and Jaffe and reject the hypothesis of no serial correlation.

Hall et al. (1992) consider the problem of testing for serial correlation in an extended disequilibrium model. They consider a model with price adjustment (see Maddala, 1983, chapter 10, for a discussion of disequilibrium models with price adjustment). Their model is:

$$D_t = a_1 P_t + b_1' X_{1t} + u_{1t}$$

$$S_t = a_2 P_t + b_2' X_{2t} + u_{2t}$$

$$P_t = a_3(D_t - S_t) + P_{t-1} + b_3' X_{3t} + u_{3t}$$

$$Q_t = \min(D_t, S_t)$$

and u_t follows a first-order vector error process

$$u_t = Ru_{t-1} + e_t.$$

They develop a score test for the hypothesis $R = 0$. Their test is again based on the estimated serial correlations and cross correlations of the generalized residuals from the disequilibrium model.

Score test for contemporaneous correlation

The preceding discussion also applies to tests for contemporaneous correlation. Consider the bivariate probit model given by

$$y_1^* = \beta_1' x_1 + u_1$$

$$y_2^* = \beta_2' x_2 + u_2.$$

Both y_1^* and y_2^* are observed only as dichotomous variables. u_1, u_2 are bivariate normal with zero means, unit variances and correlation ρ. The computation of the bivariate probit is much more complicated than the single equation probits and hence a test for $\rho = 0$ is worthwhile. (The bivariate probit model is built into packages like the LIMDEP but it has been found to give strange results in some cases.) The score vector for this model is proportional to

$$\frac{\partial L}{\partial \beta_1} = \sum x_{1i}\hat{u}_{1i}, \quad \frac{\partial L}{\partial \beta_2} = \sum x_{2i}\hat{u}_{2i}, \quad \frac{\partial L}{\partial \rho} = \sum \hat{u}_{1i}\hat{u}_{2i}$$

where $\hat{u}_{1i}$ and $\hat{u}_{2i}$ are the generalized residuals defined in (4.3) for the two probit equations. The OPG version of the score test statistic is given by nR^2 from an artificial regression of a vector of ones on ($x_1\hat{u}_1$, $x_2\hat{u}_2$, $\hat{u}_1\hat{u}_2$). Other versions of the score test can also be worked out. One simpler alternative is to compute the generalized residuals, compute their squared correlation r^2, and use nr^2 as χ_1^2.

Kiefer (1982) develops score tests for multivariate probit models.

He starts with a general assumption that the correlation matrix of the errors is R and develops a score test for the hypothesis $R = I$. He also develops score tests to test the hypothesis $\rho = 0$ when $R = (1 - \rho)I + \rho ee'$ where e is a vector of ones. This is the equicorrelated case that occurs in random effects models in panel data. However, he does not simplify his test statistics in terms of generalized residuals.

6 Tests for Selection Bias

Tests for selection bias are among the very first of the specification tests in limited dependent variable models. They were first discussed by Gronau (1974) and Heckman (1979) in the mid 1970s. Heckman viewed the sample selection problem as a bias arising from an omitted variable. The model, in its simplest form, consists of the regression equation

$$y_{1i}^* = \beta_1' x_{1i} + u_{1i} \tag{6.1}$$

and a selection equation

$$y_{2i}^* = \beta_2' x_{2i} + u_{2i} \tag{6.2}$$

y_{1i}^* is observed and equal to y_{1i} only if $y_{2i}^* > 0$. Thus y_{1i}^* is censored by the selection equation (6.2). The tobit model is a special case where the censoring is based on the sign of y_{1i}^* itself.

Since y_{2i}^* is observed only as a dichotomous variable, we normalize equation (6.2) by assuming $\text{var}(u_{2i}) = 1$. We shall assume that

$$\begin{pmatrix} u_{1i} \\ u_{2i} \end{pmatrix} \sim N\left(\begin{pmatrix} 0 \\ 0 \end{pmatrix}, \begin{pmatrix} \sigma^2 & \rho\sigma \\ \rho\sigma & 1 \end{pmatrix} \right).$$

Other nonnormal distributions can be assumed (see, for instance, Maddala, 1983, pp. 267–75; Olsen, 1982) but we shall start with this assumption. The least squares estimation of (6.1) gives biased estimates of β_1 because $E[u_{1i} | y_{2i}^* > 0] \neq 0$. This expression is given by $\rho\sigma\lambda_i$ where

$$\lambda_i = \frac{\phi(\beta_2' x_{2i})}{\Phi(\beta_2' x_{2i})} \quad \text{(see Maddala, 1983, p. 367).}$$

Thus equation (6.1), in terms of the observed y_{1i}, can be written as

$$y_{1i} = \beta_1' x_{1i} + \rho\sigma\lambda_i + e_{1i} \quad \text{where } E[e_{1i}] = 0. \tag{6.3}$$

This shows the nature of the specification error, namely the omission of the variable λ_i. Since λ_i is not observed, Heckman suggests obtaining a preliminary estimate $\hat{\lambda}_i$ based on $\hat{\beta}_2$, the probit estimate from (6.2), and estimating (6.3) by least squares. There is no selectivity bias if $\rho = 0$. Melino (1982) shows that Heckman's t-test for the significance of λ_i in (6.3) is a score test for the hypothesis $\rho = 0$. Thus, it has the same desirable asymptotic properties as the score test.

There are some cases where the two-stage method breaks down. The coefficient of $\sigma\rho$ in (6.3) is not estimable if x_{2i} contains only a constant term (in which case λ_i is constant) or if λ_i is a linear function of the components of x_{1i} (this produces multicollinearity). This occurs if x_{2i} contains only dummy variables and x_{1i} includes the same dummy variables and their interactions. For further discussion of the identifiablity conditions, see Olsen (1980). Little (1985) expresses general concerns about the instability of selection bias estimates from the two-step fitting procedure. These problems can be avoided using the ML method, but this is more sensitive to the distributional assumptions. One major problem with the ML estimation of the selection model has been that of convergence to a local maximum. It has been found that the ML estimates of the selection model using the LIMDEP program are not reliable (see Nawata, 1993a, b). Olsen (1982b) shows that the likelihood function for the selectivity model has a unique maximum, *conditional* on ρ. This suggests that one can get the ML estimates conditional on ρ and scan on ρ. This scanning procedure has been used by Nawata, who shows that it gives more reliable results than the LIMDEP program or Heckman's two-stage procedure.

Distributional tests for selectivity bias

The above-mentioned test considers the effect of a shift in the mean of the error distribution due to selection. Olsen (1982b) argues that some other consequences of selection are that the errors in the sample without the missing observations are heteroskedastic and their distribution is nonnormal. On the other hand, if the errors in the population are nonnormal, then lack of normality would be confused with selectivity bias (and the same holds for heteroskedasticity). Olsen suggests how least squares residuals can be used to test for selection by testing for shifts in their distribution. This is in contrast to the two-step procedures based on shifts in the means. Olsen's method consists of partitioning the sample into two groups, the high probability group and the low probability group, and testing for differences in the distribution of the residuals in the two groups. His tests are based on the predicted behavior of least squares residuals for the two groups if selection is present. Olsen also develops an estimator for the selection model where the population errors are not normal but instead follow a normal-truncated normal convolution.

Score tests for selectivity bias

Even if the error distributions in (6.1) and (6.2) are nonnormal, one can make some transformations to normality (see Maddala, 1983, pp. 272–5). Hence, we shall discuss the score tests for selectivity bias in the context of bivariate normality of the errors in (6.1) and (6.2).

The ML estimation of the selection model is not very complicated. However, it would be interesting to see what the score test is in this model. Lee and Maddala (1985) give a score test for selection bias, but in a more general setting than the case of bivariate normality. Lee and Chesher (1986) discuss the score test for selection bias in greater detail. They also give the information matrix (on p. 124) under the null and hence one can construct the efficient score test statistic rather than the OPG version.

As demonstrated by Melino (1982), the score test statistic for selection bias is asymptotically equivalent to the t-statistic associated with the coefficient $\sigma\rho$ in equation (6.3). Thus Heckman's two-step method of testing for selection bias is asymptotically equivalent to a score test. In cases where the two-step procedure breaks down, the score test also breaks down. Lee and Chesher suggest an "extremum test" as an extension of the score test in cases where the score test breaks down. They call this the generalized score test. This test (p. 139), based on the third derivative of the log-likelihood, is asymptotically equivalent to a test of skewness. This is intuitively appealing because if $\rho \neq 0$, the distribution of u_{1i} conditional on $y_{2i} = 1$ is not symmetric.

We shall, now, discuss the case where (6.1) is itself a probit equation. The usual discussion of selection bias is in terms of a regression equation, that is, where equation (6.1) describes a censored regression model. However, there are many cases where the selection is for a probit or logit model. Olsen (1982a) estimates such a model and discusses its identification. In the case where (6.1) describes a censored probit equation, we observe whether $y_{1t}^* > 0$ or $\leqslant 0$ only when $y_{2t}^* > 0$. The estimation of this censored bivariate probit model is not trivial (since it involves bivariate integrals). The estimation is much more complicated than for the regression model with selectivity we have discussed earlier. Hence it is useful to have a test for $\rho = 0$ in this model because then univariate probit models can be used. Dubin and Rivers (1990) show that under H_0: $\rho = 0$ the scores are proportional to:

$$\frac{\partial L}{\partial \beta_1} = \sum_{i=1}^{n} y_{2i} x_{1i} \hat{u}_{1i}$$

$$\frac{\partial L}{\partial \beta_2} = \sum_{i=1}^{n} x_{2i} \hat{u}_{2i} \quad \text{and}$$

$$\frac{\partial L}{\partial \rho} = \sum_{i=1}^{n} \hat{u}_{1i} \hat{u}_{2i}$$

where $\hat{u}_{1i}$ and $\hat{u}_{2i}$ are generalized residuals for the two probit equations for y_{1t}^* and y_{2t}^*. We defined the generalized residuals earlier in equation (4.3). However, there is an error in the last expression given by Dubin and Rivers. Note that $\hat{u}_{1i}$ is defined only for the observations $y_{2i}^* > 0$ or $y_{2i} = 1$. The correct expression for $\partial L/\partial \rho$ is

$$\frac{\partial L}{\partial \rho} = \sum_{i=1}^{n} y_{2i} \hat{u}_{1i} \hat{\phi}_{2i} / \hat{\Phi}_{2i}$$

where $\hat{\phi}_{2i} = \phi(\hat{\beta}_2 x_{2i})$ with $\hat{\Phi}_{2i}$ defined similarly.

The OPG variant of the score test would involve the artificial regression of a vector of ones on $y_{2i} x_{1i} \hat{u}_{1i}$, $x_{2i} \hat{u}_{2i}$, and $y_{2i} \hat{u}_{1i} \hat{\phi}_{2i} / \hat{\Phi}_{2i}$. Alternatively, we compute, for the observations for which $y_{2i}^* > 0$, the generalized residuals $\hat{u}_{1i}$ and find the squared correlation r^2 of $\hat{u}_{1i}$ with $\hat{\phi}_{2i}/\hat{\Phi}_{2i}$. Then nr^2 has a χ^2 distribution with 1 d.f.

In the case of probit models with selectivity, the above score test for selection bias would be very useful because if the hypothesis $\rho = 0$ is not rejected we do not have to undertake a more elaborate estimation procedure.

CM tests and CML (conditional maximum likelihood) tests for selectivity bias

The conditional moment (CM) tests for selection bias are based on the notion that $E[u_{1i} u_{2i}] = 0$ if there is no selection bias. This moment condition is replaced by $\frac{1}{n} \sum \hat{u}_{1i} \hat{u}_{2i} = 0$ where $\hat{u}_{1i}$ and $\hat{u}_{2i}$ are generalized residuals. However, care should be taken in specifying this moment condition because the summation is over the observations for which $y_{2i}^* > 0$ or $y_{2i} = 1$ (see the equation at the top of p. 9 in Lee and

Maddala, 1985). Thus, the generalized residuals are not the ones given in equations (4.2) and (4.3). Vella (1992) talks at length about the CM test but dismisses it arguing that the Monte Carlo studies in Skeels and Vella (1993a, b) and in Vella (1993) showed their performance to be poor. In any case, since the CM tests are not any better than the score tests and efficient score tests are easily computable, the CM tests are not worth pursuing.

Another alternative is the conditional maximum likelihood (CML) test. The name originates from the papers by Smith and Blundell (1986) and Rivers and Vuong (1988), who use the same technique in tests for exogeneity (these are discussed in the next section). The idea is to write

$$u_{1i} = \lambda u_{2i} + \varepsilon_i$$

where

$$\lambda = \frac{\operatorname{cov}(u_{1i}, u_{2i})}{\operatorname{var}(u_{2i})} = \rho\sigma.$$

Substituting this in equation (6.1) we get

$$y_{1i}^* = \beta_1' x_{1i} + (\rho\sigma)u_{2i} + \varepsilon_i \tag{6.4}$$

This is another omitted variable regression. Now substitute the generalized residual $\hat{u}_{2i}$ for u_{2i} in (6.4) and estimate it by OLS. Smith and Blundell (1986) show that this is asymptotically equivalent to a score test (in the case of tests for exogeneity). This idea has been used by Vella (1992) in tests for selection bias, although in this simple case the test is not different from that based on the Heckman procedure of using the Mills ratio. In more complicated models the CML method is more convenient. Vella (1993) reports that his Monte Carlo studies showed that the CML test performed much better than the CM tests and performed as well as the score test (which is more difficult to compute). However, the derivation of the asymptotic distribution of the CML test statistic is no more simple than that of the score test statistic (this is not presented in Vella's paper but is given in the papers of Smith and Blundell, and Rivers and Vuong for tests of exogeneity).

Hausman-type tests for selection bias

Verbeek and Nijman (1992, 1993) apply Hausman-type tests for selectivity bias in panel data models. In panel data with selectivity, the selection criterion produces unbalanced data with different observations missing in different time periods. From this unbalanced panel data set we can construct a balanced panel data set by discarding all observations for which we do not have complete observations across individuals and time. Verbeek and Nijman consider Hausman-type tests based on the differences between four estimators. These are from the fixed-effects and random-effects models based on the unbalanced panel and the balanced subpanel. All these estimators are consistent under H_0 (that there is no selection) but are likely to be biased with different degrees under the alternative H_1. The argument is similar to that made in Ruud (1984). Unlike the case in the standard Hausman-type tests, these estimators are all inconsistent under the alternative and, in the unlikely case that they all have the same asymptotic biases, the test will have no power. Verbeek and Nijman develop some score tests but these are much more difficult to compute. They also suggest some variable addition tests. Wooldridge (1993) develops several other variable addition tests in the context of testing for selection bias in panel data models. These tests are variants of the CML tests discussed earlier.

What do we do after these tests?

Estimates of selection bias (and the tests as well) are very sensitive to departures from normality (see Goldberger, 1983). The likelihood estimates are in fact more sensitive than the two-stage estimates. To avoid this sensitivity, one could use semiparametric methods discussed in Cosslett (1991), Newey (1988), Ahn and Powell (1993) and Donald (1994). They all allow for unknown distribution of the errors. Ahn and Powell allow for a nonparametric selection equation. Donald allows for heteroskedasticity of an unknown form and a nonparametric selection mechanism. Cosslett (1991) also studies the cost of using the semiparametric methods in a correctly specified parametric model. He reports very encouraging results about the performance of his estimator. He speculates that bootstrap methods might be used to get small sample distributions of his estimator, although their performance remains to be seen.

7 Tests for Exogeneity

In simultaneous equation models involving limited dependent variables, diagnostic tests for exogeneity are performed because under the assumption of exogeneity the estimation of the model is greatly simplified. In the case of disequilibrium models the exogeneity of the price variable is a crucial assumption, because if price is endogenous, we have an equilibrium (simultaneous equations) model. The tests for exogeneity that we shall discuss are concerned with the question of whether some of the explanatory variables in the probit or tobit equations are indeed exogenous. As with the other diagnostic tests, we have to consider the score tests, Durbin–Hausman tests, CM tests and the IM test. The IM test is an omnibus test but it has been decomposed into three components to test for normality, heteroskedasticity and exogeneity (see, for instance, Smith, 1985; Chesher et al., 1985).

Durbin–Hausman tests

Even (1988) adapts the Hausman test along the lines suggested by Nelson for the tobit model. He considers two estimators, the standard probit ML estimator that is consistent and efficient under H_0, and Amemiya's (1978) simultaneous equations probit estimator, which is consistent under H_1 but inefficient under H_0. The problem with this test is that it requires the computation of the more complicated simultaneous probit estimator. The score version of this test, such as the one considered by Peters and Smith for the Newey test, discussed in section 4, would be to substitute the probit ML estimates in the first derivatives (score vector) of the simultaneous equation probit model and test whether the scores are zero. This does not require the computation of the more complicated estimator.

Grogger (1990) considers Hausman-type exogeneity tests for the probit, logit and Poisson regression models by considering the estimation problem in a non-linear least squares (NLLS) framework. For the estimator under the alternative, he suggests using a nonlinear instrumental variable method (NLIV), using as instruments variables w_i that are uncorrelated with the errors but correlated with the endogenous regressors. However, this choice of IVs does not work with limited dependent variable models. The IVs must satisfy stronger conditions than those in the usual regression models (see Weiss, 1993, p. 170).

Rivers and Vuong (1988) also consider Hausman-type tests but the estimator they consider under the alternative, the two-stage conditional maximum likelihood (2SCML), is easier to compute than Amemiya's simultaneous equation probit estimator. Rivers and Vuong argue, on the basis of some Monte Carlo studies, that the 2SCML performs well compared to its competitors. But even this test would have a score version, where we substitute the tobit ML estimates in the score vector for the 2SCML and check whether the scores are zero.

Score tests

Smith and Blundell (1986) consider the model

$$y_{1i}^* = y_{2i}'\gamma_1 + x_{1i}'\beta_1 + u_{1i}$$

$$y_{2i}' = x_i'\pi_2 + \gamma_{2i}' + u_{2i}$$

$$\begin{aligned} y_{1i} &= y_{1i}^* \quad \text{if } y_{1i}^* > 0 \\ &= 0 \quad \text{otherwise} \end{aligned} \cdot \begin{pmatrix} u_{1i} \\ u_{2i} \end{pmatrix} \sim IN\left(\begin{pmatrix} 0 \\ 0 \end{pmatrix}, \begin{pmatrix} \sigma_{11} & \sigma_{12} \\ \sigma_{21} & \Sigma_{22} \end{pmatrix}\right). \quad (7.1)$$

y_{1i}^* is not observed.

The hypothesis to be tested is H_0: $\sigma_{12} = 0$. The method suggested by Smith and Blundell is as follows: Write $u_{1i} = v_{2i}'\lambda + \varepsilon_{1i}$ and substitute this in (7.1). Denote var(ε_{1i}) by σ_{112}. Get a consistent estimate $\hat{\pi}_2$ of π_2 and hence $\hat{v}_{2i}$. This gives

$$y_{1i}^* = y_{2i}'\gamma_1 + x_{1i}'\beta_1 + \hat{v}_{2i}'\alpha + e_{1i} \quad (7.2)$$

Now estimate (7.2) as a tobit model and test the hypothesis H_0: $\alpha = 0$. We can also write (7.2) as

$$y_{1i}^* = \hat{y}_{2i}'\gamma_1 + x_{1i}'\beta_1 + [\hat{v}_{2i}'(\alpha + \gamma_1) + e_{1i}] \quad (7.3)$$

and treat $[\hat{v}_{2i}'(\alpha + \gamma_1) + e_{1i}]$ as the composite error. However, in the presence of censoring, the two methods will give different estimates of γ_1 and β_1.

Smith and Blundell call the two estimators based on (7.2) and (7.3) the conditional and marginal ML estimators. Smith and Blundell show that their test is equivalent to a score test. Note that this test and the following tests all depend on the assumption of normality. One could avoid this by estimating the first equation in (7.1) by Powell's SCLS estimator. See Weiss (1993), who uses the CLAD (censored least absolute derivation estimator).

Rivers and Vuong (1988) consider the same model as Blundell and Smith but in the context of a probit equation. They consider four methods of estimation for equation (7.1): LIML, IVP (instrumental variable probit), G2SP (Amemiya's generalized two-stage probit) and 2SCML (two-stage conditional maximum likelihood), which is the method used by Blundell and Smith. They have detailed discussion of the properties of all these estimators. Next they suggest Wald, LR, and score tests and three Hausman-type tests. The three Hausman-type tests are H_1: for γ_1 only, H_2: for (γ_1, β_1), and H_3: for $(\gamma_1, \beta_1, \alpha)$. All tests are based on 2SCML. H_1 and H_2 did not perform well. Hence they conclude that if the Hausman-type tests are used, they should be based on a test for all parameters in (7.2).

Vella and Verbeek (1993) extend the CML methods of Smith and Blundell, and Rivers and Vuong, to the case of censored panel data. Vella (1993) extends the Smith and Blundell paper to the case where y_{2i} are also censored variables. In this case, instead of $\hat{v}_{2i}$ we have to use the generalized residuals from the tobit estimation of the equations y_{2i}. Vella suggests testing the coefficients of these generalized residuals. He calls this the AV test (the paper does not present the covariance matrix of these coefficients). He presents Monte Carlo evidence that shows that the AV test is as good as the score test (which is more difficult to compute) and that the performance of the CM test is far worse.

CM tests

The CM test for exogeneity is based on the moment condition

$$\frac{1}{n}\sum \hat{u}_{1i}\hat{v}_{2i}' = 0.$$

For $\hat{u}_{1i}$ we have to use the generalized residuals $\hat{\eta}_i$ defined in equation (4.2) for the tobit model and (4.3) for the probit model. Newey (1985, p. 1062) presents the moment condition for the CM test in the probit model, which is the same as the condition above. As described in section 2, the CM test based on the artificial regression will regress the unit vector i on the scores and the matrix of moment conditions (evaluated at the restricted MLEs). However, as pointed out by Pagan and Vella (1989, p. S-44), we need to include the scores from both the fitted equations, i.e. for y_{1i} and y_{2i} in this artificial regression.

However, the simplicity of the CM tests arises from the use of the OPG variant of the covariance matrices and it has been sufficiently documented that this produces tests whose small sample properties are quite different from those predicted by large sample asymptotic theory. As mentioned earlier, Vella (1993) found the performance of the CM tests to be very poor compared with that of the score test and his AV test (details, however, are not presented in his paper).

Tests for price exogeneity in disequilibrium models

Consider the disequilibrium model (see Maddala, 1983, chapter 10).

$$D = X_1\beta_1 + \gamma_1 P + u_1$$
$$S = X_2\beta_2 + \gamma_2 P + u_2$$
$$Q = \min(D, S). \tag{7.4}$$

If price is not exogenous, the model is misspecified. Either we have to assume that it is an equilibrium model (a simultaneous equation model with P and Q $(= D = S)$ as endogenous variables) or we have to supplement the model (7.4) with a price adjustment equation.

Write the reduced form for the price equation as

$$P = W\delta + v.$$

Hajivassiliou (1986) uses essentially the same procedure as that of Blundell and Smith. First, estimate the reduced form for P, get $\hat{v}$ and substitute it in equations (7.4). Now estimate

$$D = X_1\beta_1 + \gamma_1 P + \alpha_1\hat{v} + \varepsilon_1$$
$$S = X_2\beta_2 + \gamma_2 P + \alpha_2\hat{v} + \varepsilon_2$$
$$Q = \min(D, S)$$

Estimate this as a disequilibrium model and test whether $\alpha_1 = 0$ and $\alpha_2 = 0$. A more detailed discussion of this test and a score interpretation of the test statistic can be found in Gourieroux and Laroque (1987).

Other models

Tsurumi and Mehr (1993) consider a different model. In their model y_{1i} and y_{2i} are both censored by a *single* indicator variable I_i. If $I_i > 0$, then both y_{1i} and y_{2i} are observed. Otherwise neither variable is observed. In this model, the exogeneity test is $\text{cov}(y_{2i}, u_{1i} | I_i > 0) = 0$ versus $\text{cov}(y_{2i}, u_{1i} | I_i > 0) \neq 0$. They derive some sampling theory tests and some Bayesian tests for this hypothesis.

Measurement errors and tests for exogeneity

Consider the tobit model

$$y_i^* = \beta' x_i + u_i \quad \text{with } y_i = y_i^* \quad \text{if } y_i^* > 0$$
$$= 0 \quad \text{otherwise.}$$

Suppose x_i have measurement errors. As is well known, this produces correlation between x_i and u_i. In a sense, therefore, test for measurement errors is a test for exogeneity.

The usual problem in regression models is to find instrumental variables z_i which are uncorrelated with u_i but correlated with x_i. However, because of the nonlinearity of the model, this simple requirement for the instrumental variables is not sufficient. Weiss (1993) therefore assumes that the variables measured with error can be represented by a reduced form equation

$$x_i = \gamma' z_i + v_i.$$

Thus, the instruments are related to the variables measured with error via a reduced form equation. This condition is stronger than the usual one based on zero correlation between z_i and u_i.

Since a test for measurement error reduces to a test for exogeneity, we can use the CML procedure of Smith and Blundell (1986). The procedure is: estimate the reduced form by OLS, get $\hat{v}_i$, use it as an extra explanatory variable in the tobit equation and test the significance of its coefficient. Weiss (1993) discusses the estimation problem and tests for measurement error in the context of Powell's censored least absolute derivations (CLAD) estimator. One could also use Powell's (1986) SCLS estimator. These avoid the assumptions of normality and heteroskedasticity that are implicit in the procedures of Smith and Blundell (1986) and Rivers and Vuong (1988) discussed earlier.

8 Tests for Omitted Variables

The effect of omitted variables and the direction of the biases due to the omission of relevant variables in linear regression models are well-known. In the case of limited dependent variable models the formulas for the directions of the biases are somewhat different. Lee (1982a) discusses this problem in the context of a multinomial logit model.

If we want to know whether a variable z_i should be included or not, then a test for the omitted variable can be conducted by adding the variable z_i to the list of explanatory variables and testing whether its coefficient is zero. In regression models, in cases where z_i is not known a proxy to use is $\hat{y}_i$. In the linear regression model since $\hat{y}_i$ is collinear with the explanatory variables, a suggested procedure (this is Ramsay's test – see Maddala, 1992, pp. 477–8 and the references) is to use $\hat{y}_i^2$ and higher powers of $\hat{y}_i$ as proxies. In the limited dependent variable models, because of the nonlinearities, $\hat{y}_i$ can be used as a proxy for z_i. In the case of the logit and probit models we can take $\hat{y}_i$ as the estimate of the prob $(y_i = 1)$, that is $\hat{y}_i = \hat{F}_i$.

The CM test for omitted variables z_i discussed in Newey (1985, p. 1062) depends on the moment condition $\frac{1}{n}\sum z_i\eta_i = 0$ where η_i are the generalized residuals defined earlier in equations (4.2) and (4.4). Gourieroux et al. (1987) derive it as a score test by showing that $\frac{1}{n}\sum z_i\eta_i$ is proportional to the score of the likelihood function with respect to γ in the expanded model

$$y_i^* = \beta' x_i + \gamma' z_i + u_i.$$

As noted by Davidson and MacKinnon (1984), the score tests for heteroskedasticity discussed in section 3 can be easily modified for tests for omitted variables. It can be checked that the second equation in (3.6) and (3.8) involves z_i only instead of $(\beta' x_i)z_i$. Thus, the score test LM_2 can be used with the above modification in (3.7) to test for omitted variables. The artificial regression implied by LM_2 can be simplified as (see MacKinnon, 1992, p. 135)

$$\hat{v}_i^{-1/2}(y_i - \hat{F}_i) = \hat{v}_i^{-1/2}\hat{f}_i(x_i b + z_i c) + \text{residual}$$

where $\hat{v}_i = [\hat{F}_i(1 - \hat{F}_i)]$. After computing preliminary estimates $\hat{\beta}$ of β, we compute this artificial regression and use nR^2 from this regression as the score test statistic.

As mentioned earlier, when z_i is not known, we have to use some proxy for z_i, and one proxy is $\hat{F}_i$. In the case of omitted variables, direct tests are available, by just including the omitted variable z_i or its proxy as an additional explanatory variable, and then testing whether its coefficient is zero. Thus, in this case a simpler procedure is available instead of the elaborate test discussed above.

9 Tests for Stability: The Predictive Score Test

In the case of regression models, tests for coefficient stability form an essential battery of diagnostic tests. In the case of limited dependent variable models, such tests are much less common. Anderson (1987) is a notable exception. He advocates a comparison of the log-likelihood over the sample period with that when the model is fitted with the sample and postsample data. This is in the spirit of Chow's predictive test for stability (incidentally, this is discussed in Rao, 1973, p. 193, under the heading: "The third fundamental theorem on least squares").

In the case of the linear regression model this test can be implemented by the dummy variable method as noted by Salkever (1976). Anderson noted that this dummy variable method can be extended to the logit model but he ran into difficulties in the case of the tobit model and suggested an approximation. Hoffman and Pagan (1989) and Pagan and Vella (1989) suggest the following *predictive score test* and apply it to a tobit model.

Define the sample period as 1 to N and the postsample period as $N + 1$ to $N + n$. Then form the statistic

$$\hat{\tau} = \frac{1}{n} \sum_{t=N+1}^{N+n} \hat{d}_t$$

where $\hat{d}_t$ are the estimated scores. The mean of the postsample scores should be close to zero in the case of parameter stability. The asymptotic variance of $\hat{\tau}$ is $N(1 + k)I_{\theta\theta}$ (see Hoffman and Pagan, 1989), where $k = n/N$. Hence the test statistic will be

$$\frac{1}{N(1 + k)} \hat{\tau}' \hat{I}_{\theta\theta}^{-1} \hat{\tau}$$

which has a χ^2 distribution with d.f. n.

This predictive score test can be applied to any of the limited dependent variable models, estimated by the method of maximum likelihood.

10 Multinomial Logit Model Specification Tests

The multinomial logit model (MNL) is the most commonly used model in discrete choice modeling. It is well known that its main defect is the IIA property (independence of irrelevant alternatives), which states that the ratio of choice probabilities for alternatives j and k should be independent of how many alternatives are offered (the choice set). The multinomial probit (MNP) model does not have this restrictive assumption but it is computationally more complex, although now simulation methods have been developed.

Several tests have been suggested in the literature to test the IIA property. Hausman and McFadden (1984) suggest two types of tests. The first is a Hausman type test that compares the ML estimates from the full model with those from a model with a restricted choice set. The other is a test based on a generalization of the MNL model to the nested MNL model (NMNL). In this case one needs to estimate the more complicated NMNL model if the Wald or LR tests are used. Small and Hsiao (1985) point out problems with both these tests. In the first, the test statistics are sensitive to the choices eliminated, and the difference between the covariance matrices in the Hausman test statistic can be negative definite. With the use of the NMNL model as well, one needs to specify the nesting sequence. They therefore suggest a generalization of a ML procedure (suggested by McFadden, Train and Tye) which makes use of random subsamples to eliminate the asymptotic bias of the ML procedure of McFadden et al. (this is similar to the jack-knife procedure). But this procedure also involves some arbitrariness in dividing up the sample.

Tse (1987) suggests another alternative and a score test for the MNL model, by considering it as a special case of the dogit model. The score test does not involve computations with the more complicated dogit model suggested by Gaudry and Dagenais (1979). Tse also does a Monte Carlo study to investigate the performance of the score test (in terms of size) and its power against the MNP and NMNL. He finds that the score test compares favorably with the Hausman–McFadden tests.

Wills (1987) argues that the basic idea in all the MNL specification tests is to test whether the coefficients of the choice model are constant when there are variations in the choice set. He suggests that classical Wald, LR and score tests can be used for this problem, and using the result in Holly (1982) he shows that the Hausman test for this problem is the same as the classical test.

Chesher and Santos-Silva (1992) suggest testing the IIA property by considering a small-σ approximation to the MNL logit model with random parameters. The conventional MNL model is a special case of this model. This provides a basis for inference when neglected heterogeneity is a possibility for the violation of the IIA property. The attractive feature of this approach is that it provides an alternative way of modelling the discrete choice problem when the MNL is rejected. The test statistic can be computed as a test for omitted variables. Santos-Silva (1992) presents some simulation results about the performance of this test for the IIA property and also an illustration of the use of this model based on the 1980 budget survey from the Dutch Central Bureau of Statistics on private car ownership. This approach to testing the IIA property in the MNL model appears to be very promising.

The test for the IIA property is another example (in addition to the one in the preceding section) where the CM tests cannot be devised because there is no natural way to formulate the moment condition to test the IIA property. On the other hand, the IM test, as interpreted by Chesher (1984) as a test for neglected heterogeneity, can still be used in this case. This is a case where the IM test leads to a useful alternative.

11 Conclusions

This chapter reviews several specification tests in limited dependent variable models under the different categories: score tests, Durbin–Hausman tests, CM tests and IM tests. Overall, the most commonly used tests are the score tests. Though some authors have found it convenient to view all specification tests as CM tests, the CM approach to testing does not appear to be very promising (because of bad performance in small samples), although it is a convenient way of checking the validity of a score test. Very often it involves more tedious algebra and, except for the OPG variant, it is not any easier to compute than the score test. The IM test is also very complicated to use, except again in its OPG version, but this has been found to perform very poorly. In some cases (tests for exogeneity and selection bias) the CML (conditional ML) tests are easier to use than the score tests (and are asymptotically equivalent to the score tests). Hence they can be advocated.

In some cases, like tests for omitted variables, the tests outlined here are not worthwhile because the alternative model is so easy to estimate. At the other extreme are score tests for serial correlation which are of great practical use, because in the presence of serial correlation, estimation of limited dependent variable models is very complicated.

In many practical applications, it would be useful to have some idea of the magnitudes of the (asymptotic) biases caused by the misspecification. Yatchew and Griliches (1985) examine the effects of various types of misspecification (omitted variables, errors in variables, heteroskedasticity) on the maximum likelihood (ML) and minimum chi-square (MC) estimators of the probit model, and derive various asymptotic bias formulae. These are useful both for assessing and interpreting parameter estimates when it is suspected that the model has been misspecified, and for analyzing the power of hypothesis tests. Yatchew and Griliches also suggest a chi-square goodness of fit test and show that it is asymptotically equivalent to the Hausman specification test.

We have not discussed the problems relating to the small sample performance of the score test statistics, and their power. The evidence in this respect is sketchy and lot more work remains to be done. Pagan and Pak (1993, pp. 511–14) have some discussion on these issues in relation to tests for heteroskedasticity.

It is 48 years since the publication of C. R. Rao's seminal paper on score tests. The score principle for generalization of test statistics is becoming more pervasive than ever, and the alternatives have not reduced the usefulness of score tests. It remains, by far, the most commonly used approach to specification testing in econometrics.

Note

I would like to thank Hongyi Li for his assistance in the preparation of this chapter, and Stephen Cosslett, Stephen Donald, Lung-Fei Lee, Randy Olsen, J. Santos-Silva, and Scott Shonkwiler for helpful comments. The usual disclaimer applies.

References

Ahn, H. and Powell, J. L. (1993) Semiparametric estimation of censored selection models with a nonparametric selection mechanism. *Journal of Econometrics*, 58, 3–29.

Amemiya, T. (1978) The estimation of a simultaneous equation generalized probit model. *Econometrica*, 48, 1193–205.

Anderson, G. J. (1987) Prediction tests in limited dependent variable models. *Journal of Econometrics*, 34, 253–61.

Andrews, D. W. K. (1988) Chi-square diagnostic tests for econometric models; introduction and applications. *Journal of Econometrics*, 37, 135–56.

Arabmazar, A. and Schmidt, P. (1982) An investigation of the robustness of the tobit estimator to nonnormality. *Econometrica*, 50, 1055–63.

Bera, A. K., Jarque, C. M. and Lee, L.-F. (1984) Testing the normality assumption in limited dependent variable models. *International Economic Review*, 25, 563–78.

Bera, A. K. and McKenzie, C. R. (1986) Alternative forms and properties of the score test. *Journal of Applied Statistics*, 13, 13–25.

Bera, A. K. and Robinson, P. M. (1989) Tests for serial dependence and other specification analysis in models of markets in disequilibrium. *Journal of Business and Economic Statistics*, 7, 343–52.

Bera, A. K. and Ullah, A. (1991) Rao's score test in econometrics. *Journal of Quantitative Economics*, 7, 189–220.

Blundell, R. (ed.) (1987) Specification testing in limited and discrete dependent variable models. *Journal of Econometrics*, 34.

Blundell, R. and Meghir, C. (1986) Selection criteria for microeconomic model of labor supply. *Journal of Applied Econometrics*, 1, 55–82.

Brannas, K. and Laitila, T. (1989) Heteroskedasticity in the tobit model. *Statistical Papers*, 30, 185–96.

Breusch, T. S. and Pagan, A. R. (1980) The lagrange multiplier test and its applications to model specification in econometrics. *Review of Economic Studies*, 47, 239–53.

Brown, C. and Moffitt, R. (1983) The effect of ignoring heteroskedasticity on estimates of the tobit model. NBER Technical Working Paper, no. 27.

Burbidge, J. B. et al. (1988) Alternative transformations to handle extreme values of the dependent variable. *Journal of the American Statistical Association*, 83, 123–7.

Chesher, A. D. (1984) Testing for neglected heterogeneity. *Econometrica*, 52, 865–72.

Chesher, A. (1985) Score tests for zero covariances in recursive linear models for grouped or censored data. *Journal of Econometrics*, 28, 291–305.

Chesher, A. and Irish, M. (1987) Residual analysis in grouped data and censored normal linear model. *Journal of Econometrics*, 34, 33–62.

Chesher, A., Lancaster, T. and Irish, M. (1985) On detecting the failure of distributional assumptions. *Annales de L'INSEE*, 59, 7–44.

Chesher, A. and Santos-Silva, J. (1992) Discrete choice models without the IIA property. Dept of Economics discussion paper no. 93/12, University of Bristol.

Cosslett, S. R. (1991) Semiparametric estimation of regression model with sample selectivity. In W. A. Barnett et al. (eds), *Nonparametric and Semiparametric Methods in Econometrics and Statistics*. Cambridge: Cambridge University Press, pp. 175–97.

Cox, D. R. (1983) Some remarks on overdisperion. *Biometrika*, 70, 269–74.

Davidson, R. and MacKinnon, J. G. (1984) Convenient specification tests for logit and probit models. *Journal of Econometrics*, 25, 241–62.

Davidson, R. and MacKinnon, J. G. (1989) Testing for consistency using artificial regressions. *Econometric Theory*, 5, 363–84.

Deaton, A. S. and Irish, M. (1984) Statistical models for zero expenditures in household budgets. *Journal of Public Economics*, 23, 59–80.

Donald, S. G. (1994) Two-step estimation of sample selection models. *Journal of Econometrics*, forthcoming.

Durbin, J. (1954) Errors in variables. *Review of the International Statistical Institute*, 22, 23–32.

Durbin, J. A. and Rivers, D. (1990) Selection bias in linear regression, logit and probit models. In J. Fox and J. S. Long (eds), *Modern Methods of Data Analysis*. Newbury Park, CA: Sage, pp. 410–42.

Engle, R. F. (1984) Wald likelihood ratio and lagrange multiplier tests in econometrics. In Z. Griliches and M. D. Intrilligator (eds), *Handbook of Econometrics, volume II*. Amsterdam: North-Holland, pp. 776–828.

Even, W. (1988) Testing exogeneity in a probit model. *Economics Letters*, 26, 125–8.

Gallant, A. R. and Nychka, D. W. (1987) Semiparametric maximum likelihood estimation. *Econometrica*, 55, 363–93.

Gaudry, M. J. I. and Dagenais, M. G. (1979) The dogit model. *Transportation Research B*, 13, 105–11.

Godfrey, L. G. (1988) *Misspecification Tests in Econometrics: the Lagrangian Multiplier Principle and Other Approaches*. Cambridge: Cambridge University Press.

Goldberger, A. S. (1983) Abnormal selection bias. In Karlin, Amemiya and Goodmann (eds), *Studies in Econometrics, Time Series and Multivariate Analysis*. New York: Academic Press.

Gouriéroux, C. and Laroque, G. (1987) Testing price exogeneity in the canonical disequilibrium model. Discussion paper no. 8713, INSEE, Paris.

Gouriéroux, C. A., Monfort, E. R. and Trognon, A. (1987) Generalized residuals. *Journal of Econometrics*, 34, 5–32.

Grogger, J. (1990) A simple test for exogeneity in probit, logit and poisson regression models. *Economics Letters*, 33, 329–32.

Gronau, R. (1974) Wage comparisons: a selectivity bias. *Journal of Political Economy*, 82, 119–43.

Hajivassiliou, V. A. (1986) Two misspecification tests for the simple switching regressions disequilibrium model. *Economics Letters*, 22, 343–8.

Hall, S. G., Henry, S. G. B. and Pemberton, M. (1992) Testing a discrete switching disequilibrium model of the UK labour market. *Journal of Applied Econometrics*, 7, 83–91.

Hall, W. J. and Mathiason, D. J. (1990) On large sample estimation and testing in parametric models. *International Statistical Review*, 58, 77–97.

Hausman, J. (1978) Specification tests in econometrics. *Econometrica*, 46, 1251–71.

Hausman, J. and McFadden, D. (1984) Specification tests for the multinomial logit model. *Econometrica*, 52, 1219–40.

Heckman, J. (1979) Sample selection bias as a specification error. *Econometrica*, 47, 153–61.

Heckman, J. (1984) The chi-square goodness of fit statistic for models with parameters estimated from micro data. *Econometrica*, 52, 1543–7.

Hoffman, D. and Pagan, A. R. (1989) Post-sample prediction tests for generalized method of moments estimators. *Oxford Bulletin of Economics and Statistics*, 51, 333–44.

Holly, A. (1982) A remark on Hausman's specification test. *Econometrica*, 50, 749–59.

Holly, A. and Monfort, A. (1986) Some useful equivalence properties of Hausman test. *Economics Letters*, 20, 39–43.

Horowitz, J. L. (1986) A distribution-free least squares estimator for the consored linear regression models. *Journal of Econometrics*, 32, 59–84.

Horowitz, J. L. and Neumann, G. R. (1989) Specification testing in censored regression models: parametric and semiparametric methods. *Journal of Applied Econometrics*, 4, S61–S86.

Hurd, M. (1979) Estimation in truncated samples when there is heteroskedasticity. *Journal of Econometrics*, 11, 247–58.

Kaplan, E. L. and Meier, P. (1958) Nonparametric estimation from incomplete observations. *Journal of the American Statistical Association*, 53, 457–81.

Kiefer, N. M. (1982) Testing for dependence in multivariate probit models. *Biometrika*, 69, 161–6.

Lancaster, T. (1984) Tests of specification in econometrics. *Econometric Reviews*, 3, 211–42.

Lee, L. F. (1982a) Specification error in multinomial logit models – analysis of the omitted variable bias. *Journal of Econometrics*, 20, 197–209.

Lee, L. F. (1982b) Some approaches to the correction of selectivity bias. *Review of Economic Studies*, 49, 355–72.

Lee, L. F. (1983) A test for distributional assumptions for the stochastic frontier functions. *Journal of Econometrics*, 22, 245–67.

Lee, L. F. (1984a) Maximum likelihood estimation and a specification test for nonnormal distributional assumption for the accelerated failure time models. *Journal of Econometrics*, 24, 159–79.

Lee, L. F. (1984b) Tests for the bivariate normal distribution in the econometric models with selectivity. *Econometrica*, 52, 843–63.

Lee, L. F. (1984c) The likelihood function and a test for serial correlation in a disequilibrium market model. *Economics Letters*, 14, 195–200.

Lee, L. F. (1986) Specification test for poisson regression models. *International Economic Review*, 27, 689–706.

Lee, L. F. and Chesher, A. (1986) Specification testing when score test statistics are identically zero. *Journal of Econometrics*, 31, 121–49.

Lee, L. F. and Maddala, G. S. (1985) The common structure of tests for slectivity bias, serial correlation, heteroskedasticity and non-normality in the tobit model. *International Economic Review*, 26, 1–20.

Little, R. J. A. (1985) A note about models for selectivity bias. *Econometrics*, 53, 1469–74.

MacKinnon, J. G. (1992) Model specification tests and artificial regressions. *Journal of Economic Literature*, 30, 102–46.

Maddala, G. S. (1983) *Limited Dependent and Qualitative Variables in Econometrics*. Cambridge: Cambridge University Press.

Maddala, G. S. and Nelson, F. D. (1975) Specification errors in limited dependent variable models. NBER Working Paper Series no. 96.

Maddala, G. S. (1992) *Introduction to Econometrics*, 2nd edn. New York: MacMillan.

Melino, A. (1982) Testing for sample selection bias. *Review of Economic Studies*, 49, 151–3.

Mukerjee, R. (1993) Rao's score test: recent asymptotic results. In G. S.

Maddala, C. R. Rao and H. D. Vinod (eds), *Handbook of Statistics, volume 11: Econometrics*. Amsterdam: North-Holland, pp. 363–79.

Nawata, K. (1993a) A note on the estimation of models with sample selection biases. *Economics Letters*, 42, 15–24.

Nawata, K. (1993b) Estimation of sample selection biases models. Manuscript, Dept of Economics, University of Western Australia.

Nelson, F. D. (1981) A test for misspecification in the censored normal model. *Econometrica*, 49, 1317–29.

Newey, W. K. (1985) Maximum likelihood specification testing and conditional moment tests. *Econometrica*, 53, 1047–73.

Newey, W. K. (1987) Specification tests for distributional assumptions in the tobit model. *Journal of Econometrics*, 34, 125–45.

Newey, W. K. (1988) Two-step series estimation of sample selection models. Manuscript, Princeton University.

Olsen, R. (1980) A least squares correction for selectivity bias. *Econometrica*, 48, 1815–20.

Olsen, R. (1982a) Independence from irrelevant alternatives and attrition bias: their relation to one another in the evaluation of experimental programs. *Southern Economic Journal*, 49, 521–35.

Olsen, R. J. (1982b) Distributional tests for selectivity bias and more robust likelihood estimator. *International Economic Review*, 23, 223–40.

Orme, C. (1990) The small-sample performance of the information matrix test. *Journal of Econometrics*, 46, 309–31.

Orme, C. (1992) Efficient score tests for heteroskedasticity in micro-econometrics. *Econometric Reviews*, 11, 235–52.

Orme, C. (1993) On the use of artificial regressions in certain microeconometric models. Manuscript, York University, UK.

Pagan, A. R. and Pak, Y. (1993) Testing for heteroskedasticity. In G. S. Maddala, C. R. Rao and H. D. Vinod (eds), *Handbook of Statistics, volume 11*. Amsterdam: North-Holland, pp. 489–518.

Pagan, A. R. and Vella, F. (1989) Diagnostic tests for models based on unit record data: a survey. *Journal of Applied Econometrics*, 4, S29–S59.

Peters, S. and Smith, R. (1991) Distributional specification tests against semi-parametric alternatives. *Journal of Econometrics*, 47, 175–94.

Poirier, D. J. (1980) A lagrange multiplier test for skewness in binary logit models. *Economics Letters*, 5, 141–3.

Powell, J. L. (1986) Symmerically trimmed least squares estimation for tobit models. *Econometrica*, 54, 1435–60.

Quandt, R. E. (1988) *The Econometrics of Disequilibrium*. New York: Basil Blackwell.

Rao, C. R. (1947) Large sample tests of statistical hypotheses concerning several parameters with applications to problems of estimation. *Proceedings of the Cambridge Philosophical Society*, 44, 50–7.

Rao, C. R. (1962) Efficient estimates and optimum inference procedures in

large samples. *Journal of the Royal Statistical Society, Series B*, 24, 46–72.
Rao, C. R. (1973) *Linear Statistical Inference and Its Applications*. New York: John Wiley and Sons.
Rao, C. R. and Mitra, S. K. (1971) *Generalized Inverses of Matrices and Its Applications*, New York: Wiley.
Rao, C. R. and Mukerjee, R. (1993) Tests based on score statistics: power properties and related results. Manuscript, Center for Multivariate Analysis, Penn State University.
Reynolds, A. and Shonkwiler, J. S. (1991) Misspecification and transformation of the tobit model. *Empirical Economics*, 16, 313–23.
Rivers, D. and Vuong, Q. (1988) Limited information estimators and exogeneity tests for simultaneous probit models. *Journal of Econometrics*, 39, 347–69.
Robinson, P. M., Bera, A. K. and Jarque, C. M. (1985) Tests for serial dependence in limited dependent variable models. *International Economic Review*, 26, 629–38.
Ruud, P. A. (1984) Tests of specification in econometrics. *Econometric Reviews*, 3, 211–42.
Salkever, D. S. (1976) The use of dummy variables to compute predictions, prediction errors and confidence intervals. *Journal of Econometrics*, 4, 353–97.
Santos-Silva, J. (1992) The performance of an approximation to a random parameter multinomial logit model. Report AE 16/92, University of Amsterdam.
Silvey, S. D. (1959) The lagrangian multiplier test. *Annals of Mathematical Statistics*, 7, 389–407.
Skeels, C. L. and Vella, F. (1993a) The performance of conditional moment tests in tobit and probit models. ANU, Canberra.
Skeels, C. L. and Vella, F. (1993b) The robustness of conditional moment tests in tobit and probit models. ANU, Canberra.
Small, K. and Hsiao, C. (1985) Multinomial logit specification tests. *International Economic Review*, 26, 619–27.
Smith, R. (1985) Some tests for misspecification in bivariate limited dependent variable models. *Annales de L'INSEE*, 59/60, 97–122.
Smith, R. (1987) Testing the normality assumption in multivariate simultaneous limited dependent variable models. *Journal of Econometrics*, 34, 105–23.
Smith, R. (1989) On the use of distributional misspecification checks in limited dependent variable models. *Economic Journal*, Supplement, 99, 178–92.
Smith, R. and Blundell, R. (1986) An exogeneity test for a simultaneous equation tobit model with an application to labor supply. *Econometrica*, 54, 679–85.
Tauchen, G. (1985) Diagnostic testing and evaluation of maximum likelihood models. *Journal of Econometrics*, 30, 415–43.
Taylor, L. (1991) Testing exclusion restrictions for misspecified tobit model. *Economics Letters*, 37, 411–16.

Tse, Y. K. (1987) A diagnostic test for the multinomial logit model. *Journal of Business and Economic Statistics*, 5, 283–6.

Tsurumi, H. and Mehr, P. (1993) Exogeneity tests in a truncated structural equation. *Journal of Econometrics*, 56, 371–96.

Vella, F. (1992) Simple tests for sample selection bias in censored and discrete choice models. *Journal of Applied Econometrics*, 7, 413–21.

Vella, F. (1993) A simple estimator for simultaneous models with censored endogenous regressors. *International Economic Review*, 34, 441–57.

Vella, F. and Verbeek, M. (1993) Estimating and testing simultaneous equation panel data models with censored endogenous variables. Paper presented at the Econometric Society Meetings, Uppsala, Sweden.

Verbeek, M. and Nijman, T. (1992) Testing for selectivity bias in panel data models. *International Economic Review*, 33, 681–703.

Verbeek, M. and Nijman, T. (1993) Incomplete panels and selection bias: a survey. In L. Matyas and P. Sevestre (eds), *The Econometrics of Panel Data*. Boston: Kluwer, pp. 262–302.

Weiss, A. (1993) Some aspects of measurement error in censored regression model. *Journal of Econometrics*, 56, 169–88.

White, H. (1982) Maximum likelihood estimation of misspecified models. *Econometrica*, 50, 1–25.

White, H. (1987) Specification testing in dynamic models. In T. Bewley (ed.), *Advances in Econometrics*. Cambridge: Cambridge University Press, pp. 1–58.

Wills, H. (1987) A note on specification tests for the multinomial logit model. *Journal of Econometrics*, 34, 263–74.

Wooldridge, J. M. (1990) A unified approach to robust, regression-based specification test. *Econometric Theory*, 6, 17–43.

Wooldridge, J. M. (1993) Selection corrections for panel data models under conditional mean independence assumptions. Manuscript, Michigan State University.

Wu, D. M. (1973) Alternative tests of independence between stochastic regressors and disturbances. *Econometrica*, 41, 733–50.

Yatchew, A. and Griliches, Z. (1985) Specification errors in probit models. *Review of Economics and Statistics*, 87, 134–9.

2 The Optimality of Extended Score Tests with Applications to Testing for a Moving Average Unit Root

Katsuto Tanaka

1 Introduction

The score test was suggested by Rao (1947) and is now in wide use. An exactly equivalent test was proposed by Aitchison and Silvey (1958), now referred to as the Lagrange multiplier (LM) test. The score or LM statistic is essentially based on the partial derivative of the log-likelihood with respect to the parameter vector to be tested, where the derivative is evaluated under the null hypothesis, replacing nuisance parameters by the maximum likelihood estimators (MLEs) under the null.

The testing problem dealt with in this chapter is nonstandard in the sense that score test statistics do not tend to normality. The basic model we are concerned with is

$$y_t = x_t'\beta + u_t, \quad (t = 1, \ldots, T), \tag{1.1}$$

where (i) $\{y_t\}$ is a sequence of scalar observations, whereas $\{x_t\}$ is a $p \times 1$ nonstochastic, fixed sequence; (ii) β is a $p \times 1$ vector of unknown parameters; (iii) $\{u_t\}$ is a normal process specified later with $E(u_t) = 0$. In matrix notation we have

$$y = X\beta + u \sim N(X\beta, \sigma^2\Omega(\alpha)), \tag{1.2}$$

where X is a $T \times p$ $(T > p)$ matrix of full column rank, while α is a scalar parameter to be tested and σ^2 is an unknown scalar parameter. We assume that $\text{cov}(y) = \sigma^2\Omega(\alpha)$ is positive definite and also assume that the parameters α, β and σ^2 are functionally independent of each other.

Our testing problem is to test

$$H_0\colon \alpha = \alpha_0 \quad \text{against} \quad H_1\colon \alpha < \alpha_0, \tag{1.3}$$

or

$$H_0\colon \alpha = \alpha_0 \quad \text{against} \quad H_1\colon \alpha \neq \alpha_0, \tag{1.4}$$

treating β and σ^2 as nuisance parameters. The present problem was considered earlier by King and Hillier (1985), who derived the locally best invariant (LBI) test for (1.3) and the LBI and unbiased (LBIU) test for (1.4) following Ferguson (1967).

We defer the discussion on LBI and LBIU tests until section 2, but an important consequence of their results is that the LBI test for (1.3) is equivalent to the score test, which rejects H_0 when

$$S_{1T} = \frac{\partial L(\alpha_0, \hat{\beta}, \hat{\sigma}^2)}{\partial \alpha} < \text{constant}, \tag{1.5}$$

where

$$L(\alpha, \beta, \sigma^2) = -\frac{T}{2}\log 2\pi\sigma^2 - \frac{1}{2}\log|\Omega(\alpha)| - \frac{1}{2\sigma^2}(y - X\beta)'\Omega^{-1}(\alpha)(y - X\beta), \tag{1.6}$$

$$\frac{\partial L(\alpha, \beta, \sigma^2)}{\partial \alpha} = -\frac{1}{2}\operatorname{tr}\left(\Omega^{-1}(\alpha)\frac{d\Omega(\alpha)}{d\alpha}\right) - \frac{1}{2\sigma^2}(y - X\beta)'\frac{d\Omega^{-1}(\alpha)}{d\alpha}(y - X\beta), \tag{1.7}$$

$$\hat{\beta} = (X'\Omega^{-1}(\alpha_0)X)^{-1}X'\Omega^{-1}(\alpha_0)y, \tag{1.8}$$

$$\hat{\sigma}^2 = \frac{1}{T}(y - X\hat{\beta})'\Omega^{-1}(\alpha_0)(y - X\hat{\beta}). \tag{1.9}$$

As for the LBIU test for (1.4), we consider the situation where S_{1T} becomes constant, which is equivalent to $S_{1T} = 0$, i.e. the log-likelihood has slope zero at $\alpha = \alpha_0$. Since S_{1T} in (1.5) can be rewritten as

$$S_{1T} = \text{constant} + \frac{T}{2}\frac{\hat{u}'\Omega^{-1}(\alpha_0)\dfrac{d\Omega(\alpha_0)}{d\alpha}\Omega^{-1}(\alpha_0)\hat{u}}{\hat{u}'\Omega^{-1}(\alpha_0)\hat{u}}, \tag{1.10}$$

where $\hat{u} = y - X\hat{\beta}$, S_{1T} reduces to 0 if $d\Omega(\alpha_0)/d\alpha$ is a constant multiple of $\Omega(\alpha_0)$. This occurs if $\{u_t\}$ in (1.1) follows an MA(1) process $u_t = \varepsilon_t - \alpha\varepsilon_{t-1}$, where $\varepsilon_0, \varepsilon_1, \ldots, \varepsilon_T \sim \mathrm{NID}(0, \sigma^2)$ and $\alpha_0 = 1$, because

$$\Omega(\alpha) = \begin{pmatrix} 1+\alpha^2 & -\alpha & & 0 \\ -\alpha & 1+\alpha^2 & \ddots & \\ & \ddots & \ddots & -\alpha \\ 0 & & -\alpha & 1+\alpha^2 \end{pmatrix} = \alpha\Omega(1) + (1-\alpha)^2 I_T, \tag{1.11}$$

$$\frac{d\Omega(1)}{d\alpha} = \Omega(1). \tag{1.12}$$

This case will be discussed in section 3.

Another possibility for S_{1T} in (1.10) to be 0 is that $\hat{u}'\Omega^{-1}(\alpha_0)d\Omega(\alpha_0)/d\alpha$ is a constant multiple of $\hat{u}'$. This occurs if $\{u_t\}$ follows an AR(1) process $u_t = \alpha u_{t-1} + \varepsilon_t$ with $u_0 = 0$, $\{\varepsilon_t\} \sim \mathrm{NID}(0, \sigma^2)$ and $\alpha_0 = 1$, and the vector $d = (1, 2, \ldots, T)'$ belongs to the column space of X in (1.2). In this case $\Omega(\alpha) = C(\alpha)C'(\alpha)$, where

$$C(\alpha) = \begin{pmatrix} 1 & & & 0 \\ \alpha & \ddots & & \\ \vdots & & \ddots & \\ \alpha^{T-1} & \cdots & \alpha & 1 \end{pmatrix}, \quad C^{-1}(\alpha) = \begin{pmatrix} 1 & & & 0 \\ -\alpha & \ddots & & \\ & \ddots & \ddots & \\ 0 & & -\alpha & 1 \end{pmatrix}, \tag{1.13}$$

$$\Omega_{jk}(\alpha) = \begin{cases} \sum_{l=0}^{j-1} \rho^{k-j+2l} & (j \leqslant k), \\ \sum_{l=0}^{k-1} \rho^{j-k+2l} & (j > k), \end{cases} \tag{1.14}$$

$$\frac{d\Omega_{jk}(1)}{d\alpha} = jk - \min(j, k), \tag{1.15}$$

$$\frac{d\Omega(1)}{d\alpha} = dd' - C(1)C'(1) = dd' - \Omega(1), \tag{1.16}$$

$$\hat{u}'\Omega^{-1}(1)\frac{d\Omega(1)}{d\alpha} = y'N'(\Omega^{-1}(1)dd' - I_T). \tag{1.17}$$

Here $\Omega_{jk}(\alpha)$ is the (j, k)th element of $\Omega(\alpha)$, I_T is the $T \times T$ identity matrix and $N' = I_T - \Omega^{-1}(1)X(X'\Omega^{-1}(1)X)^{-1}X'$. Thus, if $d = Xb$ for some $p \times 1$ vector b, then we have $\hat{u}'\Omega^{-1}(1)d\Omega(1)/d\alpha = -\hat{u}'$. This case is not discussed in this chapter, but can be found in Nabeya and Tanaka (1990).

In any case, if S_{1T} in (1.5) reduces to 0, we consider a test which rejects $\alpha = \alpha_0$ when

$$S_{2T} = \frac{\partial^2 L(\alpha_0, \hat{\beta}, \hat{\sigma}^2)}{\partial \alpha_0^2} > \text{constant}. \tag{1.18}$$

We shall show in section 2 the LBIU property of the extended score test in (1.18) under the stated situation.

In the next section we first describe the derivation of the LBI and LBIU tests for the testing problems (1.3) and (1.4), and discuss the equivalence with the score tests (1.5) and (1.18) respectively. Section 3 considers the model (1.2) with $\{u_t\}$ following an MA(1) process $u_t = \varepsilon_t - \alpha\varepsilon_{t-1}$ and $\alpha_0 = 1$, where we deal with two cases concerning the initial value ε_0. The one is to assume that $\varepsilon_0 = 0$, while another $\varepsilon_0 \sim N(0, \sigma^2)$. An important feature is that the two cases yield completely different results, unlike the AR(1) process. The score test for the former leads us to the LBI test, the latter to the LBIU test. The limiting local powers of these tests as $T \to \infty$ under $\alpha = 1 - c/T$ with c (> 0) fixed are also computed by specifying the matrix X. These are extended from results obtained by Tanaka (1990), where only the model $y \sim N(0, \sigma^2\Omega(\alpha))$ was considered. Section 4 concludes this chapter by mentioning possible generalizations.

2 Equivalence of Score and Optimal Tests

We first describe briefly how to derive LBI and LBIU tests for the testing problems (1.3) and (1.4), respectively. From (1.2) it can be seen that the present problem is invariant under the group of transformations: $y \to ay + Xb$, $\beta \to a\beta + b$, $\sigma^2 \to a^2\sigma^2$ and $\alpha \to \alpha$, where $0 < a < \infty$ and b is a $p \times 1$ vector. Put $M = I_T - X(X'X)^{-1}X'$ and choose a $T \times (T - p)$ matrix H_1 such that $H_1'H_1 = I_{T-p}$ and $H_1H_1' = M$. Noting that $MX = H_1H_1'X = 0$ and thus $H_1'X = 0$, we have

$$w = H_1'y \sim N(0, \sigma^2 H_1'\Omega(\alpha)H_1). \tag{2.1}$$

The statistic $s(w) = w/\sqrt{w'w}$ is a maximal invariant under the above group of transformations. Let $P(\cdot|\alpha)$ be the distribution of $s(w)$ and $h(w|\alpha)$ the density of w under α in the parameter space, and $\sigma^2 = 1$. Then it can be shown (Wijsman, 1967; Kariya, 1980) that the Radon–Nikodym derivative or the probability density $f(s(w)|\alpha)$ of $P(\cdot|\alpha)$ with respect to $P(\cdot|\alpha_0)$ is given by

$$f(s(w)|\alpha) = \frac{\int_0^\infty a^{T-p-1}h(aw|\alpha)da}{\int_0^\infty a^{T-p-1}h(aw|\alpha_0)da} = \frac{g(w|\alpha)}{g(w|\alpha_0)}, \tag{2.2}$$

where

$$g(w|\alpha) = \frac{1}{2}\Gamma\left(\frac{T-p}{2}\right)|H_1'\Omega(\alpha)H_1|^{-1/2}[\pi w'(H_1'\Omega(\alpha)H_1)^{-1}w]^{-(T-p)/2}. \tag{2.3}$$

The LBI test for the testing problem (1.3) is now derived from Ferguson (1967) as rejecting H_0 when

$$\frac{\partial \log f(s(w)|\alpha_0)}{\partial \alpha} = \frac{\partial \log g(w|\alpha_0)}{\partial \alpha} < \text{constant}, \tag{2.4}$$

which is equivalent to

$$\frac{w'(H_1'\Omega(\alpha_0)H_1)^{-1}H_1'\dfrac{d\Omega(\alpha_0)}{d\alpha}H_1(H_1'\Omega(\alpha_0)H_1)^{-1}w}{w'(H_1'\Omega(\alpha_0)H_1)^{-1}w} < \text{constant}. \tag{2.5}$$

We now show

Theorem 1. The score test in (1.5) is identical with the LBI test in (2.4) for the testing problem in (1.3).

To prove this theorem we need

Lemma 1. Let P and Q be $T \times (T-p)$ and $T \times p$ matrices such that $R = (P, Q)$ is orthogonal. Then, for any $T \times T$ nonsingular matrix A, it holds that

$$P(P'AP)^{-1}P' = A^{-1} - A^{-1}Q(Q'A^{-1}Q)^{-1}Q'A^{-1}.$$

Proof. We first note that the $T \times T$ matrix F defined by

$$F = \begin{pmatrix} P'A \\ Q' \end{pmatrix}$$

is nonsingular, because

$$FR = \begin{pmatrix} P'A \\ Q' \end{pmatrix}(P, Q) = \begin{pmatrix} P'AP & P'AQ \\ 0 & I_p \end{pmatrix}$$

is nonsingular and R is also nonsingular. Then it is sufficient to show

$$F[P(P'AP)^{-1}P' - (A^{-1} - A^{-1}Q(Q'A^{-1}Q)^{-1}Q'A^{-1})] = 0,$$

which is certainly true, and the lemma is established. □

We now proceed to

Proof of theorem 1. We have only to show that

$$w'(H_1'AH_1)^{-1}w = \hat{u}'A^{-1}\hat{u}, \tag{2.6}$$

$$w'(H_1'AH_1)^{-1}H_1'BH_1(H_1'AH_1)^{-1}w = \hat{u}'A^{-1}BA^{-1}\hat{u}, \tag{2.7}$$

where $A = \Omega(\alpha_0)$ and $B = d\Omega(\alpha_0)/d\alpha$. Choose a $T \times p$ matrix H_2 such that $H = (H_1, H_2)$ is orthogonal, where H_1 is the $T \times (T - p)$ matrix defined before. Then, using lemma 1, we have

$$\begin{aligned} H_1(H_1'AH_1)^{-1}w &= H_1(H_1'AH_1)^{-1}H_1'y \\ &= A^{-1}Ny = N'A^{-1}Ny, \end{aligned}$$

where $N = I_T - H_2(H_2'A^{-1}H_2)^{-1}H_2'A^{-1}$. Expressing H_2 as $H_2 = XG$, where G is a $p \times p$ nonsingular matrix, it holds that $N = I_T - X(X'A^{-1}X)^{-1}X'A^{-1}$, from which (2.6) and (2.7) can be easily established by noting that $Ny = \hat{u}$. □

We next consider the LBIU test for the testing problem (1.4), which is derived from Ferguson (1967) as rejecting H_0 when

$$\frac{\partial^2 \log f(s(w)|\alpha_0)}{\partial\alpha^2} + \left(\frac{\partial \log f(s(w)|\alpha_0)}{\partial\alpha}\right)^2 > k_1 + k_2\frac{\partial \log f(s(w)|\alpha_0)}{\partial\alpha} \tag{2.8}$$

for some constants k_1 and k_2. Here we consider only the case where $\log f(s(w)|\alpha)$ has slope zero at $\alpha = \alpha_0$ so that $L(\alpha, \hat{\beta}, \hat{\sigma}^2)$ does because of theorem 1. Then the LBIU test rejects H_0 when

$$\frac{\partial^2 \log f(s(w)|\alpha_0)}{\partial\alpha^2} > \text{constant}, \tag{2.9}$$

which is equivalent, on account of (2.2) and (2.3), to

$$\frac{w'(H_1'\Omega(\alpha_0)H_1)^{-1}H_1'\dfrac{d^2\Omega(\alpha_0)}{d\alpha^2}H_1(H_1'\Omega(\alpha_0)H_1)^{-1}w}{w'(H_1'\Omega(\alpha_0)H_1)^{-1}w} > \text{constant}. \tag{2.10}$$

On the other hand the extended score test in (1.18) rejects H_0 when

$$\frac{\hat{u}'\Omega^{-1}(\alpha_0)\dfrac{d^2\Omega(\alpha_0)}{d\alpha^2}\Omega^{-1}(\alpha_0)\hat{u}}{\hat{u}'\Omega^{-1}(\alpha_0)\hat{u}} > \text{constant.} \tag{2.11}$$

Then the following theorem is an immediate consequence of theorem 1.

Theorem 2. Suppose that the log-likelihood $L(\alpha, \hat{\beta}, \hat{\sigma}^2)$ has slope zero at $\alpha = \alpha_0$. Then the extended score test in (1.18) is identical with the LBIU test in (2.9) for the testing problem in (1.4).

The score test in (1.5) and the extended score test in (1.18) are conducted in the next section to test for an MA(1) unit root.

3 Testing for an MA(1) Unit Root

Let us consider the model

$$y_t = x_t'\beta + u_t, \quad (t = 1, \ldots, T),$$
$$u_t = \varepsilon_t - \alpha\varepsilon_{t-1}, \tag{3.1}$$

where $|\alpha| \leqslant 1$ and $\varepsilon_1, \ldots, \varepsilon_T \sim \text{NID}(0, \sigma^2)$. As for the initial value ε_0, we deal with the two cases. One is to assume that $\varepsilon_0 = 0$, which we call the conditional case, while another, the unconditional case, is to assume ε_0 to follow $N(0, \sigma^2)$ and be independent of $\varepsilon_t (t \geqslant 1)$.

Our testing problem is to test

$$H_0\colon \alpha = 1 \quad \text{against} \quad H_1\colon \alpha < 1. \tag{3.2}$$

Note that $\alpha = 1$ is on the boundary of the parameter space $|\alpha| \leqslant 1$ and thus $\alpha < 1$ is equivalent to $\alpha \neq 1$. In the next subsection we deal with the conditional case and consider the score test which is LBI, while the second subsection deals with the unconditional case for which the extended score test equivalent to the LBIU test is considered. The third subsection computes the limiting local powers of these tests.

Conditional case

The model in (3.1) may be rewritten as

$$y = X\beta + u, \quad u = C^{-1}(\alpha)\varepsilon \sim N(0, \sigma^2(C'(\alpha)C(\alpha))^{-1}), \tag{3.3}$$

where $C(\alpha)$ is defined in (1.13) and $\varepsilon = (\varepsilon_1, \ldots, \varepsilon_T)$. Noting that $\Omega(\alpha) = (C'(\alpha)C(\alpha))^{-1}$ is given by

$$\Omega(\alpha) = \begin{pmatrix} 1 & -\alpha & & & 0 \\ -\alpha & 1+\alpha^2 & & & \\ & \cdot & \cdot & \cdot & \\ & & \cdot & \cdot & \cdot \\ & & \cdot & \cdot \quad \cdot & -\alpha \\ 0 & & & -\alpha & 1+\alpha^2 \end{pmatrix} = C^{-1}(\alpha)(C'(\alpha))^{-1}, \qquad (3.4)$$

so that $d\Omega(1)/d\alpha = \Omega(1) - e_1e_1'$, where $e_1 = (1, 0, \ldots, 0)'$: $T \times 1$, we have, from (1.5), (1.6), and (1.10),

$$\begin{aligned} \frac{\partial L(1, \hat{\beta}, \hat{\sigma}^2)}{\partial \alpha} &= \frac{T}{2}\frac{\hat{u}'\Omega^{-1}(\Omega - e_1e_1')\Omega^{-1}\hat{u}}{\hat{u}'\Omega^{-1}\hat{u}} \\ &= \frac{T}{2}\left[1 - \frac{\hat{u}'C'ee'C\hat{u}}{\hat{u}'C'C\hat{u}}\right], \end{aligned}$$

where $\Omega = \Omega(1)$, $C = C(1)$, $\hat{u} = y - X\hat{\beta}$ and $e = (1, \ldots, 1)'$: $T \times 1$. Thus we have the following theorem.

Theorem 3. For the model in (3.3) the score test which rejects $\alpha = 1$ when

$$S_{1T} = \frac{\hat{u}'C'ee'C\hat{u}}{\hat{u}'C'C\hat{u}} > \text{constant}, \qquad (3.5)$$

is LBI for the testing problem (3.2).

The distribution of S_{1T} in (3.5) depends on X and α because $\hat{u} = (I_T - X(X'\Omega^{-1}X)^{-1}X'\Omega^{-1})C^{-1}(\alpha)\varepsilon$. For α we suppose

$$\alpha = 1 - \frac{c}{T}, \quad c > 0, \qquad (3.6)$$

and consider the limiting distribution of S_{1T} as $T \to \infty$ under (3.6). For X we consider case 1: $X = 0$, case 2: $X = e$, case 3: $X = d$, and case 4: $X = (e, d)$, where $e = (1, \ldots, 1)'$: $T \times 1$ and $d = (1, 2, \ldots, T)'$. For these cases it can be checked easily that $\hat{u}'C'C\hat{u}'/(T\sigma^2)$ converges in probability to 1 as $T \to \infty$ under (3.6). Thus we concentrate on the behavior of the numerator of S_{1T} in (3.5).

Case 1: $X = 0$. We put $S_{1T}(1) = u'C'ee'Cu/u'C'Cu$, where $u = C^{-1}(\alpha)\varepsilon$. Then we have, from (1.13),

$$\frac{1}{T}e'CC^{-1}(\alpha)(C^{-1}(\alpha))'C'e \to \frac{3 + 3c + c^2}{3} = a_1$$

so that

$$S_{1T}(1) \to a_1\chi^2(1), \tag{3.7}$$

where $\chi^2(1)$ is a χ^2 distribution with one degree of freedom.

Case 2: $X = e$. We consider $S_{1T}(2) = 4 \times \hat{u}'C'ee'C\hat{u}/\hat{u}'C'C\hat{u}$, where $\hat{u} = NC^{-1}(\alpha)\varepsilon$ and $N = I_T - e(e'\Omega^{-1}e)^{-1}e'\Omega^{-1}$. It holds, because of the definition of $\Omega = \Omega(1)$ in (3.4), that

$$\frac{4}{T}e'CNC^{-1}(\alpha)(C^{-1}(\alpha))'N'C'e \to \frac{60 + 15c + 2c^2}{60} = a_2$$

so that

$$S_{1T}(2) \to a_2\chi^2(1). \tag{3.8}$$

Case 3: $X = d$. We consider $S_{1T}(3) = 9 \times \hat{u}'C'ee'C\hat{u}/(4 \times \hat{u}'C'C\hat{u})$, where $\hat{u} = NC^{-1}(\alpha)\varepsilon$ and $N = I_T - d(d'\Omega^{-1}d)^{-1}d'\Omega^{-1}$. It can be shown that

$$S_{1T}(3) \to \frac{126 + 56c + 9c^2}{126}\chi^2(1) = a_3\chi^2(1). \tag{3.9}$$

Case 4: $X = (e, d)$. We consider $S_{1T}(4) = 9 \times \hat{u}'C'ee'C\hat{u}/\hat{u}'C'C\hat{u}$, where $\hat{u} = NC^{-1}(\alpha)\varepsilon$ and $N = I_T - X(X'\Omega^{-1}X)^{-1}X'\Omega^{-1}$. It can be shown that

$$S_{1T}(4) \to \frac{315 + 35c + 3c^2}{315}\chi^2(1) = a_4\chi^2(1). \tag{3.10}$$

In all the cases considered above the statistics $S_{1T}(j)$ $(j = 1, 2, 3, 4)$ follow $\chi^2(1)$ asymptotically under H_0. The limiting powers under $\alpha = 1 - c/T$ can be easily computed from the above results, which will be reported later.

Unconditional case

In the present case the model in (3.1) may be rewritten as

$$y = X\beta + u, \quad u = D(\alpha)\varepsilon^* \sim N(0, \sigma^2\Omega(\alpha)), \tag{3.11}$$

where $\Omega(\alpha)$ is defined in (11), $\varepsilon^* = (\varepsilon_0, \varepsilon')'$: $(T + 1) \times 1$ and $D(\alpha)$ is a $T \times (T + 1)$ matrix defined by

$$D(\alpha) = \begin{pmatrix} -\alpha & 1 & & & & \\ & -\alpha & 1 & & 0 & \\ & & \cdot & \cdot & & \\ & & & \cdot & \cdot & \\ 0 & & & & \cdot & \cdot \\ & & & & -\alpha & 1 \end{pmatrix} = (-\alpha e_1,\ C^{-1}(\alpha)). \quad (3.12)$$

It can be easily checked that

$$\frac{\partial L(1, \hat{\beta}, \hat{\sigma}^2)}{\partial \alpha} = 0$$

so that we consider the extended score test in (2.11). Noting that $d^2\Omega(1)/d\alpha^2 = 2I_T$ and

$$\begin{aligned} \Omega^{-1}(1) &= [(C'C)^{-1} + e_1 e_1']^{-1} \\ &= C'\tilde{M}C, \end{aligned}$$

where $\tilde{M} = I_T - ee'/(T + 1)$, we have

$$\frac{\partial^2 L(1, \hat{\beta}, \hat{\sigma}^2)}{\partial \alpha^2} = T\frac{\hat{u}'\Omega^{-2}\hat{u}}{\hat{u}'\Omega^{-1}\hat{u}} = T\frac{\hat{u}'(C'\tilde{M}C)^2\hat{u}}{\hat{u}'C'\tilde{M}C\hat{u}},$$

where $\Omega = \Omega(1)$. Then we obtain the following theorem.

Theorem 4. For the model in (3.11) the extended score test which rejects $\alpha = 1$ when

$$S_{2T} = \frac{1}{T}\frac{\hat{u}'\Omega^{-2}\hat{u}}{\hat{u}'\Omega^{-1}\hat{u}} = \frac{1}{T}\frac{\hat{u}'(C'\tilde{M}C)^2\hat{u}}{\hat{u}'C'\tilde{M}C\hat{u}} > \text{constant}, \quad (3.13)$$

is LBIU for the testing problem (3.2).

Let us derive the limiting distribution of S_{2T} in (3.13) as $T \to \infty$ under (3.6) for the same cases of X as were considered above (p. 57). For these cases it can be shown that $\hat{u}'\Omega^{-1}\hat{u}/(T\sigma^2)$ converges in probability to 1 and that $\hat{u}'\Omega^{-2}\hat{u}/(T^2\sigma^2)$ converges to a nondegenerate distribution. To see this last statement note that

$$\begin{aligned} \Omega(\alpha) &= \alpha\Omega + (1 - \alpha)^2 I_T, \\ \Omega^{-1}N &= \Omega^{-1} - \Omega^{-1}X(X'\Omega^{-1}X)^{-1}X'\Omega^{-1} = B, \\ \Omega^{-1}N\Omega N'\Omega^{-1} &= B, \end{aligned} \quad (3.14)$$

and thus we have

$$\begin{aligned}\mathcal{L}(\hat{u}'\Omega^{-2}\hat{u}) &= \mathcal{L}(\varepsilon^{*\prime}D'(\alpha)N'\Omega^{-2}ND(\alpha)\varepsilon^{*}) \\ &= \mathcal{L}(\varepsilon'\Omega^{-1}N\Omega(\alpha)N'\Omega^{-1}\varepsilon) \\ &= \mathcal{L}(\varepsilon'[\alpha B + (1-\alpha)^2B^2]\varepsilon),\end{aligned}$$

where $\mathcal{L}(X)$ denotes the probability law of X.

Invoking arguments in Tanaka (1990), it can be shown that

$$\mathcal{L}\left(\frac{1}{T^2\sigma^2}\hat{u}'\Omega^{-2}\hat{u}\right) \to \mathcal{L}\left(\sum_{n=1}^{\infty}\left(\frac{1}{\lambda_n} + \frac{c^2}{\lambda_n^2}\right)\xi_n^2\right), \tag{3.15}$$

where $\{\xi_n\} \sim \text{NID}(0, 1)$ and $0 < \lambda_1 < \lambda_2 < \ldots$ are the eigenvalues of the integral equation

$$f(t) = \lambda\int_0^1 K(s, t)f(s)ds \tag{3.16}$$

for $f(t)$ and λ. Here $K(s, t)$ is a uniform limit of B/T, with B defined in (3.14), in the sense that

$$\lim_{T\to\infty}\max_{j,k}\left|K\left(\frac{j}{T}, \frac{k}{T}\right) - \frac{1}{T}B_{jk}\right| = 0,$$

where B_{jk} is the (j, k)th element of B. Moreover, the limiting characteristic function (c.f.) $\phi(\theta)$ of (3.15) is given by

$$\phi(\theta) = [D(i\theta + \sqrt{-\theta^2 + 2ic^2\theta})\,D(i\theta - \sqrt{-\theta^2 + 2ic^2\theta})]^{-1/2}, \tag{3.17}$$

where $D(\lambda)$ is the Fredholm determinant associated with the kernel $K(s, t)$ in (3.16). More specifically, for each of the four cases of X considered above, we have the following kernels $K_j(s, t)$ and Fredholm determinants $D_j(\lambda)$ associated with the limiting distributions of $S_{2T}(j)$ $(j = 1, 2, 3, 4)$, where S_{2T} is defined in (3.13). For the derivation of $K_j(s, t)$ and $D_j(\lambda)$ see Nabeya and Tanaka (1988).

Case 1: $X = 0$.

$$K_1(s, t) = \min(s, t) - st,$$

$$D_1(\lambda) = \frac{\sin\sqrt{\lambda}}{\sqrt{\lambda}}.$$

Case 2: $X = e$.

$$K_2(s, t) = \min(s, t) - st - 3st(1-s)(1-t),$$

$$D_2(\lambda) = \frac{12}{\lambda^2}(2 - \sqrt{\lambda}\sin\sqrt{\lambda} - 2\cos\sqrt{\lambda}).$$

Case 3: $X = d$.

$$K_3(s, t) = \min(s, t) - st - \frac{5}{4}st(1 - s^2)(1 - t^2),$$

$$D_3(\lambda) = \frac{45}{\lambda^3}\left(\sqrt{\lambda}\left(1 - \frac{\lambda}{3}\right)\sin\sqrt{\lambda} - \lambda\cos\sqrt{\lambda}\right).$$

Case 4: $X = (e, d)$.

$$K_4(s, t) = \min(s, t) - 9st - 48s^2t^2 - 20s^3t^3 + 18st(s + t) - 10st(s^2 + t^2) + 30s^2t^2(s + t),$$

$$D_4(\lambda) = \frac{8640}{\lambda^4}\left(2 + \frac{\lambda}{3} + \sqrt{\lambda}\left(-2 + \frac{\lambda}{12}\right)\sin\sqrt{\lambda} + \left(-2 + \frac{2\lambda}{3}\right)\cos\sqrt{\lambda}\right).$$

The limiting powers of the extended score tests for the above four cases can be computed by inverting the c.f. $\phi_j(\theta)$ defined in (3.17) with D replaced by D_j ($j = 1, 2, 3, 4$), which will be reported in the next subsection.

Computation of limiting local powers

Let $F_{jk}(x; c)$ be the limit of $P(S_{kT}(j) \leqslant x)$ as $T \to \infty$ under $\alpha = 1 - c/T$ ($j = 1, 2, 3, 4$; $k = 1, 2$). Let $x_{jk}(\gamma)$ be the upper 100γ percent point of $F_{jk}(x; 0)$, i.e. $1 - F_{jk}(x_{jk}(\gamma); 0) = \gamma$. Then the limiting local powers at the 100γ percent significance level is computed as $1 - F_{jk}(x_{jk}(\gamma); c)$. More specifically we have

$$F_{j1}(x; c) = P\left(\chi_1^2 \leqslant \frac{x}{a_j}\right), \quad (j = 1, 2, 3, 4),$$

where $\chi_1^2 \sim \chi^2(1)$ and

$$F_{j2}(x; c) = \frac{1}{\pi}\int_0^\infty \mathrm{Re}\left[\frac{1 - e^{-i\theta x}}{i\theta}\phi_j(\theta)\right]d\theta, \quad (j = 1, 2, 3, 4).$$

Table 2.1 reports limiting local powers under various values of γ and c together with significance points $x_{jk}(\gamma)$. It may be concluded from the table that

1 Powers increase as c becomes large.
2 Powers decrease as regressors are added to the model.
3 For $j = 2$ and 3, i.e. for the models with $X = e$ and d, the powers are higher for $j = 3$ in the conditional case ($k = 1$), while those are comparable in the unconditional case ($k = 2$);
4 The power behavior as a function of c is different between the

Table 2.1 Limiting local powers of score tests

	(j, k)	$x_{jk}(\gamma)$	$c = 1$	2	5	10	20	50	60
$\gamma = 0.01$									
	(1, 1)	6.6349	0.0917	0.2159	0.4963	0.6989	0.8357	0.9310	0.9422
	(2, 1)	6.6349	0.0230	0.0439	0.1424	0.3244	0.5580	0.7935	0.8252
	(3, 1)	6.6349	0.0364	0.0807	0.2497	0.4678	0.6779	0.8561	0.8787
	(4, 1)	6.6349	0.0150	0.0218	0.0544	0.1411	0.3314	0.6402	0.6909
	(1, 2)	0.7435	0.0141	0.0301	0.1772	0.4742	0.7810	0.9768	0.9880
	(2, 2)	0.2177	0.0110	0.0143	0.0476	0.2089	0.6027	0.9660	0.9848
	(3, 2)	0.2472	0.0112	0.0151	0.0549	0.2295	0.6085	0.9622	0.9824
	(4, 2)	0.1205	0.0105	0.0121	0.0265	0.1085	0.4452	0.9445	0.9758
$\gamma = 0.05$									
	(1, 1)	3.8415	0.1995	0.3464	0.6047	0.7685	0.8746	0.9475	0.9560
	(2, 1)	3.8415	0.0836	0.1251	0.2643	0.4534	0.6558	0.8421	0.8665

	(3, 1)	3.8415	0.1114	0.1838	0.3811	0.5807	0.7520	0.8903	0.9075
	(4, 1)	3.8415	0.0641	0.0808	0.1433	0.2628	0.4598	0.7221	0.7622
	(1, 2)	0.4614	0.0620	0.0994	0.3110	0.6106	0.8665	0.9909	0.9959
	(2, 2)	0.1479	0.0531	0.0629	0.1369	0.3671	0.7477	0.9873	0.9951
	(3, 2)	0.1642	0.0536	0.0649	0.1486	0.3862	0.7508	0.9859	0.9944
	(4, 2)	0.0860	0.0516	0.0566	0.0946	0.2415	0.6217	0.9782	0.9919
$\gamma = 0.1$	(1, 1)	2.7055	0.2816	0.4294	0.6640	0.8049	0.8947	0.9559	0.9631
	(2, 1)	2.7055	0.1465	0.1981	0.3489	0.5292	0.7083	0.8672	0.8878
	(3, 1)	2.7055	0.1816	0.2647	0.4623	0.6429	0.7908	0.9078	0.9224
	(4, 1)	2.7055	0.1202	0.1429	0.2194	0.3473	0.5351	0.7653	0.7995
	(1, 2)	0.3473	0.1174	0.1674	0.4019	0.6880	0.9061	0.9953	0.9980
	(2, 2)	0.1192	0.1048	0.1191	0.2169	0.4695	0.8162	0.9933	0.9976
	(3, 2)	0.1305	0.1055	0.1219	0.2301	0.4868	0.8190	0.9926	0.9973
	(4, 2)	0.0715	0.1025	0.1100	0.1639	0.3411	0.7127	0.9881	0.9960

conditional and unconditional cases. The powers are higher in the former when c is small, i.e. the alternative is close to the null, while the relationship is reversed as c becomes large, i.e. the alternative goes away from the null.

We note in passing that the limiting local powers can be used as a good approximation to the finite sample powers with the same value of $c = T(1 - \alpha)$ as was reported in Tanaka (1990).

4 Concluding Remarks

The model we have dealt with is the regression model in (1.2), where the covariance matrix of the error term is $\sigma^2\Omega(\alpha)$. We can extend the problem by considering a more general covariance matrix $\sigma^2\Omega(\alpha, \delta)$, say. This includes the case where the error process follows an ARMA process. Tanaka (1990) and Saikkonen and Luukkonen (1991) have considered this generalization for case 1, though the score tests do not enjoy the LBI or LBIU property under finite samples. We can also generalize the MA(1) unit root test to the seasonal MA(m) unit root test, where the error process follows $u_t = \varepsilon_t - \alpha_m\varepsilon_{t-m}$. The model may also be interpreted as a cross-section time-series model, and the analysis will be parallel to the MA(1) unit root test.

References

Aitchison, J. and Silvey, S. D. (1958) Maximum-likelihood estimation of parameters subject to restraints. *Annals of Mathematical Statistics*, 29, 813–28.

Ferguson, T. S. (1967) *Mathematical Statistics: a Decision Theoretic Approach*. New York: Academic Press.

Kariya, T. (1980) Locally robust tests for serial correlation in least squares regression. *Annals of Statistics*, 8, 1065–70.

King, M. L. and Hillier, G. H. (1985) Locally best invariant tests of the error covariance matrix of the linear regression model. *Journal of the Royal Statistical Society*, B, 47, 98–102.

Nabeya, S. and Tanaka, K. (1988) Asymptotic theory of a test for the constancy of regression coefficients against the random walk alternative. *Annals of Statistics*, 16, 218–35.

Nabeya, S. and Tanaka, K. (1990) Limiting power of unit-root tests in time-series regression. *Journal of Econometrics*, 46, 247–71.

Rao, C. R. (1947) Large sample tests of statistical hypotheses concerning several parameters with applications to problems of estimation. *Proceedings of Cambridge Philosophical Society*, 44, 50–7.

Saikkonen, P. and Luukkonen, R. (1993) Testing for a moving average unit root in autoregressive integrated moving average models. *Journal of the American Statistical Association*, 88, 596–601.

Tanaka, K. (1990) Testing for a moving average unit root. *Econometric Theory*, 6, 433–44.

Wijsman, R. A. (1967) Cross-sections of orbits and their application to densities of maximal invariants. *Proceedings of the Fifth Berkeley Symposium on Mathematical Statistics and Probability*, 1, 389–400.

3 Score Diagnostics for Linear Models Estimated by Two Stage Least Squares

Jeffrey M. Wooldridge

1 Introduction

Rao's (1947) score test has been a workhorse in the specification testing literature in econometrics. MacKinnon's (1992) recent extensive survey is a testament to the applications and extensions of the score principle in a variety of economic settings. Some of these extensions are to situations where a model does not entirely specify a distribution. The score principle is still applicable in such cases but the actual calculation of the test statistic often needs to be modified. One area that has not been covered exhaustively is the application of the score principle to models with endogenous explanatory variables. MacKinnon (1992) summarizes the case of testing for exclusion restrictions where the same set of instruments is used under the null and alternative models.

Specification tests for more general situations often arise in practice, especially in time series applications. In addition, the often maintained assumptions of fixed or strictly exogenous instruments, homoskedasticity of the errors, and the absence of serial correlation are often untenable. The purpose of this chapter is to give a detailed treatment of the score principle in possibly dynamic linear models estimated by two stage least squares (2SLS). The framework here allows for instruments that are not strictly exogenous, for misspecification indicators that are not linear functions of the null instruments, and for errors that are not assumed to be independent and identically distributed or even uncorrelated. This allows for simple robust tests of endogeneity, serial correlation, overidentification, nonlinearities, and other tests that are common in econometric applications.

2 Model, Assumptions, and Robust Standard Errors

Let $\{(\mathbf{w}_t, \mathbf{x}_t, y_t)$: $t = 1, 2, \ldots)$ be a strictly stationary, weakly dependent time series, where $\mathbf{w}_t$ is a $1 \times L$ vector, $\mathbf{x}_t$ is a $1 \times K$ vector, and y_t is a scalar. A special case is when the observations are independent and identically distributed. As is usual in contexts with weakly dependent data, the assumption of strict stationarity is for convenience only. The following procedures can be applied to heterogeneous data, and even to data with deterministic polynomial trends and deterministic seasonality; one would simply augment the explanatory variables, the instruments, or both with time trends and seasonal dummies wherever appropriate. For notational simplicity these possibilities are not made explicit.

Interest lies in the linear model

$$y_t = \beta_1 x_{t1} + \beta_2 x_{t2} + \ldots + \beta_K x_{tK} + u_t = \mathbf{x}_t\beta + u_t,\ t = 1, 2, \ldots \tag{2.1}$$

where β is a $K \times 1$ vector to be estimated and $\{u_t$: $t = 1, 2, \ldots\}$ is the sequence of unobserved disturbances. Typically, the first element of $\mathbf{x}_t$ is unity to allow for a nonzero intercept. Throughout we assume that all random variables have at least finite second moments.

We analyze model (2.1) under the orthogonality assumption.

Assumption A.1 $E(\mathbf{w}_t' u_t) = 0.$ □

This allows some or all of the elements of $\mathbf{x}_t$, for whatever reason, to be correlated with u_t. Generally the set of instrumental variables $\mathbf{w}_t$ and the explanatory variables $\mathbf{x}_t$ can overlap; for example, usually $\mathbf{x}_t$ and $\mathbf{w}_t$ have at least unity in common. The case $\mathbf{w}_t \equiv \mathbf{x}_t$ is a special case and so the analysis is valid for OLS when $\mathbf{x}_t$ can be treated as orthogonal to u_t.

A sufficient condition for assumption A.1 is the zero conditional mean assumption

$$E(u_t|\mathbf{w}_t) = 0. \tag{2.2}$$

Much of the time we are willing to assume (2.2) if we are willing to assume (2.1), but not always. Tests for nonlinearities necessarily maintain (2.2) under H_0, something we turn to in the examples section. Because A.1 is weaker than (2.2) we adopt it for the general analysis.

Under A.1, the two stage least squares estimator of β is consistent and $\sqrt{T}$-asymptotically normal under an identification assumption and weak regularity conditions (see, for example, White, 1984). The identification condition with strictly stationary data is

Assumption A.2 Let $\mathbf{x}_t^* \equiv L(\mathbf{x}_t|\mathbf{w}_t) = \mathbf{w}_t\Pi$, where $\Pi \equiv [E(\mathbf{w}_t'\mathbf{w}_t)]^{-1}E(\mathbf{w}_t'\mathbf{x}_t)$, and $L(\mathbf{x}|\mathbf{w})$ denotes the linear projection of $\mathbf{x}$ onto $\mathbf{w}$. Then

$$\mathbf{A} \equiv E(\mathbf{x}_t^{*\prime}\mathbf{x}_t^*) \tag{2.3}$$

is positive definite, that is, rank $\mathbf{A} = K$. □

Assumption A.2 is the standard rank condition for identification of β in equation (2.1). Necessary is the order condition $L \geqslant K$. When $\mathbf{x}_t$ is exogenous, so that $\mathbf{x}_t^* = \mathbf{w}_t = \mathbf{x}_t$, A.2 reduces to the ordinary least squares identification assumption rank $E(\mathbf{x}_t'\mathbf{x}_t) = K$.

Recall that the 2SLS estimator of β can be expressed as

$$\hat{\beta} \equiv \left(\sum_{t=1}^{T} \hat{\mathbf{x}}_t'\hat{\mathbf{x}}_t\right)^{-1}\left(\sum_{t=1}^{T} \hat{\mathbf{x}}_t' y_t\right)$$

$$= \beta + \left(T^{-1}\sum_{t=1}^{T} \hat{\mathbf{x}}_t'\hat{\mathbf{x}}_t\right)^{-1}\left(T^{-1}\sum_{t=1}^{T} \hat{\mathbf{x}}_t' u_t\right) \tag{2.4}$$

where $\hat{\mathbf{x}}_t \equiv \mathbf{w}_t\hat{\Pi}$ is the $1 \times K$ vector of fitted value for observation t from the first-stage regression

$$\mathbf{x}_t \quad \text{on} \quad \mathbf{w}_t, \quad t = 1, \ldots, T. \tag{2.5}$$

Under A.1 and A.2, finite second moment assumptions, and general weak dependence requirements,

$$\hat{\beta} \xrightarrow{p} \beta$$

by the weak law of large numbers. This is easily shown because $E(\mathbf{x}_t^{*\prime}u_t) = 0$ under A.1, $E(\mathbf{x}_t^{*\prime}\mathbf{x}_t^*)$ is nonsingular under A.2, and $\hat{\Pi} \xrightarrow{p} \Pi$. Note that nothing is assumed about the conditional variance $\text{var}(u_t|\mathbf{w}_t)$ or the serial correlation properties of $\{u_t\}$ in obtaining this result.

Now let us add the assumption that the $K \times 1$ stochastic process $\{\mathbf{s}_t \equiv \mathbf{x}_t^{*\prime}u_t\colon t = 1, 2, \ldots\}$ satisfies the central limit theorem, that is

$$T^{-1/2}\sum_{t=1}^{T} \mathbf{x}_t^{*\prime}u_t \xrightarrow{d} \text{normal}\ (\mathbf{0}, \mathbf{B}), \tag{2.6}$$

where

$$B \equiv \lim_{T\to\infty} \operatorname{var}\left(T^{-1/2}\sum_{t=1}^{T}\mathbf{x}_t^{*\prime}u_t\right)$$

$$= E(\mathbf{s}_t\mathbf{s}_t') + \sum_{j=1}^{\infty}[E(\mathbf{s}_t\mathbf{s}_{t+j}') + E(\mathbf{s}_{t+j}\mathbf{s}_t')]. \tag{2.7}$$

Then $\hat{\beta}$ has first order asymptotic representation

$$\sqrt{T}(\hat{\beta} - \beta) = \mathbf{A}^{-1}T^{-1/2}\sum_{t=1}^{T}\mathbf{x}_t^{*\prime}u_t + o_p(1). \tag{2.8}$$

Equation (2.8) shows that the fact the fitted values $\hat{\mathbf{x}}_t$ depend on the estimator $\hat{\Pi}$ does not affect the limiting distribution of the 2SLS estimator; the same limiting distribution is obtained when $\hat{\mathbf{x}}_t$ replaces $\mathbf{x}_t^*$, that is when $\hat{\Pi}$ replaces Π. Because this does not rely on the second moment or dependence properties of $\{u_t\}$, this makes it easy to obtain consistent standard errors in a variety of circumstances.

Without further assumptions

$$\sqrt{T}(\hat{\beta} - \beta) \xrightarrow{d} \text{normal}\ (\mathbf{0}, \mathbf{A}^{-1}\mathbf{B}\mathbf{A}^{-1}), \tag{2.9}$$

and so the asymptotic variance of $\hat{\beta}$ is

$$\operatorname{avar}(\hat{\beta}) = \mathbf{A}^{-1}\mathbf{B}\mathbf{A}^{-1}/T. \tag{2.10}$$

Standard 2SLS analysis imposes two additional assumptions that simplify the form of (2.10). These are the assumptions of conditional homoskedasticity and conditional uncorrelatedness of the errors. The homoskedasticity assumption is most easily stated as

Assumption A.3 (homoskedasticity). $E(u_t^2|\mathbf{w}_t) = \sigma^2$. □

Note that assumption A.3 is not always the same as $\operatorname{var}(u_t|\mathbf{w}_t) = \sigma^2$; A.3 implies that $\operatorname{var}(u_t|\mathbf{w}_t) = \sigma^2$ only under (2.2). But assumption A.3 is the relevant one for the purposes of simplifying inference. The appropriate no serial correlation assumption is

Assumption A.4 (no serial correlation). $E(u_tu_{t+j}|\mathbf{w}_t,\mathbf{w}_{t+j}) = 0$, $j \geqslant 1$. □

Because A.3 and A.4 are stated conditional on the instruments, they explicitly allow for stochastic instruments and instruments that are not strictly exogenous; in particular, for time series applications the assumptions allow for $\mathbf{w}_t$ to contain lagged endogenous and exogenous variables, without assuming *strict* exogeneity of the exogenous variables. The same assumptions are sufficient when heterogeneity and deterministic trends are allowed. Importantly, unless the $\mathbf{w}_t$ are treated as nonrandom, it is not sufficient that $E(u_t^2) = \sigma^2$ for all t and $E(u_t u_{t+j}) = 0$, $j \geq 1$. Note that A.4 is automatically satisfied for cross-section applications with independent data, but of course A.3 can be violated.

Incidentally, in the statement of A.3 and A.4, $\mathbf{w}_t$ and $\mathbf{w}_{t+j}$ can be replaced by $\mathbf{x}_t^*$ and $\mathbf{x}_{t+j}^*$; this gives slightly weaker assumptions, but the additional generality afforded is probably modest in practice.

Under the additional assumptions A.3 and A.4, the asymptotic variance of $\hat{\beta}$ reduces to the familiar form

$$\text{avar}(\hat{\beta}) = \sigma^2 \mathbf{A}^{-1}/T. \tag{2.11}$$

This expression is easily estimated. Let $\hat{u}_t \equiv y_t - \mathbf{x}_t\hat{\beta}$ denote the 2SLS residuals (as usual, these are not the same as the residuals from the second stage regression). Then a consistent estimator of σ^2 – with a degrees-of-freedom adjustment – is given by

$$\hat{\sigma}^2 \equiv (T - K)^{-1}\sum_{t=1}^{T}\hat{u}_t^2. \tag{2.12}$$

A consistent estimator of $\mathbf{A}$ is always

$$\hat{\mathbf{A}} \equiv T^{-1}\sum_{t=1}^{T}\hat{\mathbf{x}}_t'\hat{\mathbf{x}}_t = \hat{\mathbf{X}}'\hat{\mathbf{X}}/T, \tag{2.13}$$

where $\hat{\mathbf{X}}$ is the $T \times K$ matrix the tth row $\hat{\mathbf{x}}_t$. Then $\text{avar}(\hat{\beta})$ is estimated by

$$\hat{\sigma}^2(\hat{\mathbf{X}}'\hat{\mathbf{X}})^{-1}, \tag{2.14}$$

and the asymptotic standard error of $\hat{\beta}_j$ is the square root of the jth diagonal element of this matrix. This is what is printed out by all 2SLS regression packages.

The White heteroskedasticity-robust variance matrix estimator for 2SLS is easily obtained under A.1, A.2, and A.4. Let

$$\hat{\mathbf{B}} \equiv \hat{\mathbf{X}}'\hat{\mathbf{D}}\hat{\mathbf{X}}/(T - K) = (T - K)^{-1}\sum_{t=1}^{T}\hat{u}_t^2\hat{\mathbf{x}}_t'\hat{\mathbf{x}}_t, \tag{2.15}$$

where $\hat{\mathbf{D}} \equiv \text{diag}(\hat{u}_1^2, \ldots, \hat{u}_T^2)$ is a $T \times T$ matrix. Then, a heteroskedasticity-robust covariance matrix estimator of $\text{avar}(\hat{\beta})$ is

$$[T/(T - K)](\hat{\mathbf{X}}'\hat{\mathbf{X}})^{-1}(\hat{\mathbf{X}}'\hat{\mathbf{D}}\hat{\mathbf{X}})(\hat{\mathbf{X}}'\hat{\mathbf{X}})^{-1}, \tag{2.16}$$

and the asymptotic standard error of $\hat{\beta}_j$ is the square root of the jth diagonal element of (2.16) (see, for example, White, 1984). Without the leading term $T/(T - K)$ and with $\hat{\mathbf{X}} = \mathbf{X}$, (2.16) was proposed by White (1980). MacKinnon and White (1985) showed in simulations that the degrees-of-freedom adjustment generally improves finite sample performance. Their simulations also show that jack-knife estimators have better finite sample properties, but these are more difficult to compute and not often used.

For the general case that $\{\mathbf{x}_t^{*\prime}u_t\}$ might be serially correlated and $E(u_t^2|\mathbf{w}_t)$ nonconstant, the matrix $\mathbf{B}$ can be estimated using a variety of serial correlation robust matrices. Effectively, we must estimate the spectral density of $\{\mathbf{s}_t\}$ at frequency zero. Newey and West (1987) and Andrews (1991) cover several estimators that can be applied to $\{\hat{\mathbf{s}}_t\}$. The estimator proposed by Newey and West (1987) is

$$\hat{\mathbf{B}} = \hat{\Omega}_0 + \sum_{h=1}^{G} \omega(h, G)\{\hat{\Omega}_h + \hat{\Omega}_h'\} \tag{2.17}$$

where

$$\hat{\Omega}_h \equiv (T - K)^{-1} \sum_{t=h+1}^{T} \hat{\mathbf{s}}_t\hat{\mathbf{s}}_{t-h}', \quad \hat{\mathbf{s}}_t \equiv \hat{\mathbf{x}}_t'\hat{u}_t \tag{2.18}$$

and

$$\begin{aligned} \omega(h, G) &= 1 - h/(G + 1), \quad h = 1,2, \ldots, G \\ &= 0, \quad h > G. \end{aligned} \tag{2.19}$$

Under general conditions $\hat{\mathbf{B}} \xrightarrow{p} \mathbf{B}$ as $T \to \infty$ provided $G \to \infty$ and $G = o(T^{1/2})$, see Andrews (1991) and Hansen (1992) for further discussion. Avar($\hat{\beta}$) is estimated as

$$\hat{\mathbf{V}}/T \equiv (\hat{\mathbf{X}}'\hat{\mathbf{X}})^{-1}(T\hat{\mathbf{B}})(\hat{\mathbf{X}}'\hat{\mathbf{X}})^{-1}. \tag{2.20}$$

Often it is useful to have a simple method for computing a serial correlation robust standard error. The following procedure extends Wooldridge (1989, 1991).

Procedure 2.1 (1) Estimate $\hat{\beta}$ by 2SLS using instruments $\mathbf{w}_t$. This yields "se($\hat{\beta}_j$)" (the reported but generally incorrect standard errors), $\hat{\sigma}$, and the 2SLS residuals $\{\hat{u}_t: t = 1, \ldots, T\}$. Obtain the fitted values $\hat{\mathbf{x}}_t$ from the first step regression

$$\mathbf{x}_t \quad \text{on} \quad \mathbf{w}_t.$$

(2) Compute the residuals $\{\hat{r}_{tj}: t = 1, \ldots, T\}$ from the regression

$$\hat{x}_{tj} \text{ on } \hat{x}_{t1}, \ldots, \hat{x}_{t,j-1}, \hat{x}_{t,j+1}, \ldots, \hat{x}_{tK}, \quad t = 1, \ldots, T \tag{2.21}$$

(3) For a given j, set $\hat{q}_t \equiv \hat{r}_{tj}\hat{u}_t$ and run the regression

$$\hat{q}_t \quad \text{on} \quad \hat{q}_{t-1}, \ldots, \hat{q}_{t-G}, \tag{2.22}$$

where G is, say, the integer part of $T^{1/3}$. Compute Berk's (1974) autoregressive spectral density estimator

$$\hat{c}_j \equiv [T/(T-K)]\hat{\tau}_G^2/(1 - \hat{\alpha}_1 - \hat{\alpha}_2 - \ldots - \hat{\alpha}_G)^2, \tag{2.23}$$

where $\hat{\alpha}_h$, $h = 1, \ldots, G$ are the OLS coefficients from the autoregression and $\hat{\tau}_G^2$ is the square of the standard error of the regression from (2.22).

Alternatively, apply the Newey–West estimator to $\{\hat{q}_t\}$:

$$\hat{c}_j \equiv (T-K)^{-1}\sum_{t=1}^{T}\hat{q}_t^2 + 2\sum_{h=1}^{G}\omega(h, G)(T-K)^{-1}\sum_{t=h+1}^{T}\hat{q}_t\hat{q}_{t-h}, \tag{2.24}$$

where $\omega(h, G)$ is given by (2.19).

(4) Compute a valid standard error, $\text{se}(\hat{\beta}_j)$, from

$$\text{se}(\hat{\beta}_j) = [\text{"se}(\hat{\beta}_j)\text{"}/\hat{\sigma}]^2(T\hat{c}_j)^{1/2}. \quad \square \tag{2.25}$$

Note that steps 2 to 4 must be carried out for each j for which a robust standard error is desired. The standard errors from procedure 2.1 are both heteroskedasticity and serial correlation robust (as $T \to \infty$). Showing that this produces a consistent standard error follows along the lines of Wooldridge (1991). In practice, one needs to choose a lag length G (and this could be different for each coefficient), which introduces some arbitrariness into the procedure (such as taking G to be the integer part of $T^{1/3}$). There are data-based methods for choosing G that may work better than a deterministic rule. See Andrews (1991) for a general discussion.

If assumption A.4 is assumed to hold one can set

$$\hat{c}_j \equiv (T-K)^{-1}\sum_{t=1}^{T}\hat{q}_t^2.$$

This gives a degrees-of-freedom adjusted White (1980) heteroskedasticity-robust standard error for the 2SLS estimator $\hat{\beta}_j$.

Before we proceed to diagnostic tests, some comments on the use of 2SLS in the presence of heteroskedasticity or serial correlation are warranted. It is now well known (for example, White, 1984, chapter 4) that when $L > K$ – which can always be ensured if (2.2) holds, even when $\mathbf{w}_t = \mathbf{x}_t$ – there exist method of moments estimators more efficient than 2SLS (or OLS) if either A.3 or A.4 fails. Testing can then be carried out in a generalized method of moments (GMM) framework. This chapter is motivated by the popularity of 2SLS due to its availability in most econometric packages and the widespread knowledge of its properties. The use of the asymptotically more efficient GMM estimators for standard applications has been slow to catch on and is implemented in only a few econometrics packages. This may be due to the fact that researchers are often willing to nominally assume A.3 and A.4, but they want their inference to be robust to violations of them. Also, even though GMM is asymptotically more efficient than 2SLS, it can easily have worse finite sample properties. Finally, under an assumption such as (2.2), the list of instruments that can improve the asymptotic efficiency of GMM is endless even if the reduced form of the endogenous variables is linear, and there are no easy recipes for choosing the "best" set.

3 A General Class of Diagnostic Tests

Let $\mathbf{v}_t(\gamma)$ be a $1 \times Q$ vector of misspecification indicators that possibly depend on a $G \times 1$ vector of parameters γ and elements of $\{\mathbf{w}_t, y_{t-1}, \mathbf{x}_{t-1}, \mathbf{w}_{t-1}, \ldots\}$. The parameters γ need not be of particular interest, but often γ is equal to or otherwise related to β. In any case we assume the existence of an estimator $\hat{\gamma}$ such that $\sqrt{T}(\hat{\gamma} - \gamma) = O_p(1)$ (in particular, $\gamma = \operatorname{plim} \hat{\gamma}$). As shorthand, we sometimes write $\mathbf{v}_t \equiv \mathbf{v}_t(\gamma)$.

The tests we derive explicitly take the null hypothesis to be

$$H_0\colon E(\mathbf{v}_t' u_t) = 0. \tag{3.1}$$

Usually, (3.1) is simply an implication of a more restrictive hypothesis about u_t, such as a zero conditional mean assumption. A useful example to carry along is

$$\mathbf{v}_t \equiv (u_{t-1}, u_{t-2}, \ldots, u_{t-Q}), \tag{3.2}$$

in which case the null states that the errors in (2.1) are serially uncorrelated (at least up to order Q). Note that $\gamma = \beta$ here.

We now derive tests of (3.1) under assumptions that are extensions of those made in section 2; when each is used it is assumed to hold under H_0. We do not analyze the tests under fixed or local alternatives. Some comments on the power of the statistics are given in the conclusion. To state the first assumption, let $\nabla_\gamma \mathbf{v}_t(\gamma)$ denote the $G \times Q$ matrix of partial derivatives of $\mathbf{v}_t(.)$ evaluated at $\operatorname{plim} \hat{\gamma}$.

Assumption B.1 Assumption A.1 holds and, in addition,

$$\text{(i)} \quad E[\mathbf{v}_t(\gamma)'u_t] = 0$$

$$\text{(ii)} \quad E[\nabla_\gamma \mathbf{v}_t(\gamma)'u_t] = 0. \quad \square$$

Part (ii) of assumption B.1 is certainly not needed to derive a test of (3.1). But imposing it greatly simplifies construction of the test statistics without materially affecting the scope of applications. Without B.1(ii), the limiting distribution of $\sqrt{T}(\hat{\gamma} - \gamma)$ would affect the limiting distribution of the test statistics. All the example in section 4 – indeed, all examples that come to mind – satisfy B.1(ii) as well as B.1(i) under the relevant null hypothesis. If $\mathbf{v}_t(\gamma)$ is a linear function of instruments assumed to be uncorrelated with u_t then B.1 holds; this happens in tests for endogeneity and overidentification tests. For most tests of nonlinearities $\mathbf{v}_t(\gamma)$ is a nonlinear function of the null instruments $\mathbf{w}_t$, in which case B.1 holds under the natural assumption (2.2). More generally, if the null is stated as $E(u_t|\mathbf{w}_t, \mathbf{z}_t) = 0$ for some random vector $\mathbf{z}_t$, then B.1 holds whenever $\mathbf{v}_t(\gamma)$ is any function of $(\mathbf{w}_t, \mathbf{z}_t)$; this is the case for tests of serial correlation and other tests of dynamic specification.

The rank condition is now stated as

Assumption B.2 A.2 holds and, in addition, define

$$\mathbf{x}_t^+ \equiv L(\mathbf{x}_t|\mathbf{w}_t, \mathbf{v}_t). \tag{3.3}$$

Then

$$\text{rank } E(\mathbf{r}_t'\mathbf{r}_t) = Q, \tag{3.4}$$

where $\mathbf{r}_t$ is the $1 \times Q$ population residual from the linear projection of $\mathbf{v}_t$ onto $\mathbf{x}_t^+$:

$$\mathbf{r}_t \equiv \mathbf{v}_t - L(\mathbf{v}_t|\mathbf{x}_t^+). \quad \square \tag{3.5}$$

Assumption B.2 ensures that $\mathbf{v}_t$ is nonredundant with respect to $\mathbf{x}_t^+$. One implication of this is that the specification test statistics will have Q degrees of freedom. If $\mathbf{v}_t$ contains redundancies it is easiest to drop them ahead of time.

The homoskedasticity assumption must now account for $\mathbf{v}_t$:

Assumption B.3 $E(u_t^2|\mathbf{w}_t, \mathbf{v}_t) = \sigma^2$. $\square$

Under assumption B.3 the choice of $\mathbf{v}_t$ can rule out certain kinds of heteroskedasticity. For example, if $\mathbf{v}_t$ is as in (3.2) then B.3 rules out dynamic forms of conditional heteroskedasticity, such as Engle's

(1982b) ARCH model and Bollerslev's (1986) GARCH model. But if, say, $\mathbf{w}_t$ and $\mathbf{v}_t$ depend only on contemporaneous variables then B.3 allows for heteroskedasticity not related to $(\mathbf{w}_t, \mathbf{v}_t)$ – for example, certain forms of dynamic heteroskedasticity. When $\mathbf{v}_t$ is a function of $\mathbf{w}_t$ then B.3 and A.3 are identical.

The assumption of no serial correlation now reads

Assumption B.4 $E(u_t u_{t+j}|\mathbf{w}_t, \mathbf{v}_t, \mathbf{w}_{t+j}, \mathbf{v}_{t+j}) = 0, j \geqslant 1.$ □

As with A.4, assumption B.4 automatically holds in cross-section settings with independent observations. It is also very natural for a broad class of diagnostics in time series settings. To investigate this class of diagnostics we introduce a notion of dynamic completeness.

Definition 3.1 The model (2.1) is *dynamically complete* if

$$E(u_t|\mathbf{w}_t, \mathbf{x}_{t-1}, u_{t-1}, \mathbf{w}_{t-1}, \ldots) = 0. \quad \square \tag{3.6}$$

In other words, the expected value of u_t given current instruments and past values of everything (instruments, explanatory variables, and errors) is zero. (Note that that lagged u_t could be replaced with lagged y_t in (3.6).) The usefulness of this definition is that if (2.1) is dynamically complete and $\mathbf{v}_t$ is a function of $\{\mathbf{w}_t, \mathbf{x}_{t-1}, u_{t-1}, \mathbf{w}_{t-1}, \ldots\}$, then B.1 *and* B.4 necessarily hold under H_0 – this follows by the law of iterated expectations. Definition 3.1 is important because the goal of many specification tests of time series equations is to test for dynamic completeness; the null (3.1) is simply a way of operationalizing a test of the null of interest, (3.6). As we will see, when B.4 can be maintained under H_0 it greatly simplifies computation of the test statistics.

It is essential that dynamic completeness be stated in terms of a conditional expectation. The natural statement of dynamic completeness in terms of zero covariances is not sufficient to imply the relevant no serial correlation assumption B.4 under H_0. It is easy to see that assuming u_t is uncorrelated with all elements in $\{\mathbf{w}_t, \mathbf{x}_{t-1}, u_{t-1}, \mathbf{w}_{t-1}, \ldots\}$ is not sufficient for B.4, even when $\mathbf{v}_t$ is a linear function of this information set.

We now discuss regression-based tests under decreasingly restrictive assumptions. Assumptions B.1 and B.2, which state the null hypothesis, the identification condition, and a nonredundancy condition, are maintained throughout. Assumptions B.3 and B.4 are auxiliary assumptions that are often added to simplify computations. Thus, in addition to having tests under standard assumptions, we are interested in obtaining tests that are robust to failures of B.3 or B.3 and B.4.

The general approach should be familiar to those acquainted with the variable addition testing literature (see, for example, Pagan and Hall, 1983; Davidson and MacKinnon, 1990; Wooldridge, 1991). These are score-type tests because the test is based on the score of the objective function from the model estimated under H_0, as in Rao's (1948) classic article. For linear models estimated by 2SLS, this leads to (essentially) the sample covariance

$$T^{-1}\sum_{t=1}^{T}\hat{\mathbf{v}}_t'\hat{u}_t, \tag{3.7}$$

where the $\hat{u}_t$ are the 2SLS residuals and $\hat{\mathbf{v}}_t \equiv \mathbf{v}_t(\hat{\gamma})$. When $\mathbf{v}_t$ is as in (3.2), $\hat{\gamma} = \hat{\beta}$ (the 2SLS estimator) and

$$\hat{\mathbf{v}}_t = (\hat{u}_{t-1}, \hat{u}_{t-2}, \ldots, \hat{u}_{t-Q}). \tag{3.8}$$

As in Wooldridge (1990), to obtain a computationally simple test, we adjust this statistic by replacing $\hat{\mathbf{v}}_t$ with the $1 \times Q$ residuals $\hat{\mathbf{r}}_t$ from the regression

$$\hat{\mathbf{v}}_t \quad \text{on} \quad \hat{\mathbf{x}}_t, \quad t = 1, 2, \ldots, T, \tag{3.9}$$

where – and this is important – the $\hat{\mathbf{x}}_t$ are generally the $1 \times K$ fitted values from the regression

$$\mathbf{x}_t \quad \text{on} \quad \mathbf{w}_t, \hat{\mathbf{v}}_t, \quad t = 1, 2, \ldots, T. \tag{3.10}$$

We postpone a detailed discussion of why $\hat{\mathbf{v}}_t$ is included in (3.10), as well as when it can be omitted; briefly, for the test below to be valid $\hat{\mathbf{x}}_t$ must estimate the population quantity $\mathbf{x}_t^+$ (see (3.3)).

To derive the key first-order asymptotic representation, we assume only that B.1 and B.2 hold, along with the law of large numbers and CLT. Of interest is the limiting distribution of

$$T^{-1/2}\sum_{t=1}^{T}\hat{\mathbf{r}}_t'\hat{u}_t. \tag{3.11}$$

The asymptotic distribution of this $Q \times 1$ vector is straightforward to derive. The first useful observation is that, under B.1 and B.2, estimation of $\mathbf{r}_t$ does not affect the first-order asymptotic distribution:

$$T^{-1/2}\sum_{t=1}^{T}\hat{\mathbf{r}}_t'\hat{u}_t = T^{-1/2}\sum_{t=1}^{T}\mathbf{r}_t'\hat{u}_t + o_p(1)$$

under H_0; this can be verified through a mean value expansion, noting that $\hat{\mathbf{r}}_t$ is a linear function of $(\mathbf{w}_t, \mathbf{v}_t(\hat{\gamma}))$ (this is where B.1(ii) is used). Next,

$$T^{-1/2}\sum_{t=1}^{T}\mathbf{r}_t'\hat{u}_t = T^{-1/2}\sum_{t=1}^{T}\mathbf{r}_t'(u_t - \mathbf{x}_t(\hat{\beta} - \beta))$$

$$= T^{-1/2}\sum_{t=1}^{T}\mathbf{r}_t'u_t - T^{-1}\sum_{t=1}^{T}\mathbf{r}_t'\mathbf{x}_t\sqrt{T}(\hat{\beta} - \beta).$$

By the CLT, $\sqrt{T}(\hat{\beta} - \beta) = O_p(1)$. By definition of $\mathbf{x}_t^+$, $\mathbf{x}_t = \mathbf{x}_t^+ + \mathbf{g}_t$ where $E(\mathbf{w}_t'\mathbf{g}_t) = 0$, $E(\mathbf{v}_t'\mathbf{g}_t) = 0$. Therefore, $E(\mathbf{r}_t'\mathbf{g}_t) = 0$, so

$$E(\mathbf{r}_t'\mathbf{x}_t) = E(\mathbf{r}_t'\mathbf{x}_t^+) = 0;$$

the latter equality holds because $\mathbf{r}_t$ is the population residual from the regression of $\mathbf{v}_t$ onto $\mathbf{x}_t^+$. It follows by the WLLN that

$$T^{-1}\sum_{t=1}^{T}\mathbf{r}_t'\mathbf{x}_t \xrightarrow{p} 0.$$

This gives the very useful asymptotic equivalence

$$T^{-1/2}\sum_{t=1}^{T}\mathbf{r}_t'\hat{u}_t = T^{-1/2}\sum_{t=1}^{T}\mathbf{r}_t'u_t + o_p(1). \tag{3.12}$$

Note that we have relied on only B.1 and B.2 in deriving (3.12); B.3 and B.4 are not needed.

We now explain why $\hat{\mathbf{v}}_t$ is generally included in the regression (3.10). For (3.12) to be valid, $\hat{\mathbf{x}}_t$ must estimate the linear projection of $\mathbf{x}_t$ onto $(\mathbf{w}_t, \mathbf{v}_t)$ under H_0. If *under* H_0 the $\mathbf{v}_t$ are not useful additional instruments for $\mathbf{x}_t$ in the sense that

$$L(\mathbf{x}_t|\mathbf{w}_t, \mathbf{v}_t) = L(\mathbf{x}_t|\mathbf{w}_t), \tag{3.13}$$

then $\hat{\mathbf{v}}_t$ can be omitted from (3.10). If (3.13) is not true then $\hat{\mathbf{v}}_t$ should be included in (3.10) for the following procedures to be valid. If $\mathbf{v}_t$ is a linear function of $\mathbf{w}_t$ then (3.13) is trivially satisfied; this is the case studied in most of the literature (see MacKinnon, 1992). If $\mathbf{v}_t$ is a nonlinear function of $\mathbf{w}_t$ then (3.13) holds if $E(\mathbf{x}_t|\mathbf{w}_t)$ is linear. Even in more general situations (3.13) can be maintained under H_0 because, if the $\mathbf{v}_t$ were not redundant as instruments under H_0, then they (or estimates of them) would probably be included among the instrument set in an attempt to enhance efficiency. Nevertheless, we do not maintain (3.13) in deriving the specification tests.

In the context of testing for omitted variables, Engle (1982a, 1984) has noted the difficulty in applying the usual score procedure when different instruments are used under H_0 and the alternative. The previous discussion shows that in a general specification testing context it is straightforward to still apply the score procedure provided $\hat{\mathbf{x}}_t$ is obtained from (3.10) and the purging of $\hat{\mathbf{x}}_t$ from $\hat{\mathbf{v}}_t$ is carried out as in regression (3.9). This analysis also characterizes when using the usual 2SLS first-stage fitted values is valid – namely, when the redundancy condition (3.13) holds. It is not the presence of different instruments *per se* that causes difficulty for the score test; what matters is how one goes about estimating the projection of $\mathbf{x}_t$ onto $(\mathbf{w}_t, \mathbf{v}_t)$ under H_0.

The asymptotic equivalence in (3.12) makes it easy to find the limiting distribution of (3.11). Let $\mathbf{k}_t \equiv u_t\mathbf{r}_t$, a $1 \times Q$ vector, and define

$$\begin{aligned}\mathbf{C} &\equiv \lim_{T\to\infty} \operatorname{var}\left(T^{-1/2}\sum_{t=1}^{T}\mathbf{r}_t' u_t\right)\\ &= E(\mathbf{k}_t'\mathbf{k}_t) + \sum_{j=1}^{\infty}[E(\mathbf{k}_t'\mathbf{k}_{t+j}) + E(\mathbf{k}_{t+j}'\mathbf{k}_t)].\end{aligned}$$

Given a consistent estimator $\hat{\mathbf{C}}$ of $\mathbf{C}$, the test statistic proposed here is

$$\begin{aligned}\mathscr{I}_T &\equiv \left(T^{-1/2}\sum_{t=1}^{T}\hat{\mathbf{r}}_t'\hat{u}_t\right)'\hat{\mathbf{C}}^{-1}\left(T^{-1/2}\sum_{t=1}^{T}\hat{\mathbf{r}}_t'\hat{u}_t\right)\\ &= \left(\sum_{t=1}^{T}\hat{\mathbf{r}}_t'\hat{u}_t\right)'(T\hat{\mathbf{C}})^{-1}\left(\sum_{t=1}^{T}\hat{\mathbf{r}}_t'\hat{u}_t\right). \qquad (3.14)\end{aligned}$$

Under B.1, B.2, and standard regularity conditions, $\mathscr{I}_T \xrightarrow{d} \chi^2_Q$.

The actual form of the test statistic depends on the estimator used for $\mathbf{C}$. This depends on what is assumed under H_0. We begin with the simplest, albeit most restrictive, form of the test.

Under B.3, a simple application of iterated expectations gives

$$\begin{aligned}E(\mathbf{k}_t'\mathbf{k}_t) &= E(u_t^2\mathbf{r}_t'\mathbf{r}_t) = E[E(u_t^2\mathbf{r}_t'\mathbf{r}_t|\mathbf{w}_t, \mathbf{v}_t)]\\ &= E[E(u_t^2|\mathbf{w}_t, \mathbf{v}_t)\mathbf{r}_t'\mathbf{r}_t] = \sigma^2 E(\mathbf{r}_t'\mathbf{r}_t).\end{aligned}$$

Similarly, under B.4, for $j \geqslant 1$,

$$\begin{aligned}E(\mathbf{k}_t'\mathbf{k}_{t+j}) &= E(u_t u_{t+j}\mathbf{r}_t'\mathbf{r}_{t+j}) = E[E(u_t u_{t+j}\mathbf{r}_t'\mathbf{r}_{t+j}|\mathbf{w}_t, \mathbf{v}_t, \mathbf{w}_{t+j}, \mathbf{v}_{t+j})]\\ &= E[E(u_t u_{t+j}|\mathbf{w}_t, \mathbf{v}_t, \mathbf{w}_{t+j}, \mathbf{v}_{t+j})\mathbf{r}_t'\mathbf{r}_{t+j}] = 0\end{aligned}$$

Therefore, under the additional assumptions B.3 and B.3, $\mathbf{C}$ has the simple form

$$\mathbf{C} = \sigma^2 E(\mathbf{r}_t'\mathbf{r}_t).$$

The usual estimator of σ^2 in score testing contexts is based on the residuals under the null without a degrees of freedom correction (see (2.12) with $T - K$ replaced by T). If

$$\hat{\mathbf{C}} = \hat{\sigma}^2\left(T^{-1}\sum_{t=1}^{T}\hat{\mathbf{r}}_t'\hat{\mathbf{r}}_t\right), \tag{3.15}$$

and this is plugged into (3.14), $\mathscr{I}_T$ can be computed as follows.

Procedure 3.1 (valid under B.1 to B.4). (1) Obtain $\hat{u}_t$ as the residuals from the 2SLS regression

$$y_t \quad \text{on} \quad \mathbf{x}_t \text{ using instruments } \mathbf{w}_t.$$

Compute the $1 \times K$ fitted values $\hat{\mathbf{x}}_t$ from the regression of $\mathbf{x}_t$ on $\mathbf{w}_t$, $\hat{v}_t$ or, if condition (3.13) holds, from the regression of $\mathbf{x}_t$ on $\mathbf{w}_t$.

(2) Obtain $\hat{\mathbf{r}}_t$ as the $1 \times Q$ residuals from the regression

$$\hat{\mathbf{v}}_t \quad \text{on} \quad \hat{\mathbf{x}}_t, \quad t = 1, 2, \ldots, T.$$

(3) Run the regression

$$\hat{u}_t \quad \text{on} \quad \hat{\mathbf{r}}_t, \quad t = 1, 2, \ldots, T. \tag{3.16}$$

Then $\mathscr{I}_T = TR_u^2$, where R_u^2 is the uncentered r-squared from this regression. □

This statistic is fairly easy to compute, but generally it has a limiting χ_Q^2 distribution only if B.3 and B.4 hold. If either heteroskedasticity or serial correlation is present under H_0, this procedure is not ensured to be valid.

The statistic can be computed in an even simpler fashion if (3.13) is maintained under H_0 and the $\hat{\mathbf{x}}_t$ are the 2SLS fitted values from the first-stage regression

$$\mathbf{x}_t \quad \text{on} \quad \mathbf{w}_t. \tag{3.17}$$

In this case $\hat{\mathbf{x}}_t$ and $\hat{u}_t$ are orthogonal in sample, and so $\mathscr{I}_T$ can be computed as TR_u^2 from the regression

$$\hat{u}_t \quad \text{on} \quad \hat{\mathbf{x}}_t, \hat{\mathbf{v}}_t, \quad t = 1, 2, \ldots, T. \tag{3.18}$$

A simple alternative to procedure 3.1 is available if $\hat{v}_t$ is a scalar. An asymptotically standard normal statistic is the usual 2SLS t-statistic on $\hat{v}_t$ in the model

$$y_t = \mathbf{x}_t\beta + \gamma\hat{v}_t + \text{error}_t, \tag{3.19}$$

estimated using instruments $(\mathbf{w}_t, \hat{v}_t)$. This is more of a Wald-type test that is valid under B.1 to B.4.

As stated earlier, many tests in a time series context are tests of dynamic completeness, in which case B.4 necessarily holds under H_0. Still, the homoskedasticity assumption B.3 can fail in such cases. The following test is robust to violations of B.3, and is useful in cross-section and time series contexts.

Procedure 3.2 (valid under B.1, B.2, and B.4). Replace step (3) in procedure (3.1) as follows:

(3) Define the $1 \times Q$ vector $\hat{\mathbf{k}}_t \equiv \hat{u}_t \hat{\mathbf{r}}_t$, $t = 1, 2, \ldots, T$. Then $\mathcal{I}_T = TR_u^2 = T - \text{SSR}$ from the regression

$$1 \quad \text{on} \quad \hat{\mathbf{k}}_t, \quad t = 1, 2, \ldots, T, \tag{3.20}$$

where SSR is the usual sum of squared residuals from this regression. Under B.1, B.2, and B.4, T − SSR $\overset{a}{\sim} \chi^2_Q$. □

The validity of this procedure can be seen as follows. Under B.1, B.2, and B.4, a consistent estimator of $\mathbf{C}$ is

$$T^{-1} \sum_{t=1}^{T} \hat{\mathbf{k}}_t' \hat{\mathbf{k}}_t$$

Plugging this into (13.14) and comparing this with the formula for TR_u^2 from (3.20) shows that the statistics are identical.

Finally, we relax both B.3 and B.4, and derive the most robust form of the test that is useful for time series applications with incomplete dynamics.

Procedure 3.3 (valid under B.1 and B.2). Replace step (3) of procedures 3.1 and 3.2 with

(3) Set $\hat{\mathbf{k}}_t \equiv \hat{u}_t \hat{\mathbf{r}}_t$. For some integer G, run the VAR(G) regression

$$\hat{\mathbf{k}}_t \quad \text{on} \quad \hat{\mathbf{k}}_{t-1}, \ldots, \hat{\mathbf{k}}_{t-G}, \tag{3.21}$$

and save the $1 \times Q$ residuals, say $\hat{\mathbf{e}}_t$.

(4) Use $TR_u^2 = T - \text{SSR}$ from the regression

$$1 \quad \text{on} \quad \hat{\mathbf{e}}_t \tag{3.22}$$

as asymptotically χ^2_Q; in practice, T can be the actual number of observations used in this final regression. □

Unlike the previous statistics, the statistic obtained from regression (3.22) cannot be obtained directly from (3.14). A heteroskedasticity–serial correlation robust statistic that has the form (3.14) can be obtained by applying the Newey–West estimator to $(\hat{\mathbf{k}}_t')$ to obtain $\hat{\mathbf{C}}$, but this is computationally more cumbersome than needed to find a valid test. Procedure 3.3 is based on the following observation: what is really being tested is the null

$$H_0\colon E(\mathbf{k}_t) = 0. \tag{3.23}$$

The problem with using standard methods for testing that a vector has a zero mean is that $\{\mathbf{k}_t\}$ is possibly serially correlated. But, under general assumptions $\{\mathbf{k}_t\}$ can be well approximated by a VAR with a sufficient number of lags. For a given lag G, define

$$\mathbf{e}_t \equiv \mathbf{k}_t - L(\mathbf{k}_t|\mathbf{k}_{t-1}, \ldots, \mathbf{k}_{t-G}). \tag{3.24}$$

Then (3.23) holds if and only if

$$E(\mathbf{e}_t) = 0. \tag{3.25}$$

Now by choosing G large enough the serial correlation in $\{\mathbf{e}_t\}$ can be made arbitrarily small. We have assumed that it is zero in procedure 3.3, but this is valid provided G can grow with T (see Berk, 1974). The regression in (3.22) gives the statistic

$$\left(\sum_{t=G+1}^{T} \hat{\mathbf{e}}_t\right)\left(\sum_{t=G+1}^{T} \hat{\mathbf{e}}_t'\hat{\mathbf{e}}_t\right)^{-1}\left(\sum_{t=G+1}^{T} \hat{\mathbf{e}}_t\right)', \tag{3.26}$$

which has a limiting χ^2_Q distribution because the fact that the $\hat{\mathbf{e}}_t$ depend on estimates can be shown not to matter asymptotically under H_0. For more on this approach for nonlinear regression models, see Wooldridge (1991).

4 Examples

We now cover several applications of the procedures in section 3.

Example 4.1 (testing for omitted variables). Consider the model

$$y_t = \mathbf{x}_t\beta + \mathbf{q}_t\delta + u_t, \tag{4.1}$$

where the null hypothesis is

$$H_0\colon \delta = 0.$$

Both $\mathbf{x}_t$ and $\mathbf{q}_t$ can contain elements correlated with u_t. In general, the list of instruments can be different under the null and alternative models. Let $\mathbf{w}_t$ denote the instruments used under the null and let $\mathbf{z}_t$

be additional instruments used to estimate the general model; the maintained assumptions are $E(\mathbf{w}_t'u_t) = 0$ and $E(\mathbf{z}_t'u_t) = 0$. They $\hat{\mathbf{v}}_t \equiv \hat{\mathbf{q}}_t$, where $\hat{\mathbf{q}}_t$ are the fitted values from the regression

$$\mathbf{q}_t \quad \text{on} \quad \mathbf{w}_t, \mathbf{z}_t. \tag{4.2}$$

Let $\hat{u}_t = y_t - \mathbf{x}_t\hat{\beta}$ be the 2SLS residuals estimated under $\delta = 0$ using instruments $\mathbf{w}_t$. Generally, $\hat{\mathbf{x}}_t$ is obtained from the regression

$$\mathbf{x}_t \text{ on } \mathbf{w}_t, \mathbf{z}_t. \tag{4.3}$$

Depending on what else is maintained under H_0, procedure 3.1, 3.2, or 3.3 can be used. If the same instruments are used under H_0 and H_1, and B.3 and B.4 are maintained, the statistic can be obtained as TR_u^2 from the OLS regression

$$\hat{u}_t \quad \text{on} \quad \hat{\mathbf{x}}_t, \hat{\mathbf{q}}_t, \quad t = 1, 2, \ldots, T;$$

see also MacKinnon (1992). □

Example 4.2 (testing for serial correlation). Let $\hat{u}_t$ be obtained from the 2SLS regression of

$$y_t \quad \text{on} \quad \mathbf{x}_t \text{ using instruments } \mathbf{w}_t.$$

A test for AR(Q) serial correlation is obtained by choosing $\hat{\mathbf{v}}_t \equiv (\hat{u}_{t-1}, \ldots, \hat{u}_{t-Q})$, and we assume that the null hypothesis is given by (3.6) so that B.1 and B.4 hold under H_0. The $\hat{\mathbf{x}}_t$ are generally the fitted values from the regression

$$\mathbf{x}_t \quad \text{on} \quad \mathbf{w}_t, \hat{u}_{t-1}, \ldots, \hat{u}_{t-Q}, \tag{4.4}$$

or the lagged residuals can be omitted from (4.4) if they are assumed to be redundant instruments under H_0. Either procedure 3.1 or 3.2 can be used to compute a valid test statistic, with procedure 3.2 being robust to arbitrary forms of static or dynamic heteroskedasticity. Procedure 3.3 would not be used here since the null hypothesis is the absense of dynamic misspecification. □

Example 4.3 (testing for endogeneity). Let the model be partitioned as

$$y_t = \mathbf{x}_{t1}\beta_1 + \mathbf{x}_{t2}\beta_2 + u_t, \tag{4.5}$$

where $\mathbf{x}_{t1}$ is maintained to be exogenous. The issue is whether $\mathbf{x}_{t2}$ is endogenous, stated as H_0: $E(\mathbf{x}_{t2}'u_t) = 0$. The model is estimated by OLS under H_0, so let $\hat{u}_t$ denote the OLS residuals from the regression y_t on $\mathbf{x}_{t1}, \mathbf{x}_{t2}$. We test whether the fitted values of $\mathbf{x}_{t2}$ onto a set of instruments is approximately uncorrelated with $\hat{u}_t$. Note that the instruments under the null are $\mathbf{w}_t \equiv \mathbf{x}_t$, so (3.13) trivially holds. Let $\mathbf{z}_t$ denote a set of $1 \times L$ instruments, $L \geqslant K$, that includes $\mathbf{x}_{t1}$ but not $\mathbf{x}_{t2}$. A maintained assumption is $E(\mathbf{z}_t' u_t) = 0$. The (population) misspecification indicator is $\mathbf{v}_t = \mathbf{x}_{t2}^* = L(\mathbf{x}_{t2}|\mathbf{z}_t)$, and a Hausman test which compares the OLS and 2SLS estimators can be shown to be based on the sample covariance

$$T^{-1}\sum_{t=1}^{T} \hat{\mathbf{x}}_{t2}' \hat{u}_t,$$

where the $\hat{\mathbf{x}}_{t2}$ are the fitted values from the first stage regression of $\mathbf{x}_{t2}$ on $\mathbf{z}_t$. Therefore, we are really testing whether the OLS residuals are correlated with a particular linear combination of $\mathbf{z}_t$. To apply any of procedures 3.1, 3.2, or 3.3 take $\hat{\mathbf{x}}_t \equiv \mathbf{x}_t$ and $\hat{\mathbf{v}}_t \equiv \hat{\mathbf{x}}_{t2}$. The degrees-of-freedom of the test are K_2, the dimension of $\mathbf{x}_{t2}$. A test that assumes homoskedasticity and no serial correlation is based on TR_u^2 from the regression

$$\hat{u}_t \quad \text{on} \quad \mathbf{x}_t, \hat{\mathbf{x}}_{t2}. \tag{4.6}$$

This is essentially the form suggested by Hausman (1983). Procedures 3.2 and 3.3 give fairly simple robust forms of the test. □

Example 4.4 (testing overidentifying restrictions). Let the model be

$$y_t = \mathbf{x}_t\beta + u_t,$$

where $\mathbf{x}_t$ is $1 \times K$. Let $\mathbf{w}_t$ be a $1 \times L$ vector of instruments, where $L > K$. If $\hat{u}_t$ denotes the 2SLS residuals $y_t - \mathbf{x}_t\beta$, a test of overidentifying restrictions, which assumes homoskedasticity and no serial correlation under the null, is obtained as TR_u^2 from the regression of $\hat{u}_t$ on $\mathbf{w}_t$ (condition (3.13) trivially holds in this case); TR_u^2 is asymptotically distributed as χ_Q^2, where $Q \equiv L - K$. Procedure 3.2 or 3.3 is applied by taking $\hat{\mathbf{x}}_t = \mathbf{w}_t\hat{\Pi}$ and $\hat{\mathbf{v}}_t$ to be any of Q elements from $\mathbf{w}_t$ that are not also elements of $\mathbf{x}_t$. This produces a heteroskedasticity robust or heteroskedasticity–serial correlation robust test of the overidentifying restrictions. □

Example 4.5 (testing for nonlinearities). Consider the model

$$y_t = \mathbf{q}_t\alpha + \mathbf{z}_t\delta + u_t \tag{4.7}$$

$$E(u_t|\mathbf{w}_t) = 0, \tag{4.8}$$

where $\mathbf{q}_t$ is $1 \times G$ vector of endogenous variables and $\mathbf{z}_t$ is a $1 \times M$

vector of exogenous variables; therefore, $\mathbf{z}_t$ is included among the instruments $\mathbf{w}_t$. For identification, $\mathbf{w}_t$ must have at least G more elements than $\mathbf{z}_t$. A RESET-type test (Ramsey, 1969) can be obtained from the augmented model

$$y_t = \mathbf{q}_t\alpha + \mathbf{z}_t\delta + \gamma_1(\mathbf{q}_t\alpha + \mathbf{z}_t\delta)^2 + \gamma_2(\mathbf{q}_t\alpha + \mathbf{z}_t\delta)^3 + u_t. \qquad (4.9)$$

A score diagnostic is obtained as follows:

(1) Estimate model (4.7) by 2SLS using instruments $\mathbf{w}_t$. Let $\hat{u}_t$ denote the 2SLS residuals and define the 1×2 vector

$$\hat{\mathbf{h}}_t \equiv \{(\mathbf{q}_t\hat{\alpha} + \mathbf{z}_t\hat{\delta})^2, (\mathbf{q}_t\hat{\alpha} + \mathbf{z}_t\hat{\delta})^3\}, \qquad (4.10)$$

where $(\hat{\alpha}, \hat{\delta})$ are the 2SLS estimators. Note that $\hat{\mathbf{h}}_t$ depends on the endogenous variable $\mathbf{q}_t$.

(2) Augment the instruments $\mathbf{w}_t$ with some nonlinear functions of $\mathbf{w}_t$, say $\mathbf{g}_t \equiv g(\mathbf{w}_t)$. Because of the form of $\hat{\mathbf{h}}_t$, natural candidates to include in $\mathbf{g}_t$ are the squares, cubes, and various cross products of the elements of $\mathbf{w}_t$, or some subset of these. Note that (4.8) ensures that u_t is uncorrelated with any function of $\mathbf{w}_t$, including $\mathbf{g}_t$; in this example it is not sufficient to assume only $E(\mathbf{w}_t'u_t) = 0$. Obtain $\hat{\mathbf{q}}_t$ as the predicted values from the regression

$$\mathbf{q}_t \quad \text{on} \quad \mathbf{w}_t, \mathbf{g}_t \qquad (4.11)$$

and set $\hat{\mathbf{x}}_t \equiv (\hat{\mathbf{q}}_t, \mathbf{z}_t)$. Obtain the $\hat{\mathbf{v}}_t$ as the 1×2 vectors of fitted values from the regression

$$\hat{\mathbf{h}}_t \quad \text{on} \quad \mathbf{w}_t, \mathbf{g}_t. \qquad (4.12)$$

(3) $\hat{u}_t$, $\hat{\mathbf{x}}_t$, and $\hat{\mathbf{v}}_t$ can be used in procedure 3.1, 3.2, or 3.3, depending on what else is maintained under H_0.

If $L(\mathbf{q}_t|\mathbf{w}_t, \mathbf{g}_t) = L(\mathbf{q}_t|\mathbf{w}_t)$, which automatically holds if $E(\mathbf{q}_t|\mathbf{w}_t)$ is linear – a natural assumption under H_0 for many applications – then $\hat{\mathbf{q}}_t$ can be the original first-stage 2SLS fitted values from the regression $\mathbf{q}_t$ on $\mathbf{w}_t$. If, in addition, B.3 and B.4 hold then the test statistic is TR_u^2 from the regression

$$\hat{u}_t \quad \text{on} \quad \hat{\mathbf{q}}_t, \mathbf{z}_t, \hat{v}_{t1}, \hat{v}_{t2};$$

$TR_u^2 \overset{a}{\sim} \chi_2^2$ under these assumptions. The form that does not maintain linearity of $E(\mathbf{q}_t|\mathbf{w}_t)$ and the robust forms are only moderately more difficult to compute. □

5 Concluding Remarks

The procedures suggested in this chapter offer relatively simple methods for carrying out robust inference in linear models that are estimated by 2SLS. The standard errors and test statistics discussed in sections 2 to 4 are alternatives to more popular methods that model serial correlation in a parametric fashion and necessarily impose certain strict exogeneity assumptions on the explanatory variables and instruments. The robust forms of the test statistics require only very weak assumptions on the errors.

In addition to offering simple, robust tests, a useful innovation is the explicit treatment of cases where the misspecification indicator $\mathbf{v}_t$ is not a function of the instruments used under H_0. In the published literature this distinction has been made in the context of testing for exclusion restrictions but has not been adequately treated in the context of general specification tests. The analysis of section 3 derives the needed adjustment if the elements of $\mathbf{v}_t$ are not redundant as instruments under H_0; if the redundancy condition (3.13) holds then the adjustment is unnecessary.

We have said nothing about the finite sample performance of the statistics or their behavior under alternative hypotheses. It turns out that the adjustments used to make the statistics robust have no adverse affects on the asymptotic local power of the statistics if the auxiliary assumptions (B.3 and B.4) happen to be true. This is shown generally in Wooldridge (1990). When the same instruments are used under the null and alternative, the score-type tests suggested here are asymptotically equivalent to the Wald statistics suggested in Engle (1984) under local alternatives. This suggests that the statistics can be expected to have reasonable power against alternatives.

The finite sample performance of the statistics obtained from procedures 3.1 and 3.2 have been investigated by Bollerslev and Wooldridge (1992) in the context of dynamic regression models with ARCH and GARCH errors estimated by OLS (and quasi-MLE). These statistics behave quite well in terms of both actual size and power against reasonable alternatives; and, as expected from the theoretical results, the robust statistic behaves better when heteroskedasticity (ARCH or GARCH) is present but neglected. This does not mean that the statistics necessarily have good properties in the context of 2SLS, but it is suggestive.

Unfortunately, much less is known about the finite sample behavior of serial correlation robust procedures such as procedure 3.3. It seems likely that these will be less well behaved because of the nonparametric serial correlation adjustments, and the simulation results of Andrews (1991) bear this out for variance matrix estimation. Still, this remains a topic for future research.

Finally, the robust tests can be used in a specification testing strategy so that no auxiliary assumptions are maintained under the relevant null hypothesis. See Godfrey (1987) and Wooldridge (1991) for more on this.

Note

An anonymous referee and David Weaver provided helpful comments on an earlier draft. I would also like to acknowledge the generous financial support from a Sloan Foundation Research Fellowship.

References

Andrews, D. W. K. (1991) Heteroskedasticity and autocorrelation consistent covariance matrix estimation. *Econometrica*, 59, 817–58.

Berk, K. N. (1974) Consistent autoregressive spectral estimates. *Annals of Statistics*, 2, 489–502.

Bollerslev, T. (1986) Generalized autoregressive conditional heteroskedasticity. *Journal of Econometrics*, 31, 307–28.

Bollerslev, T. and Wooldridge, J. M. (1992) Quasi-maximum likelihood estimation and inference for dynamic models with time-varying covariances. *Econometric Reviews*, 11, 143–72.

Davidson, R. and MacKinnon, J. G. (1990) Specification tests based on artificial regressions. *Journal of the American Statistical Association*, 85, 220–7.

Engle, R. F. (1982a) A general approach to Lagrange multiplier diagnostics. *Journal of Econometrics*, 20, 83–104.

Engle, R. F. (1982b) Autoregression conditional heteroskedasticity with estimates of United Kingdom inflation. *Econometrica*, 50, 987–1008.

Engle, R. F. (1984) Wald, likelihood ratio, and Lagrange multiplier tests in econometrics. In Z. Griliches and M. D. Intriligator (eds), *Handbook of Econometrics, Vol. II*. Amsterdam: North-Holland, pp. 775–826.

Godfrey, L. G. (1987) Discriminating between autocorrelation and misspecification in regression analysis: an alternative test strategy. *Review of Economics and Statistics*, 69, 128–34.

Hansen, B. E. (1992) Consistent covariance matrix estimation for dependent heterogeneous processes. *Econometrica*, 60, 967–72.

Hausman, J. A. (1983) Specification and estimation of simultaneous equation models. In Z. Griliches and M. D. Intriligator (eds), *Handbook of Econometrics, Vol. I*. Amsterdam: North-Holland, pp. 391–448.

MacKinnon, J. G. (1992) Model specification tests and artificial regressions. *Journal of Economic Literature*, 30, 102–46.

MacKinnon, J. G. and White, H. (1985) Some heteroskedasticity consistent covariance matrix estimators with improved finite sample properties. *Journal of Econometrics*, 29, 305–25.

Newey, W. K. and West, K. D. (1987) A simple positive semi-definite heteroskedasticity and autocorrelation consistent covariance matrix. *Econometrica*, 55, 703–8.

Pagan, A. R. and Hall, A. D. (1983) Diagnostic tests as residual analysis. *Econometric Reviews*, 2, 159–218.

Ramsey, J. B. (1969) Tests for specification errors in classical least squares regression analysis. *Journal of the Royal Statistical Society B*, 31, 350–71.

Rao, C. R. (1947) Large sample tests of statistical hypotheses concerning several parameters with applications to problems of estimation. *Proceedings of the Cambridge Philosophical Society*, 44, 50–7.

White, H. (1980) A heteroskedasticity consistent covariance matrix estimator and a direct test for heteroskedasticity. *Econometrica*, 48, 817–38.

White, H. (1984) *Asymptotic Theory for Econometricians*. Orlando: Academic Press.

Wooldridge, J. M. (1989) A computationally simple heteroskedasticity and serial correlation robust standard error for the linear regression model. *Economics Letters*, 31, 239–43.

Wooldridge, J. M. (1990) A unified approach to robust, regression-based specification tests. *Econometric Theory*, 6, 17–43.

Wooldridge, J. M. (1991) On the application of robust, regression-based diagnostics to models of conditional means and conditional variances. *Journal of Econometrics*, 47, 5–46.

4 Asymptotic Expansions in Statistics: a Review of Methods and Applications

Rabi N. Bhattacharya and Madan L. Puri

1 Introduction

Normal approximation lies at the heart of the asymptotic theory of statistics. Cramér–Edgeworth asymptotic expansions refine this approximation and, therefore, improve classical procedures for setting confidence intervals and critical regions. They also provide the principal tools for: (a) the study of higher order asymptotic optimality theory, which discriminates among (first order) asymptotically efficient estimators and test procedures; (b) the analysis of the bootstrap methodology; (c) computation of power functions in parametric models in the neighborhood of the null hypothetical values etc. In addition, they have many applications in other fields of mathematics.

Historically, Chebyshev (1890) seems to have been the first to provide a formal expansion of the probability density function of the normalized sum S_n of n i.i.d. random variables X_j in terms of the Gaussian density and Hermite polynomials. Edgeworth (1896, 1905) independently obtained the same expansion, and went much further. In the second part of his 1905 article Edgeworth provided a scheme for expanding the density of certain statistics, which are not just linear functions of S_n, assuming appropriate decays of higher order cumulants in powers of $n^{-1/2}$. This last expansion has come to be known as the *Edgeworth expansion*. It was, however, Cramér (1928) who gave the first rigorous derivation of an asymptotic expansion (of the distribution function of S_n) in powers of $n^{-1/2}$ under the condition that the magnitude of the characteristic function (c.f.) of X_j be bounded away from one at infinity. A multidimensional extension of Cramér's result was derived in Bhattacharya (1968, 1971). Bikyalis (1968) provided an L_1-

expansion for the density of S_n under conditions which were necessarily stronger. A comprehensive account of normal approximation errors and asymptotic expansions for normalized sums of independent random vectors may be found in Bhattacharya and Ranga Rao (1976).

Since very few statistics are expressible as normalized sums, Edgeworth's formal method was still not justified in general. The importance of such a justification was laid out in a survey article by Wallace (1958). Chibishov (1972, 1973) and Bhattacharya and Ghosh (1978) provided the desired justification of the formal Edgeworth expansion for large classes of classical statistics, which included M-estimators, under readily verifiable conditions on the common distribution of the underlying i.i.d. observations. In section 2 the approach of Bhattacharya and Ghosh (1978) is explained. The latter was extended to classical test statistics, such as likelihood ratios, by Chandra and Ghosh (1979, 1980).

The approach to the derivation of Edgeworth expansions in Bhattacharya and Ghosh (1978) apply to statistics which can be expressed as, or approximated adequately (for example, using a Taylor expansion) by, smooth functions of a vector of average sample characteristics, such as a finite set of sample moments. Expansions for this class of statistics may be derived by the scheme described in section 2, making use of expansions for normalized sums S_n of random vectors such as stated in sections 2 and 3. But two important classes of statistics not covered by this scheme are U-statistics and rank-based nonparametric statistics. Expansions up to order $o(n^{-1})$ for them are given in sections 4 and 5. The main result presented for U-statistics is due to Götze and van Zwet (1991), which improves earlier results of many authors, especially Callaert et al. (1980) and Bickel et al. (1986). For nonparametric statistics the results are due to Albers et al. (1976), Bickel and van Zwet (1978), Does (1983a, b), Seoh (1983), and Puri and Seoh (1984a, b).

Section 3 deals with normalized sums S_n of weakly dependent sequences of random vectors such as arising in time series models. The main result here is due to Götze and Hipp (1983), improving and extending earlier results of Nagaev (1961) and Statulevichius (1969–70). For statistics arising from such models one may then derive Edgeworth expansions following the same route as taken in Bhattacharya and Ghosh (1978) and explained in section 2.

Among other methods proposed for deriving Edgeworth-type expansions we mention Bhattacharya and Puri (1983) and a versatile approach of Götze (1985). The powerful method of Stein (1986), which has been successful in deriving Berry–Esseen bounds under weak dependence, is yet to be applied effectively for the derivation of Edgeworth expansions.

Since the important case of lattice random vectors has been left out of the main body of the article because of lack of space, some comments about it are in order in this introduction. In the second part of his 1905 paper Edgeworth considered expanding the point masses of the multinomial. But the first general results were obtained in one of the most important papers on the subject of normal approximations by Esseen (1945). In the one-dimensional lattice case Esseen derived full local expansions, as well as expansions of distribution functions which necessarily involved jump terms. The latter was based on local expansion and the Euler–McLaurin summation formula. Extensions of these expansions to multidimension were given by Ranga Rao (1961) and, in more precise form, by Bhattacharya and Ranga Rao (1976). For sums of weakly dependent random vectors, Huang has recently obtained similar local expansions following the route taken by Götze and Hipp (1983). In his article Esseen (1945) showed that the chi-square approximation to Karl Pearson's frequency chi-square statistic under a simple null hypothesis has an error $O(n^{-k/k+1})$, where k is the degrees of freedom. In general this is the best possible error bound. Note that for $k \geqslant 2$ this is of smaller order than the Berry–Esseen bound $O(n^{-1/2})$ for Borel measurable convex sets. For this reason the classical chi-square approximation turns out to be very good for most statistical purposes, even when some expected frequencies are smaller than the proverbial "five." This is confirmed in extensive numerical comparisons carried out by Yarnold (1970) and Bhattacharya and Chan (1994). In the latter article the chi-square is seen to outperform the bootstrap in most cases.

In the concluding section (section 6) we briefly review Edgeworth type expansions in economics, often derived independently of the probability-statistics literature, and indicate how the methods described in this article are of general applicability in econometrics. Among many contributions involving multivariate analysis and time-series models arising in economics only a few are mentioned. The derivations in these articles are mostly by a direct attack on the characteristic function of the statistic concerned. In many models with Gaussian errors, this approach has yielded a great deal of detailed information, especially in the so-called dynamic (i.e. autoregressive) models (see e.g. Sargan and Satchell 1986; Phillips 1978, 1986). On the other hand, such a program is difficult, if not impossible, to implement in semiparametric models where the type of the error distribution is not completely specified.

2 Asymptotic Expansions under Independence

The present section gives an overview of methods and some of the applications of asymptotic expansions for statistics based on i.i.d. observations.

Suppose $X_1, X_2, \ldots, X_n, \ldots$ is a sequence of i.i.d. observations with values in $\mathbb{R}^k$, $EX_n = 0$, $\operatorname{cov} X_n = \Sigma$, $E|X_n|^s < \infty$ for some integer $s \geqslant 3$. Here Σ is assumed nonsingular. The characteristic function (c.f.) of $S_n = (X_1 + \ldots + X_n)/n^{1/2}$ is $\hat{Q}_n(t) = \hat{Q}_1^n(t/n^{1/2})$, where Q_1 is the distribution of X_n and Q_n that of $(X_1 + \ldots + X_n)/n^{1/2}$, and the Fourier transform of a finite (signed) measure μ is denoted by $\hat{\mu}$. The cumulant generating function of the normalized sum may then be expanded in Taylor series to yield

$$\ln \hat{Q}_n(t) = -t'\Sigma t/2 + \sum_{r=1}^{s-2} n^{-r/2}\lambda_{r+2}(it'X_1)/(r+2)! + o(n^{-(s-2)/2}) \qquad (2.1)$$

as $n \to \infty$. Here $\lambda_r(t'X_1)$ denotes the rth cumulant of the random variable $t'X_1$, and $\lambda_r(it'X_1) = i^r\lambda_r(t'X_1)$.

One may rewrite (2.1) as

$$\begin{aligned}\hat{Q}_n(t) &= \exp(-t'\Sigma t/2)\exp\left(\sum_{r=1}^{s-2} n^{-r/2}\lambda_{r+2}(it'X_1)/(r+2)!\right) \\ &\quad (1 + o(n^{-(s-2)/2})) \\ &= \exp(-t'\Sigma t/2)\left[1 + \sum_{j=1}^{s-2} n^{-j/2}P_j(it)\right] + o(n^{-(s-2)/2}), \end{aligned} \qquad (2.2)$$

where P_j is a polynomial, obtained by collecting together coefficients of $n^{-j/2}$ in the Taylor expansion of the second exponential on the right side of the first equality in (2.2). The principal part of $\hat{Q}_n$ in (2.2) is the Fourier transform of a finite signed measure $\Gamma_{s,n}$ whose density is

$$\gamma_{s,n}(x) = \left[1 + \sum_{j=1}^{s-2} n^{-j/2}P_j(-D)\right]\varphi_\Sigma(x). \qquad (2.3)$$

Here φ_V is the standard normal density with mean zero and covariance matrix V, and D is the gradient operator $D = (\partial/\partial x_1, \ldots, \partial/\partial x_k)$. Although such an expansion of Q_n in one dimension was formally proposed by Edgeworth (1905) and Chebyshev (1890) at the turn of the century, Cramér (1928) was the first to rigorously prove that the expansion

$$\sup_x \left| F_n(x) - \int_{-\infty}^{x} \gamma_{s,n}(y)dy \right| = o(n^{-(s-2)/2}) \tag{2.4}$$

for the distribution function (d.f.) F_n of Q_n holds in the one-dimensional case under the so-called *Cramér's condition*

$$\limsup_{|t|\to\infty} |E\exp(it'X_1)| < 1. \tag{2.5}$$

A more general multidimensional extension of this result may be stated as follows (see Bhattacharya and Ranga Rao, 1976, chapter 4). If (2.5) holds then

$$\sup_{B\in\mathscr{B}} \left| P(S_n \in B) - \int_B \gamma_{s,n}(y)dy \right| = o(n^{-(s-2)/2}) \tag{2.6}$$

for every class $\mathscr{B}$ of Borel sets satisfying

$$\sup_{B\in\mathscr{B}} \int_{(\partial B)^\varepsilon} \exp(-|x|^2/2)dx = o(-\ln\varepsilon)^{-r} \quad \forall r > 0 \text{ as } \varepsilon \downarrow 0. \tag{2.7}$$

Here ∂B is the boundary of B and $(\partial B)^\varepsilon$ is the ε-neighborhood of ∂B. Clearly (2.7) holds for every class $\mathscr{B}$ for which the left side is $O(\varepsilon^a)$, as $\varepsilon \downarrow 0$, for some positive a. In particular it holds for the class $\mathscr{C}$ of all Borel measurable convex subsets of $\mathbb{R}^k$ (see Bhattacharya and Ranga Rao, 1976, corollary 3.2).

Note that without the assumption (2.5) such an expansion cannot hold in general. For example, if X_j are one-dimensional lattice random variables, i.e. if there exist constants x_0 and $b > 0$ such that $P(X_j \in \{x_0 + b\mathbb{Z}\}) = 1$, then F_n has jumps of order $n^{-1/2}$.

Since few statistics are expressible as normalized sums of i.i.d. random variables or vectors, one may, at least formally, consider an analogous formal expansion for the distribution of a real-valued normalized statistic W_n whose asymptotic distributions is $\mathcal{N}(0, \sigma^2)$. Such an expansion was suggested by Edgeworth (1905). We present now an appropriate version of this scheme. Suppose there exists an approximation $\tilde{W}$ of W_n (often given by a Taylor expansion of W_n) such that

$$\sup_x |P(W_n \leqslant x) - P(\tilde{W}_n \leqslant x)| = o(n^{-(s-2)/2}). \tag{2.8}$$

Assume also that the rth cumulant of $\tilde{W}_n$ may be expressed as

$$\gamma_r(\tilde{W}_n) = \chi_{r,n} + o(n^{-(s-2)/2}), \tag{2.9}$$

where there are constants b_{rj} satisfying

$$\chi_{r,n} = \begin{cases} \Sigma_{j=1}^{s-2} n^{-j/2} b_{1j} & \text{if } r = 1, \\ \sigma^2 + \Sigma_{j=1}^{s-2} n^{-j/2} b_{2j} & \text{if } r = 2, \\ \Sigma_{j=r-2}^{s-2} n^{-j/2} b_{rj} & \text{if } 3 \leqslant r \leqslant s. \end{cases} \tag{2.10}$$

A large class of normalized statistics satisfy (2.8) to (2.10). Among them are M-estimators in regular parametric models (see Bhattacharya and Ghosh, 1978) and U-statistics (Bhattacharya and Puri, 1983). If (2.8) to (2.10) hold, then the c.f. of W_n may be expressed as

$$\begin{aligned} E\exp(itW_n) &= \exp\left(-\sum_{s=1}^{s-2} \chi_{r,n}(it)^r/r!\right) + o(n^{-(s-2)/2}) \\ &= \exp(-\sigma^2 t^2/2)\exp\left(\sum_{r=1}^{s-2} \chi_{r,n}(it)^r/r! + \sigma^2 t^2/2\right) \\ &\quad + o(n^{-(s-2)/2}) \\ &= \exp(-\sigma^2 t^2/2)\exp\left(\sum_{j=1}^{s-2} n^{-j/2} p_j(it)\right) + o(n^{-(s-2)/2}) \\ &\quad \left[p_j(it) := \sum_{r=1}^{s-2} b_{rj}(it)^r/r!\right] \\ &= \exp(-\sigma^2 t^2/2)\left[1 + \sum_{j=1}^{s-2} n^{-j/2} P_j(it)\right] + o(n^{-(s-2)/2}) \\ &= \eta_{s,n}(t) + o(n^{-(s-2)/2}) \end{aligned} \tag{2.11}$$

in a neighborhood of $t = 0$. For example,

$$\begin{aligned} &P_1(it) = p_1(it), \qquad P_2(it) = p_2(it) - p_1^2(it), \\ &P_3(it) = p_3(it) + p_1(it)p_2(it) - p_1^3(it)/3! \end{aligned} \tag{2.12}$$

Based on (2.11) one may attempt an expansion of the distribution of W_n by a signed measure $\Psi_{s,n}$ whose Fourier transform is $\eta_{s,n}$ and whose density is

$$\psi_{s,n}(x) = \left[1 + \sum_{j=1}^{s-2} n^{-j/2} P_j(-d/dx)\right]\varphi_{\sigma^2}(x). \tag{2.13}$$

Once again, such a *"formal" expansion* is not always valid. The methods for deriving valid expansions may be roughly divided into two groups. One may directly attempt to expand the c.f. f_n of W_n to show that, for some sequence $\{a_n\}$ satisfying $a_n/(\log n)^{1/2} \to \infty$,

$$\int_{\{|t| \leq a_n\}} \frac{1}{|t|} |f_n(t) - \eta_{s,n}(t)| dt = o(n^{-(s-2)/2}), \tag{2.14}$$

and, for some sequence $\Delta_n \to \infty$,

$$\int_{\{a_n < |t| \leq \Delta_n n^{(s-2)/2}\}} \frac{|f_n(t)|}{|t|} dt = o(n^{-(s-2)/2}), \tag{2.15}$$

The proof is completed by the use of Esseen's smoothing inequality (see Bhattacharya and Ranga Rao, 1976, pp. 101–2, lemma 12.2). For every $T > 0$ one has, with $M := \sup |\psi_{s,n}(x)|$,

$$\sup_x \left| F_n(x) - \int_{-\infty}^{x} \psi_{s,n}(y)\, dy \right| \leq (7/8\pi) \int_{-T}^{T} \frac{1}{|t|} |f_n(t) - \eta_{s,n}| dt + \frac{9M}{8\pi T}. \tag{2.16}$$

Asymptotic expansions for U-statistics and rank based nonparametric statistics are generally derived by this method, under appropriate assumptions on the statistic and on the common distribution of the i.i.d. observations on which the statistic is based. Such a derivation often involves ingenious estimation of the growth of the c.f. $f_n(t)$ for large values of t, and is generally provided for $s = 4$, which is adequate for many statistical purposes. In section 4 we provide some details of such estimation for rank statistics.

The second method, which is generally applicable to classical parametric as well as semiparametric statistics, expresses W_n as (or approximates it by) a polynomial $\tilde{W}_n = h_n(S_n)$ of the normalized sum $S_n = (Z_1 + \ldots + Z_n)/n^{1/2} = (S_{n1}, \ldots, S_{nk})$ with a nonvanishing leading linear term $\Sigma_i a_i S_{ni}$. Here $Z_j = (f_1(X_j), \ldots, f_k(X_j))$ is a vector function of the jth observation X_j. If the c.f. of Z_j satisfies Cramér's condition (2.5), and if the sth absolute moment of Z_j is finite, then one may apply the expansion (2.6) to get

$$\sup_x \left| P(W_n \leq x) - \int_{\{z: h_n(z) \leq x\}} \gamma_{s,n}(z) dz \right| = o(n^{-(s-2)/2}). \tag{2.17}$$

Since it is in general terribly messy and impractical to carry out the integration in (2.17), the next step is to show that this expansion is the same as the formal expansion (2.13). The details may be found in

Bhattacharya and Ghosh (1978), where it is shown, in addition, that if (a) the m-dimensional observation X_j has a nonzero absolutely continuous component with a positive density in a ball U, (b) $f_1, f_2, \ldots, f_k$ are continuously differentiable in U, (c) $1, f_1, f_2, \ldots, f_k$ are linearly independent as elements of the vector space of continuous functions on U, (d) the statistic W_n is of the form $n^{1/2}(H(\bar{Z}) - H(\mu))$ where H is $s - 1$ times continuously differentiable in a neighborhood of $\mu = EZ_j$, and (e) Z_j has a finite sth absolute moment, then

$$\sup_{B \in \mathscr{B}^1} \left| P(W_n \in B) - \int_B \psi_{s,n}(x)dx \right| = o(n^{-(s-2)/2}). \qquad (2.18)$$

where $\mathscr{B}^1$ is the class of all Borel subsets of $\mathbb{R}^1$. This result extends to vector-valued statistics W_n converging in distribution to $\mathcal{N}(0, V)$. One class of examples are maximum likelihood estimators in exponential (or curved exponential) families. More generally, under usual regularity conditions, one may show that (see Bhattacharya and Ghosh, 1978, or Bhattacharya, 1985) for normalized p-dimensional M-estimators W_n one has

$$\sup_{B \in \mathscr{B}} \left| P(W_n \in B) - \int_B \psi_{s,n}(x)dx \right| = o(n^{-(s-2)/2}). \qquad (2.19)$$

for every class $\mathscr{B}$ of Borel sets of $\mathbb{R}^p$ satisfying, for some $a > 0$,

$$\sup_{B \in \mathscr{B}} \int_{(\partial B)^\varepsilon} \exp(|x|^2/2)dx = O(\varepsilon^a) \qquad \text{as } \varepsilon \downarrow 0. \qquad (2.20)$$

This method also applies to statistics W_n of the form $n(H(\bar{Z}) - H(\mu))$, where grad H is zero at μ, and the matrix of second order derivatives does not vanish at μ (see Chandra and Ghosh, 1979, 1980). The latter case arises for likelihood ratios and chi-square statistics, for example. For some significant earlier work on asymptotic expansions for statistics we refer to Chibishov (1973).

A recent extension of the method described above has been given by Bai and Rao (1991), where for the statistic $W_n = n^{1/2}(H(\bar{Z}) - H(\mu))$ it is shown that if (a) $Z_j = (Z_{j1}, Z_{j2}, \ldots, Z_{jk})$ has a finite sth absolute moment, (b) H is $s - 1$ times continuously differentiable in a neighborhood of $\mu = EZ_j$, (c) $l_1 = (\partial/\partial x_1)H(x))_{x=\mu} \neq 0$, and (d) $\limsup_{|t| \to \infty} E|v_1(t)| < 1$, where $v_1(t) = E(\exp(itZ_{j1})|Z_{j2}, \ldots, Z_{jk})$, then the formal Edgeworth expansion for the d.f. of W_n is valid. There are statistical applications of this result where one of the components of Z_j is discrete, so that Cramér's condition is not satisfied. Of course, in general Cramér's condition for Z_j does not imply (d) either.

Since discrete observations in general, and lattice observations in particular, do not satisfy Cramér's condition, it is comforting to know that expectations of smooth functions of S_n (and of W_n, as a consequence) have asymptotic expansions under moment conditions alone. A precise statement of this result, due to Götze and Hipp (1978), is as follows. If Z_j has a finite sth absolute moment, then

$$E(f(S_n)) = \int f(x)\gamma_{s,n}(x)dx + o(n^{-(s-2)/2}) \tag{2.21}$$

for all $s - 2$ times continuously differentiable functions f such that $(1 + |x|^s)^{-1}|f(x)|$ is bounded and $(s - 2)$th order derivatives of f have at most a polynomial growth at infinity. An alternative version of this result may be found in Bhattacharya (1985).

We conclude this section with brief discussions of two types of applications of asymptotic expansions to statistics. First, consider Efron's (1979) *bootstrap distribution function* F_n^* of a normalized statistic W_n. In the case W_n is the standardized mean of n i.i.d. one-dimensional random variables, it was shown in a basic paper by Singh (1981), using asymptotic expansions, that the difference between the true distribution function F_n of W_n and F_n^* is a.s. $o(n^{-1/2})$, uniformly for all arguments of the d.f., provided the distribution of the summands is nonlattice and has a finite third moment. Thus the bootstrap provides a better approximation of the distribution of W_n than the classical normal approximation, the latter having error $o(n^{-1/2})$. The method of Singh was one-dimensional and based on Esseen's inequality (2.16), which has no proper multidimensional analogue. In a subsequent significant contribution, Babu and Singh (1984) provided an asymptotic expansion up to $o(n^{-(s-2)/2})$ for a normalized multivariate sample mean $\bar{Z}$ under Cramér's condition for Z_j. It follows in particular that the bootstrap distribution function F_n^* of the Student's statistic approximates the true d.f. F_n with an error $o(n^{-1/2})$ a.s., uniformly for all arguments. It is shown in Bhattacharya and Qumsiyeh (1989) that the bootstrap approximation for studentized statistics is superior to even a two-term empirical Edgeworth expansion. A comprehensive account of the bootstrap and its relations with the Edgeworth expansion may be found in the monograph by Hall (1992).

Turning to *higher order asymptotics*, in a parametric model satisfying the usual regularity conditions the m.l.e. (i.e. a consistent solution of the likelihood equation) is asymptotically efficient in the sense of Fisher; namely, its asymptotic variance attains the information lower bound. There are, however, many such estimators. For example, a one-step Newton–Raphson approximation to the solution of the likelihood equation, starting with any $n^{1/2}$-consistent estimator, is asymptotically efficient, or what is now called first order efficient. A notion of *second order efficiency* may be used to discriminate among first order efficient estimators. Roughly speaking, if the m.l.e. is bias-corrected up to $o(n^{-1})$, then it has the smallest expected squared error among all similarly bias-corrected estimators if terms of order $o(n^{-2})$ are neglected. Fisher (1925) himself suggested that the m.l.e. itself is second order efficient in this sense. The theory of higher order efficiency was developed much further in a series of papers by Rao (1961, 1962, 1963). More modern treatments as well as extensions were given by Ghosh and Subramanyam (1974), Efron (1975), Pfanzagl (1980), and Akahira and Takeuchi (1981). An insightful account of this and many other aspects of higher order asymptotics may be found in the recent book by Ghosh (1994).

An expository derivation of the basic expansions discussed in this section, along with a number of statistical applications, may be found in Bhattacharya and Denker (1990).

3 Expansions under Weak Dependence

For notational convenience, the symbols c, d below will denote positive constants, not always the same, which do not vary with the variable indices n, m, i, j, r, etc.

We begin with a description of the basic structure of the Fourier analytic method for the derivation of an asymptotic expansion of the nth normalized partial sum $S_n = n^{-1/2}(X_1 + \ldots + X_n)$ of a sequence of k-dimensional random vectors $X_1, X_2, \ldots$ satisfying

$$EX_j = 0 \text{ for all } j, \quad \beta_{s+1} := \sup_n E|X_n|^{s+1} < \infty. \tag{3.1}$$

For technical purposes it is necessary to consider truncated random vectors $Z_j' = X_j \cdot 1(|X_j| \leqslant n^{\beta})$, $Z_j = Z_j' - EZ_j'$, $S_n' = n^{-1/2}(Z_1' + \ldots + Z_n')$, $S_n^* = n^{-1/2}(Z_1 + \ldots + Z_n)$. Here $\beta \in (0, \frac{1}{2}]$ is an appropriate constant. Let Σ_n denote the covariance matrix of S_n^*, and let $\lambda_\nu(S_n^*)$ denote its νth cumulant for a multi-index $\nu = (\nu_1, \ldots, \nu_k)$. Let δ_n be the smallest eigenvalue of Σ_n. Assume there exist positive constants c_2, c_r such that

$$\liminf \delta_n \geqslant c_2, \ \limsup n^{(r-2)/2}|\lambda_\nu(S_n^*)| \leqslant c_r \quad \text{for } 2 \leqslant r \leqslant s+1, \tag{3.2}$$

where $r = \nu_1 + \ldots + \nu_k$. The *formal Cramér–Edgeworth expansion* of the c.f. $\hat{Q}_n(t)$ of the distribution Q_n of S_n^* is defined as follows. Write

$$\exp\left(\sum_{r=3}^{s} \frac{\lambda_r(it'S_n^*)}{r!}\right) = \exp\left(\sum_{r=1}^{s-2} n^{-r/2} \frac{(n^{r/2}\lambda_{r+2}(it'S_n^*))}{r+2!}\right)$$

$$= 1 + \sum_{r=1}^{s-2} n^{-r/2} P_{r,n}(it) + R_n, \tag{3.3}$$

obtained by a Taylor expansion. In other words,

$$P_{r,n}(it) = r!\left[(d^r/du^r)\exp\left(\sum_{r=1}^{s-2} u^r a_{r+2,n}(it)\right)\right]_{u=0},$$

$$a_{r+2,n}(it) := n^{r/2}\lambda_{r+2}(it'S_n^*)/(r+2)!. \tag{3.4}$$

Lemma 3.1 If (3.1) and (3.2) hold, then for all multi-indices $\alpha = (\alpha_1, \ldots, \alpha_k)$, $\Sigma_i \alpha_i \leqslant s + 1 + k$, there exist positive constants c, c', c'', such that for $|t| \leqslant c'' n^{1/2}$ one has

$$\left| D^\alpha\left[\exp\left(\sum_{r=2}^{s} \frac{\lambda_r(it'S_n^*)}{r!}\right) - \exp\left(-\frac{t'\Sigma_n t}{2}\right)\left(1 + \sum_{r=1}^{s-2} n^{-r/2} P_{r,n}(it)\right)\right]\right|$$

$$\leqslant c' n^{-(s-1)/2} \exp(-c|t^2|). \quad \square \tag{3.5}$$

The proof of lemma 3.1 is the same as in the classical case, and only uses Taylor expansion and Cauchy's estimate for derivatives of analytic functions (see Bhattacharya and Ranga Rao, 1976, lemmas 9.7, 9.8). The formal Edgeworth expansion of the c.f. of S_n^* is now given by

$$\hat{\gamma}_{s,n}(t) = \exp(-t'\Sigma_n t/2)\left(1 + \sum_{r=1}^{s-2} n^{-r/2} P_{r,n}(it)\right), \tag{3.6}$$

and the signed measure $\Gamma_{s,n}$ having Fourier transform $\hat{\gamma}_{s,n}(it)$ has density

$$\gamma_{s,n}(x) = \left(1 + \sum_{r=1}^{s-2} n^{-r/2} P_{r,n}(-D)\right)\phi_{\Sigma_n}(x). \tag{3.7}$$

Lemma 3.2 Assume that (3.1) and (3.2) hold, and that (a continuous extension of) the logarithm of the c.f. $\hat{Q}_n(it)$ satisfies, for all α, $\Sigma\alpha_i \leqslant s + 1 + k$,

$$\left| D^\alpha\left(\log \hat{Q}_n(it) - \sum_{r=2}^{s} \lambda_r(it'S_n^*)/r!\right)\right| \leqslant c n^{-(s-2+\varepsilon_1)/2} q_1(t) \tag{3.8}$$

for $|t| \leqslant c' n^{\varepsilon_2}$. Here q_1 is a polynomial which does not vary with n, and

ε_1 and ε_2 are positive constants, $\varepsilon_2 \leqslant \frac{1}{2}$. Then there exist positive constants c_1', c_2', c_3', ε_3 ($\leqslant \varepsilon_2$) such that

$$\left| D^\alpha \left[\hat{Q}_n(t) - \exp\left(\sum_{r=2}^{s} \frac{\lambda_r(it'S_n^*)}{r!} \right) \right] \right| \leqslant c_1' n^{-(s-2+\varepsilon_1)} \exp(-c_2'|t|^2) \quad (3.9)$$

for $|t| \leqslant c_3' n^{\varepsilon_3}$ and for $\Sigma \alpha_i \leqslant s + 1 + k$. □

The proof of lemma 3.2 is quite analogous to that of the corresponding result in the classical case, and once again requires little beyond Taylor expansion and Cauchy's estimate (see lemma 9.3 in Bhattacharya and Ranga Rao, 1976).

Assume next that the following estimate for large values of t holds for $D^\alpha \hat{Q}_n(t)$:

$$\sup_{\substack{|t| \geqslant c_3' n^{\varepsilon_3} \\ \Sigma \alpha_i \leqslant s+1+k}} |D^\alpha \hat{Q}_n(t)| = o(n^{-r}) \quad \text{for all } r > 0. \quad (3.10)$$

Theorem 3.1 Assume (3.10) and the hypothesis of lemma 3.2. Assume also that

$$P(S_n \neq S_n') = o(n^{-(s-2)/2}), \quad |ES_n'| = o(n^{-(s-2)/2}). \quad (3.11)$$

Then

$$\sup_{B \in \mathscr{B}} \left| P(S_n \in B) - \int_B \gamma_{s,n}(x) dx \right| = o(n^{-(s-2)/2}) \quad (3.12)$$

for every class $\mathscr{B}$ of Borel sets satisfying, for some positive constant a,

$$\sup_{B \in \mathscr{B}} \int_{(\partial B)^\varepsilon} \exp\left(\frac{-|x|^2}{2} \right) dx = O(\varepsilon^a), \quad \text{as } \varepsilon \downarrow 0. \quad □ \quad (3.13)$$

Proof. By corollary 11.3 in Bhattacharya and Ranga Rao (1976), for every Borel set B and every $\varepsilon > 0$, one has

$$|Q_n(B) - \Gamma_{s,n}(B)| \leqslant \frac{1}{2} \| (Q_n - \Gamma_{s,n}) * K_\varepsilon \| + \int_{(\partial B)^{2\varepsilon}} |\gamma_{s,n}(x)| dx. \quad (3.14)$$

Here $\| \cdot \|$ denotes variation norm and K_ε is the distribution of εZ, with Z satisfying

$$P(|Z|) \leqslant 1) \equiv K_1(\{x : |x| \leqslant\}) = 1. \quad (3.15)$$

Choose K_1 to satisfy (see Bhattacharya and Ranga Rao, 1976, corollary 10.4)

$$|D^{\alpha}\hat{K}_1(t)| \leqslant c_{\alpha}\exp(-|t|^{1/2}) \quad (t \in \mathbb{R}^k), \quad \forall\alpha. \tag{3.16}$$

By lemma 11.6 in Bhattacharya and Ranga Rao (1976), writing $|\beta| = \Sigma\beta_i$,

$$\begin{aligned} \|(Q_n - \Gamma_{s,n})K_{\varepsilon}\| &\leqslant c(k) \max_{|\beta|=0,k+1} \int |D^{\beta}[(\hat{Q}_n(t) - \hat{\gamma}_{s,n}(t))\hat{K}_1(\varepsilon t)]|dt \\ &\leqslant c'(k) \max_{\substack{(\alpha_1,\alpha_2):\alpha_1+\alpha_2=\beta, \\ |\beta|=0,k+1}} \int |D^{\alpha_1}(\hat{Q}_n(t) - \hat{\gamma}_{s,n}(t)) \cdot D^{\alpha_2}\hat{K}_1(\varepsilon t)|dt. \end{aligned} \tag{3.17}$$

Denoting the above integral by I, one has

$$\begin{aligned} I \leqslant & \int_{|t| \leqslant c_3' n^{\varepsilon_3}} |D^{\alpha_1}(\hat{Q}_n(t) - \hat{\gamma}_{s,n}(t))|dt + \int_{|t| > c_3' n^{\varepsilon_3}} |D^{\alpha_1}\hat{\gamma}_{s,n}(t)|dt \\ & + \int_{|t| > c_3' n^{\varepsilon_3}} |D^{\alpha_1}\hat{Q}_n(t) \cdot D^{\alpha_2}\hat{K}_1(\varepsilon t)|dt \\ = & \; I_1 + I_2 + I_3, \quad \text{say}. \end{aligned} \tag{3.18}$$

By lemmas 3.1 and 3.2,

$$I_1 = o(n^{-(s-2)/2}). \tag{3.19}$$

Since $\hat{\gamma}_{s,n}(t) \to 0$ exponentially fast as $|t| \to \infty$,

$$I_2 = o(n^{-(s-2)/2}). \tag{3.20}$$

By (3.10) and (3.16),

$$I_3 = o(n^{-(s-2)/2}). \tag{3.21}$$

if $\varepsilon = n^{-\gamma}$ for some $\gamma > 0$. The proof is now complete from (3.13), (3.14) if one takes, for example, $\gamma = (s-2)/a$. □

We now state the main result for sums of weakly dependent random vectors due to Götze and Hipp (1983). Let $X_1, X_2, \ldots,$ be a sequence of k-dimensional random vectors defined on a probability space $(\Omega, \mathscr{F}, P)$. In addition to (3.1), we assume the following conditions:

(A1) $\liminf \delta_n > 0$, $\limsup \|\mathfrak{X}_n\| < \infty$.

(A2) There exist a sequence of σ-fields $\mathscr{D}_n$ $(n = 0, \pm 1, \pm 2, \ldots)$ and positive constants c, d such that, for each pair (r, m) of positive integers, there is a random vector $X_{r,m}$ measurable with respect to $\mathscr{D}_{r-m}^{r+m}$ satisfying

$$E|X_r - X_{r,m}| \leqslant ce^{-dm}.$$

Here $\mathscr{D}_p^q := \sigma\{\mathscr{D}_n : p \leqslant n \leqslant q\}$.

(A3) There exist positive constants c, d such that for all n, m,

$$\sup_{A \in \mathscr{D}^{n}_{-\infty}, B \in \mathscr{D}^{\infty}_{n+m}} |P(A \cap B) - P(A)P(B)| \leqslant ce^{-dm}.$$

(A4) There exist positive constants $d_1 < 1$ and d_2 such that for all positive integers $m < n$ and for all t satisfying $|t| \geqslant d_2$,

$$E|E(\exp(it'(X_{n-m} + X_{n-m+1} + \ldots + X_{n+m}))|\mathscr{D}j : j \neq n)| \leqslant d_1. \tag{3.22}$$

(A5 There exist positive constants d_3, d_4 such that for all m, r, p and $B \in \mathscr{D}^{r+p}_{r-p}$

$$E|P(B|\mathscr{D}_j : j \neq r) - P(B|\mathscr{D}_j : 0 < |r - j| \leqslant m + p)| \leqslant d_3 \exp(-d_4 m).$$

Under assumptions (3.1), (A2), (A3), it may be easily shown that for all β sufficiently near 1/2 the normalized sum S_n^* of truncated random vectors Z_j introduced above satisfies (3.2), (3.11). In this case the formal Edgeworth expansion (3.12) of the distribution of S_n^* is the same as that of S_n.

Theorem 3.2 (Götze and Hipp, 1983). Under the assumptions (3.1), (A1) to (A5), the formal Edgeworth expansion (3.12) stated in theorem 3.1 is valid. □

In order to prove this theorem one needs to verify the hypotheses of theorem 3.1. Assume for the sake of simplicity that X_j is measurable with respect to $\mathscr{D}^{j+r}_{j-r}$ for some fixed r. In this case it is enough that the inequality in (3.22) in assumption (A4) holds for a fixed m. Now the hypotheses of lemmas 3.1, 3.2 may be verified using assumptions (3.1), (A3), and the fact that the smallest eigenvalue of Σ_n is bounded away from zero. A crucial step in such a derivation is an algebraic identity involving cumulants and moments of arbitrary random variables (see Bulinskii and Zhurbenko, 1976; Jensen, 1989a): Define the *simple cumulant* of the random variables $V_1, V_2, \ldots, V_r$ as

$$\operatorname{cum}(V_1, V_2, \ldots, V_r) := i^{-r}\left[\frac{\partial^r}{\partial\varepsilon_1 \ldots \partial\varepsilon_r} \log E \exp\left(i\sum_{j=1}^{r} \varepsilon_j V_j\right)\right]_{\varepsilon_1 = \ldots = \varepsilon_r = 0} \tag{3.23}$$

Write $I = \{1, 2, \ldots, r\}$. Let I', II'' be nonempty and disjoint, $I = I' \cup I''$. For a given partition $\{I_1, I_2, \ldots, I_\nu\}$ of I, define $I'_j = I_j \cap I'$, $I''_j = I_j \cap I''$,

$$M_j = E\prod_{i \in I_j} V_i, \qquad M'_j = E\prod_{i \in I'_j} V_i, \qquad M''_j = E\prod_{i \in I''_j} V_i,$$

$$L_j = M_j' M_j'', \qquad D_j = M_j - L_j. \tag{3.24}$$

Then one has the identity

$$\mathrm{cum}(V_1, \ldots, V_r) = \sum{}^* \frac{(-1)^{\nu-1}}{\nu} \sum_{j=1}^{\nu} L_1 \ldots L_{j-1} D_j M_{j+1} \ldots M_\nu, \tag{3.25}$$

where L_0, as well as any empty product, equals one, and Σ^* denotes summation over all partitions $\{I_1, I_2, \ldots, I_\nu\}$ such that $\max\{i : i \in I_j\} < \min\{i : i \in I_{j+1}\}$ for all j.

Now take $V_j = Z_{i_j}$ where $\{i_1, i_2, \ldots, i_r\} \subset \{1, 2, \ldots, n\}$ and $i_1 < i_2 < \ldots < i_r$. Choose p and $I' = \{i_1, i_2, \ldots, i_p\}$ such that the gap $i_{p+1} - i_p$ is maximal. If this gap is large, then D_j is small. From this and (A3) one may deduce (3.2), and by a similar argument also derive (3.8).

To derive (3.10), one uses the Cramér-type condition (A4) as well as the technical looking assumption (A5). The role of (A5) becomes clear when one attempts to take a conditional expectation of $\exp(it'S_n^*)$, given all summands except those involved in the sum appearing in the exponent in (3.22). In view of (A5), the conditional expectation of the exponential in (3.22) may be replaced by that given a rather small subset. One may repeat this process for N block sums such as appearing in (3.22), but widely separated, and then use the strong mixing type condition (A3) to approximate the c.f. of S_n by that of a sum of N independent random vectors each satisfying a Cramér type condition. A similar estimation holds for evaluating derivatives of $\hat{Q}_n$. Finally an appropriate choice of N completes the verification of (3.10). For details see Götze and Hipp (1983) or Jensen (1989a).

The following are a set of important examples in which all the assumptions (3.1), (A1) to (A5) are satisfied (see Götze and Hipp, 1983, 1994). The random variables X_j below are to be centered, or S_n has to be centered.

Example 3.1 (m-dependent sequences). Let Y_j ($j = 1, 2, \ldots$) be a sequence of i.i.d. random variables having a density g with respect to the Lebesgue measure. Let

$$X_j := h(Y_j, Y_{j+1}, \ldots, Y_{j+m-1}). \tag{3.26}$$

Here h is a measurable function on $\mathbb{R}^m$ satisfying

$$\sum_{r=1}^{m} \left(\frac{\partial h(x_1, \ldots, x_m)}{\partial x_r} \right)_{(x_1, \ldots, x_m) = (y_1, \ldots, y_m)} \neq 0, \tag{3.27}$$

for all y_r ($1 \leqslant r \leqslant m$) in an interval $(-c, c)$ on which g is positive. The sequence X_j ($j = 1, 2, \ldots$) is strictly stationary. Assume that X_j has a finite moment of order $s + 1$. The assumptions (A1) to (A5) are satisfied if one takes $\mathscr{D}_j$ to be the σ-field generated by Y_j. Most m-dependent sequences, although not all, are of the form (3.26).

Example 3.2 (moving averages). Let Y_j ($j = 0, \pm 1, \pm 2, \ldots$) be a sequence of i.i.d. random variables, and

$$X_j := \sum_{r=-\infty}^{\infty} c_r Y_{j+r} \tag{3.28}$$

where c_r go to zero exponentially fast as $r \to \pm\infty$, and $\Sigma\, c_r \neq 0$. If Y_j has a finite moment of order $s + 1$ and satisfies Cramér's condition (2.5), then all the assumptions are satisfied. Once again take $\mathscr{D}_j$ to be $\sigma\{Y_j\}$ and m in (A4) such that $c_{-n} + \ldots + c_n \neq 0$ for all $n \geqslant m$.

Example 3.3 (autoregressive and ARMA models). Let Y_j ($j = 0, \pm 1, \pm 2, \ldots$) be a sequence of i.i.d. real-valued random variables as in the preceding example, satisfying Cramér's condition (2.5). Given, $X_1, \ldots, X_p$, let X_j be recursively defined by

$$X_j := \sum_{r=1}^{p} a_r X_{j-r} + \sum_{r=1}^{q} b_r Y_{j-r} + Y_j, \quad (j = p + 1, p + 2, \ldots) \tag{3.29}$$

where b_r are arbitrary constants, $a_p \neq 0$, and the roots of the equation

$$z^p = \sum_{r=1}^{p} a_r z^{p-r} \tag{3.30}$$

all lie in the unit circle $\{z : |z| < 1\}$. In the case b_r are all zero, the X_j's define an autoregressive process of order p, or an AR(p) process. If $b_q \neq 0$, the process is called an autoregressive moving average model of order (p, q) (ARMA(p, q)). One may assume (3.29) to hold for all $j = 0, \pm 1, \pm 2, \ldots$, and express X_j in the form (3.28). The case of arbitrary initial $X_1, \ldots, X_p$ (with finite $(s + 1)$th moments) may then be dealt with by a direct comparison. It is also possible to deal with these processes by Markovian methods (see example 3.4 below).

Example 3.4 (functions of Markov processes). Let Y_j ($j = 0, 1, \ldots$) be a Markov process with stationary transition probability $p(y, dz)$ satisfying

$$\sup |p(y, B) - p(y', B)| < 1. \tag{3.31}$$

where the supremum is over all measurable sets B and all y and y'. For example, (3.31) is satisfied when there exists a positive measure μ such that $p(y, B) \geqslant \mu(B)$ for all y and all B. Let now

$$X_j := h(Y_j) \tag{3.32}$$

where h is a measurable real valued function such that, under the (unique) stationary initial distribution, X_1 satisfies Cramér's condition (2.5). If X_1 has a finite moment of order $s + 1$, then all the assumptions are satisfied, if one takes $\mathscr{D}_j = \sigma\{Y_j\}$. As remarked in example 3.3, the stable ARMA(p, q) models may be dealt with from this Markovian point of view.

Among other important classes that may be treated by the present theorem are functionals of nonlinear autoregressive processes (Götze and Hipp, 1994) and of stationary Gaussian processes.

Remark. Writing U_j for X_j in (3.28) or (3.29), one may consider $X_j := h(U_j, \ldots, U_{j+p-1})$ for a continuously differentiable $h: \mathbb{R}^p \to \mathbb{R}^k$ such that $E\|D_i h(U_j, \ldots, U_{j+p-1})\| < \infty$ (D_i being the derivative with respect to the ith argument). If, in addition, Y_j has a continuous and positive density then (A1) to (A5) hold provided some obvious degeneracy (such as $X_j := U_j - U_{j-1}$) does not occur. Also, for expansions of distributions of statistics of the form considered in section 2, but based on weakly dependent observations such as considered in this section, the same technique as before applies (Götze and Hipp, 1994).

Theorem 3.2 is very useful in the statistical analysis of stationary time series. As an example we cite Bose (1988), who used the above expansion to analyze the bootstrap methodology in stable AR(p) models. Taniguchi (1983, 1991) derived asymptotic expansions for Gaussian ARMA processes and used them for the study of higher order efficiencies of estimators.

The moment condition (3.1) and the exponential decay in (A3) have been relaxed by Lahiri (1993). Replacing the Cramér type condition (A4) by an appropriate lattice condition, Huang (1994) has recently obtained asymptotic expansions for lattice random vectors analogous to those under independence as given, for example, in Bhattacharya and Ranga Rao (1976, chapter 5).

Among other significant contributions under dependence we mention Nagaev (1961), Statulevichius (1969–70), and Jensen (1989b).

4 Edgeworth Expansions for Nonparametric Statistics

Let X_{ni} ($1 \leqslant i \leqslant n$) be independent r.v.s. (random variables) with continuous distribution functions (df) $\{F_{ni}(x), 1 \leqslant i \leqslant n\}$. Let R_{ni} be the rank of X_{ni} in the partial sequence $X_{n1}, \ldots, X_{nn}$; R_{ni}^+, the rank of $|X_{ni}|$ in the partial sequence $|X_{n1}|, \ldots, |X_{nn}|$. Let $\operatorname{sgn} x_i = 1$ if $x_i \geqslant 0$, and -1 if $x_i < 0$. Consider the following statistics:

$$S_n = \sum_{i=1}^{n} c_{ni} a_n(R_{ni}), \quad S_n^+ = \sum_{i=1}^{n} c_{ni} a_n(R_{ni}^+) \operatorname{sgn} X_{ni}. \tag{4.1}$$

Here $\{c_{ni}, 1 \leqslant i \leqslant n\}$ are known constants; $\{a_n(i), 1 \leqslant i \leqslant n\}$ are "scores" generated by a known function $J(t)$, $0 < t < 1$ in either of the following two ways:

$$a_n(i) = E[J(U_{n:i})], \quad 1 \leqslant i \leqslant n \quad \text{(exact scores)} \tag{4.2}$$

or

$$a_n(i) = J[E(U_{n:i})] \quad \text{(approximate scores)} \tag{4.3}$$

where $U_{n:i}$ is the ith order statistic in a random sample of size n from a uniform distribution over (0, 1). Scores given by (4.2) give rise to locally most powerful rank tests whereas the scores given by (4.3) have the appeal of simplicity although in both cases they lead to asymptotically most powerful rank tests. In the nonparametric literature, S_n is called a *simple linear rank statistic*; S_n^+ is called a *signed rank statistic*. These statistics are often used in nonparametric inference problems.

Example 4.1 (regression problem). Let $F_{ni}(x) = F(x - \Delta c_{ni})$, $1 \leqslant i \leqslant n$. Then, for testing the hypothesis $H_0 : \Delta = 0$ against the one-sided alternative $H_1 : \Delta > 0$, the locally most powerful rank test is based on the statistic S_n with scores $a_n(i)$ given by

$$a_n(i) = E\{-f'(F^{-1}(U_{n:i}))/f(F^{-1}(U_{n:i}))\}, \quad 1 \leqslant i \leqslant n \quad \text{(exact scores)}, \tag{4.4}$$

and a locally asymptotically most powerful test is based on

$$a_n(i) = -f'[F^{-1}(EU_{n:i})]/f[F^{-1}(EU_{n:i})], \quad 1 \leqslant i \leqslant n \quad \text{(approximate scores)}, \tag{4.5}$$

where $f = F'$ is absolutely continuous with derivative (a.e.) f' such that $\int |f'(x)| dx < \infty$ and $F^{-1}(u) = \inf\{x : F(x) \geqslant u\}$.

Similarly, for testing the hypothesis $H_0^* : \Delta = 0$ and F is symmetric, against the alternative $H_1^* : \Delta > 0$ and F is symmetric, the locally most powerful rank test is based on the statistic S_n^+ with the scores $a_n(i)$ given by

$$a_n(i) = -E\{f'_+(F_+^{-1}(U_{n:i}))/f_+(F_+^{-1}(U_{n:i}))\}, \quad 1 \leqslant i \leqslant n, \tag{4.6}$$

and the locally asymptotically most powerful test has scores $a_n(i)$ given by

$$a_n(i) = -f'_+[F_+^{-1}(EU_{n:i})]/f_+[F_+^{-1}(EU_{n:i})], \quad 1 \leqslant i \leqslant n, \qquad (4.7)$$

where $F_+(x) = P[|X| \leqslant x] = 2F(x) - 1$ if $x > 0$, and 0 if $x \leqslant 0$, and $f_+(x) = F'_+(x)$ is absolutely continuous with derivative (a.e.) f'_+ such that $\int |f'_+(x)| dx < \infty$.

Example 4.2 (two-sample problem). Let $F_{n1} = \ldots = F_{nm} \equiv F$ and $F_{n,m+1} = \ldots = F_{n,n} \equiv G$. Then, for testing $H_0 : F = G$, many rank tests are based on the statistic $S'_n = \Sigma_{i=1}^m a_n(R_{ni})$ which is a specialization of S_n when $c_{ni} = 1$ if $1 \leqslant i \leqslant m$, and $c_{ni} = 0$ if $m + 1 \leqslant i \leqslant n$.

Example 4.3 (one-sample problem). Let $F_1 = \ldots = F_n \equiv F$. Then, for testing $H_0 : F(x)$ is symmetric about 0, many rank tests are based on the statistic $S_n^+ = \Sigma_{i=1}^n a_n(R_{ni}^+) \operatorname{sgn} X_{ni}$ which is a specialization of S_n^+ when $c_{ni} \equiv 1$, $1 \leqslant i \leqslant n$.

For more examples, see Hájek and Sidàk (1967).

Let us now write $S_n^* = (S_n - a_n)/b_n$ and $S_n^{+*} = (S_n^+ - a_n^+)/b_n^+$ where a_n, a_n^+, b_n and b_n^+ are normalizing constants, and let us give a generic name T_n to any of these statistics. Then it is well known that under suitable assumptions T_n has asymptotically, as $n \to \infty$, the standard normal distribution, i.e. $\lim_{n\to\infty} \sup_x |P(T_n \leqslant x) - \Phi(x)| = 0$ where $\Phi(x) = (2\pi)^{-1/2} \int_{-\infty}^{x} e^{-t^2/2} dt$. The results of this type justify the use of normal approximation to compute the critical values of the test procedures when n is large. They also enable us to compute the limiting powers of the test procedures and make efficiency comparisons on that basis.

However, quite often, one needs information more precise than the asymptotic normality can provide. On the one hand one may need more accurate numerical approximations; on the other hand one may wish to compare the performance of one procedure with other procedures with the same limiting powers (cf. Hodges and Lehmann, 1970). For this purpose it is enough to derive Edgeworth expansions (or higher order asymptotics) with remainder $o(n^{-1})$. They provide some qualitative insight into the regions of unreliability of the first order results. The first general results (for rank statistics) in the case of the standard one-sample problem were obtained by Albers et al. (1976). They established the Edgeworth expansion under the hypothesis of symmetry as well as under contiguous location alternatives. The same programme was carried out for the two-sample problem in

Bickel and van Zwet (1978). Under the null hypothesis, a similar result was proved by Robinson (1978). (See also Robinson, 1980, where an asymptotic expansion for rank tests for several samples is established.) Extensions of these results to the cases of simple linear rank statistics S_N and signed rank statistic S_N^+ were carried out by Does (1983a, b), and Seoh (1983) and Puri and Seoh (1984a, b) respectively.

Our attention is mainly focused on simple signed rank statistics with regression constants, the Edgeworth expansion for which was derived by Seoh (1983) and Puri and Seoh (1984a, b) with remainder $o(n^{-1})$. Parallel to this study is the work of Does (1983a, b), which deals with unsigned rank statistics with regression constants. Since the results are qualitatively the same, we shall deal with the Edgeworth expansion for signed rank statistics.

Denote $F_n(x) = P((S_n^+ - E(S_n^+))\tilde{\sigma}_n^{-1} \leqslant x)$, $x \in (-\infty, \infty)$ where $\tilde{\sigma}_n$ is either the exact standard deviation of S_n^+ or some normalizing constant.

We make the following assumptions on regression constants and score generating functions:

Assumption A. $X_{n1}, \ldots, X_{nn}$ are i.i.d. symmetrically distributed about zero, and the regression constants $c_{n1}, \ldots, c_{nn}$ satisfy

$$\sum_{i=1}^{n} c_{ni}^2 = 1, \quad \max_{1 \leqslant i \leqslant n} |c_{ni}| = O(n^{-1/2}). \tag{4.8a}$$

Assumption B. The score generating function J is non-constant, $\int_0^1 J^2(t)dt = 1$, and is three times differentiable and

$$|J'''(t)| \leqslant \Gamma\{t(1-t)\}^{-3-(1/4)+\delta}, \quad t \in (0, 1), \quad \delta < \frac{1}{14} \tag{4.8b}$$

and Γ is some positive number.

Since $(t(1-t))^{-\beta} \leqslant (t(1-t))^{-\gamma}$, $t \in (0, 1)$, for $0 < \beta \leqslant \gamma$, assumption (4.8b) is satisfied if $|J'''(t)| \leqslant \Gamma\{t(1-t)\}^{-\alpha}$ for some α, $0 < \alpha < 3 + \frac{1}{14}$.

By the symmetry assumption it is clear that $ES_n^+ = 0$ and

$$\sigma_n^2 = \operatorname{var} S_n^+ = \frac{1}{n}\sum_{i=1}^{n} J^2(i/(n+1)).$$

Define, for each $n \geqslant 1$ and real x,

$$S_n^* = \sigma_n^{-1} S_n^+, \quad F_n^*(x) = P(S_n^* \leqslant x), \quad -\infty < x < \infty, \tag{4.9}$$

and

$$\tilde{F}_n(x) = \Phi(x) - \varphi(x)\kappa_{4n}(x^3 - 3x)/24, \tag{4.10}$$

where Φ denotes the standard normal distribution function, φ is its density function and κ_{4n} is given by

$$\kappa_{4n} = \sum_{i=1}^{n} c_{ni}^4 \left\{ \int_0^1 J^4(t)\,dt - 3 \right\} - 3n^{-1} \left\{ \int_0^1 J^4(t)\,dt - 1 \right\}. \tag{4.11}$$

Our main theorem is as follows.

Theorem 4.1 Under the assumptions A and B we have, as $n \to \infty$,

$$\sup_x |F_n^*(x) - \tilde{F}_n(x)| = o(n^{-1}). \quad \square$$

Since $\tilde{F}_n(x) = \Phi(x) + O(n^{-1})$ uniformly in x, we have an improvement of the Berry–Esseen bound of Puri and Seoh (1985) under stronger assumptions.

Corollary 4.1 Under assumptions A and B we have, as $n \to \infty$,

$$\sup_x |F_n^*(x) - \Phi_n(x)| = O(n^{-1}). \quad \square$$

We note that the third cumulant of S_n^* is zero and that κ_{4n} is an asymptotic expansion for the fourth cumulant of S_n^* where terms of order $o(n^{-1})$ have been neglected. Hence $\tilde{F}_n$ may be said to constitute a genuine Edgeworth expansion for F_n^*. It may be noted that the assumption B allows score generating functions tending to infinity in the neighborhood 0 and 1 at the rate of $\{t(1 - t)\}^{-1/14+\varepsilon}$ for some $\varepsilon > 0$. Clearly this includes the chi-quantile function.

From now on, for simplicity of notation, we shall omit indices n in X_{ni}, R_{ni}^+ and $\operatorname{sgn} X_{ni}$, etc.

In order to prove theorem 4.1 we first derive a bound for the variance of S_n^+. Then we study the behavior of the characteristic function of S_n^* for large values of the argument.

Lemma 4.1 If the score generating function J satisfies the assumption B, then

$$\sigma_n^2 = \frac{1}{n} \sum_{i=1}^{n} J^2\left(\frac{i}{n+1}\right) = 1 + O(n^{-6/7-2\delta}). \tag{4.12}$$

Proof. Note that the assumption B ensures that for some positive number Γ_0,

$$|J^{(i)}(t)| \leqslant \Gamma_0 \{t(1 - t)\}^{-i-1/14+\delta}, \quad i = 0, 1, 2, 3. \tag{4.13}$$

Hence the lemma follows by mean value theorems for derivatives and integrals. □

The behavior of the characteristic function of S_n^* for large values of the argument is given by lemma 4.2 below, whose proof we omit (see Seoh, 1983).

Lemma 4.2 Suppose that the assumptions of theorem 4.1 are satisfied and let $\psi_n(t) = E\exp(itS_n^*)$. Then there are positive numbers B, β and γ such that, for $\log n \leqslant |t| \leqslant \gamma n^{3/2}$, $n \geqslant 1$,

$$|\psi_n(t)| \leqslant Bn^{-\beta\log n}. \quad \square$$

To prove theorem 4.1, we start with an application of Esseen's smoothing lemma (2.16), which implies that, for all $\gamma > 0$,

$$\sup_x |F_n^*(x) - \tilde{F}_n(x)| \leqslant \frac{1}{\pi}\int_{|t|\leqslant\gamma n^{3/2}} |\psi_n(t) - \lambda_n(t)|/|t|\,dt + O(n^{-3/2}) \tag{4.14}$$

where ψ_n denotes the characteristic function of S_n^* and λ_n denotes the Fourier–Stieltjes transform of $\tilde{F}_n$, i.e.

$$\lambda_n(t) = \int_{-\infty}^{\infty} e^{itx}d\tilde{F}_n(x) = e^{-t^2/2}\{1 + \kappa_{4n}t^4/24\}. \tag{4.15}$$

Since derivatives of $\psi_n(t)$ and $\lambda_n(t)$ are uniformly bounded and $\psi_n(0) = \lambda_n(0) = 1$, we have

$$\int_{|t|\leqslant n^{-3/2}} |\psi_n(t) - \lambda_n(t)|/|t|\,dt = O(n^{-3/2}). \tag{4.16}$$

Furthermore, lemma 4.2 and (4.15) ensure that

$$\int_{\log n\leqslant|t|\leqslant\gamma n^{3/2}} |\psi_n(t) - \lambda_n(t)|/|t|\,dt = O(n^{-3/2}). \tag{4.17}$$

Thus it follows from (4.14), (4.16), and (4.17) that, in order to prove theorem 4.1, it suffices to show that

$$\int_{n^{-3/2}\leqslant|t|\leqslant\log n} |\psi_n(t) - \lambda_n(t)|/|t|\,dt = O(n^{-1}). \tag{4.18}$$

To prove this one uses a conditioning argument as in Bickel and van Zwet (1978) or Does (1983a, b).

Omitting the details of computations (see Seoh, 1983), we obtain (uniformly for $|t| \leqslant \log n$)

$$\psi_n(t) = e^{-t^2/2}\left[1 + \frac{t^4}{24\sigma_n^4}\kappa_{4n}\right] + O(n^{-22/15})$$
$$+ o(n^{-1}|t|P(t)e^{-\theta t^2}) + O(n^{-1-\varepsilon}|t|P(t)) \qquad (4.19)$$

where $0 < \theta < \frac{1}{2}$, $\varepsilon > 0$, and $P(t)$ is a polynomial which does not involve n. □

Theorem 4.1 justifies the validity of the expansion with terms up to order n^{-1} used by Fellingham and Stoker (1964) who investigated the performance of the formal Edgeworth series with terms taken to order n^{-1} and n^{-2}. They compared their approximations with normal approximations and demonstrated that the approximation by an Edgeworth series is considerably more accurate in the range of upper 5 percent probability and for $n \geqslant 10$. For the performance of the formal Edgeworth expansion taken to terms of order n^{-1} in the case of absolute normal scores statistic, the reader is referred to Thompson et al. (1967).

Next, we provide the main result dealing with the two-term Edgeworth expansion for the signed rank statistic S_n^+ under near location alternatives.

Let $\{X_{ni}, 1 \leqslant i \leqslant n\}$ be independent r.v.s. such that $X_{ni} = \theta_{ni} + e_{ni}$, $1 \leqslant i \leqslant n$, where e_{ni}, $1 \leqslant i \leqslant n$, are i.i.d. r.v.s. with a common continuous df $F(x)$, and θ_{ni}, $1 \leqslant i \leqslant n$, are location parameters.

We assume that

1 The regression constants c_{ni}s satisfy the assumption (4.8), and $\Sigma_{i=1}^n \theta_{ni}^2 = O(1)$.
2 $f(x) = F'(x)$ is symmetric about 0, and $f'(x)$ satisfies $\int|f'(x)|dx < \infty$.
3 The function J (see assumption B) is nonconstant and twice differentiable on (0, 1), and its second derivative J'' satisfies the Lipschitz condition of order δ, $0 < \delta \leqslant 1$, i.e. $|J''(s) - J''(t)| \leqslant \Delta|s - t|^\delta$, $0 < s, t < 1$ for some constant Δ. Furthermore $\int_0^1 J^2(t)dt = 1$.

Denote

$$\tau_n^2 = \text{var}(S_n^+), \quad S_n^* = \tau_n^{-1}(S_n^* - ES_n^+) \quad \text{and let } F^+(x) = P[|e_{ni}| \leqslant x].$$

Furthermore, let

$$A_n(x) = \Phi(x) - \phi(x)\left\{\frac{k_{3n}}{6}(x^2 - 1) + \frac{k_{4n}}{24}(x^3 - 3x)\right\} \qquad (4.20)$$

where

$$k_{3n} = \sum_{i=1}^{n} c_{ni}^{3} \int_{-\infty}^{\infty} \{J^{3}(F^{+}(|x|)) - 3J(F^{+}(|x|))\}$$
$$\operatorname{sgn} x\{f(x - \theta_{ni}) - f(x)\}\,dx$$
$$- \frac{3}{n} \sum_{i=1}^{n} c_{ni} \int_{-\infty}^{\infty} \{J^{3}(F^{+}(|x|)) - J(F^{+}(|x|))\}$$
$$\operatorname{sgn} x\{f(x - \theta_{ni}) - f(x)\}\,dx \tag{4.21}$$

and

$$k_{4n} = \sum_{i=1}^{n} c_{ni}^{4} \left\{ \int_{0}^{1} J^{4}(t)\,dt \right\} - 3\left\{ \int_{0}^{1} J^{4}(t)\,dt - 1 \right\}. \tag{4.22}$$

Then.

Theorem 4.2 Under assumptions 1 through 3, we have

$$\sup_{x} |P(S_n^* \leqslant x) - A_n(x)| = o(n^{-1}), \quad \text{as } n \to \infty. \quad \square$$

Since $A_n(x) = \Phi(x) + O(n^{-1})$, uniformly in x, we have

Corollary 4.2 Under assumptions 1 through 3, we have

$$\sup_{x} |P(S_n^* \leqslant x) - \Phi(x)| = O(n^{-1}), \quad \text{as } n \to \infty. \quad \square$$

We now define for each $n > 1$ and real x

$$\tilde{A}_n(x) = \Phi(x) - \phi(x)\left\{ \frac{1}{6}\tilde{k}_{3n}(x^2 - 1) + \frac{k_{4n}}{24}(x^3 - 3x) \right\}$$

where

$$\tilde{k}_{3n} = \sum_{i=1}^{n} c_{ni}^{3}\theta_{ni} \int_{-\infty}^{\infty} \{J^{3}(F^{+}(|x|)) - 3J(F^{+}(|x|))\} \operatorname{sgn} x f'(x)\,dx$$
$$+ \frac{3}{n} \sum_{i=1}^{n} c_{ni}\theta_{ni} \int_{-\infty}^{\infty} \{J^{3}(F^{+}(|x|)) - J(F^{+}(|x|))\} \operatorname{sgn} x f'(x)\,dx.$$

Note that if $f(x)$ has the second integrable Radon–Nikodym derivative f'', then Taylor's expansion exsures that $\sup_x |A_n(x) - \tilde{A}_n(x)| = O(n^{-3/2})$. This proves

Corollary 4.3 Under assumptions 1 through 3, we have

$$\sup_{x} |P(S_n^* \leqslant x) - \tilde{A}_n(x)| = o(n^{-1}), \quad \text{as } n \to \infty$$

if $f(x)$ has the second integrable Radon–Nikodym derivative. □

For proofs of these results, see Seoh (1983) or Puri and Seoh (1984b).

Theorem 4.2 provides the Edgeworth expansion with natural parameters $E(S_n^+)$ and $\operatorname{var}(S_n^+)$. In Seoh (1983), the Edgeworth expansion is also derived for simple normalizing constants under somewhat stronger assumptions on location parameters θ_{ni}, $1 \leqslant i \leqslant n$, namely, $\Sigma_{i=1}^n |\theta_{ni}|^3 = O(n^{-1/2})$, and on f (for details, see Seoh, 1983; Puri and Seoh, 1984b).

Finally, we present very briefly Edgeworth expansion up to the order $o(n^{-1})$ for the df of simple linear rank statistics S_n (defined in (2.1)) under the null hypothesis. The results are due to Does (1983a). The methods in the derivation of the results are the same as in the symmetry problem discussed earlier.

Let $\{X_{ni}, 1 \leqslant i \leqslant n\}$ be i.i.d. r.v.s. with a common continuous df $F(x)$. Let R_{ni}, $1 \leqslant i \leqslant n$ be the rank of X_{ni} among $\{X_{nk}, 1 \leqslant k \leqslant n\}$. Then, Does (1983a) considers the statistics of the form $S_n = \Sigma_{i=1}^n c_{ni} a_n(R_{ni})$ where c_{ni}, $1 \leqslant i \leqslant n$ are known constants, and $a_n(i) = J(i/(n+1))$ as defined in (4.3).

We assume that the cs satisfy (4.8a) and $\Sigma_{j=1}^n c_{jn} = 0$. Furthermore, the score generating function J satisfies (4.8b), and $\limsup_{t\to 0,1} t(1-t)|J''(t)/J'(t)| < 2$. Finally, we assume (without loss of generality) that $\int_0^1 J(t) = 0$ and $\int_0^1 J^2(t)dt = 1$. It is clear that

$$E(S_n) = 0, \quad \text{and} \quad \sigma_n^2 = \operatorname{var}(S_n) = \frac{1}{n-1} \sum_{i=1}^n \left(J\left(\frac{i}{n+1}\right) - \bar{J} \right)^2$$

where

$$\bar{J} = \sum_{i=1}^n J\left(\frac{i}{n+1}\right) \Big/ n.$$

Define for each $n \geqslant 2$, $S_n^{**} = \sigma_n^{-1} S_n$, and $F_n^{**}(x) = P(S_n^{**} \leqslant x)$ and

$$\tilde{F}_n^*(x) = \Phi(x) - \phi(x)\left\{\frac{k_{3n}}{6}(x^2 - 1) + \frac{k_{4n}}{24}(x^3 - 3x) + \frac{k_{3n}^2}{72}(x^5 - 10x^3 + 15x)\right\}$$

where

$$k_{3n} = \sum_{i=1}^n c_{in}^3 \left\{ \int_0^1 J^3(t)dt \right\}$$

and

$$k_{4n} = \sum_{i=1}^{n} c_{in}^4 \left\{ \int_0^1 J^4(t)dt - 3 \right\} - \frac{3}{n} \left\{ \int_0^1 J^4(t)dt - 1 \right\}.$$

Then

Theorem 4.3 $\sup_x |F_n^{**}(x) - \tilde{F}_n^*(x)| = o(n^{-1})$ as $n \to \infty$. □

Note that k_{3n} and k_{4n} are asymptotic expressions for the third and fourth cumulants of S_n^{**} where terms of order $o(n^{-1})$ have been neglected. Thus $\tilde{F}_n^*$ constitutes a genuine Edgeworth expansion for $\tilde{F}_n^{**}$. Furthermore, note that the characteristic function of S_n^{**} behaves exactly as in lemma 4.2. The proof of the theorem is similar to that of theorem 4.1 and is dealt with in Does (1983a, b). We may mention that the asymptotic expansions given in theorems 4.1 and 4.2 can be used to derive deficiencies in the sense of Hodges and Lehmann (1970) for S_n^+ and S_n with respect to their parametric competitors. To the best of our knowledge this problem has not been studied thus far.

5 *U*-Statistics

Most classical statistics U_n based on i.i.d. observations $X_1, X_2, \ldots, X_n$ may be cast in the form

$$U_N := \binom{n}{r}^{-1} \sum_{1 \leq i_1 < i_2 < \ldots < i_r \leq n} h(X_{i_1}, X_{i_2}, \ldots, X_{i_r}), \tag{5.1}$$

where h is real-valued, measurable, and symmetric in its r arguments. The statistic U_n in (5.1) is called a *U-statistic of order r*. Often such statistics may be expressed as, or approximated by, statistics of the form $H(\bar{Z})$ as described in section 2, and in such cases they are better dealt with by the (multivariate) method described earlier. There are, however, many instances where such a representation is not possible.

Example 5.1 (Wilcoxon one-sample statistic). This is related to Example 4.3. Here

$$\begin{aligned} U_n &= \binom{n}{2}^{-1} \sum_{1 \leq i < j \leq n} 1_{\{X_i + X_j > 0\}} \\ &= \frac{1}{n(n-1)} \sum_{i=1}^{n} R_{ni}^+ \operatorname{sgn} X_i + \frac{1}{2}\left(\frac{n+1}{n-1}\right) - \binom{n}{2}^{-1} \sum_{i=1}^{n} 1_{\{X_i > 0\}}. \end{aligned} \tag{5.2}$$

Example 5.2 (Gini's mean difference). The statistic

$$U_n = \binom{n}{2}^{-1} \sum_{1 \leqslant i < j \leqslant n} |X_i - X_j| \tag{5.3}$$

is sometimes used as a measure of concentration.

For such examples ingenious estimations of the c.f. of the normalized U_n are necessary, followed by the use of Esseen's inequality (2.16). For simplicity we assume $r = 2$. Assume, by centering, that $Eh(X_1, X_2) = 0$. Projecting U_n onto the closure of the linear space spanned by functions of single variables X_j, $1 \leqslant j \leqslant n$, one has the *Hoeffding decomposition*

$$\begin{aligned} U_n &= \frac{2}{n} \sum_{j=1}^{n} g(X_j) + \frac{1}{\binom{n}{2}} \sum_{1 \leqslant i < j \leqslant n} (h(X_i, X_j) - g(X_i) - g(X_j)), \\ &= \frac{2}{n} \sum_{j=1}^{n} g(X_j) + \binom{n}{2}^{-1} \sum_{1 \leqslant i < j \leqslant n} \Psi(X_i, X_j), \quad \text{say}, \end{aligned} \tag{5.4}$$

where $g(x) = Eh(X_1, x)$. By orthogonality, one has

$$\theta_n^2 := \operatorname{var}(U_n) = \frac{4}{n} Eg^2(X_1) + \binom{n}{2}^{-1} E(h(X_1, X_2) - g(X_1) - g(X_2))^2. \tag{5.5}$$

Assume

$$\sigma^2 := Eg^2(X_1) > 0, \tag{5.6}$$

$$E|h(X_1, X_2)|^p < \infty \quad \text{for some } p > 4, \tag{5.7}$$

and the Cramér condition

$$\limsup_{|t| \to \infty} |E \exp(itg(X_1))| < 1. \tag{5.8}$$

Theorem 5.1 (Götze and van Zwet, 1991). Under assumptions (5.6), (5.7), (5.8), one has

$$\begin{aligned} \sup_x \Bigg| P(\theta_n^{-1} U_n \leqslant x) - \Phi(x) - \Bigg\{ n^{-1/2} \frac{\kappa_3}{6}(x^2 - 1) + n^{-1} \frac{\kappa_4}{24}(x^3 - 3x) \\ + n^{-1} \frac{\kappa_3^2}{72}(x^5 - 10x^3 + 15x) \Bigg\} \varphi(x) \Bigg| = o(n^{-1}) \end{aligned} \tag{5.9}$$

where $\Phi(x)$ is the standard normal distribution function and $\varphi(x)$ its density, and

$$\kappa_3 = \sigma^{-3}[Eg^3(X_1) + 3Eg(X_1)g(X_2)\psi(X_1, X_2)],$$
$$\kappa_4 = \sigma^{-4}[Eg^4(X_1) - 3\sigma^4 + 12Eg^2(X_1)g(X_2)\psi(X_1, X_2) + 12Eg(X_1)g(X_2)\psi(X_1, X_3)\psi(X_2, X_3)]. \quad \square \tag{5.10}$$

This result is an improvement on earlier results of Callaert et al. (1980) and Bickel et al. (1986).

6 Expansions in Econometrics and General Remarks

One of our aims in this survey has been to present those main results and techniques for deriving Edgeworth expansions which are widely applicable in statistics and economics.

When valid, Edgeworth expansions provide good approximations to distributions of statistics, thereby providing confidence intervals for estimates and critical values for tests corresponding more precisely to the desired levels than given by the classical procedures based on normal approximation. This aspect of Edgeworth expansions is currently often superseded by the bootstrap methodology of Efron (1979). But the most convincing demonstration of the effectiveness of the bootstrap is provided only by Edgeworth expansions (Singh, 1981; Bhattacharya and Qumsiyeh, 1989; Hall, 1992).

Expansions are also important theoretical tools for gaining insight into what the economists call the "finite sample theory" (Phillips, 1980), i.e. inference based on moderate sample sizes. It has been shown in a number of studies that the asymptotically efficient maximum likelihood estimator (m.l.e.) is not always superior to some other competing estimators (see Berkson, 1980) if the sample size is not large. An insight into this is often provided by an expansion of the distribution, or of the expected loss, which goes beyond the first approximation on which asymptotic efficiency considerations are based. For example, it may be shown using expansions that the m.l.e. in a one-parameter exponential family, when properly bias-corrected, is still at least as good as any other (similarly bias-corrected) estimate (see Ghosh, 1994) up to any order; but when not corrected appropriately for bias it may be outdone by other competitors. Similar aspects of "finite sample approximation" of much significance in economics are discussed in Bergstrom (1962) and Sawa (1969). For expansions related to the so-called k-class estimators and Nagar approximations see Kadane (1971) and Sargan (1975).

Due to special structures of models that often arise in economics, econometricians have often derived expansions which are particularly suited to their problems. In most of these models, e.g. regression models, with or without lagged variables (or autoregression), the disturbances or error terms are generally taken to be Gaussian. Anderson and Sawa (1973) and Anderson (1976) obtain asymptotic expansions of distributions of the m.l.e., ordinary least squares, and two-stage least squares estimates in a regression model in which the means of the independent bivariate observations have a linear functional relationship and both variables are subject to uncorrelated normal errors with a common variance. This is applied to the distribution of estimates in a simultaneous equations model. For dynamic models with endogenous lagged variables, Sargan and Satchell (1986) and Phillips (1980, 1986) give detailed and ingenious calculations of the c.f. of the normalized statistic under consideration, in order to check its necessary integrability properties. A theorem of Chambers (1967), when properly corrected, now gives an L_1-expansion of the density of the normalized statistic. Since this theorem of Chambers has been used rather often in the literature, perhaps a word of caution is in order. The theorem in question (see Chambers, 1967, p. 369) asserts a valid expansion of the density with an error $o(n^{-(r+1)/2+\varepsilon})$ for some $\varepsilon > 0$, provided (i) the cumulants of the statistic up to order $r + 3$ have the same order of magnitude as those of the normalized sum S_n of i.i.d. random variables, and (ii) the c.f. f_n of the (normalized) statistic satisfies, for all $\alpha \in (0, \frac{1}{2})$

$$\int_{|t|>n^{\alpha}} |f_n(t)|\,dt = o(n^{-(r+1)/2+\varepsilon}). \tag{6.1}$$

As explained in section 2 (see 2.4), for a valid expansion of the distribution function, or the density, one must provide (a) an expansion of the c.f. $f_n(t)$ for $|t| \leqslant a_n$ where a_n is at least of order $(\log n)^{1/2}$, and (b) an appropriate rate of decay of $f_n(t)$ for $|t| \geqslant n^{1/2}$. While the assumption (ii) takes care of the requirement (b), one can only derive an Edgeworth expansion of $f_n(t)$ for $|t| \leqslant \delta$ for some $\delta > 0$ by using (i). This clearly is not enough for (a). Most expansions derived in the econometrics literature which allude to the above theorem of Chambers (1967) are, however, accompanied with such detailed analyses of the c.f. of the statistic that the condition (a) above would be easy to check using standard techniques similar to those in the case of S_n. Alternatively, one may apply the methods of sections 2 and 3.

Taniguchi (1983, 1991) has derived expansions for estimators in Gaussian time series models, by a direct attack.

In regression type models in economics, with nonstochastic (exogenous) regressors, with or without lagged endogenous variables, and with Gaussian disturbances, the statistic may still be expressed in the form $H(\bar{Z})$ where $Z_j = (f_i(X_j), \ldots, f_k(X_j))$; but the observations X_j are not identically distributed. It is often possible to apply to such problems multivariate expansions analogous to those discussed in sections 2 and 3. Notice, for example, that theorem 3.2 does not require stationarity. For the case of independent but not identically distributed observations see Skovgaard (1981). In the classical regression model with nonstochastic regressors and i.i.d. errors, expansions for least squares estimators may be found in Qumsiyeh (1990). Similar expansions may be derived in dynamic models where endogenous lagged variables are involved. The algorithm for computing the terms in the Edgeworth expansion as described in section 2 still works. One advantage of the general approaches considered in this article is that expansions hold for non-Gaussian errors as well.

The method of expansions considered in this chapter extends to the multisample case.

There are some specialized techniques for approximating probabilities associated with statistics which have not been discussed in this chapter. For probabilities in the tails, *large deviation methods*, originally due to Cramér (1938), are useful (see Phillips, 1986, for econometric applications). In parametric models one may also sometimes use the so-called *saddlepoint approximations* of Daniels (1954), Barndorff-Nielsen and Cox (1979) and Phillips (1978). The terms of the Edgeworth expansion, on the other hand, depend only on cumulants, or moments, of the underlying distribution, making these expansions reasonably robust in semiparametric models.

Note

The authors wish to thank Professor P. C. B. Phillips and two anonymous referees for their helpful suggestions. The research of R.N.B. was supported in part by NSF Grant DMS 9206937. The research of M.L.P. was supported by the Office of Naval Research Contract N00014-91-J-1020.

References

Akahira, M. and Takeuchi, K. (1981) *Asymptotic Efficiency of Statistical Estimators: Concepts and Higher Order Efficiency*. Lecture Notes in Statistics 7. New York: Springer-Verlag.

Albers, W., Bickel, P. J. and Van Zwet, W. R. (1976) Asymptotic expansions for the power of distribution free tests in the one-sample problem. *Annals of Statistics*, 4, 108–56.

Anderson, T. W. and Sawa, T. (1973) Distribution of estimates of coefficients of a single equation in a simultaneous system and their asymptotic expansions. *Econometrica*, 41, 683–714.

Anderson, T. W. (1976) Estimation of linear functional relationships: approximate distributions and connections with simultaneous equations in econometrics. *Journal of the Royal Statistical Society B*, 38, 1–36.

Babu, G. J. and Singh, K. (1984) On one-term Edgeworth correction by Efron's bootstrap. *Sankhya A*, 46, 219–32.

Bai, Z. D. and Rao, C. R. (1991) Edgeworth expansion of a function of sample means. *Annals of Statistics*, 19, 1295–315.

Barndorff-Nielsen, O. E. and Cox, D. R. (1979) Edgeworth and saddle-point approximations with statistical applications (with discussion). *Journal of the Royal Statistical Society B*, 41, 279–312.

Bergstrom, A. R. (1962) The exact sampling distributions at least squares and maximum likelihood estimators of the marginal propensity to consume. *Econometrica*, 30, 480–90.

Berkson, J. (1980) Minimum chi-square, not maximum likelihood (with discussion). *Annals of Statistics*, 8, 457–87.

Bhattacharya, R. N. (1968) Berry–Esseen bounds for the multi-dimensional central limit theorem. *Bulletin of the American Mathematical Society*, 75, 285–7.

Bhattacharya, R. N. (1971) Rates of weak convergence and asymptotic expansions for classical central limit theorems. *Annals of Mathematical Statistics*, 42, 241–59.

Bhattacharya, R. N. (1985) Some recent results on Cramér–Edgeworth expansions with applications. In P. R. Krishnaiah (ed.), *Multivariate Analysis VI*. Amsterdam: North-Holland, pp. 57–75.

Bhattacharya, R. N. and Chan, N. H. (1994) Comparisons of chisquare, Edgeworth expansions and bootstrap approximations to the distribution of the frequency chi square. *Sankhya*, in the press.

Bhattacharya, R. N. and Denker, M. (1990) *Asymptotic Statistics*. Boston: Birkhauser.

Bhattacharya, R. N. and Ghosh, J. K. (1978) On the validity of the formal Edgeworth expansion. *Annals of Statistics*, 6, 434–51.

Bhattacharya, R. N. and Puri, M. L. (1983) On the order of magnitude of cumulants of von Mises functionals and related statistics. *Annals of Probability*, 11, 346–54.

Bhattacharya, R. N. and Qumsiyeh, M. (1989) Second order and L_p-comparisons between the bootstrap and empirical Edgeworth expansion methodologies. *Annals of Statistics*, 17, 160–9.

Bhattacharya, R. N. and Ranga Rao, R. (1976) *Normal Approximation and Asymptotic Expansions*. New York: Wiley. Second reprint with supplement (1986), Florida: Krieger, Malabar.

Bickel, P. J., Götze, F. and van Zwet, W. R. (1986) The Edgeworth expansion for U-statistics of degree two. *Annals of Statistics*, 14, 1463–84.

Bickel, P. J. and Van Zwet, W. R. (1978) Asymptotic expansions for the power of distribution free tests in the two-sample problem. *Annals of Statistics*, 6, 937–1004.

Bikyalis, A. (1968) Asymptotic expansions of distribution functions and density functions of sums of independent and identically distributed random vectors. *Litov. Mat. Sb.*, 8, 405–22 (in Russian).

Bose, A. (1988) Edgeworth correction by bootstrap in autoregressions. *Annals of Statistics*, 16, 1709–22.

Bulinskii, A. V. and Zhurbenko, I. G. (1976) The central limit theorem for random fields. *Soviet Math. Dokl.*, 17, 14–17.

Callaert, H., Janssen, P. and Veraverbeke, N. (1980) An Edgeworth expansion for *U*-statistics. *Annals of Statistics*, 8, 299–312.

Chambers, J. M. (1967) On methods of asymptotic approximation for multivariate distributions. *Biometrika*, 54, 367–83.

Chandra, T. K. and Ghosh, J. K. (1979) Valid asymptotic expansions for the likelihood ratio statistic and other perturbed chisquare variables. *Sankhya A*, 41, 22–47.

Chandra, T. K. and Ghosh, J. K. (1980) Valid asymptotic expansions for the likelihood ratio and other statistics under contiguous alternatives. *Sankhya A*, 42, 170–84.

Chebyshev, P. L. (1890) Sur deux théorèmes relatifs aux probabilités. *Acta Mathematica*, 14, 305–15.

Chibishov, D. M. (1972) An asymptotic expansion for the distribution of a statistic admitting an asymptotic expansion. *Theor. Probab. Appl.*, 17, 620–30.

Chibishov, D. M. (1973) An asymptotic expansion for a class of estimators containing the maximum likelihood estimators. *Theor. Probab. Appl.*, 18, 295–303.

Cramér, H. (1928) On the composition of elementary errors. *Skand. Aktuarietidskr.*, 11, 13–74, 141–80.

Cramér, H. (1938) Sur un nouveau théorème-limite de théorie des probabilités. *Actualités Sci. et Ind.*, 736, 5–23.

Daniels, H. E. (1954) Saddlepoint approximations in statistics. *Annals of Mathematical Statistics*, 25, 631–50.

Does, R. J. M. M. (1983a) An Edgeworth expansion for simple linear rank statistics under the null hypothesis. *Annals of Statistics*, 11, 607–24.

Does, R. J. M. M. (1983b) Asymptotic expansions for simple linear rank statistics under contiguous alternatives. In P. Mandl and M. Huskova (eds), *Proceedings of the Third Prague Symposium on Asymptotic Statistics*. Amsterdam/New York: Elsevier, pp. 221–30.

Edgeworth, F. Y. (1896) The asymmetrical probability curve. *Philosophical Magazine*, 5th series, 41, 90–9.

Edgeworth, F. Y. (1905) The law of error. *Transactions of the Cambridge*

Philosophical Society, 20, 36–65, 113–41.

Efron, B. (1975) Defining the curvature of a statistical problem (with applications to second order efficiency). *Annals of Statistics*, 3, 1189–242.

Efron, B. (1979) Bootstrap methods: another look at the jackknife. *Annals of Statistics*, 7, 1–26.

Esseen, C. G. (1945) Fourier analysis of distribution functions. A mathematical study of the Laplace–Gaussian law. *Acta Mathematica*, 77, 1–125.

Fellingham, S. A. and Stoker, D. J. (1964) An approximation for the exact distribution of Wilcoxon test for symmetry. *J. Amer. Statist.*, 19, 899–905.

Fisher, R. A. (1925) Theory of statistical estimation. *Proceedings of the Cambridge Philosophical Society*, 22, 700–25.

Ghosh, J. K. (1994) *Higher Order Asymptotics*. Hayward, CA: Institute of Mathematical Statistics.

Ghosh, J. K. and Subramanyam, K. (1974) Second order efficiency of maximum likelihood estimators. *Sankhya A*, 36, 325–58.

Götze, F. (1985) Asymptotic expansions in functional central limit theorems. *Journal of Multivariate Analysis*, 16, 1–20.

Götze, F. and Hipp, C. (1978) Asymptotic expansions in the central limit theorem under moment conditions. *Z. Wahrsch. Verw. Geb.*, 42, 67–87.

Götze, F. and Hipp, C. (1983) Asymptotic expansions for sums of weakly dependent random vectors. *Z. Wahrsch. Verw. Geb.*, 64, 211–39.

Götze, F. and Hipp, C. (1994) Asymptotic distribution of statistics in time series. *Annals of Statistics*, in the press.

Götze, F. and Van Zwet, W. (1991) Edgeworth expansion for asymptotically linear statistics. Preprint 91-034, University of Bielefeld.

Hájek, J. and Šidák, Z. (1967) *Theory of Rank Tests*. New York: Academic Press.

Hall, P. G. (1992) *Bootstrap and Edgeworth Expansion*. Second Edition, New York: Springer-Verlag.

Hodges, J. L. and Lehmann, E. L. (1970) Deficiency. *Annals of Mathematical Statistics*, 41, 783–801.

Huang, F. (1994) Berry–Esseen bounds and asymptotic expansions under dependence. Thesis in progress, Indiana University, Bloomington.

Jensen, J. L. (1989a) A note on the work of Götze and Hipp concerning asymptotic expansions for sums of weakly dependent random vectors. In P. Mandl and M. Huškovà (eds), *Proceedings of the Fourth Prague Symposium on Asymptotic Statistics*. Prague: Charles University, pp. 295–303.

Jensen, J. L. (1989b) Asymptotic expansions for strongly mixing Harris recurrent Markov chains. *Scandinavian Journal of Statistics*, 16, 47–64.

Kadane, J. B. (1971) Comparison of *k*-class estimators when the disturbances are small. *Econometrica*, 39, 723–37.

Lahiri, S. N. (1993) Refinements in asymptotic expansions for sums of weakly dependent random vectors. *Annals of Probability*, 21, 791–9.

Nagaev, S. V. (1961) More exact statements of limit theorems for homogeneous Markov chains. *Theor. Probab. Appl.*, 6, 62–81.

Pfanzagl, J. (1980) Asymptotic expansions in parametric statistical theory. In P. R. Krishnaiah (ed.), *Developments in Statistics, volume 3*. New York: Academic Press, pp. 1–97.

Phillips, P. C. B. (1978) Edgeworth and saddle point approximations in the first order noncircular autoregression. *Biometrika*, 65, 91–8.

Phillips, P. C. B. (1980) Finite sample theory and the distributions of alternative estimators of the marginal propensity to consume. *Rev. Econ. Studies*, 47, 183–224.

Phillips, P. C. B. (1986) Large deviation expansions in econometrics. *Advances in Econometrics*, 5, 199–226.

Puri, M. L. and Seoh, M. (1984a) Edgeworth expansions for signed linear rank statistics with regression constants. *J. Statist. Plann. Inference*, 10, 137–49.

Puri, M. L. and Seoh, M. (1984b) Edgeworth expansions for signed linear rank statistics under near location alternatives. *J. Statist.* Plann. Inference, 10, 289–309.

Puri, M. L. and Seoh, M. (1985) Berry–Esseen for signed linear rank statistics with regression constants. In P. Révész (ed.), *Colloquium on Limit Theorems in Probability Statistics*. Amsterdam: North-Holland, pp. 875–905.

Qumsiyeh, M. (1990) Edgeworth expansion in regression models. *Journal of Multivariate Analysis*, 35, 86–101.

Ranga Rao, R. (1961) On the central limit theorem in $\mathbb{R}_k$. *Bulletin of the American Mathematical Society*, 67, 359–61.

Rao, C. R. (1961) Asymptotic efficiency and limiting information. *Proceedings of the Fourth Berkeley Symposium on Mathematical Statistics and Probability*, 1, 531–46.

Rao, C. R. (1962) Efficient estimates and optimum inference procedures in large samples. *Journal of the Royal Statistical Society B*, 24, 46–63.

Rao, C. R. (1963) Criteria of estimation in large samples. *Sankhya*, 25, 189–206.

Robinson, J. (1978) An asymptotic expansion for samples from a finite population. *Annals of Statistics*, 6, 1005–11.

Robinson, J. (1980) An asymptotic expansion for permutation tests with several samples. *Annals of Statistics*, 8, 851–64.

Sargan, J. D. (1975) Gram–Charlier approximations applied to t-ratios of k-class estimators. *Econometrica*, 43, 327–46.

Sargan, J. D. and Satchell, S. E. (1986) A theorem of validity of Edgeworth expansions. *Econometrica*, 54, 189–214.

Sawa, T. (1969) The exact sampling distribution of ordinary least squares and two stage least squares estimator. *Journal of the American Statistical Association*, 64, 923–36.

Seoh, M. (1983) Rate of convergence to normality and Edgeworth expansions for signed linear rank statistics with regression constants. PhD thesis, Indiana University.

Singh, K. (1981) On the asymptotic theory of Efron's bootstrap. *Annals of Statistics*, 9, 1187–95.

Skovgaard, Ib. M. (1981) Edgeworth expansions of the distributions of maximum likelihood estimators in the general (non i.i.d.) case. *Scandinavian Journal of Statistics*, 8, 227–36.

Statulevichius, V. (1969–70) Limit theorems for sums of random variables related to a Markov chain. *Litovsk Mat. Sb.*, 9, 10 (in Russian).

Stein, C. (1986) *Approximate Computation of Expectations*. IMS Lecture Notes Monograph Series 7. Hayward, CA: Institute of Mathematical Statistics.

Taniguchi, M. (1983) On the second order asymptotic efficiency of estimators of Gaussian ARMA processes. *Annals of Statistics*, 11, 157–69.

Taniguchi, M. (1991) *Higher Order Asymptotic Theory for Time Series Analysis*. Lecture Notes in Statistics 68. New York: Springer-Verlag.

Thompson, R., Govindarajulu, Z. and Doksum, K. (1967) Distribution and power of the absolute normal scores test. *Journal of the American Statistical Association*, 62, 966–75.

Wallace, D. L. (1958) Asymptotic approximations to distributions. *Annals of Mathematical Statistics*, 29, 635–54.

Yarnold, J. K. (1970) The minimum expectation in χ^2 goodness of fit tests and the accuracy of approximation for the null distribution. *Journal of the American Statistical Association*, 65, 864–86.

5 An Asymptotic Expansion for the Distribution of Test Criteria Which Are Asymptotically Distributed as Chi-squared under Contiguous Alternatives

Alberto Holly and Lucien Gardiol

1 Introduction

In practice, most of the test criteria are based on sequences of random vectors which converge to a p-variate normal distribution with nonzero mean under contiguous alternatives. This is notably the case for the likelihood ratio statistic and the statistics proposed by Wald (1943) and Rao (1947) (Rao's efficient score, or, equivalently, the Lagrange multiplier statistic proposed by Silvey, 1959). There is a general statistical theory based on refined asymptotic methods, using asymptotic expansions rather than normal approximations (see, for example, Pfanzagl, 1980, and Bhattacharya, 1990, for an account of this theory). However, explicit general formulae to compute the asymptotic local power up to order $o(T^{-1})$, where T is the sample size, for test sequences which are asymptotically distributed as noncentral chi-squared distributions under contiguous alternatives do not seem to be available in the literature. The purpose of this chapter is to attempt to remedy this situation.

At the outset, we would like to emphasize that we are mainly concerned in this chapter with the explicit algebraic computation of expansions of the Edgeworth type in order to compute the asymptotic local power up to order $o(T^{-1})$ under contiguous alternatives of test statistics, and not by the proof of the validity of these expansions under general sufficient conditions.

Let ξ_T be a test statistic whose asymptotic distribution under contiguous alternatives is a noncentral chi-square with p degrees of freedom. Here, like in Phillips and Park (1988), we assume that the test statistics sequences satisfy the regularity conditions which guarantee the existence of a stochastic expansion up to order $O_p(T^{-3/2})$. From a practical point of view, this assumption is justified by the fact that test sequences obtained by the usual principles (maximum likelihood, Wald, Rao's efficient score – or, equivalently, Lagrange multipliers) are of this type. The main result shown in this chapter is that the probability density function (p.d.f.) of ξ_T under contiguous alternatives possesses an expansion in powers of $T^{-1/2}$, the leading term being a noncentral chi-square with r degrees of freedom, $r \leq p$. Note that there is a difference between the result presented in this chapter and the theoretical one derived in Chandra and Ghosh (1980). Indeed, we consider general stochastic expansions of test statistics sequences up to order $O_p(T^{-3/2})$, which are not necessarily derived from a Taylor's expansion of a sequence of smooth functions. For this reason, the coefficients of $T^{-1/2}$ and T^{-1} that we obtain are not only linear combinations of noncentral chi-squares with the same noncentrality parameters as in Chandra and Ghosh (1980), but also of derivatives of the noncentral chi-square with r degrees of freedom. In fact, there is a similar difference between the papers of Chandra and Ghosh (1979) and Phillips and Park (1988) for the null distributions, and our chapter could be considered as an extension of the latter under contiguous alternatives.

In applications, the main result we have just mentioned could be applied to compute the asymptotic local power up to order $o(T^{-1})$ under contiguous alternatives of the usual test statistics mentioned above.[1]

To obtain the main result of this chapter, we have adopted and developed classical conventions of multilinear algebra, such as those exposed in Marcus (1973), in order to use vector and tensor power notation, which we find of great help in the case of sequences of random vectors. Employing such vector and tensor power notation, the multivariate versions of formulae for the moments, Hermite polynomials, and Edgeworth expansions are not any more complicated than the univariate ones.

This chapter is organized as follows. Section 2 presents some results on differential calculus using vector and tensor power notation. These results are used to derive expressions for multivariate Hermite polynomials, multivariate vector moments of a noncentral normal distribution, and multivariate Edgeworth expansion in tensor power notation. These expressions should be useful in many situations beside those considered in the present chapter. Section 3 develops formulae for the asymptotic expansion of the distribution of ξ_T under contiguous alternatives. Some particular cases of interest are considered in section 4.

There is a gigantic number of algebraic computations involved in obtaining the multivariate Edgeworth expansion to order $o(T^{-1})$ derived in sections 3 and 4. However, these computations are well-suited for symbolic manipulation on the computer, i.e. for computer algebra (see Pavelle et al., 1981). As already noted by many researchers (e.g. Merckens and Wansbeek, 1989), computer algebra will provide statistics and econometrics with a powerful tool. This chapter also illustrates how computer algebra can be effectively applied in econometrics, with the help of *Mathematica*.[2]

The notation $\mathscr{D}$ and $\mathscr{AD}$ is used throughout to mean the distribution and asymptotic distribution, respectively, of a random variable or a random vector. The noncentral chi-square distribution with r degrees of freedom and noncentrality parameter λ^2 is defined as the distribution of the scalar product of a random r-dimensional normal vector with covariance equal to the identity matrix and mean vector having a norm of λ, and is denoted by $\chi^2_r(\lambda^2)$.

2 Multivariate Edgeworth Expansion of a Density in a Vector Form

Phillips and Park (1988, appendix B) should be credited for being the first to use a Taylor expansion in vector form to derive formulae for the Edgeworth expansion up to $o(T^{-1})$ under the null hypothesis. The purpose of this section is to provide an alternative formulation based on vector Hermite polynomials and vector multivariate cumulants for contiguous alternatives.

Before we do so, we need to indicate some complementary results on differential calculus on $\mathbb{R}^p$. The notions presented in this section are interesting for their own sake; they may be used in other situations. For an alternative presentation, along the same lines, see Holmquist (1985b).

Complements on differential calculus on $\mathbb{R}^p$

We shall assume the reader to be familiar with the notion of Fréchet derivative. Nonetheless, we begin with a review of certain concepts associated with the theory of Fréchet derivative largely to fix notation and terminology. A standard reference for differential calculus is Dieudonné (1969).

Let E, F be Banach spaces and D an open subset of E. We denote by $\mathscr{L}(E, F)$ the vector space of all continuous linear mappings from E into F. A mapping u: $D \subset E \rightarrow F$ is Fréchet differentiable at $x_0 \in D$ if there exists a linear transformation $du(x_0)$: $E \rightarrow F$ such that

$$\lim_{\|h\|_E \to 0} \frac{\| u(x + h) - u(x) - du(x_0)h \|_F}{\| h \|_E} = 0$$

If u is Fréchet differentiable at every $x \in D$ then u is Fréchet differentiable on D, and u is called a Fréchet differentiable mapping, and $du(x)h$ is said to be the Fréchet differential of u at x with increment h. The linear transformation $du(x_0) \in \mathscr{L}(E, F)$ is the Fréchet derivative at x_0 of first order.

Now we know that $\mathscr{L}(E, F)$ is a Banach space, and hence we may consider the Fréchet differential of du(.): $E \rightarrow \mathscr{L}(E, F)$. If this differential exists we will denote it by $d^2u(x)$ and it is clear that $d^2u(x) \in \mathscr{L}(E, \mathscr{L}(E, F))$. However, it can be shown that $\mathscr{L}(E, \mathscr{L}(E, F))$ is isometrically isomorphic to $\mathscr{L}(E \times E, F)$, so that we may think of $d^2u(x)$ as an element of $\mathscr{L}(E \times E, F)$ and $d^2u(.)$: $E \rightarrow \mathscr{L}(E \times E, F)$. We may obviously continue this process so that

$$d^n u(.): E \rightarrow \mathscr{L}(E \times E \times \ldots \times E, F)$$

The evaluation of the map $d^n u(x_0)$ at the point $(h_1, h_2, \ldots, h_n)$ is $d^n u(x_0)(h_1, h_2, \ldots, h_n)$. The symbol $d^n u(x_0)h^n$ is used to represent $d^n u(x_0)(h_1, h_2, \ldots, h_n)$ when $h_1 = h_2 = \ldots = h_n = h$.

It is important to observe that, because of the linearity of the Fréchet derivative, $d^n u(x)$ is a symmetric multilinear operator. That is to say that for any permutation σ in $\mathscr{S}_n$, the symmetry group of degree n, we have

$$d^n u(x_0)(h_1, h_2, \ldots, h_n) = d^n u(x_0)(h_{\sigma(1)}, h_{\sigma(2)}, \ldots, h_{\sigma(n)})$$

As is well known, the higher order differentials lead to an extension of Taylor's theorem to Banach spaces. Specifically, let E, F be Banach spaces and D an open subset of E. Then if u: $D \subset E \rightarrow F$ is n-times Fréchet differentiable at $x_0 \in D$,

$$u(x_0 + h) = u(x_0) + du(x_0)h + \frac{1}{2!}d^2u(x_0)h^2 + \ldots + \frac{1}{n!}d^nu(x_0)h^n + o(\| h \|_E^n) \qquad (2.1)$$

We now assume that $E = \mathbb{R}^p$ and $F = \mathbb{R}$. We wish to write (2.1) in vector form. Before we do so, we introduce some notation.

Let

$$\bigotimes_{i=1}^{m} A_i \stackrel{\text{def}}{=} A_1 \otimes A_2 \otimes \ldots \otimes A_m$$

for any matrices $A_1, A_2, \ldots, A_m$ and

$$\bigotimes^{m} A \stackrel{\text{def}}{=} \underbrace{A \otimes A \otimes \ldots \otimes A}_{m \text{ times}}$$

for any matrix A.

One can show that there exists a unique n^p-dimensional vector $u^{(n)}(x_0)$ which is a coordinate space representation of the linear transformation $d^nu(x_0)$; that is,

$$d^nu(x_0)h^n = \left(\bigotimes^{n} h\right)' u^{(n)}(x_0) \qquad (2.2)$$

Of course, the vector $u^{(n)}(x_0)$ satisfies the following condition of symmetry

$$\left(\bigotimes_{i=1}^{n} h_i\right)' u^{(n)}(x_0) = \left(\bigotimes_{i=1}^{n} h_{\sigma^{-1}(i)}\right)' u^{(n)}(x_0) \qquad (2.3)$$

for any permutation σ in $\mathscr{S}_n$. It is convenient to write (2.3) in terms of a permutation operator. We denote by $P_{p,n}(\sigma)$ the unique linear map in $\mathscr{L}(\otimes^n \mathbb{R}^p, \otimes^n \mathbb{R}^p)$ satisfying

$$P_{p,n}(\sigma)\left(\left(\bigotimes_{i=1}^{n} x_i\right)\right) = \left(\bigotimes_{i=1}^{m} x_{\sigma^{-1}(i)}\right) \qquad (2.4)$$

Also, let

$$S_{p,n} \stackrel{\text{def}}{=} \frac{1}{n!} \sum_{\sigma \in \mathscr{S}_n} P_{p,n}(\sigma) \qquad (2.5)$$

be the completely symmetric operator defined on $\otimes^n \mathbb{R}^p$. For the properties of $P_{p,n}(\sigma)$ and $S_{p,n}$ see Marcus (1973). The explicit expressions for the $P_{p,n}(\sigma)$s are given in Holmquist (1985b, p. 70, 1988) as a particular case of the *direct product permuting matrices* (DPPM) investigated in Holmquist (1985a). Alternatively, one could express the $P_{p,n}(\sigma)$s by means of the permutation matrices F_j and R_s introduced in Balestra and Holly (1990). All the permutation matrices we have just mentioned are matrix representations of permutation operators on tensor spaces, and are extensions of the so-called commutation matrix defined, among other places, in Balestra (1976) and Magnus and Neudecker (1979). For a review of definitions, notations and alternative names for the commutation matrix, see Henderson and Searle (1981).

It follows from (2.3) that

$$\left(\bigotimes_{i=1}^{n} x_i\right)' u^{(n)}(x_0) = \left(\bigotimes_{i=1}^{n} x_i\right)' S_{p,n} u^{(n)}(x_0) \tag{2.6}$$

Equation (2.6) will be of considerable interest to us in deriving $u^{(n)}(x_0)$.

Now, suppose that $u\colon D \subset \mathbb{R}^p \to \mathbb{R}$ is n-times differentiable at $x_0 \in D$. Using (2.2), we can write Taylor's theorem (2.1) in the following vector form,

$$u(x_0 + h) = u(x_0) + h'u^{(1)}(x_0) + \frac{1}{2!}(h \otimes h)'u^{(2)}(x_0) + \dots$$
$$+ \frac{1}{n!}\left(\bigotimes^{n} h\right)' u^{(n)}(x_0) + o(\|h\|^n_{\mathbb{R}^p})$$

This vector form of Taylor's theorem is extremely convenient as it can be easily combined with the general formulae for moments of multivariate normal distribution which have been obtained, among others, by Magnus and Neudecker (1979), Holly (1986), Neudecker and Wansbeek (1987), Phillips and Park (1988), Balestra and Holly (1990), and Holmquist (1988).

It is also useful to represent the symmetric multilinear operator $d^n u(x)$ in the following differential form

$$d^n u(x) = \left(\bigotimes^{n} dx\right)' u^{(n)}(x) \tag{2.7}$$

The differential (2.7) extends to higher orders than the standard first and second differentials and may be conveniently used, in combination with (2.6), to derive the expression for the vectors $u^{(n)}(x)$. This will be illustrated in the following subsection.

Multivariate Hermite polynomials in vector form

The objective of this subsection is to derive formulae for multivariate Hermite polynomials associated with a multivariate normal distribution with mean μ and nonsingular covariance matrix V. These formulae are in vector form and believed to be published for the first time.

Let us start with a definition of multivariate Hermite polynomials in vector form. Let x be a p-dimensional random vector such that $\mathscr{D}(x) = \mathscr{N}(\mu, V)$. Throughout this chapter we shall denote the density function of x by $\varphi(x; \mu, V)$.

We define the multivariate Hermite polynomials of order n to be the vectors $\mathscr{H}^{(n)}(x; \mu, V)$ which are related to the differentials of $\varphi(x; \mu, V)$ as follows.

$$(-1)^n\left(\bigotimes^n dx\right)'\mathscr{H}^{(n)}(x; \mu, V) \overset{\text{def}}{=} \frac{1}{\varphi(x; \mu, V)} d^n\varphi(x; \mu, V) \qquad (2.8)$$

where $d^n\varphi(x; \mu, V)$ the differential of order n of $\varphi(x; \mu, V)$.

Let

$$\text{ch.f.}(t; \mu, V) \overset{\text{def}}{=} \exp[it'\mu - \frac{1}{2}t'Vt] \qquad (2.9)$$

be the characteristic function of x. We have,

$$d^n\varphi(x; \mu, V) = \frac{1}{(2i\pi)^n}\int (-i)^n(t'dx)^n e^{-it'x}\,\text{ch.f.}(t; \mu, V)dt \qquad (2.10)$$

from which it follows, using (2.8) that

$$\varphi(x; \mu, V)\mathscr{H}^{(n)} = \frac{(-i)^n}{(2i\pi)^n}\int \left(\bigotimes^n t\right)e^{-it'x}\text{ch.f.}(t; \mu, V)dt \qquad (2.11)$$

The multivariate Hermite polynomials $\mathscr{H}^{(n)}(x; \mu, V)$ may be obtained by successive differentiation of $\varphi(x; \mu, V)$ and by using the differential formula (2.7) together with (2.6). Alternatively, one may adopt a two-stage derivation which is described below.

In order to avoid notational burden, it is more convenient to change notation, as in Holmquist (1985b), and define

$$y^{\langle r\rangle} \overset{\text{def}}{=} \left(\bigotimes^r y\right)$$

for the rth tensor power of $y \in \mathbb{R}^p$.

Now, for deriving the expression for $\mathscr{H}^{(n)}(x; \mu, V)$, we first assume that $\mu = 0$. It can be shown, by successive differentiation of $\varphi(x; 0, V)$, that

$$\mathscr{H}^{(n)}(x; 0, V) = S_{p,n}\left(\sum_{i=0}^{[n/2]}(-1)^i\frac{n!}{i!(n-2i)!2^i}(\text{vec}\, V^{-1}x)^{\langle n-2i\rangle} \otimes (\text{vec}\, V^{-1})^{\langle i\rangle}\right) \quad (2.12)$$

It is interesting to note that the Hermite polynomials given in (2.12) are the vector form versions of the formula in index notation given in Amari and Kumon (1983) (see also Holly, 1986; Barndorff-Nielsen and Cox, 1990).

Replacing $\text{vec}\, V^{-1}$ by $\text{vec}\,(V^{-1}VV^{-1})$, we can write (2.12) as

$$\mathscr{H}^{(n)}(x; 0, V) = (V^{-1})^{\langle n\rangle}S_{p,n}\left(\sum_{i=0}^{[n/2]}(-1)^i\frac{n!}{i!(n-2i)!2^i}x^{\langle n-2i\rangle} \otimes (\text{vec}\, V)^{\langle i\rangle}\right) \quad (2.13)$$

In the second stage, we replace x by $x - \mu$ in (2.13). By using the multinomial expansion formula given in Holmquist (1985b, equation (2.6)), and the properties of symmetrizers defined by groups of permutations included in $\mathscr{S}_n$, we obtain:

$$\mathscr{H}^{(n)}(x; \mu, V) = (V^{-1})^{\langle n\rangle}S_{p,n}\left[\sum_{i=0}^{[n/2]}(-1)^i\frac{n!}{i!(n-2i)!2^i}\left(\sum_{j=0}^{n-2i}(-1)^j\frac{1}{i!(n-2i-j)!j!}x^{\langle n-2i-j\rangle} \otimes \mu^{\langle j\rangle}\right) \otimes (\text{vec}\, V)^{\langle i\rangle}\right]$$

For future reference we shall give the expression of $\mathscr{H}^{(n)}(x; \mu, V)$ for $n = 1, 2, \ldots, 6$. (2.14)

$$\mathscr{H}^{(1)}(x; \mu, V) = V^{-1}(x - \mu)$$

$$\mathscr{H}^{(2)}(x; \mu, V) = (V^{-1})^{\langle 2\rangle}S_{p,2}[x^{\langle 2\rangle} - 2x \otimes \mu + \mu^{\langle 2\rangle} - \text{vec}\, V]$$

$$\mathscr{H}^{(3)}(x; \mu, V) = (V^{-1})^{\langle 3\rangle}S_{p,3}[x^{\langle 3\rangle} - 3x^{\langle 2\rangle} \otimes \mu + 3x \otimes \mu^{\langle 2\rangle} - 3x \otimes \text{vec}\, V - \mu^{\langle 3\rangle} + 3\mu \otimes \text{vec}\, V]$$

$$\mathscr{H}^{(4)}(x; \mu, V) = (V^{-1})^{\langle 4\rangle}S_{p,4}[x^{\langle 4\rangle} - 4x^{\langle 3\rangle} \otimes \mu + 6x^{\langle 2\rangle} \otimes \mu^{\langle 2\rangle} - 6x^{\langle 2\rangle} \otimes \text{vec}\, V - 4x \otimes \mu^{\langle 3\rangle} + 12x \otimes \mu \otimes \text{vec}\, V + \mu^{\langle 4\rangle} - 6\mu^{\langle 2\rangle} \otimes \text{vec}\, V + 3(\text{vec}\, V)^{\langle 2\rangle}]$$

$$\begin{aligned}\mathscr{H}^{(5)}(x;\mu,V) = (V^{-1})^{\langle 5\rangle}S_{p,3}[&x^{\langle 5\rangle} - 5x^{\langle 4\rangle}\otimes\mu + 10x^{\langle 3\rangle}\otimes\mu^{\langle 2\rangle}\\
&- 10x^{\langle 3\rangle}\otimes \operatorname{vec} V\\
&- 10x^{\langle 2\rangle}\otimes\mu^{\langle 3\rangle} + 30x^{\langle 2\rangle}\otimes\mu\otimes\operatorname{vec} V\\
&+ 5x\otimes\mu^{\langle 4\rangle}\\
&- 30x\otimes\mu^{\langle 2\rangle}\otimes\operatorname{vec} V + 15x\otimes(\operatorname{vec} V)^{\langle 2\rangle}\\
&- \mu^{\langle 5\rangle} + 10\mu^{\langle 3\rangle}\otimes\operatorname{vec} V - 15\mu\otimes(\operatorname{vec} V)^{\langle 2\rangle}]\end{aligned}$$

$$\begin{aligned}\mathscr{H}^{(6)}(x;\mu,V) = (V^{-1})^{\langle 6\rangle}S_{p,6}[&x^{\langle 6\rangle} - 6x^{\langle 5\rangle}\otimes\mu + 15x^{\langle 4\rangle}\otimes\mu^{\langle 2\rangle}\\
&- 15x^{\langle 4\rangle}\otimes\operatorname{vec} V\\
&- 20x^{\langle 3\rangle}\otimes\mu^{\langle 3\rangle} - 4x^{\langle 3\rangle}\otimes\mu\otimes\operatorname{vec} V\\
&+ 15x^{\langle 2\rangle}\otimes\mu^{\langle 4\rangle} + 6x^{\langle 2\rangle}\otimes\mu^{\langle 2\rangle}\otimes\operatorname{vec} V\\
&+ 45x^{\langle 2\rangle}\otimes(\operatorname{vec} V)^{\langle 2\rangle} - 6x\otimes\mu^{\langle 5\rangle}\\
&- 4x\otimes\mu^{\langle 3\rangle}\otimes\operatorname{vec} V\\
&- 2x\otimes\mu\otimes(\operatorname{vec} V)^{\langle 2\rangle} + \mu^{\langle 6\rangle}\\
&+ \mu^{\langle 4\rangle}\otimes\operatorname{vec} V + \mu^{\langle 2\rangle}\otimes(\operatorname{vec} V)^{\langle 2\rangle} - 15(\operatorname{vec} V)^{\langle 3\rangle}]\end{aligned}$$

Multivariate Edgeworth expansion of a density in vector form

We first introduce a definition of multivariate cumulants in vector form.

Let x be a p-dimensional random vector with characteristic function $\text{ch.f.}_x(t)$ and suppose for simplicity that all the moments exist. We define the vector cumulants of order n by the relation

$$t^{\langle n\rangle\prime}\kappa^{(n)} \overset{\text{def}}{=} d^n[\log \text{ch.f.}_x(t)]p^n \tag{2.15}$$

A similar definition is proposed by Holmquist (1985b). Note that $\kappa^{(n)}$ may be viewed as a coordinate space representation of a completely symmetric operator defined on $\otimes^n\mathbb{R}^p$, which, following the suggestion made by Holmquist (1985b), may be called a cumulant operator. We refer the reader to Holmquist (1985b) for a detailed discussion of the cumulant operators and their coordinate space representations.

Let $\{x_T;\ T \geqslant 1\}$ be a sequence of p-dimensional random vectors such that

$$E(\sqrt{T}x_T) = \mu$$

and

$$V(\sqrt{T}x_T) = V_T$$

We also assume that the cumulant $\kappa^{(n)}$ of $\sqrt{T}x_T$ exist for $n \geqslant 3$ and is of order $T^{-(n/2-1)}$, a case fairly common.

Define

$$\lambda^{(n)} \overset{\text{def}}{=} T^{1-n/2}\kappa^{(n)}$$

Assume now that $\mathscr{AD}(\sqrt{T}x_T) = \mathscr{N}(\mu, V)$ where V is nonsingular and $\| V_T - V\| \rightarrow 0$ as $T \rightarrow \infty$.

We also assume that the characteristic function of $\sqrt{T}x_T$ may be written as

$$\text{ch.f.}_{\sqrt{T}x_T}(t) = \zeta_T(t) + o(T^{-1}) \tag{2.16}$$

where

$$\zeta_T(t) = \exp\left\{it'\mu - \frac{1}{2}t'Vt\right\}\left[1 + \frac{1}{\sqrt{T}}\frac{(i)^3}{6}\lambda^{(3)\prime}t^{\langle 3\rangle}\right] + \frac{1}{T}\left[\frac{(i)^4}{24}\lambda^{(4)\prime}t^{\langle 4\rangle} + \frac{(i)^6}{72}\lambda^{(3)\langle 2\rangle\prime}t^{\langle 6\rangle}\right] + o(T^{-1}) \tag{2.17}$$

By term by term Fourier inversion of (2.17), and using (2.11), we obtain the following Edgeworth approximation in vector form to $\text{pdf}_{\sqrt{T}x_T}(x)$, the probability density function of $\sqrt{T}x_T$,

$$= \varphi(x; \mu, V)\left\{1 + \frac{1}{6\sqrt{T}}\lambda^{(3)\prime}\mathscr{H}^{(3)} + \frac{1}{T}\left[\frac{1}{24}\lambda^{(4)\prime}\mathscr{H}^{(4)} + \frac{1}{72}\lambda^{(3)\langle 2\rangle\prime}\mathscr{H}^{(6)}\right]\right\} \tag{2.18}$$

We now assume that the sequence $\{\sqrt{T}x_T;\ T \geqslant 1\}$ satisfies conditions which are sufficient to ensure that the Edgeworth approximation given in (2.18) are, in fact, asymptotic expansions. In other words, we implicitly assume in the statement of the results presented in sections 3 and 4, that the following expansion is valid:

$$\text{pdf}_{\sqrt{T}x_T}(x) = \varphi(x; \mu, V)\left\{1 + \frac{1}{6\sqrt{T}}\lambda^{(3)\prime}\mathscr{H}^{(3)} + \frac{1}{T}\left[\frac{1}{24}\lambda^{(4)\prime}\mathscr{H}^{(4)} + \frac{1}{72}\lambda^{(3)\langle 2\rangle\prime}\mathscr{H}^{(6)}\right]\right\} + o(T^{-1}) \tag{2.19}$$

Compare the above expression with Barndorff-Nielsen and Cox (1979, equation (4.4)). Note the similarity of (2.19) in vector form with the Edgeworth expansion in the univariate case.

To conclude this section, we would like to make a comment on the conditions which are sufficient to ensure the validity of the Edgeworth expansion (2.19). In the applications we have in mind, Tx_T is not necessarily the sum of T independent and identically distributed (i.i.d.) random vectors. Therefore, very general conditions are needed to show that the probability density function of $\sqrt{T}x_T$ will admit a valid Edgeworth expansion. In fact, one should be able to establish this validity from appropriate modifications of assumptions and arguments given, among other places, in Phillips (1977), Sargan (1975, 1980), Sargan and Satchell (1986), and Skovgaard (1981, 1986). For an i.i.d sequence of random vectors, see Bhattacharya and Rao (1976), Bhattacharya and Ghosh (1978), Chandra and Ghosh (1979, 1980), and Bhattacharya (1990).

3 Edgeworth Expansion for Contiguous Alternatives

Consider the sequence $\{x_T;\ T \geqslant 1\}$ of p-dimensional random vectors already introduced, such that $\mathscr{AD}(\sqrt{T}x_T) = \mathscr{N}(\mu,\ V)$ under contiguous alternatives, where V is nonsingular.

At this stage, is convenient to change notation and define

$$\bar{q} \overset{\text{def}}{=} \sqrt{T}x_T$$

Consider now a test statistic ξ_T which admits a stochastic expansion of the vector form

$$\xi T = \bar{q}'A\bar{q} + T^{-1/2}b'\bar{q}^{\langle 3\rangle} + T^{-1}c'\bar{q}^{\langle 4\rangle} + O_p(T^{-3/2}) \qquad (3.1)$$

where A is a symmetric $p \times p$ matrix, b is a p^3-dimensional vector, and c a p^4-dimensional vector. It is further assumed that the matrix A is such that

$$(AV)^2 = AV \quad \text{and} \quad \operatorname{rank}(AV) = \operatorname{tr}(AV) = r$$

that is,

$$\mathscr{AD}\,(\bar{q}'A\bar{q}) = \chi_r^2(\mu'A\mu)$$

The characteristic function of ξ_T can be written as

$$\text{ch.f.}_{\xi_T}(t)$$
$$= (2\pi)^{-p/2}(\det V)^{-1/2}\int_{\mathbb{R}^p} \exp\Big[it\bar{q}'A\bar{q}$$

$$- \left(\frac{1}{2}\right)(\bar{q} - \mu)'V^{-1}(\bar{q} - \mu)\Bigg]$$

$$\Bigg\{1 + \frac{1}{\sqrt{T}}[(it)b'\bar{q}^{\langle 3\rangle} + \frac{1}{6}\lambda^{(3)\prime}\mathscr{H}^{(3)}]$$

$$+ \frac{1}{T}\Bigg[(it)c'\bar{q}^{\langle 4\rangle} + (it)^2 b^{\langle 2\rangle\prime}\bar{q}^{\langle 6\rangle}$$

$$+ (it)\frac{1}{6}(b \otimes \lambda^{(3)})'[\bar{q}^{\langle 3\rangle} \otimes \mathscr{H}^{(3)}] + \frac{1}{24}\lambda^{(4)\prime}\mathscr{H}^{(4)}$$

$$+ \frac{1}{72}\lambda^{(3)\langle 2\rangle\prime}\mathscr{H}^{(6)}\Bigg]\Bigg\}d\bar{q} + o(T^{-1}) \tag{3.2}$$

This integral is more easily computed if we modify the exponential term as follows.

We have

$$(2\pi)^{-p/2}(\det V)^{-1/2}\exp\left[it\bar{q}'A\bar{q} - \left(\frac{1}{2}\right)(\bar{q} - \mu)'V^{-1}(\bar{q} - \mu)\right]$$

$$= (2\pi)^{-p/2}(\det V)^{-1/2}\exp\left(-\frac{1}{2}\mu'V^{-1}\mu\right)$$

$$\times \exp\left[-\frac{1}{2}\bar{q}'(I_p - 2itAV)V^{-1}\bar{q} + \mu'V^{-1}\bar{q}\right] \tag{3.3}$$

To evaluate the second exponential in (3.3), define

$$W^{-1} \stackrel{\text{def}}{=} (I_p - 2itAV)V^{-1}$$

Thus,

$$-\frac{1}{2}\bar{q}'[I_p - 2itAV]V^{-1}\bar{q} + \mu'V^{-1}\bar{q} = -\frac{1}{2}\bar{q}'W^{-1}\bar{q} + \mu'V^{-1}\bar{q}$$

$$= \frac{1}{2}\mu'V^{-1}WV^{-1}\mu - \frac{1}{2}(\bar{q} - WV^{-1}\mu)'W^{-1}(\bar{q} - WV^{-1}\mu)$$

Now, by using the fact that $(AV)^2 = AV$, it is easy seen that

$$W = V\left((I_p - AV) + \frac{1}{1 - 2it}AV\right) \tag{3.4}$$

By using (3.4), and rearranging terms, we can write:

$$\mu'V^{-1}WV^{-1}\mu = \mu'V^{-1}\mu + \frac{2it}{1 - 2it}\mu'A\mu \tag{3.5}$$

and

$$WV^{-1}\mu = (I_p - AV)\mu + \frac{1}{1-2it}VA\mu \tag{3.6}$$

Inserting (3.5) and (3.6) in (3.3) yields

$$\begin{aligned}
&(2\pi)^{-p/2}(\det V)^{-1/2}\exp\left[it\bar{q}'A\bar{q} - \left(\frac{1}{2}\right)(\bar{q}-\mu)'V^{-1}(\bar{q}-\mu)\right] \\
&\quad = (2\pi)^{-p/2}(\det V)^{-1/2}\exp\left(-\frac{2it}{1-2it}\frac{\mu'A\mu}{2}\right) \\
&\quad\quad \times \exp\left[-\frac{1}{2}(\bar{q} - WV^{-1}\mu)'W^{-1}(\bar{q} - WV^{-1}\mu)\right]
\end{aligned} \tag{3.7}$$

Let us modify equation (3.7) by multiplying the first line of the r.h.s. by $(\det W)^{1/2}$ and the second line by $(\det W)^{-1/2}$ to obtain

$$\begin{aligned}
&(2\pi)^{-p/2}(\det V)^{-1/2}\exp\left[it\bar{q}'A\bar{q} - \left(\frac{1}{2}\right)(\bar{q}-\mu)'V^{-1}(\bar{q}-\mu)\right] \\
&\quad = (2\pi)^{-p/2}(\det V)^{-1/2}(\det W)^{1/2}\exp\left(-\frac{2it}{1-2it}\frac{\mu'A\mu}{2}\right) \\
&\quad\quad \times (\det W)^{-1/2}\exp\left[-\frac{1}{2}(\bar{q} - WV^{-1}\mu)'W^{-1}(\bar{q} - WV^{-1}\mu)\right]
\end{aligned} \tag{3.8}$$

Now, note that

$$\begin{aligned}
(\det V)^{-1/2}(\det W)^{1/2} &= [\det(I_p - 2itAV)]^{-1/2} \\
&= (1-2it)^{-r/2}
\end{aligned}$$

and hence, equation (3.8) may be written as

$$\begin{aligned}
&(2\pi)^{-p/2}(\det V)^{-1/2}\exp\left[it\bar{q}'A\bar{q} - \left(\frac{1}{2}\right)(\bar{q}-\mu)'V^{-1}(\bar{q}-\mu)\right] \\
&\quad = (2\pi)^{-p/2}(1-2it)^{-r/2}\exp\left(-\frac{2it}{1-2it}\frac{\mu'A\mu}{2}\right) \\
&\quad\quad \times (\det W)^{-1/2}\exp\left[-\frac{1}{2}(\bar{q} - WV^{-1}\mu)'W^{-1}(\bar{q} - WV^{-1}\mu)\right]
\end{aligned} \tag{3.9}$$

Using (3.9), we can write the characteristic function of ξ_T given in (3.2) as:

$$\text{ch.f.}_{\xi_T}(t) = (1-2it)^{-r/2}\exp\left(-\frac{2it}{1-2it}\frac{\mu'A\mu}{2}\right)(2\pi)^{-p/2}$$

$$(\det W)^{-1/2}\int_{\mathbb{R}^p} \exp\left[-\frac{1}{2}(\bar{q} - WV^{-1}\mu)'W^{-1}(\bar{q} - WV^{-1}\mu)\right]$$

$$\left\{1 + \frac{1}{\sqrt{T}}\left[(it)b'\bar{q}^{\langle 3\rangle} + \frac{1}{6}\lambda^{(3)\prime}\mathcal{H}^{(3)}\right]\right.$$

$$+ \frac{1}{T}\left[(it)c'\bar{q}^{\langle 4\rangle} + (it)^2 b^{\langle 2\rangle\prime}\bar{q}^{\langle 6\rangle}\right.$$

$$+ (it)\frac{1}{6}(b \otimes \lambda^{(3)})'[\bar{q}^{\langle 3\rangle} \otimes \mathcal{H}^{(3)}] + \frac{1}{24}\lambda^{(4)\prime}\mathcal{H}^{(4)}$$

$$\left.\left. + \frac{1}{72}\lambda^{(3)\langle 2\rangle\prime}\mathcal{H}^{(6)}\right]\right\}d\bar{q} + o(T^{-1}) \tag{3.10}$$

The leading term of this expansion is the characteristic function of a $\chi^2_r(\mu' A\mu)$. But we still have to evaluate the $1/\sqrt{T}$ and $1/T$ terms of the series.

It is clear that these terms depend, among other things, on the moments of a normal distribution $\mathcal{N}(WV^{-1}\mu, W)$, where $WV^{-1}\mu$ and W are given by (3.6) and (3.4) respectively.

At this stage, it is necessary to describe the method used to evaluate these moments. This is done in three steps as follows:

In the first step, we need to derive the expectations $E(x^{\langle n\rangle})$ for $n = 1, 2, \ldots, 6$, when $\mathscr{D}(x) = \mathcal{N}(\mu, V)$. There are several ways of doing it. One possibility is to obtain the $E(x^{\langle n\rangle})$s by vectorizing the expressions for the corresponding moments given in Balestra and Holly (1990). Alternatively, one could adopt the method used in Balestra and Holly (1990) to directly derive these expressions. However, it seems more appropriate, in relation to the exposition on differential calculus given in section 2, to evaluate the $E(x^{\langle n\rangle})$s by differentiation of the characteristic function of x.

We have

$$E(x^{\langle n\rangle}) = (-i)^n \,\text{ch.f.}(t;\, \mu,\, V)^{(n)}|_{t=0}$$

where $\text{ch.f.}(t;\, \mu,\, V)^{(n)}$ is the coordinate space representation of the linear transformation $d^n\text{ch.f.}(t;\, \mu,\, V)$. This is the approach adopted by Holmquist (1988), where the moment generating function is used instead of the characteristic function. In our notation, Holmquist (1988) obtained the following general result (cf. equation (2.12)):

$$E(x^{\langle n\rangle}) = S_{p,n}\left(\sum_{i=0}^{[n/2]} \frac{n!}{i!(n-2i)!2^i}\mu^{\langle n-2i\rangle} \otimes (\text{vec}\, V)^{\langle i\rangle}\right) \tag{3.11}$$

For easy reference, we now give the expression of $E(x^{\langle n \rangle})$ for $n = 1, \ldots, 6$.

$$\begin{aligned}
E(x) &= \mu \\
E(x^{\langle 2 \rangle}) &= S_{p,2}[\mu^{\langle 2 \rangle} + \operatorname{vec} V] \\
E(x^{\langle 3 \rangle}) &= S_{p,3}[3\mu \otimes \operatorname{vec} V + \mu^{\langle 3 \rangle}] \\
E(x^{\langle 4 \rangle}) &= S_{p,4}[6\mu^{\langle 2 \rangle} \otimes \operatorname{vec} V + \mu^{\langle 4 \rangle} + 3(\operatorname{vec} V)^{\langle 2 \rangle}] \\
E(x^{\langle 5 \rangle}) &= S_{p,5}[10\mu^{\langle 3 \rangle} \otimes \operatorname{vec} V + \mu^{\langle 5 \rangle}4 + 15\mu \otimes (\operatorname{vec} V)^{\langle 2 \rangle}] \\
E(x^{\langle 6 \rangle}) &= S_{p,6}[15\mu^{\langle 4 \rangle} \otimes \operatorname{vec} V + \mu^{\langle 6 \rangle} \\
&\quad + 45\mu^{\langle 2 \rangle} \otimes (\operatorname{vec} V)^{\langle 2 \rangle} + 15(\operatorname{vec} V)^{\langle 3 \rangle}] \qquad (3.12)
\end{aligned}$$

In the second step, we compute the expectation of the $1/\sqrt{T}$ and $1/T$ terms of the expansion (3.10) using (3.12), for a normal distribution with mean $WV^{-1}\mu$ and variance W given by (3.6) and (3.4) respectively.

The third step consists in decomposing the fractions, of the form $(2it)^q/(1-2it)^s$ for $s \geqslant 1$, which appear in the expectations obtained at the earlier step into rational decompositions of the form

$$\frac{(2it)^q}{(1-2it)^s} = \sum_{\upsilon=0}^{s} \frac{a_{s,\upsilon}}{(1-2it)^{\upsilon}}$$

The second and third steps we have just described are formidable tasks to do "by hand." They are, however, well suited for being performed by symbolic manipulation languages on the computer. As indicated in the introduction, we used *Mathematica* to perform this computer algebra.

After these three steps, one obtains that the characteristic function of ξ_T given by (3.10) may be written as

$$\begin{aligned}
\text{ch.f.}_{\xi_T}(t) &= (1-2it)^{-r/2} \exp\left(-\frac{2it}{1-2it}\frac{\mu' A \mu}{2}\right) \\
&\left\{1 + \frac{1}{\sqrt{T}}\left[\pi'(it) + \sum_{q=0}^{3} \pi^{(q)} \frac{1}{(1-2it)^q}\right]\right. \\
&\left. + \frac{1}{T}\left[\rho''(it)^2 + \rho'(it) + \sum_{s=0}^{6} \rho^{(s)} \frac{1}{(1-2it)^s}\right]\right\} + o(T^{-1}) \qquad (3.13)
\end{aligned}$$

Upon Fourier inversion of (3.13) we obtain approximations to the sequence of probability density functions of ξ_T for contiguous alternatives.

We implicitly assume in the statement of the results presented in this section and the following one that general assumptions are being made which are sufficient to ensure that these approximations are, in fact, valid asymptotic expansions up to $o(T^{-1})$. The form of this expansion is given in the following theorem.

Theorem 1. The asymptotic expansion of the density function of ξ_T up to $o(T^{-1})$ for contiguous alternatives is given by

$$\begin{aligned} f_{\xi_T}(x) &= f_{\chi^2}(x; r, \mu' A\mu) \\ &\quad + \frac{1}{\sqrt{T}}\left[\pi' f'_{\chi^2}(x; r, \mu' A\mu) + \sum_{q=0}^{3} \pi^{(q)} f_{\chi^2}(x; r + 2q, \mu' A\mu)\right] \\ &\quad + \frac{1}{T}\left[\rho'' f''_{\chi^2}(x; r, \mu' A\mu) + \rho' f'_{\chi^2}(x; r, \mu' A\mu)\right. \\ &\quad \left. + \sum_{s=0}^{6} \rho^{(s)} f_{\chi^2}(x; r + 2s, \mu' A\mu)\right] + o(T^{-1}) \end{aligned} \tag{3.14}$$

where $f_{\chi^2}(x; v, \lambda)$ denotes the density of the noncentral chi-squared distribution with v degrees of freedom and noncentrality parameter λ, and $f'_{\chi^2}(x; v, \lambda)$, $f''_{\chi^2}(x; v, \lambda)$ its first and second order derivatives respectively. □

Below, we shall only give the expression for the coefficients π' and $\pi^{(q)}$ for $q = 0, 1, 2, 3$. The general expression for the coefficients ρ'', ρ' and $\rho^{(s)}$ for $s = 0, 1, \ldots, 6$ are quite lengthy and are given in the supplement to this chapter.[3] Some particular cases are dealt with in the next section. Note that there is a difference between the result presented in this chapter and the one derived in Chandra and Ghosh (1980) in which the derivatives of the p.d.f. of the noncentral chi-square distribution do not appear since it does not use a stochastic expansion up to order $O_p(T^{-3/2})$ of the form given in (3.1).

To simplify the notation, we define

$$\tilde{\lambda}^{(n)} \overset{\text{def}}{=} (V^{-1})^{\langle n \rangle} \lambda^{(n)}$$

We have,

$$\begin{aligned} \pi' &= 3b'(\mu \otimes (VA\mu)^{\langle 2 \rangle}) + 3b'(\mu \otimes (\operatorname{vec} V)) \\ &\quad - 3b'(\mu \otimes (\operatorname{vec} VAV)) - 3b'((VA\mu) \otimes (\operatorname{vec} V)) \\ &\quad + 3b'((VA\mu) \otimes (\operatorname{vec} VAV)) - 3b'(\mu^{\langle 2 \rangle} \otimes (VA\mu)) \\ &\quad + b'(\mu^{\langle 3 \rangle}) - b'((VA\mu)^{\langle 3 \rangle}) \end{aligned}$$

$$\pi^{(0)} = 3b'(\mu \otimes (VA\mu)^{\langle 2\rangle}) - 3b'(\mu \otimes (\mathrm{vec}\, VAV))/2$$
$$- 3b'((VA\mu) \otimes (\mathrm{vec}\, V))/2 + 3b'((VA\mu) \otimes (\mathrm{vec}\, VAV))$$
$$- 3b'(\mu^{\langle 2\rangle} \otimes (VA\mu))/2 - 3b'((VA\mu)^{\langle 3\rangle})/2$$
$$- \tilde{\lambda}^{(3)\prime}((VA\mu) \otimes \mu^{\langle 2\rangle})/2 + \tilde{\lambda}^{(3)\prime}((VA\mu) \otimes (\mathrm{vec}\, VAV))/2$$
$$+ \tilde{\lambda}^{(3)\prime}(\mu^{\langle 2\rangle} \otimes (VA\mu))/2 - \tilde{\lambda}^{(3)\prime}((VA\mu)^{\langle 3\rangle})/6$$

$$\pi^{(1)} = -9b'(\mu \otimes (VA\mu)^{\langle 2\rangle})/2 + 3b'(\mu \otimes (\mathrm{vec}\, VAV))/2$$
$$+ 3b'((VA\mu) \otimes (\mathrm{vec}\, V))/2 - 9b'((VA\mu) \otimes (\mathrm{vec}\, VAV))/2$$
$$+ 3b'(\mu^{\langle 2\rangle} \otimes (VA\mu))/2 + 3b'((VA\mu)^{\langle 3\rangle})$$
$$+ \tilde{\lambda}^{(3)\prime}((VA\mu) \otimes \mu^{\langle 2\rangle})/2 - \tilde{\lambda}^{(3)\prime}((VA\mu) \otimes (\mathrm{vec}\, VAV))$$
$$- \tilde{\lambda}^{(3)\prime}(\mu^{\langle 2\rangle} \otimes (VA\mu))/2 + \tilde{\lambda}^{(3)\prime}((VA\mu)^{\langle 3\rangle})/2$$

$$\pi^{(2)} = 3b'(\mu \otimes (VA\mu)^{\langle 2\rangle})/2 + 3b'((VA\mu) \otimes (\mathrm{vec}\, VAV))/2$$
$$- 2b'(VA\mu)^{\langle 3\rangle} + \tilde{\lambda}^{(3)\prime}((VA\mu) \otimes (\mathrm{vec}\, VAV))/2$$
$$- \tilde{\lambda}^{(3)\prime}(VA\mu)^{\langle 3\rangle}/2$$

$$\pi^{(3)} = b'((VA\mu)^{\langle 3\rangle}/2 + \tilde{\lambda}^{(3)\prime}((VA\mu)^{\langle 3\rangle})/6$$

4 Some Special Cases of Interest

We consider in this section two special cases of interest, namely when $\mu = 0$, and when $A = V^{-1}$.

The case where $\mu = 0$

The case where $\mu = 0$ corresponds to the asymptotic expansion of the distribution function of ξ_T under the null hypothesis. One can calculate the critical value of the distribution function of ξ_T up to order $o(T^{-1})$ in terms of the critical value of the χ^2_p distribution at the level α.

By setting $\mu = 0$, we see that the $1/\sqrt{T}$ term in the expansion of the distribution function of ξ_T is equal to zero. In addition, the coefficients $\rho^{(4)}$, $\rho^{(5)}$, and $\rho^{(6)}$ are equal to zero. Therefore, we have:

Corollary 1. The asymptotic expansion of the density function of ξ_T up to $o(T^{-1})$ under the null hypothesis is given by

$$f_{\xi_T}(x) = f_{\chi^2}(x; r) + \frac{1}{T}\Bigg[\rho''_{\{\mu=0\}} f''_{\chi^2}(x; r) + \rho'_{\{\mu=0\}} f'_{\chi^2}(x; r)$$
$$+ \sum_{s=0}^{3} \rho^{(s)}_{\{\mu=0\}} f_{\chi^2}(x; r + 2s)\Bigg] + o(T^{-1}) \qquad (4.1)$$

where $f_{\chi^2}(x;\ \nu)$ denotes the density of the central chi-squared distribution with ν degrees of freedom, and $f'_{\chi^2}(x;\ \nu)$, $f''_{\chi^2}(x;\ \nu)$ its first and second order derivatives respectively.

Upon integration of equation (4.1) we obtain the cumulative distribution function (cdf) of ξ_T up to order $o(T^{-1})$ which we denote by $\mathrm{cdf}_{\xi_T}(x)$. The critical value of $\mathrm{cdf}_{\xi_T}(x)$ at the level α up to order $o(T^{-1})$ is given by the solution of

$$\mathrm{cdf}_{\xi_T}(x_{\xi_T,\alpha}) = \alpha$$

Remark. The case considered by Phillips and Park (1988) is a particular case in which the vector b in the stochastic expansion (3.1) is the derivative of $\mathrm{vec}\,(A)$. One can verify that we obtain exactly the same coefficients as in Phillips and Park (1988, appendix B). In particular, the coefficient $\rho''_{\{\mu=0\}}$ is equal to zero.

The case where $A = V^{-1}$

In the particular case where the null hypothesis is that the vector of true parameters is equal to zero, we have $A = V^{-1}$. This particular case has been studied in detail by Peers (1971) for the following three test criteria: likelihood ratio, Wald, and Rao's efficient score. The case of composite alternatives has also been examined by Hayakawa (1975, 1977) and Harris and Peers (1980).

We find in this case that $\pi' = 0$, $\rho'' = 0$ and $\rho' = 0$.

Hence, we have:

Corollary 2. Suppose $A = V^{-1}$. Then, the asymptotic expansion of the density function of ξ_T up to $o(T^{-1})$ for contiguous alternatives is given by

$$\begin{aligned} f_{\xi_T}(x) &= f_{\chi^2}(x;\, p,\, \mu' V^{-1}\mu) \\ &\quad + \frac{1}{\sqrt{T}}\left[\sum_{q=0}^{3} \pi^{(q)}_{\{A=V^{-1}\}} f_{\chi^2}(x;\, p+2q,\, \mu' V^{-1}\mu)\right] \\ &\quad + \frac{1}{T}\left[\sum_{s=0}^{6} \rho^{(s)}_{\{A=V^{-1}\}} f_{\chi^2}(x;\, p+2s,\, \mu' V^{-1}\mu)\right] + o(T^{-1}) \qquad (4.2) \end{aligned}$$

Corollary 2 extends the results given in Peers (1971), Hayakawa (1975, 1977) and Harris and Peers (1980) by including the $1/T$ term in the expansion of the density function of ξ_T when $A = V^{-1}$.

$$\pi^{(0)}_{\{A=V^{-1}\}} = \bar{\lambda}^{(3)\prime}(\mu \otimes (\mathrm{vec}\, V))/2 - \bar{\lambda}^{(3)\prime}(\mu^{\langle 3\rangle})/6$$

$$\pi^{(1)}_{\{A=V^{-1}\}} = -3b'(\mu \otimes (\operatorname{vec} V))/2 - \tilde{\lambda}^{(3)\prime}(\mu \otimes (\operatorname{vec} V)) + \tilde{\lambda}^{(3)\prime}(\mu^{\langle 3\rangle})/2$$

$$\begin{aligned}\pi^{(2)}_{\{A=V^{-1}\}} = {} & 3b'(\mu \otimes (\operatorname{vec} V))/2 - b'(\mu^{\langle 3\rangle})/2 \\ & + \tilde{\lambda}^{(3)\prime}(\mu \otimes (\operatorname{vec} V))/2 - \tilde{\lambda}^{(3)\prime}(\mu^{\langle 3\rangle})/2\end{aligned}$$

$$\pi^{(3)}_{\{A=V^{-1}\}} = b'(\mu^{\langle 3\rangle})/2 + \tilde{\lambda}^{(3)\prime}(\mu^{\langle 3\rangle})/6$$

To conclude, we would like to remark that the general explicit form of the expansion under contiguous alternatives up to $o(T^{-1})$ derived in this chapter are very useful, upon specialization, for the computation of the asymptotic local power of test statistics and the comparison of competing tests.

Appendix: expression for the ρ coefficients when $\mu = 0$

Here, we give the complete expression for the coefficients when $\mu = 0$.

$$\begin{aligned}\rho''_{\{\mu=0\}} = {} & -45b^{\langle 2\rangle\prime}S_{p,6}((\operatorname{vec} V)^{\langle 2\rangle} \otimes (\operatorname{vec} VAV))/2 \\ & + 45b^{\langle 2\rangle\prime}S_{p,6}((\operatorname{vec} V) \otimes (\operatorname{vec} VAV)^{\langle 2\rangle})/2 \\ & + 15b^{\langle 2\rangle\prime}S_{p,6}((\operatorname{vec} V)^{\langle 3\rangle})/2 \\ & - 15b^{\langle 2\rangle\prime}S_{p,6}((\operatorname{vec} VAV)^{\langle 3\rangle})/2\end{aligned}$$

$$\begin{aligned}\rho'_{\{\mu=0\}} = {} & -6c'((\operatorname{vec} V) \otimes (\operatorname{vec} VAV)) \\ & + 3c'((\operatorname{vec} V)^{\langle 2\rangle}) \\ & + 3c'((\operatorname{vec} VAV)^{\langle 2\rangle}) \\ & + 3(b \otimes \tilde{\lambda}^{(3)})'(S_{p,4} \otimes I_{p^2})((\operatorname{vec} V) \otimes (\operatorname{vec} VAV) \otimes (\operatorname{vec} V)) \\ & - 3(b \otimes \tilde{\lambda}^{(3)})'(S_{p,4} \otimes I_{p^2})((\operatorname{vec} VAV)^{\langle 2\rangle} \otimes (\operatorname{vec} V))/2 \\ & - 3(b \otimes \tilde{\lambda}^{(3)})'(S_{p,4} \otimes I_{p^2})((\operatorname{vec} V)^{\langle 3\rangle})/2 \\ & - 15(b \otimes \tilde{\lambda}^{(3)})'S_{p,6}((\operatorname{vec} V)^{\langle 2\rangle} \otimes (\operatorname{vec} VAV))/2 \\ & + 15(b \otimes \tilde{\lambda}^{(3)})'S_{p,6}((\operatorname{vec} V) \otimes (\operatorname{vec} VAV)^{\langle 2\rangle})/2 \\ & + 5(b \otimes \tilde{\lambda}^{(3)})'S_{p,6}((\operatorname{vec} V)^{\langle 3\rangle})/2 \\ & - 5(b \otimes \tilde{\lambda}^{(3)})'S_{p,6}((\operatorname{vec} VAV)^{\langle 3\rangle})/2 \\ & - 45b^{\langle 2\rangle\prime}S_{p,6}((\operatorname{vec} V)^{\langle 2\rangle} \otimes (\operatorname{vec} VAV))/4 \\ & + 45b^{\langle 2\rangle\prime}S_{p,6}((\operatorname{vec} V) \otimes (\operatorname{vec} VAV)^{\langle 2\rangle})/2 \\ & - 45b^{\langle 2\rangle\prime}S_{p,6}((\operatorname{vec} VAV)^{\langle 3\rangle})/4\end{aligned}$$

$$\begin{aligned}\rho^{(0)}_{\{\mu=0\}} = {} & -3c'((\operatorname{vec} V) \otimes (\operatorname{vec} VAV)) \\ & + 3c'((\operatorname{vec} VAV)^{\langle 2\rangle}) \\ & + \tilde{\lambda}^{(4)\prime}((\operatorname{vec} VAV)^{\langle 2\rangle})/8 \\ & + 3(b \otimes \tilde{\lambda}^{(3)})'(S_{p,4} \otimes I_{p^2})((\operatorname{vec} V) \otimes (\operatorname{vec} VAV) \otimes (\operatorname{vec} V))/2\end{aligned}$$

$$
\begin{aligned}
& - 3(b \otimes \tilde{\lambda}^{(3)})'(S_{p,4} \otimes I_{p^2})((\operatorname{vec} VAV)^{\langle 2\rangle} \otimes (\operatorname{vec} V))/2 \\
& - 15(b \otimes \tilde{\lambda}^{(3)})' S_{p,6}((\operatorname{vec} V)^{\langle 2\rangle} \otimes (\operatorname{vec} VAV))/4 \\
& + 15(b \otimes \tilde{\lambda}^{(3)})' S_{p,6}((\operatorname{vec} V) \otimes (\operatorname{vec} VAV)^{\langle 2\rangle})/2 \\
& - 15(b \otimes \tilde{\lambda}^{(3)})' S_{p,6}((\operatorname{vec} VAV)^{\langle 3\rangle})/4 \\
& - 45 b^{\langle 2\rangle\prime} S_{p,6}((\operatorname{vec} V)^{\langle 2\rangle} \otimes (\operatorname{vec} VAV))/8 \\
& + 135 b^{\langle 2\rangle\prime} S_{p,6}((\operatorname{vec} V) \otimes (\operatorname{vec} VAV)^{\langle 2\rangle})/8 \\
& - 45 b^{\langle 2\rangle\prime} S_{p,6}((\operatorname{vec} VAV)^{\langle 3\rangle})/4 \\
& - 5(\tilde{\lambda}^{(3)\langle 2\rangle})' S_{p,6}((\operatorname{vec} VAV)^{\langle 3\rangle})/4
\end{aligned}
$$

$$
\begin{aligned}
\rho^{(1)}_{\{\mu=0\}} = {} & 3c'((\operatorname{vec} V) \otimes (\operatorname{vec} VAV)) \\
& - 9c'((\operatorname{vec} VAV)^{\langle 2\rangle})/2 \\
& - \tilde{\lambda}^{(4)\prime}((\operatorname{vec} VAV)^{\langle 2\rangle})/4 \\
& - 3(b \otimes \tilde{\lambda}^{(3)})'(S_{p,4} \otimes I_{p^2})((\operatorname{vec} V) \\
& \otimes (\operatorname{vec} VAV) \otimes (\operatorname{vec} V))/2 \\
& + 9(b \otimes \tilde{\lambda}^{(3)})'(S_{p,4} \otimes I_{p^2})((\operatorname{vec} VAV)^{\langle 2\rangle} \otimes (\operatorname{vec} V))/4 \\
& + 15(b \otimes \tilde{\lambda}^{(3)})' S_{p,6}((\operatorname{vec} V)^{\langle 2\rangle} \otimes (\operatorname{vec} VAV))/4 \\
& - 45(b \otimes \tilde{\lambda}^{(3)})' S_{p,6}((\operatorname{vec} V) \otimes (\operatorname{vec} VAV)^{\langle 2\rangle})/4 \\
& + 15(b \otimes \tilde{\lambda}^{(3)})' S_{p,6}((\operatorname{vec} VAV)^{\langle 3\rangle})/2 \\
& + 45 b^{\langle 2\rangle\prime} S_{p,6}((\operatorname{vec} V)^{\langle 2\rangle} \otimes (\operatorname{vec} VAV))/8 \\
& - 45 b^{\langle 2\rangle\prime} S_{p,6}((\operatorname{vec} V) \otimes (\operatorname{vec} VAV)^{\langle 2\rangle})/2 \\
& + 75 b^{\langle 2\rangle\prime} S_{p,6}((\operatorname{vec} VAV)^{\langle 3\rangle})/4 \\
& + 15(\tilde{\lambda}^{(3)\langle 2\rangle})' S_{p,6}((\operatorname{vec} VAV)^{\langle 3\rangle})/4
\end{aligned}
$$

$$
\begin{aligned}
\rho^{(2)}_{\{\mu=0\}} = {} & 3c'((\operatorname{vec} VAV)^{\langle 2\rangle})/2 \\
& + \tilde{\lambda}^{(4)\prime}((\operatorname{vec} VAV)^{\langle 2\rangle})/8 \\
& - 3(b \otimes \tilde{\lambda}^{(3)})'(S_{p,4} \otimes I_{p^2})((\operatorname{vec} VAV)^{\langle 2\rangle} \otimes (\operatorname{vec} V))/4 \\
& + 15(b \otimes \tilde{\lambda}^{(3)})' S_{p,6}((\operatorname{vec} V) \otimes (\operatorname{vec} VAV)^{\langle 2\rangle})/4 \\
& - 5(b \otimes \tilde{\lambda}^{(3)})' S_{p,6}((\operatorname{vec} VAV)^{\langle 3\rangle}) \\
& + 45 b^{\langle 2\rangle\prime} S_{p,6}((\operatorname{vec} V) \otimes (\operatorname{vec} VAV)^{\langle 2\rangle}))/8 \\
& - 75 b^{\langle 2\rangle\prime} S_{p,6}((\operatorname{vec} VAV)^{\langle 3\rangle})/8 \\
& - 15(\tilde{\lambda}^{(3)\langle 2\rangle})' S_{p,6}((\operatorname{vec} VAV)^{\langle 3\rangle})/4
\end{aligned}
$$

$$
\begin{aligned}
\rho^{(3)}_{\{\mu=0\}} = {} & 5(b \otimes \tilde{\lambda}^{(3)})' S_{p,6}((\operatorname{vec} VAV)^{\langle 3\rangle})/4 \\
& + 15 b^{\langle 2\rangle\prime} S_{p,6}((\operatorname{vec} VAV)^{\langle 3\rangle})/8 \\
& + 5(\tilde{\lambda}^{(3)\langle 2\rangle})' S_{p,6}((\operatorname{vec} VAV)^{\langle 3\rangle})/4
\end{aligned}
$$

$$\rho^{(4)}_{\{\mu=0\}} = 0$$

$$\rho^{(5)}_{\{\mu=0\}} = 0$$

$$\rho^{(6)}_{\{\mu=0\}} = 0$$

Notes

We would like to thank three anonymous referees and Peter C. B. Phillips for reading the first version and for their helpful comments towards its improvement. We would also like to thank Jayalakshmi Krishnakumar for having been kind enough to read this chapter and make suggestions for corrections as regards the English, which has made it more readable. All errors remain our responsibility.

1 Some examples taken from the econometric literature are: Sargan (1980), Rothenberg (1984), Cavanagh (1984), and Magee (1989).
2 We used $\mathrm{T_EX}$ to produce the manuscript of this chapter. One additional advantage of using *Mathematica* is that one obtains formulae which can be transformed into a $\mathrm{T_EX}$ file. Note, however, that *Mathematica* has serious limitations in producing these $\mathrm{T_EX}$ files and has to be complemented with another programming language, like Pascal.
3 This supplement is available from the authors upon request.

References

Amari, S.-I. and Kumon, M. (1983) Differential geometry of Edgeworth expansions in curved exponential family. *Annals of the Institute of Statistical Mathematics*, *A*, 35, 1–24.

Balestra, P. (1976) *La dérivation matricielle*. Collection de l'IME no. 12, Université de Dijon, France.

Balestra, P. and Holly, A. (1990) A general Kronecker formula for the moments of the multivariate normal distribution. *Cahiers de recherches économiques*, 9002, University of Lausanne.

Barndorff-Nielsen, O. and Cox, D. R. (1979) Edgeworth and saddlepoint approximations with statistical applications. *Journal of the Royal Statistical Society B*, 41, 279–312.

Barndorff-Nielsen, O. and Cox, D. R. (1990) *Asymptotic Techniques for Use in Statistics*. London: Chapman and Hall.

Bhattacharya, R. N. (1990) Asymptotic expansions in statistics. In R. N. Bhattacharya and M. Denker (eds), *Asymptotic Statistics*. Berlin: Birhäuser Verlag.

Bhattacharya, R. N. and Ghosh, J. K. (1978) On the validity of the formal Edgeworth expansions. *Annals of Statistics*, 6, 434–51.

Bhattacharya, R. N. and Rao, R. R. (1976) *Normal Approximation and Asymptotic Expansions*. New York: John Wiley & Sons.

Cavanagh, C. L. (1984) Comparing alternative tests in nonlinear regression models. Discussion paper series number 113, Harvard Institute of Economic Research.

Chandra, T. K. and Ghosh, J. K. (1979) Valid asymptotic expansions for the likelihood ratio statistic and other perturbed chi-square variables. *Sankhya A*, 41, 22–47.

Chandra, T. K. and Ghosh, J. K. (1980) Valid asymptotic expansions for the likelihood ratio and other statistics under contiguous alternatives. *Sankhya A*, 42, 170–84.

Dieudonné, J. (1969) *Foundations of Modern Analysis*. New York: Academic Press.

Harris, P. and Peers, H. W. (1980) The local power of the efficient scores test statistic. *Biometrika*, 67, 525–9.

Hayakawa, T. (1975) The likelihood ratio criterion for composite hypothesis under a local alternative. *Biometrika*, 62, 451–60.

Hayakawa, T. (1977) The likelihood ratio criterion and the asymptotic expansion of its distribution. *Annals of the Institute of Statistical Mathematics, A*, 29, 359–78.

Henderson, H. V. and Searle, S. R. (1981) The vec-permutation matrix, the vec operator and Kronecker products. A review. *Linear and Multilinear Algebra*, 9, 271–88.

Holly, A. (1986) Tensor components of multivariate Hermite polynomials and moments of a multivariate normal distribution. Instituto de Matemática Pura e Aplicada (IMPA), Rio de Janeiro, and *Cahiers de Reherches Economiques*, 8701, Département d'économétrie et d'économie politique, University of Lausanne.

Holmquist, B. (1985a) The direct product permuting matrices. *Linear and Multilinear Algebra*, 17, 117–41.

Holmquist, B. (1985b) Moments and cumulants from generating functions of Hilbert space-valued random variables and an application to the Wishart distribution. University of Lund and Lund Institute of Technology, Department of Mathematical Statistics, Statistical Research Report, 3, 1–86.

Holmquist, B. (1988) Moments and cumulants of the multivariate normal distribution. *Stochastic Analysis and Applications*, 6, 273–8.

Magee, L. (1989) An Edgeworth test size correction for the linear model with AR(1) errors. *Econometrica*, 57, 661–74.

Magnus, J. R. and Neudecker, H. (1979) The commutation matrix: some properties and applications. *Annals of Statistics*, 7, 381–94.

Marcus, M. (1973) *Finite Dimensional Multilinear Algebra, Part 1*. New York: Marcel Dekker.

Merckens, A. and Wansbeek, T. (1989) Formula manipulation in statistics on the computer: evaluating the expectation or higher-degree functions of normally distributed matrices. *Computational Statistics and Data Analysis*, 8, 189–200.

Neudecker, H. and Wansbeek, T. (1987) Fourth-order properties of normally distributed random matrices. *Linear Algebra and Its Applications*, 97, 13–21.

Pavelle, R., Rothstein, M. and Fitch, J. (1981) Computer algebra. *Scientific American*, 245, 102–13.

Peers, H. W. (1971) Likelihood ratio and associated test criteria. *Biometrika*, 58, 577–87.

Pfanzagl, J. (1980) Asymptotic expansions in parametric decision theory. In P. R. Krishnaiah (ed.), *Developements in Statistics, volume 3*. New York: Academic Press, pp. 1–97.

Phillips, P. C. B. (1977) A general theorem in the theory of asymptotic expansions as approximations to finite sample distributions of econometric estimators. *Econometrica*, 45, 453–86.

Phillips, P. C. B. and Park, J. Y. (1988) On the formulation of Wald tests of nonlinear restrictions. *Econometrica*, 56, 1065–83.

Rao, C. R. (1947) Large sample tests of statistical hypotheses concerning several parameters with applications to problems of estimation. *Proceedings of the Cambridge Philosophical Society*, 44, 50–7.

Rothenberg, T. J. (1984) Hypothesis testing in the linear model when the error covariance matrix is nonscalar. *Econometrica*, 52, 827–42.

Sargan, J. D. (1975) Gram–Charlier approximations applied to t-ratios of k-class estimators. *Econometrica*, 43, 327–46.

Sargan, J. D. (1980) Some approximations to the distribution of econometric criteria which are asymptotically distributed as chi-squared. *Econometrica*, 48, 1107–38.

Sargan, J. D. and Satchell, S. E. (1986) A theorem of validity for Edgeworth expansions. *Econometrica*, 54, 189–213.

Silvey, S. D. (1959) The Lagrangian multiplier test. *Annals of Mathematical Statistics*, 30, 389–407.

Skovgaard, Ib. M. (1981) Transformation of an Edgeworth expansion by a sequence of smooth functions. *Scandinavian Journal of Statistics*, 8, 207–17.

Skovgaard, Ib. M. (1986) On multivariate Edgeworth expansions. *International Statistical Review*, 54, 169–86.

Wald, A. (1943) Tests of statistical hypotheses concerning several parameters when the number of observations is large. *Transactions of the American Mathematical Society*, 54, 426–82.

6 Estimation in Semiparametric Models: a Review

Oliver Linton

1 Introduction

Nonparametric and semiparametric methods have been the focus of much interest in the econometric and statistical literatures. The motivation for adopting these methods is that the potential costs of misspecifying parametric models can be high – inefficient or even inconsistent parameter estimates as well as test statistics with low asymptoctic power or even incorrect size. There have already been a number of survey papers that review various aspects of this material. The exhaustive but as yet unfinished monograph of Bickel et al. (1992), hereafter BKRW, develops a comprehensive theory of inference for a large number of semiparametric models, although mostly within i.i.d. sampling. Robinson (1988b) reviews aspects of estimation in semiparametric models for econometricians. Newey (1990a) reviews efficiency-bound calculations in semiparametric models.

We review recent work on estimation in semiparametric models. We believe that a proper evaluation of the higher order properties of semiparametric estimators is necessary if reliable inference is to be carried out in semiparametric situations. We therefore emphasize some recent work on the higher order properties of semiparametric procedures.

Our notions of first order and higher order efficiency owe a great deal to the early work of C. R. Rao. The Cramér–Rao (Cramér, 1946; Rao, 1945) lower bound is an important benchmark against which to measure the performance of alternative estimators in fully parametric situations. The efficiency bounds of Begun et al. (1983), henceforth

BHHW, BKRW, Chamberlain (1986, 1987), and Newey (1990a) extend this theory to semiparametric models.

Rao (1962, 1963) also contributed extensively to the development of the higher order theory of parametric estimators. We believe that this theory can and should be extended to semiparametric situations and would provide a more realistic appraisal of the properties of these procedures.

In section 2 we give some general definitions and review a number of models that have been treated semiparametrically. In section 3 we review the construction of semiparametric estimators, while in section 4 we examine their asymptotic properties. Section 5 concludes.

2 Semiparametric Models

General framework

Classical statistical theory is set in the context of i.i.d. sampling schemes, in which the data is described by a probability measure P_{θ_0}, where $\{P_\theta;\ \theta \in \Theta \subseteq \Re^P\}$ is a parametric family. We consider the more general semiparametric situation where the data are described by a sequence of probability measures P_{n,θ_0,G_0}, where for each n: $\{P_{n,\theta,G};\ \theta \in \Theta \subseteq \Re^P,\ G(.) \in \Gamma\}$ is a semiparametric family of probability measures, i.e. Γ is a function space such as L_2. In the remainder of this section we introduce some background definitions adopting the notation appropriate for i.i.d. models.

Consider the enlarged parametric model P_ϕ, where $\phi = (\theta, \eta)$ in which $G(*;\ \eta)$ is a parameterization of G. Let $l(*;\ \phi)$ be the log-likelihood function, $S_\phi(*;\ \phi) \equiv \partial l/\partial\phi$ be the score function, and $I_{\phi\phi}(\phi)$ the information in P_ϕ, where

$$I_{\phi\phi}(\phi) \equiv E\left[\frac{\partial l}{\partial \phi}\frac{\partial l}{\partial \phi^T}\right] = \begin{pmatrix} I_{\theta\theta} & I_{\theta\eta} \\ I_{\eta\theta} & I_{\eta\eta} \end{pmatrix}. \tag{2.1}$$

In the presence of unknown η, the Cramer–Rao lower bound for estimating θ is (the inverse efficient information):

$$I^*_{\theta\theta}(\phi)^{-1} = [I_{\theta\theta}(\phi) - I_{\theta\eta}(\phi)I^{-1}_{\eta\eta}(\phi)I_{\eta\theta}(\phi)]^{-1}, \tag{2.2}$$

which is larger (to the extent that $I_{\theta\eta}$ departs from zero) than when η is known in which case the lower bound is $I^{-1}_{\theta\theta}$. It is convenient to define the efficient score function

$$S^*_\theta(*;\ \phi) = S_\theta(*;\ \phi) - I_{\theta\eta}I^{-1}_{\eta\eta}S_\eta(*,\ \phi), \tag{2.3}$$

which can be interpreted as the projection of $S_\theta(*; \phi)$ onto $S_\eta(*, \phi)$.

The theory developed in BKRW closely parallels the classical results. In particular, they define the efficient information in the semiparametric model as

$$I^*_{\theta\theta}(\theta; G) = \inf[I_{\theta\theta} - I_{\theta\eta}I^{-1}_{\eta\eta}I_{\eta\theta}], \tag{2.4}$$

where the infimum is taken over all finite dimensional parameterizations $G(*; \eta)$ that pass through the given G, while the efficient score function $S^*_\theta(*; \theta, G)$ is the $L_2(P)$ projection of $S_\theta(*; \theta, G)$ onto the closed linear subspace of $L_2(P)$ generated by all score functions $S_\eta(*; \phi)$ derived from feasible parameterizations η. BKRW show how to calculate $S^*_\theta(*; \theta, G)$ and $I^*_{\theta\theta}(\theta; G)$ for a large number of semiparametric models, although mostly in iid settings. Chamberlain (1986, 1987) and Newey (1990a) calculate these quantities in a number of econometric models, some under heterogeneous sampling, while Hansen and Singleton (1991) deal with these issues under dependent sampling. In many cases, these projections take the form of conditional expectations.

BKRW establish a generalization of the Cramer–Rao theorem for semiparametric models. They show that $I^*_{\theta\theta}(\theta, G)^{-1}$ is a lower bound for the variance of any regular estimator of θ constructed in $P_{n,\theta,G}$. There is always more information in the parametric model, although in a number of important cases $I^*_{\theta\theta}(\theta, G) = I_{\theta\theta}(\theta, G)$ and $S^*_\theta(*; \theta, G) = S_\theta(*; \theta, G)$: this is referred to as an *adaptive* situation. In this case, one can in principle estimate θ as well when G is known as when it has to be estimated.

We examine a number of semiparametric models that fit this general framework. We concentrate on situations where $I^*_{\theta\theta}(\theta, G) > 0$, which excludes a number of important examples under study by econometricians, notably, some limited dependent variable models in which only conditional moment or quantile restrictions are maintained, but the data distribution is otherwise unrestricted. Newey (1990a) discusses a number of such situations and relates the different conditions. See also Kim and Pollard (1990).

We order our presentation by the type of unknown nuisance function G: densities, spectral densities, hazard rates, and regression functions.

Density function

In a number of situations one would like to treat the density function of an unobservable error process nonparametrically, while retaining a parametric structure for other features of the model.

The symmetric location model first treated in Stein (1956) and subsequently by Stone (1975) is the classical problem. There has been much recent interest in this specification following Bickel (1982), who gives a comprehensive analysis of the theoretical problems involved and treats a number of more complicated examples, such as the linear regression with general error distribution. A number of further generalizations have appeared: Manski (1984) allows the mean to be nonlinear, Kreiss (1987) considers the ARMA(p, q) model with symmetric errors, and Kreiss (1988) considers AR processes with general error density. Bickel and Ritov (1987) consider the errors in variables model.

Censored regression

Many economic datasets include dependent variables that have been censored in some fashion. The classic example is due to Tobin (1958), who considers data on consumer durable purchase in which many individuals spent zero dollars on these commodities. The following model could describe his dataset:

$$y_i^* = \beta^T x_i + \varepsilon_i; \quad y_i = y_i^* 1 \quad (y_i^* > 0), \quad i = 1, 2, \ldots, n, \qquad (2.5)$$

where only $\{(y_i, x_i)\}_{i=1}^n$ is observed, while ε is i.i.d., symmetric about zero with density $f(.)$ of unknown functional form. Furthermore, ε is independent of x.

Maximum likelihood estimation of β based on the normal distribution is discussed in Amemiya (1985): unfortunately, if the error distribution is not normal, this estimator is inconsistent. Powell (1984) showed that least absolute deviation estimators of β are consistent whatever distribution ε (provided only the median of ε conditional on x is zero) has, although this procedure is inefficient in general. Newey and Powell (1987) and Newey (1991) consider efficient estimation in a number of versions of this semiparametric model, allowing more general conditions on the conditional distribution of ε given x. They also investigate the truncated regression model in which both x and y are lost when the censoring event occurs. Ritov (1990) considers the more general setting where the censoring occurs at a random point c_i.

GARCH

Engle's (1982) seminal paper introduced the autoregressive conditional heteroskedastic (ARCH) model and generated interest in a large new class of nonlinear time series models, including the GARCH model of Bollerslev (1986). This class of models has been used extensively to model financial time series (see Bollerslev et al., 1992, for references). The semiparametric model is

$$y_t = \beta^T x_t + \varepsilon_t \sigma_t, \quad \sigma_t^2 = \alpha_0 + \sum_{j=1}^{p} \alpha_j \sigma_{t-j}^2 + \sum_{k=1}^{q} \gamma_k \varepsilon_{t-k}^2 \sigma_{t-k}^2,$$
$$t = 1, 2, \ldots, T, \tag{2.6}$$

where ε is independent of x, iid with density $f(.)$ of unknown functional form.

Weiss (1986), Lumsdaine (1991), and Bollerslev and Wooldridge (1992), establish that Gaussian MLEs of the unknown parameters $\theta = (\beta^T, \alpha^T, \gamma^T)^T$ are consistent and asymptotically normal under general conditions. However, they are inefficient in general. Engle and Gonzalez-Rivera (1990) investigate the properties of the above semiparametric model. Linton (1993) constructs a semiparametric estimator of β and ratios of the α parameters that are equivalent to the MLE when f is symmetric about zero.

Hazard function

In recent years, there has been a considerable amount of interest in duration or survival data, especially in the biostatistics literature. In economics, these data arise primarily in connnection with unemployment duration (see, for example, Nickell, 1979).

Proportional hazards I

Following Cox (1972, 1975), the proportional hazard specification has been a dominant paradigm for empirical investigations of this type of data. Suppose that we observe a sample $(t_i; x_i)$, $i = 1, 2, \ldots, n$ of durations t_i and covariates x_i. The "Cox model" is

$$\lambda(t_i; x_i) = \lambda_0(t_i) \exp(\beta^T x_i), \quad i = 1, 2, \ldots, n, \tag{2.7}$$

where the baseline hazard $\lambda_0(.)$ is of unknown functional form, while β is a finite dimensional parameter of interest. As shown in BHHW, this is an adaptive situation with regard to β.

Proportional hazards II

An alternative model allows the effect of the covariates to be of unknown functional form, while restricting the baseline hazard to be parametric, for example the Weibull. This model is

$$\lambda(t_i; x_i) = \lambda_0(t_i; \theta) g(x_i), \quad i = 1, 2, \ldots, n, \tag{2.8}$$

where θ is a finite dimensional parameter of interest, while $g(.)$ is of unknown form. See, for example, Sasieni (1992).

Spectral density

Serial correlation is frequently apparent in the residuals from estimated time series models, although it is often difficult to pin down its precise form. This motivates a semiparametric approach in which one allows the spectral density of the error process to be of arbitrary form. The original treatment of this problem is due to Hannan (1963), who considers a linear regression model with stationary errors whose spectrum is of unknown functional form. Hansen and Singleton (1991) and Robinson (1991a) also consider a number of semiparametric time series models.

Triangular cointegrated system

Many economic time series are believed to be integrated, i.e. stochastically trending, and yet combinations of them appear to be stationary, i.e. are cointegrated. Introduced in Granger (1983) and formalized in Engle and Granger (1987), this property has been investigated in many applications. Recently, Johansen (1991) and Phillips (1991b) have developed a comprehensive theory for inference in these models. Consider the following triangular system:

$$y_{1t} = \beta^T y_{2t} + \varepsilon_t; \quad \Delta y_{2t} = \eta_t, \quad t = 1, 2, \ldots, T, \tag{2.9}$$

where Δ denotes the time series difference operator, and $\{u_t\}_{t=1}^T$, where $u_t = (\varepsilon_t, \eta_t)^T$, is a dependent Gaussian process with spectral density $f_{uu}(.)$ of unknown functional form.

The costs of not accounting for serial correlation are more serious than efficiency loss – the asymptotic distribution of the parameter estimates is otherwise nonstandard with a complicated nuisance parameter dependency (see Phillips, 1991b). Philips (1991a) shows how to extend the Hannan procedure to the nonstationary system.

Regression function

Linear regression models are the basis of much empirical work in econometrics. In many datasets, however, there is evidence of nonlinearity which would lead to incorrect inferences if the usual methods were applied. This motivates a semiparametric approach.

Average derivative

A common problem in demand analysis is to estimate the average response of demand to some conditioning variable. If an inappropriate functional form is chosen, then inference may be misleading. Let (y_i, x_i), $i = 1, 2, \ldots, n$ be a random sample from (y, x), where

$$g(x) = E[y_i | x_i = x], \quad i = 1, 2, \ldots, n \tag{2.10}$$

is of unknown form. Stoker (1986), Härdle and Stoker (1989), and Powell et al. (1989) consider estimation of the average derivative parameter $\alpha(g) = E[g'(x)]$.

The partially linear model

This specification is a useful means of dimensionality reduction. Engle et al. (1986) use this model to estimate the effects of temperature on electricity demand, while Stock (1991) models the effect of the proximity of toxic waste on house prices. In both cases, the effect is highly nonlinear, while the large number of covariates make a fully nonparametric analysis infeasible. The model is

$$y_i = \beta^T x_i + r(z_i) + \varepsilon_i; \quad x_i = g(z_i) + \eta_i, \quad i = 1, 2, \ldots, n \tag{2.11}$$

where $r(.)$ and $g(.)$ are of unknown functional form. The parameters of interest are β and functionals of $r - \alpha(r)$. This specification also arises from various sample selection models (see Ahn and Powell, 1991; Lee et al., 1992).

Heckman (1986), Robinson (1988a), and Chen (1988) have all established the first order asymptotic properties of various estimators of β. This is not an adaptive situation – when the errors are normal:

$$I^*_{\beta\beta} = \text{var}[\varepsilon]\,\text{var}[x|z] \leqslant I_{\beta\beta} = \text{var}[\varepsilon]\text{var}\,[x]. \tag{2.12}$$

Heteroskedastic nonlinear regression

Heteroskedasticity is a common problem in applied econometric studies, both in time series and in cross-sectional datasets. A semiparametric approach allows one to take account of this without imposing unwarranted structure on this second moment phenomenon. Consider the following nonlinear regression model:

$$y_i = \tau(x_i; \beta) + \varepsilon_i \sigma(x_i), \quad i = 1, 2, \ldots, n, \tag{2.13}$$

where $\tau(.; \beta)$ is known, while $\sigma^2(.)$ is of unknown functional form.

Carroll (1982) and Robinson (1987) examine the situation where

$\tau(x; \beta) = \beta^T x$. They establish (under i.i.d. sampling) the first order properties of feasible GLS estimators that use nonparametric estimators of the unknown function as weights. Extensions of this model to the multivariate nonlinear $\tau(.; \beta)$ case are considered in Delgado (1992), while Hidalgo (1992b) allows both heteroskedasticity and serial correlation of unknown form.

Binary choice model

Data on consumer choice among a discrete number of alternatives are widely available. A number of parametric models suitable for this type of data are given in Cox (1970) – see also Amemiya (1985). Consider the following specification:

$$y_i = 1(\beta^T x_i + u_i \geqslant 0),$$

where (x, u) are i.i.d. with distribution G. There are many treatments of this model, following the seminal paper of Manski (1975) in which a slightly more general specification was considered. Chamberlain (1986) shows that if only $Med(u|x) = 0$ is assumed, then $I^*_{\beta\beta} = 0$, i.e. β is not estimable at rate $\sqrt{n}$ (see also Cosslett, 1983; Manski, 1985; Ruud, 1986; Horowitz, 1992). If u is assumed to be independent of x with unknown distribution function $F(.)$, then $I^*_{\beta\beta} > 0$. Efficient estimation in this case is discussed in Klein and Spady (1993). In this situation,

$$\begin{aligned} \Pr[y_i = 1|x_i] &= F(\beta^T x_i), \\ \Pr[y_i = 0|x_i] &= 1 - F(\beta^T x_i), \quad i = 1, 2, \ldots, n, \end{aligned} \tag{2.14}$$

and note that $\Pr[y_i = 1|x_i] = E[y_i|x_i]$, i.e. $F(.)$ is a regression function. See also Ichimura (1988) and Ichimura and Lee (1991).

3 Semiparametric Estimation

We now discuss efficient estimation of θ. Any such procedure involves approximations to the log-likelihood function, the efficient score function, or the efficient influence function $\Psi^*_\theta(*; \theta, G)$, where

$$\Psi^*_\theta(*; \theta, G) \equiv I^*_{\theta\theta}(\theta, G)^{-1} S^*_\theta(*; \theta, G), \tag{3.1}$$

and $E[S^*_\theta(*; \theta, G)] = 0 = E[\Psi^*_\theta(*; \theta, G)]$, while $E[\Psi^*_\theta(*; \theta, G)\Psi^*_\theta(*; \theta, G)^T] = I^*_{\theta\theta}(\theta, G)^{-1}$. In practice these quantities all depend on the unknown function G, which must be estimated.

There are numerous nonparametric methods suitable for estimating

G, such as kernels, nearest neighbors, splines, and orthogonal series. One aspect these methods have in common is the presence of a smoothing parameter h, frequently called the bandwidth, which controls the effective number of nuisance parameters fitted to G. We refer the reader to the monographs of Silverman (1986), Prakasa Rao (1983), Müller (1987), and Härdle (1990) for a more detailed discussion of these and other methods. A number of modifications to the textbook procedures, discussed in the sequel, may be necessary in semiparametric contexts, including: (a) trimming, (b) sample splitting, (c) bias reduction, and (d) under smoothing.

Suppose that $\hat{\theta}(*; G)$, a solution of $S_\theta^*(*; \theta, G) = 0$, can be written down explicitly in terms of the data and G only, and suppose also that G can itself be estimated from the observed data by $\hat{G}$. Substituting $\hat{G}$ for G in $S_\theta^*(*; \theta, G)$ provides a plausible estimator of θ. An example is the partially linear regression model of Robinson (1988a). When the errors are normally distributed, the efficient score function is

$$\begin{aligned} S_\beta^*(*; \beta, G) &\equiv S_\beta(*; \beta) - E[S_\beta(*; \beta)|z] \\ &= \{(y - E[y|z]) - \beta^T(x - E[x|z])\}(x - E[x|z]), \end{aligned}$$

which can be solved for β with observable data replacing random variables so that

$$\bar{\beta} = \left[\sum_{i=1}^n (x_i - E[x_i|z_i])(x_i - E[x_i|z_i])^T\right]^{-1} \left[\sum_{i=1}^n (x_i - E[x_i|z_i])(y_i - E[y_i|z_i])\right].$$

Robinson (1988a) constructed a semiparametric estimator of β by replacing $E[x_i|z_i]$ and $E[y_i|z_i]$ by nonparametric estimates:

$$\hat{E}[y_i|z_i] = \sum_{j=1}^n w_{ij} y_j; \quad \hat{E}[x_i|z_i] = \sum_{j=1}^n w_{ij} x_j, \quad i = 1, 2, \ldots, n, \tag{3.2}$$

where the weights $\{w_{ij}\}_{j=1}^n$ are from the fixed window Nadaraya–Watson[1] kernel scheme, i.e.

$$w_{ij} = \frac{K\left(\frac{z_i - z_j}{h}\right)}{\sum_{j=1}^n K\left(\frac{z_i - z_j}{h}\right)}, \quad j = 1, 2, \ldots, n, \tag{3.3}$$

where K is a density function with zero first and bounded second moments. Robinson (1988a) modified the kernel estimators *by trimming*, i.e. throwing away observations in the sparse tails of z's distribution. The Hannan regression model and Phillips (1991a, b) triangular cointegrated system are also situations where the finite dimensional parameters can be estimated in this way.

A closed-form expression for solutions of $S^*_\theta(*;\ \theta,\ G) = 0$ is the exception rather than the rule. However, one frequently has preliminary estimates of both θ and G. In this case, one can use a two-step Newton–Raphson procedure based on an estimate of the efficient influence function $\Psi^*_\theta(*;\ \theta,\ G)$. Let $\tilde{\theta}$ be an initial $\sqrt{n}$ consistent estimator of θ and let $\hat{G}$ be an initial estimator of G, possibly constructed from residuals. Then, define the two step estimator

$$\hat{\theta} = \tilde{\theta} - \Psi^*_{n\theta}(*;\ \tilde{\theta},\ \hat{G}), \tag{3.4}$$

where the standardized sample efficient influence function $\Psi^*_{n\theta}(*;\ \theta,\ G)$ is typically a sample average. This procedure is especially useful when G is an error density – see, for example, Bickel (1982), Kreiss (1987), Newey (1991), Hidalgo (1992a), and Linton (1992c). For example, in the symmetric location model of Bickel (1982):

$$\hat{\Psi}^*_{n\theta}(*;\ \tilde{\theta}, \hat{f}, \hat{f}') = \hat{I}^{-1}\frac{1}{n}\sum_{i=1}^{n}\frac{\hat{f}'}{\hat{f}}(\tilde{\varepsilon}_i);\quad \hat{I} = \frac{1}{n}\sum_{i=1}^{n}\left[\frac{\hat{f}'}{\hat{f}}(\tilde{\varepsilon}_i)\right]^2, \tag{3.5}$$

where $\hat{f}$ and $\hat{f}'$ are suitable nonparametric estimates of f and f' *constructed from the residuals* $\tilde{\varepsilon}_i = y_i - \tilde{\theta}$, for example, the kernel estimate

$$\hat{f}(z) = \frac{1}{nh}\sum_{i=1}^{n}K\left(\frac{z - \tilde{\varepsilon}_i}{h}\right).$$

Bickel modified the nonparametric estimates in a number of ways. First, observations where $\hat{f}/\hat{f}(\tilde{\varepsilon}_i)$ was too large were trimmed out. Second, Bickel (1982)[2] found it convenient to employ *sample splitting*, i.e. half of the sample was used to estimate $\hat{f}'/\hat{f}(.)$ and the other half were used to construct $\hat{\Psi}^*_{n\theta}$. Kreiss (1987) dispensed with this modification.

Andrews (1991a, b) examines "MINPIN" estimators $\hat{\theta}$ that minimize a general criterion function $Q_n(*;\ \theta,\ \hat{G})$, where $\hat{G}$ is a preliminary estimator of G. An important special case of Andrews's scheme is where $Q_n(*;\ \theta,\ \hat{G})$ is the quasi log-likelihood function $l_n(*;\ \theta,\ \hat{G})$. The parameters β in example (2.13) can be estimated by this method. In the multivariate version considered by Delgado (1992), the standardized quasi log-likelihood function is, apart from a constant not depending on β,

$$Q_n(*;\beta,\hat{\Sigma}(.)) = \frac{1}{n}\sum_{i=1}^{n}[y_i - \tau(x_i;\beta)]^T\hat{\Sigma}_i^{-1}[y_i - \tau(x_i;\beta)], \quad (3.6)$$

where $\hat{\Sigma}_i = \Sigma_{j=1}^{n} w_{ij}\tilde{u}_j\tilde{u}_j^T$ is a preliminary estimate of the covariance matrix Σ_i with weights $\{w_{ij}\}_{j=1}^{n}$ defined as in (3.3), for example, and $\tilde{u}_j = y_j - \tau(x_i;\tilde{\beta})$ residuals obtained from a preliminary consistent estimate $\tilde{\beta}$. The semiparametric estimator $\hat{\beta}$ minimizes $Q_n(*;\beta,\hat{\Sigma})$ or equivalently solves the vector of first order conditions $Q_{n\beta}(*;\hat{\beta},\hat{\Sigma}) = 0$, where $Q_{n\beta}(*;\beta,\hat{\Sigma})$ is the vector of partial derivatives of $Q_n(*;\beta,\hat{\Sigma})$ with respect to β. These equations can be solved by standard numerical methods as described in Harvey (1981).

A slight extension of the MINPIN method in which the function G is estimated simultaneously with θ is also of some practical importance. In this case, let $\hat{\theta}$ be the minimiser of $Q_n(*;\theta,\hat{G}(*;\theta))$, where $\hat{G}(*;\theta)$ is a profiled "estimate" of G in which $\hat{G}(*;\theta)$ depends on the unknown parameter θ in addition to the data. In other words, $\hat{G}(*;\theta)$ itself is not a feasible estimator of G. Klein and Spady (1993) use this method to estimate β in the binary choice model. In their case, the quasi log-likelihood function (the log-likelihood with $\hat{F}$ replacing F) is

$$Q_n(*;\hat{F}(*;\beta)) = \sum_{i=1}^{n}\{y_i\ln[\hat{F}(\beta^Tx_i)] + (1-y_i)\ln[1-\hat{F}(\beta^Tx_i)]\}, \quad (3.7)$$

involving the profiled estimator:

$$\hat{F}(\beta^Tx_i) = \sum_{j=1}^{n} w_{ij}(\beta)y_j, \quad i = 1, 2, \ldots, n, \quad (3.8)$$

where for each β the weights $\{w_{ij}(\beta)\}_{i,i=1}^{n}$ are as in (3.3) but are constructed from the derived data series $\{\beta^Tx_i\}_{i=1}^{n}$. This "MINPROFIN" estimator is constructed by an iterative scheme.

4 Properties of Semiparametric Estimators

First order properties

The properties of semiparametric estimators have mostly been worked out on a case by case basis. Robinson (1987, 1988a), Härdle and Stoker (1989), and Newey (1988) are excellent examples of this type of asymptotic theory.

There are also, however, a number of recent papers that have attempted to provide a general theory. In particular, Andrews (1989a,

b) and BKRW provide conditions under which various semiparametric estimators $\hat{\theta}$ satisfy

$$\sqrt{n}(\hat{\theta} - \theta_0) \Rightarrow N(0, I^*_{\theta\theta}(\theta_0, G_0)^{-1}). \tag{4.1}$$

BKRW, building on earlier work of Bickel (1982) and Shick (1986), establish the asymptotic properties of two step Newton–Raphson type estimators in general semiparametric models. They impose two local regularity conditions on the parametric submodels. First, they require P_{n,θ_n,G_0} to be contiguous[3] to P_{n,θ_0,G_0} for each fixed sequence $\theta_n = \theta_0 + cn^{-1/2}$ and for each θ_0 and G_0. Second, they require the following asymptotic linearity condition:

$$\sqrt{n}\,[\Psi^*_{n\theta}(*;\, \theta_n,\, G_0) - \Psi^*_{n\theta}(*;\, \theta,\, G_0) + \theta_n - \theta] = o_P(1). \tag{4.2}$$

They also require that the efficient influence function can be estimated suitably well. In particular,

$$B1)\quad \sqrt{n}\Psi^*_{n\theta}(*;\, \theta_n,\, \hat{G}) = o_P(1);$$

$$B2)\quad |\Psi^*_{n\theta}(*;\, \theta_n,\, \hat{G}) - \Psi^*_{n\theta}(*;\, \theta_n,\, G)|^2 = o_P(1). \tag{4.3}$$

The contiguity condition is implied by the following local asymptotic normality (LAN) condition of Le Cam (1960):

$$\Lambda_n(\theta_n,\, \theta_0) - c^T S_{n\theta}(*;\, \theta_0) + \frac{1}{2}c^T I_{\theta\theta}(\theta_0)c \to 0 \text{ in } P_{n,\theta_0} \text{ probability,} \tag{4.4}$$

where $\Lambda_n(\theta_n, \theta_0)$ is the log-likelihood ratio in the parametric model $P_{n,\theta} = P_{n,\theta,G_0}$. The LAN property can be established in many parametric models – even those involving dependent heterogeneous processes – using the primitive conditions of Le Cam (1960), Roussas (1979), or Swensen (1985). To verify the asymptotic linearity condition usually requires some additional "smoothness" (see, for example, Kreiss, 1987, 1988; Hidalgo, 1992a; Linton, 1992c).

Andrews (1989a) gives several sets of sufficient conditions[4] under which MINPIN estimators are $\sqrt{n}$ consistent[5] and asymptotically normal. In one version, Andrews requires that both $Q_{n\theta}(*;\, \theta,\, G)$ and $Q_{n\theta\theta}(*;\, \theta,\, G)$ obey uniform laws of large numbers in some neighborhood $(\theta, G) \in \mathfrak{N}_0 \subseteq \Theta \times \Gamma$ of (θ_0, G_0). He also requires the following *stochastic equicontinuity* assumption:

$$\forall\varepsilon,\ \exists\eta > 0,\ \mathbb{N}_0\colon\ \overline{\lim_{n\to\infty}}\, P^*(\sup_{\mathfrak{N}_0}|\nu_n(\theta, G) - \nu_n(\theta_0, G_0)| > \eta) < \varepsilon \tag{4.5}$$

of the process

$$\nu_n(\theta, G) = \sqrt{n}\{Q_{n\theta}(*; \theta, G) - E[Q_{n\theta}(*; \theta, G)]\}, \tag{4.6}$$

where P^* denotes outer probability measure in the event that the relevant process is not measurable. Andrews gives primitive conditions on the data and on the criterion function that imply these properties.

Finally, Andrews assumes that $\sqrt{n}Q_{n\theta}(*; \hat{\theta}, \hat{G}) \xrightarrow{P} 0$, which is essentially the same requirement as assumption B1 of BKRW. This property depends on the criterion function, but also on how well $\hat{G}$ approximates G. Consider the special case

$$\sqrt{n}Q_{n\theta}(*; \theta_0, \hat{G}) = \frac{1}{\sqrt{n}}\sum_{i=1}^{n} q(X_i; \theta_0, \hat{G}(X_i)). \tag{4.7}$$

Expanding about G_0 one obtains

$$\frac{1}{\sqrt{n}}\sum_{i=1}^{n} q_{0i} + \frac{1}{\sqrt{n}}\sum_{i=1}^{n} q_{0Gi}[\hat{G}(X_i) - G_0(X_i)] + \frac{1}{\sqrt{n}}\sum_{i=1}^{n} q_{0GGi}[\hat{G}(X_i) - G_0(X_i)]^2 + \ldots, \tag{4.8}$$

where $q_{0i} = q(X_i; \theta_0, G_0(X_i))$, while G subscripts denote the corresponding partial derivatives of q with respect to its third argument. The leading term is a standardized single sum, while further terms consist of a deterministic "bias" and random variables of the general form

$$\sum_{i_1=1}^{n}\sum_{i_2=1}^{n} \cdots \sum_{i_m=1}^{n} \varphi_n(X_{i_1}, X_{i_2}, \ldots, X_{i_m}) \tag{4.9}$$

for some mean zero function φ_n dependent on the smoothing parameter $h(n)$. This is a U-statistic of order m. Definitions and properties of such random variables can be found in the monograph of Lee (1990); they occur frequently in asymptotic theory for semiparametric models.

The main problem occurs with the third term in the expansion. In non *adaptive* situations $E[q_{GGi}] \neq 0$; in this case the bias of $\hat{G}$ must be $o(n^{-1/4})$, otherwise B1 clearly is violated. To establish this it may be necessary to employ *bias reduction* techniques such as the higher order kernels of Bartlett (1963) or to *undersmooth* $\hat{G}$, i.e. to use a bandwidth that is narrower than warranted by the properties of $\hat{G}$ itself, especially when the design is high dimensional or if derivatives have to be estimated (see, for example, Robinson, 1988a; Powell et al., 1989). In *adaptive* situations, one usually has $E[q_{GGi}] = 0$. In this case, one can usually avoid imposing a rate condition on $\hat{G}$ (see, for example, Bickel, 1982; Robinson, 1987).

When does this method fail? Clearly, when $I^*_{\theta\theta}(\theta, G) = 0$ one cannot obtain $\sqrt{n}$ consistent estimators of θ. This is the case if θ is actually nonparametric, i.e. if θ is the value of a density function at a single point. This situation also occurs through lack of identification of parameters that may be estimable in a parametric submodel, as discussed in Bickel (1982). However, there are further reasons that can prevent $\sqrt{n}$ consistent estimation even when $I^*_{\theta\theta}(\theta, G) > 0$ everywhere. Specifically, if G is not sufficiently smooth or if its domain is too high dimensional one cannot obtain $\hat{G}$ that converges sufficiently fast. Therefore, in nonadaptive situations, (4.7) will not be $o_P(1)$. In fact, Bickel and Ritov (1987) show that in the partially linear model, there exists no $\sqrt{n}$ consistent estimator of β when $r(.)$ is insufficiently smooth.

Higher order properties

The first order properties of semiparametric estimators are quite promising, especially in adaptive situations. In this case, despite having to estimate the unknown function G, one obtains estimators of θ that have the same asymptotic distribution as the MLE. One may view these results with some scepticism. In particular, having to estimate the function G must impose some small sample cost on the performance of $\hat{\theta}$. Some documentation of poor small sample performance of semiparametric estimators is available in the Monte Carlo evidence presented in Stock (1989) and Stoker (1990), where quite substantial biases were found in certain cases (see also Engle and Gardiner, 1976; Hsieh and Manski, 1987). A perhaps more serious problem is that the first order theory does not reflect the bandwidth h, while in practice one may obtain very different estimators of θ depending on the value of h chosen. A number of monte carlo studies report performance very sensitive to bandwidth, including Hsieh and Manski (1987) and Delgado (1992).

Some recent analytical work has investigated the speed at which semiparametric estimators approach their limiting distributions. Robinson (1991b) establishes a Berry–Esseen type result for fixed G, showing that the rate of convergence to normality of $\sqrt{n}(\hat{\theta} - \theta)$ is $O(n^{-\gamma} \log n)$, where γ depends on various properties of G including its dimensionality and its smoothness class. This compares unfavorably with the standard rate $O(n^{-1/2})$ obtained in parametric models.

Furthermore, Klaassen (1980) shows, in the context of the symmetric location model, that the convergence is not uniform over all $G \in \Gamma$ – there are densities for which the rate of convergence is arbitrarily slow.

These techniques only supply rather limited qualitative information. An alternative approach that has proved useful in other contexts is to develop higher order asymptotic expansions. These have been employed extensively in parametric situations: see Rothenberg (1984) for an exposition of these methods and useful references.

If $\hat{\theta}$ is explicitly defined, an $o_p(n^{-1})$ stochastic expansion for the standardized estimator $T = \sqrt{n}(\hat{\theta} - \theta)$ can be obtained by straightforward Taylor expansion, while if $\hat{\theta}$ is implicitly defined as the minimiser of a smooth criterion function Q_n, one can proceed to the same result by expanding out Q_n as in (4.8) and then inverting, as in Bhattacharya and Ghosh (1978). Collecting terms, one obtains

$$T = A_0 + \sum_{r=1}^{d} \frac{A_r(h)}{n^{a_r}} + R_n(h) \equiv T^*(h) + R_n(h), \tag{4.10}$$

where the random variables A_r, $r = 0, 1, \ldots, d$ are $O_P(1)$, while $0 < a_1 < \ldots < a_d < 1$. The magnitude of a_r and the number of terms in the expansion clearly depends on $h(n)$ and on the required degree of approximation as measured by the stochastic order of magnitude of $R_n(h)$.

The cumulants of T^* can be readily calculated from (4.10). These depend on h and on various other aspects of the estimation problem including the dimensionality of the domain of G and the smoothness of G. In particular,

$$\begin{aligned} E[T^*] &= \frac{\kappa_1(\theta_0, \zeta)}{n^{\mu_1}} + o(n^{-\mu_1}); \\ \operatorname{var}[T^*] &= I^*_{\theta\theta}(\theta, G)^{-1} + \frac{\kappa_2(\theta_0, \zeta)}{n^{\mu_2}} + o(n^{-\mu_2}), \end{aligned} \tag{4.11}$$

where the constants μ_j depend on the order of magnitude of the bandwidth, while $\zeta(G)$ depends on G in a simple fashion, usually through the derivatives of G. The quantities μ_j and κ_j measure the efficiency loss resulting from not knowing G. The second order correction is, in general, of larger order of magnitude than n^{-1}, since $\mu_j < 1/2$. The information contained in (4.11) can be used to define higher order optimality with respect to quadratic loss for example. In the sequel, second order optimality is to be measured relative to this criterion.

Härdle et al. (1992b), hereafter HHMT, examine the second order properties of an average derivative estimator. They show that when a bandwidth $h(n) = O(n^{-2/7})$ is used such that $hn^{2/7} \to \gamma$, then $\mu_2 = 2\mu_1 = 1/7$, which rate is optimal for $\hat{\theta}$. This entails undersmoothing[6] the function estimates. Furthermore, the asymptotic MSE of $\hat{\alpha}$ is determined by $\kappa_1 = (\gamma^2 a_1/2)\zeta_1$ and $\kappa_2 = (a_2/\gamma^3)\zeta_2$, where a_j are known constants, and

$$\zeta_1 = \int \frac{g(x)}{f(x)}[f'(x)f''(x) - f(x)f''(x)]dx; \quad \zeta_2 = \int \sigma^2(x)dx, \quad (4.12)$$

where $\sigma^2(x) = \text{var}[y|x]$ and f is the marginal density[7] of x. Similar approximations are obtained by Carroll and Härdle (1989), Cavanagh (1989), and Linton (1992b) for the heteroskedastic linear regression model, although in this case the optimal bandwidth is $O(n^{-1/5})$ for scalar design which is the same order of magnitude as is optimal for pointwise estimation of G (see, for example, Härdle, 1990). Similar calculations are carried out in Hall and Marron (1987) and Falk (1983a, b) for various functionals of G.

Bandwidth choice

The main methods of bandwidth choice in nonparametric estimation include cross validation, plug-in, and bootstrap, and useful reviews can be found in Härdle (1990) for nonparametric regression, and Marron (1988). A standard measure of optimality used in nonparametric estimation is the integrated mean squared error (IMSE) of the function estimate. Under this criterion, the above methods can provide optimal bandwidths as discussed in Härdle (1990). There has been an enormous amount of research into improved bandwidth selection methods in nonparametric estimation, in particular by Chiu (1991), Hall et al. (1991), Jones et al. (1991), and Hall and Johnstone (1992).

There has also been some recent work extending these methods to semiparametric situations. Ideally, an automatic bandwidth selection method for $\hat{\theta}(h)$ should result in bandwidths that deliver estimators with optimal second order properties not merely first order optimality.

Härdle et al. (1992a) examine the cross validation method in the single index model of Ichimura (1988), where $\{y_i, x_i\}_{i=1}^n$ is a random sample from $(y, x^T)^T$ with $g(x|\beta) = E[y_i|\beta^T x_i = x]$. They show that

$$CV(\beta, h) = \sum_{i=1}^{n}[y_i - \hat{g}_i(\beta^T x_i|\beta)]^2 = S(\beta) + CV_g(h) + R_n(\beta; h), \quad (4.13)$$

where $\hat{g}_i(\beta^T x_i|\beta)$ is a "leave-one-out"[8] estimate of $g(x|\beta)$, and

$$S(\beta) = \sum_{i=1}^{n} [y_i - g(\beta^T x_i|\beta)]^2; \quad CV_g(h) = \sum_{i=1}^{n} [g(\beta_0^T x_i) - \hat{g}_i(\beta_0^T x_i|\beta_0)]^2, \tag{4.14}$$

where $CV_g(h)$ is precisely the least squares cross-validating criterion used in nonparametric regression (see Härdle, 1990), while the remainder $R_n(\beta; h)$ consists of terms that are of smaller order or do not depend on β. Therefore, if $\hat{\beta}$ and $\hat{h}$ minimize $CV(\beta, h)$, then $\hat{\beta}$ is asymptotically normal with the same distribution that would obtain were h deterministic, while $\hat{h}$ is asymptotically optimal with respect to an asymptotic IMSE criterion of the function estimate $\hat{g}$.

A natural generalization of the least squares criterion suitable for general semiparametric models is the quasi log-likelihood criterion suggested in Robinson (1991a). For example, in the heteroskedastic linear regression model one chooses β and h simultaneously to minimize

$$CV_{LIK}(\beta; h) = \sum_{i=1}^{n} \hat{\sigma}^{i-2}(h)[y_i - \beta^T x_i]^2 + \sum_{i=1}^{n} \log \hat{\sigma}_i^2(h), \tag{4.15}$$

where $\hat{\sigma}_i^2(h)$ is the "leave one out" estimator of $\sigma^2(x_i)$. Park (1992) establishes a similar result to Härdle et al. (1992a) when using this method of bandwidth choice in the symmetric location model of Bickel (1982).

These procedures are automatic and simple to implement, although it is uncertain what optimality properties, if any, this method of bandwidth choice has in general. In particular, if the properties of $\hat{\beta}(h)$ are considered, it seems implausible that this method will provide optimal bandwidths. In general, the quasi-likelihood criterion $CV_{LIK}(\theta; h)$ reflects the properties of some functional of $\hat{G}$ itself, rather than the properties of $\hat{\theta}$. Therefore, if it is optimal to undersmooth $\hat{G}$, as in the partially linear model, then clearly the objectives of estimating G and estimating θ are incompatible. In this case, the quasi-likelihood cross-validated bandwidths will tend to be too large.

The plug-in method appears more promising if one wants to optimize the properties of $\hat{\theta}$. In this method, one first obtains a formula for the optimal bandwidth h_{opt} from the second order moment approximations. This depends on G only through the functionals ζ. Let $\hat{\zeta}$ be an estimate of ζ. A feasible second stage estimator of θ is then constructed using the estimated optimal bandwidth $\hat{h}_{opt} = h_{opt}(\hat{\zeta})$. HHMT employ this method for the average derivative estimator, while Andrews (1991b) uses it to determine bandwidth in the estimation of robust covariance matrices (see also Hall and Horowitz, 1990). This procedure should provide estimators $\hat{\theta}(\hat{h})$ that are second order efficient, provided $\hat{\zeta} \to \zeta$ suitably fast (see Linton, 1991b). The results of Andrews (1991a) – in which the asymptotic properties of series-based estimators of various linear and nonlinear functionals of G are established – should be useful in establishing the properties of $\hat{\zeta}$.

5 Conclusion

Semiparametric models can be specified and estimated in a variety of situations of interest to econometricians. The resulting procedures have desirable first order asymptotic properties in a wide range of sampling schemes. There have been many successful applications of these methods to economic datasets.

Nevertheless, some residual supicion may remain about the merits of the semiparametric approach. This may be because the procedures are quite complex to understand and to implement. It may also be because practitioners are suspicious of the "now you see it now you don't" nature of the first order asymptotic theory. In particular, it is frequently claimed that these methods couldn't possibly work unless one has very large sample sizes.

This is somewhat misleading. Any semiparametric procedure essentially involves fitting a parametric model to the given dataset. The parametric model is embedded in a sequence of such models, where the number of "pseudo-parameters" increases with sample size. For a given sample size and dataset, one can choose a large or small number of parameters to describe G. In this sense, semiparametric methods themselves are indistinguishable from parametric methods. Unless the way the data were generated depends on which procedure is chosen, it is hard to see how semiparametric methods *per se* can be more or less reliable than "parametric" ones.

The main problem with semiparametric estimators is the quality of information provided by the first order asymptotic theory. This approximation does not reflect the small sample cost of choosing a particular number of "pseudo-parameters," nor does it give any information about how to choose an appropriate number of "pseudo-parameters" for a given dataset. The same concerns are equally relevant in semiparametric testing problems (see Robinson, 1989; Andrews, 1989b; Delgado and Stengos, 1990).

Second order theory – as developed in HHMT, Carroll and Härdle (1989), Cavanagh (1989), Linton (1991a, 1992b), and Härdle et al. (1992a) – at least addresses these issues, and, it is hoped, will facilitate better inference in semiparametric models.

Notes

1 Alternative weighting schemes can be found in Priestley and Chao (1972), Gasser and Muller (1979), Cleveland (1979), and Fan (1992).

2 In addition, Bickel (1982) symmetrized the density estimates, i.e. $\tilde{f}(z) = \frac{1}{2}[(\tilde{f}(z) + \tilde{f}(-z)]$ was used in place of $\tilde{f}(z)$.

3 P_{n,θ_n,G_0} and P_{n,θ_0,G_0} are contiguous if for each event A, $P_{n,\theta_n,G_0}(A) \to 0 \Leftrightarrow P_{n,\theta_0,G_0}(A) \to 0$. If it is necessary to use residuals derived from an initial $\sqrt{n}$ consistent estimator when constructing G, then contiguity allows one to proceed in many respects as if one had used the true errors.

4 He considers a quite general dependent heterogeneous sampling scheme, and allows nonsmooth criterion functions in some cases. We shall only discuss applications to smooth criterion functions.

5 The conditions needed to establish consistency of the estimator are similar to those needed in fully parametric problems (see, for example, Amemiya, 1985). It is clearly fundamental that $\hat{G} \to G_0$, where G_0 is the true function, and $\psi_\theta^*(*; \theta, \hat{G}) = o_P(1)$.

6 That is, to use a bandwidth $h(n)$ which is narrower than would be optimal for estimating G.

7 They assume that (y, x) are i.i.d., and calculate the moments unconditionally.

8 That is, to use weights as in (3.3), except that $w_{ii} = 0$.

References

Ahn, H. and Powell, J. L. (1991) Estimation of censored selection models with a nonparametric selection mechanism. Unpublished manuscript, University of Wisconsin.

Amemiya, T. (1985) *Advanced Econometrics*. Cambridge, MA: Harvard University Press.

Andrews, D. W. K. (1989a) Semiparametric econometric models: I, estimation. Cowles Foundation discussion paper no. 908.

Andrews, D. W. K. (1989b) Semiparametric econometric models: II, testing. Manuscript, Cowles Foundation.

Andrews, D. W. K. (1991a) Asymptotic normality of series estimators for nonparametric and semiparametric regression models. *Econometrica*, 59, 307–46.

Andrews, D. W. K. (1991b) Heteroskedasticity and autocorrelation consistent covariance matrix estimation. *Econometrica*, 59, 817–58.

Bartlett, M. S. (1963) Statistical estimation of density functions. *Sankhya A*, 25, 145–54.

Begun, J. M., Hall, W. J., Huang, W. and Wellner, J. A. (1983) Information and asymptotic efficiency in parametric-nonparametric models. *Annals of Statistics*, 11, 432–52.

Bhattacharya, R. N. and Ghosh, J. K. (1978) On the validity of the formal Edgeworth expansion. *Annals of Statistics*, 6, 434–51.

Bickel, P. J. (1982) On adaptive estimation. *Annals of Statistics*, 10, 647–71.

Bickel, P. J. and Ritov, Y. (1987) Efficient estimation in the errors in variables model. *Annals of Statistics*, 15, 513–40.

Bickel, P. J. and Ritov, Y. (1990) Achieving information bounds in non and semiparametric models. *Annals of Statistics*, 18, 925–38.

Bickel, P. J., Klaassen, C. A. J., Ritov, Y. and Wellner, J. A. (1992) *Efficient and Adaptive Inference in Semiparametric Models*. Baltimore: Johns Hopkins University Press.

Bierens, H. J. (1987) Kernel estimators of regression fuctions. In T. F. Bewley (ed.), *Advances in Econometrics: Fifth World Congress, volume 1*. Cambridge: Cambridge University Press.

Bollerslev, T. (1986) Generalized autoregressive conditional heteroskedasticity. *Journal of Econometrics*, 31, 307–27.

Bollerslev, T., Chou, R. Y. and Kroner, K. F. (1992) ARCH modelling in finance. *Journal of Econometrics* 52, 5–59.

Bollerslev, T. and Wooldridge, J. M. (1992) Quasi-maximum likelihood estimation of dynamic models with time varying covariates. *Econometric Reviews*, 11, 143–72.

Brillinger, D. R. (1980) *Time Series, Data Analysis and Theory*. San Francisco: Holden-Day.

Carroll, R. J. (1982) Adapting for heteroskedasticity in linear models. *Annals of Statistics*, 10, 1224–33.

Carroll, R. J. and Härdle, W. (1989) Second order effects in semiparametric weighted least squares regression. *Statistics*, 20, 179–186.

Cavanagh, C. J. (1989) The cost of adapting for heteroskedasticity in linear regression models. Preprint, Harvard University.

Chamberlain, G. (1986) Asymptotic efficiency in semiparametric models with censoring. *Journal of Econometrics*, 32, 189–218.

Chamberlain, G. (1987) Asymptotic efficiency in estimation with moment restrictions. *Journal of Econometrics*, 34, 305–34.

Chen, H. (1988) Convergence rates for parametric components in a partly linear model. *Annals of Statistics*, 16, 136–46.

Chiu, S. T. (1991) Bandwidth selection for kernel density estimation. *Annals of Statistics*, 19, 1883–905.

Cleveland, W. S. (1979) Robust locally weighted regression and smoothing scatterplots. *Journal of the American Statistical Association*, 74, 829–36.

Cosslett, S. J. (1983) Distribution free maximum likelihood estimation of the binary choice model. *Econometrica*, 51, 765–82.

Cosslett, S. J. (1991) Semiparametric estimation of a regression model with sample selectivity. In Barnett, Powell and Tauchen (eds), *Nonparametric and Semiparametric Methods in Econometrics and Statistics*. Cambridge: Cambridge University Press.

Cox, D. R. (1970) *Analysis of Binary Data*. London: Chapman and Hall.

Cox, D. R. (1972) Regression models and life-tables, with discussions. *Journal of the Royal Statistical Society B*, 34, 187–220.

Cox, D. R. (1975) Partial likelihood. *Biometrika*, 62, 269–76.

Cramer, H. (1946) *Mathematical Methods of Statistics*. Princeton, NJ: Princeton University Press.

Das, S. (1990) A semiparametric structural analysis of the idling of cement kilns. *Journal of Econometrics*, 50, 235–56.

Delgado, M. (1992) Semiparametric generalised least squares in the multivariate nonlinear regression model. *Econometric Theory*, 8, 203–22.

Delgado, M. and Stengos, T. (1990) Semiparametric specification testing. Working paper no. 778, Queens University.

Engle, R. F. (1982) Autoregressive conditional heteroskedasticity with estimates of the variance of UK inflation. *Econometrica*, 50, 987–1008.

Engle, R. F. and Gardiner, R. (1976) Some finite sample properties of spectral estimators of a linear regression. *Econometrica*, 44, 149–65.

Engle, R. F. and Gonzalez-Rivera, G. (1990) Semiparametric ARCH models. *Journal of Business and Economic Statistics*, 9, 345–60.

Engle, R. F. and Granger, C. W. J. (1987) Co-integration and error correction: representation, estimation and testing. *Econometrica*, 55, 251–76.

Engle, R. F., Granger, C. W. J., Rice, J. and Weiss, A. (1986) Semiparametric estimates of the relationship between weather and electricity sales. *Journal of the American Statistical Association*, 81, 310–20.

Falk, M. (1983a) Relative efficiency and deficiency of kernel type estimators of smooth distribution fuctions. *Statistica Neerlandica*, 37, 73–83.

Falk, M. (1983b) Relative deficiency of kernel type estimators of quantiles. *Annals of Statistics*, 12, 261–8.

Fan, J. (1992) Design-adaptive nonparametric regression. *Journal of the American Statistical Association*, 87, 998–1004.

Gallant, A. R., Hsieh, D. A. and Tauchen, G. E. (1991) On fitting a recalcitrant series: the pound/dollar exchange rate, 1974–1983. In Barnett, Powell and Tauchen (eds), *Nonparametric and Semiparametric Methods in Econometrics and Statistics*. Cambridge: Cambridge University Press.

Gasser, T. and Müller, H. G. (1979) Kernel estimation of regression functions. In Gasser and Rosenblatt (eds), *Smoothing Techniques for Curve Estimation*. New York: Springer-Verlag.

Granger, C. W. J. (1983) Co-integrated variables and error-correcting models. UCSD discussion paper 83-13a.

Hall, P. and Horowitz, J. L. (1990) Bandwidth selection in semiparametric estimation of censored linear regression models. *Econometric Theory*, 6, 123–50.

Hall, P. and Johnstone, I. (1992) Empirical functionals and efficient smoothing parameter selection. *Journal of the Royal Statistical Society Series B*, 54, 475–530.

Hall, P. and Marron, J. S. (1987) Estimation of integrated squared density derivatives. *Statistics and Probability Letters*, 6, 109–15.

Hall, P., Sheather, S. J., Jones, M. C. and Marron, J. S. (1991) On optimal data-based bandwidth selection in kernel density estimation. *Biometrika*, 78, 263–9.

Hannan, E. J. (1963) Regression for time series. In M. Rosenblatt (ed.), *Time Series Analysis*. New York: John Wiley.

Hansen, L. P. and Singleton, K. J. (1991) Computing semiparametric efficiency bounds for linear time series models. In Barnett, Powell and Tauchen (eds), *Nonparametric and Semiparametric Methods in Econometrics and Statistics*. Cambridge: Cambridge University Press.

Härdle, W. (1990) *Applied Nonparametric Regression*. Cambridge: Cambridge University Press.

Härdle, W., Hall, P. and Ichimura, H. (1992a) Opimal smoothing in single index models. CORE discussion paper no. 9107.

Härdle, W., Hall, P. and Marron, J. S. (1988) How far are automatically chosen regression smoothing parameters from their optimum. *Journal of the American Statistical Association*, 83, 86–101.

Härdle, W., Hart, J., Marron, J. S., and Tsybakov, A. B. (1992b) Bandwidth choice for average derivative estimation. *Journal of the American Statistical Association*, 87, 218–26.

Härdle, W. and Marron, J. S. (1988) Optimal bandwidth selection in non-parametric regression function estimation. *Annals of Statistics*, 16, 1465–81.

Härdle, W. and Stoker, T. M. (1989) Investigating smooth multiple regression by the method of average derivatives. *Journal of the American Statistical Association*, 84, 986–95.

Harvey, A. C. (1981) *The Econometric Analysis of Time Series*. Oxford: Philip Allan.

Heckman, N. E. (1986) Spline smoothing in a partly linear model. *Journal of the Royal Statistical Society Series B*, 48, 244–8.

Hidalgo, J. (1992a) Adaptive estimation in the presence of autocorrelation of unknown form. *Journal of Time Series Analysis*, 13, 47–78.

Hidalgo, J. (1992b) Adaptive estimation in time series models with hetero-skedasticity of unknown form. *Econometric Theory*, 8, 161–87.

Horowitz, J. L. (1992) A smoothed maximum score estimator for the binary response model. *Econometrica*, 60, 505–32.

Horowitz, J. L. and Neumann, G. R. (1987) Semiparametric estimation of employment duration models. *Econometric Reviews*, 6, 5–40.

Hsieh, D. A. and Manski, C. F. (1987) Monte Carlo evidence on adaptive maximum likelihood estimation of a regression. *Annals of Statistics*, 15, 541–51.

Ichimura, H. (1988) Semiparametric least squares estimation of single index models. Preprint, Department of Economics, University of Minnesota, Minneapolis.

Ichimura, H. and Lee, L. F. (1991) Semiparametric least squares estimation of multiple index models: single equation estimation. In Barnett, Powell and Tauchen (eds), *Nonparametric and Semiparametric Methods in Econometrics and Statistics*. Cambridge: Cambridge University Press.

Johansen, S. (1991) Estimation and hypothesis testing of cointegrating vectors in Gaussian vector autoregressive models. *Econometrica*, 59, 1551–80.

Jones, M. C., Marron, J. S. and Park, B. U. (1991) A simple root n bandwidth selector. *Annals of Statistics*, 19, 1919–32.

Kim, J. and Pollard, D. (1990) Cube root asymptotics. *Annals of Statistics*, 18, 191–219.

Klaassen, C. A. J. (1980) Statistical performance of location estimators. PhD thesis, University of Amsterdam.

Klein, R. W. and Spady, R. H. (1993) An efficient semiparametric estimator for binary choice models. *Econometrica*, 61, 387–421.

Kreiss, J. P. (1987) On adaptive estimation in stationary ARMA processes. *Annals of Statistics*, 15, 112–33.

Kreiss, J. P. (1988) On adaptive estimation in autoregressive models when there are nuisance functions. *Statistics and Decisions*, 5, 59–76.

Le Cam, L. (1960) Locally asymptotically normal families of distributions. *University of California Publications in Statistics*, 3, 267–84.

Lee, A. J. (1990) *U-statistics: Theory and Practice*. New York; Marcel Dekker.

Lee, L. F. (1992) Semiparametric minimum distance estimation. CREST working paper no. 92-08.

Lee, L. F., Rosenzweig, M. R. and Pitt, M. M. (1992) The effects of improved nutrition, sanitation and water purity on child health in high-mortality populations. Unpublished manuscript.

Linton, O. B. (1991a) Edgeworth approximation in semiparametric regression models. PhD thesis, Department of Economics, University of California at Berkeley.

Linton, O. B. (1991b) Second order approximation in the partially linear model. Forthcoming in *Econometrica*.

Linton, O. B. (1992a) Edgeworth approximation for generalised minimum contrast estimators in semiparametric regression models. Forthcoming in *Econometric Theory*.

Linton, O. B. (1992b) Small sample properties of adaptive GLS estimators. Forthcoming in *Econometric Reviews*.

Linton, O. B. (1993) Adaptive estimation in ARCH models. *Econometric Theory*, 9, 539–69.

Lumsdaine, R. L. (1991) Asymptotic properties of the quasi-maximum likelihood estimator in GARCH (1, 1) and IGARCH (1, 1) models. Manuscript, Harvard University.

Manski, C. F. (1975) Maximum score estimation of the stochastic utility model of choice. *Journal of Econometrics*, 3, 205–28.

Manski, C. F. (1984) Adaptive estimation of nonlinear regression models. *Econometric Review*, 3, 145–94.

Manski, C. F. (1985) Semiparametric analysis of discrete response: asymptotic properties of the maximum score estimator. *Journal of Econometrics*, 27, 313–33.

Marron, J. S. (1985) An asymptotically efficient solution to the bandwidth problem of kernel density estimation. *Annals of Statistics*, 13, 1011–23.

Marron, J. S. (1988) Automatic smoothing parameter selection: a survey. *Empirical Economics*, 13, 187–208.

Marron, J. S. and Wand, M. P. (1992) Exact mean integrated squared error. *Annals of Statistics*, 20, 712–36.

Müller, H. G. (1987) *Nonparametric Regression Analysis of Longitudinal Data*. Heidelberg/New York: Springer-Verlag.

Newey, W. K. (1988) Adaptive estimation of regression models via moment restrictions. *Journal of Econometrics*, 38, 301–39.

Newey, W. K. (1990a) Semiparametric efficiency bounds. *Journal of Applied Econometrics*, 5, 99–135.

Newey, W. K. (1990b) Efficient instrumental variables estimation of nonlinear models. *Econometrica*, 58, 809–37.

Newey, W. K. (1991) Efficient estimation of tobit models under conditional symmetry. In Barnett, Powell and Tauchen (eds), *Nonparametric and Semiparametric Methods in Econometrics and Statistics*. Cambridge: Cambridge University Press.

Newey, W. K. and Powell, J. L. (1987) Efficient estimation of linear and censored regression models under conditional quantile restrictions. Econometric research program, Princeton University, no. 331.

Newey, W. K., Powell, J. L. and Walker, J. R. (1990) Semiparametric estimation of selection models: some empirical results. *American Economic Review Papers and Proceedings*, 80, 324–8.

Nickell, S. (1979) Estimating the probability of leaving unemployment. *Econometrica*, 47, 1249–66.

Nielsen, J. P. (1990) Kernel estimation of densities and hazards: a counting process approach. PhD thesis, University of California at Berkeley.

Pagan, A. R. and Hong, Y. S. (1991) Nonparametric estimation and the risk premium. In Barnett, Powell and Tauchen (eds), *Nonparametric and Semiparametric Methods in Econometrics and Statistics*. Cambridge: Cambridge University Press.

Park, B. U. (1992) A cross-validatory choice of smoothing parameter in adaptive location estimation CORE discussion paper no. 9230.

Pfanzagl, J. (1980) Asymptotic expansions in parametric statistical theory. In P. R. Krishnaiah (ed.), *Developments in Statistics, volume 3*. New York: Academic Press.

Phillips, P. C. B. (1991a) Spectral regression for cointegrated time series. In

Barnett, Powell and Tauchen (eds), *Nonparametric and Semiparametric Methods in Econometrics and Statistics*. Cambridge: Cambridge University Press.

Phillips, P. C. B. (1991b) Optimal inference in cointegrated systems. *Econometrica*, 59, 283–306.

Powell, J. L. (1984) Least absolute deviations estimation for the censored regression model. *Journal of Econometrics*, 25, 303–25.

Powell, J. L., Stock, J. H. and Stoker, T. M. (1989) Semiparametric estimation of index coefficients. *Econometrica*, 57, 1403–30.

Prakasa Rao, B. L. S. (1984) *Nonparametric Functional Estimation*. New York: Academic Press.

Priestley, M. B. and Chao, M. T. (1972) Nonparametric function fitting. *Journal of the Royal Statistical Society Series B*, 34, 385–92.

Ramlau-Hansen, H. (1983) Smoothing counting process intensities by means of kernel functions. *Annals of Statistics*, 11, 453–66.

Rao, C. R. (1945) Information and accuracy attainable in the estimation of statistical parameters. *Bulletin of the Calcutta Mathematical Society*, 37, 81–91.

Rao, C. R. (1962a) Asymptotic efficiency and limiting information. *Proceedings of the Fourth Berkeley Symposium on Mathematical Statistics and Probability*, pp. 531–45.

Rao, C. R. (1962b) Efficient estimates and optimum inference procedures in large samples. *Journal of the Royal Statistical Society Series B*, 46–72.

Rice, J. (1986) Convergence rates for partially splined models. *Statistics and Probability Letters*, 4, 203–8.

Ritov, Y. (1990) Estimation in a linear regression model with censored data. *Annals of Statistics*, 18, 301–28.

Robinson, P. M. (1987) Asymptotically efficient estimation in the presence of heteroscedasticity of unknown form. *Econometrica*, 56, 875–91.

Robinson, P. M. (1988a) Root-*N*-consistent semiparametric regression. *Econometrica*, 56, 931–54.

Robinson, P. M. (1988b) Semiparametric econometrics: a survey. *Journal of Applied Econometrics*, 3, 35–51.

Robinson, P. M. (1989) Hypothesis testing in semiparametric and nonparametric models for economic time series. *Review of Economic Studies*, 56, 511–34.

Robinson, P. M. (1990) Nonparametric estimators for time series. *Journal of Time Series Analysis*, 11, 185–208.

Robinson, P. M. (1991a) Automatic frequency domain inference on semiparametric and nonparametric models. *Econometrica*, 59, 1329–64.

Robinson, P. M. (1991b) Best nonlinear three-stage least squares estimation of certain econometric models. *Econometrica*, 59, 755–86.

Rothenberg, T. (1984) Approximating the distributions of econometric estimators and test statistics. In Z. Griliches and M. Intriligator (eds), *Handbook of Econometrics, volume 2*. Amsterdam: North-Holland.

Roussas, G. G. (1979) Asymptotic distribution of the log-likelihood function for stochastic processes. *Zeitschrift für Wahrscheinlichkeitstheorie und verwandte Gebiete*, 43, 31–46.

Ruud, P. A. (1986) Consistent estimation of limited dependent variable models despite misspecification of distribution. *Journal of Econometrics*, 32, 157–87.

Sasieni, P. (1992) Information bounds for the conditional hazard ratio in a nested family of regression models. *Biometrika*, 54, 617–36.

Shick, A. (1986) On asymptotically efficient estimation in semiparametric models. *Annals of Statistics*, 14, 1139–51.

Speckman, P. (1988) Kernel smoothing in partial linear models. *Journal of the Royal Statistical Society Series B*, 50, 413–36.

Silverman, B. W. (1986) *Density Estimation for Statistics and Data Analysis*. London: Chapman and Hall.

Stein, C. (1956) Efficient nonparametric testing and estimation. *Proceedings of the Third Berkeley Symposium on Mathematical Statistics and Probability, Volume 1*. University of California at Berkeley.

Stock, J. H (1989) Nonparametric policy analysis. *Journal of the American Statistical Association*, 84, 567–76.

Stock, J. H. (1991) Nonparametric policy analysis: an application to estimating hazardous waste cleanup benefits. In Bernett, Powell and Tauchen (eds), *Nonparametric and Semiparametric Methods in Econometrics and Statistics*. Cambridge: Cambridge University Press.

Stoker, T. M. (1986) Consistent estimation of scaled coefficients. *Econometrica*, 54, 1461–81.

Stoker, T. M. (1990) Smoothing bias in derivative estimation. Unpublished manuscript, Sloan School of Management.

Stone, C. (1975) Adaptive maximum likelihood estimation of a location parameter. *Annals of Statistics*, 3, 267–84.

Swensen, A. R. (1985) The asymptotic distribution of the likelihood ratio for autoregressive time series with a regression trend. *Journal of Multivariate Analysis*, 16, 54–70.

Tobin, J. (1958) Estimation of relationships for limited dependent variables. *Econometrica*, 26, 24–36.

Weiss, A. (1986) Asymptotic theory for ARCH models: estimation and testing. *Econometric Theory*, 2, 107–31.

Whistler, D. (1988) Semiparametric ARCH estimation of intra-daily exchange rate volatility. Manuscript, London School of Economics.

7 Pooling Nonparametric Estimates of Regression Functions with a Similar Shape

C. A. P. Pinkse and P. M. Robinson

1 Objective

Given two nonparametric estimates for the same regression function based on different samples, intuitively one expects that combining, or *pooling*, the two estimates will – by virtue of the larger number of observations used – lead to a gain in precision. In this chapter we wish to establish that this is indeed the case, not only for regression functions that are identical but also for those that are just similar in shape. We will also give a procedure on how to optimally combine the two kernel regression estimates.

When we say "*similar in shape*" (or when we speak of "*shape-invariant modelling*") we mean that we know two transformations (one for the argument and one for the function value), up to a finite number of parameters, which transform one regression function into the other. If the parameters were known, one could simply transform one of the kernel estimates, such that we have two estimates of the same regression function. If the parameters are unknown, but can be estimated suitably efficiently, we show that the resulting pooled nonparametric regression estimate is asymptotically as efficient as employing known parameter values.

The related literature is not very extensive and generally has a somewhat different goal. It is in general not concerned with the improvement of the nonparametric estimates but rather with the estimation of the above parameters. It further generally assumes deterministic regressors, in particular ones with support on the unit interval and which depend on N, the number of observations, in order for the asymptotic theory to go through: the applications envisaged are mostly in physical and biometric experiments. An obvious application can be found in the estimation of human growth curves (see Gasser et al., 1984; a parametric application of growth curves can be found in Rao, 1977); all humans have a similar growth pattern, but the exact location of peaks and such may vary. In other disciplines, for instance in economics, the argument for deterministic regressors is much less convincing. Shape-invariant modelling is, however, also relevant in these disciplines; for instance, in the estimation of so-called *Engle-curves*, i.e. curves that represent the relationship between income and food expenditure. Another interesting setting in which shape-invariant modelling can be of interest is panel data. If, for instance, we have observed a panel with a large number of "individuals" but over a limited number of time periods, say two, it makes sense to assume that the relationship to be estimated in both periods is similar in shape, and hence shape-invariant modelling may be of interest. In effect, practitioners usually prescribe a linear relationship between the regressand and regressors in both time periods. If the number of regressors is the same in both equations, this would imply shape invariance. If one knows that the relationship between regressands and regressors is linear, however, nonparametric regression estimates are inefficient, and in such a setting this chapter would be of little relevance. If, on the other hand, one is uncertain about linearity, nonparametric regression estimation may be the only way to appropriately explain the relationship between the above variables. In practice, the present approach seems most useful when the regression functions of interest are identical up to scale and location parameter. To be particularly relevant in an econometric context, the results in this chapter may need to be extended to allow for more regressors. It is important to point out, though, that the precision of nonparametric estimates deteriorates rather quickly with an increase in the number of regressors.

We will use scalar random regressors and will consider two main cases, which we shall label $\mathscr{C}_1$ and $\mathscr{C}_2$. In $\mathscr{C}_1$ all regressors and disturbances are mutually independent and all regressors are identically distributed. Further, the conditional expectation of any disturbance conditional on any regressor is zero. The regressors in both samples are also assumed to admit the same density. In $\mathscr{C}_2$ the regressors in one sample may be differently distributed from those in the other and we will allow for limited dependencies between regressors in different samples. In section 2 we show that parameter estimates are $\sqrt{N}$-consistent and asymptotically normal in case of $\mathscr{C}_1$, that they converge at a rate faster than that of the nonparametric regression estimates in case of $\mathscr{C}_2$ and that whether we know or estimate the true parameters makes no difference for the pooling procedure. In section 3 we demonstrate and justify optimal pooling of two kernel regression estimates for the same regression function. The nonparametric regression methods used are kernel-based, and some useful but standard asymptotic properties of the kernel estimates, which we employ, are presented in the appendix.

2 Parameter Estimation

Models

In this subsection we will give a general outline of the models we wish to estimate. We will leave the full description of the regularity conditions to the next subsection.

We are concerned with the estimation of the following regression models:

$$Y_i = m(X_i) + U_i, \quad i = 1, \ldots, N,$$

$$Z_i = m_a(W_i) + V_i, \quad i = 1, \ldots, N_a,$$

where X_i, Y_i, W_i, Z_i are scalar observables and m and m_a are nonparametric functions, with $E[U_i|X_j] = E[V_i|W_j] = 0$, almost surely for all i, j. We assume that two transformations S and T exist such that for all x.

$$m(x) = S(\xi_0, m_a(T(\mu_0, x))),$$

and that these transformations are known except for the column parameter vector $\theta_0 = [\xi_0^\tau, \mu_0^\tau]^\tau$, where $^\tau$ indicates transposition. Later on we will estimate θ_0 by $\hat{\theta} = [\hat{\xi}^\tau, \hat{\mu}^\tau]^\tau$. In section 4, we briefly discuss the impact of incorrectly specifying the above parametric transformation.

Härdle and Marron (1990) suggest estimating θ_0 by minimizing the following function with respect to θ:

$$\int [m(x) - S(\xi, \hat{m}_a(T(\mu, x)))]^2 w(x)dx,$$

where w is a bounded function that is positive on the interior of a compact interval and zero elsewhere and $\hat{m} = \hat{r}/\hat{f}$ and $\hat{m}_a = \hat{r}_a/\hat{f}_a$ are Nadaraya–Watson kernel estimates for $m = r/f$ and $m_a = r_a/f_a$, respectively (where f and f_a are the densities of X_1 and W_1, respectively), such that

$$\hat{f}(x) = \frac{1}{Nh}\sum_i k_h(x - f_i), \quad \hat{r}(x) = \frac{1}{Nh}\sum_i k_h(x - X_i)Y_i,$$

where h denotes a bandwidth, $k_h(u) = k(u/h)$, with k an even kernel; $\hat{f}_a$ and $\hat{r}_a$ are similarly defined. When deterministic regressors are involved this approach is satisfactory, but with random regressors it is rather cumbersome, because the kernel regression estimate is then a ratio of random variables and taking expectations is awkward. We will only examine the most important case, namely when S is linear in both arguments, in contrast to Härdle and Marron (1991). Then we can write

$$\begin{aligned} m(x) &= \xi_{01} + \xi_{02}m_a(T(\mu_0, x)) \\ &\Leftrightarrow f_a(T(\mu_0, x))r(x) = \xi_{01}f(x)f_a(T(\mu_0, x)) + \xi_{02}f(x)r_a(T(\mu_0, x)), \end{aligned}$$

for all x. We thus define $\hat{\theta}$ as the value of θ that minimizes the loss function

$$L_N(\theta) = \int \Lambda_N^2(x, \theta)w(x)dx,$$

where

$$\Lambda_N(x, \theta) = \hat{f}_a(T(\mu, x))\hat{r}(x) - \xi_1\hat{f}(x)\hat{f}_a(T(\mu, x)) - \xi_2\hat{f}(x)\hat{r}_a(T(\mu, x)).$$

We require w to be also twice boundedly differentiable (besides being positive only on the interior a compact interval and zero elsewhere).

In $\mathscr{C}_1$ we will show that $\hat{\theta}$ is $\sqrt{N}$-consistent for θ_0 and asymptotically normal, and in $\mathscr{C}_2$ that $\hat{\theta} - \theta_0 = o_p(N^{-2/5})$. We have chosen this specific rate because the optimal kernel regression estimate that does not use higher order kernels converges at rate $N^{-2/5}$ and we only need to show that the parameter estimates converge faster. Thus, were we to use higher order kernels, the required convergence rate would be higher, but as the higher order kernels could then also be used to estimate $\hat{\theta}$, a higher convergence rate is then also more easily achievable.

Assumptions

In this subsection we will state the assumptions required for the results of the present section to go through. Throughout, a superscript (j)

denotes the jth derivative, but we will also – when we feel it improves clarity – use the usual (‴ is third derivative) notation.

First, we define two useful function classes.

Definition 1. The class $\mathscr{G}_l$ comprises all functions g that are l times boundedly differentiable. □

The functions g that we have in mind are all multiples of a function of interest and a probability density, so many cases in which the function of interest is unbounded are included.

Definition 2. The class $\mathscr{K}_l$ comprises all l times boundedly differentiable functions k that are even, integrate to one and satisfy

$$\int |k^{(i)}(u)|^2 du < \infty, \quad i = 0, \ldots, l, \quad \int |k(u)|u^2 du < \infty.$$

$$k(x) = \int K(u)e^{iux} du,$$

for all x, where

$$\int |u^i K(u)| du < \infty, \quad i = 0, \ldots, l. \quad \square$$

Assumption A. It is assumed that all (U_i, V_i) pairs are mutually independent, and that U_i and V_i both have finite second moments. We assume $E[U_i|X_j] = E[V_i|W_j] = 0$ for all i, j. We require that the X_i's are i.i.d. with density $f \in \mathscr{G}_2$ and that the W_i's are i.i.d. with density $f_a \in \mathscr{G}_2$. We also assume that $r \in \mathscr{G}_2$, $r_a \in \mathscr{G}_2$, $q = m^2 f \in \mathscr{G}_0$ and $q_a = m_a^2 f_a \in \mathscr{G}_0$. Further, an unknown vector $\theta_0 = [\xi_0, \mu_0]^\tau \in \theta$, with θ a bounded and open set, and two functions S and T exist such that for all x, $m(x) = S(\xi_0, m_a(T(\mu_0, x)))$. We assume that S is linear in both arguments. We also assume that N_a and N increase at the same rate. In $\mathscr{C}_1$ and $\mathscr{C}_2$ respectively we require:

1 $f \equiv f_a$ and $T(\mu_0, x) = x$, for all $x \in \Xi$, where Ξ is defined in assumption B below and $\{X_i\}$, $\{W_i\}$ are mutually independent.

2 X_i may depend on W_i but (X_i, W_i) is independent of (X_j, W_j) for $i \neq j$, X_1 and W_1 may have different densities but the transformation T is twice boundedly differentiable on $\theta \times \Xi$. Moreover, a function T^{-1} exists such that for all x: $x = T^{-1}(\mu, T(\mu, x))$. It is also assumed that T_2, the partial derivative of T with respect to its second argument, is bounded away from zero on $\Theta \times \Xi$. □

To simplify notation we assume $N_a = N$, but all results go through when N_a and N are related only in the way described in the assumption.

Assumption B. The twice boundedly differentiable weight function w, is nonnegative and positive only on the interior of a compact interval Ξ. For all points $x \in \Xi$ we have that $f(x) > 0$ and for all $(\theta, x) \in \Theta \times \Xi$ that $f_a(T(\mu, x)) > 0$. No parameter vector $\theta \neq \theta_0$ exists such that $m(x) = S(\xi, m_a(T(\mu, x)))$ for almost all $x \in \Xi$. □

There is a variety of ways to choose w and Ξ. One way is to choose w to be polynomial on Ξ, such that w and w' are zero at the boundaries of their support. We have chosen to limit Ξ to be compact, which makes the proofs somewhat easier. If one is willing to impose certain additional conditions on w, it is likely that a similar result could be obtained for $\Xi = \Re$. In practice, one will usually prefer to numerically integrate over a bounded area, though. One could dispense with numerical integration altogether by using either regressor density, instead of w. Indeed, in such a situation, one would try to estimate $E\Lambda^2(X_1, \theta)$, with $\Lambda(x, \theta) = f_a(T(\mu, x))r(x) - \xi_1 f(x) f_a(T(\mu, x)) - \xi_2 f(x) r_a(T(\mu, x))$. Such an estimate could take the form $L_{NE}(\theta) = (1/N)\Sigma_i\{\hat{f}_a(T(\mu, X_i))\hat{r}(X_i) - \xi_1\hat{f}(X_i)\hat{f}_a(T(\mu, X_i)) - \xi_2\hat{f}(X_i)\hat{f}_a(T(\mu, X_i))\}^2$, in which case $\hat{\theta}$ would be defined as the value of θ, for which $L_{NE}(\theta)$ is minimised. The obvious advantage is the ease of computation. There is, however, no reason why f should be a better weight function than other allowed choices of w. Indeed, one might choose w to be some other density, and draw random numbers from that distribution. Obviously, there is any number of possibilities.

Assumption C. We assume that both estimates employ the same kernel $k \in \mathscr{K}_2$ □

An example of such a kernel is the Gaussian density, $k(x) = (2\pi)^{-1/2}\exp(-x^2/2)$.

Assumption D. We assume that both estimates employ the same bandwidth h, where

$$Nh^5 \to \infty, \quad Nh^6 \to 0, \quad \text{as } N \to \infty, \quad \text{for } \mathscr{C}_1.$$

$$Nh^{10/3} \to \infty, \quad Nh^5 \to 0, \quad \text{as } N \to \infty, \quad \text{for } \mathscr{C}_2. \quad \square$$

Convergence of parameter estimates

In the theorem below, we need first and second order partial derivatives of L_N with respect to θ. The partial derivative of L_N with respect to θ is

$$\left.\frac{\partial L_N}{\partial \theta}\right|_{\theta} = \int \Lambda_N(x, \theta)\lambda_N(x, \theta)w(x)dx, \tag{2.1}$$

where (omitting arguments)

$$\lambda_N = -2\begin{bmatrix} \hat{f}\hat{f}_a \\ \hat{f}\hat{r}_a \\ (\xi_1\hat{f}\hat{f}'_a + \xi_2\hat{f}\hat{r}'_a - \hat{f}'_a\hat{r})T_1 \end{bmatrix}, \tag{2.2}$$

where T_1 denotes the partial derivative of T with respect to its first argument. The Hessian of $L_N(\theta)$ is given by

$$\left.\frac{\partial^2 L_N}{\partial\theta\partial\theta^\tau}\right|_{\theta} = \int \lambda_N\lambda_N^\tau w - 2\int \Lambda_N \begin{bmatrix} 0 & 0 & \hat{f}\hat{f}'_a T_1^\tau \\ 0 & 0 & \hat{f}\hat{r}'_a T_1^\tau \\ \hat{f}\hat{f}'_a T_1 & \hat{f}\hat{r}'_a T_1 & \lambda_N^* \end{bmatrix} w, \tag{2.3}$$

where $\lambda_N^* = (\xi_1\hat{f}\hat{f}''_a + \xi_2\hat{f}\hat{r}''_a - \hat{f}''_a\hat{r})T_1T_1^\tau + (\xi_1\hat{f}\hat{f}'_a + \xi_2\hat{f}\hat{r}'_a - \hat{f}'_a\hat{r})T_{11}$, with $T_{11} = \partial^2 T/(\partial\mu\partial\mu^\tau)$.

Theorem 1. Under assumptions A–D

$$N^{1/2}(\hat{\theta} - \theta_0) \xrightarrow{\mathscr{C}} N(0, \Sigma), \text{ in } \mathscr{C}_1,$$

for some finite variance matrix Σ and

$$N^{2/3}(\theta - \theta_0) \xrightarrow{P} 0, \text{ in } \mathscr{C}_2. \quad \square$$

Parameters can be replaced by their estimates

In this subsection we will show that it makes no difference asymptotically whether one uses the true paraneter values or their estimates. Suppose we have obtained an estimate $\hat{\theta}$ for θ_0 on the basis of the procedure described above. By theorem 1, we have $\hat{\theta} - \theta_0 = o_p(N^{-2/5})$. The kernel estimates used to obtain $\hat{\theta}$ need not use the same bandwidth as the kernel estimates we will use in section 3 to obtain our pooled estimate. Therefore, the kernel estimates used in this section are not subject to assumption D. Indeed, we will allow $\hat{r}$ and $\hat{f}$ to use a bandwidth different from the one used by $\hat{r}_a$ and $\hat{f}_a$.

Assumption E. h and h_a converge at the same rate, $Nh^3 \to \infty$ and $h \to 0$, as $N \to \infty$. $\square$

Assumption E ensures that $\hat{r}_a$ and $\hat{f}_a$ converge to r_a and f_a respectively, uniformly in $\theta \in \Theta$ and for all $x \in \Xi$, by Lemmas 1 and 2; this follows from an argument similar to the one applying to expression (A.5).

Theorem 2. Let assumptions A–C, E hold. If $\hat{\theta} - \theta_0 = o_p(N^{-2/5})$, and if $\hat{m}(x, \theta)$ denotes $S(\xi, \tilde{m}_a(T(\mu, x)))$, for all x, θ, then

$$\tilde{m}(x, \hat{\theta}) - \tilde{m}(x, \theta_0) = o_p(N^{-2/5}),$$

for all $x \in \Xi$. □

3 Pooling Kernel Estimates

Setting

In the present setting we will show that pooling kernel regression estimates leads to a smaller asymptotic mean squared error. The formula for the asymptotic mean squared error of a kernel regression estimate, not involving a higher order kernel, is (see Mack, 1981)

$$\text{Bias}^2 + \text{Variance} = \left[\frac{c_1 h^2\{m''(x)f(x) + 2m'(x)f'(x)\}}{2f(x)}\right]^2 + \left[\frac{c_2\sigma^2(x)}{Nhf(x)}\right], \tag{3.1}$$

where $c_1 = \int k(u)u^2du$, $c_2 = \int k^2(u)du$ and $\sigma^2(x) = E[U_1^2|X_1 = x]$. After renorming, the first term in (3.1) is the squared expectation of the asymptotic distribution of $\hat{m} - m$, and the second term the variance. The bias-term is based on a Taylor expansion, where all the terms of smaller order of probability are dropped. Obviously, if $Nh^5 \to 0$, the first term in (3.1) is of lower order than the second, and as a consequence the expectation of the asymptotic distribution is zero. By the same token, if $Nh^5 \to \infty$, the asymptotic distribution will be degenerate, because its variance is zero.

There are reasons for using the asymptotic mean squared error rather than, for instance, the asymptotic variance or the (normal) mean squared error ($E[\hat{m}(x) - m(x)]^2$). Because $\hat{f}$, the denominator of $\hat{m}$, can be arbitraily close to, or even equal to, zero the expectation $E[\hat{m}(x) - m(x)]^2$ need not exist for any finite N. This makes the mean squared error undesirable as a tool in the present setting, as we wish to keep the class of allowed kernel regression estimates as large as possible. The asymptotic variance is – as we have seen above – only suitable if $Nh^5 \to 0$. This restriction on the bandwidth may not always be desirable. Indeed, for the infeasible choice of bandwidth that minimizes the asymptotic mean squared error, for instance, we have that $Nh^5 \to c$, for some c with $0 < c < \infty$. There may also be other reasons to have the bandwidth converge at a slower rate, depending on the implementation of the kernel estimates in question. If $Nh^5 \nrightarrow 0$, however, we will need extra restrictions on the model for our results to go through, as will become evident further below.

Because of theorem 2 we can act as if the parameter vector θ_0 is fully known. Thus, if $Y_i^* = (Y_i - \xi_{01})/\xi_{02}$, $X_i^* = T(\mu_0, X_i)$ and $U_i^* = U_i/\xi_{02}$, then we can write

$$Y_i^* = m_a(X_i^*) + U_i^* \quad i = 1, \ldots, N$$

$$Z_i = m_a(W_i) + V_i \quad i = 1, \ldots, N_a.$$

We define

$$m_a^*(x) = \frac{\hat{r}_*(x)}{\hat{f}_*(x)},$$

where

$$f_*(x) = \frac{1}{Nh}\sum_i k_h(x - X_i^*), \quad \hat{r}_*(x) = \frac{1}{Nh}\sum_i k_h(x - X_i^*)Y_i^*.$$

Let x be the point at which we wish to estimate m_a. We will require that assumptions A (for $\mathscr{C}_2$) and C hold. We also need the following two assumptions.

Assumption F. Let $f_*(u) = f(T^{-1}(\mu_0, u))$, for all u. The joint density of (X_1^*, W_1) is not degenerate and both f and f_* are strictly positive at x. □

Assumption F is to ensure that $\text{cov}(\hat{m}_a^*, \hat{m}_a)$ tends to zero faster than both $V\hat{m}_a^*$ and $V\hat{m}_a$. Let h_a denote the bandwidth used by $\hat{m}_a$ and h that used by $\hat{m}_a^*$.

Assumption G. We require that assumptions C and E hold. Further, at least one of the following three conditions holds.

- $\mathscr{C}_3$: At the point x at which we wish to estimate m_a, we have that either both $f_*'(x)/f_*(x) - f_a'(x)/f_a(x) = 0$ and $h \sim h_a$, as $N \to \infty$, or that $m_a''(x)$ is known.
- $\mathscr{C}_4$: $Nh^5 \to 0$, as $N \to \infty$.
- $\mathscr{C}_5$: $Nh^5 \to \infty$, as $N \to \infty$ and m_a'' satisfies a Lipschitz-condition of degree one at x. □.

The reasons for each of the three conditions in assumption G will become apparent in theorem 3.

Results

In theorem 3 below we derive the optimal (in terms of the asymptotic mean squared error) linear combination of $\hat{m}_a$ and $\hat{m}_a^*$. In case $f_a(x) = f_*(x)$, almost everywhere, one might also consider $\hat{m}_d(x) = \{c_1\hat{r}_*(x) + c_2\hat{r}_a(x)\}/\{c_1\hat{f}_*(x) + c_2\hat{f}_a(x)\}$, with $c_1 + c_2 = 1$. This will not generally lead to an improvement of the asymptotic mean squared error. In the special case that $N_a = N$, and $m_a(x) = m(x)$, $V[Z_i|W_i = x] = V[U_i|X_i = x]$, and all regressors are independent, within and across samples, the squared asymptotic bias will in both cases be equal to the first term on the right hand side in (3.1) and the asymptotic variance to the second, divided by two, because $\hat{m}_d$ is, under the present circumstances, just a kernel regression estimate based on twice the number of observations, while $V[\{\hat{m}_a(x) + \hat{m}(x)\}/2] = V[\hat{m}(x)]/2$.

Theorem 3. Under Assumptions F and G the linear combination of $\hat{m}_a^*$ and $\hat{m}_a$ that minimises 3.1 is given by

$$\hat{m}_{p,\Omega^*}(x) = \Omega^*\hat{m}_a^*(x) + (1 - \Omega^*)\hat{m}_a(x),$$

where

$$\Omega^* = \frac{\mathcal{V} - \mathcal{B}(\mathcal{B}_* - \mathcal{B})}{(\mathcal{B}_* - \mathcal{B})^2 - \mathcal{V}_* + \mathcal{V}}, \tag{3.2}$$

where $\mathcal{V} = V\hat{m}_a(x) = c_2\sigma_a^2(x)/(Nhf_a(x))$, $\mathcal{V}_* = V\hat{m}_a^*(x) = c_2\sigma_*^2(x)/(Nhf_*(x))$, $\mathcal{B} = E\hat{m}_a(x) - m_a(x) = c_1h^2\{m_a''(x)f_a(x) + 2m_a'(x)f_a'(x)\}/(2f_a(x))$ and $\mathcal{B}_* = E\hat{m}_a^*(x) - m_a(x) = c_1h^2\{m_a''(x)f_*(x) + 2m_a'(x)f_*'(x)\}/(2f_*(x))$, where f_* is the density of X_1^* and σ_*^2 the variance of U_1^* given $X_1^* = x$. □

The above result is interesting, perhaps even surprising, in at least one respect: the optimal weight can be less than zero or greater than one! It is not a situation that is likely to arise very often in practice, though. The asymptotic variances and biases used in theorem 3 are unknown, but we may estimate them.

Theorem 4. Under the conditions of the previous subsection, the weight Ω^* defined in theorem 3 can be consistently estimated (by $\hat{\Omega}$, say) and the feasible pooled estimate, $\hat{m}_{p,\hat{\Omega}}(x) = \hat{\Omega}\hat{m}_a^*(x) + (1 - \hat{\Omega})\hat{m}_a(x)$, is as efficient – in terms of the asymptotic mean squared error, as given by (3.1) – as the infeasible pooled estimate $\hat{m}_{p,\Omega^*}(x)$. □

There is one important question that remains; namely, how precise must $\hat{\Omega}$ be to improve on not doing any pooling at all? Or, in other words, just how robust is our gain against poor estimation? We will get some insight in this from the corollary to the theorem below. In the theorem, we derive, for given Ω_0, the interval, in every point of which the asymptotic mean squared error M_p – defined by $M_p(\Omega) = [\mathcal{V}_* + \mathcal{V} + (\mathcal{B}_* - \mathcal{B})^2]\Omega^2 + 2[\mathcal{B}(\mathcal{B}_* - \mathcal{B}) - \mathcal{V}]\Omega + [\mathcal{B}^2 + \mathcal{V}]$ – is less than or equal to $M_p(\Omega_0)$. In the corollary, we establish the circumstances under which the pooled estimate is better than both "marginal" estimates, and also better than their naive average, $\hat{m}_m(x) = (\hat{m}_a(x) + \hat{m}_a^*(x))/2$. We wish to point out that the asymptotic mean squared error ignores the impact of the estimation of θ_0. It is thus hazardous to make strong assertions on the basis of the below theorem or its corollary.

Theorem 5. Given Ω_0, the set $\Upsilon(\Omega_0)$, consisting of all values of $\Omega \in \mathbf{R}$ such that $M_p(\Omega) \leqslant M_p(\Omega_0)$, is given by$\Upsilon(\Omega_0) = [\Omega_0, 2\Omega^* - \Omega_0]$, when $\Omega^* \geqslant \Omega_0$, and by $[2\Omega^* - \Omega_0, \Omega_0]$, otherwise. □

Corollary 1. The pooled regression estimate reduces to either marginal kernel regression estimate, when $\Omega = 0$, or $\Omega = 1$, and it is the naive pooled estimate $\hat{m}_m$, when $\Omega = \frac{1}{2}$. For $\Omega^* \in (0, 1)$, it has an asymptotic mean squared error no higher than that of both the marginal estimates, when $\Omega \in \Upsilon(0) \cap \Upsilon(1) = [2\Omega^* - 1, 2\Omega^*\}$, and for any $\Omega^* \in \mathbf{R}$ it is at least as good as $\hat{m}_m$, if and only if $\Omega \in \Upsilon(\frac{1}{2})$. □

In the next subsection we will examine ways to estimate the conditional variance of V_1 given W_1.

Variance estimation

In theorem 4 we temporarily ignored the issue of how to estimate σ_*^2 and σ_a^2. We will now present ways to estimate $\sigma^2(x) = E[U_1^2|X_1]$, where $\sigma_a^2(x)$ and $\sigma_*^2(x)$ can be estimated in the same fashion.

A standard estimate is

$$\hat{\sigma}^2(x) = \frac{\Sigma_i k_h(x - X_i)(Y_i - \hat{m}(x))^2}{\Sigma_i k_h(x - X_i)}. \tag{3.3}$$

A disadvantage of the estimate in (3.3) is that it is rather sensitive to changes in the scale of m. This can be most easily seen when we write (omitting arguments) $\hat{\sigma}^2 = \Sigma k_h U^2/\Sigma k_h + \Sigma k_h\{(m - \hat{m})^2 + 2(m - \hat{m})U\}/\Sigma k_h$. The latter term in the above expansion is a nuisance term and is the obvious cause of the afore-mentioned sensitivity to changes in scale of m.

For homoskedastic disturbances a procedure of Hall and Titterington (1988) for nonstochastic regressors can be modified to the stochastic regressor case, as follows.

Theorem 6. Denote by N_D the number of X_i lying in a given interval $[a, b]$ in the support of X_1. Denote by $X_{(1)}, \ldots, X_{(N_D)}$, the order statistics of the X_i within $[a, b]$ and denote by $Y_{(i)}$, $U_{(i)}$, the Y and U corresponding to $X_{(i)}$. Then

$$\hat{\sigma}^2 = \frac{2}{N_D} \sum_{i=1}^{N_D} (Y_{(i)} - Y_{(i-1)})^2. \tag{3.4}$$

is a consistent estimate of σ^2. □

4 Other Issues

An issue we have completely ignored so far is that when the true transformation is not of the form envisaged, the resulting pooled estimates will not be consistent. One thus needs to be fairly confident of the existence of the imposed relationship between the two regression functions. It is possible to test whether the two regression functions do have the shape similarity expected. When there is shape-invariance, $L(\theta_0) = 0$. The converse is not generally true, although if w is positive on a sufficiently wide interval, a srnall value of $L_N(\theta)$ would be very reassuring.

Indeed, if one would extend theorem 1 to include the case $\Xi = \mathbf{R}$, for certain w, a consistent test could be created, i.e. a test that always rejects asymptotically whenever the null hypothesis does not hold, and always accepts when it does. For, in such a case $L(\theta_0) = 0$ if and only if there is shape invariance of the specified form, and $L_N(\theta)$ would be a consistent estimate of $L(\theta_0)$ if the above extension were feasible.

5 Summary

In this chapter we have established a way to estimate shape invariance parameters, in the presence of random regressors, with sufficient efficiency to obtain asymptotically efficient pooled nonparametric regression estimates.

We have considered two basic cases, one in which the regressor densities are identical and there are no dependencies, and one in which regressor densities may differ and limited dependencies are allowed for. In the former case, we establish that the parameter estimates are $\sqrt{N}$-consistent with a normal asymptotic distribution, whereas in the latter case the parameter estimates are shown to converge faster than the nonparametric regression estimates. This enables us to substitute the estimates for the true parameter values without asymptotic significance, allowing us to use data from both data sets to estimate both regression equations simultaneously. We have also examined which was the most efficient (in terms of the asymptotic mean squared error) way of pooling the two data sets, and have pointed out under which circumstances the (asymptotically) optimally pooled estimate is better than both "marginal" nonparametric regression estimates and a naive pooled estimate (i.e. their unweighted average). We have also provided a more robust way of estimating conditional variances in a nonparametric regression setting, and have given some guidelines to how a test for the correctness of the parametric specification of the transformations could be created.

Appendix 1: proofs of theorems

Proof of theorem 1

Applying the mean value theorem to the first order partial derivative of L at θ we get

$$\left.\frac{\partial L_N}{\partial \theta}\right|_{\hat{\theta}} = \left.\frac{\partial L_N}{\partial \theta}\right|_{\theta_0} + \widetilde{\frac{\partial^2 L_N}{\partial \theta \partial \theta^\tau}}(\hat{\theta} - \theta_0),$$

where the tilde indicates that each of the rows of $\partial^2 L_N/(\partial\theta\partial\theta^\tau)$ is evaluated at a (possibly different) point in $(\hat{\theta}, \theta_0)$. The quantity on the left hand side in the last displayed equation is zero by the definition of $\hat{\theta}$ and hence

$$\hat{\theta} - \theta_0 = \left[\widetilde{\frac{\partial^2 L_N}{\partial \theta \partial \theta^\tau}}\right]^{-1} \left.\frac{\partial L_N}{\partial \theta}\right|_{\theta_0},$$

provided that the inverse exists. Thus, the theorem is proved if we can establish the following six properties.

1 An open and bounded set Θ exists to which θ_0 belongs.
2 L_N is a measurable function in the observations for all $\theta \in \Theta$. Further, $\partial L_N/\partial\theta$ (see (2.1)) exists and is continuous on Θ.
3 $L_N(\theta)$ converges to a nonstochastic function $L(\theta)$ in probability uniformly in $\theta \in \Theta$ and $L(\theta)$ attains a strict global minimum at θ_0.
4 The Hessian of L_N, which is given in (2.3), exists and is continuous on Θ.
5 The above Hessian evaluated at θ_N converges to a nonsingular matrix

$$A(\theta_0) = \lim E \left.\frac{\partial^2 L_N}{\partial \theta \partial \theta^\tau}\right|_{\theta_0}$$

in probability for any sequence θ_N that converges in probability to θ_0.
6 As $N \to \infty$,

$$N^{1/2}\frac{\partial L_N}{\partial \theta}\bigg|_{\theta_0} \xrightarrow{\mathcal{L}} N(0, B(\theta_0)), \text{ in } \mathscr{C}_1,$$

where

$$B(\theta_0) = \lim E\frac{\partial L_N}{\partial \theta}\frac{\partial L_N}{\partial \theta^\tau}\bigg|_{\theta_0},$$

and

$$N^{2/5}\frac{\partial L_N}{\partial \theta}\bigg|_{\theta_0} \xrightarrow{P} 0, \text{ in } \mathscr{C}_2.$$

If all the above conditions are satisfied, then as $N \to \infty$

$$N^{1/2}(\hat{\theta} - \theta_0) \to N(0, A^{-1}(\theta_0)B(\theta_0)A^{-1}(\theta_0)), \text{ in } \mathscr{C}_1,$$

and

$$N^{2/5}(\hat{\theta} - \theta_0) \xrightarrow{P} 0, \text{ in } \mathscr{C}_2.$$

We will establish the above six properties step by step.

1 This is assumed in assumption A.

2 The partial derivative, $(\partial L_N/\partial\theta)|_{(\theta)}$, is continuous if k and T are continuously differentiable, which was assumed in assumptions C and A respectively.

3 Define

$$L(\theta) = \int \Lambda^2(x, \theta)w(x)dx,$$

where

$$\Lambda(x, \theta) = r(x)f_a(T(\mu, x)) - \xi_1 f(x)f_a(T(\mu, x)) - \xi_2 r_a(T(\mu, x))f(x).$$

We will first show that

$$L_N(\theta) - L(\theta) = o_p(1), \tag{A.1}$$

uniformly in θ over any bounded interval. We have

$$L_N(\theta) - L(\theta) = \int \{\Lambda_N^2(x, \theta) - \Lambda^2(x, \theta)\}w(x)dx.$$

Now, $\Lambda_N^2 - \Lambda^2 = (\Lambda_N - \Lambda)^2 + 2(\Lambda_N - \Lambda)\Lambda$, so for (A.1) it suffices to show that

$$\sup_{\theta\in\Theta}\sup_{x\in\Xi}|\Lambda_N(x, \theta) - \Lambda(x, \theta)| = o_p(1). \tag{A.2}$$

Because Θ is bounded, so are ξ_1 and ξ_2 in the expansions of Λ_N and Λ and these therefore play no role of importance. We write

$$\Lambda_n - \Lambda = (\hat{r}\hat{f}_a - rf_a) - \xi_1(\hat{f}\hat{f}_a - ff_a) - \xi_2(\hat{f}\hat{r}_a - fr_a). \tag{A.3}$$

We will now show that

$$\sup_{\theta\in\Theta}\sup_{x\in\Xi}|\hat{r}_a\hat{f} - r_a f| = o_p(1), \tag{A.4}$$

where the other terms in (A.3) can be dealt with in a similar manner. We can rewrite (A.4) as

$$\sup_{\theta\in\Theta}\sup_{x\in\Xi}|(\hat{r}_a - r_a)(\hat{f} - f) + (\hat{r}_a - r_a)f + (\hat{f} - f)r_a| = o_p(1). \tag{A.5}$$

θ appears only in the argument of r_a and $\hat{r}_a$ in (A.5) and because lemmas 1 and 2 (all lemmas as stated and proved in appendix 2) hold uniformly on **R**, (A.5) holds also. That L attains a strict global minimum at θ_0 is implied by $L(\theta_0) = 0 \leqslant L(\theta)$ for all θ, assumption B and the obvious fact that $L(\theta)$ can only be zero if $m(x) = S(\xi, m_a(T(\mu, x)))$, for almost all $x \in \Xi$.

4 Existence and continuity are implied by existence and continuity of the second order derivatives of T and k and the compactness of Ξ.

5 We will show that the matrix $A(\theta_0)$ is given by

$$A(\theta_0) = \int \lambda(x, \theta_0)\lambda(x, \theta_0)^\tau w(x)(dx),$$

where

$$\lambda(x, \theta) := -2\begin{bmatrix} ff_a \\ fr_a \\ (\xi_1 ff'_a + \xi_2 fr'_a - f'_a r)T_1 \end{bmatrix}$$

It is sufficient to show that

$$\int \{\lambda_N(x, \theta_N)\lambda_N^\tau(x, \theta_N) - \lambda(x, \theta_N)\lambda^\tau(x, \theta_N)\}w(x)dx = o_p(1), \tag{A.6}$$

$$\int \{\lambda(x, \theta_N)\lambda^\tau(x, \theta_N) - \lambda(x, \theta_0)\lambda^\tau(x, \theta_0)\}w(x)dx = o_p(1), \tag{A.7}$$

and if we call the matrix under the second integral in (2.3) M_N,

$$\int \{\Lambda_N(x, \theta_N)M_N(x, \theta_N) - \Lambda(x, \theta_N)EM_N(x, \theta_N)\}w(x)dx = o_p(1), \tag{A.8}$$

$$\int \Lambda(x, \theta_N)EM_N(x, \theta_N)w(x)dx = o_p(1). \tag{A.9}$$

We will prove (A.6) through (A.9) by demonstrating that the results hold for every element in the matrices. For (A.6) we need to show that $\int(\hat{f}^2\hat{f}_a^2 - f^2 f_a^2)w = o_p(1)$, $\int(\hat{f}^2\hat{f}_a\hat{r}_a - f^2 f_a r_a)w = o_p(1), \ldots, \int\{(\hat{f}'_a)^2\hat{r}^2 - (f'_a)^2 r^2\}T_1 T_1^\tau w = o_p(1)$. All these conditions can be established in similar fashion. Because convergence of derivative estimates is slower than of estimates of the original function, we will show convergence of a term which includes a derivative estimate. Consider $Q = \int(\hat{f}\hat{r}\hat{f}'_a\hat{r}'_a - frf'_a r'_a)T_1 w$. Because we know the convergence properties of the separate estimates, we will split Q up using the basic algebraic property

$$\prod_{j=1}^{4} \hat{D}_{4j} - \prod_{j=1}^{4} D_{4j} = \sum_{i_1=0}^{1} \sum_{i_2=0}^{1} \sum_{i_3=0}^{1} \sum_{i_4=0}^{3-i_2-i_2-i_3} \prod_{j} \mathrm{D}_{4_j}^{i_j} (\hat{D}_{4j} - D_{4j})^{1-i_j}.$$

We know from lemma 3 and assumption D that $\sup_x|\hat{f} - f| + \sup_x|\hat{r} - r| = O_p(h^2 + N^{-1/2}h^{-1}) = o_p(1)$. We also know that f, r, f'_a, r'_a are all bounded. It is therefore sufficient to show that

$$\int [(\hat{f}'_a - f_a)'(\hat{r}'_a - r'_a) - (\hat{f}'_a - f'_a) + (\hat{r}'_a - r'_a)]\zeta = o_p(1),$$

for any bounded function ζ. By the inequality of Cauchy–Schwarz we only need to show that

$$\int (\hat{f}'_a - f'_a)^2 \zeta = o_p(1), \quad \int (\hat{r}'_a - r'_a)^2 \zeta = o_p(1).$$

We will only show that the last of these two conditions holds. Taking the expectation leads to

$$\int E[\hat{r}'_a - r'_a]^2 \zeta = \int \{V[\hat{r}'_a] + (E[\hat{r}'_a] - r'_a)^2\}\zeta = O(h^2 + N^{-1}h^{-3}),$$

by lemmas 1 and 4.

Condition (A.7) follows from Slutsky's theorem, from the fact that $\int \lambda\lambda^\tau w$ is continuous in θ and from $\theta_N - \theta_0 = o_p(1)$. To show (A.8) note that

$$\begin{aligned} \Lambda_N M_N - \Lambda E M_N = (\Lambda_N - \Lambda)(M_N - EM_N) + \Lambda(M_N - EM_N) \\ + EM_N(\Lambda_N - \Lambda). \end{aligned} \qquad \text{(A.10)}$$

We will restrict ourselves to showing convergence of the second term on the right hand side in (A.10), arguably the hardest part. The other terms follow by a similar argument. We will prove convergence of each element in M_N separately. Because second order derivatives converge slowest, we will just show convergence for an element involving a second order derivative; the rest of the elements can be handled in identical fashion. We will thus show that $\int(\hat{f}\hat{r}''_a - E[\hat{f}\hat{r}''_a])\Lambda w = o_p(1)$. By lemma 6 it suffices to show that: $\int(\hat{f}\hat{r}''_a - E\hat{f}E\hat{r}''_a)\Lambda w = o_p(1)$ because $E[\hat{f}\hat{r}''_a] - E\hat{f}E\hat{r}''_a = O(N^{-1}h^{-3}) = o(1)$. Because $\sup_x|\hat{f}(x) - E\hat{f}(x)| = o_p(1)$, by lemma 2 and assumption D, we need to show that

$$\int (\hat{r}''_a - E\hat{r}''_a) E\hat{f}\Lambda w = o_p(1). \qquad \text{(A.11)}$$

Because $\hat{r}''_a = (1/Nh^3)\Sigma_i k''_h(T(\mu_N, x) - W_i)Z_i$, we are interested in

$$\int k''_h(T(\mu_N, x) - W_i)\Lambda(\theta_N, x)E\hat{f}(x)w(x)dx = \int k''_h(u - W_i)\xi(u)du, \qquad \text{(A.12)}$$

where the equality follows from the substitution of $u = T(\mu_N, x)$, and the fact that T_2 is assumed bounded away from zero on $\Theta \times \Xi$, defining $\xi(u)$ by

$$\xi(u) = \frac{\Lambda(\theta_N, T^{-1}(\mu_N, u))Ef(T^{-1}(\mu_N, u))w(T^{-1}(\mu_N, u))}{T_2(T^{-1}(\mu_N, u))}.$$

Because w (and hence w') is zero outside Ξ, ξ and ξ' are zero outside $T(\mu_N, \Xi)$. We rewrite (A.12) as (using partial integration twice)

$$-h[k_h'(u - W_i)\xi(u)]_{-\infty}^{\infty} + h^2[k_h(u - W_i)\xi'(u)]_{-\infty}^{\infty} + h^2\int k_h(u - W_i)\xi''(u)du. \tag{A.13}$$

As noted before ξ and ξ' are zero outside the integration area, so the first two terms in (A.13) are zero. Substitution of $v = (u - W_i)/h$ in the last term in (A.13) gives

$$h^3\int k(v)\xi''(W_i - hv)dv = h^3\rho(W_i),$$

which implicitly defines ρ. By the boundedness of ξ'', $\rho(W_i)$ is bounded. The left hand side in (A.11) now reads

$$\begin{aligned}&\frac{1}{Nh^3}\sum_i\int k_h''(T(\mu_N, x) - W_i)\Lambda(x, \theta_N)E\hat{f}(x)w(x)dxZ_i\\ &- E\left[\frac{1}{Nh^3}\sum_i\int k_h''(T(\mu_N, x) - W_i)\Lambda(x, \theta_N)E\hat{f}(x)w(x)dxZ_i\right]\\ &= \frac{1}{N}\sum_i\rho(W_i)Z_i - E[\rho(W_1)Z_1] = O_p(N^{-1/2}),\end{aligned}$$

because the $\rho(W_i)Z_i$ are i.i.d. with finite variance. So (A.11) holds and so does (A.8). All that is left is (A.9). By lemma 1, $E\hat{r}_a'' = O(1)$ uniformly in x and hence so is EM_N. So all we really need to do is to show that

$$\int\Lambda(x, \theta_N)w(x)dx - \int\Lambda(x, \theta_0)w(x)dx = o_p(1), \tag{A.14}$$

noting that $\Lambda(x, \theta_0) = 0$ for all x. But because $\int\Lambda(x, \theta)w(x)dx$ is a continuous function and because $\theta_N - \theta_0 = o_p(1)$ Slutsky's theorem gives (A.14).

6 For $\mathscr{C}_2$ we need to prove that:

$$\int\Lambda_N(x, \theta_0)\lambda_N(x, \theta_0)w(x)dx = o_p(N^{-2/5}), \tag{A.15}$$

We shall do this by proving the following three conditions that are together sufficient for (A.15).

$$\int\Lambda_N(x, \theta_0)\{\lambda_N(x, \theta_0) - \lambda(x, \theta_0)\}w(x)dx = o_p(N^{-2/5}), \tag{A.16}$$

$$E\int\Lambda_N(x, \theta_0)\lambda(x, \theta_0)w(x)dx = o(N^{-2/5}), \tag{A.17}$$

$$\int \Lambda_N(x, \theta_0)\lambda(x, \theta_0)w(x)dx - E\left[\int \Lambda_N(x, \theta_0)\lambda(x, \theta_0)w(x)dx\right] = o_p(N^{-2/5}). \tag{A.18}$$

We first consider (A.16). We define $D_1 = [r, f, f]^\tau$, $D_2 = [f_a, f_a, r_a]^\tau$, $d_1 = [1, -\zeta_{01}, -\zeta_{02}]^\tau$, $D_3 = [f, f, f, f, r]^\tau$, $D_4 = [f_a, r_a, f_a', r_a', f_a']^\tau$, $d_2 = [-2, -2, \zeta_{01}\|T_1\|, \zeta_{02}\|T_1\|, -\|T_1\|]^\tau$, so that we can write

$$\Lambda_N - \Lambda = \sum_{j=1}^{3} d_{1j}(\hat{D}_{1j}\hat{D}_{2j} - D_{1j}D_{2j}).$$

$$\lambda_N - \lambda = \left[d_{21}(\hat{D}_{31}\hat{D}_{41} - D_{31}D_{41}),\ d_{22}(\hat{D}_{32}\hat{D}_{42} - D_{32}D_{42}),\right.$$
$$\left.\sum_{j=3}^{5} d_{2j}(\hat{D}_{3j}\hat{D}_{4j} - D_{3j}D_{4j})\right]^\tau.$$

Thus,

$$\left|\int \Lambda_N(\lambda_N - \lambda)w\right|$$
$$\leqslant \int \sqrt{(\Lambda_N - \Lambda)^2 \|\lambda_N - \lambda\|^2}\, w$$
$$\leqslant C\int \sqrt{\sum_{j=1}^{3}\left\{(\hat{D}_{1j} - D_{1j})^2(\hat{D}_{2j} - D_{2j})^2 + D_{1j}^2(\hat{D}_{2j} - D_{2j})^2 + D_{2j}^2(\hat{D}_{1j} - D_{1j})^2\right\}}$$
$$\times \sqrt{\sum_{j=1}^{5}\left\{(\hat{D}_{3j} - D_{3j})^2(\hat{D}_{4j} - D_{4j})^2 + D_{4j}^2(\hat{D}_{3j} - D_{3j})^2 + D_{3j}^2(\hat{D}_{4j} - D_{4j})^2\right\}}\, w,$$

for some large $C > 0$. Because $\sup_{x,j}|\hat{D}_{1j} - D_{1j}| + \sup_{x,j}|(\hat{D}_{2j} - D_{2j}| + \sup_{x,j}|(\hat{D}_{3j} - D_{3j}| + \sup_{x,j}|(\hat{D}_{4j} - D_{4j}| = o_p(1)$, $(\hat{D}_{1j} - D_{1j})^2(\hat{D}_{2j} - D_{2j})^2$ and $(\hat{D}_{3j} - D_{3j})^2(\hat{D}_{4j} - D_{4j})^2$ are of lower order than $D_{1j}^2(\hat{D}_{2j} - D_{2j})^2 + D_{2j}^2(\hat{D}_{1j} - D_{1j})^2$ and $D_{3j}^2(\hat{D}_{4j} - D_{4j})^2 + D_{4j}^2(\hat{D}_{3j} - D_{3j})^2$ respectively. So we only need to look at

$$C\int \sqrt{\sum_{j=1}^{3}\left\{D_{1j}^2(\hat{D}_{2j} - D_{2j})^2 + D_{2j}^2(\hat{D}_{1j} - D_{1j})^2\right\}}$$
$$\times \sqrt{\sum_{j=1}^{5}\left\{D_{4j}^2(\hat{D}_{3j} - D_{3j})^2 + D_{3j}^2(\hat{D}_{4j} - D_{4j})^2\right\}}\, w. \tag{A.19}$$

By lemmas 1 and 4 we know that

$$\sup_{x,j} E[\hat{D}_{1j} - D_{1j}]^2 + \sup_{x,j} E[\hat{D}_{2j} - D_{2j}]^2 = O(h^4 + (Nh)^{-1}),$$
$$\sup_{x,j} E[\hat{D}_{3j} - D_{3j}]^2 + \sup_{x,j} E[\hat{D}_{4j} - D_{4j}]^2 = O(h^2 + N^{-1}h^{-3}),$$

and hence the expectation of (A.19) is of order $O(h^3 + N^{-1}h^{-2}) = o(N^{-2/5})$. Now consider (A.17). Lemma 6 implies that we can proceed as if the kernel estimates are all based on completely independent samples. Using again $\Lambda(x, \theta_0) = 0$ for all x we write (using lemma 6)

$$E\Lambda_N - \Lambda = E\hat{r}E\hat{f}_a - rf_a - \xi_{01}(E\hat{f}E\hat{f}_a - ff_a) - \xi_{02}(E\hat{f}E\hat{r}_a - fr_a) + O(N^{-1}h^{-1}), \qquad \text{(A.20)}$$

uniformly in x. We will deal with each of the terms in (A.20) separately. We will just demonstrate the procedure for the first term, where the proof for the other terms follows trivially. We write

$$E\hat{r}E\hat{f}_a - rf_a = (E\hat{r} - r)(E\hat{f}_a - f_a) + r(E\hat{f}_a - f_a) + f_a(E\hat{r} - \mathrm{r}). \qquad \text{(A.21)}$$

By lemma 1, (A.21) is $O(h^2)$, uniformly in x, which with assumption D implies that (A.21) is $o(N^{-2/5})$. So (A.17) holds. Expression (A.18) is fairly straightforward to deal with. We will limit ourselves to proving

$$\int \{\hat{r}(x)\hat{f}_a(T(\mu_0, x)) - E[\hat{r}(x)\hat{f}_a(T(\mu_0, x))]\}\lambda(x, \theta_0)w(x)dx = O_p(N^{-1/2}), \qquad \text{(A.22)}$$

where the result for the other terms can be obtained in the same fashion. Lemma 6 states that $E[\hat{r}\hat{f}_a] - E\hat{r}E\hat{f}_a = O(N^{-1}h^{-1})$. Further,

$$\hat{r}\hat{f}_a - E\hat{r}E\hat{f}_a = (\hat{r} - E\hat{r})(\hat{f}_a - E\hat{f}_a) + (\hat{f}_a - E\hat{f}_a)E\hat{r} + (\hat{r} - E\hat{r})E\hat{f}_a. \qquad \text{(A.23)}$$

The first term on the right hand side in (A.23) is of lower order as seen when verifying (A.16). We will now deal with the last term on the right hand side in (A.23) where the middle term can be dealt with in the very same way. Note that for any bounded functions ζ,

$$\int k_h(x - X_i)\zeta(x)dx = h\int k(u)\zeta(X_i + hu)du = h\rho(X_i),$$

which implicitly defines ρ. We define ζ by $\zeta(x) = \lambda(x, \theta_0)w(x)E\hat{f}_a(T(\mu_0, x))$. Hence

$$\begin{aligned}
&\int \{\hat{r}(x) - E\hat{r}(x)\}E\hat{f}_a(T(\mu_0, x))\lambda(x, \theta_0)w(x)dx \\
&= \int \{\hat{r}(x) - E\hat{r}(x)\}\zeta(x)dx \\
&= \frac{1}{Nh}\sum_i \int k_h(x - X_i)\zeta(x)dxY_i - E\left[\frac{1}{Nh}\sum_i \int k_h(x - X_i)\zeta(x)dxY_i\right] \\
&= \frac{1}{N}\sum_i \rho(X_i)Y_i - E[\rho(X_1)Y_1] = O_p(N^{-1/2}). \qquad \text{(A.24)}
\end{aligned}$$

This procedure can be applied in turn to all terms in the expansion of the left hand side of (A.18) and so (A.18) holds. This concludes the proof of (A.15). The proof for $\mathscr{C}_1$ is not very different. We have to show that the left hand sides in (A.16) and (A.17) are $o(N^{-1/2})$ and that the left hand side in (A.18) times $\sqrt{N}$ converges to a normal distribution. The proof of the first of these three conditions is simple; just apply the bandwidth restrictions of $\mathscr{C}_1$ to the proof of (A.16) for case $\mathscr{C}_2$. The second is not hard either. Note that

$$\begin{aligned} E\hat{r} &= \frac{1}{Nh}\sum_i E[k_h(x - X_i)Y_i] = \frac{1}{h}E[k_h(x - X_1)\{\xi_{01} + \xi_{02}m_a(X_1)\}] \\ &= \xi_{01}E\hat{f} + \xi_{02}E\hat{r}_a, \end{aligned}$$

and hence

$$E\Lambda_N(x, \theta_0) = E\hat{r}E\hat{f}_a - \xi_{01}E\hat{f}E\hat{f}_a - \xi_{02}E\hat{f}E\hat{r}_a = 0.$$

For the third we again refer to the proof for $\mathscr{C}_2$. From (A.24) and the discussion preceding it, it follows that the left hand side of (A.18) times $\sqrt{N}$ can be written

$$\frac{1}{\sqrt{N}}\sum_i \left\{\sum_{j=1}^{J} (\rho_j(X_i) - E\rho_j(X_1))\right\} \tag{A.25}$$

where J is some finite positive integer. By the Lindeberg–Levy central limit theorem, (A.25) is asymptotically normal with a finite variance. □

Proof of theorem 2

Because Θ is an open set and $\hat{\theta}$ is a consistent estimate of $\theta_0 \in \Theta$, $\hat{\theta}$ will (for sufficiently large N) lie in Θ a.s.. So we can assume that $\hat{\theta} \in \Theta$ and that no $\theta \notin \Theta$ exists such that $\|\theta - \theta_0\| < \|\hat{\theta} - \theta_0\|$. Because S, T, m_a are all differentiable we use the mean value theorem to obtain

$$\tilde{m}(x, \theta) - \tilde{m}(x, \theta_0) = (\hat{\theta} - (\theta_0)^{\tau}\begin{bmatrix} S_1(\xi^*, \hat{m}_a(T(\mu^*, x))) \\ T_1(\mu^*, x)\hat{m}_a'(T(\mu^*, x))S_2(\xi^*, \hat{m}_a(T(\mu^*, x))) \end{bmatrix}, \tag{A.26}$$

where subscripts indicate to which argument the partial derivative was taken and θ^* – which may depend on x – lies between θ and θ_0 and hence in Θ. As a result of the argument just preceding this theorem and of Slutsky's theorem, the second factor on the right hand side in (A.26) is bounded in probability. As assumed, the first factor is $o_p(n^{-2/5})$. □

Proof of theorem 3

The asymptotic mean squared error, as defined in (3.1), of the pooled estimate, as a function of Ω reads

$$\begin{aligned} M_p(\Omega) &= \mathscr{B}_p^2(\Omega) + \mathscr{V}_p(\Omega) \\ &= [\Omega\mathscr{B}_* + (1 - \Omega)\mathscr{B}]^2 + \Omega^2\mathscr{V}_* + (1 - \Omega)^2\mathscr{V} \\ &\quad + 2\Omega(1 - \Omega)\text{as cov}(\hat{m}_a^*, \hat{m}_a). \end{aligned}$$

The asymptotic covariance in the last displayed equation is of lower order than the two variances, which are $O(N^{-1}h^{-1})$; we will not prove this, but a heuristic argument is easy to give. The principal reason that the above statement is true is that $E[k_h^2(x - X_1)] = O(h)$ and $E[k_h(x - X_1)k_h(x - W_1)] = O(h^2)$, unless the density of (X_1, W_1) is degenerate. Thus, ignoring the last term, expanding the last displayed equation leads to

$$M_p(\Omega) = [\mathscr{V}_* + \mathscr{V} + (\mathscr{B}_* - \mathscr{B})^2]\Omega^2 + 2[\mathscr{B}(\mathscr{B}_* - \mathscr{B}) - \mathscr{V}]\Omega + [\mathscr{B}^2 + \mathscr{V}]. \qquad (A.27)$$

Minimizing $M_p(\Omega)$ with respect to Ω gives (3.2). □

Proof of theorem 4

Note first that $\mathscr{V}$ and $\mathscr{V}_*$ can be consistently estimated if f_a, f_*, σ_a^2 and σ_*^2 can, where σ_a^2 and σ_*^2 correspond to σ^2 in (3.1). f_* and f_a can be consistently estimated, as follows from lemma 5. The estimation of σ_a^2 and σ_*^2 is discussed in the text. In case $\mathscr{C}_3$, $(\mathscr{B}_* - \mathscr{B}) = 0$, and hence Ω^* is a function of $\mathscr{V}_*$ and $\mathscr{V}$ only, which are estimable. In case $\mathscr{C}_4$, h^4 tends to zero faster than $(Nh)^{-1}$ and hence the squared bias terms are of lower order than the variance terms and again Ω^* depends (for large N) only on the variances. In case $\mathscr{C}_5$, $f_a, f_a', f_a'', r_a, r_a', r_a'', f_*, f_*', f_*'', r_*, r_*', r_*''$ can all be estimated consistently in view of lemma 5 and hence so can m_a, m_a'', m_*, m_*'' and thence $\mathscr{B}, \mathscr{B}_*, \mathscr{V}, \mathscr{V}_*$.

It remains to be shown that a consistent estimate for Ω^* automatically leads to the same efficiency. We have

$$\begin{aligned}\hat{m}_{p,\Omega}(x) &= \{\hat{\Omega}x) - \Omega^*(x)\}\hat{m}_a^*(x) + \{\Omega^*(x) - \hat{\Omega}(x)\}\hat{m}_a(x) + \hat{m}_{p,\Omega^*}(x)\\ &= \{\Omega(x) - \Omega^*(x)\}\{\hat{m}_a^*(x) - \hat{m}_a(x)\} + \hat{m}_{p,\Omega^*}(x)\\ &= \hat{m}_{p,\Omega^*}(x) + o_p(|\hat{m}_a^*(x) - m_a(x)\}| + |\hat{m}_a(x) - m_a(x)|),\end{aligned}$$

because $\hat{m}_a^*$ and $\hat{m}_a$ converge at the same rate to m_a and Ω is consistent for Ω^*. □

Proof of theorem 5

Because M_p (defined as in (A.27)) is quadratic in Ω, there are two (possibly coinciding) solutions to $M_p(\Omega) = M_p(\Omega_0)$, one of them being $\Omega = \Omega_0$, where we shall call the other one Ω_e. Thus, $M_p(\Omega) - M_p(\Omega_0) = 0$ is equivalent to

$$\begin{aligned}&\{\mathscr{V}_* + \mathscr{V} + (\mathscr{B}_* - \mathscr{B})^2\}\{\Omega^2 - \Omega_0^2\} + 2\{\mathscr{B}(\mathscr{B}_* - \mathscr{B}) - \mathscr{V}\}\{\Omega - \Omega_0\} = 0\\ &\Leftrightarrow \{\mathscr{V}_* + \mathscr{V} + (\mathscr{B}_* - \mathscr{B})^2\}\{\Omega - \Omega_0\}\{\Omega + \Omega_0\}\\ &+ 2\{\mathscr{B}(\mathscr{B}_* - \mathscr{B}) - \mathscr{V}\}\{\Omega - \Omega_0\} = 0,\end{aligned}$$

such that $\Omega_e = 2\Omega^* - \Omega_0$. If $\Omega^* \geqslant (\leqslant)\ \Omega_0$, $2\Omega^* - \Omega_0 \geqslant (\leqslant)\ \Omega_0$, and because $\Omega^* \in [\Omega_0, 2\Omega^* - \Omega_0]$ $(\Omega^* \in [2\Omega^* - \Omega_0, \Omega_0])$, $M_p(\Omega)$ is less than $M_p(\Omega_0)$, in all points on the afore-mentioned interval. □

Proof of theorem 6

Expanding (3.4), we have

$$\hat{\sigma}^2 = \frac{2}{N_D}\sum_{i=1}^{N_D}\{m(X_{(i)}) - m(X_{(i-1)})\}^2$$

$$+ \frac{4}{N_D}\sum_{i=1}^{N_D}\{m(X_{(i)}) - m(X_{(i-1)})\}\{U_{(i)} - U_{(i-1)}\}$$
$$+ \frac{2}{N_D}\sum_{i=1}^{N_D}\{U_{(i)} - U_{(i-1)}\}^2. \tag{A.28}$$

By $E[U_i|X_j] = 0$, for all i, j, and independence across U_i, the last term in (A.28) is $\sigma^2 + o_p(1)$, as $N \to \infty$. On the other hand, by the mean value theorem, the first term on the right of (A.28) is

$$O\left(\frac{1}{N_D}\sum_{i=1}^{N_D}(X_{(i)} - X_{(i-1)})^2\right) = O_p(N_D^{-1}),$$

and if f is positive on $[a, b]$ this is $O_p(N^{-1})$. From these properties and the Cauchy inequality, the intermediary term in (A.28) is $O_p(N_D^{-1/2})$. It follows that

$$\hat{\sigma}^2 \xrightarrow{P} \sigma^2, \quad \text{as } N \to \infty \quad \square$$

Appendix 2: some technical lemmas

The lemmas in this appendix are fairly standard. The assumptions made in the main body of this chapter, in so far as they concern r, k, and f, and the conditions on the various variables and the way they are related apply here as well. In this section Ξ should just be read as any compact set on which f is bounded away from zero.

Lemma 1. We have

$$\sup_{x\in\mathcal{R}}|Er^{(l)}(x) - r^{(l)}(x)| = O_p(h^{2-l}), \quad l = 0, 1, 2.$$

Proof.

We write

$$\sup_x|E\hat{r}^{(l)}(x) - r^{(l)}(x)| = \sup_x\left|\frac{1}{h^{l+1}}E[k_h^{(l)}(x - X_1)m(X_1)] - r^{(l)}(x)\right|$$
$$= \sup_x\left|\frac{1}{h^{l+1}}\int k_h^{(l)}(x - u)r(u)du - r^{(l)}(x)\right|.$$

For $l > 0$ the partial integration rule can be applied to obtain

$$\sup_x\left|-\frac{1}{h^l}[k_h^{(l-1)}(x - u)r(u)]_{-\infty}^{\infty} + \frac{1}{h^l}\int k_h^{(l-1)}(x - u)r^{(l)}(u)du - r^{(l)}(x)\right|. \tag{A.29}$$

Because $r \in \mathcal{G}_2$, r is bounded and because k integrates to one, $k_h(-\infty) = k_h(\infty) = 0$. Therefore, the first term in (A.29) is zero. For $l = 2$ this step can be repeated. This leaves

$$\sup_x\left|\frac{1}{h}\int k_h(x - u)r^{(l)}(u)du - r^{(l)}(x)\right| = \sup_x\left|\int k(v)[r^{(l)}(x - hv) - r^{(l)}(x)]dv\right|. \tag{A.30}$$

If $l = 2$ the boundedness of r'' implies that the above expression is $O(1)$. For $l = 0$ we get by a first order Taylor expansion

$$\sup_x \left| \int k(v)[hvr'(x) + h^2v^2r''(x - hv; x)]dv \right|,$$

where $(x - hv; x)$ is some number between $x - hv$ and x. Because $k \in \mathcal{K}_2$, $\int k(v)vdv = 0$ and thus by $k \in \mathcal{K}_2$ and $r \in \mathcal{G}_2$ the last displayed expression is $O(h^2)$. For $l = 1$ we write using the mean value theorem

$$h \sup_x \left| \int k(v)[vr''(x - hv; x)]dv \right|.$$

Again, by the assumed boundedness of r'' the last displayed expression is $O(h)$. □

A remark that should be made is that if r'' is first order Lipschitz-continuous, (A.30) is $O(h)$, and therefore so is $Er''(x) - r''(x)$.

Obviously, the above lemma can just as well be applied to $\hat{f}$. This also holds for the following uniform convergence result:

Lemma 2. We have

$$\sup_x |\hat{r}^{(l)}(x) - E\hat{r}^{(l)}(x)| = O_p(N^{-1/2}h^{-l-1}),\ l = 0, 1, 2. \tag{A.31}$$

Proof.

We write the left hand side of (A.31) as

$$\sup_x \left| \frac{1}{Nh^{l+1}} \sum_j [k_h^{(l)}(x - X_j)Y_j - E(k_h^{(l)}(x - X_j)Y_j)] \right|.$$

Using $k(x) = \int K(u)e^{iux}$, we obtain

$$\sup_x \left| \frac{1}{Nh^{l+1}} \sum_j \int u^l K(u) \{e^{iu((x-X_j)/h)}Y_j - E(e^{iu((x-X_j)/h)}Y_j)\} du \right|. \tag{A.32}$$

After substitution of $v = u/h$, (A.32) can be bounded by

$$\int |v^l K(hv)| \sup_x |e^{ivx}| \left| \frac{1}{N} \sum_j \{e^{-ivX_j}Y_j - E(e^{-ivX_j}Y_j)\} \right| dv. \tag{A.33}$$

The expression in (A.33) is nonnegative, so it suffices to show that its expectation is $O(N^{-1/2}h^{-l-1})$ or

$$\int |v^l K(hv)| \sup_x |e^{ivx}| E \left| \frac{1}{N} \sum_j \{e^{-ivX_j}Y_j - E(e^{-ivX_j}Y_j)\} \right| dv = O(N^{-1/2}h^{-l-1}). \tag{4.34}$$

But $\sup_x |e^{ivx}| = 1$ and

$$\int |v^l K(hv)| dv = \frac{1}{h^{l+1}} \int |u^l K(u)| du = O(h^{-l-1}),$$

by the assumption that $k \in \mathcal{K}_2$, so we only need to show that the expectation in (A.34) is $O(N^{-1/2})$ uniformly in v. Thus, by the inequality of Cauchy–Schwarz

$$\sup_v E\left|\frac{1}{N}\sum_j \{e^{-ivX_j}Y_j - E(e^{-ivX_j}Y_j)\}\right| \leqslant \sup_v \sqrt{E\left|\frac{1}{N}\sum_j \{e^{-ivX_j}Y_j - E(e^{-ivX_j}Y_j)\}\right|^2}$$
$$= O(N^{-1/2}). \quad \square$$

Lemma 3. We have:

$$\sup_{x\in\Xi}|\hat{r}^{(l)}(x) - r^{(l)}(x)| = O_p(N^{-1/2}h^{-l-1} + h^{2-l})$$

Proof.
Is a trivial combination of lemmas 1 and 2. $\square$

Lemma 4. We have

$$\sup_{x\in\Xi} V\hat{r}^{(l)}(x) = O(N^{-1}h^{-2l-1}), \quad \sup_{x\in\Xi} V\hat{f}^{(l)}(x) = O(N^{-1}h^{-2l-1}).$$

Proof.

We will only show the first result. We have

$$V\hat{r}^{(l)}(x) = E[\hat{r}^{(l)}(x)]^2 - E^2\hat{r}^{(l)}(x)$$
$$= \frac{1}{N^2h^{2l+2}}\sum_i \{E[k_h^{(l)}(x - X_i)(m(X_i) + U_i)]^2$$
$$- E[k_h^{(l)}(x - X_i)(m(X_i) + U_i)]\}. \quad \text{(A.35)}$$

The last expectation on the right hand side in the above equation is by lemma 1, $O(h^2)$. Because $E[U_1|X_1] = 0$, (A.35) is

$$\frac{1}{Nh^{2l+2}}\{E[(k_h^{(l)}(x - X_1))^2\, m^2(X_1)]$$
$$+ E[(k_h^{(l)}(x - X_1))^2E[U_1^2|X_1]]\} + O(N^{-1}h^{-2l}).$$

Expanding the first expectation in the above expression we obtain (using the conditions on q and k)

$$\int [k_h^{(l)}(x - v)]^2m^2(v)f(v)dv = h\int [k^{(l)}(u)]^2q(x - hu)du = O(h). \quad \square$$

Lemma 5. We have at any point $x \in \Xi$

$$\hat{r}^{(l)}(x) - r^{(l)}(x) = O_p(N^{-1/2}h^{-l-1/2} + h^{2-l})$$

and if r'' is first order Lipschitz-continuous, $\hat{r}^{(2)}(x) - r^{(2)}(x) = O_p(N^{-1/2}h^{-5/2} + h)$.

Proof.

Follows immediately from lemmas 1 (and the remark immediately after it) and 4. □

Of course lemma 5 holds also for $\hat{f}$ with respect to f.

Lemma 6. Suppose we have for all x that $\hat{r}_{\omega}(x) = \hat{r}^{(\omega_1)}(x)\hat{r}^{(\omega_2)}(x)$, where $\omega_1, \omega_2 \leqslant 2$. Let $\tilde{\omega} = \omega_1 + \omega_2 + 2$. Let $r \in \mathscr{G}_2$ and let the kernel be $k \in \mathscr{K}_2$. Then

$$E\hat{r}_{\omega}(x) - E\hat{r}^{(\omega_1)}(x)E\hat{r}^{(\omega_2)}(x) = O(N^{-1}h^{1-\tilde{\omega}}),$$

for all x.

Proof.

$$\begin{aligned}
&E[\hat{r}^{(\omega_1)}(x)\hat{r}^{(\omega_2)}(x)] - E\hat{r}^{(\omega_1)}(x)E\hat{r}^{(\omega_2)}(x)\\
&= \frac{1}{N^2h^{\tilde{\omega}}}\sum_i\sum_j\{E[k_h^{(\omega_1)}(x - X_i)Y_i k_h^{(\omega_2)}(x - X_j)Y_j]\\
&\quad - E[k_h^{(\omega_1)}(x - X_i)Y_i]\,E[k_h^{(\omega_2)}(x - X_j)Y_j]\}\\
&= \frac{1}{N^2h^{\tilde{\omega}}}\sum_i \operatorname{cov}(k_h^{(\omega_1)}(x - X_i)Y_i,\ k_h^{(\omega_2)}(x - X_i)Y_i)\\
&= O(N^{-1}h^{1-\tilde{\omega}}). \quad \square
\end{aligned}$$

Note

This chapter is based on research funded by the Economic and Social Research Council (ESRC), reference number R000233609. It is part of the PhD thesis at the London School of Economics of the first author under the supervision of the second author. We thank two anonymous referees for their valuable comments. The first author thanks the Foreign and Commonwealth Office and his parents for financial support.

References

Amemiya, T. (1985) *Advanced Econometrics*. Oxford: Basil Blackwell.

Gasser, T., Müller, H.-G., Köhler, W., Molinari, L. and Prader, A. (1984) Non-parametric regression analysis of growth curves. *Annals of Statistics*, 12, 210–29.

Hall, P. and Titterington, M. (1988) On confidence bands in nonparametric density estimation and regression. *Journal of Multivariate Analysis*, 27, 228–54.

Härdle, W. (1990) *Applied Nonparametric Regression*. Cambridge: Cambridge University Press.

Härdle, W. and Marron, J. S. (1990) Semiparametric comparison of regression curves. *Annals of Statistics*, 18, 63–89.

Kendall, M. G. and Stuart, A. (1967) *The Advanced Theory of Statistics, volume 2*, 2nd edn. London: Charles Griffin & Co.

Mack, Y. P. (1981) Local properties of k-NN regression estimates. *SIAM Journal of Algebraic and Discrete Methods*, 2, 311–23.

Prakasa Rao, B. L. S. (1983) *Nonparametric functional estimation*. New York: Academic Press.

Rao, C. R. (1977) Prediction of future observations with special reference to linear models. In P. R. Krishnaiah (ed.), *Multivariate Analysis IV*. Amsterdam: North-Holland, pp. 193–208.

8 On the Theory of Testing Covariance Stationarity under Moment Condition Failure

Peter C. B. Phillips and Mico Loretan

1 Introduction

Diagnostic testing is now a familiar facet of regression analysis in econometrics. Among the many different procedures in general use, one of the most useful principles for the construction of diagnostics is Rao's (1947) score test, which is popularly known in the econometrics literature as the LM test, following the work of Silvey (1959), and using a terminology that is appealing to the econometrician's fondness for shadow prices and Lagrange multipliers. The score test enables us to assess the adequacy of a given convenient specification against that of a more general maintained hypothesis. Diagnostics that help to determine the adequacy of convenient assumptions are, of course, useful outside the immediate context of regression theory and maximum likelihood estimation.

The context of diagnostic evaluation that concerns us in the present chapter is time series, where it is often both customary and convenient to transform series to "achieve stationarity" before subsequent analysis. For instance, we frequently difference the logarithms of financial time series to produce a time series of financial returns. Such differencing will indeed remove a stochastic trend when there is a unit root in the time series, but it does not mean that the resulting series of returns is covariance stationary. Further diagnostic analysis that focuses attention on the properties of the second moments of the return data are needed for this purpose. This is the type of diagnostic evaluation that is the subject of the present chapter.

A feature of stock market data that has recently come to light is the apparent nonstationarity in the unconditional variance of stock returns. For instance, Pagan and Schwert (1990a, b) present some strong evidence that stock return data over long periods cannot be assumed to be covariance stationary. In their 1990a paper they plot reursive estimates of the variance of monthly stock returns from 1835 to 1987 and point to the dramatic increase in the variance in the decade after 1930. Figure 8.1 reproduces this plot of

$$\hat{\mu}_2(t) = t^{-1}\Sigma_1^t(\hat{u}_k - \bar{u}_t)^2, \quad \bar{u}_t = t^{-1}\Sigma_1^t\hat{u}_k \tag{1.1}$$

where $\hat{u}_t$ is the difference between the actual stock return in period t and an estimate of its conditional mean (calculated by taking the residuals from a regression on monthly dummies, as described in section 2.2 of Pagan and Schwert, 1990a). The distinctive pattern of this plot makes it highly unlikely that the data are covariance stationary. In their 1990b paper, Pagan and Schwert formally test this hypothesis using a postsample prediction test, a cusum test and a modified scaled range test. The results show strong evidence of departure from the null of covariance stationarity.

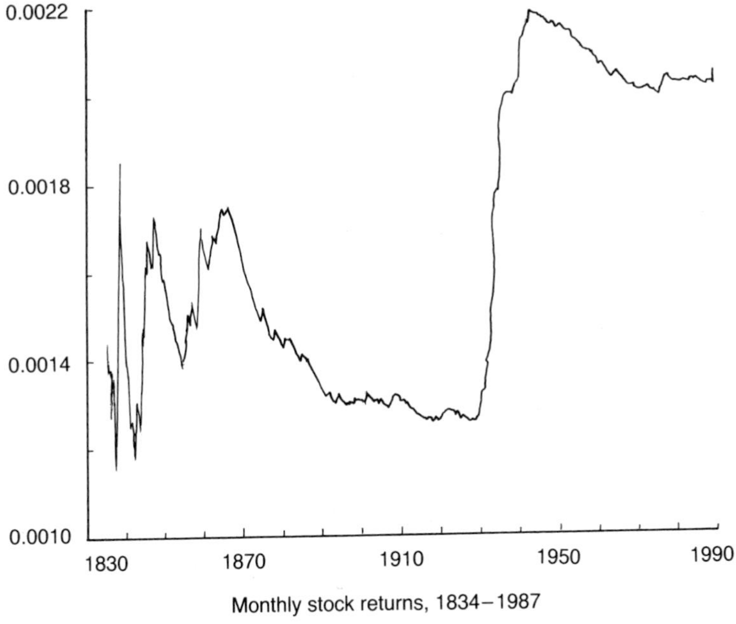

Figure 8.1 Recursive variance: monthly stock returns 1834–1987.

The idea of calculating the recursive variance (1.1) is due to Mandelbrot (1963), who suggested recursive variance plots as a useful diagnostic for the nonexistence of second order moments. When population variances do not exist, the behavior of the recursive sample variance is very different from that of a covariance stationary process. Figures 8.2 and 8.3 illustrate these differences by plotting recursive sample variances of sequences of i.i.d. draws from standard symmetric stable and Gaussian distributions, respectively. As is apparent from these plots the recursive sample variance of a stable process with exponent $\alpha < 2$ is subject to jumps and shows no tendency to settle down to a particular value as the sample size increases. In fact, for random draws from a stable law with exponent $\alpha < 2$ we have $\hat{\mu}_2(t) \rightarrow_{\text{a.s.}} \infty$. Such behavior is quite distinct from that of a Gaussian or other finite variance process where the recursive sample variance converges a.s. to the population variance as $t \rightarrow \infty$.

In the light of these differences it is natural to ask whether rejections of covariance stationarity for stock returns in formal statistical tests are simply a byproduct of thick tails in the generating mechanism. Most asymptotic distribution theory that is used in empirical econometric research relies on moment conditions that carefully

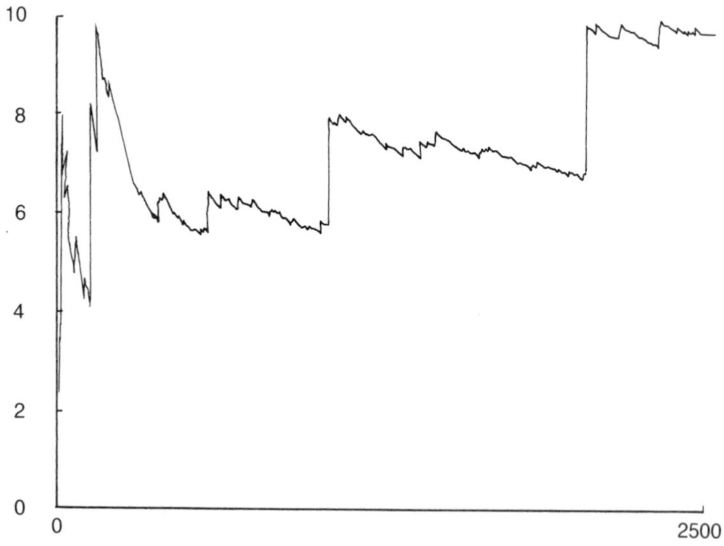

Figure 8.2 Recursive variance: i.i.d. symmetric, stable variates, $\alpha = 1.5$, $n = 2500$.

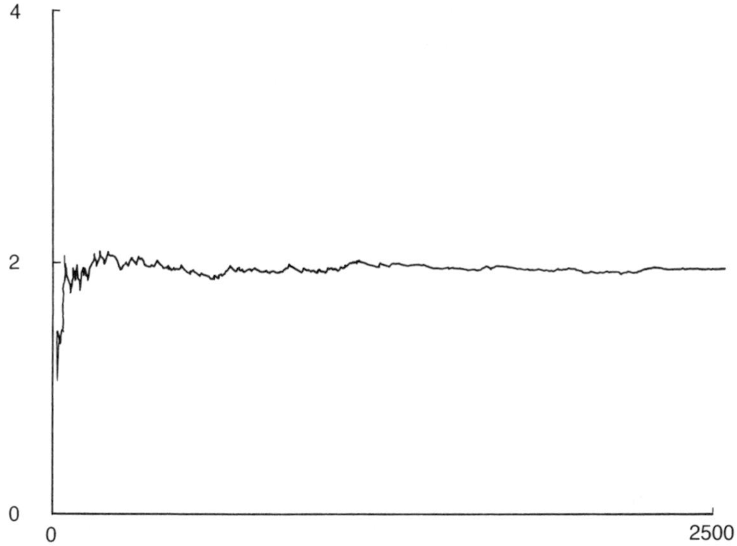

Figure 8.3 Recursive variance: i.i.d. Gaussian variates, $\sigma^2 = 2$, $n = 2500$.

control outlier occurrences. Indeed, it is not unusual, and in many cases it is quite reasonable, to see conditions of the type "let all required moments exist." However, in financial and commodity market time series the extent of the outlier activity casts doubt on the suitability of generic moment existence assumptions and this concern motivated Mandelbrot's original investigation. In the present case, it is important to note that since the recursive sample *variance* (1.1) is the object under study, conventional asymptotic distribution theory for this quantity calls for the existence of at least fourth order moments of the underlying data in the maintained hypothesis. This seems like a tall order when the series is common stock returns.

The present chapter seeks to determine the effect on the asymptotic theory for statistics such as the recursive sample variance (1.1) when there is a relaxation in moment conditions on the underlying data. Our attention will concentrate on tests for covariance stationarity that involve sample second moments of the data. Principal among these are sample split prediction tests for constant variance, cusum of squares tests, and modified scaled range tests. These tests were used by Pagan and Schwert (1990b) in their study of monthly stock returns and we will attempt to reevaluate their empirical findings in the light of the new asymptotic theory. There are many other applications of our theory that are relevant to diagnostic testing methods in econometrics, such as LM tests for ARCH and GARCH effects which also rely on fourth moment conditions.

The chapter is organized as follows. Section 2 presents some preliminary theory concerning the asymptotic distribution of sample second moments when fourth moments may not be finite. This theory is employed in section 3 to develop an asymptotic theory for various tests of covariance stationarity. Conventional theory for these tests involves standard normal and Brownian bridge asymptotics. When fourth moment conditions fail we show that the new limit theory involves asymmetric stable processes and, in particular, a stable–Levy bridge process in place of the usual Brownian bridge and a quadratic variation process in place of the usual normalizing constant. It is also shown that conventional tests for homogeneous variances have reduced asymptotic power when fourth moments are infinite and are actually inconsistent when the variance is infinite. We therefore propose a new test of heterogeneity that is consistent in the infinite variance case. This test involves the use of consistent estimates of the scale coefficient and characteristic exponent of the tail of a distribution of the asymptotic Pareto–Levy type. The estimate of the characteristic exponent may also be used to construct a consistent test about the size of the maximal moment exponent, for instance whether the fourth moment is finite. Some concluding remarks are made in section 4.

2 Some Preliminary Discussion of Heavy-tailed Innovations and Limit Theory for Sample Second Moments

Let (ε_t) be an i.i.d. sequence whose tail behavior is of the Pareto–Levy form, viz.

$$P(\varepsilon > x) = d_1 x^{-\alpha}(1 + \alpha_1(x)), \quad x > 0, \quad d_1 > 0$$
$$P(\varepsilon < -x) = d_2 x^{-\alpha}(1 + \alpha_2(x)), \quad x > 0, \quad d_2 > 0 \qquad \text{(C1)}$$

where $\alpha_i(x) \to 0$ $(i = 1, 2)$ as $x \to \infty$. When $0 < \alpha < 2$, (C1) ensures that ε lies in the normal domain of attraction of a stable law with characteristic exponent parameter α and we shall write $\varepsilon \in \mathcal{N}\mathcal{D}(\alpha)$ to signify this fact (the reader is referred to Ibragimov and Linnik, 1971, or Brieman, 1992, for an introduction to the theory of domains of attraction and stable laws). When $\alpha > 2$, ε is in the normal domain of attraction of a normal distribution. In the latter case it is important to note that when $2 < \alpha < 4$ we have $\varepsilon^2 \in \mathcal{ND}(\alpha/2)$, so that partial sums of ε^2 are no longer in the domain of attraction of a normal distribution. Obviously, such a distinction can play an important role in the asymptotic behavior of tests that are based on quantities like the recursive sample variance (1.1).

We add the following centering condition:

$$\begin{aligned}&\text{If } \alpha > 1 \text{ in (C1) then we require } E(\varepsilon) = 0.\\ &\text{If } \alpha = 1 \text{ we require } \varepsilon =_d -\varepsilon \\ &\text{(i.e. } \varepsilon \text{ is symmetrically distributed about the origin).}\end{aligned} \tag{C2}$$

Note that, when $\alpha < 1$ in (C1), no centering will be required. But this case is unlikely to be of importance in stock market data for which point estimates of α have typically been in the range $1.2 < \alpha < 2.0$ (see Fama, 1965, and more recent work by Blattberg and Gonedes, 1974, and Fielitz and Rozelle, 1982; and see So, 1987, Loretan, 1991, and Loretan and Phillips, 1994, on estimates of α for exchange rate series). However, when $\alpha < 2$, no centering will be needed for partial sums of $\varepsilon_t^2 \in \mathcal{ND}(\alpha/2)$ and this turns out to have very important implications on the asymptotic properties of tests based on (1.1), as we shall see in section 3.

If the observed series is generated by the linear process

$$y_t = \sum_{j=0}^{\infty} c_j \varepsilon_{t-j} \tag{2.1}$$

where ε_t satisfies (C1) and (C2), then the series for y_t is convergent a.s., provided the coefficients c_j satisfy a suitable summability condition. We shall employ the following condition

$$\Sigma_1^{\infty} j |c_j|^p < \infty \quad \text{for } 0 < p < \alpha, \quad p \leqslant 1 \tag{C3}$$

because it is useful in the development of our asymptotic theory. Note that the series (2.1) converges a.s. provided $\Sigma_1^{\infty} |c_j|^p < \infty$ for $0 < p < \alpha$, $p \leqslant 1$ (see Brockwell and Davis, 1991, p. 536), so that (C3) is stronger than is necessary for (2.1) to be well defined. But note also that (C3) holds whenever y_t is generated by a stationary ARMA process because then the coefficients in (2.1) decline geometrically and thereby trivially satisfy (C3). Thus, (C3) is sufficiently general to cover many cases of interest.

If $\varepsilon_t \in \mathcal{ND}(\alpha)$ with $0 < \alpha < 2$ we also have $y_t \in \mathcal{VD}(\alpha)$; and if ε_t follows a symmetric stable law then so too does y_t and we have the following distributional equivalence:

$$y_t =_d [\Sigma_{j=0}^{\infty}|c_j|^{\alpha}]^{1/\alpha}\varepsilon_t.$$

For these and many other aspects of the linear processes and heavy-tailed innovations the reader is referred to the books by Brockwell and Davis (1991, chapter 13.2) and by Ibragimov and Linnik (1971, chapter 2). The limit theory for sample means and covariances of time series generated as in (2.1) was developed by Davis and Resnick (1985a, b, 1986) and a recent treatment is given in Phillips and Solo (1992).

As remarked above, under (C3), (2.1) includes all stationary ARMA processes and in what follows it will be convenient for us to explicitly work with the AR(p) process

$$y_t = \Sigma_{i=1}^{p}\varphi_i y_{t-i} + \varepsilon_t \tag{2.2}$$

where the roots of $z^p - \Sigma_{i=1}^{p}\phi_i z^{p-i} = 0$ all lie inside the unit circle.

Under (C1) and (C2) with $0 < \alpha < 2$ we have the normalizing sequence

$$a_n = \inf\{x: P(|\varepsilon| > x) \leqslant n^{-1}\} = dn^{1/\alpha} \tag{2.3}$$

for some constant d. When we parameterize the scale coefficients in (C1) as $d_1 = pa^{\alpha}$, $d_2 = qa^{\alpha}$ (with $p + q = 1$) we find that the constant coefficient in (2.3) is $d = a$ and then $a_n = an^{1/\alpha}$. With this normalization sequence (in place of the usual $n^{1/2}$ for finite variance models) we have the following limit laws for $0 < \alpha < 2$:

$$a_n^{-1}\Sigma_1^n\varepsilon_t \to_d U_\alpha(1),\ a_n^{-1}\Sigma_1^{[nr]}\varepsilon_t \to_d U_\alpha(r), \tag{2.4}$$

$$[a_n^{-1}\Sigma_1^{[nr]}\varepsilon_t,\ a_n^{-2}\Sigma_1^{[nr]}\varepsilon_t^2] \to_d (U_\alpha(r),\ \textstyle\int_0^r(dU_\alpha)^2). \tag{2.5}$$

Here $U_\alpha(r)$ is the Levy α-stable process and $\int_0^r(dU_\alpha)^2 = [U_\alpha]_r$ is its quadratic variation process. The first result of (2.4) is classical (e.g. Ibragimov and Linnik, 1971, chapter 2), the second is its functional version, and (2.5) is a joint functional limit law for first and second sample moments that is proved in Resnick (1986, pp. 94–5). Some typical sample trajectories of a symmetric stable Levy process $U_\alpha(r)$ are plotted in Phillips (1990).

When $2 < \alpha < 4$ we have both $n^{-1}\Sigma_1^n\varepsilon_t \to_{\text{a.s.}} 0$ and $n^{-1}\Sigma_1^n\varepsilon_t^2 \to_{\text{a.s.}} \sigma_\varepsilon^2 = E(\varepsilon_t^2)$. However, since $\varepsilon_t^2 \in \mathcal{ND}(\alpha/2)$ we also have a stable limit distribution theory for the sample second moments. In particular, we have

$$a_n^{-2}\Sigma_1^n(\varepsilon_t^2 - \sigma_\varepsilon^2) \to_d U_{\alpha/2}(1),\ a_n^{-2}\Sigma_1^{[nr]}(\varepsilon_t^2 - \sigma_\varepsilon^2) \to_d U_{\alpha/2}(r) \tag{2.6}$$

$$[a_n^{-2}\Sigma_1^{[nr]}(\varepsilon_t^2 - \sigma_\varepsilon^2),\ a_n^{-4}\Sigma_1^{[nr]}(\varepsilon_t^2 - \sigma_\varepsilon^2)^2] \to_d [U_{\alpha/2}(r),\ \textstyle\int_0^r(dU_{\alpha/2})^2]. \tag{2.7}$$

Since the distribution of $\varepsilon_t^2 - \sigma_\varepsilon^2$ is asymmetric with a finite left extremity $(-\sigma_\varepsilon^2)$ the limit law represented by $U_{\alpha/2}(r)$ in (2.6) is an asymmetric stable process. The asymmetry coefficient in the limit stable law is given by $\beta = 1$. Moreover, as $\alpha \searrow 2$ the asymmetry of the limit process becomes more heavily accentuated. Ultimately, when $\alpha < 2$ we have

$$a_n^{-2}\Sigma_1^{[nr]}\varepsilon_t^2 \rightarrow_d U_{\alpha/2}^{+}(r)$$

and in this case $U_{\alpha/2}^{+}(r)$ is a positive stable process on $D[0, 1]$, i.e. the increments of $U_{\alpha/2}^{+}(r)$ are independent and follow a strictly positive stable law.

Finally, we observe that if y_t is generated by the AR(p) (2.2) the coefficients are consistently estimated by the OLS regression

$$y_t = \Sigma_{i=1}^{p}\hat{\phi}_i y_{t-i} + \hat{\varepsilon}_t \tag{2.8}$$

irrespective of the value of α (e.g. see Kanter and Steiger, 1974; Hannan and Kanter, 1977). Correspondingly, the OLS residual $\hat{\varepsilon}_t$ is consistent for ε_t for all $\alpha > 0$. When $\alpha > 2$, $\sigma_\varepsilon^2 = E(\varepsilon_t^2) < \infty$ and we have $\hat{\sigma}_\varepsilon^2 = n^{-1}\Sigma_1^n\hat{\varepsilon}_t^2 \rightarrow_p \sigma_\varepsilon^2$. Moreover, the following limit theory applies to sample variances of the residuals $\hat{\varepsilon}_t$.

Lemma 2.1. Let (C1), (C2) and (2.2) hold and $\hat{\varepsilon}_t$ be the residuals from (2.8).

(a) If $\alpha > 4$ and $v_\varepsilon = E(\varepsilon_t^2 - \sigma_\varepsilon^2)^2 = \kappa_4 + 2\sigma^4$ then

$$(nv_\varepsilon)^{-1/2}\Sigma_1^{[nr]}(\hat{\varepsilon}_t^2 - \hat{\sigma}_\varepsilon^2) \rightarrow_d B(r),$$

a standard Brownian bridge on $C[0, 1]$.

(b) If $0 < \alpha < 4$ then

$$a_n^{-2}\Sigma_1^{[nr]}(\hat{\varepsilon}_t^2 - \hat{\sigma}_\varepsilon^2) \rightarrow_d U_{\alpha/2}(r) - rU_{\alpha/2}(1) = K_{\alpha/2}(r)$$

a stable–Levy bridge or tied down stable Levy process on $D[0, 1]$. When $2 \leqslant \alpha < 4$, $U_{\alpha/2}(r)$ is a two-tailed asymmetric stable process. When $0 < \alpha < 2$, $U_{\alpha/2}(r)$ is a positive stable process, i.e. a stable process whose increments are independent and follow a positive stable law with parameter $\alpha/2$. □

3 Asymptotic Theory for Tests of Covariance Stationarity

In what follows our focus will be on the unconditional variance of a time series because our main concern is covariance stationarity, not the presence or absence of conditional heterogeneity. There are several ways of testing for homogeneity in the unconditional variance of a time series. We shall look first at the tests suggested in Pagan and Schwert (1990b) and later consider some others that look promising. Two general approaches are possible. The first is to work with the observed series y_t itself. For stock return data the series is nearly random but there is some evidence of moving average effects, which Pagan and Schwert (1990a) suggest may be due to nonsynchronous data and calendar effects. Thus, a second approach is to work with a general model like (2.1) and (2.2) that accommodates temporal dependence and use the residuals obtained from a suitable regression. Clearly, AR models offer a convenient choice for this approach and the OLS residuals $\hat{\varepsilon}_t$ from regressions like (2.8) consistently estimate the time series innovations ε_t for all $\alpha > 0$.

We shall examine both these approaches below.

Sample split prediction tests for covariance stationarity

Here we split the sample into two eras according to $n = n_1 + n_2$ with $n_1 = k_n n_2$ and consider the hypothesis that

$$H_0\colon E\hat{\mu}_2^{(1)} = E\hat{\mu}_2^{(2)}$$

where

$$\hat{\mu}_2^{(1)} = n_1^{-1}\Sigma_1^{n_1} y_t^2, \quad \hat{\mu}_2^{(2)} = n_2^{-1}\Sigma_{n_1+1}^{n} y_t^2.$$

Pagan and Schwert (1990b) set $k_n = 1$, define $\hat{\tau} = \hat{\mu}_2^{(1)} - \hat{\mu}_2^{(2)}$ and estimate the variance of $\hat{\tau}$ nonparametrically by $2\hat{v}$ where

$$\hat{v} = \hat{\gamma}_0 + 2\Sigma_{j=1}^{l}(1 - j/(l + 1))\hat{\gamma}_j,$$

corresponding to the use of Bartlett weights in the estimation of the spectrum. In the formula for $\hat{v}$, $\hat{\gamma}_j$ is the jth serial covariance of y_t^2 and l is a suitable lag truncation number ($l = 8$ in their empirical application). We assume that $l \to \infty$ as $n \to \infty$ in such a way that $l/n \to 0$. Then, when $\alpha > 4$, $\hat{v}$ is a consistent estimator of v by conventional theory under quite general conditions (see Andrews, 1991; Newey and West, 1987; Phillips, 1987).

We shall consider the general case where $k_n \to k$ with $k > 0$. Then $k/(1 + k)$ (respectively, $1/(1 + k)$) is the fraction of the overall sample in the limit that is in the first (second) era. A t-ratio test statistic for a sample split in the variance between the two eras can then be constructed on the basis of anticipated normal asymptotics for $\hat{\tau}$. Indeed, when fourth moments are finite we have from the proof of part (a) of theorem 3.1 below that

$$n_1^{1/2}\hat{\tau} \rightarrow_d N(0, (1 + k)v).$$

This leads to the statistic

$$V_k(\tau) = n_1^{1/2}\hat{\tau}/[(1 + k_n)\hat{v}]^{1/2}. \tag{3.1}$$

When $k = 1$, $V_1(\tau) = n_1^{1/2}\hat{\tau}/(2\hat{v})^{1/2}$ is the statistic suggested in Pagan and Schwert (1990b). When $k \neq 1$, $V_k(\tau)$ enables us to look at eras of unequal length.

The asymptotic distribution of $V_k(\tau)$ depends on the value of the parameter α as shown in the following:

Theorem 3.1. Assume (C1) to (C3) hold and $k_n \rightarrow k$ as $n \rightarrow \infty$ with $k > 0$ fixed. Then:

(a) If $\alpha > 4$, $V_k(\tau) \rightarrow_d N(0, 1)$.

(b) If $0 < \alpha < 4$,

$$V_k(\tau) \rightarrow_d [k\textstyle\int_0^1(dU_{\alpha/2})^2]^{-1/2}[(1 + k)U_{\alpha/2}(k/(1 + k)) - kU_{\alpha/2}(1)]$$
$$= \bar{V}_k, \text{ say.} \tag{3.2}$$

In (b) $U_{\alpha/2}(r)$ is an asymmetric stable process with characteristic exponent $\alpha/2$ when $2 \leqslant \alpha < 4$ and a positive stable process when $0 < \alpha < 2$. □

Remarks.

(i) When $\alpha > 4$, the limit distribution of $V_k(\tau)$ is standard normal, so that conventional critical values from the $N(0, 1)$ distribution can be used in testing H_0 under this maintained hypothesis that moments of the data are finite up to at least the fourth order.

(ii) When $\alpha < 4$ the limit distribution of $V_k(\tau)$ is a ratio of correlated stable variates. The limit distribution simplifies considerably when the length of the eras is the same in the limit, i.e. $k_n \rightarrow 1$.

Corollary 3.2. Suppose $k = 1$ and $0 < \alpha < 4$. Then

$$V_1(\tau) \rightarrow_d [\textstyle\int_0^1(dU^s_{\alpha/2})^2]^{-1/2}U^s_{\alpha/2}(1), \tag{3.3}$$

where $U^s_{\alpha/2}(r)$ is a symmetric stable process with characteristic exponent $\alpha/2$ on $D[0, 1]$. □

The limit distribution given by (3.3) is, in fact, the same as the limit distribution of a self normalized sum (or t-ratio) formed from an i.i.d. sequence of variates in the domain of attraction of a stable law with exponent parameter $\alpha/2$. Logan et al. (1973), Resnick (1986), and Phillips (1990) give various representations of this limit distribution – see Phillips (1990, equation 46) for the representation given here. It is known to be bimodal (Logan et al., 1973), and Phillips are Hajivassiliou, 1987, provide graphical plots), and nominal critical values from the $N(0, 1)$ distribution are known to be conservative at the conventional levels 1 and 5 percent, but to lead to reductions in power (see Efron, 1968). Thus, when $\alpha < 4$ we can expect that tests based on $V_1(\tau)$ and standard normal critical values will suffer power reductions compared with the case where $\alpha > 4$. This will be explored further below when we consider the limit behavior of power functions of this test.

(iii) When $\alpha > 4$, $U_{\alpha/2}(r)$ is standard Brownian motion $W(r)$ and since $(dW)^2 = dr$ a.s. we have

$$\int_0^1 (dU_{\alpha/2})^2 = 1 \text{ a.s.}$$

for the denominator of (3.2). A small calculation shows that

$$k^{-1/2}[W(k/(1 + k)) - k\{W(1) - W(k/(1 + k))\}] =_d N(0, 1)$$

so that the limit result (3.2) also yields part (a) as $\alpha \nearrow 4$.

(iv) When $k \neq 1$ and $\alpha < 4$, the limit distribution of $V_k(\tau)$ depends on k. This is because the construction of $V_k(\tau)$ is based on the explicit behavior of $n^{1/2}\hat{\tau}$ when $\alpha > 4$ (see 3.1) and ignores the random limit of the denominator of $V_k(\tau)$ when $\alpha < 4$. The use of subsample estimates also leads to a dependence on k in the limit. To see this, let $\hat{v}_1$ and $\hat{v}_2$ be estimates of v constructed just as $\hat{v}$ but based on the two separate data sets $\{y_t^2 \colon t = 1, \ldots, n_1\}$ and $\{y_t^2 \colon t = n_1 + 1, \ldots, n\}$. The composite estimate of v is now

$$\tilde{v} = \hat{v}_1 + k_n \hat{v}_2.$$

When $\alpha > 4$ we have $\hat{v}_1, \hat{v}_2 \rightarrow_p v$ and, hence, $\tilde{v} \rightarrow (1 + k)v$, the same limit as that of $\hat{v}$. Use of the composite variance estimate $\tilde{v}$ leads to the modified t-ratio statistic

$$\tilde{V}_k(\tau) = n_1^{1/2}\hat{\tau}/\tilde{v}^{1/2}.$$

The asymptotic distribution of $\tilde{V}_k(\tau)$ is as follows:

Theorem 3.3. Under the same conditions and with the same notation as theorem 3.1 we have:

(a) if $\alpha > 4$, $\tilde{V}_k(\tau) \rightarrow_d N(0, 1)$;

(b) if $0 < \alpha < 4$

$$\tilde{V}_k(\tau) \to_d \left[\int_0^{k/(1+k)} (dU_{\alpha/2})^2 + k^2 \int_{k/(1+k)}^1 (dU_{\alpha/2})^2 \right]^{-1/2}$$

$$\times [U_{\alpha/2}(k/(1+k)) - k\{U_{\alpha/2}(1) - U_{\alpha/2}(k/(1+k))\}] \quad (3.4)$$

$$\tilde{V}_1(\tau) \to_d [\textstyle\int_0^1 (dU^s_{\alpha/2})^2]^{-1/2} U^s_{\alpha/2}(1). \quad (3.5)$$

In (3.5) $U^s_{\alpha/2}(r)$ is a symmetric stable process with characteristic exponent $\alpha/2$ as in corollary 3.2. □

Analogous results to those of theorem 3.1 and 3.2 apply to split sample tests that are based on the residuals $\hat{\varepsilon}_t$ from the fitted model (2.8). We shall work below with the analogue of $\tilde{V}_k(\tau)$. Define

$$\hat{\tau}_\varepsilon = n_1^{-1}\Sigma_1^{n_1}\hat{\varepsilon}_t^2 - n_2^{-1}\Sigma_{n_1+1}^n\hat{\varepsilon}_t^2 = \hat{\sigma}_{1\varepsilon}^2 - \hat{\sigma}_\varepsilon^2,$$

$$\hat{v}_{1\varepsilon} = n_1^{-1}\Sigma_1^{n_1}(\hat{\varepsilon}_t^2 - \hat{\sigma}_{1\varepsilon}^2)^2, \quad \hat{v}_{2\varepsilon} = n_2^{-1}\Sigma_{n_1+1}^n[\hat{\varepsilon}_t^2 - \hat{\sigma}_{2\varepsilon}^2]^2,$$

$$\hat{v}_\varepsilon = n^{-1}\Sigma_1^n[\hat{\varepsilon}_t^2 - \hat{\sigma}_\varepsilon^2]^2, \quad \tilde{v}_\varepsilon = \hat{v}_{1\varepsilon} + k_n\tilde{v}_{2\varepsilon},$$

and construct the t-statistics

$$V_k(\tau_\varepsilon) = n_1^{1/2}\hat{\tau}_\varepsilon/\hat{v}_\varepsilon^{1/2}, \quad \tilde{V}_k(\tau_\varepsilon) = n_1^{1/2}\hat{\tau}_\varepsilon/\tilde{v}_\varepsilon^{1/2}.$$

The asymptotic theory for these statistics is as follows:

Theorem 3.4. If (2.2) is the generating mechanism for y_t and if (C1) and (C2) hold, then $V_k(\tau_\varepsilon)$ (respectively, $\tilde{V}_k(\tau_\varepsilon)$) is asymptotically equivalent to $V_k(\tau)$ ($\tilde{V}_k(\tau)$) and has the same limit theory as that given in theorem 3.1 (3.3). □

To examine the consistency of these tests we relax H_0. Let $(\varepsilon_t)_{-\infty}^{\infty}$ be split into the two half series of iid variates $(\varepsilon_t)_{-\infty}^{n_1}$ and $(\varepsilon_t)_{n_1+1}^{\infty}$ that individually follow (C1) but with different scale coefficients. For the finite variance case ($\alpha > 2$) we shall employ

$$H_1: \sigma_\varepsilon^2 \neq \sigma_{\varepsilon+}^2$$

where $\sigma_\varepsilon^2 = E(\varepsilon_t^2)$ for $t \leq n_1$ and $\sigma_{\varepsilon+}^2 = E(\varepsilon_t^2)$ for $t > n_1$. Under H_1 we have

$$E(y_t^2) = \sigma_y^2 = (\Sigma_0^\infty c_j^2)\sigma_\varepsilon^2, \quad t \leq n_1$$

$$E(y_t^2) = \sigma_{ys}^2 = (\Sigma_{j=0}^{s-1}c_j^2)\sigma_{\varepsilon+}^2 + (\Sigma_{j=s}^\infty c_j^2)\sigma_\varepsilon^2, \quad t = n_1 + s > n_1.$$

For the infinite variance case ($\alpha < 2$) we introduce heterogeneity through the scale coefficient in the tail of the distributions, as prescribed by (C1). We do so by using the scale coefficients (d_1, d_2) for $(\varepsilon_t)_{-\infty}^{n_1}$ and (d_1^+, d_2^+) for $(\varepsilon_t)_{n_1+1}^{\infty}$. If we assume that ε_t is symmetrically distributed then we can write $d_1 = d_2 = (1/2)a^\alpha$, $d_1^+ = d_2^+ = (1/2)a_+^\alpha$. The alternative hypothesis is then simply expressed as

$$H_1': a \neq a_+.$$

The following result gives the properties of the covariance stationarity tests $V_k(\tau)$, $\tilde{V}_k(\tau)$ and $\tilde{V}_k(\tau_\varepsilon)$ under these alternatives, H_1 and H_1'.

Theorem 3.5. Assume (C1) to (C3) hold and $k > 0$. Two cases apply.

(a) $\alpha > 2$: Under H_1, the statistics $V_k(\tau)$ and $\tilde{V}_k(\tau)$ diverge as $n \to \infty$ and tests based on these statistics are consistent. Specifically, the rates of divergence as $n \to \infty$ are given by:

$$V_k(\tau),\ \tilde{V}_k(\tau) = O_p(n^{1/2}), \quad \text{for } \alpha > 4 \tag{3.6}$$

$$V_k(\tau),\ \tilde{V}_k(\tau) = O_p(n^{1-2/\alpha}), \quad \text{for } 2 < \alpha \leqslant 4. \tag{3.7}$$

(b) $0 < \alpha < 2$: Under H_1', tests based on the statistics $V_k(\tau)$ and $\tilde{V}_k(\tau)$ are inconsistent. Specifically, as $n \to \infty$:

$$V_k(\tau),\ \tilde{V}_k(\tau) = O_p(1). \tag{3.8}$$

If (C1) and (C2) and (2.2) hold then identical results apply for the tests based on the statistic $V_k(\tau_\varepsilon)$ and $\tilde{V}_k(\tau_\varepsilon)$. □

Remarks.

(i) The $V_k(\tau)$ and $V_k(\tau_\varepsilon)$ tests are consistent provided $\alpha > 2$. But note from (3.7) that the rate of divergence of $V_k(\tau)$ under the alternative slows as $\alpha \searrow 2$. We can therefore expect the power properties of the test to be very unsatisfactory when α is close to 2.

(ii) When $0 < \alpha < 2$ the tests are inconsistent. Thus, all of these tests have no real discriminatory power in identifying heterogeneity in the sample observations under conditions of infinite variance. If we seek to determine whether heterogeneity is present in such cases, other tests are required.

The cusum of squares test for covariance stationarity

This test is based on the cumulative sums of $y_t^2 - \hat{\mu}_2$ where $\hat{\mu}_2 = n^{-1}\Sigma_1^n y_t^2$, leading to the statistic

$$\psi_n(r) = (n\hat{v})^{-1/2}\Sigma_1^{[nr]}(y_t^2 - \hat{\mu}_2).$$

Alternatively, we can use deviations of the squared residuals, $\hat{\varepsilon}_t^2 - \hat{\sigma}_\varepsilon^2$, leading to the statistic

$$\psi_n^\varepsilon(r) = (n\hat{v}_\varepsilon)^{-1/2}\Sigma_1^{[nr]}(\varepsilon_t^2 - \hat{\sigma}_\varepsilon^2).$$

Both $\psi_n(r)$ and $\psi_n^{\varepsilon}(r)$ are studentized cusum of squares statistics. In this sense they differ from the original cusum of squares statistic suggested in Brown et al. (1975). The original cusum of squares statistic is known to be not robust to departures from normality and its asymptotic distribution is sensitive to fourth moments. This is usually overcome by estimating fourth moments and studentizing the statistic, as suggested in Ploberger and Krämer (1986). The resulting statistic is entirely analogous to $\psi_n^{\varepsilon}(r)$. The statistic $\psi_n(r)$ is similar in form but involves the estimate $\hat{v}$ of the "long-run" fourth moment of the data (i.e. the spectrum of y_t^2 at the origin) rather than simply the fourth moment of y_t itself. Pagan and Schwert (1990b) employ $\psi_n(r)$ in their empirical work.

Sample realizations of $\psi_n(r)$ and $\psi_n^{\varepsilon}(r)$ lie in the function space $D[0, 1]$ and a limit distribution theory must be worked out by using suitable weak convergence methods on this space. For models where y_t^2 has finite variance ($\alpha > 4$) this presents no difficulty and the limit process of $\psi_n(r)$ and $\psi_n^{\varepsilon}(r)$ is a standard Brownian bridge, whose sample paths lie almost surely in $C[0, 1]$. When $\alpha < 4$ the limit process is different, is no longer confined to $C[0, 1]$ and weak convergence in $D[0, 1]$ does not always obtain in the J_1-Skorohod topology due to possible serial dependence in y_t^2 (see Avram and Taqqu, 1986, 1989). For this reason, it is especially convenient to work with the cusum statistic $\psi_n^{\varepsilon}(r)$ that is based on the squared residuals $\hat{\varepsilon}_t^2$ from the autoregression (2.8). For, under (2.2), $\hat{\varepsilon}_t$ is consistent to ε_t and is thereby serially independent asymptotically. In this case, weak convergence of $\psi_n^{\varepsilon}(r)$ does apply in $D[0, 1]$ and $\psi_n^{\varepsilon}(r)$ can form the basis of a suitable cusum test.

We give the following limit theory.

Theorem 3.6. Assume (C1) to (C3) hold. Then:

(a) If $\alpha > 4$

$$\psi_n(r),\ \psi_n^{\varepsilon}(r) \rightarrow_d B(r) \tag{3.9}$$

a standard Brownian bridge on $C[0, 1]$.

(b) If $0 < \alpha < 4$

$$\psi_n(r) \rightarrow_{\text{f.d.d.}} L\alpha_{/2}(r) = K_{\alpha/2}(r)/[\textstyle\int_0^1 (dU_{\alpha/2})^2]^{1/2} \tag{3.10}$$

$$\psi_n^{\varepsilon}(r) \rightarrow_d L\alpha_{/2}(r) = K_{\alpha/2}(r)/[\textstyle\int_0^1 (dU_{\alpha/2})^2]^{1/2} \tag{3.11}$$

where $K_{\alpha/2}(r) = U_{\alpha/2}(r) - rU_{\alpha/2}(1)$ is a stable–Levy bridge on $D[0, 1]$ and $\rightarrow_{\text{f.d.d.}}$ signifies weak convergence of the finite dimensional distributions of the process. □

Remarks.

(i) When $\alpha > 4$, the limit distribution of both cusums $\psi_n(r)$ and $\psi_n^\varepsilon(r)$ is the standard Brownian bridge. Pagan and Schwert (1990b) use bands that are based on critical values of the finite dimensional distributions, i.e. $B(r) =_d N(0, r(1 - r))$ for inference in graphical plots of their cusum statistic $\psi_n(r)$. These bands differ from those originally envisaged by Brown et al. (1975) for the cusum of squares statistic and by Durbin (1969) for the accumulated periodogram. In these papers the bands are designed so that the probability that the statistic hits the barrier at some point in its trajectory is controlled at the size of the test. This means that the probability that the trajectory is ever on or beyond the barrier corresponds to the level of the test. The situation is quite different for the finite dimensional distributions (f.d.d.) bands that are based on critical values of $B(r) =_d N(0, r(1 - r))$ for fixed r. In this case, the probability that a sample trajectory lies outside the f.d.d. bands is greater than the nominal size, leading to a liberal test. This is because, for example, $P[B(r) > c] \leqslant P[\sup_s B(s) > c]$ for all r. The f.d.d. bands do tell us something: if the sample trajectory lies inside the bands then nonrejection is certainly the right decision. But these f.d.d. bands do understate the extremes of sample trajectories and thereby lead to size distortions in testing stationarity by overrejection under the null.

(ii) When $\alpha < 4$ the limit theory is quite different. First, for $\psi_n(r)$, only the finite dimensional distributions converge (written as "$\rightarrow_{\text{f.d.d.}}$" in (3.10)) when the underlying data are serially dependent and we cannot in general assert that the random function $\psi_n(r)$ converges in $D[0, 1]$. As shown in Avram and Taqqu (1992), serial dependence in the process leads to successive jumps in the trajectories of the process which usually prevent convergence of partial sum processes like $\psi_n(r)$ in the J_1-Skorohod topology. This means that mass of the distribution escapes as the partial sums fluctuate too wildly for the sequence of probability measures associated with $\psi_n(r)$ to be tight. For this reason, it seems inappropriate to use $\psi_n(r)$ as a statistic for testing covariance stationarity. However, the statistic $\psi_n^\varepsilon(r)$ that is based on regression residuals does converge in $D[0, 1]$ when $0 < \alpha < 4$. The limit process (3.11) is a ratio of the stable – Levy bridge on $D[0, 1]$ represented by $K_{\alpha/2}(r)$ and the correlated, positive stable process represented by the multiple stochastic integral $\int_0^1 (dU_{\alpha/2})^2$. Bands that are based on critical values of the finite dimensional distributions of $L_{\alpha/2}(r)$ and its extrema $\sup_r$, $\inf_r L_{\alpha/2}(r)$ can be used for inference in the cusum plot for $\psi_n^\varepsilon(r)$.

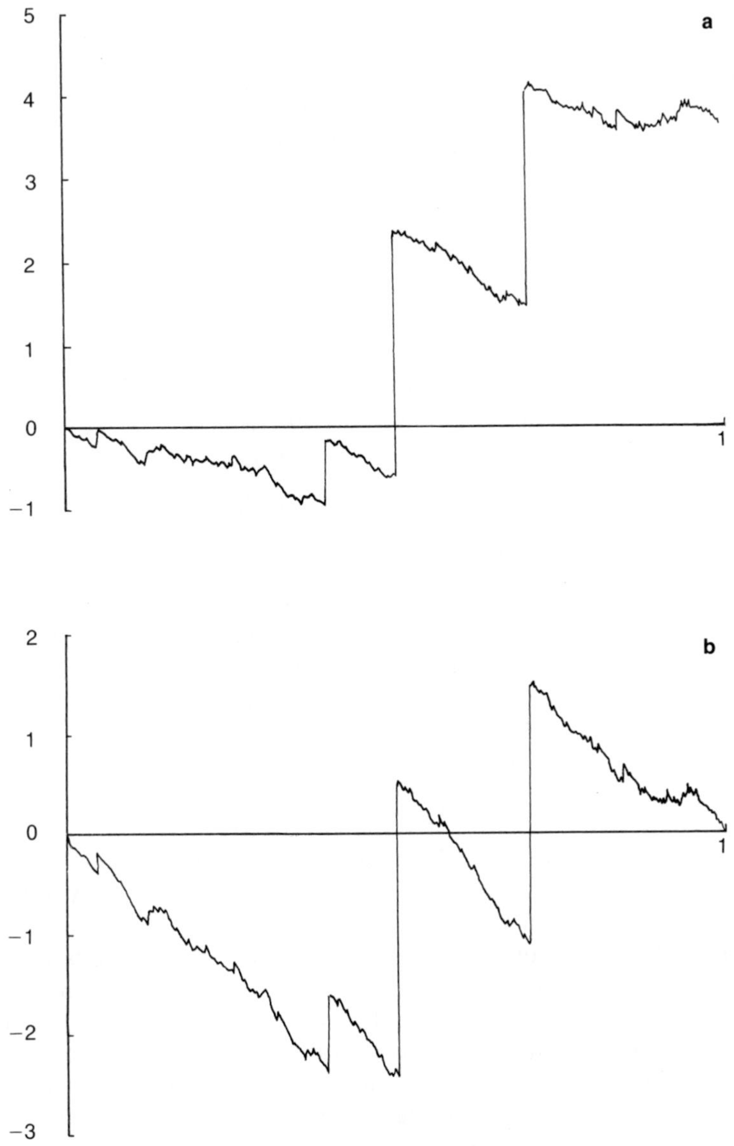

Figure 8.4 **a**, Asymmetric stable process, $n = 2500$, $\alpha/2 = 1.5$. **b**, Asymmetric stable bridge, $n = 2500$, $\alpha/2 = 1.5$.

They are computed and applied in sections 4 and 5 of Loretan and Phillips (1994).

(iii) The stable process $U_{\alpha/2}(r)$ that appears in (3.11) is asymmetric for $2 \leqslant \alpha \leqslant 4$ and strictly positive when $0 < \alpha < 2$. Examples of the sample trajectories of such processes and the associated bridge process $K_{\alpha/2}(r)$ are illustrated in figure 8.4. The distribution of the bridge process $K_{\alpha/2}(r)$ is skew symmetric in the sense that

$$K_{\alpha/2}(r) =_d -K_{\alpha/2}(1 - r).$$

To prove this we write

$$\begin{aligned} K_{\alpha/2}(r) &= U_{\alpha/2}(r) - rU_{\alpha/2}(1) = \textstyle\int_0^r dU_{\alpha/2} - r\int_0^1 dU_{\alpha/2} \\ &= \textstyle\int_0^1 dU_{\alpha/2} - \int_r^1 dU_{\alpha/2} - r\int_0^1 dU_{\alpha/2} \\ &= (1-r)\textstyle\int_0^1 dU_{\alpha/2} - \int_r^1 dU_{\alpha/2} \\ &= -\{\textstyle\int_r^1 dU_{\alpha/2} - (1-r)\int_0^1 dU_{\alpha/2}\} \\ &=_d -\{\textstyle\int_0^{1-r} dU_{\alpha/2} - (1-r)\int_0^1 dU_{\alpha/2}\} \\ &= -\{U_{\alpha/2}(1-r) - (1-r)U_{\alpha}(1)\} \\ &= -K_{\alpha/2}(1-r). \end{aligned}$$

Note that the skew symmetry of $K_{\alpha/2}(r)$ implies that of the limit process $L_{\alpha/2}(r)$ in (3.11) and this is reflected in the confidence contours for this process that we compute in section 4. Note also that the skew symmetry of $K_{\alpha/2}(r)$ also implies the following distributional equivalence

$$\bar{V}_k =_d -\bar{V}_{1/k}$$

for the limit variate of the $V_k(\tau)$ statistic given in theorem 3.1. This latter property generalizes the result given earlier in corollary 3.2 that $\bar{V}_k$ is symmetric when $k = 1$.

(iv) Consistency properties of the cusum of square tests can be studied in the same way as the sample split prediction tests. Since $\psi_n^{\varepsilon}(r)$ has a functional limit law for all $\alpha > 0$ we focus on the power properties of this test below. It is seen that the rates of divergence are comparable with those of the samle split prediction tests given in theorem 3.5. In particular, the cusum test has decreasing power as $\alpha \searrow 2$ and is inconsistent of $0 < \alpha < 2$.

Theorem 3.7. Suppose (C1) and (C2) and (2.2) hold. Then we have:

(a) $\alpha > 2$: Under H_1 tests based on $\psi_n^{\varepsilon}(r)$ are consistent with the following rates of divergence:

$$\psi_n^{\varepsilon}(r) = O_p(n^{1/2}), \quad \text{for } \alpha > 4 \tag{3.12}$$

$$\psi_n^\varepsilon(r) = O_p(n^{1-2/\alpha}), \quad \text{for } 2 < \alpha \leqslant 4. \tag{3.13}$$

(b) $0 < \alpha < 2$: Under H_1', tests based on $\psi_n^\varepsilon(r)$ are inconsistent and we have $\psi_n^\varepsilon(r) = O_p(1)$. □

The modified scaled range test

This test is based on the extent of the observed maximum fluctuation in the cusum of squares statistic. We define

$$R_n = \sup_r \psi_n(r) - \inf_r \psi_n(r)$$

$$R_n^\varepsilon = \sup_r \psi_n^\varepsilon(r) - \inf_r \psi_n^\varepsilon(r).$$

These are functionals of $\psi_n(r)$ and $\psi_n^\varepsilon(r)$ on $D(0, 1]$. Using theorem 3.6 and the continuous mapping theorem (both sup and inf are continuous functionals in the J_1-Skorohod topology) we get

(a) for $\alpha > 4$

$$R_n, R_n^\varepsilon \rightarrow_d \sup_r B(r) - \inf_r B(r) = R_B, \quad \text{say}$$

(b) for $0 < \alpha < 4$

$$R_n^\varepsilon \rightarrow_d \sup_r L_{\alpha/2}(r) - \inf_r L_{\alpha/2}(r) = R_L, \quad \text{say.}$$

Critical values for R_B are tabulated in, for example, Lo (1991, table II) and critical values for R_L are tabulated in Loretan and Phillips (1994). Observe that there is no corresponding limit for R_n in case (b) since the random element $\psi_n(r)$ is not weakly convergent in $D[0, 1]$ in the J_1-Skorohod topology, as earlier discussed.

Using theorem 3.4 we deduce that tests based on R_n^ε are consistent when $\alpha > 2$ but inconsistent when $\alpha < 2$. Tests based on R_n are consistent when $\alpha > 4$ but inconsistent when $\alpha < 4$, due to the failure of R_n to converge in this case.

A consistent test for heterogeneity in the infinite variance case

When $0 < \alpha < 2$ all the statistics considered earlier lead to inconsistent tests under heterogeneity of the data. Since the data have infinite variance when $0 < \alpha < 2$ it might be argued that there is little point in testing for heterogeneity using sample variances. This is certainly borne out by theorems 3.5 and 3.7. However, if the focus of interest is the more general hypothesis of stationarity (rather than constant variance or covariance stationarity) and it is suspected that this hypothesis breaks down over the sampling period, then we would expect such a breakdown to become evident in some characteristics of the data, if not the sample variances.

One way to test H_1' under $0 < \alpha < 2$ is to work directly with consistent estimates of the scale coefficients that appear in (C1). These may be constructed using order statistics in the following manner. Let $(\hat{\varepsilon}_t)_1^n$ be the residuals from (2.8) and let $\hat{\varepsilon}_{n1} \leqslant \hat{\varepsilon}_{n2} \leqslant \ldots \leqslant \hat{\varepsilon}_{nn}$ be the order statistics corresponding to this sample of residuals. Next, define

$$\hat{\alpha}_s = [s^{-1}\Sigma_{j=1}^s \ln \hat{\varepsilon}_{n,n-j+1} - \ln \hat{\varepsilon}_{n,n-s}]^{-1} \tag{3.14}$$

$$\hat{d}_s = sn^{-1}(\hat{\varepsilon}_{n,n-s})^{\hat{\alpha}_s} \tag{3.15}$$

for some integer s. It is assumed that n is large enough and s/n small enough so that $\hat{\varepsilon}_{n,n-s} > 0$ and thus $\hat{\alpha}_s$ and $\hat{d}_s$ are well defined real quantities. These estimators were originally suggested by Hill (1975) as conditional maximum likelihood estimators of the characteristic exponent parameter α and the scale coefficient $d = d_1$ in (C1). The asymptotic theory for them in the general case of a distribution whose tails have the asymptotic Pareto–Levy form (C1) is due to Hall (1982), who shows that it is optimal, at least in terms of the asymptotic bias and variance of these estimates, to choose the integer $s = s(n)$ so that it tends to infinity with n and is of order $n^{2\gamma/(2\gamma+\alpha)}$ when $\alpha_i(x) = O(x^{-\gamma})$ in C(1).

There is some advantage to choosing $s(n)$ so that $s/n^{2\gamma/(2\gamma+\alpha)} \to 0$ as $n \to \infty$. For, in this case we have from theorem 2 of Hall (1982)

$$s^{1/2}(\hat{\alpha}_s - \alpha) \to_d N(0, \alpha^2) \tag{3.16}$$

and

$$s^{1/2}[\ln(n/s)]^{-1}(\hat{d}_s - d) \to_d N(0, d^2). \tag{3.17}$$

These asymptotics apply at a slightly reduced rate, i.e. $s^{1/2}$ and $s^{1/2}[\ln(n/s)]^{-1}$ rather than the rates $n^{\gamma/(2\gamma+\alpha)}$ and $n^{\gamma/(2\gamma+\alpha)}[\ln(n)]^{-1}$ which apply when $s(n) = O(n^{2\gamma/(2\gamma+\alpha)})$. But they have the advantage that the limit distributions (3.16) and (3.17) involve only scale nuisance parameters which are easily eliminated in statistical tests.

Suppose, for example, we wish to mount a sample split prediction test using (3.17). We split the sample into two eras, $(\hat{\varepsilon}_t)_1^{n_1}$ and $(\hat{\varepsilon}_t)_{n_1+1}^n$, of approximately equal length and let $\hat{d}_s^{(1)}$, $\hat{d}_s^{(2)}$ be the corresponding scale coefficient estimators obtained by applying (3.15) to each of these subsamples. Next define the deviation

$$\tau_d = \hat{d}_s^{(1)} - \hat{d}_s^{(2)}$$

and the t-statistic

$$\tilde{V}(\tau_d) = s^{1/2}[\ln(n_1/s)]^{-1}\tau_d/[\hat{d}_s^{(1)^2} + \hat{d}_s^{(2)^2}]^{1/2}. \tag{3.18}$$

The asymptotic theory for $\tilde{V}(\tau_d)$ yields a standard $N(0, 1)$ test. We have:

Theorem 3.8. Let (C1), (C2), and (2.2) hold and suppose $k_n \to k = 1$ as $n \to \infty$. Assume that $a_i(x) = O(x^{-\gamma})$ for $i = 1, 2$ in (C1) for some $\gamma > 0$. Let $s \to \infty$ and $s/n_1^{2\gamma/(2\gamma+\alpha)} \to 0$ as $n_1 \to \infty$. Then, for all $\alpha > 0$,

$$\tilde{V}(\tau_d) \to_d N(0, 1). \quad \square \tag{3.19}$$

Remarks.

(i) Tests for heterogeneity in the sample that are based on $\tilde{V}(\tau_d)$ may be applied easily using critical values from the $N(0, 1)$ distribution. In constructing the statistic (3.18), however, a choice must be made in selecting s, the number of order statistics that are employed in formulae (3.14) and (3.15). If the tails are strictly Pareto (with $\gamma = \infty$) then $s = o(n_1)$ will suffice in theorem 3.8. If the tails are not strictly Pareto (which seems more likely) but are well represented by an asymptotic series in $x^{-\alpha}$, then $\gamma = \alpha$ and we require $s = o(n_1^{2/3})$. An adaptive (data-based) procedure for choosing s has been given by Hall and Welsh (1985) and applied recently in MacFarland et al. (1993) and Phillips (1993).

(ii) Note that the standard $N(0, 1)$ asymptotics (3.19) apply for all values of $\alpha > 0$. Thus, the test may be applied irrespective of the value of the tail exponent α in (C1) and therefore provides an alternative to the sample split prediction tests $V(\tau)$ and $V(\tau_\varepsilon)$. However, when $\alpha > 4$ the order statistic test $V(\tau_\alpha)$ will have lower power than $V(\tau)$ and $V(\tau_\varepsilon)$. Indeed, rates of divergence under H_1' are given in the following result.

Theorem 3.9. Let the same conditions as those of theorem 3.8 apply. Then, under H_1', the test based on $\tilde{V}(\tau_d)$ is consistent for all $\alpha > 0$. Specifically, as $n \to \infty$ we have the following rate of divergence under H_1':

$$\tilde{V}(\tau_d) = O_p(s^{1/2}/\ln(n_1/s)). \quad \square \tag{3.20}$$

(iii) Suppose we have $s = n_1^{2/3}/\ln(\ln n_1)$, as suited for tails with an asymptotic series representation in power of $x^{-\alpha}$. This choice leads to a divergence rate under H_1' of $O_p(n^{1/3}/\ln(n)(\ln\ln(n))^{1/2})$. Comparing these results with (3.7) we see that the order statistic test $\tilde{V}(\tau_d)$ will have greater asymptotic power whenever $\alpha < 3$. Thus, the test statistic $\tilde{V}(\tau_d)$ would seem to be worth using even in the finite variance case provided the tails are not too thin.

(iv) Observe that tests based on $\tilde{V}(\tau_d)$ may be applied to both the right and left tails of the distribution. In the latter case we simply use the order statistics for the alternate series $\eta_t = -\hat{\varepsilon}_t$.

(v) Subsample tests of heterogeneity may also be constructed for the characteristic exponent α. In this case we may employ estimates of α based on the use of (3.14) for the two eras. Let these estimates be $\hat{\alpha}_s^{(1)}$ and $\hat{\alpha}_s^{(2)}$, respectively. Again we shall assume that the eras are of approximately equal length. Define

$$\tau_\alpha = \hat{\alpha}_s^{(1)} - \hat{\alpha}_s^{(2)}$$

and construct the *t*-statistic

$$\tilde{V}(\tau_\alpha) = s^{1/2}\tau_\alpha/[\hat{\alpha}_s^{(1)^2} + \hat{\alpha}_s^{(2)^2}]^{1/2}.$$

This leads to a test of the hypothesis

$$H_0^\alpha\colon \alpha^{(1)} = \alpha^{(2)} = \alpha$$

that the characteristic exponents $\alpha^{(1)}$ and $\alpha^{(2)}$ in (C1) are the same in the two eras. Again, the test is an asymptotic $N(0, 1)$ test and is easy to implement. We have:

Theorem 3.10. Let the same conditions as those of theorem 3.8 apply. Then under the null hypothesis H_0^α we have

$$\tilde{V}(\tau_\alpha) \to_d N(0, 1) \tag{3.21}$$

and under the alternative hypothesis $H_1^\alpha\colon \alpha^{(1)} \neq \alpha^{(2)}$ we have

$$\tilde{V}(\tau_\alpha) = O_p(s^{1/2}) \tag{3.22}$$

and tests based on $\tilde{V}(\tau_\alpha)$ are consistent. □

Testing hypotheses about the maximal moment exponent

The maximal moment exponent of a distribution whose tails satisfy (C1) is given by the parameter α since $\alpha = \sup_q\{E|\varepsilon|^q < \infty\}$. Of course, α is unknown in applications and it will often be useful to combine estimation of α with a test of the hypothesis that it has a particular value, say

$$H_0\colon \alpha = \alpha_0$$

against the one-sided alternative that

$$H_1\colon \alpha < \alpha_0.$$

Of prominent interest will be the two cases $\alpha_0 = 4$ and $\alpha_0 = 2$. For then, the alternative H_1' corresponds to the cases of moment condition failure that we have studied earlier where different asymptotic theory comes into play. A suitable test is based on the studentized statistic

$$V(\alpha) = s^{1/2}(\hat{\alpha}_s - \alpha_0)/\hat{\alpha}_s,$$

or its LM version

$$V_0(\alpha) = s^{1/2}(\hat{\alpha}_s - \alpha_0)/\alpha_0.$$

Under H_0 we have, from (3.16), the same limit theory for both statistics, i.e.

$$V(\alpha),\ V_0(\alpha) \rightarrow_d N(0, 1),$$

leading to one-tailed tests based on the standard normal distribution. These tests are easy to apply and may form part of the preliminary diagnostic checking of the data characteristics. Their use is illustrated in Loretan and Phillips (1994).

4 Conclusion

The limit theory given here makes is possible to conduct asymptotic tests of covariance stationarity in the presence of heavy-tailed distributions. The sample split prediction tests and studentized cusum of squares tests that we consider are based on estimates of second and fourth moments of the data. When the usual fourth moment condition holds, we can rely on standard normal and Brownian bridge asymptotics. When fourth moments are infinite, the limit laws of these tests involve functionals of stable processes instead of Gaussian processes. Critical values for the tests that are based on the new limit theory have been computed by simulation and are reported in Loretan and Phillips (1994). Both these tests for covariance stationarity are consistent as long as second moments are finite. When second moments are infinite as well, the tests are inconsistent.

This chapter gives a new test for heterogeneity which is robust to moment condition failure. Instead of relying on estimated moments, the test is based on direct estimation of the tail parameters of a family of distributions with Pareto-like tails. The test suggested is particularly simple to use and relies on the standard normal limiting distribution.

The "cost" of its robustness is that it has lower power than moments-based tests when moment condition failure is not at issue.

In an empirical application of the methods given here Loretan and Phillips (1994) test whether several financial time series (daily and monthly stock market returns and exchange rate returns) are covariance stationary. None of the series they considered passed the tests for covariance stationarity, a finding that corroborates the work of Pagan and Schwert (1990a) on stock returns and casts some doubt on the validity and descriptive accuracy of econometric models that assume the unconditional variance of financial time series to be constant.

Mathematical appendix

Proof of lemma 2.1

(a) Set $x_t' = (y_{t-1}, \ldots, y_{t-p})$ and write $\hat{\varepsilon}_t = \varepsilon_t + (\varphi - \hat{\varphi})'x_t$. Then

$$\begin{aligned}\hat{\varepsilon}_t^2 - \hat{\sigma}_\varepsilon^2 &= \varepsilon_t^2 - \sigma_\varepsilon^2 + (\sigma_\varepsilon^2 - \hat{\sigma}_\varepsilon^2) + 2(\varphi - \hat{\varphi})'x_t\varepsilon_t \\ &\quad + (\varphi - \hat{\varphi})'x_t x_t'(\varphi - \hat{\varphi}).\end{aligned} \tag{A.1}$$

$$\begin{aligned}(nv_\varepsilon)^{-1/2}\Sigma_1^{[nr]}(\hat{\varepsilon}_t^2 - \hat{\sigma}_\varepsilon^2) &= (nv_\varepsilon)^{-1/2}\Sigma_1^{[nr]}(\varepsilon_t^2 - \sigma_\varepsilon^2) \\ &\quad - ([nr]/n)(nv_\varepsilon)^{-1/2}\Sigma_1^n(\varepsilon_t^2 - \sigma_\varepsilon^2) \\ &\quad + 2(\varphi - \hat{\varphi})'[(nv_\varepsilon)^{-1/2}\Sigma_1^{[nr]}x_t\varepsilon_t] \\ &\quad + (\varphi - \hat{\varphi})'[(nv)^{-1/2}\Sigma_1^{[nr]}x_t x_t'](\varphi - \hat{\varphi}) \\ &\quad - ([nr]/n)\{2(\varphi - \hat{\varphi})'[(nv_\varepsilon)^{-1/2}\Sigma_1^n x_t\varepsilon_t] \\ &\quad + (\varphi - \hat{\varphi})'[(nv)^{-1/2}\Sigma_1^n x_t x_t'](\varphi - \hat{\varphi})\}\end{aligned} \tag{A.2}$$

and by Donsker's theorem for partial sums of i.i.d. variates (e.g. Billingsley, 1968, p. 137) it follows that

$$\begin{aligned}&(nv_\varepsilon)^{-1/2}\Sigma_1^{[nr]}(\varepsilon_t^2 - \sigma_\varepsilon^2) - ([nr]/n)(nv_\varepsilon)^{-1/2}\Sigma_1^n(\varepsilon_t^2 - \sigma_\varepsilon^2) \\ &\quad \to_d W(r) - rW(1) = B(r).\end{aligned} \tag{A.3}$$

Thus, we deduce

$$(nv_\varepsilon)^{-1/2}\Sigma_1^{[nr]}(\hat{\varepsilon}_t^2 - \hat{\sigma}_\varepsilon^2) \to_d B(r) \tag{A.4}$$

from (A.2) and (A.3) provided

$$\sup_r|2(\varphi - \hat{\varphi})'(nv_\varepsilon)^{-1/2}\Sigma_1^{[nr]}x_t\varepsilon_t + (\varphi - \hat{\varphi})'[(nv)^{-1/2}\Sigma_1^{[nr]}x_t x_t'](\varphi - \hat{\varphi})| \to_p 0. \tag{A.5}$$

This follows if

$$(\varphi - \hat{\varphi})'\max_k[(nv_\varepsilon)^{-1/2}\Sigma_1^k x_t\varepsilon_t] \to_p 0 \tag{A.6}$$

$$(\varphi - \hat{\varphi})'\max_k[(nv_\varepsilon)^{-1/2}\Sigma_1^k x_t x_t'](\varphi - \hat{\varphi}) \to_p 0. \tag{A.7}$$

But $\Sigma_1^k x_t \varepsilon_t$ is a martingale and by the martingale maximal inequality (e.g. Hall and Heyde, 1980, p. 14)

$$P[\max_k |n^{-3/4}\Sigma_1^k x_t \varepsilon_t| > \delta] < \delta^{-2} n^{-3/2} \Sigma_1^n \sigma_\varepsilon^2 E(x_t' x_t) = p\delta^{-2} n^{-1/2} \sigma_\varepsilon^2 \sigma_y^2 \rightarrow 0$$

for all $\delta > 0$. Thus,

$$(\varphi - \hat{\varphi})' \max_k [(nv_\varepsilon)^{-1/2} \Sigma_1^k x_t \varepsilon_t] = n^{1/4} (\varphi - \hat{\varphi})' \max_k [n^{-3/4} v_\varepsilon^{-1/2} \Sigma_1^k x_t \varepsilon_t] \rightarrow_p 0,$$

since $n^{1/2}(\hat{\varphi} - \varphi) = O_p(1)$, and (A.6) holds. (A.7) is immediate since the left side is dominated by

$$v_\varepsilon^{-1/2} (\varphi - \hat{\varphi})' [n^{-1} \Sigma_1^n x_t x_t'] n^{1/2} (\varphi - \hat{\varphi})$$

which tends to zero in probability. Hence (A.5) holds and we have (A.4) as required.

(b) We consider three cases.

Case (i) $2 < \alpha < 4$. Here $\sigma_\varepsilon^2 = E(\varepsilon_t^2) < \infty$ and we have a decomposition that is analogous to (A.2), i.e.

$$\begin{aligned} a_n^{-2} \Sigma_1^{[nr]} (\hat{\varepsilon}_t^2 - \hat{\sigma}_\varepsilon^2) = {} & a_n^{-2} \Sigma_1^{[nr]} (\varepsilon_t^2 - \sigma_\varepsilon^2) \\ & - ([nr]/n) a_n^{-2} \Sigma_1^n (\varepsilon_t^2 - \sigma_\varepsilon^2) + 2(\varphi - \hat{\varphi})' [a_n^{-2} \Sigma_1^{[nr]} x_t \varepsilon_t] \\ & + (\varphi - \hat{\varphi})' [a_n^{-2} \Sigma_1^{[nr]} x_t x_t'] (\varphi - \hat{\varphi}) \\ & - ([nr]/n) \{ 2(\varphi - \hat{\varphi})' [a_n^{-2} \Sigma_1^n x_t x_t'] \\ & + (\varphi - \hat{\varphi})' [a_n^{-2} \Sigma_1^n x_t x_t' (\varphi - \hat{\varphi}) \}. \end{aligned} \quad \text{(A.8)}$$

Now

$$a_n^{-2} \Sigma_1^{[nr]} (\varepsilon_t^2 - \sigma_\varepsilon^2) \rightarrow_d U_{\alpha/2}(r) \quad \text{(A.9)}$$

by (2.5), since $\varepsilon_t^2 \in \mathcal{ND}(\alpha/2)$ and $\varepsilon_t^2 - \sigma_\varepsilon^2$ is an i.i.d. sequence with zero mean. It follows from (A.8) and (A.9) that

$$a_n^{-2} \Sigma_1^{[nr]} (\hat{\varepsilon}_t^2 - \hat{\sigma}_\varepsilon^2) \rightarrow_d U_{\alpha/2}(r) - rU_{\alpha/2}(1) \quad \text{(A.10)}$$

provided

$$\sup_r |2(\varphi - \hat{\varphi})' (a_n^{-2} \Sigma_1^{[nr]} x_t \varepsilon_t) + (\varphi - \hat{\varphi})' (a_n^{-2} \Sigma_1^{[nr]} x_t x_t') (\varphi - \hat{\varphi})| \rightarrow_p 0, \text{(A.11)}$$

since (A.11) implies that the corresponding Skorohod distance necessarily converges to zero in probability. Thus, (A.10) converges weakly to the limit process $U_{\alpha/2}(r)$ in $D[0, 1]$ in the J_1-Skorohod topology if (A.11) holds. But (A.11) follows if

$$(\varphi - \hat{\varphi})' \max_k |a_n^{-2} \Sigma_1^k x_t \varepsilon_t| \rightarrow_p 0, \quad \text{(A.12)}$$

since the contribution from the second term inside the sup is dominated by a quantity that tends to zero in probability because $\hat{\varphi} - \varphi \rightarrow_p 0$, i.e.

$$(\varphi - \hat{\varphi})' \max_k [a_n^{-2} \Sigma_1^k x_t x_t'] (\varphi - \hat{\varphi}) \leqslant (\varphi - \hat{\varphi})' [a_n^{-2} \Sigma_1^n x_t x_t'] (\varphi - \hat{\varphi}) \rightarrow_p 0.$$

However,

$$P[\max_k|a_n^{-2}\Sigma_1^k x_t\varepsilon_t| > \delta] < \delta^{-2}a_n^{-4}\Sigma_1^n\sigma_\varepsilon^2 E(x_t'x_t)) = p\delta^{-2}\sigma_\varepsilon^2\sigma_y^2(n/a_n^4) \to 0$$

and (A.12) holds, giving (A.10) as required.

Case (ii) $\alpha = 2$. In this case we set $\sigma_{\varepsilon n}^2 = E[\varepsilon_t^2 1(\varepsilon_t^2 < a_n^2)]$. The decomposition (A.8) has the same form as before with $\sigma_{\varepsilon n}^2$ replacing σ_ε^2. In place of (A.9) we have

$$a_n^{-2}\Sigma_1^k(\varepsilon_t^2 - \sigma_{\varepsilon n}^2) \to_d U_{\alpha/2}(r)$$

and (A.10) follows since (A.11) holds as in case (i).

Case (iii) $0 < \alpha < 2$. In this case, no centering is required and the first two terms on the right side of (A.8) are replaced by

$$a_n^{-2}\Sigma_1^k\varepsilon_t^2 - ([nr]/n)a_n^{-2}\Sigma_1^n\varepsilon_t^2 \to_d U_{\alpha/2}(r) - rU_{\alpha/2}(1).$$

Here, the limit process $U_{\alpha/2}(\mathrm{r})$ is a positive stable process on $D[0, 1]$. As in case (i), (A.11) holds if (A.12) does. But

$$\max_k|a_n^{-2}\Sigma_1^k x_t\varepsilon_t| \leqslant a_n^{-2}\Sigma_1^n|x_t\varepsilon_t| \leqslant [a_n^{-2}\Sigma_1^n x_t^2]^{-1/2}[a_n^{-2}\Sigma_1^n\varepsilon_t^2]^{1/2} = O_p\ (1)$$

since $\varepsilon_t^2, x_t^2 \in \mathscr{D}(\alpha/2)$. Finally, by Hannan and Kanter (1977), $n^{1/\delta}(\hat{\varphi} - \varphi) \to_{\text{a.s.}} 0$ for any $\delta > \alpha$, so that $\hat{\varphi} - \varphi \to_{\text{a.s.}} 0$ as (A.12) holds, giving the required result (A.10) with $U_{\alpha/2}(r)$ being a positive stable process in this case.

Proof of theorem 3.1

(a) From theorem 3.8 of Phillips and Solo (1992) we have the following CLT for variances under (C1) to (C3) and $\alpha > 4$:

$$n^{-1/2}\Sigma_1^n(y_t^2 - \sigma_y^2) \to_d N(0, v) \qquad \text{(A.13)}$$

where $\sigma_y^2 = E(y_t^2) = \sigma_\varepsilon^2\Sigma_0^\infty c_j^2$ and

$$v = \kappa_4[\Sigma_0^\infty c_j^2]^2 + 2\sigma_\varepsilon^4\Sigma_{-\infty}^\infty[\Sigma_{s=0}^\infty c_s c_{s+j}]^2. \qquad \text{(A.15)}$$

Note that κ_4 is the fourth cumulant of ε_t and the series that appear in v converge under (C3) by lemma 3.5 of Phillips and Solo (1992). Next, observe that

$$n_1^{1/2}\hat{\tau} = n_1^{-1/2}\Sigma_1^{n_1}(y_t^2 - \sigma_y^2) - (n_1/n_2)^{1/2}n^{-1/2}\Sigma_{n_1+1}^n(y_t^2 - \sigma_y^2)$$

and, by assumption, $k_n = n_1/n_2 \to k$ as $n \to \infty$. The two sums that appear in this expression are asymptotically independent under (C3) and again by theorem 3.7 of Phillips and Solo (1992) we deduce that

$$n_1^{1/2}\tau \to_d N(0, (1 + k)v).$$

Finally, $\hat{v} \to_p v$ since $\hat{v}$ is the usual Bartlett estimate of the long run variance of y_t^2 and this estimate is consistent under the stated conditions. The required result, i.e. $V_k(\tau) \to_d N(0, 1)$, now follows directly.

(b) Suppose $2 < \alpha < 4$, so that $E(y_t^2) = \sigma_y^2 = (\Sigma_0^\infty c_j^2)\sigma_\varepsilon^2 < \infty$. Set $a_n = an^{1/\alpha}$, $r = k/(1+k)$ and note that

$$\frac{n_1}{n} = \frac{k_n}{1+k_n} = \frac{[nr]}{n} + o(1) \to r,$$

$$\frac{n_2}{n} = \frac{1}{1+k_n} = \frac{n-[nr]}{n} + o(1) \to 1-r.$$

Next, observe that

$$\begin{aligned} y_t^2 &= \Sigma_0^\infty c_j^2 \varepsilon_{t-j}^2 + \Sigma_{j=0}^\infty \Sigma_{r=-j,\neq 0}^\infty c_j c_{j+r} \varepsilon_{t-j}\varepsilon_{t-j-r} \\ &= f_0(L)\varepsilon_t^2 + \Sigma_{r=-\infty,\neq 0}^\infty f_r(L)\varepsilon_t\varepsilon_{t-r} \end{aligned} \tag{A.15}$$

where $f_h(L) = \Sigma_0^\infty c_j c_{j+h}$. We use the following decomposition of the lag polynomial $f_h(L)$ (see equation (23) and lemma 2.1 of Phillips and Solo, 1992):

$$f_h(L) = f_h(1) - (1-L)\tilde{f}_h(L) \tag{A.16}$$

where

$$\tilde{f}_h(L) = \Sigma_{k=0}^\infty \tilde{f}_{hk} L^k, \quad \tilde{f}_{hk} = \Sigma_{s=k+1}^\infty f_{hs} = \Sigma_{s=k+1}^\infty c_s c_{s+h}.$$

Employ (A.16) in (A.15) and note that $\varepsilon_t^2 \in \mathcal{ND}(\alpha/2)$ so that $a_n^{-2}\Sigma_1^{[nr]}(\varepsilon_t^2 - \sigma_\varepsilon^2) \to_d U_{\alpha/2}(r)$ by (2.4); while for $s \neq 0$ $\varepsilon_t\varepsilon_{t-s} \in \mathcal{ND}(2)$ and we have $a_n^{-2}\Sigma_1^{n_1}\varepsilon_t\varepsilon_{t-s} = o_p(1)$. Combining these results we obtain

$$\begin{aligned} a_n^{-2}\Sigma_1^{n_1}(y_t^2 - \sigma_y^2) &= a_n^{-2}\Sigma_1^{[nr]}(y_t^2 - \sigma_y^2) + o_p(1) \\ &= f_0(1)[a_n^{-2}\Sigma_1^{[nr]}(\varepsilon_t^2 - \sigma_t^2)] + o_p(1) \\ &\to_d U_{\alpha/2}(r), \end{aligned} \tag{A.17}$$

with $r = k/(1+k)$ fixed and

$$\sigma^2 = f_0(1) = \Sigma_0^\infty c_j^2.$$

In a similar way we deduce

$$a_n^{-2}\Sigma_{n_1+1}^n(y_t^2 - \sigma_y^2) \to_d \sigma^2[U_{\alpha/2}(1) - U_{\alpha/2}(r)]. \tag{A.18}$$

It follows from (A.17) and (A.18) that

$$\begin{aligned} n_1 a_n^{-1}\hat{\tau} &= a_n^{-2}\Sigma_1^{n_1}(y_t^2 - \sigma_y^2) - k_n a_n^{-2}\Sigma_{n_1+1}^n(y_t^2 - \sigma_y^2) \\ &\to_d \sigma^2\{U_{\alpha/2}(r) - k[U_{\alpha/2}(1) - U_{\alpha/2}(r)]\} \\ &= \sigma^2\{(1+k)U_{\alpha/2}(k/(1+k)) - kU_{\alpha/2}(1)\}. \end{aligned} \tag{A.19}$$

Turning to the denominator of $V_k(\tau)$ and using the same arguments as those in Phillips (1990, section 2.3) we find

$$na_n^{-4}\hat{v} \to_d \sigma^4 \textstyle\int_0^1 (dU_{\alpha/2})^2, \tag{A.20}$$

so that

$$n_1(1 + k_n)a_n^{-4}\hat{v} = k_n(na_n^{-4}\hat{v}) \to_d k\sigma^4\textstyle\int_0^1(dU_{\alpha/2})^2. \tag{A.21}$$

It follows that

$$\begin{aligned} V_k(\tau) &= [(1 + k_n)\hat{v}]^{-1/2}(n_1^{1/2}\tau) = [n_1(1 + k_n)a_n^{-4}\hat{v}]^{-1/2}(n_1a_n^{-2}\hat{\tau}) \\ &\to_d [k\textstyle\int_0^1(dU_{\alpha/2})^2]^{-1/2}[(1 + k)U_{\alpha/2}(k/(1 + k)) - kU_{\alpha/2}(1)] \end{aligned}$$

as required.

When $\alpha = 2$ we may center on $\sigma_{yn}^2 = E[y_t^2 1(y_t^2 < a_n^2)]$, giving

$$\begin{aligned} n_1a_n^{-2}\hat{\tau} &= a_n^{-2}\Sigma_1^{n_1}(y_t^2 - \sigma_{yn}^2) - k_na_n^{-2}\Sigma_{n_1+1}^n(y_t^2 - \sigma_{yn}^2) \\ &\to_d \sigma^2\{U_{\alpha/2}(r) - k[U_{\alpha/2}(1) - U_{\alpha/2}(r)]\} \end{aligned}$$

as in (A.19). (A.21) continues to hold when $\alpha = 2$, and this covers the case $\alpha = 2$.

When $0 < \alpha < 2$ we note that $\alpha/2 < 1$ and so no centering is needed in the numerator of the statistic. In this case we have

$$n_1a_n^{-2}\hat{\tau} = a_n^{-2}\Sigma_1^{n_1}y_t^2 - k_na_n^{-2}\Sigma_{n_1+1}^n y_t^2 \to_d \sigma^2[U_{\alpha/2}^+(r) - k\{U_{\alpha/2}^+(1) - U_{\alpha/2}^+(r)\}]$$

where $U_{\alpha/2}^+(r)$ is a positive stable process with exponent $\alpha/2$, i.e. increments in $U_{\alpha/2}^+(r)$ are independent and are distributed as a positive stable variate with characteristic exponent $\alpha/2$. (A.21) holds as before and this establishes part (b). □

Proof of corollary 3.2

We need to show that the limit variate given by (3.2) is equivalent in distribution to (3.3). First observe that the variates $U_{\alpha/2}(r) - U_{\alpha/2}(r/2)$ and $U_{\alpha/2}(r/2)$ are stable, independent and equivalent in distribution, i.e.

$$U_{\alpha/2}(r) - U_{\alpha/2}(r/2) =_d U_{\alpha/2}(r/2).$$

Hence

$$U_{\alpha/2}(r/2) - \{U_{\alpha/2}(r) - U_{\alpha/2}(r/2)\} =_d -[U_{\alpha/2}(r/2) - \{U_{\alpha/2}(r) - U_{\alpha/2}(r/2)\}]$$

and

$$U_{\alpha/2}^s(r) = U_{\alpha/2}(r/2) - \{U_{\alpha/2}(r) - U_{\alpha/2}(r/2)\}$$

is a symmetric stable process on $D[0, 1]$. It follows that

$$U_{\alpha/2}(1/2) - U_{\alpha/2}(1) = U_{\alpha/2}(1/2) - \{U_{\alpha/2}(1) - U_{\alpha/2}(1/2)\} = U_{\alpha/2}^s(1)$$

as required for the numerator of (3.3).

Now let $V_{\alpha/2}(r/2) = U_{\alpha/2}(r) - U_{\alpha/2}(r/2)$ and write

$$U_{\alpha/2}^s(r) = U_{\alpha/2}(r/2) - V_{\alpha/2}(r/2)$$

as the difference of the two independent stable processes $U_{\alpha/2}$ and $V_{\alpha/2}$. Increments in these processes are also independent and we have

$$dU_{\alpha/2}^s(r) = dU_{\alpha/2}(r/2) - dV_{\alpha/2}(r/2) =_d (1/2)^{2/\alpha}dU_{\alpha/2}(r) - (1/2)^{2/\alpha}dV_{\alpha/2}(r).$$

Next observe that

$$dU_{\alpha/2}(r), \quad dV_{\alpha/2}(r) \in \mathcal{ND}(\alpha/2)$$

and hence

$$(dU_{\alpha/2}(r))^2, \quad (dV_{\alpha/2}(r))^2 \in \mathcal{ND}(\alpha/4).$$

However, in view of the independence of $U_{\alpha/2}(r)$ and $V_{\alpha/2}(r)$ products of increments in these processes are in $\mathcal{D}(\alpha/2)$ and hence

$$dU_{\alpha/2}(r)dV_{\alpha/2}(r) = 0 \text{ a.s.}$$

Thus

$$\begin{aligned}(dU^s_{\alpha/2}(r))^2 &=_d (1/2)^{4/\alpha}(dU_{\alpha/2}(r))^2 + (1/2)^{4/\alpha}(dV_{\alpha/2}(r))^2 \\ &=_d [(1/2) + (1/2)]^{4/\alpha}(dU_{\alpha/2}(r))^2 \\ &= (dU_{\alpha/2}(r))^2.\end{aligned}$$

It follows that

$$[\textstyle\int_0^1(dU_{\alpha/2})^2]^{-1/2}[2U_{\alpha/2}(1/2) - U_{\alpha/2}(1)] =_d [\int_0^1(dU^s_{\alpha/2})^2]^{-1/2}U^s_{\alpha/2}(1)$$

thereby establishing (3.3) as required.

Proof of theorem 3.3

(a) When $\alpha > 4$, we have $\hat{v}_1$, $\hat{v}_2 \to_p v$ and $\hat{v}_1 + k_n\hat{v}_2 \to_p (1 + k)v$. Further, $n_1^{1/2}\hat{\tau} \to_d N(0, (1 + k)v)$ as before and part (a) follows directly.

(b) When $0 < \alpha < 4$ the numerator of

$$\tilde{V}_k(\tau) = n_1^{1/2}\hat{\tau}/\tilde{v}^{1/2} = (n_1a_n^{-2}\hat{\tau})/(n_1a_n^{-4}\tilde{v})^{1/2}$$

has the same limit behavior as before, i.e.

$$n_1a_n^{-2}\hat{\tau} \to_d \sigma^2[U_{\alpha/2}(r) - k\{U_{\alpha/2}(1) - U_{\alpha/2}(r)\}] \qquad \text{(A.22)}$$

where $r = k/(1 + k)$. The denominator behaves as follows:

$$\begin{aligned}n_1a_n^{-4}\tilde{v} &= n_1a_n^{-4}\hat{v}_1 + k_n^2(a_n^{-4}n_2\hat{v}_2) \\ &\to_d \sigma^4\{\textstyle\int_0^r(dU_{\alpha/2})^2 + k^2\int_r^1(dU_{\alpha/2})^2\}.\end{aligned} \qquad \text{(A.23)}$$

Combining (A.22) and (A.23) we get the first expression given in part (b). The distributional equivalence of (3.4) and (3.5) when $k = 1$ follows just as in corollary 3.2.

Proof of theorem 3.4

In all cases (i.e. $0 < \alpha < 4$ and $\alpha \geqslant 4$) we have $\hat{\varphi} \to_p \varphi$. Next, when $\alpha > 2$ we have $\hat{\sigma}^2_{1\varepsilon}$, $\hat{\sigma}^2_{2\varepsilon} \to_p \sigma^2_\varepsilon$; and when $\alpha > 4$ we have:

$$\begin{aligned}\hat{v}_{1\varepsilon} &= n_1^{-1}\Sigma_1^{n_1}[\hat{\varepsilon}_t^2 - \hat{\sigma}^2_{1\varepsilon}]^2 = n_1^{-1}\Sigma_1^{n_1}[\varepsilon_t^2 - \sigma^2_\varepsilon]^2 + o_p(1) \\ &\to_p v_\varepsilon = \kappa_4 + 2\sigma^4_\varepsilon\end{aligned}$$

and, similarly, $\hat{v}_{2\varepsilon} \to_p v_\varepsilon$. Thus, when $\alpha > 4$, we have $\tilde{v} \to_p (1 + k)v_\varepsilon$ and

$$n_1^{-1/2}\hat{\tau}_\varepsilon = n_1^{-1/2}\Sigma_1^{n_1}(\hat{\varepsilon}_t^2 - \hat{\sigma}_{1\varepsilon}^2) - k_n^{1/2}n_2^{-1/2}\Sigma_{n_1+1}^{n}(\hat{\varepsilon}_t^2 - \sigma_\varepsilon^2)$$
$$\to_d N(0, (1 + k)v_\varepsilon).$$

It follows that when $\alpha > 4$ we have

$$\tilde{V}_k(\tau_\varepsilon) \to_d N(0, 1)$$

as required.

When $2 < \alpha < 4$ we employ lemma 2.1, set $r = k/(1 + k)$ and find that

$$n_1 a_n^{-2}\hat{\tau}_\varepsilon = a_n^{-2}\Sigma_1^{n_1}(\hat{\varepsilon}_t^2 - \sigma_\varepsilon^2) - k_n a_n^{-2}\Sigma_{n_1+1}^{n}(\hat{\varepsilon}_t^2 - \sigma_\varepsilon^2)$$
$$= a_n^{-2}\Sigma_1^{[nr]}(\hat{\varepsilon}_t^2 - \sigma_\varepsilon^2) - k_n a_n^{-2}\Sigma_{[nr]+1}^{n}(\hat{\varepsilon}_t^2 - \sigma_\varepsilon^2) + o_p(1) \tag{A.24}$$
$$\to_d \sigma^2\{U_{\alpha/2}(r) - k[U_{\alpha/2}(1) - U_{\alpha/2}(r)]\} \tag{A.25}$$

and

$$n_1 a_n^{-4}\tilde{v}_\varepsilon = n_1 a_n^{-4}\hat{v}_{1\varepsilon} + k_n^2(a_n^{-4}n_2\hat{v}_{2\varepsilon})$$
$$\to_d \sigma^4\{\textstyle\int_0^r(dU_{\alpha/2})^2 + k^2\int_r^1(dU_{\alpha/2})^2\} \tag{A.26}$$

as in (A.19) and (A.23). When $\alpha = 2$ we center on $\sigma_{\varepsilon n}^2 = E(\varepsilon_1^2 1(\varepsilon_t^2 < a_n))$ in the sums in (A.24) and, when $0 < \alpha < 2$, no centering of the sums in (A.24) is required. In both cases (A.25) holds, as does (A.26). Writing

$$\tilde{V}_k(\tau_\varepsilon) = n_1 a_n^{-2}\tilde{\tau}_\varepsilon/[n_1 a_n^{-4}\tilde{V}_\varepsilon]^{1/2}$$

and using (A.25), (A.26) and joint weak convergence we obtain the required asymptotic equivalence of $\tilde{V}_k(\tau_\varepsilon)$ and $\tilde{V}_k(\tau)$. Similar derivations yield the asymptotic equivalence of $V_k(\tau_\varepsilon)$ and $V_k(\tau)$. □

Proof of theorem 3.5

(a) Under H_1 we have

$$\hat{\tau} = n_1^{-1}\Sigma_1^{n_1}(y_t^2 - \sigma_y^2) - n_2^{-1}\Sigma_{s=1}^{n_2}(y_{n_1+s}^2 - \sigma_{ys}^2)$$
$$+ \sigma_y^2 - n_2^{-1}\Sigma_{s=1}^{n_2}\sigma_{ys}^2, \tag{A.27}$$

so that

$$n_1^{1/2}\hat{\tau} = n_1^{-1/2}\Sigma_1^{n_1}(y_t^2 - \sigma_y^2) - k_n^{1/2}n_2^{-1/2}\Sigma_{s=1}^{n_2}(y_{n_1+s}^2 - \sigma_{ys}^2)$$
$$+ k_n^{1/2}n_2^{-1/2}\Sigma_{s=1}^{n_2}(\sigma_y^2 - \sigma_{ys}^2).$$

Now $k_n \to k$ as $n \to \infty$ and

$$n_2^{-1/2}\Sigma_{s=1}^{n_2}(\sigma_y^2 - \sigma_{ys}^2) = n_2^{-1/2}\Sigma_{s=1}^{n_2}\Sigma_{j=0}^{s-1}c_j^2(\sigma_\varepsilon^2 - \sigma_{\varepsilon+}^2)$$
$$= (\sigma_\varepsilon^2 - \sigma_{\varepsilon+}^2)n_2^{-1/2}\Sigma_{j=0}^{n_2}(n_2 - j)c_j^2$$
$$= (\sigma_\varepsilon^2 - \sigma_{\varepsilon+}^2)n_2^{1/2}\Sigma_{j=0}^{n_2}(1 - j/n_2)c_j^2$$
$$= O(n^{1/2}).$$

Hence, $n_1^{1/2}\hat{\tau} = O_p(n^{1/2})$. The denominators of $V_k(\hat{\tau})$ and $\tilde{V}_k(\hat{\tau})$ depend on $\hat{v}$ and $\tilde{v}$ and

$$\hat{v} \rightarrow_p v = \lim_{n\to\infty}\{n^{-1}E[\Sigma_1^n(y_t^2 - E(y_t^2))]^2\},$$

$$\tilde{v} = \hat{v}_1 + k_n\hat{v}_2 \rightarrow_p \lim_{n\to\infty} n_1^{-1}E[\Sigma_1^{n_1}(y_t^2 - E(y_t^2))]^2 + k \lim_{n\to\infty} n_2^{-1}E[\Sigma_{n_1+1}^n(y_t^2 - E(y_t^2))]^2.$$

These limits exist under (C3) since fourth moments of ε_t are finite and bounded. It follows that $V_k(\tau)$, $\tilde{V}_k(\tau) = O_p(n^{1/2})$ as required and these tests are consistent under H_1. In an entirely analogous way we find that $V_k(\tau_\varepsilon)$, $\tilde{V}_k(\tau_\varepsilon) = O_p(n^{1/2})$. This establishes the rates of divergence under H_1' given in (3.6) for $\alpha > 4$.

Expression (A.27) continues to hold when $2 < \alpha < 4$ and we have

$$n_1a_n^{-2}\tau = a_n^{-2}\Sigma_1^{n_1}(y_t^2 - \sigma_y^2) - k_na_n^{-2}\Sigma_{s=1}^{n_2}(y_{n_1+s}^2 - \sigma_{ys}^2) + k_na_n^{-2}\Sigma_1^{n_2}(\sigma_y^2 - \sigma_{ys}^2).$$

Now we find

$$a_n^{-2}\Sigma_1^{n_2}(\sigma_y^2 - \sigma_{ys}^2) = (\sigma_\varepsilon^2 - \sigma_{\varepsilon+}^2)(n_2a_n^{-2})\Sigma_{j=0}^{n_2}(1 - j/n_2)c_j^2 = O(n^{1-2/\alpha}).$$

But

$$V_k(\tau) = [n_1(1 + k_n)a_n^{-4}\hat{v}]^{-1/2}[n_1a_n^{-2}\hat{\tau}] \tag{A.28}$$

and the denominator $n_1(1 + k_n)a_n^{-4}\hat{v} = O_p(1)$ as in the null case. Thus, $V_k(\tau) = O_p(n^{1-2/\alpha})$ as asserted in (3.7). The same rate of divergence under H_1 applies to $\tilde{V}_k(\tau)$, $V_k(\tau_\varepsilon)$ and $\tilde{V}_k(\tau_\varepsilon)$, thereby establishing part (a).

(b) Observe that both ε_t^2 and y_t^2 lie in $\mathcal{ND}(\alpha/2)$. When $0 < \alpha < 2$, neither ε_t^2 nor y_t^2 has finite mean and no centering is required for the limit theory. Further, for $r = k/(1 + k)$ fixed, we have

$$n_1a_n^{-2}\hat{\tau} = a_n^{-2}\Sigma_1^{n_1}y_t^2 - k_na_n^{-2}\Sigma_{n_1+1}^n y_t^2 \rightarrow_d \sigma^2\{U_{\alpha/2}^+(r) - kf^2[U_{\alpha/2}^+(1) - U_{\alpha/2}^+(r)]\} \tag{A.29}$$

where $\sigma^2 = \Sigma_0^\infty c_j^2$, as before, and $f = a_+/a$. To verify (A.29) we employ (A.15) as in the proof of theorem 3.1, giving

$$a_n^{-2}\Sigma_1^{n_1}y_t^2 = \sigma^2(a_n^{-2}\Sigma_1^{n}\varepsilon_t^2) + o_p(1) \rightarrow_d \sigma^2U_{\alpha/2}^+(r)$$

and

$$a_n^{-2}\Sigma_{n_1+1}^n y_t^2 = \sigma^2(a_{+,n}/a_n)^2(a_{+,n}^{-2}\Sigma_{n_1+1}^n\varepsilon_t^2) + o_p(1) \rightarrow_d \sigma^2f^2\{U_{\alpha/2}^+(1) - U_{\alpha/2}^+(r)\}$$

as required, where $a_{+,n} = a_+n^{1/\alpha}$ is the normalizing constant for the upper half sequence $(\varepsilon)_{n_1+1}^\infty$.

For the denominator of $V_k(\tau)$ in (A.28) we find

$$\begin{aligned} na_n^{-4}\hat{v} &= \sigma^4 a_n^{-4}\Sigma_1^n \varepsilon_t^2 + o_p(1) \\ &= \sigma^4\{a_n^{-4}\Sigma_1^{n_1}\varepsilon_t^2 + (a_{+,n}/a_n)^4(a_{+,n}^{-4}\Sigma_{n_1+1}^n \varepsilon_t^2)\} + o_p(1) \\ &\rightarrow_d \sigma^4\{\textstyle\int_0^r [dU_{\alpha/2}^+]^2 + f^4 \int_r^1 (dU_{\alpha/2})^2\}. \end{aligned}$$

Hence

$$n_1(1 + k_n)a_n^{-4}\hat{v} \rightarrow_d k\sigma^4\{\textstyle\int_0^r [dU_{\alpha/2}^+]^2 + f^4 \int_r^1 (dU_{\alpha/2})^2\}.$$

We deduce that under H_1'

$$\begin{aligned} V_k(\tau) \rightarrow_d & [k\{\textstyle\int_0^r [dU_{\alpha/2}^+]^2 + f^4 \int_r^1 [dU_{\alpha/2}^+]^2\}]^{-1/2} \\ & [U_{\alpha/2}^+(r) - kf^2\{U_{\alpha/2}^+(1) - U_{\alpha/2}(r)\}] \end{aligned}$$

and, hence, $V_k(\tau) = O_p(1)$, leading to an inconsistent test. Similar derivations show that $\tilde{V}_k(\tau)$, $V_k(\tau_\varepsilon)$ and $\tilde{V}_k(\tau_\varepsilon)$ are $O_p(1)$ as $n \rightarrow \infty$ and these tests are also inconsistent under H_1', thereby establishing part (b). □

Proof of theorem 3.6

(a) Write

$$\begin{aligned} \psi_n(r) &= (n\hat{v})^{-1/2}\Sigma_1^{[nr]}(y_t^2 - \sigma_y^2 + \sigma_y^2 - \hat{\mu}_2) \\ &= (n\hat{v})^{-1/2}\Sigma_1^{[nr]}(y_t^2 - \sigma_y^2) + [nr](n\hat{v})^{-1/2}(\sigma_y^2 - \hat{\mu}_2) \\ &= (v/\hat{v})^{1/2}[(nv)^{-1/2}\Sigma_1^{[nr]}(y_t^2 - \sigma_y^2) \\ &\quad - ([nr]/n)(nv)^{-1/2}\Sigma_1^n(y_t^2 - \sigma_y^2)] \\ &\rightarrow_d W(r) - rW(1) \end{aligned}$$

by theorem 3.7 of Phillips and Solo (1992), since $\hat{v}/v \rightarrow_p 1$. The limit process $B(r) = W(r) - rW(1)$ is a Brownian bridge on $C[0, 1]$.

Similarly, we have

$$\psi_n^\varepsilon(r) = (n\hat{v}_\varepsilon)^{-1/2}\Sigma_1^{[nr]}(\hat{\varepsilon}_t^2 - \hat{\sigma}_\varepsilon^2) = (v_\varepsilon/\hat{v}_\varepsilon)^{1/2}[(nv_\varepsilon)^{-1/2}\Sigma_1^{[nr]}(\hat{\varepsilon}_t^2 - \hat{\sigma}_t^2)] \rightarrow_d B(r)$$

since $\hat{v}_\varepsilon \rightarrow_p v_\varepsilon$ and $(nv_\varepsilon)^{-1/2}\Sigma_1^{[nr]}(\hat{\varepsilon}_t^2 - \hat{\sigma}_\varepsilon^2) \rightarrow_d B(r)$ by lemma 2.1(a).

(b) When $0 < \alpha < 4$ we have, as in the proof of part (b) of theorem 3.1, the weak convergence for *fixed r*

$$\begin{aligned} a_n^{-2}\Sigma_1^{[nr]}(y_t^2 - \hat{\mu}_2) &= a_n^{-2}\Sigma_1^{[nr]}(y_t^2 - \sigma_y^2) - ([nr]/n)a_n^{-2}\Sigma_1^n(y_t^2 - \sigma_y^2) \\ &\rightarrow_d \sigma^2[U_{\alpha/2}(r) - rU_{\alpha/2}(1)] = \sigma^2 K_{\alpha/2}(r). \end{aligned}$$

Similarly, for fixed r_1 and r_2, we have the joint weak convergence

$$[a_n^{-2}\Sigma_1^{[nr]}(y_t^2 - \hat{\mu}_2), a_n^{-2}\Sigma_1^{[nr_2]}(y_t^2 - \hat{\mu}_2)] \rightarrow_d [\sigma^2 K_{\alpha/2}(r_1), \sigma^2 K_{\alpha/2}(r_2)]$$

and the same applies to the higher finite dimensional distributions. Thus

$$a_n^{-2}\Sigma_1^{[nr]}(y_t^2 - \hat{\mu}_2) \rightarrow_{\text{f.d.d.}} \sigma^2 K_{\alpha/2}(r). \tag{A.30}$$

Combining (A.30) and (A.20) we have:

$$\psi_n(r) = (n\hat{v})^{-1/2}\Sigma_1^{[nr]}(y_t^2 - \hat{\mu}_2) = [na_n^{-4}\hat{v}]^{-1/2}a_n^{-2}\Sigma_1^{[nr]}(y_t^2 - \hat{\mu}_2)$$

$$\to_{\text{f.d.d.}} [U_{\alpha/2}(r) - rU_{\alpha/2}(1)]/[\int_0^1 (dU_{\alpha/2})^2]^{1/2},$$

as required for (3.10).

To prove (3.11) we first write

$$\psi_n^{\varepsilon}(r) = [na^{-4}\hat{v}_{\varepsilon}]^{-1/2}[a_n^{-2}\Sigma_1^{[nr]}(\hat{\varepsilon}_t^2 - \hat{\sigma}_{\varepsilon}^2)]. \tag{A.31}$$

By lemma 2.1(b) we have

$$a_n^{-2}\Sigma_1^{[nr]}(\hat{\varepsilon}_t^2 - \hat{\sigma}_{\varepsilon}^2) \to_d K_{\alpha/2}(r). \tag{A.32}$$

The denominator of (A.31) is handled by treating the following three cases.

Case (i) $2 < \alpha < 4$.

$$\begin{aligned}\hat{v}_{\varepsilon} = n^{-1}\Sigma_1^n[\hat{\varepsilon}_t^2 - \hat{\sigma}_{\varepsilon}^2]^2 &= n^{-1}\Sigma_1^n[\hat{\varepsilon}_t^2 - \sigma_{\varepsilon}^2]^2 \\ &+ 2n^{-1}\Sigma_1^n(\hat{\varepsilon}_t^2 - \sigma_{\varepsilon}^2)(\sigma_{\varepsilon}^2 - \hat{\sigma}_{\varepsilon}^2) + [\sigma_{\varepsilon}^2 - \hat{\sigma}_{\varepsilon}^2]^2\end{aligned} \tag{A.33}$$

Then

$$\begin{aligned}na_n^{-4}\hat{v}_{\varepsilon} &= a_n^{-4}\Sigma_1^n[\hat{\varepsilon}_t^2 - \hat{\sigma}_{\varepsilon}^2]^2 + 2a_n^{-4}\Sigma_1^n(\hat{\varepsilon}_t^2 - \hat{\sigma}_{\varepsilon}^2)(\sigma_{\varepsilon}^2 - \hat{\sigma}_{\varepsilon}^2) \\ &+ [a_n^{-2}(\sigma_{\varepsilon}^2 - \hat{\sigma}_{\varepsilon}^2)]^2 \to_d \int_0^1(dU_{\alpha/2})^2\end{aligned} \tag{A.34}$$

since $\varepsilon_t^2 \in \mathcal{ND}\ (\alpha/2)$ and $\hat{\sigma}_{\varepsilon}^2 \to_p \sigma_{\varepsilon}^2$. Using (A.32) and (A.34) in (A.31) we obtain the required result (3.11).

Case (ii) $\alpha = 2$. In this case we recenter on $\sigma_{\varepsilon n}^2 = E[\varepsilon_t^2 1(\varepsilon_t^2 < a_n^2)]$ in place of σ_{ε}^2 in (A.33). Observe that

$$a_n^{-2}(\sigma_{\varepsilon n}^2 - \hat{\sigma}_{\varepsilon}^2) = -a_n^{-2}n^{-1}\Sigma_1^n(\hat{\varepsilon}_t^2 - \sigma_{\varepsilon n}^2) = O_p(n^{-1})$$

$$a_n^{-4}\Sigma_1^n[\hat{\varepsilon}_t^2 - \sigma_{\varepsilon n}^2]^2 = -a_n^{-4}\Sigma_1^n(\varepsilon_t^2 - \sigma_{\varepsilon n}^2) + o_p(1) \to_d \int_0^1(dU_{\alpha/2})^2$$

and then

$$na_n^{-4}\hat{v}_{\varepsilon} \to_d \int_0^1(dU_{\alpha/2})^2$$

leading again to (3.11) in conjunction with (A.31) and (A.32).

Case (iii) $0 < \alpha < 2$. Here, no centering is required and we have

$$\begin{aligned}na_n^{-4}\hat{v}_{\varepsilon} &= a_n^{-4}\Sigma_1^n\hat{\varepsilon}_t^4 - na_n^{-4}\hat{\sigma}_{\varepsilon}^4 \\ &= a_n^{-4}\Sigma_1^n\hat{\varepsilon}_t^4 - n^{-1}[a^{-2}\Sigma_1^n\hat{\varepsilon}_t^2] \\ &= a_n^{-4}\Sigma_1^n\hat{\varepsilon}_t^4 + O_p(n^{-1}) \\ &\to_d \int_0^1(dU_{\alpha/2})^2\end{aligned}$$

which again leads to the required result. □

Proof of theorem 3.7

This is similar to theorem 3.5. We write

$$\psi_n^{\varepsilon}(r) = (v_{\varepsilon}/\hat{v}_{\varepsilon})^{1/2}n^{-1/2}\{\Sigma_1^{[nr]}(\hat{\varepsilon}_t^2 - \sigma_{\varepsilon}^2) - ([nr]/n)\Sigma_1^n(\hat{\varepsilon}_t^2 - \sigma_{\varepsilon}^2)\}$$

$$= (v_\varepsilon/\hat{v}_\varepsilon)^{1/2}\{n^{-1/2}\Sigma_1^{[nr]}(\hat{\varepsilon}_t^2 - \sigma_\varepsilon^2) - ([nr]/n)[n^{-1/2}\Sigma_1^{n_1}(\hat{\varepsilon}_t^2 - \sigma_\varepsilon^2)$$
$$+ n^{-1/2}\Sigma_{n_1+1}^{n}(\hat{\varepsilon}_t^2 - \sigma_\varepsilon^2)] + n_2 n^{-1/2}(\sigma_{\varepsilon+}^2 - \sigma_\varepsilon^2)\}. \tag{A.35}$$

Now suppose that $\alpha > 4$. Since $v_\varepsilon/\hat{v}_\varepsilon = O_p(1)$ and $\sigma_\varepsilon^2 \neq \sigma_{\varepsilon+}^2$ under H_1 it is easy to see that all the finite dimensional distributions of $\psi_n^\varepsilon(r)$ diverge under H_1. For $r \leqslant r_k = k/(1+k)$ we have from (A.35) that $\psi_n^\varepsilon(r) = O_p(n_2 n^{-1/2}) = O_p(n^{1/2})$ as $n \to \infty$. A similar decomposition for $\psi_n^\varepsilon(r)$ applies when $r > r_k$ leading to the same rate of divergence over the interval $(r_k, 1]$ and we have (3.12) as required.

When $2 < \alpha < 4$ we have in place of (A.35) the decomposition

$$a_n^{-2}\Sigma_1^{[nr]}(\hat{\varepsilon}_t^2 - \hat{\sigma}_\varepsilon^2) = a_n^{-2}\Sigma_1^{[nr]}(\hat{\varepsilon}_t^2 - \sigma_\varepsilon^2) + ([nr]/n)a_n^{-2}(\hat{\varepsilon}_t^2 - \sigma_\varepsilon^2)$$
$$= a_n^{-2}\Sigma_1^{[nr]}(\hat{\varepsilon}_t^2 - \sigma_\varepsilon^2) - ([nr]/n)a_n^{-2}[\Sigma_1^{n_1}(\hat{\varepsilon}_t^2 - \sigma_\varepsilon^2)$$
$$+ \Sigma_{n_1+1}^{n_2}(\hat{\varepsilon}_t^2 - \sigma_{\varepsilon t}^2) + n_2(\sigma_{\varepsilon+}^2 - \sigma_\varepsilon^2)].$$

Then, taking $r \leqslant r_k$ we have

$$\psi_n^\varepsilon(r) = (na_n^{-4}\hat{v}_\varepsilon)^{-1/2}a_n^{-2}\Sigma_1^{[nr]}(\hat{\varepsilon}_t^2 - \sigma_\varepsilon^2)$$
$$= O_p(n_2 a_n^{-2}) = O_p\,(n^{1-2/\alpha})$$

as required for (3.13). Again the same rate of divergence applies when $r > r_k$.

Finally, when $\alpha < 2$ we write

$$a_n^{-2}\Sigma_1^{[nr]}(\hat{\varepsilon}_t^2 - \hat{\sigma}_\varepsilon^2) = a_n^{-2}\Sigma_1^{[nr]}\hat{\varepsilon}_t^2 - ([nr]/n)a_n^{-2}\Sigma_1^{n}\hat{\varepsilon}_t^2$$
$$= a_n^{-2}\Sigma_1^{[nr]}\hat{\varepsilon}_t^2 - ([nr]/n)\{a_n^{-2}\Sigma_1^{n_1}\hat{\varepsilon}_t^2 + a_n^{-2}\Sigma_{n_1+1}^{n}\hat{\varepsilon}_t^2\}$$
$$= O_p(1),$$

and $na_n^{-4}\hat{v}_\varepsilon = O_p(1)$ as in the proof of theorem 3.5. Thus, we find

$$\psi_n^\varepsilon(r) = (na_n^{-4}\hat{v}_\varepsilon)^{-1/2}a_n^{-2}\Sigma_1^{[nr]}(\hat{\varepsilon}_t^2 - \hat{\sigma}_\varepsilon^2) = O_p(1)$$

and the test is inconsistent in this case.

Proof of theorem 3.8

Using (3.17) we have

$$s^{1/2}[\ln(n_1/s)]^{-1}\tau_d$$
$$= s^{1/2}[\ln(n_1/s)]^{-1}(\hat{d}_s^{(1)} - d) - s^{-1/2}\ln(n_1/s)]^{-1}(\hat{d}_s^{(2)} - d)$$
$$\to_d N(0, 2d^2)$$

and $\tilde{V}(\tau_d) = s^{1/2}[\ln(n_1/s)]^{-1}\tau_d/[\hat{d}_s^{(1)^2} + \hat{d}_s^{(2)^2}]^{1/2} \to_d N(0, 1)$

as required. Note that we may proceed as if $\hat{\varepsilon}_{n,j}$ is replaced by $\varepsilon_{n,j}$ in (3.14) and (3.15) since $\hat{\varepsilon}_t$ (and hence $\hat{\varepsilon}_{n,j}$) is consistent for ε_t (respectively $\varepsilon_{n,j}$) under both the null and alternative hypotheses.

Proof of theorem 3.9

Under H_1 we have

$$\begin{aligned} s^{1/2}[\ln(n_1/s)]^{-1}\tau_d &= s^{1/2}[\ln(n_1/s)]^{-1}(\hat{d}_s^{(1)} - d^{(1)}) \\ &\quad - s^{1/2}[\ln(n_1/s)]^{-1}(\hat{d}_s^{(2)} - d^{(2)}) \\ &\quad + s^{1/2}[\ln(n_1/s)]^{-1}(d^{(1)} - d^{(2)}) \\ &= O_p(s^{1/2}[\ln(n_1/s)]^{-1}). \end{aligned}$$

The same divergence rate applies to $\tilde{V}(\tau_d)$ as $n \to \infty$ since $\hat{d}_s^{(1)} \to_p d^{(1)}$ and $\hat{d}_s^{(2)} \to_p d^{(2)}$.

Proof of theorem 3.10

Using (3.16) we have under H_0^α

$$s^{1/2}(\hat{\alpha}_s^{(1)} - \hat{\alpha}_s^{(2)}) = s^{1/2}(\hat{\alpha}_s^{(1)} - \alpha) - s^{1/2}(\hat{\alpha}_s^{(2)} - \alpha) \to_d N(0, 2\alpha^2)$$

and (3.21) follows directly. Similarly under H_1^α we have

$$\begin{aligned} s^{1/2}(\hat{\alpha}_s^{(1)} - \hat{\alpha}_s^{(2)}) &= s^{1/2}(\hat{\alpha}_s^{(1)} - \alpha^{(1)}) - s^{1/2}(\hat{\alpha}_s^{(2)} - \alpha^{(2)}) + s^{1/2}(\alpha^{(1)} - \alpha^{(2)}) \\ &= O_p(s^{1/2}) \end{aligned}$$

as required for (3.22).

Notes

This chapter is a revised version of the theoretical parts of an earlier paper by the authors entitled "Testing covariance stationarity under moment condition failure with an application to common stock returns." Our thanks go to Glena Ames for wordprocessing and to the NSF for research support under Grant Nos SES 8821180 and SES 9122142.

References

Andrews, D. W. K. (1991) Heteroskedasticity and autocorrelation consistent covariance matrix estimation. *Econometrica*, 59, 817–58.

Avram, F. and Taqqu, M. S. (1986) Weak convergence of moving averages with infinite variance. In E. Eberlain and M. S. Taqqu (eds), *Dependence in Probability and Statistics: a Survey of Recent Results*. Boston: Birkhäuser.

Avram, F. and Taqqu, M. S. (1989) Probability bounds for M-Skorohod oscillations. *Stochastic Processes and Their Applications*, 33, 63–72.

Avram, F. and Taqqu, M. S. (1992) Weak convergence of sums of moving averages in the α-stable domain of attraction. *Annals of Probability*, 20, 483–503.

Billingsley, P. (1968) *Convergence of Probability Measures*. New York: John Wiley.

Blattberg, R. C. and Gonedes, N. J. (1974) A comparison of the stable and student distributions as statistical models for stock prices. *Journal of Business*, 47, 244–80.

Bollerslev, T. (1986) Generalized autoregressive conditional heteroskedasticity. *Journal of Econometrics*, 31, 307–27.

Brieman, L. (1992) *Probability*. Philadelphia: SIAM

Brockwell, P. J. and Davis, R. A. (1991) *Time Series: Theory and Methods*, 2nd edn. New York: Springer-Verlag.

Brown, R. L., Durbin, J. and Evans, J. M. (1975) Techniques for testing the constancy of regression relationships ofer time. *Journal of the Royal Statistical Society B*, 37, 149–63.

Davis, R. A. and Resnick, S. I. (1985a) Limit theory for moving averages of random variables with regularly varying tail probabilities. *Annals of Probability*, 13, 179–95.

Davis, R. A. and Resnick, S. I. (1985b) More limit theory for sample correlation functions of moving averages. *Stochastic Processes and Their Applications*, 20, 257–79.

Davis, R. A. and Resnick, S. I. (1986) Limit theory for the sample covariance and correlation functions of moving averages. *Annals of Statistics*, 14, 533–58.

Durbin, J. (1969) Tests for serial correlation in regression analysis based on the periodogram of least squares residuals. *Biometrika*, 56, 1–15.

Efron, B. (1969) Student's *t*-test under symmetry conditions. *Journal of the American Statistical Association*, 63, 1278–302.

Fama, E. F. (1965) The behavior of stock market prices. *Journal of Business*, 38, 34–105.

Fielitz, B. D. and Rozelle, J. P. (1982) Stable distributions and mixtures of distributions hypotheses for common stock returns. *Journal of the American Statistical Association*, 78, 28–36.

Hall, P. (1982) On some simple estimates of an exponent of regular variation. *Journal of the Royal Statistical Society B*, 44, 37–42.

Hall, P. and Heyde, C. C. (1980) *Martingale Limit Theory and Its Application*. New York: Academic Press.

Hall, P. and Welsh, A. H. (1985) Adaptive estimates of parameters of regular variation. *Annals of Statistics*, 13, 331–41.

Hannan, E. J. and Kanter, M. (1977) Autoregressive processes with infinite variance. *Journal of Applied Probability*, 14, 411–15.

Hill, B. M. (1975) A simple general approach to inference about the tail of a distribution. *Annals of Mathematical Statistics*, 3, 1163–74.

Ibragimov, I. A. and Linnik, Yu. V. (1971) *Independent and Stationary Sequences of Random Variables*. Groningen: Wolters-Noordhof.

Kanter, M. and Steiger, W. L. (1974) Regression and autoregression with infinite variance. *Advances in Applied Probability*, 6, 768–83.

Lo, A. W. (1991) Long-term memory in stock market prices. *Econometrica*, 59, 1279–313.

Logan, B. F., Mallows, C. L., Rice, S. O. and Shepp, L. A. (1973) Limit distributions of selfnormalized sums. *Annals of Probability*, 1, 788–809.

Loretan, M. (1991) Testing covariance stationarity of heavytailed economic time series. Unpublished PhD dissertation, Yale University.

Loretan, M. and Phillips, P. C. B. (1994) Testing the covariance stationarity of heavytailed time series: an overview of the theory with applications to several financial data sets. *Journal of Empirical Finance*, 1, 211–48.

Mandelbrot, B. B. (1963) The variation of certain speculative prices. *Journal of Business*, 36, 394–419.

McFarland, J. W., McMahon, P. C. and Phillips, P. C. B. (1993) Robust tests of forward exchange market efficiency with empirical evidence from the 1920s. Mimeo, Yale University.

Newey, W. K. and West, K. D. (1987) A simple, positive, demi-definite, heteroskedasticity and autocorrelation consistent covariance matrix. *Econometrica*, 55, 703–8.

Pagan, A. R. and Schwert, G. W. (1990a) Testing for covariance stationarity in stock market data. *Economics Letters*, 33, 165–70.

Pagan, A. R. and Schwert, G. W. (1990b) Alternative models for conditional stock volatility. *Journal of Econometrics*, 45, 267–90.

Phillips, P. C. B. (1987) Time series regression with a unit root. *Econometrica*, 55, 277–301.

Phillips, P. C. B. (1990) Time series regression with a unit root and infinite variance errors. *Econometric Theory*, 6, 44–62.

Phillips, P. C. B. (1993) Forward exchange market unbiasedness: the case of the Australian dollar since 1984. Cowles Foundation discussion paper no. 1055.

Phillips, P. C. B. and Hajvassiliou, V. A. (1987) Bimodal t-ratios. Cowles Foundation discussion paper no. 842, July.

Phillips, P. C. B. and Solo, V. (1992) Asymptotics for linear processes. *Annals of Statistics*, 20, 971–1001.

Ploberger, W. and Krämer, W. (1986) On studentizing a test for structural change. *Economics Letters*, 20, 341–4.

Rao, C. R. (1947) Large sample tests of statistical hypotheses concerning several parameters with applications to problems of estimation. *Proceedings of the Cambridge Philosophical Society*, 44, 50–7.

Resnick, S. I. (1986) Point processes regular variation and weak convergence. *Advances in Applied Probability*, 18, 66–138.

Schwert, G. W. (1989) Business cycles, financial crises, and stock volatility. *Carnegie-Rochester Conference Series*, 31, 83–129.

Silvey, S. D. (1959) The Lagrange multiplier test. *Annals of Mathematical Statistics*, 30, 387–407.

So, J. (1987) The sub-Gaussian distribution of currency futures: stable Paretian or nonstationary? *Review of Economics and Statistics*, 69, 100–7.

9 Pattern Identification of ARMA Models

T. W. Anderson

1 Introduction

A family of models frequently used for the statistical analysis of stationary time series consists of autoregressive moving average processes. In fitting such a process to a set of data an important problem is to determine the orders of the autoregressive and moving average parts. Many approaches to this problem have been suggested. Among these are methods that exploit the Yule–Walker equations of the process. Some features of these equations are summarized by functions of the autocovariances; inference can be based on the same functions of the sample autocovariances.

In chapter 5 of his book *ARMA Model Identification*, Byoung Seon Choi (1992) presents about a dozen methods proposed by several statisticians. The purpose of the present chapter is to organize these methods coherently and relate them to each other. The "different" functions employed are essentially variations on a single function; in fact, many methods are based on the function in various forms. This chapter is restricted to consideration of the process autocovariances without further regard to statistical inference.

Let $\{y_t\}$ be a stationary stochastic process with mean $\mathscr{E}y_t = 0$ and autocovariances $\sigma(h) = \mathscr{E}y_t y_{t+h}$, $h = \ldots, -1, 0, 1, \ldots$, satisfying

$$\sum_{j=0}^{p} \beta_j y_{t-j} = \sum_{g=0}^{q} \alpha_g v_{t-g}, \quad t = \ldots, -1, 0, 1, \ldots, \tag{1.1}$$

where $\beta_0 = \alpha_0 = 1$ and $\{v_t\}$ consists of uncorrelated random variables with mean $\mathscr{E}v_t = 0$ and variance $\mathscr{E}v_t^2 = \sigma^2$. The zeros of $\Sigma_{j=0}^{p}\beta_j x^{p-j}$ associated with the autoregressive part have absolute values less than 1 and are distinct from the zeros of $\Sigma_{g=0}^{p}\alpha_g x^{q-g}$ associated with the moving average part. We shall call this model ARMA (p, q). The question studied here is how to determine p and q of the model generating $\{y_t\}$ on the basis of the sequence $\{\sigma(h)\}$. We assume $\beta_p \neq 0$ and $\alpha_q \neq 0$ so that the orders are nontrivial.

The process has the moving average representation

$$y_t = \sum_{r=0}^{\infty} \psi_r v_{t-r}, \tag{1.2}$$

where ψ_r is the coefficient of z^r in $\Sigma_{g=0}^{q}\alpha_g z^g / \Sigma_{j=0}^{p}\beta_j z^j$. Multiplying (1.1) by y_{t-s} and taking expectation yields the Yule–Walker equations. Dividing these by $\sigma(0)$ yields

$$\begin{aligned}\sum_{j=0}^{p}\beta_j\rho_{s-j} &= \frac{\sigma^2}{\sigma(0)}\sum_{g=s}^{q}\alpha_g\psi_{g-s}, \quad s = 1, \ldots, q,\\ &= 0, \quad s = q+1, q+2, \ldots,\end{aligned} \tag{1.3}$$

where $\rho_h = \sigma(h)/\sigma(0)$. These equations will form the basis for determination of the orders.

2 Ranks of Relevant Matrices

Define an $r \times c$ Toeplitz matrix and a $(p+1)$-vector by

$$\mathbf{R}(r, c, i) = \begin{bmatrix} \rho_i & \rho_{i-1} & \cdots & \rho_{i-c+1} \\ \rho_{i+1} & \rho_i & \cdots & \rho_{i-c+2} \\ \vdots & \vdots & & \vdots \\ \rho_{i+r-1} & \rho_{i+r-2} & \cdots & \rho_{i+r-c} \end{bmatrix}, \tag{2.1}$$

$$\boldsymbol{\beta}_{p+1} = \begin{bmatrix} 1 \\ \beta_1 \\ \vdots \\ \beta_p \end{bmatrix} = \begin{bmatrix} 1 \\ -\boldsymbol{\phi}_p \end{bmatrix} = \begin{bmatrix} 1 \\ -\phi_1 \\ \vdots \\ -\phi_p \end{bmatrix}. \tag{2.2}$$

Then the second set of Yule–Walker equations in (1.3) can be written

$$\mathbf{R}(\infty, p+1, q+1)\boldsymbol{\beta}_{p+1} = \mathbf{0}. \tag{2.3}$$

In fact,

$$\mathbf{R}(\infty, c, q+1)\begin{pmatrix} \boldsymbol{\beta}_{p+1} \\ \mathbf{0} \end{pmatrix} = \mathbf{0} \tag{2.4}$$

for $c \geqslant p + 1$, where the subvector $\mathbf{0}$ has $c - (p + 1)$ components. This implies that $\mathbf{R}(r, c, i)$ has rank $< c$ for $r \geqslant 1$, $c \geqslant p + 1$, $i \geqslant q + 1$. In particular, this implies that

$$|\mathbf{R}(k, i)| = 0, \quad k \geqslant p + 1, \quad i \geqslant q + 1, \tag{2.5}$$

where $\mathbf{R}(k, i) = \mathbf{R}(k, k, i)$.

Proposition 1. The rank of $\mathbf{R}(r, p, q)$, $r = p, p + 1, \ldots$, is p.

Proof. Let $\boldsymbol{\rho}(p, i) = (\rho_{i+1}, \ldots, \rho_{i+p})'$ and $\tilde{\boldsymbol{\rho}}(p, i) = (\rho_{i+p}, \ldots, \rho_{i+1})'$. (Throughout this chapter the tilde symbol reverses the order of the components of the vector.) Note that

$$\mathbf{R}(k, i) = [\boldsymbol{\rho}(k, i - 1), \boldsymbol{\rho}(k, i - 2), \ldots, \boldsymbol{\rho}(k, i - k)]$$
$$= \begin{bmatrix} \tilde{\boldsymbol{\rho}}'(k, i - k) \\ \tilde{\boldsymbol{\rho}}(k, i - k + 1) \\ \vdots \\ \tilde{\boldsymbol{\rho}}(k, i - 1) \end{bmatrix}. \tag{2.6}$$

If the rank of $\mathbf{R}(p, p, q) = \mathbf{R}(p, q)$ were less than p, there would exist a vector $\boldsymbol{\gamma}$ such that $\mathbf{R}(p, p, q)\boldsymbol{\gamma} = \mathbf{0}$. Since

$$\begin{aligned} \mathbf{0} &= \tilde{\boldsymbol{\beta}}'_{p+1}\mathbf{R}(p + 1, p, q) \\ &= (-\tilde{\boldsymbol{\phi}}_p, 1)\begin{bmatrix} \mathbf{R}(p, p, q) \\ \tilde{\boldsymbol{\rho}}'(p, q)' \end{bmatrix} \\ &= -\tilde{\boldsymbol{\phi}}_p R(p, p, q) + \tilde{\boldsymbol{\rho}}'(p, q), \end{aligned} \tag{2.7}$$

we have $\boldsymbol{\rho}'(p, q)\boldsymbol{\gamma} = 0$ and

$$\mathbf{0} = \begin{bmatrix} \mathbf{R}(p, p, q) \\ \boldsymbol{\rho}'(p, q) \end{bmatrix}\boldsymbol{\gamma} = \mathbf{R}(p + 1, p, q)\boldsymbol{\gamma}. \tag{2.8}$$

By induction $\mathbf{R}(r, p, q)\boldsymbol{\gamma} = \mathbf{0}$, $r \geqslant p$. However, this would imply that y_t is an ARMA $(p - 1, q)$ process, contrary to the assumption that $\beta_p \neq 0$. □

It follows that

$$|\mathbf{R}(p, i)| \neq 0, \quad i = q, q + 1, \ldots. \tag{2.9}$$

Now consider $\mathbf{R}(k, q)$ for $k > p$. Let

$$\mathbf{v}(k, 1) = \begin{bmatrix} \boldsymbol{\beta}_{p+1} \\ \mathbf{0} \end{bmatrix}, \quad \mathbf{v}(k, j) = \begin{bmatrix} \mathbf{0} \\ \boldsymbol{\beta}_{p+1} \\ \mathbf{0} \end{bmatrix}, \quad j = 2, \ldots, k - p - 1,$$
$$\mathbf{v}(k, k - p) = \begin{bmatrix} \mathbf{0} \\ \boldsymbol{\beta}_{p+1} \end{bmatrix}, \tag{2.10}$$

where the first $\mathbf{0}$ in $\mathbf{v}(k, j)$ has $j - 1$ components, $j = 2, \ldots, k - p - 1$. Let $\mathbf{M} = [\mathbf{v}(k, 1), \ldots, \mathbf{v}(k, k - p)]$, and let $\mathbf{N} = (\mathbf{0}, \mathbf{I}_p)'$. Then $|\mathbf{M}, \mathbf{N}| = 1$ and

$$\mathbf{R}(k, q)[\mathbf{M}, \mathbf{N}] = \begin{bmatrix} \mathbf{A} & \mathbf{B} \\ \mathbf{0} & \mathbf{R}(p, q) \end{bmatrix}, \tag{2.11}$$

where $\mathbf{A}$ is upper triangular with diagonal elements $\sigma^2\alpha_q/\sigma(0)$ and $\mathbf{R}(p, q)$ is nonsingular. Thus $\mathbf{R}(k, q)$ is nonsingular, and

$$|\mathbf{R}(k, q)| \neq 0, \quad k = p + 1, p + 2, \ldots. \tag{2.12}$$

Since $\mathbf{R}(p, q)$ is nonsingular, the set of linear equations (1.3) for $s = q + 1, \ldots, q + p$ can be solved for $\beta_1, \ldots, \beta_p$. Then $\Sigma_{j=0}^{p}\beta_j y_{t-j} = w_t$, say, can be generated. From $\mathscr{E} w_t w_{t-i}$, $i = 0, 1, \ldots, q$, a set of coefficients for the moving average process $\Sigma_{\alpha=0}^{q}\alpha_g v_{t-g}$ can be found since $\mathscr{E} w_t w_{t-i} = 0$, $i = q + 1, q + 2, \ldots$ (Anderson, 1971, section 5.7). The coefficients are uniquely determined if this moving average process is invertible and the solution is required to be invertible; if it is not invertible, an arbitrary rule on the unit roots can be imposed to make the solution unique. This shows that there can be only one pair of p and q that will satisfy the Yule–Walker equations.

The orders p and q have the properties

(i) rank $[\mathbf{R}(\infty, p + 1, q + 1)] = p$,
(ii) rank $[\mathbf{R}(\infty, p + 1, q)] = p + 1$,
(iii) rank $[\mathbf{R}(\infty, p, q)] = p$.

Property (i) implies the Yule–Walker equations for $s = q + 1, q + 2, \ldots$; it implies the existence of p and q. Property (ii) implies that the order of the moving average part is not less than q. Property (iii) implies that the order of the autoregressive part is not less than p when the order of the moving average part is at least q.

Given $\{\sigma(h)\}$ or $\{\rho_h\}$ a procedure is to determine c and r so that rank $[\mathbf{R}(\infty, c + 1, r + 1)] = c$, rank $[\mathbf{R}(\infty, c + 1, r)] = c + 1$, and rank $[\mathbf{R}(\infty, c, r)] = c$. Then conclude that $p = c$ and $q = r$. In practice the values of c and r have to be limited; it may assumed that $p \leqslant P$ and $q \leqslant Q$, where P and Q are specified in advance.

Many methods of identification determine the ranks of the relevant matrices by various functions of the correlations.

3 Methods of Identification

Determinants of $\mathbf{R}(k, i)$*: the "corner method"*

Perhaps the simplest criterion of rank is the determinant of a square matrix. Let

$$I_{rs} = \{(k, s)|k = r, r + 1, \ldots\} \cup \{(r, i)|i = s, s + 1, \ldots\}, \quad (3.1)$$

$$J_{rs} = \{(k, i)|k = r, r + 1, \ldots, i = s, s + 1, \ldots\}. \quad (3.2)$$

Note that $J_{rs} = I_{rs} \cup J_{r+1,s+1}$ and $I_{rs} \cap J_{r+1,s+1} = 0$. The pattern of determinants for ARMA (p, q) is (Beguin et al., 1980)

$$\begin{aligned} |\mathbf{R}(k, i)| &\neq 0, \quad (k, i) \in I_{pq}, \\ &= 0, \quad (k, i) \in J_{p+1,q+1}. \end{aligned} \quad (3.3)$$

The relationships (3.3) can be expressed in alternative, but equivalent ways. Let $\mathrm{ch}_{\min}(\mathbf{A})$ denote the minimum characteristic root of a square matrix $\mathbf{A}$. Then (3.3) is alternatively stated as

$$\begin{aligned} \mathrm{ch}_{\min}\mathbf{R}(k, i) &\neq 0, \quad (k, i) \in I_{pq}, \\ &= 0, \quad (k, i) \in J_{p+1,q+1}, \end{aligned} \quad (3.4)$$

$$\begin{aligned} \mathrm{ch}_{\min}\mathbf{R}(k, i)\mathbf{R}'(k, i) &\neq 0, \quad (k, i) \in I_{pq}, \\ &= 0, \quad (k, i) \in J_{p+1,q+1}, \end{aligned} \quad (3.5)$$

$$\begin{aligned} \mathrm{ch}_{\min}\mathbf{R}'(k, i)\mathbf{R}^{-1}(k, 0)\mathbf{R}(k, i) &\neq 0, \quad (k, i) \in I_{pq}, \\ &= 0, \quad (k, i) \in J_{p+1,q+1}, \end{aligned} \quad (3.6)$$

$$\begin{aligned} \mathrm{ch}_{\min}[\mathbf{R}^{-1}(k, 0)\mathbf{R}'(k, i)\mathbf{R}^{-1}(k, 0)\mathbf{R}(k, i)] &\neq 0, \quad (k, i) \in I_{pq}, \\ &= 0, \quad (k, i) \in J_{p+1,q+1}. \end{aligned} \quad (3.7)$$

Choi refers to (3.4), (3.5), and (3.6) (proposed by Akaike, 1974) as "eigen-analysis" and (3.7) as SCAN. Let $\mathbf{y}_t^{(k)} = (y_t, y_{t-1}, \ldots, y_{t-k+1})'$. The characteristic roots of $\mathbf{R}^{-1}(k, 0)\mathbf{R}'(k, i)\mathbf{R}(k, 0)^{-1}\mathbf{R}(k, i)$ are the squares of the canonical correlations between $\mathbf{y}_t^{(k)}$ and $\mathbf{y}_{t-i}^{(k)}$ (proposed by Tsay and Tiao, 1985).

Generalized partial correlations

The partial correlation between y_t and y_{t-k-1} conditioned on $\mathbf{y}_{t-1}^{(k)} = (y_{t-1}, \ldots, y_{t-k})'$ is

$$\mathrm{PACF}(k + 1) = \frac{\mathscr{E}(y_t - \boldsymbol{\phi}'(k, 0)\mathbf{y}_{t-1}^{(k)})(y_{t-k-1} - \tilde{\boldsymbol{\phi}}(k, 0)\mathbf{y}_{t-1}^{(k)})}{\mathscr{E}(y_t - \phi'(k, 0)\mathbf{y}_{t-1}^{(k)})^2}$$

$$= \frac{\begin{array}{c}\sigma(k+1) - \phi'(k,0)\tilde{\boldsymbol{\sigma}}(k,0) - \\ \boldsymbol{\phi}'(k,0)\boldsymbol{\sigma}(k,0) + \boldsymbol{\phi}'(k,0)\boldsymbol{\Sigma}(k,0)\tilde{\boldsymbol{\phi}}(k,0)\end{array}}{\begin{array}{c}\sigma(0) - 2\boldsymbol{\phi}'(k,0)\boldsymbol{\sigma}(k,0) \\ + \boldsymbol{\phi}'(k,0)\boldsymbol{\Sigma}(k,0)\boldsymbol{\phi}(k,0)\end{array}}$$

$$= \frac{\rho_{k+1} - \tilde{\rho}'(k,0)\mathbf{R}^{-1}(k,0)\boldsymbol{\rho}(k,0)}{1 - \boldsymbol{\rho}'(k,0)\mathbf{R}^{-1}(k,0)\boldsymbol{\rho}(k,0)}$$

$$= (-1)^k \frac{\begin{vmatrix}\boldsymbol{\rho}(k,0) & \mathbf{R}(k,0) \\ \rho_{k+1} & \tilde{\boldsymbol{\rho}}'(k,0)\end{vmatrix}}{\begin{vmatrix}1 & \boldsymbol{\rho}'(k,0) \\ \boldsymbol{\rho}(k,0) & \mathbf{R}(k,0)\end{vmatrix}}$$

$$= (-1)^k \frac{|\mathbf{R}(k+1),1)|}{|\mathbf{R}(k+1,0)|}, \tag{3.8}$$

where $\boldsymbol{\sigma}(k, 0) = [\sigma(1), \ldots \sigma(k)]'$ and $\phi(k, 0)$ consists of the coefficients of the regression of y_t on $\mathbf{y}_{t-1}^{(k)}$ and of y_{t-k-1} on $\tilde{\mathbf{y}}_{t-1}^{(k)}$, namely

$$\boldsymbol{\phi}(k,0) = \mathbf{R}^{-1}(k,0)\boldsymbol{\rho}(k,0), \quad \tilde{\boldsymbol{\phi}}(k,0) = \mathbf{R}^{-1}(k,0)\tilde{\boldsymbol{\rho}}(k,0), \tag{3.9}$$

where $\boldsymbol{\rho}(k, 0) = (\rho_1, \ldots, \rho_k)'$ and $\tilde{\boldsymbol{\rho}}(k, 0) = (\rho_k, \ldots, \rho_1)'$, throughout this chapter (see, for example, section A.3 of Anderson (1984) for explanation of the penultimate equality in (3.8)).

For the AR(p) = ARMA (p, 0) process PACF($k + 1$) = 0, $k + 1 = p + 1, p+ 2, \ldots$. For ARMA($p$, q) generally define

$$\boldsymbol{\phi}(k,i) = \mathbf{R}^{-1}(k,i)\boldsymbol{\rho}(k,i). \tag{3.10}$$

Then

$$\boldsymbol{\rho}(k,i) = \mathbf{R}(k,i)\boldsymbol{\phi}(k,i)$$

$$= [\boldsymbol{\rho}(k,i-1), \boldsymbol{\rho}(k,i-2), \ldots, \boldsymbol{\rho}(k,i-k)]\begin{bmatrix}\phi_{k1}^{(i)} \\ \phi_{k2}^{(i)} \\ \vdots \\ \phi_{kk}^{(i)}\end{bmatrix}, \tag{3.11}$$

and

$$\tilde{\boldsymbol{\rho}}(k,i) = [\tilde{\boldsymbol{\rho}}(k,i-k), \ldots, \tilde{\boldsymbol{\rho}}(k,i-1)]\begin{bmatrix}\phi_{kk}^{(i)} \\ \vdots \\ \phi_{k1}^{(i)}\end{bmatrix} = \mathbf{R}'(k,i)\tilde{\phi}(k,i). \tag{3.12}$$

Thus $\tilde{\boldsymbol{\phi}}(k, i) = [\mathbf{R}'(k, i)]^{-1}\tilde{\boldsymbol{\rho}}(k, i)$. The equation (3.10) gives the solution to the Yule–Walker equations (1.3) for $s = q + 1, \ldots, q + p$

when $k = p$ and $i = q$. Note $\boldsymbol{\beta}_{p+1} = (1, -\boldsymbol{\phi}'(p, q))'$. Then

$$\boldsymbol{\beta}'_{p+1}\mathbf{y}_t^{(p+1)} = y_t - \boldsymbol{\phi}'(p, q)\mathbf{y}_{t-1}^{(p)} = \sum_{g=0}^{q} \alpha_g v_{t-g} \tag{3.13}$$

and

$$\begin{aligned}\tilde{\boldsymbol{\beta}}'_{p+1}\mathbf{y}_{t-q-1}^{(p+1)} &= \mathbf{y}_{t-p-q-1} - \tilde{\boldsymbol{\phi}}'(p, q)\mathbf{y}_{t-q-1}^{(p)} \\ &= \sum_{j=0}^{p} \beta_j y_{t-q-p-1+j} \\ &= \sum_{j=0}^{p}\sum_{r=0}^{\infty} \beta_j \psi_r v_{t-q-p-1+j-r}\end{aligned} \tag{3.14}$$

are uncorrelated. In fact, $\boldsymbol{\beta}'_{p+1}\mathbf{y}_t^{(p+1)}$ and $\tilde{\boldsymbol{\beta}}'_{p+1}\mathbf{y}_{t-i-1}^{(p+1)}$ are uncorrelated for $i = q, q + 1, \ldots$. Note that $\tilde{\boldsymbol{\phi}}'(k, i)\tilde{\mathbf{y}}_{t-i-1}^{(k)} = \boldsymbol{\phi}'(k, i)\tilde{\mathbf{y}}_{t-i-1}^{(k)}$.

The covariance between $y_t - \boldsymbol{\phi}'(k, i)\mathbf{y}_{t-1}^{(k)} = y_t - \Sigma_{j=1}^{k}\phi_{kj}^{(i)}y_{t-j}$ and $y_{t-k-i-1} - \tilde{\boldsymbol{\phi}}'(k, i)\mathbf{y}_{t-i-1}^{(k)} = y_{t-k-i-1} - \Sigma_{j=1}^{k}\phi_{k,k-j+1}^{(i)}y_{t-i-j}$ is

$$\begin{aligned}&\mathscr{E}[y_t - \boldsymbol{\phi}'(k, i)\mathbf{y}_{t-1}^{(k)}][y_{t-k-i-1} - \tilde{\boldsymbol{\phi}}'(k, i)\mathbf{y}_{t-i-1}^{(k)}] \\ &\quad= \sigma(0)[\rho_{i+k+1} - \tilde{\boldsymbol{\phi}}'(k, i)\boldsymbol{\rho}(k, i) - \tilde{\boldsymbol{\rho}}(k, i)\boldsymbol{\phi}(k, i) \\ &\qquad + \tilde{\boldsymbol{\phi}}'(k, i)\mathbf{R}(k, i)\boldsymbol{\phi}(k, i)] \\ &\quad= \sigma(0)[\rho_{i+k+1} - \tilde{\boldsymbol{\rho}}'(k, i)\mathbf{R}^{-1}(k, i)\boldsymbol{\rho}(k, i)] \\ &\quad= (-1)^k\sigma(0)\frac{\begin{vmatrix}\boldsymbol{\rho}(k, i)\mathbf{R}(k, i) \\ \rho_{i+k+1} \quad \tilde{\boldsymbol{\rho}}'(k, i)\end{vmatrix}}{|\mathbf{R}(k, i)|} \\ &\quad= (-1)^k\sigma(0)\frac{|\boldsymbol{R}(k + 1, i + 1)|}{|\boldsymbol{R}(k, i)|}\end{aligned} \tag{3.15}$$

if $|\mathbf{R}(k, i)| \neq 0$. Takemura (1984) divided this covariance by the variance of $y_t - \boldsymbol{\phi}'(k, i)y_{t-1}^{(k)}$ (which is also the variance of $y_{t-k-i-1} - \tilde{\boldsymbol{\phi}}'(k, i)\mathbf{y}_{t-i-1}^{(k)}$) to obtain

$$\begin{aligned}&T(k + 1, i + 1) \\ &= (-1)^k \frac{|\mathbf{R}(k + 1, i + 1)|}{|\mathbf{R}(k, i)|[1, -\boldsymbol{\phi}'(k, i)]\mathbf{R}(k + 1, 0)][1, -\boldsymbol{\phi}'(k, i)]'} \\ &= \frac{\rho_{k+i+1} - \tilde{\boldsymbol{\rho}}'(k, i)\mathbf{R}^{-1}(k, i)\boldsymbol{\rho}(k, i)}{1 - 2\boldsymbol{\rho}'(k, 0)\mathbf{R}^{-1}(k, i)\boldsymbol{\rho}(k, i) - \boldsymbol{\rho}'(k, i) [\mathbf{R}'(k, i)]^{-1}\mathbf{R}(k, 0)\mathbf{R}^{-1}(k, i)\boldsymbol{\rho}(k, i)}\end{aligned} \tag{3.16}$$

if $|\mathbf{R}(k, i)| \neq 0$. (Choi denotes $T(k + 1, i + 1)$ by $\tau(k, i)$.) From (3.3) we deduce that $T(k+1, i+1) \neq 0$ for $(k+1, i+1) \in I_{pq}$ and $T(k+1, i+1) = 0$ for $(k + 1, i + 1) \in I_{p+1,q+1}$.

Since $T(k + 1, i + 1)$ is a correlation coefficient, $|T(k, i)| < 1$. When $k = 0$, $T(1, i) = \rho_i$, and when $i = 0$, $T(k + 1, 1) = \text{PACF}(k)$. (Choi incorrectly reports $\tau(0, i) = T(1, i) = \rho_{i+1}$.) Thus $T(k, i)$ is a generalization of the autocorrelation coefficient and the partial autocorrelation coefficient.

Now we turn to the case of $|\mathbf{R}(k, i)| = 0$. Suppose $k > p$ and $i > q$. The upper left-hand submatrix of

$$\mathbf{R}(k, i) = \begin{bmatrix} \mathbf{R}(p, i) & \mathbf{R}(p, k - p, i - p) \\ \mathbf{R}(k - p, p, i + p) & \mathbf{R}(k - p, i) \end{bmatrix} \tag{3.17}$$

is nonsingular by proposition 1.

Proposition 2. If $0 < k - p \leqslant i - q$,

$$\mathbf{R}(k, i)\mathbf{v}(k, j) = 0, \quad j = 1, \ldots, k - p. \tag{3.18}$$

Proof. The hth row of (3.18) is $\Sigma_{g=0}^{p} \beta_g \rho_{i+h-j-g}$. The coefficient of $\beta_0 = 1$ has index $i + h - j$, which is minimized by $h = 1$ and $j = k - p$. The index $s = i + 1 - (k - p) \geqslant q + 1$ and hence the Yule–Walker equation (1.3) has right hand side 0. □

Proposition 3. If $0 < i - q \leqslant k - p$,

$$\mathbf{R}(k, i)\mathbf{v}(k, j) = \mathbf{0}, \quad j = 1, \ldots, i - q. \tag{3.19}$$

Proof. The upper right-hand submatrix of

$$\mathbf{R}(k, i) = \begin{bmatrix} \mathbf{R}(k - i + q, i - q, i) & \mathbf{R}(k - i + q, q) \\ \mathbf{R}(i - q, k + q) & \mathbf{R}(i - q, k - i + q, k - i + 2q) \end{bmatrix} \tag{3.20}$$

is nonsingular by (2.12). The coefficient of β_0 in the hth row of $\mathbf{R}(k, i)\mathbf{v}(k, j)$ is minimized by $h = 1$ and $j = i - q$. The index is $s = i + 1 - (i - q) \geqslant q + 1$. □

Proposition 4. The rank of $\mathbf{R}(k, i)$ is $\max(p, k - i + q)$.

Proof. Propositions 3 and 4. □

Note that by (2.6)

$$\mathbf{R}'(k, i)\tilde{\mathbf{v}}(k, j) = \mathbf{0}, \quad j = 1, \ldots, \min(k - p, i - q). \tag{3.21}$$

Now consider

$$\mathbf{R}(k, i)\boldsymbol{\phi}(k, i) = \boldsymbol{\rho}(k, i) \tag{3.22}$$

when $|\mathbf{R}(k, i)| = 0$; that is, when $k > p$ and $i > q$. Denote any generalized inverse of $\mathbf{R}(k, i)$ as $\mathbf{R}^{-}(k, i)$. Then

$$\boldsymbol{\phi}(k, i) = \mathbf{R}^{-}(k, i)\boldsymbol{\rho}(k, i). \tag{3.23}$$

As shown in the appendix, any solution (3.23) can be written as

$$\boldsymbol{\phi}(k, i) = \boldsymbol{\phi}_0 + \mathbf{Mh}, \tag{3.24}$$

where $\boldsymbol{\phi}_0$ is a specified solution and $\mathbf{h}$ depends on $\mathbf{R}^{-}(k, i)$ and $\boldsymbol{\phi}_0$. It is convenient to take

$$\boldsymbol{\phi}_0 = \begin{bmatrix} \mathbf{R}^{-1}(p, i)\boldsymbol{\rho}(p, i) \\ \mathbf{0} \end{bmatrix} = \begin{bmatrix} \boldsymbol{\phi}(p, q) \\ \mathbf{0} \end{bmatrix}. \tag{3.25}$$

Then

$$\tilde{\boldsymbol{\phi}}(k, i) = \tilde{\boldsymbol{\phi}}_0 + \tilde{\mathbf{M}}\mathbf{h}, \tag{3.26}$$

where $\tilde{\mathbf{M}} = [\tilde{\mathbf{v}}(k, i), \ldots, \tilde{v}(k, \min(k-p, i-q)]$. We have

$$\begin{aligned} y_t - \boldsymbol{\phi}'(k, i)\mathbf{y}_{t-1}^{(k)} &= y_t - \boldsymbol{\phi}_0'\mathbf{y}_{t-1}^{(k)} - \mathbf{h}'\mathbf{M}'\mathbf{y}_{t-1}^{(k)} \\ &= \boldsymbol{\beta}_{p+1}'\mathbf{y}_t^{(p+1)} - \mathbf{h}'\mathbf{M}'\mathbf{y}_{t-1}^{(h)}, \end{aligned} \tag{3.27}$$

$$\begin{aligned} y_{t-k-i-1} - \tilde{\boldsymbol{\phi}}'(k, i)\mathbf{y}_{t-i-1}^{(k)} &= y_{t-k-i-1} - \tilde{\boldsymbol{\phi}}_0'\mathbf{y}_{t-i-1}^{(k)} - \mathbf{h}'\tilde{\mathbf{M}}'\mathbf{y}_{t-i-1}^{(k)} \\ &= \tilde{\boldsymbol{\beta}}_{p+1}\mathbf{y}_{t-i-k+p-1}^{(p+1)} - \mathbf{h}'\tilde{\mathbf{M}}'\,\mathbf{y}_{t-i-1}^{(k)}. \end{aligned} \tag{3.28}$$

Their covariance is

$$\mathscr{E}[y_t - \boldsymbol{\phi}'(k, i)\mathbf{y}_{t-1}^{(k)}][y_{t-k-i-1} - \tilde{\boldsymbol{\phi}}'(k, i)\mathbf{y}_{t-i-1}^{(k)}] = 0. \tag{3.29}$$

Thus

$$\begin{aligned} T(k, i) &\neq 0, \quad (k, i) \in I_{pq}, \\ &= 0, \ (k, i) \in J_{p+1,q+1}. \end{aligned} \tag{3.30}$$

Glasbey (1982) proposed a statistic with the same numerator but with denominator the square root of

$$\sum_{j=-i}^{i} \left[\sum_{m=0}^{\min(k,i-j)} \sum_{l=0}^{k} \phi_{km}^{(i)} \phi_{kl}^{(i)} \rho_{i+m-l} \right]^2. \tag{3.31}$$

It would seem that this is defined only for $k \leqslant p$. Since (3.31) is a sum of squares, it will usually be positive. The pairs of (k, i) for which Glasbey's statistic is 0 or alternatively different from 0 are the pairs for which $T(k+1, i+1) = 0$ or $T(k+1, i+1) \neq 0$, respectively.

Woodward and Gray (1981) have suggested $\phi_{kk}^{(i)}$ as a generalized partial autocorrelation since $\phi_{kk}^{(k)} = \text{PACF}(k)$. Use of Cramer's rule for (3.22) that

$$\phi_{kk}^{(i)} = (-1)^{k-1} \frac{|\mathbf{R}(k, i+1)|}{|\mathbf{R}(k, i)|} \tag{3.32}$$

if $\mathbf{R}(k, i)| \neq 0$. We define

$$W(k, i) = \phi_{kk}^{(i-1)} = (-1)^{k-1} \frac{|\mathbf{R}(k, i)|}{|\mathbf{R}(k, i-1)|}. \tag{3.33}$$

Then

$$W(k, q) = \phi_{kk}^{(q-1)}, \quad k = p, p+1, \ldots, \tag{3.34}$$

$$W(p, i) = \phi_p, \quad i = q+1, q+2, \ldots, \tag{3.35}$$

$$W(k, q+1) = 0, \quad k = p+1, p+2, \ldots. \tag{3.36}$$

If $k > p$ and $i < q + 1$, the statistic is undefined.

Choi's "three-pattern" method

Choi (1992) has defined

$$\begin{aligned}\Theta(k+1, i+1) &= \rho_{i+k+1} - \tilde{\boldsymbol{\rho}}'(k, i)\mathbf{R}^{-1}(k, i)\boldsymbol{\rho}(k, i) \\ &= (-1)^k \frac{|\mathbf{R}(k+1, i+1)|}{|\mathbf{R}(k, i)|},\end{aligned} \tag{3.37}$$

$$\begin{aligned}H(k+1, i-1) &= \rho_{i-k-1} - \tilde{\boldsymbol{\rho}}'(k, i-k-1)\mathbf{R}^{-1}(k, i)\boldsymbol{\rho}(k, i-k-1) \\ &= (-1)^k \frac{|\mathbf{R}(k+1, i-1)|}{|\mathbf{R}(k, i)|},\end{aligned} \tag{3.38}$$

$$\begin{aligned}\Lambda(k+1, i) &= \rho_i - \tilde{\boldsymbol{\rho}}'(k, i-k-1)\mathbf{R}^{-1}(k, i)\boldsymbol{\rho}(k, i) \\ &= \frac{|\mathbf{R}(k+1, i)|}{|\mathbf{R}(k, i)|},\end{aligned} \tag{3.39}$$

if $\mathbf{R}(k, i)$ is nonsingular. (Choi's notation is $\theta(k, i)$, $\eta(k, i)$ and $\lambda(k, i)$, respectively.) In that case $\Theta(k, i) \neq 0$ if $(k, i) \in I_{p,q}$ and $\Theta(k, i) = 0$ if $(k, i) \in J_{p+1,q+1}$; $H(k, i) \neq 0$ if $(k, i) \in I_{p,q}$ and $H(k, i) = 0$ if $(k, i) \in J_{p+1,q+1}$; and $\Lambda(k, i) \neq 0$ if $(k, i) \in I_{p,q}$ and $\Lambda(k, i) = 0$ if $(k, i) \in J_{p,q}$. However, $\mathbf{R}(k, i)$ is singular if $(k, i) \in J_{p+1,q+1}$. In cases where both the numerator and denominator are 0 the value of the ratio of determinants is undefined. Then according to Choi's definition

$$\Theta(k+1, i+1) = \rho_{i+k+1} - \tilde{\boldsymbol{\rho}}'(k, i)\mathbf{R}^{-}(k, i)\boldsymbol{\rho}(k, i), \tag{3.40}$$

$$H(k+1, i-1) = \rho_{i-k-1} - \tilde{\boldsymbol{\rho}}'(k, i-k-1)\mathbf{R}^{-}(k, i)\boldsymbol{\rho}(k, i-k-1), \tag{3.41}$$

$$\Lambda(k+1, i) = \rho_i - \tilde{\boldsymbol{\rho}}'(k, i-k-1)\mathbf{R}^{-}(k, i)\boldsymbol{\rho}(k, i), \tag{3.42}$$

where $\mathbf{R}^{-}(k, i)$ is a generalized inverse of $\mathbf{R}(k, i)$.

As noted above, $\Theta(k, i)$ is the numerator of $T(k, i)$ and is 0 for $(k, i) \in J_{p+1,q+1}$; it does not depend on which generalized inverse is used because $\tilde{\boldsymbol{\rho}}'(k, i)\mathbf{M} = \mathbf{0}$. Thus

$$\begin{aligned} \Theta(k, i) &\neq 0, \quad (k, i) \in I_{pq}, \\ &= 0, \quad (k, i) \in J_{p+1,q+1}. \end{aligned} \tag{3.43}$$

The behavior of $\Theta(k, i)$ similar to that of $T(k, i)$ and $|\mathbf{R}(k, i)|$.

Now consider $\Lambda(k, i)$. If $k = p$ and $i \geqslant q$, $\mathbf{R}(k, i) = \mathbf{R}(p, i)$ is nonsingular and

$$\Lambda(p+1, i) = \frac{|\mathbf{R}(p+1, i)|}{|\mathbf{R}(p, i)|}, \tag{3.44}$$

where

$$|\mathbf{R}(p+1, i)| = \begin{vmatrix} \rho_i & \rho_{i-1} & \cdots & \rho_{i-p} \\ \rho_{i+1} & \rho_i & \cdots & \rho_{i-p+1} \\ \vdots & \vdots & & \vdots \\ \rho_{i+p} & \rho_{i+p-1} & \cdots & \rho_i \end{vmatrix}, \tag{3.45}$$

which is 0 if $i > q$. If $0 < k - p < i - q$, $\mathbf{R}(k, i)$ has rank p, and $\mathbf{R}(p, i)$ is nonsingular. ($0 < i - q$ is equivalent to $q < i$.) Then (3.23) is a solution to (3.22) with $\boldsymbol{\phi}_0$ given by (3.24), and

$$\Lambda(k+1, i) = \rho_i - (\rho_{i-1}, \ldots, \rho_{i-k})\boldsymbol{\phi}_0 \tag{3.46}$$

$$\begin{aligned} &= \rho_i - (\rho_{i-1}, \ldots, \rho_{i-p})\boldsymbol{\phi}(p, q) \\ &= 0 \end{aligned} \tag{3.47}$$

because $(\rho_{i-1}, \ldots, \rho_{i-k})\mathbf{M} = \tilde{\boldsymbol{\rho}}'(k, i-k-1)\mathbf{M} = \mathbf{0}$ if $0 < k - p < i - q$. If $0 < k - p = i - q$, $(\rho_{i-1}, \ldots, \rho_{i-k})\mathbf{M} \neq \mathbf{0}$; $\mathbf{R}^{-}(k, i)\boldsymbol{\rho}(k, i)$ depends on which $\mathbf{R}^{-}(k, i)$ is used, and (3.47) no longer holds. The same is true in case $0 < k - p < i - q$.

Now consider $H(k, i)$. If $k = p$ and $i > q$, $\mathbf{R}(k, i) = \mathbf{R}(p, i)$ is nonsingular and

$$H(p+1, i-1) = (-1)^p \frac{|\mathbf{R}(p+1, i-1)|}{|\mathbf{R}(k, i)|}, \tag{3.48}$$

where

$$|\mathbf{R}(p+1, i-1)| = \begin{vmatrix} \rho_{i-1} & \rho_{i-2} & \cdots & \rho_{i-p-1} \\ \rho_i & \rho_{i-1} & \cdots & \rho_{i-p} \\ \vdots & \vdots & & \vdots \\ \rho_{i+p-1} & \rho_{i+p-2} & \cdots & \rho_{i-1} \end{vmatrix}, \tag{3.49}$$

which is 0 if $i > q + 1$. Note that the equation for $\mathbf{R}^{-}(p, i)\boldsymbol{\rho}(p, i - p - 1)$ is

$$\mathbf{R}(p,i)\boldsymbol{\delta} = \begin{bmatrix} \rho_i & \cdots & \rho_{i-p+1} \\ \vdots & & \vdots \\ \rho_{i+p-1} & \cdots & \rho_i \end{bmatrix} \begin{bmatrix} \delta_1 \\ \vdots \\ \delta_p \end{bmatrix} = \begin{bmatrix} \rho_{i-p} \\ \vdots \\ \rho_{i-1} \end{bmatrix} = \boldsymbol{\rho}(p, i-p-1). \tag{3.50}$$

Since $0 = (\rho_j, \ldots, \rho_{j-p})\boldsymbol{\beta}_{p+1} = \rho_j - \Sigma_{l=1}^{p}\phi_i\rho_{j-l}$, $j \geqslant q + 1$, the solution $\boldsymbol{\delta}$ is

$$\boldsymbol{\delta} = \frac{1}{\phi_p}\begin{bmatrix} 1 \\ -\phi_1 \\ \vdots \\ -\phi_{p-1} \end{bmatrix} \tag{3.51}$$

and

$$\begin{aligned} H(p+1, i-1) &= \rho_{i-p-1} - (\rho_{i-1}, \ldots, \rho_{i-p})\boldsymbol{\delta} \\ &= -\frac{1}{\phi_p}\left(\rho_{i-1} - \sum_{l=1}^{p} \phi_l \rho_{i-1-l}\right) \\ &= 0 \end{aligned} \tag{3.52}$$

for $i \geqslant q + 2$ as stated above.

If $0 < k - p < i - q - 1$, $\mathbf{R}(k, i)$ has rank p and $\mathbf{R}(p, i)$ is nonsingular. Instead of (3.50) the equation for $\mathbf{R}^{-}(k, i)\boldsymbol{\rho}(k, i - k - 1)$ is

$$\mathbf{R}(k,i)\boldsymbol{\delta} = \begin{bmatrix} \rho_i & \cdots & \rho_{i-k+1} \\ \vdots & & \vdots \\ \rho_{i+k-1} & \cdots & \rho_i \end{bmatrix} \begin{bmatrix} \delta_1 \\ \vdots \\ \delta_k \end{bmatrix} = \begin{bmatrix} \rho_{i-k} \\ \vdots \\ \rho_{i-1} \end{bmatrix} = \boldsymbol{\rho}(k, i-k-1), \tag{3.53}$$

which has a solution

$$\boldsymbol{\delta}_0 = \frac{1}{\phi_p}\begin{bmatrix} 0 \\ \vdots \\ 0 \\ 1 \\ -\phi_1 \\ \vdots \\ -\phi_{p-1} \end{bmatrix}. \tag{3.54}$$

Then

$$\begin{aligned} H(k+1, i-1) &= \rho_{i-k-1} - (\rho_{ip-1}, \ldots, \rho_{i-k})\boldsymbol{\delta}_0 \\ &= \rho_{i-k-1} - (\rho_{i-k+p-1}, \ldots, \rho_{i-k})\begin{pmatrix} 1 \\ -\phi_1 \\ \vdots \\ -\phi_{p-1} \end{pmatrix}\frac{1}{\phi_p} \\ &= 0 \end{aligned} \tag{3.55}$$

for $i - k + p - 1 \geqslant q + 1$, which is implied by $0 < k - p < i - q - 1$. Now suppose $0 < k - p = i - q - 1$. Then $(\rho_{i-1}, \ldots, \rho_{i-k})\mathbf{M} = \mathbf{0}$ and

$$\begin{aligned} H(k+1, i-1) &= \rho_{i-k-1} - (\rho_{i-k+p-1}, \ldots, \rho_{i-k})\begin{pmatrix} 1 \\ -\phi_1 \\ \vdots \\ -\phi_{p-1} \end{pmatrix}\frac{1}{\phi_p} \\ &= -\frac{1}{\phi_p}(\rho_{i-k+p-1} - \phi_1\rho_{i-k+p-2} - \cdots - \phi_p\rho_{i-k-1}) \\ &= -\frac{\sigma_2^q\alpha_q}{\sigma(0)\phi_p} \neq 0. \end{aligned} \tag{3.56}$$

If $0 < i - q - 1 < k - p$, $(\rho_{i-1}, \ldots, \rho_{i-k})\mathbf{M} \neq \mathbf{0}$ and the equations (3.53) are inconsistent; that is, there is no solution $\mathbf{R}^{-}(k, i)\boldsymbol{\rho}(k, i-k-1)$ and $H(k, i)$ is undefined.

The extended sample autocorrelation function

Tsay and Tiao (1984) have proposed a procedure of iterated regressions to estimate the coefficients of the autoregressive part of an ARMA (p, q) model; the procedure also identifies the orders p and q. Since the study in this chapter concerns identification on the basis of knowledge of $\{\rho_h\}$, we modify the ESACF method to use ρ_hs instead of r_hs. We assume $p \leqslant P$ and $q \leqslant Q$. In these terms the method consists of the following steps. For a given k (possibly a trial value of p) regress y_t on $\mathbf{y}_{t-1}^{(k)}$ to obtain the equation

$$\mathbf{R}(k, 0)\mathbf{\Phi}(k|0) = \boldsymbol{\rho}(k, 0). \tag{3.57}$$

If $k = p$ and $q = 0$, $\mathbf{\Phi}(k|0) = \boldsymbol{\phi}(p, 0)$ and the residual

$$e_{kt}^{(0)} = y_t - \mathbf{\Phi}'(k|0)\mathbf{y}_{t-1}^{(k)} \tag{3.58}$$

is $y_t - \boldsymbol{\phi}'(p, 0)\mathbf{y}_{t-1}^{(p)} = v_t$, the residuals have autocorrelations 0. If $k = p$ and $q > 0$, some autocorrelations of $e_{kt}^{(0)}$ are different from 0. In that case the next step is to regress y_t on $\mathbf{y}_{t-1}^{(k)}$ and $e_{k,t-1}^{(0)}$ to obtain the coefficients $\mathbf{\Phi}(k|1)$ and $\beta_1(k|1)$ with residuals

$$e_{kt}^{(1)} = y_t - \mathbf{\Phi}'(k|1)\mathbf{y}_{t-1}^{(k)} - \beta_1(k|1)e_{k,t-1}^{(0)}. \tag{3.59}$$

Note that the regressors include $y_{t-1}, \ldots, y_{t-k-1}$ in terms of linear combinations. At the ith step regress y_t on $\mathbf{y}_{t-1}^{(k)}$, $e_{k,t-i}^{(0)}, e_{k,t-i+1}^{(1)}, \ldots, e_{k,t-1}^{(i-1)}$ to obtain coefficients $\mathbf{\Phi}(k|i)$, $\beta_1(k|i), \ldots, \beta_{i-1}(k|i)$ with residuals

$$e_{kt}^{(i)} = y_t - \mathbf{\Phi}'(k|i)\mathbf{y}_{t-1}^{(k)} - \sum_{j=0}^{i-1} \beta_j(k|i)e_{k,t-i+j}^{(j)}. \tag{3.60}$$

The regressors include $y_{t-1}, \ldots y_{t-k-i}$. Note that $\mathscr{E}e_{k,t-i+j}^{(j)}\mathbf{y}_{t-i-1}^{(k)} = \mathbf{0}$, $j = 0, 1, \ldots, i - 1$. The regression equations are equivalent to $\mathscr{E}e_{kt}^{(i)}y_{t-j} = 0$, $j = 1, \ldots, k + i$. A subset of these is

$$\begin{aligned}\mathbf{0} = \mathscr{E}e_{kt}^{(i)}\mathbf{y}_{t-i-1}^{(k)} &= \mathscr{E}y_{t-i-1}^{(k)} - \mathscr{E}\,\mathbf{y}_{t-i-1}^{(k)}\mathbf{y}_{t-1}^{(k)\prime}\,\mathbf{\Phi}(k|i)\\ &= \boldsymbol{\rho}(k, i) - \mathbf{R}(k, i)\mathbf{\Phi}(k|i).\end{aligned} \tag{3.61}$$

If $k = p$ and $i \geqslant q$, $\mathbf{\Phi}(k|i) = \boldsymbol{\phi}(p, q)$, and the residuals $y_t - \mathbf{\Phi}'(k|i)\mathbf{y}_{t-1}^{(k)} = y_t - \boldsymbol{\phi}'(p, q)\mathbf{y}_{t-1}^{(k)} = \Sigma_{g=0}^{q}\alpha_g v_{t-g}$, which is an MA($q$) process. The autocorrelations of order $q + 1$ and greater are 0. If $k < p$, these iterations will not lead to residuals $y_i - \mathbf{\Phi}'(k|i)\mathbf{y}_{t-1}^{(k)}$ that are uncorrelated for $i \leqslant Q$. Then a larger value of k must be tried.

Other pattern methods

The *R* and *S* arrays

The R and S arrays (Gray et al., 1978) are based on determinants of matrices

$$\mathbf{G}_k(i) = \begin{bmatrix} \rho_i & \rho_{i+1} & \cdots & \rho_{i+k-1} \\ \rho_{i+1} & \rho_{i+2} & \cdots & \rho_{i+k} \\ \vdots & \vdots & & \vdots \\ \rho_{i+k-1} & \rho_{i+k} & \cdots & \rho_{i+2k-2} \end{bmatrix} = \mathbf{R}(k, i+k-1)\mathbf{P}_k, \quad (3.62)$$

$$\mathbf{G}_{k+1}(1|i) = \begin{bmatrix} 1 & 1 & \cdots & 1 \\ \rho_i & \rho_{i+1} & \cdots & \rho_{i+k} \\ \vdots & \vdots & & \vdots \\ \rho_{i+k-1} & \rho_{i+k} & \cdots & \rho_{i+2k-1} \end{bmatrix}$$
$$= \begin{bmatrix} \boldsymbol{\varepsilon}' & 1 \\ \mathbf{G}_k(i) & \boldsymbol{\rho}(k, i+k-1) \end{bmatrix}$$
$$= \begin{bmatrix} 1 & \boldsymbol{\varepsilon}' \\ \boldsymbol{\rho}(k, i+k-1) & \mathbf{R}(k, i+k-1) \end{bmatrix} \mathbf{P}_{k+1}, \quad (3.63)$$

where

$$\mathbf{P}_k = \begin{bmatrix} 0 & 0 & \cdots & 0 & 1 \\ 0 & 0 & \cdots & 1 & 0 \\ \vdots & \vdots & & \vdots & \vdots \\ 0 & 1 & \cdots & 0 & 0 \\ 1 & 0 & \cdots & 0 & 0 \end{bmatrix}, \quad \mathbf{P}_{k+1} = \begin{bmatrix} 0 & P_k \\ 1 & 0 \end{bmatrix} \quad (3.64)$$

are permutation matrices and $\boldsymbol{\varepsilon}' = (1, 1, \ldots, 1)$. Define

$$S_{k,i} = \frac{|\mathbf{G}_{k+1}(1|i)|}{|\mathbf{G}_k(i)|} = -\frac{\begin{vmatrix} 1 & \boldsymbol{\varepsilon}' \\ \boldsymbol{\rho}(k, i+k-1) & \mathbf{R}(k, i+k-1) \end{vmatrix}}{|\mathbf{R}(k, i+k-1)|}$$
$$= -[1 - \boldsymbol{\varepsilon}'\mathbf{R}^{-1}(k, i+k-1)\boldsymbol{\rho}(k, i+k-1)]$$
$$= -[1 - \boldsymbol{\varepsilon}'\boldsymbol{\phi}(k, i+k-1)]$$
$$= -[1 - \sum_{j=0}^{k} \phi_{kj}^{(i+k-1)}] \quad (3.65)$$

when $\mathbf{R}(k, i+k-1)$ is nonsingular. To make it easier to compare with previous criteria we define

$$S_{ki}^* = S_{k,i-k+1}$$
$$= \frac{\begin{vmatrix} 1 & \boldsymbol{\varepsilon}' \\ \boldsymbol{\rho}(k, i) & \mathbf{R}(k, i) \end{vmatrix}}{|\mathbf{R}(k, i)|}$$
$$= -[1 - \boldsymbol{\varepsilon}'\boldsymbol{\phi}(k, i)]$$
$$= -[1 - \sum_{j=0}^{k} \phi_{kj}^{(i)}] \quad (3.66)$$

when $\mathbf{R}(k, i)$ is nonsingular, in particular, for $k = p, i \geqslant q$ and $k \geqslant p, i = q$. Then for $i \geqslant q$

$$S^*_{pi} = -[1 - \sum_{j=0}^{p} \phi^{(i)}_{kj}] = - \sum_{j=0}^{p} \beta_j \neq 0. \tag{3.67}$$

If $i = q$ and $k < p$, $\mathbf{R}(k, q)$ is nonsingular and

$$\begin{aligned} S^*_{pt} &= -[1 - \varepsilon'\mathbf{R}^{-1}(k, q)\boldsymbol{\rho}(k, q)] \\ &= -[1 - \boldsymbol{\varepsilon}'\boldsymbol{\phi}(k, q)] \\ &= -[1 - \boldsymbol{\varepsilon}'\boldsymbol{\phi}(p, q)] = - \sum_{j=0}^{p} \beta_j. \end{aligned} \tag{3.68}$$

Thus $S^*_{ki} \neq 0$, $(k, i) \in I_{pq}$. If $(k, i) \in J_{p+1,q+1}$, $R(k, i)$ is singular; while $\mathbf{R}^{-1}(k, i)\boldsymbol{\rho}(k, i)$ can be replaced by $\mathbf{R}^{-}(k, i)\boldsymbol{\rho}(k, i)$, $\boldsymbol{\varepsilon}'\mathbf{R}^{-}(k, i)\boldsymbol{\rho}(k, i)$ would depend on which $\mathbf{R}^{-}(k, i)$ is used because $\boldsymbol{\mu}'\mathbf{M} \neq \mathbf{0}$.

The other criterion is defined by $\mathbf{R}_{ki} = |G_k(i)|/|G_k(1|i)|$ and can be analyzed in a similar manner.

Inversion

The ARMA process has the spectral density

$$\begin{aligned} f(\lambda) &= \frac{1}{2\pi} \sum_{h=-\infty}^{\infty} \sigma(h) \cos \lambda h = \frac{1}{2\pi} \sum_{h=-\infty}^{\infty} \sigma(h) e^{i\lambda h} \\ &= \frac{\sigma^2}{2\pi} \frac{|\Sigma_{g=0}^{q} \alpha_g e^{i\lambda(q-g)}|^2}{|\Sigma_{j=0}^{p} \beta_j e^{i\lambda(p-j)}|^2}. \end{aligned} \tag{3.69}$$

If no zero of $\Sigma_{g=0}^{q} \alpha_g x^{q-g}$ has absolute value 1, $f(\lambda) > 0 \ \forall \lambda$. Then

$$\frac{1}{(2\pi)^2 f(\lambda)} = \frac{1}{2\pi\sigma^2} \frac{|\Sigma_{j=0}^{p} \beta_j e^{i\lambda(q-g)}|^2}{|\Sigma_{g=0}^{q} \alpha_g e^{i\lambda(q-g)}|^2} \tag{3.70}$$

is the spectral density of an ARMA (q, p) process with autocorrelations obtained from (3.70). Thus, given $\{\sigma(h)\}$, construct $f(\lambda) = (1/2\pi)\Sigma_{h=-\infty}^{\infty} \sigma(h)e^{i\lambda h}$; and define $\sigma i(h)$ by

$$\sigma i(h) = \frac{1}{(2\pi)^2} \int_{-\pi}^{\pi} \frac{1}{f(\lambda)} d\lambda. \tag{3.71}$$

The question is for what ARMA (q, p) are the $\sigma i(h)$ the autocovariances.

The MA and AR representations

The process (1.1) has the moving average representation (1.2). The coeficients $\{\psi_r\}$ satisfy a difference equation similar to the Yule-

Walker equations (Anderson, 1971, section 5.8). However, this approach does not seem useful since the $\{\sigma_h\}$ do not determine $\{\psi_r\}$ directly.

4 Discussion

In practice a method of identification is applied to an observed time series, $y_1, \ldots, y_T$. The methods reviewed in this chapter are based on knowledge of the sequence of autocorrelations $\{\rho_h\}$. In data analysis this sequence is replaced by a finite set of sample autocorrelations $r_1, \ldots, r_{T-1}$; a set of functions of the ρ_hs is replaced by a corresponding (necessarily finite) set of r_hs. When identification is based on the parameters, it can be determined whether a criterion is 0, but when sample quantities are used, statistical inference is involved. A criterion will typically not be exactly 0. Choi (1992) has shown that most of the criteria are asymptotically normally distributed and has given the standard errors.

For the process autocorrelations, a systematic sequence of operations can be specified. First, inspect $\rho_1, \ldots, \rho_Q$ to see if $\rho_j = 0$, $j = q + 1, \ldots, Q$, for some q $(0 \leqslant q < Q)$; if so conclude the process is MA(q) = ARMA(0, q). If $\rho_j \neq 0$, $j = 1, \ldots, Q$, check the two-component sequence (ρ_j, ρ_{j-1}). If the two sequences $\{\rho_j\}$ and $\{\rho_{j-1}\}$ are linearly dependent, $j = q + 1, \ldots, Q$, for some q $(0 \leqslant q < Q - 1)$, conclude that the process is ARMA (1, q). Linear dependence may verified by computing $|R(2, j)|$. If $|R(2, j)| \neq 0$, $j = 1, \ldots, Q - 1$, go on to check the three-component sequence $(\rho_j, \rho_{j-1}, \rho_{j-2})$ and deter-mine if linear dependence exists for j greater than some q. If no linear dependence is found, go on to look for linear dependence in four sequences. In turn more sequences can be considered up to P in number.

When sample autocorrelations are involved, statistical inference is needed. Then instead of proceeding sequentially a table of values of a criterion for (k, i), $k = 0, 1, \ldots, P$, $i = 0, 1, \ldots, Q$, is studied for a pattern described in previous sections. The variables in such a table of a given criterion will be dependent. In principle the joint distribution or asymptotic joint distribution of all the entries in the table should enter the decision process, but such a distribution is usually unavailable or is unwieldly. The choice of criterion will depend on its statistical properties. However, consideration of these matters is beyond the scope of this chapter.

Appendix: the solutions of a degenerate equation

Consider

$$\mathbf{Ax} = \mathbf{y}, \tag{A.1}$$

where $\mathbf{A}$ is singular and the equation is consistent (that is, there exists an $\mathbf{x}^*$ such that $\mathbf{Ax}^* = \mathbf{y}$). By the singular value decomposition

$$\mathbf{A} = \mathbf{PDQ} = (\mathbf{P}_1, \mathbf{P}_2)\begin{pmatrix} \mathbf{D}_1 & \mathbf{0} \\ \mathbf{0} & \mathbf{0} \end{pmatrix}\begin{pmatrix} \mathbf{Q}_1 \\ \mathbf{Q}_2 \end{pmatrix}, \tag{A.2}$$

where $\mathbf{P}$ and $\mathbf{Q}$ are orthogonal and $\mathbf{D}$ and $\mathbf{D}_1$ are diagonal with the order of $\mathbf{D}_1$ equal to the rank of $\mathbf{A}$. Then (1.1) is transformed to

$$\mathbf{DQx} = \mathbf{P}'\mathbf{y}. \tag{A.3}$$

If

$$\mathbf{Qx} = \mathbf{z}, \quad \mathbf{P}'\mathbf{y} = \mathbf{w}, \tag{A.4}$$

(A.3) is

$$\mathbf{Dz} = \begin{pmatrix} \mathbf{D}_1 & \mathbf{0} \\ \mathbf{0} & \mathbf{0} \end{pmatrix}\begin{pmatrix} \mathbf{z}_1 \\ \mathbf{z}_2 \end{pmatrix} = \begin{pmatrix} \mathbf{D}_1\mathbf{z}_1 \\ \mathbf{0} \end{pmatrix} = \mathbf{w} = \begin{pmatrix} \mathbf{w}_1 \\ \mathbf{w}_2 \end{pmatrix}. \tag{A.5}$$

For consistency the condition $\mathbf{w}_2 = \mathbf{P}_2'\mathbf{y} = \mathbf{0}$ must be satisfied; then $\mathbf{z}_2$ is any vector. Thus (A.5) reduces to

$$\mathbf{D}_1\mathbf{z}_1 = \mathbf{w}_1 \tag{A.6}$$

with solution $\mathbf{z}_1 = \mathbf{D}_1^{-1}\mathbf{w}_1 = \mathbf{D}_1^{-1}\mathbf{P}_1'\mathbf{y}$. Then a solution to (A.1) is

$$\begin{aligned} \mathbf{x} &= \mathbf{Q}'\mathbf{z} = (\mathbf{Q}_1', \mathbf{Q}_2')\begin{pmatrix} \mathbf{D}_1^{-1}\mathbf{w}_1 \\ \mathbf{z}_2 \end{pmatrix} \\ &= \mathbf{Q}_1'\mathbf{D}_1^{-1}\mathbf{P}_1'\mathbf{y} + \mathbf{Q}_2'\mathbf{z}_2. \end{aligned} \tag{A.7}$$

Then

$$\begin{aligned} \mathbf{Ax} &= \mathbf{PDQ}(\mathbf{Q}_1'\mathbf{D}_1^{-1}\mathbf{P}_1'\mathbf{y} + \mathbf{Q}_2'\mathbf{z}_2) \\ &= \mathbf{P}_1\mathbf{D}_1\mathbf{Q}_1\mathbf{Q}_1'\mathbf{D}_1^{-1}\mathbf{P}_1'\mathbf{y} \\ &= \mathbf{P}_1\mathbf{P}_1'\mathbf{y} = \mathbf{y} \end{aligned} \tag{A.8}$$

because $\mathbf{y} = \mathbf{Pw} = \mathbf{P}_1\mathbf{w}_1$.

Now consider

$$\mathbf{A}'\tilde{\mathbf{x}} = \tilde{\mathbf{y}}, \tag{A.9}$$

where $\tilde{\mathbf{y}}$ is an arbitrary vector (not necessarily $\mathbf{y}$ with components reversed) and $\tilde{\mathbf{x}}$ is a solution. Then (A.9) can be written as

$$\mathbf{DP}'\tilde{\mathbf{x}} = \mathbf{Q}\tilde{\mathbf{y}}. \tag{A.10}$$

If

$$\mathbf{P}'\tilde{\mathbf{x}} = \mathbf{z}, \quad \mathbf{Q}\tilde{\mathbf{y}} = \tilde{\mathbf{w}}, \tag{A.11}$$

then

$$\mathbf{D}\tilde{\mathbf{z}} = \begin{pmatrix} \mathbf{D}_1 & \mathbf{0} \\ \mathbf{0} & \mathbf{0} \end{pmatrix} \begin{pmatrix} \tilde{\mathbf{z}}_1 \\ \tilde{\mathbf{z}}_2 \end{pmatrix} = \begin{pmatrix} \mathbf{D}_1 \tilde{\mathbf{z}}_1 \\ \mathbf{0} \end{pmatrix} = \tilde{\mathbf{w}} = \begin{pmatrix} \tilde{\mathbf{w}}_1 \\ \tilde{\mathbf{w}}_2 \end{pmatrix}. \tag{A.12}$$

For consistency we require $\tilde{\mathbf{w}}_2 = \mathbf{Q}_2\tilde{\mathbf{y}} = \mathbf{0}$ and $\tilde{\mathbf{z}}_2$ is any vector. Then (A.12) reduces to

$$\mathbf{D}_1\tilde{\mathbf{z}}_1 = \tilde{\mathbf{w}}_1 \tag{A.13}$$

with solution $\tilde{\mathbf{z}}_1 = \mathbf{D}_1^{-1}\tilde{\mathbf{w}}_1 = \mathbf{D}_1^{-1}\mathbf{Q}_1\tilde{\mathbf{y}}$, and solution to (A.9) is

$$\begin{aligned} \tilde{\mathbf{x}} = \mathbf{P}\tilde{\mathbf{z}} &= \mathbf{P}_1\mathbf{D}_1^{-1}\mathbf{w}_1 + \mathbf{P}_2\tilde{\mathbf{z}}_2 \\ &= \mathbf{P}_1\mathbf{D}_1^{-1}\mathbf{Q}_1\tilde{\mathbf{y}} + \mathbf{P}_2\tilde{\mathbf{z}}_2. \end{aligned} \tag{A.14}$$

Then

$$\begin{aligned} \tilde{\mathbf{x}}'\mathbf{A}\mathbf{x} &= \tilde{\mathbf{x}}'\mathbf{P}_1\mathbf{P}_1'\mathbf{y} = \tilde{\mathbf{y}}'\mathbf{Q}_1'\mathbf{D}_1^{-1}\mathbf{P}_1'\mathbf{P}_1\mathbf{P}_1'\mathbf{y} \\ &= \tilde{\mathbf{y}}'\mathbf{Q}_1'\mathbf{D}_1^{-1}\mathbf{P}_1\mathbf{y}. \end{aligned} \tag{A.15}$$

Note that this bilinear form does not depend on $\mathbf{z}_2$ and $\tilde{\mathbf{z}}_2$. Thus $\tilde{\mathbf{x}}'\mathbf{A}\mathbf{x}$ does not depend on which solutions to (A.1) and (A.9) are used. Since

$$\begin{aligned} \mathbf{A}\mathbf{Q}_1'\mathbf{D}_1^{-1}\mathbf{P}_1'\mathbf{A} &= \mathbf{P}\mathbf{D}\mathbf{Q}\mathbf{Q}_1'\mathbf{D}_1^{-1}\mathbf{P}_1'\mathbf{P}\mathbf{D}\mathbf{Q}_1 \\ &= \mathbf{P}_1\mathbf{D}_1\mathbf{Q}_1 = \mathbf{P}\mathbf{D}\mathbf{Q} \\ &= \mathbf{A}, \end{aligned} \tag{A.16}$$

$\mathbf{Q}_1'\mathbf{D}_1^{-1}\mathbf{P}_1' = \mathbf{A}^-$ is a generalized inverse of (A.2), and (A.15) is

$$\tilde{\mathbf{x}}'\mathbf{A}\mathbf{x} = \tilde{\mathbf{y}}'\mathbf{A}^-\tilde{\mathbf{y}}. \tag{A.17}$$

Note that every solution $\mathbf{x}$ given by (A.7) is of the form $\mathbf{x}_0 + \mathbf{M}\mathbf{h}$, where $\mathbf{M}$ satisfies $\mathbf{A}\mathbf{M} = \mathbf{0}$ and has rank equal to the nullity of $\mathbf{A}$ (the order of $\mathbf{A}$ less its rank). For more of the properties of generalized inverses, see Rao and Mitra (1971).

Note

The author is indebted to Akimichi Takemura for helpful comments; his technical report (Takemura, 1984) proved to be very useful in preparing the exposition in section 3 on "General partial correlations."

References

Akaike, H. (1974) Markovian representation of stochastic processes and its application to the analysis of autoregressive moving average processes. *Annals of the Institute of Statistics and Mathematics*, 26, 363–87.

Anderson, T. W. (1971) *The Statistical Analysis of Time Series*. New York: John Wiley & Sons.

Anderson, T. W. (1984) *An Introduction to Multivariate Statistical Analysis*, 2nd edn. New York: John Wiley & Sons.

Beguin, J. M., Gouriéroux, C. and Monfort, A. (1980) Identification of a mixed autoregressive-moving average process: the corner method. In O. D. Anderson (ed.), *Time Series*. Amsterdam: North-Holland, pp. 423–36.

Choi, B. S. (1992) *ARMA Model Identification*. New York: Springer-Verlag.

Glasbey, C. A. (1982) A generalization of partial autocorrelations useful in identifying ARMA models. *Technometrics*, 24, 223–8.

Gray, H. L., Kelley, G. D. and McIntire, D. D. (1978) A new approach to ARMA modelling *Communications in Statistics*, B7, 1–77.

Rao, C. R. and Mitra, S. K. (1971) *Generalized Inverse of Matrices and Its Applications*. New York: John Wiley & Sons.

Takemura, A. (1984) A generalization of autocorrelation and partial autocorrelation function useful for identification of ARMA (p, q) process. Technical report no. 11, ARO contract no. DAAG 29-82-K-0156, Stanford University Department of Statistics.

Tsay, R. S. and Tiao, G. C. (1984) Consistent estimates of autoregressive parameters and extended sample autocorrelation fuction for stationary and nonstationary ARMA models. *Journal of the American Statistical Association*, 79, 84–96.

Tsay, R. S. and Tiao, G. C. (1985) Use of canonical analysis in time series model identification. *Biometrika*, 72, 299–315.

Woodward, W. A. and Gray, H. L. (1981) On the relationship between the S array and the Box-Jenkins method of ARMA model identification. *Journal of the American Statistical Association*, 76, 579–87.

10 Convergence Rates for Series Estimators

Whitney K. Newey

1 Introduction

Least squares projections of a random variable y on functions of a random vector x provide a useful way of describing the relationship between y and x. The simplest example is linear regression, the least squares projection on the set of linear combinations of x, as exemplified in Rao (1973, chapter 4). An interesting nonparametric example is the conditional expectation, the projection on the set of all functions of x with finite mean square. There are also a variety of projections that fall in between these two polar cases, where the set of functions is larger than all linear combinations but smaller than all functions. One example is an additive regression, the projection on functions that are additive in the different elements of x. This case is motivated partly by the difficulty of estimating conditional expectations when x has many components (see Zeldin and Thomas, 1977; Breiman and Stone, 1978; Friedman and Stuetzle, 1981; Breiman and Friedman, 1985; Stone, 1985). A generalization that includes some interaction terms is the projection on functions that are additive in some subvectors of x. Another example is random linear combinations of functions of x, as suggested by Riedel (1992) for growth curve estimation.

One simple way to estimate nonparametric projections is by regression on a finite dimensional subset, with dimension allowed to grow with the sample size (e.g. as in Agarwal and Studden, 1980; Gallant 1981; Stone, 1985; Cox, 1988; Andrews, 1991), which will be referred to here as series estimation. This type of estimator may not be good at recovering the "fine structure" of the projection relative to other smoothers, (see Buja et al., 1989), but is computationally simple. Also, projections often show up as nuisance functions in semiparametric estimation, where the fine structure is less important.

This chapter derives convergence rates for series estimators of projections. Convergence rates are important because they show how dimension affects the asymptotic accuracy of the estimators (e.g. Stone, 1982, 1985). Also, they are useful for the theory of semiparametric estimators that depend on projection estimates (e.g. Newey 1993a). The chapter gives mean-square rates for estimation of the projection and uniform convergence rates for estimation of functions and derivatives. Fully primitive regularity conditions are given for power series and regression splines, as well as more general conditions that may apply to other types of series.

Previous work on convergence rates for series estimates includes Agarwal and Studden (1980), Stone (1985, 1990), Cox (1988), and Andrews and Whang (1990). This chapter improves on many previous results in the convergence rate or generality of regularity conditions. Uniform convergence rates for functions and their derivatives are given and some of the results allow for a data-based number of approximating terms, unlike all but Cox (1988). Also, the projection does not have to equal the conditional expectation, as in Stone (1985, 1990) but not the others.

2 Series Estimators

The results of this chapter concern estimators of least squares projections that can be described as follows. Let z denote a data observation, y and x (measurable) functions of z, with x having dimension r. Let $\mathcal{G}$ denote a mean-squared closed, linear subspace of the set of all functions of x with finite mean-square. The projection of y on $\mathcal{G}$ is

$$g_0(x) = \text{argmin}_{g \in \mathcal{G}} E[\{y - g(x)\}^2]. \tag{2.1}$$

An example is the conditional expectation, $g_0(x) = E[y|x]$, where $\mathcal{G}$ is the set of all measurable functions of x with finite mean-square. Two further examples will be used as illustrations, and of interest in their own right.

Additive-interactive projections When x has more than a few distinct components it is difficult to estimate $E[y|x]$, a feature often referred to as the "curse of dimensionality." This problem motivates projections that are additive in functions of subvectors of x, so that the individual components have smaller dimension than x. One general way to describe these is to let $\tilde{x}_l$, $(l = 1, \ldots, L)$ be distinct subvectors of x, and specify the space of functions as

$$\mathscr{G} = \{\Sigma_{l=1}^{L} g_l(\tilde{x}_l): E[g_l(\tilde{x}_l)^2] < \infty\}. \tag{2.2}$$

For example, if $L = r$ and each $\tilde{x}_l$ is just a component of x, the set $\mathscr{G}$ consists of additive functions. The projection on $\mathscr{G}$ generalizes linear regression to allow for nonparametric nonlinearities in individual regressors. The set of equation (2.2) is a further generalization that allows for nonlinear interactive terms. For example, if each $\tilde{x}_l$ is just one or two dimensional, then this set would allow for just pairwise interactions.

Covariate interactive projections As discussed in Riedel (1992), problems in growth curve estimation motivate considering projections that are random linear combinations of functions. To describe these, suppose $x = (w, u)$, where $w = (w_1, \ldots, w_L)'$ is a vector of covariates and let $\mathscr{H}_l$, $(l = 1, \ldots, L)$ be sets of functions of u. Consider the set of functions

$$\mathscr{G} = \{\Sigma_{l=1}^{L} w_l h_l(u): h_l \in \mathscr{H}_l\}, \tag{2.3}$$
$$E[ww'|u] \text{ is nonsingular with probability one.}$$

In a growth curve application u represents time, so that each $h_l(u)$ represents a covariate coefficient that is allowed to vary over time in a general way.

The estimators of $g_0(x)$ considered here are sample projections on a finite dimensional subspace of $\mathscr{G}$, which can be described as follows. Let $p^K(x) = (p_{1K}(x), \ldots, p_{KK}(x))'$ be a vector of functions, each of which is an element of $\mathscr{G}$. Denote the data observations by y_i and x_i, $(i = 1, 2, \ldots)$, and let $y \equiv (y_1, \ldots, y_n)'$ and $p^K \equiv [p^K(x_1), \ldots, p^K(x_n)]$, for sample size n. An estimator of $g_0(x)$ is

$$\hat{g}(x) = p^K(x)'\hat{\pi}, \quad \hat{\pi} = (p^{K\prime}p^K)^- p^{K\prime}y, \tag{2.4}$$

where $(.)^-$ denotes a generalized inverse, and K subscripts for $\hat{g}(x)$ and $\hat{\pi}$ have been suppressed for notational convenience. The matrix $p^{K\prime}p^K$ will be asymptotically nonsingular under conditions given below, making the choice of generalized inverse asymptotically irrelevant.

The idea of sample projection estimators is that they should approximate $g_0(x)$ if K is allowed to grow with the sample size. The two key features of this approximation are that (a) each component of $p^K(x)$ is an element of $\mathscr{G}$, and (b) $p^K(x)$ "spans" $\mathscr{G}$ as K grows (i.e. for any function in $\mathscr{G}$, K can be chosen big enough that there is a linear combination of $p^K(x)$ that approximates it arbitrarily closely in mean square). Under (a), $\hat{\pi}$ estimates $\pi \equiv (E[p^K(x)p^K(x)'])^{-1}E[p^K(x)y] = (E[p^K(x)p^K(x)'])^{-1}E[p^K(x)g_0(x)]$, the coefficients of the projection of $g_0(x)$ on $p^K(x)$. Thus, under (a) and (b), $p^K(x)'\pi$ will approximate $g_0(x)$. Consequently, when the estimation error in $\hat{\pi}$ is small, $\hat{g}(x)$ should approximate $g_0(x)$.

Two types of approximating functions will be considered in detail. They are power series and splines.

Power series Let $\lambda = (\lambda_1, \ldots, \lambda_r)'$ denote an r-dimensional vector of nonnegative integers, i.e. a multi-index, with norm $|\lambda| = \Sigma_{j=1}^r \lambda_j$, and let $x^\lambda \equiv \Pi_{l=1}^r x_l^{\lambda_l}$. For a sequence $(\lambda(k))_{k=1}^\infty$ of distinct such vectors, a power series approximation corresponds to

$$p_k K(x) = x^{\lambda(k)}, \quad (k = 1, 2, \ldots). \tag{2.5}$$

Throughout the chapter it will be assumed that $\lambda(k)$ are ordered so that $|\lambda(k)|$ is monotonically increasing. For estimating the conditional expectation $E[y|x]$, it will also be required that $(\lambda(k))_{k=1}^\infty$ include all distinct multi-indices. This requirement is imposed so that $E[y|x]$ can be approximated by a power series. Additive–interactive projections can be estimated be restricting the multi-indices so that each term $p_{kK}(x)$ is an element of $\mathcal{G}$. This can be accomplished by requiring that the only $\lambda(k)$ that are included are those where indices of nonzero elements are the same as the indices of a subvector $\tilde{x}_l$ for some l. In addition, covariate interactive terms can be estimated by taking the multi-indices to have the same dimension as u and specifying the approximating functions to be $p_{kK}(x) = w_{l(k)}u^{\lambda(k)}$, where $l(k)$ is an integer that selects a component of w.

Power series have a potential drawback of being sensitive to outliers. It may be possible to make them less sensitive by using power series in a bounded, one-to-one transformation of the original data. An example would be to replace each component of x by a logit transformation $1/(1 + e^x)$.

The theory to follow uses orthogonal polynomials, which may help to alleviate the well known multicollinearity problem for power series. If each $x^{\lambda(k)}$ is replaced with the product of orthogonal polynomials of order corresponding to components of $\lambda(k)$, with respect to some weight function on the range of x, and the distribution of x_i is similar to this weight, then there should be little collinearity among the different $x^{\lambda(k)}$. The estimator will be numerically invariant to such a replacement (because $|\lambda(k)|$ is monotonically increasing), but it may alleviate the well known multicollinearity problem for power series.

Regression splines A regression spline is a series estimator where the approximating function is a smooth piecewise polynomial with fixed knots (join points). They have some attractive features relative to power series, including being less sensitive to singularities in the function being approximated and less oscillatory. A disadvantage is that the theory requires that knots be placed in the support and be nonrandom (as in Stone, 1985), so that the support must be known. The power series theory does not require a known support.

To describe regression splines it is convenient to begin with the one-dimensional x case. For convenience, suppose that the support of x is $[-1, 1]$ (it can always be normalized to take this form) and that the knots are evenly spaced. Let $(.)_+ = 1(. > 0)(.)$. An mth degree spline with $L + 1$ evenly spaced knots on $[-1, 1]$ is a linear combination of

$$p_{kL}(v) = \begin{cases} v^k, \ 0 \leqslant k \leqslant m, \\ \{[v + 1 - 2(k - m)/(L + 1)]_+\}^m, \ m + 1 \leqslant k \leqslant m + L \end{cases} \tag{2.6}$$

Multivariate spline terms can be formed by interacting univariate ones for different components of x. For a set of multi-indices $\{\lambda(k)\}$, with $\lambda_j(k) \leqslant m + L - 1$ for each j and k, the approximating functions will be products of univariate splines, i.e.

$$\Pi_{j=1}^{r} p_{\lambda_j}(k), \quad L^{(x_j)}, \quad (k = 1, \ldots K). \tag{2.7}$$

Note that corresponding to each K there is a number of knots for each component of x and a choice of which multiplicative components to include. Throughout the chapter it will be assumed that each ratio of numbers of knots for a pair of elements of x is bounded above and below. For estimating the conditional expectation $E[y|x]$, it will also be required that $(\lambda(k))_{k=1}^{\infty}$ include all distinct multi-indices. This requirement is imposed so that $E[y|x]$ can be approximated by interactive splines. Additive–interactive projections can be estimated by restricting the multi-indices in the same way as for power series. Also, covariate interactive terms can be estimated by forming the approximating functions as products of elements of w with splines in u analogously to the power series case.

The theory to follow uses B-splines, which are a linear transformation of the above basis that is nonsingular on $[-1, 1]$ and has low multicollinearity. The low multicollinearity of B-splines and recursive formula for calculation also lead to computational advantages (e.g. see Powell, 1981).

Series estimates depend on the choice of the number of terms K, so that it is desirable to choose K based on the data. With a data-based choice of K, these estimates have the flexibility to adjust to conditions in the data. For example, one might choose K by delete one cross validation, by minimizing the sum of squared residuals $\Sigma_{i=1}^{n}[y_i - \hat{g}_{-iK}(x_i)]^2$, where $\hat{g}_{-iK}(x_i)$ is the estimate of the regression function computed from all the observations but the ith. Some of the results to follow will allow for data-based K.

3 General Convergence Rates

This section derives some convergence rates for general series estimators. To do this it is useful to introduce some conditions. Let $u = y - h_0(x)$, $u_i = y_i - h_0(x_i)$. Also, for a matrix D let $\| D \| = [\text{trace}(D'D)]^{1/2}$, for a random matrix Y, $\| Y \|_v = \{E[\| Y \|^v]\}^{1/v}$, $v < \infty$, and $\| Y \|_\infty$ the infimum of constants C such that prob($\| Y \| < C$) = 1.

Assumption 3.1. $\{(y_i, x_i)\}$ is i.i.d. and $E[u^2|x]$ is bounded on the support of x_i.

The bounded second conditional moment assumption is quite common in the literature (e.g. Stone, 1985). Apparently it can be relaxed only at the expense of affecting the convergence rates, so to avoid further complication this assumption is retained.

The next Assumption is useful for controlling the second moment matrix of the series terms.

Assumption 3.2. For each K there is constant, nonsingular matrix A such that for $P^K(x) = Ap^K(x)$, the smallest eigenvalue of $E[P^K(x)P^K(x)']$ is bounded away from zero uniformly in K.

Since the estimator $\hat{g}(x)$ is invariant to nonsingular linear transformations, there is really no need to distinguish between $p^K(x)$ and $P^K(x)$ at this point. An explicit transformation A is allowed for in order to emphasize that assumption 3.2 is only needed for some transformation. For example, assumption 3.2 will not apply to power series, but will apply to orthonormal polynomials.

Assumption 3.2 is a normalization that leads to the series terms having specific magnitudes. The regularity conditions will also require that the magnitude of $P^K(x)$ not grow too fast with the sample size. The size of $P^K(x)$ will be quantified by

$$\zeta_d(K) = \sup_{|\lambda|=d, x\in\mathscr{X}} \| \partial^\lambda P^K(x) \| \tag{3.1}$$

where $\mathscr{X}$ is the support of x, $\| D \| = [\text{trace}(D'D)]^{1/2}$ for a matrix D, λ denotes a vector of nonnegative integers, and

$$|\lambda| = \Sigma_{j=1}^r \lambda_r, \quad \partial^\lambda P^K(x) = \partial^{|\lambda|} P^K(x)/\partial x_1^{\lambda_1} \ldots \partial x_r^{\lambda_r}.$$

That is, $\zeta_d(K)$ is the supremum of the norms of derivatives of order d.

The following condition places some limits on the growth of the series magnitude. Also, it allows for data-based choice of K, at the expense of imposing that series terms are nested.

Assumption 3.3. There are $\underline{K}(n)$ and $\bar{K}(n)$ such that $\underline{K}(n) \leqslant \hat{K} \leqslant \bar{K}(n)$ with probability approaching one and either (a) $p^K(x)$ is a subvector of $p^{K+1}(x)$ for all K with $\underline{K}(n) \leqslant K < K + 1 \leqslant \bar{K}(n)$ and $\Sigma_{K=\underline{K}}^{\bar{K}} \zeta_0(K)^4/n \to 0$, or; (b) the $P^K(x)$ of assumption 3.2 is a subvector of $P^{K+1}(x)$ for all K with $\underline{K}(n) \leqslant K < K + 1 \leqslant \bar{K}(n)$ and $\zeta_0(\bar{K}(n))^4/n \to 0$.

As previously noted, a series estimate is invariant to nonsingular linear transformations of $p^K(x)$, so that in part (a) it suffices that any such transformation form a nested sequence of vectors. Part (b) is more restrictive, in requiring that the $\{P^K(x)\}$ from assumption 3.2 be nested, but imposes a less stringent requirement on the growth rate of K. Also, if K is nonrandom, so that $\underline{K}(n) = \hat{K} = \bar{K}(n)$, the nested sequence requirement of both parts (a) and (b) will be satisfied, because that requirement is vacuous when $\underline{K} = \bar{K}$.

In order to specify primitive hypotheses for assumptions 3.2 and 3.3 it must be possible to find $p^K(x)$ satisfying the eigenvalue condition, and having known values for, or bounds on, $\zeta_0(K)$. That is, one needs explicit bounds on series terms where the eigenvalues are bounded away from zero. It is possible to derive such bounds for both power series and regression splines, when x is continuously distributed with a density that is bounded away from zero. These bounds lead to the requirements that $\bar{K}^4/n \to 0$ for power series and $K^2/n \to 0$ for regression splines with nonrandom K. These results are described in sections 5 and 6. It is also possible to derive such results for Fourier series, but this is not done here because they are most suitable for approximation of periodic functions, which have fewer applications. It may also be possible to derive results for Gallant's (1981) Fourier flexible form, although this is more difficult, as described in Gallant and Souza (1991). In terms of this chapter, the problem with the Fourier flexible form is that the linear and quadratic terms can be approximated extremely quickly by the Fourier terms, leading to a multicollinearity problem so severe that simultaneous satisfaction of assumptions 3.2 and 3.3 would impose very slow growth rates on K.

Assumptions 3.1 to 3.3 are useful for controlling the variance of a series estimator. The bias is the error from the finite dimensional approximation. A supremum Sobolev norm will be used to quantify this approximation. For a measurable function $f(x)$ defined on $\mathscr{X}$ and a nonnegative integer d, let

$$|f|_d = \max_{|\lambda| \leq d} \max_{x \in \mathscr{X}} |\partial^\lambda f(x)|,$$

and $|f|_d$ equal to infinity if $\partial^\lambda f(x)$ does not exist for some $|\lambda| \leq d$ and $x \in \mathscr{X}$. Many of the results will be based on the following polynomial approximation rate condition.

Assumption 3.4. There is a nonnegative integer d and constants C, $\alpha > 0$ such that for all K there is π with $|g - p^{K\prime}\pi|_d \leq CK^{-\alpha}$.

This condition is not primitive, but is known to be satisfied in many cases. Typically, the higher the degree of derivative of $g(x)$ that exists, the bigger α and/or d can be chosen. This type of primitive condition will be explicitly discussed for power series in section 5 and for splines in section 6. It is also possible to obtain results when the approximation rate is for an L_p norm, rather than the sup norm. However, this generalization leads to much more complicated results, and so is not given here.

These assumptions will imply both mean-square and uniform convergence rates for the series estimate. The first result gives mean-square rates. Let $F(x)$ denote the CDF of x.

Theorem 3.1. If assumptions 3.1 to 3.4 are satisfied for $d = 0$ then

$$\Sigma_{i=1}^n [\hat{g}(x_i) - g_0(x_i)]^2/n = O_p(\bar{K}/n + \underline{K}^{-2\alpha}),$$

$$\int [\hat{g}(x) - g_0(x)]^2 dF(x) = O_p(\bar{K}/n + \underline{K}^{-2\alpha}). \quad \square$$

The two terms in the convergence rate essentially correspond to variance and bias. The first conclusion, on sample mean-square error, is similar to those of Andrews and Whang (1991) and Newey (1993b), but the hypotheses are different. Here the number of terms $\hat{K}$ is allowed to depend on the data, and the projection residual u need not satisfy $E[u|x] = 0$, at the expense of requiring assumptions 3.2 and 3.3, that were not imposed in these other papers. Also, the second conclusion, on integrated mean-square error, has not been previously given at this level of generality, although Stone (1985) gave specific results for spline estimation of an additive projection.

The next result gives uniform convergence rates.

Theorem 3.2. If assumptions 3.1, 3.2, 3.3(b), and 3.4 are satisfied for a nonnegative integer d then

$$|\hat{g} - g_0|_d = O_p(\zeta_d(\bar{K})[(\bar{K}/n)^{1/2} + \underline{K}^{-\alpha}]). \quad \square$$

There does not seem to be in the literature any previous uniform convergence results that cover derivatives and general series in the way this one does. Furthermore, for the univariate power series case, the convergence rate that is implied by this result improves on that of Cox (1988), as further discussed in section 4. These uniform rates do not attain Stone's (1982) bounds, although they do appear to improve on previously known rates.

For specific classes of functions $\mathcal{G}$ and series approximations, more primitive conditions for assumptions 3.2 to 3.4 can be specified in order to derive convergence rates for the estimators. These results are illustrated in the next two sections, where convergence rates are derived for power series and regression spline estimators of additive–interactive and covariate interactive functions.

4 Additive–Interactive Projections

This section gives convergence rates for power series and regression spline estimators of additive–interactive functions. The first regularity condition restricts x to be continuously distributed.

Assumption 4.1. x is continuously distributed with a support that is a cartesian product of compact intervals, and bounded density that is also bounded away from zero.

This assumption is useful for showing that the set of additive–interactive functions is closed. Also, this condition leads to assumptions 3.2 and 3.3 being satisfied with explicit formulae for $\zeta_0(K)$. For power series it is possible to generalize this condition, so that the density goes to zero on the boundary of the support. For simplicity this generalization is not given here, although the lemmas given in the appendix can be used to verify the section 3 conditions in this case.

It is also possible to allow for a discrete regressor with finite support, by including all dummy variables for all points of support of the regressor, and all interactions. Because such a regressor is essentially parametric, and allowing for it does not change any of the convergence rate results, this generalization will not be considered here.

Under assumption 4.1 the following condition will suffice for assumptions 3.2 and 3.3

Assumption 4.2. Either (a) $p_{kK}(x)$ is a power series with $\bar{K}^4/n \to 0$, or (b) $p_{kK}(x)$ are splines, the support of x is $[-1, 1]^r$, $\bar{K}(n) = \underline{K}(n) = K$, and $K^2/n \to 0$.

It is possible to allow for data-based K for splines and obtain similar mean-square convergence rates to those given below. This generalization is not given here because it would further complicate the statement of results.

A primitive condition for assumption 3.4 is the following one.

Assumption 4.3. Each of the components $g_{l0}(\tilde{x}_l)$, $(l = 1, \ldots, L)$, is continuously differentiable of order s on the support of x_i.

Let $\varkappa$ denote the maximum dimension of the components of the additive–interactive function. This condition can be combined with known results on approximation rates for power series and splines to show that assumption 3.4 is satisfied for $d = 0$ and $\alpha = s/\varkappa$ and with $\alpha = h - d$ when $\varkappa = 1$. The details are given in the appendix.

These conditions lead to the following result on mean-square convergence.

Theorem 4.1. If assumptions 3.1 and 4.1 to 4.3 are satisfied, then

$$\Sigma_{i=1}^{n}[\hat{g}(x_i) - g_0(x_i)]^2/n = O_p(\bar{K}/n + \underline{K}^{-2s/\varkappa}),$$
$$\int[\hat{g}(x) - g_0(x)]^2 dF(x) = O_p(\bar{K}/n + \underline{K}^{2s/\varkappa}). \quad \square$$

The integrated mean-square error result for splines that is given here has previously been derived by Stone (1990). The rest of this result is new, although Andrews and Whang (1990) give the same conclusion for the sample mean-square error of power series under different hypotheses. An implication of theorem 4.1 is that power series will have an optimal integrated mean-square convergence rate if the number of terms is chosen randomly between certain bounds. If there are $C \geq c > 0$ such that $\underline{K} = cn^{\gamma}$, $\bar{K} = Cn^{\gamma}$, where $\gamma = \varkappa/(2s + \varkappa)$, and $s > 3\varkappa/2$, then the mean-square convergence rate is $n^{-s/(2s+\varkappa)}$, which attains Stone's (1982) bound. The side condition that $s > 3\varkappa/2$ is needed to ensure that $\bar{K} = Cn^{\varkappa/(2s+\varkappa)}$ satisfies assumption 4.2.

A similar side condition is present for the spline version of Stone (1990), but it has the less strigent form of $s > r/2$.

Theorem 3.2 can be specialized to obtain uniform convergence rates for power series and spline estimators.

Theorem 4.2. If assumptions 3.1 and 4.1 to 4.3 are satisfied, then for power series

$$|\hat{g} - g_0|_0 = O_P(\bar{K}[(\bar{K}/n)^{1/2} + \underline{K}^{-s/r}]),$$

and for regression splines,

$$|\hat{g} - g_0|_0 = O_P(K^{1/2}[(K/n)^{1/2} + K^{-s/r}]). \quad \square$$

Obtaining uniform convergence rates for derivatives is more difficult, because approximation rates are difficult to find in the literature. When the argument of each function is only one-dimensional, an approximation rate follows by a simple integration argument (e.g. see Lemma A.12 in the appendix). This approach leads to the following convergence rate for the one-dimensional (i.e. additive model) case.

Theorem 4.3. If assumptions 3.1 and 4.1 to 4.3 are satisfied, $r = 1$, $d < s$, $p_{kK}(x)$ is a power series or a regression spline with $m \geq d$, $h - d$, then for power series,

$$|\hat{g} - g_0|_d = O_P(\bar{K}^{1+2d}\{[\bar{K}/n]^{1/2} + \underline{K}^{-s+d}\}),$$

and for splines

$$|\hat{g} - g_0|_d = O_P(K^{1/2+d}\{[K/n]^{1/2} + K^{-s+d}\}). \quad \square$$

In the case of power series, it is possible to obtain an approximation rate by a Taylor expansion argument when the derivatives do not grow too fast with their order. The rate is faster than any power of K, leading to the following result.

Theorem 4.4. If assumptions 3.1 and 4.1 to 4.3 are satisfied, $p_{kK}(x)$ is a power series, and there is a constant C such that for each multi-index λ, the λth partial derivative of each additive component of $g(x)$ exists and is bounded by $C^{|\lambda|}$, then for any positive integers α and d,

$$|\hat{g} - g_0|_d = O_P(\bar{K}^{1+2d}\{[\bar{K}/n]^{1/2} + \underline{K}^{-\alpha}\}). \quad \square$$

The uniform convergence rates are not optimal in the sense of Stone (1982), but they improve on existing results. For the one regressor, power series case theorem 4.2 improves on Cox's (1988) rate of $O_p(K^2\{[K/n]^{1/2} + K^{-s}\})$. For the other cases there do not seem to be any existing results in the literature, so that theorems 4.2 to 4.4 give the only uniform convergence rates available. It would be interesting to obtain further improvements on these results, and investigate the possibility of attaining optimal uniform convergence rates for series estimators of additive interactive models.

5 Covariate–Interactive Projections

Estimation of random coefficient projections provides a second example of how the general results of section 3 can be applied to specific estimators. This section gives convergence rates for power series and regression spline estimators of projections on the set $\mathcal{G}$ described in equation (2.3). For simplicity, results will be restricted to mean-square and uniform convergence rates for the function, but not for its derivatives. Also, the $\mathcal{H}_l$ in equation (2.3) will each be taken as equal to the set of all functions of u with finite mean-square.

Convergence rates can be derived under the following analogue to the conditions of section 4.

Assumption 5.1. (i) u is continuously distributed with a support that is a cartesian product of compact intervals, and bounded density that is also bounded away from zero. (ii) K is restricted to be a multiple of $\mathcal{L}$ and $p^K(x) = w \otimes p^{K/\mathcal{L}}(u)$ where either $p_{kK}(u)$ is a power series with $\bar{K}^4/n \to 0$, or (b) $p_{kK}(u)$ are splines, the support of u is $[-1, 1]^r$, $\bar{K}(n) = \underline{K}(n) = K$, and $K^2/n \to 0$. (iii) Each of the components $h_{l0}(u)$, $(l = 1, \ldots, L)$, is continuously differentiable of order $\mathfrak{s}$ on the support of u_i; (iv) w is bounded, and $E[ww'|u]$ has the smallest eigenvalue that is bounded away from zero on the support of u_i.

These conditions lead to the following result on mean-square convergence.

Theorem 5.1. If assumptions 3.1 and 5.1 are satisfied, then

$$\Sigma_{i=1}^n[\hat{g}(x_i) - g_0(x_i)]^2/n = O_p(\bar{K}/n + \underline{K}^{-2\mathfrak{s}/r}),$$
$$\int[\hat{g}(x) - g_0(x)]^2 dF(x) = O_p(\bar{K}/n + \underline{K}^{-2\mathfrak{s}/r}).$$

Also, for power series and splines respectively,

$$|\hat{g} - g_0|_0 = O_p(\bar{K}[(\bar{K}/n)^{1/2} + \underline{K}^{-\mathfrak{s}/r}]),$$
$$|\hat{g} - g_0|_0 = O_p(K^{1/2}[(K/n)^{1/2} + K^{-\mathfrak{s}/r}]). \quad \square$$

An important feature of this result is that the convergence rate does not depend on $\mathscr{L}$, but is controlled by the dimension of the coefficient functions and their degree of smoothness. This feature is to be expected, since the nonparametric part of the projection is the coefficient functions.

Appendix: proofs of theorems

Throughout, let C be a generic positive constant and $\lambda_{\min}(B)$ and $\lambda_{\max}(B)$ be minimum and maximum eigenvalues of a symmetric matrix B. A number of lemmas will be useful in proving the results. First, some lemmas on mean-square closure of certain spaces of functions are given.

Lemma A.1. If $\mathscr{H}$ is linear and closed and $E[\|w\|^2] < \infty$ then $\{w'\alpha + h(x): h \in \mathscr{H}\}$ is closed.

Proof. Let $u = w - P(w|\mathscr{H})$, so that $w'\alpha + h(x) = u'\alpha + h(x) + P(w|\mathscr{H})'\alpha$. Therefore, it suffices to assume that w is orthogonal to $\mathscr{H}$. It is well known that finite dimensional spaces are closed, and that direct sums of closed orthogonal subspaces are closed, giving the conclusion. □

Lemma A.2. Consider sets $\mathscr{H}_j$, $(j = 1, \ldots, J)$, of functions of a random vector x. If each $\mathscr{H}_j$ is closed and w is a $J \times 1$ random vector such that $\Omega(x) = E[ww'|x]$ is bounded and has the smallest eigenvalue bounded away from zero, then $\{\Sigma_{j=1}^J w_j h_j(x): h_j \in \mathscr{H}_j\}$ is closed.

Proof. By iterated expectations, $E[\{w'h(x)\}^2] = E[h(x)'\Omega(x)h(x)] \geqslant CE[h(x)'h(x)]$ □

Lemma A.3. Suppose that (i) for each $\tilde{x}_l$, $(l = 1, \ldots, L)$, if $\tilde{x}$ is a subvector of $\tilde{x}_l$ then $\tilde{x} = \tilde{x}_{l'}$ for some l', and (ii) There exists a constant $c > 1$ such that for each l, with the partitioning $x = (\tilde{x}_l', \tilde{x}_l^{c\prime})'$, for any $a(x) > 0$, $c\int a(x)d[F(\tilde{x}_l) \cdot F(\tilde{x}_l^c)] \geqslant E[a(x)] \geqslant c^{-1}\int a(x)d[F(\tilde{x}_l) \cdot F(\tilde{x}_l^c)]$. Then $\{\Sigma_{l=1}^L \tilde{h}_l(\tilde{x}_l): E[\tilde{h}_l(\tilde{x}_l)^2] < \infty, l = 1, \ldots, L\}$ is closed in mean-square.

Proof. Let $\mathscr{H} = \{\Sigma_{l=1}^L \tilde{h}_l(\tilde{x}_l)\}$ and $\|a\|_2 = [\int a(x)^2 dF(x)]^{1/2}$. By proposition 2 of section 4 of the appendix of Bickel et al. (1993), $\mathscr{H}$ is closed if and only if there is a constant C such that for each $h \in \mathscr{H}$, $\|h\|_2 \geqslant C\max_l\{\|\tilde{h}_l\|_2\}$ for some h_l (note $\tilde{h}_l$ need not be unique). Following Stone (1990, lemma 1), suppose that the maximal dimension of $\tilde{x}_l$ is r, and suppose that this property holds whenever the maximal dimension of the $\tilde{x}_l$ is $r - 1$ or less. Then there is a unique decomposition $h = \Sigma_{l=1}^L h_l(\tilde{x}_l)$, such that for all $\tilde{x}_{l'}$ that are strict subvectors of $\tilde{x}_l$, $E[h_l(\tilde{x}_l)\delta(\tilde{x}_{l'})] = 0$ for all measurable functions of $\tilde{x}_{l'}$ with finite mean-square. Consequently, it suffices to show that for any "maximal" $\tilde{x}_l$, that is not a proper subvector of any other $\tilde{x}_l$, there is a constant $c > 1$ such that $E[h(x)^2] \geqslant c^{-1}E[h_k(\tilde{x}_k)^2]$. To show this property, note that that holding fixed the vector of components $\tilde{x}_k^c$ of x that are not components of $\tilde{x}_k$ each $l \neq k$, $h_l(\tilde{x}_l)$ is a function of a strict subvector of $\tilde{x}_k$. Then,

$$E[h(x)^2] \geqslant c^{-1}\int\{h_k(\tilde{x}_k) + \Sigma_{l\neq k}h_l(\tilde{x}_l)\}^2 dF(\tilde{x}_k)dF(\tilde{x}_k^c)$$
$$= c^{-1}\int[\int\{h_k(\tilde{x}_k) + \Sigma_{l\neq k}h_l(\tilde{x}_l)\}^2 dF(\tilde{x}_k)]dF(\tilde{x}_k^c)$$
$$= c^{-1}\int[\int\{h_k(\tilde{x}_k)^2 + \{\Sigma_{l\neq k}h_l(\tilde{x}_l)\}^2 dF(\tilde{x}_k)]dF(\tilde{x}_k^c)$$
$$\geqslant c^{-1}\int[\int h_k(\tilde{x}_k)^2 dF(\tilde{x}_k)]dF(\tilde{x}_k^c) = c^{-1}E[h_k(\tilde{x}_k)^2]. \quad \square$$

The next few lemmas consist of useful convergence results for random matrices with dimension that can depend on sample size. Let $\hat{\Sigma}$ and Σ denote symmetric matrices such matrices, and $\lambda_{\max}(.)$ and $\lambda_{\min}(.)$ the smallest and largest eigenvalues respectively.

Lemma A.4. If $\lambda_{\min}(\Sigma) \geqslant C$ with probability approaching one (w.p.a.1) and $\|\hat{\Sigma} - \Sigma\| = o_p(1)$ then $\lambda_{\min}(\hat{\Sigma}) \geqslant C$ w.p.a.1.

Proof. For a conformable vector μ, it follows by $\|\,.\,\|$ a matrix norm that $\lambda_{\min}(\hat{\Sigma}) = \min_{\|\mu\|=1}\{\mu'\Sigma\mu + \mu'(\hat{\Sigma} - \Sigma)\mu\} \geqslant \lambda_{\min}(\Sigma) - \lambda_{\max}(\hat{\Sigma} - \Sigma) \geqslant \lambda_{\min}(\Sigma) - \|\hat{\Sigma} - \Sigma\| \geqslant C - o_p(1)$. Therefore, $\lambda_{\min}(\hat{\Sigma}) \geqslant C/2$ w.p.a.1. $\square$

Lemma A.5. If $\lambda_{\min}(\Sigma) \geqslant C$ w.p.a.l, $\|\hat{\Sigma} - \Sigma\| = o_p(1)$, and D_n is a conformable matrix such that $\|\Sigma^{-1/2}D_n\| = O_p(\epsilon_n)$ for some ϵ_n, then $\|\hat{\Sigma}^{-1/2}D_n\| = O_p(\epsilon_n)$.

Proof. It is easy to show that for any conformable matrices A and B, $\|AB\| \leqslant \|A\| \cdot \|B\|$, $\|A'BA\| \leqslant \|B\| \circ \|A'A\|$, and that if B is positive semi-definite, $\mathrm{tr}(A'BA) \leqslant \|A\|^2\lambda_{\max}(B)$, $\|AB\| \leqslant \|A\|\lambda_{\max}(B)$ and $\|BA\| \leqslant \|A\|\lambda_{\max}(B)$. Let $\Sigma^{-1/2}$ be the symmetric square root of Σ^{-1} which is equal to $U\Lambda U'$ where U is an orthogonal matrix and Λ a diagonal matrix consisting of the square roots of the eigenvalues of Σ^{-1}. Note that $\Sigma^{-1/2}$ is positive definite and $\lambda_{\max}(\Sigma^{-1/2}) = [\lambda_{\max}(\Sigma^{-1})]^{1/2}$. Also by lemma A.4, $\lambda_{\max}(\hat{\Sigma}^{-1}) = O_p(1)$. Then

$$\begin{aligned}\|\hat{\Sigma}^{-1/2}D_n\|^2 &= \mathrm{tr}(D_n'[\hat{\Sigma}^{-1}-\Sigma^{-1}]D_n)\\ &\leqslant \|\Sigma^{-1/2}D_n\|^2(1 + \|\Sigma^{-1/2}[\Sigma - \hat{\Sigma}]\Sigma^{-1/2}\|) + \|(\Sigma - \hat{\Sigma})\Sigma^{-1}D_n\|^2\lambda_{\max}(\hat{\Sigma}^{-1})]\\ &\leqslant O_p(\epsilon_n^2)[1 + o_p(1)O_p(1) + \|\Sigma - \hat{\Sigma}\|^2\lambda_{\max}(\Sigma^{-1/2})^2 O_p(1)] = O_p(\epsilon_n^2). \quad \square\end{aligned} \tag{A.1}$$

Let $\mathrm{tr}(A)$ denote the trace of a square matrix A and u a random matrix with n rows.

Lemma A.6. Suppose $\lambda_{\min}(\Sigma) \geqslant C$, $\bar{P}$ is a $\bar{K} \times n$ random matrix such that $\|\bar{P}'\bar{P}/n - \Sigma\| = o_p(1)$ and $\|\Sigma^{-1/2}\bar{P}'u/\sqrt{n}\| = O_p(\varepsilon_n)$, and $p = \bar{P}A$ where A is a random matrix. Then $\mathrm{tr}(u'p(p'p)^{-}p'u/n) = O_p(\varepsilon_n^2)$.

Proof. Let $\bar{W} = \bar{P}(\bar{P}'\bar{P})^{-}\bar{P}'$ and $W = p(p'p)^{-}p'$ be the orthogonal projection operators for the linear spaces spanned by the columns of $\bar{P}$ and p respectively. Since the space spanned by p is a subset of the space spanned by $\bar{P}$, $\bar{W} - W$ is positive semi-definite. Let $\hat{\Sigma} = \bar{P}'\bar{P}/\mathrm{n}$. Then by lemma A.5, $\mathrm{tr(u}'Wu/n) \leqslant \mathrm{tr}(u'\bar{W}u/n) = \|\hat{\Sigma}^{-1/2}\bar{P}'u/\sqrt{n}\|^2 = O_p(\varepsilon_n^2)$. $\square$

Let Y and G denote random matrices with the same number of columns and n rows, and let $u = Y - G$. For a matrix p let $\hat{\pi} = (p'p)^{-}p'Y$ and $\hat{G} = p\hat{\pi}$.

Lemma A.7. If $\mathrm{tr}(u'p(p'p)^{-}p'u/n) = O_p(\varepsilon_n^2)$. Then for any conformable matrix π, $\|\hat{G} - G\|^2/n \leqslant O_p(\varepsilon_n^2) + \|G - p\pi\|^2/n$.

Proof. For W and $\bar{W}$ as in the proof of lemma A.6, by $Wp = p$, and $I - W$ idempotent,

$$\begin{aligned}\|\hat{G} - G\|^2/n &= \mathrm{tr}[Y'WY - Y'WG - G'WY + G'G]/n \\ &= \mathrm{tr}[u'Wu + G'(I - W)G]/n \\ &\leqslant \mathrm{tr}[u'Wu + (G - p\pi)'(I - W)(G - p\pi)]/n \\ &\leqslant O_p(\varepsilon_n^2) + \|G - p\pi\|^2/n. \quad \square\end{aligned}$$

Lemma A.8. If $\lambda_{\min}(\Sigma) \geqslant C$, $\|p'p/n - \Sigma\| = o_p(1)$, and $\mathrm{tr}[u'p(p'p)^{-}p'u/n] = O_p(\varepsilon_n^2)$, then for any conformable matrix π,

$$\|\hat{\pi} - \pi\|^2 \leqslant O_p(\varepsilon_n^2) + O_p(1)\|G - p\pi\|^2/n,$$

$$\mathrm{tr}[(\hat{\pi} - \pi)'\Sigma(\hat{\pi} - \pi)] \leqslant O_p(\varepsilon_n^2) + O_p(1)\|G - p\pi\|^2/n.$$

Proof. By lemma A.4, $\lambda_{\min}(p'p/n) \geqslant C$ w.p.a.1, so $\lambda_{\min}(p'p/n)^{-1} = O_p(1)$. Therefore, for $\tilde{G} = p\pi$,

$$\begin{aligned}&\|\hat{\pi} - \pi\|^2 \leqslant \lambda_{\min}(p'p/n)^{-1}\mathrm{tr}[(\hat{\pi} - \pi)'(p'p/n)(\hat{\pi} - \pi)] \\ &\quad = O_p(1)\mathrm{tr}[Y'WY - Y'W\tilde{G} - \tilde{G}'WY + \tilde{G}'\tilde{G}]/n \\ &\quad \leqslant O_p(1)[\mathrm{tr}(u'Wu/n) + \|\tilde{G} - G\|^2/n] = O_p(\varepsilon_n^2) + O_p(1)\|\tilde{G} - G\|^2/n.\end{aligned}$$

To prove the second conclusion, note that by the triangle inequality and the same arguments as for the previous equation,

$$\begin{aligned}&\mathrm{tr}[(\hat{\pi} - \pi)'\Sigma(\hat{\pi} - \pi)] \\ &\quad = \mathrm{tr}[(\hat{\pi} - \pi)'[\Sigma - p'p/n](\hat{\pi} - \pi)] + (\hat{\pi} - \pi)'(p'p/n)(\hat{\pi} - \pi) \\ &\qquad \leqslant \|\hat{\pi} - \pi\|^2\|\Sigma - p'p/n\| + O_p(\varepsilon_n^2) + O_p(1)\|\tilde{G} - G\|^2/n \\ &\quad = O_p(\varepsilon_n^2) + O_p(1)\|\tilde{G} - G\|^2/n. \quad \square\end{aligned}$$

Lemma A.9. If $z_1, \ldots, z_n$ are i.i.d. then for any vector of functions $a^K(z) = a_{1K}(z), \ldots, a_{KK}(z))'$ and $K = K(n)$,

$$\|\Sigma_{i=1}^n a^{K(n)}(z_i)/n - E[a^{K(n)}(z)]\| = O_p(\{E[a^{K(n)}(z)'a^{K(n)}(z)]/n\}^{1/2}).$$

Proof. Let $K = K(n)$. By the Cauchy–Schwartz inequality,

$$\begin{aligned}&E[\|\Sigma_{i=1}^n a^K(z_i)/n - E[a^K(z)]\|] \leqslant \{E[\|\Sigma_{i=1}^n a^K(z_i)/n - E[a^K(z)]\|^2]\}^{1/2} \\ &\quad \leqslant \{E[\|a^K(z)\|^2/n]\}^{1/2},\end{aligned}$$

so the conclusion follows by the Markov inequality. $\square$

Now let $\hat{\Sigma} = \Sigma_{i=1}^n P^{\hat{K}}(x_i)P^{\hat{K}}(x_i)'/n$ and $\Sigma = \int P^{\hat{K}}(x)P^{\hat{K}}(x)'dF(x)$.

Lemma A.10. Suppose that assumptions 3.1 to 3.3 are satisfied. If assumption 3.3 (a) is also satisfied

$$\|\hat{\Sigma} - \Sigma\| = O_p([\Sigma_{K=\underline{K}}^{\bar{K}} \zeta_0(K)^4/n]^{1/2}) = o_p(1).$$

If assumption 3.3 (b) is also satisfied then

$$\|\hat{\Sigma} - \Sigma\| = O_p([\zeta_0(\bar{K})^4/n]^{1/2}) = o_p(1).$$

Proof. Let $\hat{\Sigma}_K = \Sigma_{i=1}^n P^K(x_i)P^K(x_i)'/n$ and $\Sigma_K = \int P^K(x)P^K(x)'dF(x)$. To show the first conclusion, note that by the Cauchy–Schwartz inequality, for $a^{K^2}(z) = P^K(x) \otimes P^K(x)$,

$$\begin{aligned} E[\max_{\underline{K}\leqslant K\leqslant \bar{K}} \|\hat{\Sigma}_K - \Sigma_K\|] &\leqslant \{E[\Sigma_{\underline{K}\leqslant K\leqslant \bar{K}} \|\hat{\Sigma}_K - \Sigma_K\|^2]\}^{1/2} \\ &= \{\Sigma_{\underline{K}\leqslant K\leqslant \bar{K}} E[\| \Sigma_{i=1}^n a^{K^2}(z_i)/n - E[a^{K^2}(z_i)]\|]\}^{1/2} \\ &\leqslant \{\Sigma_{\underline{K}\leqslant K\leqslant \bar{K}} E[\| a^{K^2}(z)\|^2]/n\}^{1/2} \\ &= \{\Sigma_{\underline{K}\leqslant K\leqslant \bar{K}} E[\| P^K(x)\|^4]/n\}^{1/2} \leqslant [\Sigma_{\underline{K}\leqslant K\leqslant \bar{K}} \zeta_0(K)^4/n]^{1/2}. \end{aligned}$$

Then by the Markov inequality, $\max_{\underline{K}\leqslant K\leqslant \bar{K}} \|\hat{\Sigma}_K - \Sigma_K\| = O_p([\Sigma_{\underline{K}\leqslant K\leqslant \bar{K}} \zeta_0(K)^4/n]^{1/2})$. The first conclusion then follows by $\|\hat{\Sigma} - \Sigma\| \leqslant \max_{\underline{K}\leqslant K\leqslant \bar{K}} \|\hat{\Sigma}_K - \Sigma_K\|$ w.p.a.1. To show the second conclusion, note that w.p.a.1, $\hat{\Sigma}$ and Σ are submatrices of $\hat{\Sigma}_{\bar{K}}$ and $\Sigma_{\bar{K}}$ respectively, whence $\|\hat{\Sigma} - \Sigma\| \leqslant \|\hat{\Sigma}_{\bar{K}} - \Sigma_{\bar{K}}\|$. The conclusion then follows from lemma A.9. □

Let $y = (y_1, \ldots, y_n)'$, $g = (g_0(x_1), \ldots, g_0(x_n))'$, and $p = [p^{\hat{K}}(x_1), \ldots, p^{\hat{K}}(x_n)]'$.

Lemma A.11. If assumptions 3.1 to 3.3 are satisfied, then

$$(y - g)'p(p'p)^- p'(y - g)/n = O_p(\bar{K}/n).$$

Proof. Let $u \equiv y - g$, $P_i = P^{\bar{K}}(x_i)$, $\bar{P} = [P_1, \ldots, P_n]'$, and $\Sigma = E[\bar{P}'\bar{P}]/n$. By assumption 3.3, there is a random matrix A such that $p = \bar{P}A$. Also, by lemma A.9 and an argument like that of the proof of Lemma A.10, $\|\bar{P}'\bar{P}/n - \Sigma\| \xrightarrow{p} 0$. Also, by assumption 3.1, $\lambda_{\min}(\Sigma) \geqslant C$. Also, $E[P_iu_i] = 0$ by each element of P_i in $\mathscr{G}$, and $E[P_iP_i'u_i^2] = E[P_iP_i'E[u_i^2|x_i]] \leqslant C\Sigma$, so by the data i.i.d.,

$$\begin{aligned} E[\|\Sigma^{-1/2}\bar{P}'u/n\|^2] &= E[\text{tr}(u'\bar{P}\Sigma^{-1}\bar{P}'u)]/n^2 \\ &= \text{tr}(\Sigma^{-1/2}(\Sigma_{i=1}^n \Sigma_{j=1}^n E[P_iu_iP_j'u_j])\Sigma^{-1/2})/n^2 \\ &= \text{tr}(\Sigma^{-1/2}E[P_iP_i'u_i^2]\Sigma^{-1/2})/n \leqslant \text{tr}(CI_{\bar{K}})/n \leqslant C\bar{K}/n. \end{aligned}$$

Therefore, by the Markov inequality, $\|\Sigma^{-1/2}\bar{P}'u/n\| = O_p((\bar{K}/n)^{1/2})$. The conclusion then follows by lemma A.6. □

The next few lemmas give approximation rate results for power series and splines.

Lemma A.12. For power series, if the support $\mathscr{X}$ of x_i is a compact box in $\mathbb{R}^r$ and $f(x)$ is continuously differentiable of order $\mathscr{s}$, then there are α, $C > 0$ such that for each K there is π with $|f - p^{K\prime}\pi|_d < CK^{-\alpha}$, where $\alpha = \mathscr{s}/r$ for when $d = 0$, and $\alpha = \mathscr{s} - d$ when $r = 1$ and $d \leqslant \mathscr{s}$.

Proof. For the first conclusion, note that by $|\lambda(K)|$ monotonic increasing, the set of all linear combinations of $p^K(x)$ will include the set of all polynomials of degree $CK^{1/r}$ for some C small enough, so theorem 8 of Lorentz (1986) applies. For $r = 1$, note that $\partial^d p^{K+d}(x)/\partial x^d$ is a spanning vector for power series up to order K. By the first conclusion, there exists C such that for all k there is π such that, for $f_K(x) = P^{K+d}(x)'\pi$, it is the case that $\sup_{\mathscr{X}}|\partial^d f(x)/\partial x^d - \partial^d f_K(x)/\partial x^d| \leqslant C \cdot K^{-\ell+d}$. The second conclusion then follows by integration and boundedness of the support. For example, for $d = 1$, $\underline{x}$ the minimum of the support, and the constant coefficient chosen so that $f(\underline{x}) = f_K(\underline{x})$, equal to the minimum of the support x, $|f(x) - f_K(x)| \leqslant \int_{\underline{x}}^{x}|\partial f(\tilde{x})/\partial x - \partial f_K(\tilde{x})/\partial x|d\tilde{x} \leqslant CK^{-\ell+1}$. □

Lemma A.13. For power series, if $\mathscr{X}$ is star-shaped and there is C such that $f(x)$ is continuously differentiable of all orders and for all multi-indices λ, $\max_{\mathscr{X}}|\partial^\lambda f(x)| \leqslant C^{|\lambda|}\}$, then for all α, $d > 0$ there is $C > 0$ such that for all K there is π with $|f - p^{K\prime}\pi|_d \leqslant CK^{-\alpha}$.

Proof. By $\mathscr{X}$ star-shaped, there exists $\bar{x} \in \mathscr{X}$ such that for all $x \in \mathscr{X}$, $\beta x + (1 - \beta)\bar{x} \in \mathscr{X}$ for all $0 \leqslant \beta \leqslant 1$. For a function $f(x)$ let $P(f, m, x)$ denote the Taylor series up to order m for an expansion around $\bar{x}$. Note $\partial P(f, m, x)/\partial x_j = P(\partial f/\partial x_j, m - 1, x)$, so that by induction $\partial^\lambda P(f, m, x) = P(\partial^\lambda f, m - |\lambda|, x)$. Also, $\partial^\lambda f(x)$ also satisfies the hypotheses, so that by the intermediate value form of the remainder,

$$\max_{x \in \mathscr{X}}|\partial^\lambda f(x) - P(\partial^\lambda f, m - |\lambda|, x)| \leqslant C^m/[(m - d)!].$$

Next, let $m(K)$ be the largest integer such that $P(f, m, x)$ is a linear combination of $p^K(x)$, and let $f_K(x) = P(f, m(K), x)$. By the "natural ordering" hypothesis, there are constants C_1 and C_2 such that $C_1 m(K)^r \leqslant K \leqslant C_2 m(K)^r$, so that for any $\alpha > 0$, $C^{m(K)}/[(m(K) - d)!] \leqslant CK^{-\alpha}$, and

$$\begin{aligned}\sup_{|\lambda| \leqslant d, \mathscr{X}}|\partial^\lambda f(x) - \partial^\lambda f_K(x)| &= \sup_{|\lambda| \leqslant d, \mathscr{X}}|\partial^\lambda f(x) - P(\partial^\lambda f, m(K) - |\lambda|, x)| \\ &\leqslant CK^{-\alpha}. \quad \square\end{aligned}$$

Lemma A.14. For splines, if $\mathscr{X}$ is a compact box and $f(x)$ is continuously differentiable of order ℓ, then there are α, $C > 0$ such that for all K there is π $|f - p^{K\prime}\pi|_d < CK^{-\alpha}$, where $\alpha = \ell - d$ for $r = 1$ and $d \leqslant m - 1$ and $\alpha = \ell/r$ for $d = 0$.

Proof. The result for $d = 0$ follows by theorem 12.8 of Schumaker (1981). For the other case, note that $\partial^d p^K(x)/\partial x^d$ is a spanning vector for splines of degree $m - d$, with knot spacing bounded by CK^{-1} for K large enough and some C. Therefore, by Powell (1981), there exists π_K such that for $f_K(x) = p^K(x)'\pi_K$, $\sup_{\mathscr{X}}|\partial^d f(x)/\partial x^d - \partial^d f_K(x)/\partial x^d| \leqslant C \cdot K^{-\ell+d}$. The conclusion then follows by integration, similarly to the proof of lemma A.12. □

The next two lemmas show that for power series and splines, there exists $P^K(x)$ such that assumption 3.2 is satisfied, and give explicit bounds on the series and their derivatives.

Lemma A.15. For power series, if the support of x is a Cartesian product of compact intervals, say of unit intervals, with density bounded below $C\Pi_{l=1}^{r}(x_l)^{v}(1 - x_l)^{v}$, then assumptions 3.2 and equation (3.1) are satisfied, with $\zeta_d(K) \leqslant CK^{1+v+2d}$ and $P^K(x)$ is a subvector of $P^{K+1}(x)$ for all $K \geqslant 1$.

Proof. Following the definitions in Abramowitz and Stegun (1972, chapter 22), let $C_k^{(\alpha)}(x)$ denote the ultraspherical polynomial of order k for exponent α, $h_k^{(\alpha)} \equiv \pi 2^{1-2\alpha}\Gamma(k + 2\alpha)/\{k!(k + \alpha)[\Gamma(\alpha)]^2\}$, and $p_k^{(\alpha)}(x) = [h_k^{(\alpha)}]^{-1/2}C_k^{(\alpha)}(x)$. Also, let $x_j(x_j) = (2x_j - x_j^1 - x_j^2)/(x_j^2 - x_j^1)$ and define

$$P_k(x) = \Pi_{j=1}^{r} p_{\lambda_j(k)}^{(v_j+0.5)}(x_j(x_j)).$$

$P^K(x)$ is a nonsingular combination of $p^K(x)$ by the "natural ordering" assumption (i.e. by $|\lambda(k)|$ monotonic increasing). Also, for $\tilde{P}(x)$ absolutely continuous on $\mathscr{X} = \Pi_{j=1}^{r}[x_j^1, x_j^2]$ with p.d.f. proportional to $\Pi_{j=1}^{r}[(x_j^2 - x_j)(x_j - x_j^1)]^{v_j}$, and by the change of variables there is a constant C with

$$\begin{aligned}&\lambda_{\min}(\textstyle\int P^K(x)P^K(x)'dP(\tilde{x}))\\ &\quad\geqslant \lambda_{\min}(\textstyle\int \otimes_{j=1}^{r}[\bar{p}_M^{(v_j+0.5)}(x_j(x_j))\bar{p}_M^{(v_j+0.5)}(x_j(x_j))']d\tilde{P}(x)) = C,\end{aligned}$$

where the inequality follows by $P^K(x)$ a subvector of $\otimes_{j=1}^{r}[\bar{p}_M^{(v_j+0.5)}(x_j(x_j))$ for $M = \max_{k\leqslant K}|\lambda(k)|$ and $\bar{p}_M^{(\alpha)}(x) = (p_0^{(\alpha)}(x), \ldots, p_M^{(\alpha)}(x))$.

Next, by differentiating 22.5.37 of Abramowitz and Stegun (for m there equal to v here) and solving, it follows that for $l \leqslant k$, $d^l C_k^{(v+0.5)}(x)/dx^l = C \cdot C_{k-l}^{(v+l+0.5)}(x)$ so that by 22.14.2 of Abramowitz and Stegun, for $\lambda(k - s)$ as in equation (2.3),

$$\begin{aligned}|\partial^{\lambda}P_{kK}(x)| &\leqslant C\Pi_{j=1}^{r}[1 + \lambda_j(k - s)]^{0.5+v_j+2\lambda_j}\\ &\leqslant C|\lambda(k - s)|^{r(0.5+\bar{v}+\bar{\lambda})} \leqslant C \cdot K^{0.5+\bar{v}+2\bar{\lambda}},\end{aligned}$$

where the last equality follows by $|\lambda(k - s)| \leqslant CK^{1/r}$. □

Lemma A.16. For splines, if assumption 4.1 is satisfied then assumptions 3.2 and equation (3.1) are satisfied, with $\zeta_d(K) \leqslant CK^{(1/2)+d}$.

Proof. First, consider the case where $x = x_2$ and let $\mathscr{X} = \Pi_{l=1}^{r}[-1, 1]$. Let $B_{jL}^m(x)$, be the B-spline of order m, for the knot sequence $-1 + 2j/[L + 1]$, $j = \ldots, -1, 0, -1, \ldots$ with left end-knot j, and let

$$\begin{aligned}&P_{lk}(x_l) \equiv (L_l/2)^{1/2}B_{k-m-1,L_l}^m(x_l), \quad (k = 1, \ldots, L_l + m + 1, l = 1, \ldots, r),\\ &P_{kK}(x) = \Pi_{l=1}^{r}1(\lambda_l(k) > 0)P_{l,\lambda_l(k)}(x_l).\end{aligned}$$

Then existence of a nonsingular matrix A such that $P^K(x) = Ap^K(x)$ for $x \in \mathscr{X}$ follows by inclusion in $p^K(x)$ of all multiplicative interactions of splines for components of x corresponding to components of $h(x)$ and the usual basis result for B-splines (e.g. theorem 19.2 of Powell, 1981).

Next, a well known property of B-splines is that for all x, the number of elements of $P^K(x) = (P_{1K}(x), \ldots, P_{KK}(x))$ that are nonzero are bounded, uniformly in K. Also, when the elements of x are i.i.d. uniform random variables, and noting that $[2(m + 1)/L_l][L_l/2]^{-1/2}P_{lk}(x_l)$ are the so-called normalized B-splines with evenly spaced knots, it follows by the argument of Burman and Chen (1989, p. 1587) that for $P_{l,L}(x) = (P_{l1}(x_l), \ldots, P_{l,L+m+1}(x_l))$, there is C with $\lambda_{\min}(\int_{-1}^{1} P_{l,L}(x)P_{l,L}(x)'dx) \geqslant C$ for all positive integers L. Therefore, the boundedness away from zero of the smallest eigenvalue follows by $P^K(x)$ a subvector of $\otimes_{l=1}^{r} P_{l,L_l}(x_l)$, analogously to the proof of lemma A.14. Also, since changing even knot spacing is equivalent to rescaling the argument of B-splines, $\sup_{\mathbb{R}}|\partial^d B_{jL}^m(x)/\partial x^d| \leqslant CL^d$, $d \leqslant m$, implying the bounds on derivatives given in the conclusion. The proof when x_1 is present follows as in the proof of lemma 8.4. □

Proof of theorem 3.1. For each K let π be that from assumption 3.4 with $d = 0$, so that there is C such that

$$\Sigma_{i=1}^{n}[g_0(x_i) - p^{\hat{K}}(x_i)'\pi]^2/n \leqslant \sup_{x\in\mathscr{X}}|g_0(x) - p^{\hat{K}}(x)'\pi|^2 \leqslant C\hat{K}^{-2\alpha} = O_p(\underline{K}^{-2\alpha}). \tag{A.2}$$

Also, by lemma A.11, the hypothesis of lemma A.7 is satisfied with $\epsilon_n = (\bar{K}/n)^{1/2}$. The first conclusion then follows by the conclusion of lemma A.7.

The second conclusion is proven using lemma A.8. In the hypotheses of lemma A.8, let $\Sigma = \int P^{\hat{K}}(x)P^{\hat{K}}(x)'dF(x)$ and $p = [P^{\hat{K}}(x_1), \ldots, P^{\hat{K}}(x_n)]'$. By assumption 3.2 and lemmas A.10 and A.11, the hypotheses of lemma A.8 are satisfied with $\epsilon_n = (\bar{K}/n)^{1/2}$. For each K let π be as above, except with $P^K(x)$ replacing $p^K(x)$. Then (A.2) is satisfied (with $P^K(x)$ replacing $p^K(x)$) and $\int[g_0(x) - P^{\hat{K}}(x)'\pi]^2 dF(x) \leqslant \sup_{x\in\mathscr{X}}|g_0(x) - P^{\hat{K}}(x)'\pi|^2 = O_p(\underline{K}^{-2\alpha})$. Then by the second conclusion of lemma A.8,

$$\begin{aligned}\int[g_0(x) - \hat{g}(x)]^2 dF(x) &\leqslant 2\int[g_0(x) - P^{\hat{K}}(x)'\pi]^2 dF(x) + 2(\hat{\pi} - \pi)'\Sigma(\hat{\pi} - \pi)\\ &\leqslant O_p(\underline{K}^{-2\alpha}) + O_p(\bar{K}/n) + O_p(1)\Sigma_{i=1}^{n}[g_0(x_i) - P^{\hat{K}}(x_i)'\pi]^2/n\\ &= O_p(\bar{K}/n + \underline{K}^{-2\alpha}). \quad \square\end{aligned} \tag{A.3}$$

Proof of Theorem 3.2. Because $P^K(x)$ is a constant nonsingular linear transformation of $p^K(x)$, assumption 3.4 will be satisfied for $P^K(x)$ replacing $p^K(x)$. Also, by assumption 3.3 (b), when $\hat{K} \geqslant \bar{K}$, π can be chosen so that $|g_0(x) - P^{\hat{K}}(x)'\pi|_d \leqslant |g_0(x) - P^{\underline{K}}(x)'\pi|_d$, so that $|g_0(x) - P^{\hat{K}}(x)'\pi|_d = O_p(\underline{K}^{-\alpha})$. Also, it follows as in the proof of theorem 3.1 that (A.2) and the hypotheses of lemma A.8 are satisfied. Then by the first conclusion of lemma A.8 and the triangle inequality,

$$\begin{aligned}|g_0 - \hat{g}|_d &\leqslant |g_0 - P^{\hat{K}\prime}\pi|_d + |P^{\hat{K}\prime}(\hat{\pi} - \pi)|_d \leqslant O_p(\underline{K}^{-\alpha}) + \zeta_d(\hat{K})\,\|\,\hat{\pi} - \pi\,\|\\ &= O_p(\underline{K}^{-\alpha}) + \zeta_d(\bar{K})O_p((\bar{K}/n)^{1/2} + \underline{K}^{-\alpha}) = O_p(\zeta_d(\bar{K})[(\bar{K}/n)^{1/2} + \underline{K}^{-\alpha}]). \quad \square\end{aligned} \tag{A.4}$$

Proof of theorem 4.1. By assumption 4.1 it follows that the hypotheses of lemma A.3 are satisfied. Therefore, by the conclusion of lemma A.3 there exists a representation $g_0(x) = \Sigma_l g_{0l}(x_l)$, where for each l the dimension of x_l is less than or equal to $\mathscr{r}$. Then by lemmas A.12 and A.14 it follows that for each K there is π^l with $|g_{0l} - p^{K\prime}\pi|_0 \leqslant CK^{-\mathscr{s}/\mathscr{r}}$. Then by the triangle inequality, for $\pi = \Sigma_l \pi_l$, assumption 3.4 is satisfied with $d = 0$ and $\alpha = \mathscr{s}/\mathscr{r}$. Also, by lemma A.15, assumptions 3.2 and equation (3.1) are satisfied, and assumption 4.2 implies that assumption 3.3 holds. Then the conclusion follows by theorem 3.1 with $d = 0$ and $\zeta_0(K) = K$ for power series and $\zeta_0(K) = K^{1/2}$ for splines. □

Proof of theorem 4.2. It follows as in the proof of theorem 4.1 that assumptions 3.1 to 3.4 are satisfied, with $\zeta_0(K) = K$ for power series and $\zeta_0(K) = K^{1/2}$ for splines. The conclusion then follows by theorem 3.2. □

Proof of theorem 4.3. Follows as in the proof of theorem 4.2, except that assumption 3.4 is now satisfied with $\alpha = -\mathscr{s} + d$ by lemmas A.12 and A.14, and assumption 3.2 and equation (3.1) are now satisfied with $\zeta_d(K) = K^{1+2d}$ for power series, by lemma A.15, and with $\zeta_d(K) = K^{(1/2)+d}$ for splines, by lemma A.16. □

Proof of theorem 4.4. Follows as in the proof of theorem 4.3, except that lemma A.13 is applied to show that assumption 3.4 holds for any $\alpha > 0$. □

Proof of theorem 5.1. The proof is similar to that of theorems 4.1 and 4.2. By w bounded and lemmas A.12 and A.14, assumption 3.4 is satisfied with $\alpha = \mathscr{s}/r$. Also, note that assumption 4.1 is satisfied with u replacing x. Let $P^K(x) = w \otimes P^{K/\mathscr{L}}(u)$ for $P^K(u)$ equal to the vector from the conclusion of lemmas A.15 or A.16, for power series and splines respectively. Then by the smallest eigenvalue of $E[ww'|u]$ bounded away from zero, $E[P^K(x)P^K(x)'] \geqslant C(I \otimes E[P^{K/\mathscr{L}}(u)P^{K/\mathscr{L}}(u)'])$ in the positive semi-definite sense, so the smallest eigenvalue of $E[P^K(x)P^K(x)']$ is bounded away from zero. Also, bounds on elements of $P^K(x)$ are the same, up to a constant multiple, as bounds on elements of $P^{K/\mathscr{L}}(u)$, so that assumption 3.3 will hold. The conclusion then follows by the conclusions to theorems 3.1 and 3.2. □

Note

This chapter consists of part of a paper originally titled "Consistency and asymptotic normality of nonparametric projection estimators." Helpful comments were provided by Andreas Buja and financial support by the NSF and the Sloan Foundation.

References

Abramowitz, M. and Stegun, I. A. (eds) (1972) *Handbook of Mathematical Functions*, Washington, DC: Commerce Department.

Agarwal, G. and Studden, W. (1980) Asymptotic integrated mean square error using least squares and bias minimizing splines. *Annals of Statistics*, 8, 1307–25.

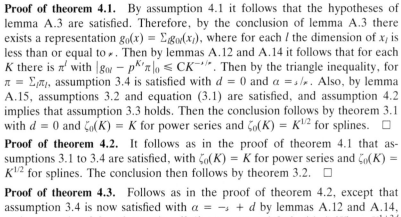

Andrews, D. W. K. (1991) Asymptotic normality of series estimators for various nonparametric and semiparametric models. *Econometrica*, 59, 307–45.

Andrews, D. W. K. and Whang, Y. J. (1990) Additive interactive regression models: circumvention of the curse of dimensionality. *Econometric Theory*, 6, 466–79.

Bickel, P., Klaassen, C. A. J., Ritov, Y. and Wellner, J. A. (1993) *Efficient and Adaptive Inference in Semiparametric Models*. Baltimore: Johns Hopkins University Press.

Breiman, L. and Friedman, J. H. (1985) Estimating optimal transformations for multiple regression and correlation. *Journal of the American Statistical Association*, 80, 580–98.

Breiman, L. and Stone, C. J. (1978) Nonlinear additive regression. Note.

Buja, A., Hastle, T. and Tibshirani, R. (1989) Linear smoothers and additive models. *Annals of Statistics*, 17, 453–510.

Burman, P. and Chen, K. W. (1989) Nonparametric estimation of a regression function. *Annals of Statistics*, 17, 1567–96.

Cox, D. D. (1988) Approximation of least squares regression on nested subspaces. *Annals of Statistics*, 16, 713–32.

Friedman, J. and Stuetzle, W. (1981) Projection pursuit regression. *Journal of the American Statistical Association*, 76, 817–23.

Gallant, A. R. (1981) On the bias in flexible functional forms and an essentially unbiased form: the Fourier flexible form. *Journal of Econometrics*, 76, 211–45.

Gallant, A. R. and Souza, G. (1991) On the asymptotic normality of Fourier flexible form estimates. *Journal of Econometrics*, 50, 329–53.

Lorentz, G. G. (1986) *Approximation of Functions*. New York: Chelsea Publishing Company.

Newey, W. K. (1988) Adaptive estimation of regression models via moment restrictions. *Journal of Econometrics*, 38, 301–39.

Newey, W. K. (1993a) The asymptotic variance of semiparametric estimators. Preprint, MIT Department of Economics.

Newey, W. K. (1993b) Series estimation of regression functionals. *Econometric Theory*, 10, 1–28.

Powell, M. J. D. (1981) *Approximation Theory and Methods*. Cambridge: Cambridge University Press.

Rao, C. R. (1973) *Linear Statistical Inference and Its Applications*. New York: Wiley.

Riedel, K. S. (1992) Smoothing spline growth curves with covariates, preprint. New York University, Courant Institute.

Schumaker, L. L. (1981) *Spline Fuctions: Basic Theory*. New York: Wiley.

Stone, C. J. (1982) Optimal global rates of convergence for nonparametric regression. *Annals of Statistics*, 10, 1040–53.

Stone, C. J. (1985) Additive regression and other nonparametric models. *Annals of Statistics*, 13, 689–705.

Stone, C. J. (1990) L_2 rate of convergence for interaction spline regression. Technical report no. 268, University of California at Berkeley.

Wahba, G. (1984) Cross-validated spline methods for the estimation of multivariate functions from data on fuctionals. In H. A. David and H. T. David (eds), *Statistics: an Appraisal. Proceedings 50th Anniversary Conference Iowa State Statistical Laboratory*. Ames: Iowa State University Press.

Zeldin, M. D. and Thomas, D. M. (1977) Ozone trends in the Eastern Los Angeles basin corrected for meteorological variations. *Proceedings International Conference on Environmental Sensing and Assessment, 2*, September 14–19, Las Vegas.

11 Generalized Least Squares with Nonnormal Errors

Christopher L. Cavanagh and
Thomas J. Rothenberg

1 Introduction

Regression models are often fit by generalized least squares where an estimate of the error covariance matrix obtained from the residuals of a preliminary regression is used in place of the true covariance matrix. In many cases the error introduced by using the estimated covariance matrix is of second order in the sense that it has no effect on the asymptotic distributions of regression estimates and test statistics but only modifies higher-order terms in the asymptotic expansions of their distribution functions. Indeed, with normal errors, Rothenberg (1984a) and Phillips (1993) show that the effect is often minimal even to second order: estimating the covariance matrix generally increases variance but otherwise has no effect on the approximate distribution of regression estimates. Carroll et al. (1988), however, show that these second-order results need not follow when the errors are nonnormal.

The second-order analysis under normality relies on the fact that covariance parameters estimated from regression residuals are distributed independently of the nonfeasible GLS estimate. However, in the absence of normality, this independence does not necessarily hold. In the present chapter, we show that most of the analysis goes through under the weaker condition that the covariance estimates are asymptotically uncorrelated with the GLS estimate. This condition is not typically satisfied in heteroskedastic models, but is satisfied in many time-series models. Thus, even in the absence of normality, there is a large class of cases where estimating the error covariance matrix has no effect on the shape of the distribution of GLS regression coeficient estimates.

2 The Model

We consider the linear model $y = X\beta + u$ where X in an $n \times K$ nonrandom design matrix having rank K and u is an n-dimensional vector of unobserved random errors with mean zero and nonsingular covariance matrix. If Ω, the inverse of the error covariance matrix, is known, the best linear unbiased estimate of β is obtained by generalized least squares and can be written as $\bar{\beta} = (X'\Omega X)^{-1}X'\Omega y$. Suppose, however, that Ω depends on an unknown p-dimensional parameter vector θ and is written as $\Omega = \Omega(\theta)$. If a reasonable estimator $\hat{\theta}$ exists, it is natural to estimate β by $\hat{\beta} = (X'\hat{\Omega}X)^{-1}X'\hat{\Omega}y$, where $\hat{\Omega} = \Omega(\hat{\theta})$. We investigate how inference based on $\bar{\beta}$ differs from inference based on $\hat{\beta}$ when Ω is a smooth function of θ and the sample size n is large relative to p and K.

To simplify the algebra, we shall concentrate on the scalar case and consider inference for an arbitrary linear combination of the elements of β. For any K-dimensional vector of constants c, the scalar $c'\bar{\beta}$ is an unbiased estimate of $c'\beta$ with variance $c'(X'\Omega X)^{-1}c$. Let Γ be an $n \times n$ lower triangular matrix such that $\Gamma'\Gamma = \Omega$. The standardized GLS estimator of $c'\beta$ (which has mean zero and variance one) can then be written as

$$A = \frac{c'(\bar{\beta} - \beta)}{[c'(X'\Omega X)^{-1}c]^{1/2}} = \frac{x'\varepsilon}{\sqrt{n}} \tag{2.1}$$

where $x = \sqrt{n}\Gamma X(X'\Omega X)^{-1}c[c'(X'\Omega X)^{-1}c]^{-1/2}$ and $\varepsilon = \Gamma u$. By construction, x is nonrandom with $x'x = n$ and the elements of ε are uncorrelated, mean zero random variables with unit variance. In section 3 we shall develop asymptotic approximations which allow us to compare the distribution of A with the distribution of the corresponding standardized estimator based on $\hat{\beta}$,

$$\hat{A} = \frac{c'(\hat{\beta} - \beta)}{[c'(X'\Omega X)^{-1}c]^{1/2}}. \tag{2.2}$$

In sections 4 to 6 specific results are derived for some important special cases. Finally, in section 7, we compare the distributions of the t-statistics based on $\bar{\beta}$ and $\hat{\beta}$.

To develop approximations, we contemplate an infinite sequence of problems with increasing sample size. In that sequence, the p-dimensional parameter vector θ and the K-dimensional parameter vector β remain fixed while the matrices X and Ω grow in size as n

tends to infinity with $X'\Omega X/n$ converging to a positive definite matrix. Suppose $\hat{\theta}$ is a consistent estimate of θ such that the vector $d = \sqrt{n}(\hat{\theta} - \theta)$ has a limiting normal distribution. If the elements of $\Omega(\theta)$ are differentiable in θ up to the third order, the standardized feasible GLS estimator can be expanded in a (stochastic) Taylor series

$$\hat{A} = A + \frac{b'd}{\sqrt{n}} + \frac{d'Cd}{n} + R \tag{2.3}$$

where typically the remainder term R is $O_p(n^{-3/2})$, and the p-dimensional vector $b = \partial\hat{A}/\partial\hat{\theta}$ and the $p \times p$ matrix $C = \frac{1}{2}\partial^2\hat{A}/\partial\hat{\theta}\partial\hat{\theta}'$ (the derivatives evaluated at the true value θ) are stochastically bounded as n tends to infinity. Explicit expressions for b and C are given in Rothenberg (1984b) but will not be needed here. It is sufficient to note that they are linear in ε with typical elements of the form

$$b_i = \frac{z_i'\varepsilon}{\sqrt{n}} \quad c_{ij} = \frac{z_{ij}'\varepsilon}{\sqrt{n}} \tag{2.4}$$

where the n-dimensional vectors z_i and z_{ij} are nonrandom and orthogonal to x. Hence, we have the key fact that b and C are uncorrelated with A.

With normally distributed errors, the variables A, b, and C are also normal; if the remainder term R in (2.3) is well behaved and can be ignored,[1] the distribution of $\hat{A}$ can easily be approximated to order n^{-1} using the asymptotic distribution of d. The analysis is only slightly more complicated with nonnormal errors as long as the joint distribution of A, b, C, and d is asymptotically normal and possesses an Edgeworth expansion. Formally, we make the following assumption:

Assumption A. The remainder term R in the stochastic expansion (2.3) satisfies $\Pr[n \log n|R| > 1] = o(n^{-1})$ and the elements of the vectors x, z_i, and z_{ij} appearing in (2.1) and (2.4) are uniformly bounded as n tends to infinity. The error vector ε possesses moments up to the fourth order and the vector η consisting of the distinct elements of (A, b, C, d) possesses a valid Edgeworth expansion to order n^{-1}. That is, the joint density function for η has the approximation

$$\phi_\Sigma(\eta)\left[1 + \frac{\Sigma\alpha_i\eta_i + \Sigma\alpha_{ijk}\eta_i\eta_j\eta_k}{\sqrt{n}} + \frac{\gamma(\eta)}{n}\right] + o(n^{-1}) \tag{2.5}$$

where ϕ_Σ is the density function of a normal random vector with mean zero and covariance matrix Σ; $\gamma(\eta)$ is an even order polynomial whose coefficients, along with the αs, are uniformly bounded scalars.

These regularity conditions appear to be appropriate for many models employed in applied work and imply that an approximation to the distribution of $\hat{A}$ with error $o(n^{-1})$ can be calculated from the moments of the approximate distribution of η. Considerable weakening of the conditions is undoubtedly possible but will not be pursued here.

3 A General Result on the Distribution of $\hat{A}$

The $o(n^{-1})$ approximate distribution of $\hat{A}$ will generally be complicated since, when the errors are nonnormal, even the leading term A in (2.3) is nonnormal. However, the $o(n^{-1})$ approximation to the *difference* between the distribution of $\hat{A}$ and the distribution of A turns out to be quite simple. We rely on the fact, derived in Cavanagh (1983) and discussed in Rothenberg (1984b, 1988), that the distribution of $\hat{A}$ is the same, to order n^{-1}, as the distribution of

$$A + \frac{1}{\sqrt{n}}E(b'd|A) + \frac{1}{n}\left[E(d'Cd|A) + \frac{1}{2}\left(A - \frac{\partial}{\partial A}\right)\text{var}(b'd|A)\right]$$

where the conditional moments are calculated from the Edgeworth approximation (2.5) (see also Barndorff-Nielsen and Cox, 1989, p. 78). To obtain $o(n^{-1})$ approximations, the moments in the final term can be calculated using the asymptotic normal distribution of η. To approximate $E(b'd|A)$ to order $n^{-1/2}$, we use the formulas given in Barndorff-Nielsen and Cox (1979) for the multivariate Edgeworth expansion of a conditional density function. Recall that A is asymptotically independent of b and C. Let the $p \times p$ matrices Σ_{bb}, Σ_{dd}, and Σ_{bd} denote the asymptotic variance and covariance matrices for the vectors b and d and let the p-dimensional column vector σ_{Ad} denote the asymptotic covariance between A and d. After some calculation, we find

$$E(b'd|A) = \text{tr}\Sigma_{bd} + A \cdot E(Ab'd) + \frac{1}{2}(A^3 - 3A) \cdot E(A^2b'\sigma_{Ad}) + o(n^{-1/2})$$

$$E(d'Cd|A) = 2A \cdot E(d'C\sigma_{Ad}) + o(1)$$

$$\text{var}(b'd|A) = \text{tr}(\Sigma_{bb}\Sigma_{dd} + \Sigma_{bd}^2) + (A^2 - 1)\sigma_{Ad}'\Sigma_{bb}\sigma_{Ad} + o(1).$$

Thus, Â has the same approximate distribution as

$$A + \frac{1}{\sqrt{n}}\text{tr}\Sigma_{bd} + \frac{1}{2n}[\rho A + [\sigma_{Ad}'\Sigma_{bb}\sigma_{Ad} + \sqrt{n}E(A^2b'\sigma_{Ad})]A^3] \quad (3.1)$$

where

$$\rho = \text{var}(b'd) - 3\sigma'_{Ad}\Sigma_{bb}\sigma_{Ad} + 4E(d'C\sigma_{Ad})$$
$$+ \sqrt{n} \cdot E(2Ab'd - 3A^2b'\sigma_{Ad}).$$

Recall that A has mean zero and its higher-order odd moments are $o(1)$. Furthermore, (3.1) is a linear function of A when $\sigma_{Ad} = 0$. Thus, If skewness is measured by the third cumulant and kurtosis by the fourth cumulant, we find:

Proposition 1. Based on moments of the $o(n^{-1})$ Edgeworth approximation to the distributions.

(a) the skewness of $\hat{A}$ is always the same as the skewness of A;
(b) if $\Sigma_{bd} = 0$, the mean of $\hat{A}$ is the same as the mean of A;
(c) if $\sigma_{Ad} = 0$, the kurtosis of $\hat{A}$ is the same as the kurtosis of A.

To a second order of approximation, the difference in location and shape between the $\bar{\beta}$ and $\hat{\beta}$ distributions depends only on the asymptotic covariances σ_{Ad} and Σ_{bd}. In Rothenberg (1984a) it is shown that, with normal errors and residual-based estimates of θ, d is necessarily independent of A and b and hence the two estimates of β have approximate distributions differing only in variance. Proposition 1 says that the same result holds with nonnormal errors as long as d is *asymptotically* independent of A and b. In any given application σ_{Ad} and Σ_{bd} should be easy to compute since only first-order asymptotics is involved. Indeed, even with nonnormal errors, there is a large class of cases where no additional calculations are needed since the asymptotic covariances are generically zero. In the next section we derive some sufficient conditions for this to occur.

4 Residual-based Estimates of θ

If the covariance parameters are not related to β, it is common to estimate θ from residuals $\tilde{u} = y - X\tilde{\beta}$, where $\tilde{\beta}$ is some preliminary consistent estimate of β. Furthermore, since $\Omega(\theta)$ determines the variance matrix for u, most estimates of θ are based on quadratic functions of such residuals. For example, $\hat{\theta}$ often satisfies an estimating equation such as

$$g(\hat{\theta}, s_1, \ldots, s_q) = 0 \tag{4.1}$$

where g is a vector of p functions and

$$s_i = \tilde{u}'B_i(\hat{\theta})\tilde{u} \quad (i = 1, \ldots, q) \tag{4.2}$$

with the $n \times n$ matrices $B_1, \ldots, B_q$ possibly depending on $\hat{\theta}$. As shown in section 6, such equations arise from normal maximum likelihood or minimum distance estimation methods. Typically the functions in (4.1) and (4.2) are smooth and can be expanded in Taylor series to give simple asymptotic representations for $\sqrt{n}(\hat{\theta} - \theta)$ in terms of quadratic functions of ε. With this motivation, we assume henceforth that the θ estimates satisfy the following condition:

Assumption B. The elements of d have stochastic expansions

$$d_k = \sqrt{n}(\hat{\theta}_k - \theta_k) = \sum_{i=1}^{q} \pi_{ki} e_i + R_k \quad (k = 1, \ldots, p)$$

where the remainder R_k satisfies $\Pr[\log n \, |R_k| > 1] = o(n^{-1})$ and the variables $e_1, \ldots, e_q$ are jointly asymptotically normal of the form

$$e_i = (\varepsilon' D_i \varepsilon - \operatorname{tr} D_i)/\sqrt{n} \quad (i = 1, \ldots, q).$$

The coefficients π_{ij} and the elements of the $n \times n$ symmetric matrices $D_1, \ldots, D_q$ are nonrandom and uniformly bounded as n tends to infinity.

Note that Σ_{bd} and σ_{Ad} are necessarily zero when $\hat{\theta}$ satisfies assumption B and the third moments of the error distribution are all zero. Even with nonzero third moments, simple general results can be obtained if the transformed error vector ε satisfies

Assumption C. The n random variables $\varepsilon_1, \ldots, \varepsilon_n$ are mutually independent with mean zero, unit variance, and uniformly bounded third and fourth cumulants $\kappa_{3t} = E(\varepsilon_t^3)$ and $\kappa_{4t} = E(\varepsilon_t^4) - 3$.

Under independence, σ_{Ad} and Σ_{bd} are linear combinations of terms such as

$$E(Ae_i) = \frac{1}{n}\sum_{t=1}^{n} x_t d_{tt}^i \kappa_{3t} \quad \text{and} \quad E(b_k e_i) = \frac{1}{n}\sum_{t=1}^{n} z_t^k d_{tt}^i \kappa_{3t}, \tag{4.3}$$

where d_{tt}^i is the tth diagonal element of D_i and z_t^k is the tth element of the vector z_k. These terms vanish if the D_i have zero diagonals. In fact, we have:

Proposition 2. Suppose $\hat{\beta}$, $\hat{\theta}$, and the errors ε_t satisfy assumptions A and B. Then the vector d is asymptotically uncorrelated with A and b if either (a) the third moments of the errors are all zero *or* (b) assumption C is also satisfied and $\lim n^{-1}\Sigma_t |d_{tt}^i| = 0$ for $i = 1, \ldots, q$. In both cases, the distribution of $\hat{\beta}$ has, to a second order of approximation, the same location and shape as the distribution of $\bar{\beta}$.

The third moments will be zero if, for example, the distribution of the error vector u is symmetric about the origin. We shall show in section 6 that the diagonal elements of the D_i are typically zero when the errors are a stationary time series. Hence, the results previously derived for normal errors hold much more generally.

5 The Effect of Estimated Weights on the Variance of β

With normal errors, the variance of $\hat{\beta}$ is necessarily greater than the variance of $\bar{\beta}$ when θ is estimated from regression residuals. Furthermore, to second order, the variance of $\hat{\beta}$ does not depend on the $\tilde{\beta}$ used in the preliminary regression. In the context of a model with heteroskedasticity, Carroll et al. (1988) demonstrate that these conclusions need not follow when errors are nonnormal. They produce examples where the choice of preliminary estimator matters and where the variance of $\hat{\beta}$ is less than the variance of $\bar{\beta}$.

If A is asymptotically uncorrelated with d, we have

$$\text{var}(\hat{A}) \cong \text{var}(A) + \frac{\text{var}(b'd)}{n} + \frac{2\sqrt{n}E(Ab'd)}{n}.$$

The approximate variance of $\hat{\beta}$ is necessarily greater than the variance of $\bar{\beta}$ if the final term is nonnegative. This term, however, depends on second-order asymptotic properties of the distribution of $\hat{\theta}$ which in turn depend on the particular estimate of β used to form the residuals $\tilde{u}$. We shall consider estimators of the form $(W'X)^{-1}W'y$ where W is an $n \times K$ matrix of observations on K nonrandom instrumental variables with the property that $EW'u = 0$ and $W'X$ has rank K. The instrumental variable residual vector can then be written as

$$\tilde{u} = y - X\tilde{\beta} = [I - X(W'X)^{-1}W']\Gamma^{-1}\varepsilon \equiv M_W\varepsilon.$$

Of course, one possible choice for W is the regressor matrix X, in which case $\tilde{u}$ is the (unweighted) least-squares residual vector. Suppose $\hat{\theta}$ satisfies an estimating equation such as (4.1). Then the s_i are of the form $\varepsilon' M_W' B_i(\hat{\theta}) M_W\varepsilon$ and behave, to first order, as $\varepsilon'\Gamma'^{-1}B_i\Gamma^{-1}\varepsilon$. Under suitable smoothness, an additional term in the Taylor expansion of $\hat{\theta}$ can be taken and assumption B strengthened as follows:

Assumption B′. The elements of d have stochastic expansions

$$d_k = \sum_{i=1}^{q}\pi_{ki}e_i + n^{-1/2}\sum_{i=1}^{q}\sum_{j=1}^{r}\delta_{ij}^{k}e_i\bar{e}_j + n^{-1/2}\pi_{k0} + \bar{R}_k \quad (k = 1, \ldots, p)$$

where the remainder $\bar{R}_k$ satisfies $\Pr[\sqrt{n}\log n\,|R_k| > 1] = o(n^{-1})$; the random variables e_i and $\bar{e}_j$ are quadratic functions of ε of the form

$$e_i = n^{-1/2}(\varepsilon' D_i \varepsilon - \mathrm{tr} D_i) \quad \bar{e}_j = n^{-1/2}(\varepsilon' \bar{D}_j \varepsilon - \mathrm{tr}\bar{D}_j).$$

where $D_i = M_W' B_i M_W$ and $\bar{D}_j = M_W' \bar{B}_j M_W$ for $n \times n$ matrices B_i and $\bar{B}_j$. The coefficients π_{ij}, δ_{ij}^k and the elements of the matrices D_i and $\bar{D}_j$ are nonrandom and uniformly bounded as n tends to infinity. Further, $\lim n^{-1}\mathrm{tr}(D_i - B_i\Omega^{-1})^2 = \lim n^{-1}\mathrm{tr}(\bar{D}_i - \bar{B}_i\Omega^{-1})^2 = 0$.

Assuming the ε_t are mutually independent, we find

$$\begin{aligned}\sqrt{n}E(Ab'd) &= \sum_{k=1}^{p}\sum_{i=1}^{q}\sum_{j=1}^{r}\delta_{ij}^{k}\Big(\frac{1}{n}\sum_{t=1}^{n}x_t d_{tt}^{i}\kappa_{3t}\Big)\Big(\frac{1}{n}\sum_{t=1}^{n}z_t^k \bar{d}_{tt}^{j}\kappa_{3t}\Big) \\ &+ \sum_{k=1}^{p}\sum_{i=1}^{q}\sum_{j=1}^{r}\delta_{ij}^{k}\Big(\frac{1}{n}\sum_{t=1}^{n}x_t \bar{d}_{tt}^{i}\kappa_{3t}\Big)\Big(\frac{1}{n}\sum_{t=1}^{n}z_t^k d_{tt}^{j}\kappa_{3t}\Big) \\ &+ \frac{1}{n}\sum_{k=1}^{p}\sum_{i=1}^{q}\pi_{ki}\Big[2z_k' D_i x + \sum_{t=1}^{n}x_t z_t^k d_{tt}^{i}\kappa_{4t}\Big] + o(1) \quad (5.1)\end{aligned}$$

where d_{tt}^{i} and $\bar{d}_{tt}^{j}$ are diagonal elements of D_i and $\bar{D}_j$, respectively. From the definitions of x and M_W, we have $D_i x = M_W' B_i M_W x = 0$. Thus, $\sqrt{n}E(Ab'd)$ will be $o(1)$ if the diagonals elements of the D_i matrices are all zero. In fact, we have the stronger result:

Proposition 3. Under assumptions A, B′, and C, the second-order approximation to the variance of $\hat{\beta}$ does not depend on the instruments employed in the preliminary regression. A sufficient condition for the approximate variance of $\hat{\beta}$ to be greater than the variance of $\bar{\beta}$ is $\lim n^{-1}\Sigma_t|d_{tt}^{i}| = 0$.

6 Stationary Errors

Generalized least squares is often employed in time-series regression where the errors $u_1, \ldots, u_n$ are assumed to be the realization of a stationary random process. An example is the first-order autoregressive error model with initial condition $u_1 = \sigma(1 - \theta^2)^{-1/2}\varepsilon_1$ and

$$u_t = \theta u_{t-1} + \sigma\varepsilon_t \quad (t = 2, \ldots, n)$$

where $|\theta| < 1$ and the ε_t are i.i.d. innovations with zero mean and unit variance. The covariance between u_i and u_j is then $\theta^{|i-j|}\sigma^2/(1 - \theta^2)$ and the error vector is related to the innovation vector by $\varepsilon = \Gamma u$, where Γ and Γ^{-1} are the $n \times n$ lower triangular matrices

$$\Gamma = \frac{1}{\sigma}\begin{bmatrix} \lambda^{-1} & & & & \\ -\theta & 1 & & & \\ 0 & -\theta & \ddots & & \\ \vdots & & \ddots & \ddots & \\ \vdots & & & 1 & \\ 0 & 0 & \dots & -\theta & 1 \end{bmatrix} \qquad \Gamma^{-1} = \sigma\begin{bmatrix} \lambda & & & & \\ \lambda\theta & 1 & & & \\ \lambda\theta^2 & \theta & \ddots & & \\ \vdots & \vdots & \ddots & \ddots & \\ \vdots & \vdots & & \ddots & 1 \\ \lambda\theta^{n-1} & \theta^{n-2} & \dots & \theta & 1 \end{bmatrix}$$

with $\lambda = (1 - \theta^2)^{-1/2}$. Suppose θ is estimated by regressing preliminary residuals on their lagged values. If Δ_i is the $(n - 1) \times n$ matrix obtained by deleting the ith row of an $n \times n$ identity matrix, the least-squares estimate of θ based on the residual vector $\tilde{u}$ can be expressed as $\hat{\theta} = \tilde{u}'\Delta_n'\Delta_1\tilde{u}/\tilde{u}'\Delta_n'\Delta_n\tilde{u}$. If instrumental variable residuals $\tilde{u} = M_W\varepsilon$ are used, we obtain the stochastic expansion

$$\begin{aligned} d = \sqrt{n}(\hat{\theta} - \theta) &= \sqrt{n}\tilde{u}'\Delta_n'(\Delta_1 - \theta\Delta_n)\tilde{u}/\tilde{u}'\Delta_n'\Delta_n\tilde{u} \\ &= \pi\frac{\varepsilon'D\varepsilon - \operatorname{tr}D}{\sqrt{n}}\left[1 - \pi^2\frac{\varepsilon'\bar{D}\varepsilon - \operatorname{tr}\bar{D}}{n}\right] + \frac{\pi\operatorname{tr}D}{\sqrt{n}} + O_p(n^{-1}) \quad (6.1) \end{aligned}$$

where $D = M_W'BM_W$, $\bar{D} = M_W'\Delta_n'\Delta_nM_W$, $\pi = n/\operatorname{tr}\bar{D}$, and B is the $n \times n$ band matrix

$$B = \frac{1}{2}(\Delta_n'\Delta_1 + \Delta_1'\Delta_n - 2\theta\Delta_n'\Delta_n) = -\frac{1}{2}\begin{bmatrix} 2\theta & -1 & & & & \\ -1 & 2\theta & -1 & & & \\ & -1 & 2\theta & -1 & & \\ & & \ddots & \ddots & \ddots & \\ & & & -1 & 2\theta & -1 \\ & & & & -1 & 0 \end{bmatrix}.$$

Simple calculation shows that $D_0 \equiv \Gamma'^{-1}B\Gamma^{-1}$ has zero diagonal. Furthermore, if the data matrices X and W are well-behaved, $\operatorname{tr}(D - D_0)^2$ is $O(1)$. Hence, if the regularity conditions in assumptions A and B′ are satisfied, the conclusions of proposition 2 and 3 follow.

The same results hold for quite general stationary linear error processes when the parameters are estimated by minimizing the sum of squared innovations or by pseudomaximum likelihood. The derivation, unfortunately, is rather lengthy so we shall restrict ourselves to a sketch of the argument for the latter case. If the regression errors were normally distributed, the log likelihood function would be

$$L(\theta, \beta) = \frac{1}{2}\log|\Omega| - \frac{1}{2}(y - X\beta)'\Omega(y - X\beta).$$

Even if the errors are nonnormal, one can still estimate θ by maximizing $L(\theta, \tilde{\beta})$ for some preliminary estimate $\tilde{\beta}$. If instrumental variables W are used to obtain the preliminary estimate, $y - X\tilde{\beta} = M_W\varepsilon$ and the first-order conditions are of the form

$$\mathrm{tr}\hat{\Omega}^{-1}\hat{\Omega}_i - \varepsilon' M_W' \hat{\Omega}_i M_W \varepsilon = 0 \quad i = 1, \ldots, p \tag{6.2}$$

where $\Omega_i = \partial\Omega/\partial\theta_i$. Under suitable regularity conditions, the left-hand side of equation (6.2) can be expanded in a Taylor series around the true value θ yielding an expansion for $d = \sqrt{n}(\hat{\theta} - \theta)$ satisfying assumption B′ with $p = q$ and $D_i = M_W'\Omega_i(\theta)M_W$. Again, if X and W are well behaved, $\mathrm{tr}(D_i - \Gamma'^{-1}\Omega_i\Gamma^{-1})^2$ is $O(1)$. But, $\Omega_i = \Gamma'\Gamma_i + \Gamma_i'\Gamma$ where $\Gamma_i = \partial\Gamma/\partial\theta_i$. Thus, we need only show that (except for a few end points) the diagonal elements of $\Gamma_i\Gamma^{-1}$ are zero.

When the errors are stationary, Ω^{-1} is a Toeplitz matrix with constant values along all the diagonals. Moreover, if the autocorrelation function is square summable, Γ itself is approximately Toeplitz with a constant on the main diagonal.[2] Since the GLS estimator is unaffected by scale, this constant need not be estimated and the diagonal elements of Γ_i may be taken to be zero. But Γ is triangular, so the diagonal elements of $\Gamma_i\Gamma^{-1}$ are also zero. Thus, the conclusions of propositions 2 and 3 hold when θ is estimated by pseudo maximum likelihood.

Strict stationarity of the errors is not crucial to the argument. For example, in the simple AR(1) example, the initial error u_1 can be set arbitrarily without changing the result. Thus, for example, in time-series regression where the errors are generated by a stable ARMA process with arbitrary initial conditions and i.i.d. innovations, the GLS estimator using an Ω estimated from the residuals of a preliminary instrumental variables regression generally has an approximate distribution with the same shape and location as that of the GLS estimator $\bar{\beta}$ but with larger variance. This variance does not, to second order, depend on the particular variables used as instruments in the preliminary regression. These conclusions hold without any assumption on the third and fourth cumulants of the error distribution (except that they exist).

7 The Distribution of the *t*-Ratio

Inference about $c'\beta$ is typically based on the ratio of $c'(\hat{\beta} - \beta)$ to its estimated standard deviation. If the errors are normal and Ω is known except for a proportionality factor, this ratio is distributed as Student's t. If additional parameters determining Ω have to be estimated or if the errors are nonnormal, the Student distribution is no longer exact, although it is often valid asymptotically. Rothenberg (1988) studies the effect of using an estimated Ω on the distribution of the t-ratio assuming normal errors. Here we shall investigate second-order approximations to the distribution of the t-ratio allowing for both nonnormal errors and an estimated covariance matrix.

It will be useful to define a scale parameter σ and let θ represent the remaining parameters which determine Ω. Thus we write the inverse of the error covariance matrix as $\Omega = \sigma^{-2}\Psi(\theta) = \sigma^{-2}\bar{\Gamma}'\bar{\Gamma}$, where $\bar{\Gamma}(\theta)$ is a lower triangular matrix now scaled so that $\mathrm{tr}\bar{\Gamma} = n$. If θ were known, the scale parameter would be estimated by $\tilde{\sigma}^2 = \tilde{\varepsilon}'\tilde{\varepsilon}/(n\text{-}K)$, where $\tilde{\varepsilon}$ is the residual vector from a regression of $\bar{\Gamma}y$ on $\bar{\Gamma}x$. If only an estimate $\hat{\theta}$ were available, residuals $\hat{\varepsilon}$ from a regression of $\bar{\Gamma}(\hat{\theta})y$ on $\bar{\Gamma}(\hat{\theta})x$ would be used to form the estimate $\hat{\sigma}^2 = \hat{\varepsilon}'\hat{\varepsilon}/(n\text{-}K)$.

Let T^* be the t-ratio for $c'\beta$ when the parameter θ is known and let T be the t-ratio when the estimate $\hat{\theta}$ is used in place of θ. We can then write:

$$
\begin{aligned}
T^* &= \frac{\tilde{\sigma}c'(\tilde{\beta} - \beta)}{[c'(X'\Psi X)^{-1}c]^{1/2}} = A\frac{\tilde{\sigma}}{\sigma} \\
T &= \frac{c'(\hat{\beta} - \beta)}{[c'(X'\hat{\Omega}X)^{-1}c]^{1/2}} = \hat{A}\frac{\hat{\sigma}}{\sigma}\left[\frac{c'(X'\hat{\Psi}X)^{-1}c}{c'(X'\Psi X)^{-1}c}\right]^{-1/2}.
\end{aligned}
\tag{7.1}
$$

In the appendix we sketch the derivation of the secord-order approximation to the distribution function for T in terms of corresponding approximate distribution function for T^*. Here we shall present some specific results for the special case examined in section 6 where the θs are autocorrelation parameters of a stationary error process. In their study of inference in nonnormal regression, Cavanagh and Rothenberg (1990) find that considerable simplification occurs in the common case where the regression has an intercept but only slope coefficients are included in $c'\beta$. We shall restrict our attention to that case here.

As argued in section 6, when the errors are a stationary time series, we can, with asymptotically negligible error, assume that the triangular matrix Γ is Toeplitz. Then, under our normalization, $\bar{\Gamma}$ has ones on the diagonal. This implies that the leading term in the expansions of both $e \equiv \sqrt{n}(\hat{\sigma}^2 - \sigma^2)/\sigma^2$ and $e^* \equiv \sqrt{n}(\tilde{\sigma}^2 - \sigma^2)/\sigma^2$ are of the form $n^{-1/2}(\varepsilon' D_0 \varepsilon - \mathrm{tr}D_0)$, where D_0 is an identity matrix. In contrast, each of the D_i matrices appearing in the leading term of the stochastic expansion of $d = \sqrt{n}(\hat{\theta} - \theta)$ has zero diagonal. As demonstrated in the Appendix, these facts imply:

Proposition 4. Suppose $\Omega = \sigma^{-2}\bar{\Gamma}'\bar{\Gamma}$, where σ is a scale parameter and $\bar{\Gamma}$ is a lower triangular Toeplitz matrix with ones on the main diagonal and the remaining elements depending on the parameter vector θ. Assume further that $\hat{\theta}$ is based on quadratic functions of instrumental variable residuals and that assumptions A, B$'$, and C are satisfied. Finally, assume that one of the columns of X is a vector of ones and that the corresponding element of c is zero. Then, the approximate distribution of T is

$$\Pr[T < t] = F\left[t\left(1 - \frac{(1 + t^2)r + s}{24n}\right)\right] + o(n^{-1}) \qquad (7.2)$$

where F is the distribution function for T^*. The parameters r and s do not depend on the error distribution so the effect of estimating θ is the same as previously shown for normal errors.

Equation (7.2) implies that, to order $o(n^{-1})$, the mean and skewness of T are the same as the mean and skewness of T^*. As shown in the appendix, r is necessarily positive so the kurtosis of T is greater than that of T^*. The sign of s depends on the particular problem so no general conclusion can be drawn about the relative variances of T and T^*.

Cavanagh and Rothenberg (1990) consider second-order approximations to the distribution of T^* with nonnormal errors. They note that, if the ε_t are i.i.d. and if the sample skewness and kurtosis coefficients for the transformed regressors $\bar{\Gamma}X$ are zero, the usual t-ratio for a linear combination of slope coefficients is approximately distributed as Student's t for any error distribution having finite fourth cumulant. If Ω is Toeplitz, then the skewness and kurtosis of the transformed regressors ΓX will be approximately zero whenever the skewness and kurtosis of the regressors X are zero. Combining these facts with those above, we find a surprisingly simple result for time-series models.

Proposition 5. Suppose, in addition to the assumptions in proposition 4, the exogenous regressors X have zero sample skewness and kurtosis. Then, no matter what the skewness and kurtosis of the error distribution, the $o(n^{-1})$ approximate distribution of the t-statistic T for testing slope coefficients is given by (7.2) where F is the distribution function of Student's t with $n - K$ degrees of freedom.

In other words, normality of the regressors can replace normality of the errors in deriving the second-order approximation to the distribution of the GLS t-ratio in stationary time-series models.

8 Conclusion

If Ω is estimated from residuals of a preliminary least squares or instrumental variables regression, the second-order properties of the feasible GLS estimator $\hat{\beta}$ are quite simple to calculate even when the errors are not normal. The resulting approximate distribution is not normal but often differs from the distribution of $\bar{\beta}$ only in variance. In particular, if the errors are a linear stationary process with independent innovations, the effect of estimating Ω is essentially the same as that under normality. Similar results hold for the usual t-ratio.

These conclusions seem to differ substantially from those obtained by Carroll et al. (1988), but there is no contradiction. These authors consider the case where Ω may be a function of β and hence study Ω estimates that are functions of more than just residuals. Furthermore, they consider preliminary estimates $\tilde{\beta}$ that are not necessarily of the instrumental variable form. Finally, they concentrate on heteroskedastic models and do not explore the implications of stationarity. If the class of estimators and problems considered is restricted somewhat, their results simplify. Our analysis suggests that, at least for some common examples, many second-order results derived previously for the normal special case hold even with nonnormal errors.

Appendix: the distribution of the t-ratio when Ω is Toeplitz

We first find stochastic expansions for the statistics T and T^* defined in (7.1). Writing

$$\frac{\hat{\sigma}^2}{\sigma^2} \equiv 1 + \frac{e}{\sqrt{n}} \quad \text{and} \quad \frac{c'(X'\hat{\Psi}X)^{-1}c}{c'(X'\Psi X)^{-1}c} \cong 1 + \frac{\lambda' d}{\sqrt{n}} + \frac{d'\Lambda d}{n},$$

where the elements of the p-dimensional vector λ and the $p \times p$ matrix Λ are standardized derivatives of $c'(X'\hat{\Psi}X)^{-1}c$ with respect to $\hat{\theta}$, we find

$$T = A + \frac{2b'd - \lambda' dA + eA}{2\sqrt{n}} + \frac{d'(8C - 4b\lambda' + 3\lambda\lambda' A - 4\Lambda A)d + e^2 A}{8n} + R_T.$$

We shall assume that the elements of λ and Λ are uniformly bounded as n tends to infinity. We assume further that the remainder term R_T satisfies the condition $\Pr[n \log n \, |R_T| > 1] = o(n^{-1})$ and therefore can be ignored in deriving second-order approximations.

By the same argument used in section 3, the distribution of T is, to order n^{-1}, the same as the distribution of

$$A + \frac{1}{\sqrt{n}} E\left[\left(b'd - \frac{1}{2}A \cdot \lambda'd\right) \middle| A\right] + \frac{1}{2n}\left(A - \frac{\partial}{\partial A}\right) \mathrm{Var}\left[\left((b'd - \frac{1}{2}A \cdot \lambda'd\right) \middle| A\right]$$

$$+ \frac{1}{8n} E[(8d'Cd - 4d'b\lambda'd + 3d'\lambda\lambda'd \cdot A - 4d'\Lambda d \cdot A)|A].$$

If the first component of θ is the scale parameter, then the first component of b is zero. If the regression contains an intercept and only slope coefficients are being tested, the x_i necessarily sum to zero. Hence, from (4.3), we see that σ_{Ad} is zero when the innovations are i.i.d. and the D_i have constants on the main diagonal. In fact, when Ω is Toeplitz, the D_i have zeros on the diagonal when $i > 1$ so that Σ_{bd} is also zero. When $\sigma_{Ad} = 0$, we find after further calculation

$$E(\lambda'd|A) = E(\lambda'd) + \frac{1}{2}(A^2 - 1) \cdot \mathrm{cov}(\lambda'd, A^2) + o(n^{-1/2})$$

$$\mathrm{var}(\lambda'd|A) = \lambda'\Sigma_{dd}\lambda + o(1), \quad \mathrm{cov}(\lambda'd, b'd|A) = o(1)$$

$$E(d'\Lambda d|A) = \mathrm{tr}\Lambda\Sigma_{dd} + o(1)$$

But, under our assumptions on the D_i, $\mathrm{cov}(\lambda'd, A^2) = E(Ab'd) = o(n^{-1/2})$. Hence, T has the same approximate distribution as

$$A\left[1 + \frac{\mathrm{var}(b'd) - \sqrt{n}E(\lambda'd) - \mathrm{tr}\Lambda\Sigma_{dd} + \frac{1}{4}\lambda'\Sigma_{dd}\lambda \cdot (A^2 + 1)}{2n}\right],$$

the result obtained in Rothenberg (1988) for the case of normal errors.

Notes

Starting with his classic paper on second-order efficiency (Rao, 1961), C. R. Rao has been a pioneer in the use of higher-order asymptotics in point estimation theory. In addition, he has written extensively on the estimation of error variances and on the theory of generalized least squares. Like so much recent work in econometric theory, our research is strongly influenced by his past contributions to the subject.

1 Robinson (1988) discusses some sufficient conditions for ignoring the remainder term in deriving approximate distributions.
2 That is, there exists a triangular Toeplitz matrix Γ such that $\Omega - \Gamma'\Gamma$ is asymptotically negligible. For details, see Iohvidov (1982, p. 148) and Gray (1972). Note that in the AR(1) example above, only one element of Γ need be changed to make it of Toeplitz form.

References

Barndorff-Nielsen, O. and Cox, D. R. (1979) Edgeworth and saddlepoint approximations with statistical applications. *Journal of the Royal Statistical Society B*. 41, 279–312.

Barndorff-Nielsen, O. and Cox, D. R. (1989) *Asymptotic Techniques for Use in Statistics*. London: Chapman and Hall.

Carroll, R. J., Wu, C. F. and Ruppert, D. (1988) The effect of estimating weights in weighted least squares. *Journal of the American Statistical Association*, 83, 1045–54.

Cavanagh, C. L. (1983) Hypothesis testing in models with discrete dependent variables. PhD thesis, University of California at Berkeley.

Cavanagh, C. L. and Rothenberg, T. J. (1990) Linear regression with non-normal errors. Working paper, Department of Economics, University of California at Berkeley.

Gray, R. M. (1972) On the asymptotic eigenvalue distribution of Toeplitz matrices. *IEEE Transactions on Information Theory*, 18, 725–30.

Iohvidov, I. S. (1982) *Hankel and Toeplitz Matrices and Forms: Algebraic Theory*. Boston: Birkhäuser.

Phillips, P. C. B. (1993) Operational algebra and regression *t*-tests. In P. C. B. Phillips (ed.), *Models, Methods and Applications of Econometrics*. Oxford: Blackwell.

Rao, C. R. (1961) Asymptotic efficiency and limiting information. *Proceedings of the Fourth Berkeley Symposium on Mathematical Statistics and Probability, volume 1*. Berkeley: University of California Press.

Robinson, P. M. (1988) The stochastic difference between econometric statistics. *Econometrica*, 56, 531–48.

Rothenberg, T. J. (1984a) Approximate normality of generalized least squares estimates. *Econometrica*, 52, 811–25.

Rothenberg, T. J. (1984b) Approximating the distributions of econometric estimators and test statistics. In Z. Griliches and M. Intriligator (eds), *Handbook of Econometrics, volume 2*. Amsterdam: North-Holland.

Rothenberg T. J. (1988) Approximate power functions for some robust tests of regression coefficients. *Econometrica*, 56, 997–1019.

12 Factor Analysis under More General Conditions with Reference to Heteroskedasticity of Unknown Form

John G. Cragg and Stephen G. Donald

1 Preliminaries

It is usual in latent-variable models and particularly factor analysis to assume that the underlying, unobserved random quantities are homoskedastic. In many cases this is implausible at least with respect to the idiosyncratic disturbances. The standard methods of inference as developed by Lawley (1940), Rao (1955), and Anderson and Rubin (1956) *inter alia* are remarkably robust (at least asymptotically) to specifications about the distributions of the random quantities, as shown in Amemiya et al. (1987) and Anderson and Amemiya (1988).

The standard approach uses a particular objective function as a criterion on which to base estimation.[1] Once we leave models with independent, identically normally distributed (i.i.n.d.) variables, the criterion has no great appeal. We therefore contrast it with a generalized least squares approach which produces asymptotically more efficient estimators. This leads in the homoskedastic case directly to feasible estimates. In the case of heteroskedasticity, the problem is more difficult since we need consistent estimates of the variances of the elements of the sample covariance matrix, especially of its off-diagonal elements, before we can proceed. We suggest that such estimates may be obtained by relying on some additional assumptions and by combining one set of consistent estimates with another.

We consider the standard factor-analysis specification for a G-element observable vector x_t:

$$x_t = \mu + \Lambda f_t + \varepsilon_t, \quad t = 1, \ldots, T, \tag{1.1}$$

where μ is a G-vector of constants, Λ is a $G \times K$ matrix of factor loadings, f_t is a K-vector of values of the factors and ε_t is a G-vector of random disturbances with $E(\varepsilon_t) = 0$. Everything on the right hand side of (1.1) is unobservable.

Critical to virtually all forms of the model is the assumption

$$E(\varepsilon_t f_t') = 0.$$

Although there are useful forms of the model which allow a weaker restriction (and very different forms of estimation; see Cragg and Donald, 1992b) it is also standard to assume, defining the G-vector $\xi' = \{\xi_1 \ldots \xi_G\}$, that

$$E(\varepsilon_t \varepsilon_t') = \Xi = \mathrm{diag}(\xi)$$

where diag(a) designates the square matrix formed with the elements of the vector a on the diagonal and all off-diagonal elements zero. With both Λ and f_t unobserved, there is an identification problem in that for any non-singular $K \times K$ matrix F, $\Lambda^* = \Lambda F$ and $f_t^* = F^{-1} f_t$ would do equally well. While there are times when it is appropriate to treat the f_t as fixed, it will be convenient to treat them for the moment as random with $E(f_t) = 0$ and $E(f_t f_t') = \Phi$. If there are no *a priori* restrictions on Λ and/or f_t, it is usual to specify that

$$\Phi = I. \tag{1.2}$$

Identification of the parameters can then be achieved by specifying

$$\Lambda' \Xi^{-1} \Lambda = Q = \mathrm{diag}(q), \tag{1.3}$$

with the value of the K-vector q left unspecified. It is also possible to achieve identification by specifying that certain values of Λ are known. For example,

$$\Lambda' = [I_K \quad \Lambda_2] \tag{1.4}$$

can replace specification (1.2) and (1.3). This of course presumes that it is known that the first K of the y_ts do all depend on the factors so that the leading $K \times K$ submatrix of Λ is of full rank. For our purposes normalization (1.3) is inconvenient since it involves the parameters of the ε process in the definition of parameters involving only the connection of the x_t with f_t. With identification in form (1.4), the model is commonly referred to as the multivariate errors-in-variables model. Nothing in our approach precludes there being further, substantive restrictions on either Φ or Λ, though we shall presume that the model can be expressed in a form where there are no *a priori* connections between Ξ and these parameters.

It is usually assumed that there are no useful restrictions on the parameter vector[2] $\mu = E(x_t)$, which is estimated by $\bar{x} = \Sigma_{t=1}^{T} x_t/T$. The inference problem therefore tends to be how to draw information on the model from the sample covariance matrix of the x_t:

$$\hat{\Sigma} = \sum_{t=1}^{T} (x_t - \bar{x})(x_t - \bar{x})'/T.$$

Let Σ be the covariance matrix of x_t. Impose the identifying restrictions on Λ and Φ and any other known restrictions by using them explicitly to reduce the number of unknown parameters to J, which we designate by the J-vector ψ. It must be the case that $J \leqslant G(G - 1)/2$, but with typical generic forms of identifying restrictions J may be a good-deal smaller[3] (see Anderson and Rubin, 1956). Then with $\Sigma = \Lambda\Phi\Lambda' + \Xi$ expressed as functions of $\theta' = \{\xi' \ \psi'\}$, the standard approach is to estimate θ as $\hat{\theta} = \text{argmax}_{\theta}[-(T/2)(\log|\Sigma| + \text{trace}\,\hat{\Sigma}\Sigma^{-1})]$. This yields the maximum-likelihood estimator when the random quantities are i.i.n.d. Furthermore, as shown by Amemiya et al. (1987) and Anderson and Amemiya (1988), the estimator is consistent and asymptotically normally distributed with a covariance matrix for which consistent estimates can be developed under much wider conditions. As Jöreskog and Goldberger (1972) and Dahm and Fuller (1986) suggest, GLS also provides a way of obtaining estimates.

Analysis of the model, at least since Anderson and Rubin (1956), typically proceeds under one or both of two approaches to the unobserved f_t. The first treats them as random; the second as fixed parameters (or conditions on them.) The same methods of inference may be used in each case, but the distribution of estimates can differ between them and so can the form of test statistics. One critical aspect of making non-standard assumptions such as heteroskedastic f_t is that in some cases, even though the f_t may in some sense "really" be random, only the conditional approach is feasible. In turn this means that only inferential procedures or statistics which do not depend (at least under the null hypothesis) on the conditioning values are of much interest.

It will be convenient to introduce two matrix operators which help in notation and focus attention on the critical aspects of inference.

These concern extracting the lower triangle and the sub-diagonal triangle from a square matrix. Define for an $N \times N$ matrix A

$$\text{vecl}(A)' = \{a_{21}\, a_{32} \ldots a_{N,N-1} \quad a_{31}\, a_{42} \ldots a_{N,N-2} \ldots a_{N1}\}$$

and

$$\begin{aligned}\text{vecd}(A)' &= \{a_{11}\, a_{22} \ldots a_{NN} \quad a_{21}\, a_{32} \ldots a_{N,N-1} \ldots a_{N1}\} \\ &= \{a_{11}\, a_{22} \ldots a_{NN} \quad \text{vecl}(A)'\}.\end{aligned}$$

vecd(A) is simply a permutation of the more usual vech(A) and standard results, such as those for differentiation of functions of square symmetric matrices as in Henderson and Searle (1979), hold with suitable re-ordering. In particular, for A symmetric, there is a unique matrix, say B, whose elements are units and zeros of dimension $N^2 \times N(N+1)/2$ and rank $N(N+1)/2$ such that $\text{vec}(A) = B\,\text{vecd}(A)$ so that, of course, $\text{vecd}(A) = (B'B)^{-1}B'\,\text{vec}(A)$. Similarly, we can write $\text{vec}(A) = C\,\text{vech}(A)$ so that $\text{vecd}(A) = (B'B)^{-1}B'C\,\text{vech}(A)$. The relationship of vecl(A) to the others is equally straightforward: $\text{vecl}(A) = [0_N \quad I_{N(N-1)/2}]\,\text{vecd}(A)$. There is no inverse relationship.

2 Nonnormal Factor Analysis

We now widen the assumptions of model (1.1) by making

Assumption 1. Using the notation developed in the previous section, and letting $\rho[.]$ designate the rank of a matrix, suppose

(a) $x_t = \Lambda f_t + \varepsilon_t$, with $E(\varepsilon_t) = 0$ and $E(f_t) = 0$.
(b) $E(x_t - \mu)(x_t - \mu)' = \Sigma_t = \Lambda E(f_t f_t')\Lambda' + E(\varepsilon_t \varepsilon_t') = \Lambda \Phi_t \Lambda' + \Xi_t$.
(c) $E(\varepsilon_t \varepsilon_t') = \Xi_t = \text{diag}(\xi_t)$ where ξ_t is a G-vector for whose elements, ξ_{it}, $0 < \kappa \leqslant \xi_{it} \leqslant \Delta < \infty$.
(d) $\lim_{T\to\infty} \xi(T) = \xi^{\circ}$ where $\xi(T) = \Sigma_{t=1}^{T} \xi_t / T$.
(e) $E(f_t f_t') = \Phi_t$ is a $K \times K$ positive semidefinite matrix for which $\Sigma_{t=1}^{T} \Phi_t / T = \Phi(T)$ with $\Phi(T)$ a positive-definite matrix whose roots, υ_i, satisfy $0 < \kappa \leqslant \upsilon_i \leqslant \Delta < \infty$. For convenience of notation we assume that $\lim_{T\to\infty} \Phi(T) = \Phi^{\circ}$, a positive-definite matrix whose roots have the same property. $\Lambda'\Lambda$ is also positive definite with similarly bounded roots.
(f) Λ and $\Phi(T)$ are functions of J parameters denoted $\psi(T)$. Define $\theta(T)' = \{\xi(T)' \quad \psi(T)'\}$ so that $\sigma(T) = \text{vecd}\,\Sigma(T) = \sigma(\theta(T))$ where $\Sigma(T) = \Sigma_{t=1}^{T} \Sigma_t / T$. Then designating the population value of parameters by a superscript$^{\circ}$, assume that $\theta^{\circ}(T) \in \text{int}\{\Theta\}$,

where $\Theta \subset \mathcal{R}^{\mathcal{J}+\mathcal{G}}$ is the parameter space providing the properties specified in (e) and that $\sigma(\theta(T))$ is twice continuously differentiable within a neighborhood of $\theta^\circ(T)$ and that at all points within the neighborhood, $\rho[\partial\sigma(T)/\partial\theta(T)] = J + G$. Furthermore, assume that for any $\theta(T) \in \Theta \neq \theta^\circ(T)$, $\sigma(\theta(T)) \neq \sigma(\theta^\circ(T))$. These properties also hold at $\sigma^\circ = \text{vecd}(\Sigma^\circ) = \sigma(\theta^\circ)$ where $\Sigma^\circ = \lim_{T\to\infty} \Sigma(T)$.

Several things may be noted about these assumptions. First, the upper bounds in 1(c) and 1(e) (whose values do not need to be specified) simply ensure that the x_t do have finite second moments and are not otherwise used. The lower bound in 1(c) similarly is needed so that in a neighborhood of ξ° the diagonal of $\Xi(T)$ is positive while that in 1(e) ensures that $\Phi(T)$ is positive-definite in a neighborhood of $\Phi^\circ(T)$. These bounds in practice do not have to be known. Second, with many convenient normalizations to ensure identifiability we would need differing $\Lambda(T)$ as well as $\Phi(T)$ and $\Xi(T)$. The critical aspect of the specification is that $\rho[\Sigma(T) - \Xi(T)] = K$. Cases with variable $\Lambda(T)$ are covered provided that there is some normalization (not necessarily the one used) for which the assumed structure holds. Third, assumption 1(f) provides the identifiability condition. It suffices when normalizations such as those in equation (1.4) are used for identification, but might need to be supplemented by further identification conditions (such as ordering or sign rules) when the identifiability conditions are stated as in equations (1.2) and (1.3). Finally, note that 1(e) and 1(f) both imply that $\rho[\Lambda] = K$. Indeed, the lower bounds on the roots of $\Lambda'\Lambda$ in 1(e) are redundant in view of 1(f). The upper bound is largely needed to guarantee that Σ° is finite. Finally, 1(b) implies that $E(f_t\varepsilon_t') = 0$. When not needed for clarity of exposition, we shall drop the (T) argument on various quantities for simplicity.

The data-generating assumption we use concerns the properties of the estimated covariance matrix, $\hat{\Sigma}(T) = \Sigma_{t=1}^{T}(x_t - \bar{x})(x_t - \bar{x})'/T$ or more particularly of $\hat{\sigma} = \text{vecd}(\hat{\Sigma}(T))$. These are

Assumption 2. Assume that f_t and ε_t are such that

(a) $\text{plim}\, \hat{\sigma} = \sigma^\circ$.
(b) $\sqrt{T}(\hat{\sigma} - E(\hat{\sigma})) \xrightarrow{d} N(0, \Omega)$ where Ω is a $G(G+1)/2 \times G(G+1)/2$ positive-definite matrix.
(c) There is available an estimate, $\check{\Omega}$, such that $\text{plim}\, \check{\Omega} = \Omega$.

Assumption 2 covers most cases that have been analyzed so far. Any number of substantive assumptions about the processes generating

x_t or f_t and ε_t will produce these conditions. To be useful, feasible consistent estimation of Ω has to be possible and at that point more substantive restrictions on the data-generating process will need to be invoked. As we shall see, extending the analysis to heteroskedasticity largely involves assuming conditions such that assumption 2 holds.

The setup provided by assumption 2 puts factor analysis in the same mould as a large number of other problems of inference. In particular, it suggests estimation of the parameters by generalized least squares and performing tests about them in this framework. This leads to

Lemma 1. Consider the estimator

$$\tilde{\theta} = \underset{\theta}{\operatorname{argmin}}(\hat{\sigma} - \sigma(\theta))'\check{\Omega}^{-1}(\hat{\sigma} - \sigma(\theta)) \tag{2.1}$$

and let $C = \partial\sigma/\partial\theta_{|\theta=\theta^\circ}$. Under assumptions 1 and 2

(a) $\operatorname{plim}\tilde{\theta} = \theta^\circ$.
(b) $\sqrt{T}(\tilde{\theta} - \theta^\circ) \xrightarrow{d} N(0, [C'\Omega^{-1}C]^{-1})$.

Proof. (a) Assumptions 1 and 2 and the form of the objective function guarantee the standard consistency of extremum estimators (Amemiya, 1985).

(b) Using assumption 1(f), expand the first-order conditions for a minimum in Taylor series about $\theta = \theta^\circ$:

$$\begin{aligned} 0 &= \sqrt{T}\partial(\hat{\sigma} - \sigma(\theta))'\check{\Omega}^{-1}(\hat{\sigma} - \sigma(\theta))/\partial\theta_{|\theta=\tilde{\theta}} \\ &= -2\sqrt{T}\,[C'\check{\Omega}^{-1}(\hat{\sigma} - E(\hat{\sigma})) - C^{*\prime}\check{\Omega}^{-1}C^*(\tilde{\theta} - \theta^\circ)] + O_p(T^{-1/2}) \end{aligned}$$

where C^* is $\partial\sigma/\partial\theta_{\theta=\theta^*}$ with θ^* between $\tilde{\theta}$ and θ° and the remainder involves terms of the form $\sqrt{T}(\hat{\sigma}_i - E(\hat{\sigma}_i))(\tilde{\theta}_j - \theta_j^\circ)$ times elements of $\check{\Omega}^{-1}$ and of $\partial^2\sigma/\partial\theta\partial\theta'_{|\theta=\theta^*}$. Hence by assumption 1(f), which guarantees that $\operatorname{plim} C^* = C$ and assumption 2(c),

$$\sqrt{T}(\tilde{\theta} - \theta^\circ) = (C'\Omega^{-1}C)C'\Omega^{-1}\sqrt{T}(\hat{\sigma} - E(\hat{\sigma})) + O_p(T^{-1/2}).$$

Therefore using assumption 2(b), $\sqrt{T}(\tilde{\theta} - \theta^\circ) \xrightarrow{d} N(0, [C'\Omega^{-1}C]^{-1})$. □

Lemma 1 with appropriate change in notation is found in Dahm and Fuller (1986). The proof is given for completeness and because it leads directly to other propositions.

The types of properties established in lemma 1 hold for the standard maximum-likelihood estimator. In particular,

Lemma 2. Consider

$$\hat{\theta} = \underset{\theta}{\operatorname{argmin}}[\log|\Sigma| + \operatorname{trace}\hat{\Sigma}\Sigma^{-1}]. \tag{2.2}$$

Then under assumptions 1 and 2,

(a) $\operatorname{plim}\hat{\theta} = \theta^\circ$.
(b) $\sqrt{T}(\hat{\theta} - \theta^\circ) \xrightarrow{d} N(0, Q\Omega Q')$ where $Q = \partial\hat{\theta}(T)/\partial\hat{\sigma}_{|\hat{\sigma}=\sigma^\circ}$.

Proof. (a) The consistency proof follows directly the equivalent proof in Amemiya et al. (1987) since by assumptions 1 and 2 $\operatorname{plim}\hat{\sigma} = \sigma^\circ = \sigma(\theta^\circ)$. It can also follow from the argument establishing (a) of lemma 1.

(b) The proof is essentially the same as that in Anderson and Amemiya (1988, theorem 2) with appropriate change in notation. The criterion of minimizing $c = [\log|\Sigma| + \operatorname{trace}\hat{\Sigma}\Sigma^{-1}]$ gives, via the first-order conditions,

$$\partial c/\partial\theta_{|\theta=\tilde{\theta}} = 0,$$

an implicit function with explicit solution $\hat{\theta} = \hat{\theta}(\hat{\sigma})$. Through assumptions 1(c) and 1(f), $\hat{\theta}(\hat{\sigma})$ has continuous derivatives w.r.t. $\hat{\sigma}$ in a neighborhood of $E(\hat{\sigma})$. Therefore, from assumption 2(a), and part (a) of this proposition, we can in a neighborhood of $E(\hat{\sigma})$ expand $\hat{\theta}$ about $E(\hat{\sigma})$ to give $\hat{\theta} = \hat{\theta}(E(\hat{\sigma})) + \partial\hat{\theta}(\sigma)/\partial\sigma_{|\sigma=\sigma^*}(\hat{\sigma} - E(\hat{\sigma}))$, with σ^* between $\hat{\sigma}$ and $E(\hat{\sigma})$. Hence, since by (a) $\hat{\theta}(\sigma^\circ) = \theta^\circ$ and by assumption 2(a) $\operatorname{plim}\hat{\sigma} = \sigma^\circ$,

$$\operatorname{plim}\sqrt{T}(\hat{\theta} - \theta^\circ) = \partial\hat{\theta}/\partial\hat{\sigma}_{|\hat{\sigma}=\sigma^\circ}\operatorname{plim}\sqrt{T}(\hat{\sigma} - E(\hat{\sigma})). \quad \square$$

Though, as lemma 2 shows, the ML estimator provides an alternative way of estimating the model, there is no question as to which is preferable. In particular,

Proposition 1. Under assumptions 1 and 2, $\tilde{\theta}$ is asymptotically more efficient than $\hat{\theta}$ in the sense that for any J-vector α,

$$\begin{aligned}&\alpha' E[\operatorname{plim}\sqrt{T}(\tilde{\theta} - \theta^\circ)\operatorname{plim}\sqrt{T}(\tilde{\theta} - \theta^\circ)']\alpha \\ &\quad \leqslant \alpha' E[\operatorname{plim}\sqrt{T}(\hat{\theta} - \theta^\circ)\operatorname{plim}\sqrt{T}(\hat{\theta} - \theta^\circ)']\alpha.\end{aligned}$$

Proof. One estimator, $\tilde{\beta}$ of β°, is more efficient asymptotically than another one, say $\hat{\beta}$, iff

$$\begin{aligned}&E[\operatorname{plim}\sqrt{T}(\hat{\beta} - \beta^\circ)\operatorname{plim}\sqrt{T}(\hat{\beta} - \beta^\circ)'] \\ &\quad - E[\operatorname{plim}\sqrt{T}(\tilde{\beta} - \beta^\circ)\operatorname{plim}\sqrt{T}(\tilde{\beta} - \beta^\circ)']\end{aligned}$$

is positive semi-definite. For this to be the case, it suffices that

$$E[\text{plim}\,\sqrt{T}(\hat{\beta} - \beta^\circ)\,\text{plim}\,\sqrt{T}(\tilde{\beta} - \beta^\circ)'] \\ = E[\text{plim}\,\sqrt{T}(\tilde{\beta} - \beta^\circ)\,\text{plim}\,\sqrt{T}(\tilde{\beta} - \beta^\circ)'].$$

To see this let $a = \sqrt{T}(\tilde{\beta} - \beta^\circ)$, $b = \sqrt{T}(\hat{\beta} - \beta^\circ)$ and $d = b - a$ so that $b = a + d$. Also let $M = E[\text{plim}\,a\,\text{plim}\,a']$ and $N = E[\text{plim}\,b\,\text{plim}\,a']$ so that $E(\text{plim}\,d\,\text{plim}\,a') = N - M$. Now

$$E[\text{plim}\,b\,\text{plim}\,b'] - E[\text{plim}\,a\,\text{plim}\,a'] \\ = E(\text{plim}\,d\,\text{plim}\,d') + N - M + N' - M' + M - M \\ = E(\sqrt{T}\,\text{plim}\,d\sqrt{T}\,\text{plim}\,d') \quad \text{if } N = M.$$

Let $A = (C'\Omega^{-1}C)^{-1}C'\Omega^{-1}$ and let B be the matrix such that $\text{vec}(\Sigma) = B\,\text{vecd}(\Sigma)$ (see Henderson and Searle, 1979). Then (see Anderson and Amemiya, 1988) $Q = V^{-1}F$ where $F = C'B'[(\Sigma^\circ)^{-1} \otimes (\Sigma^\circ)^{-1}]B$ and $V = \text{plim}\,\partial^2 c/(\partial\theta)(\partial\theta)'_{|\theta=\theta^\circ}$ where taking the probability limit entails evaluating the derivative using $\hat{\sigma} = \sigma^\circ$. Tedious but straightforward manipulation yields that

$$V = C'B'[(\Sigma^\circ)^{-1} \otimes (\Sigma^\circ)^{-1}]BC.$$

Hence

$$E[\sqrt{T}\,\text{plim}\,(\hat{\theta} - \theta^\circ)\sqrt{T}\,\text{plim}\,(\tilde{\theta} - \theta^\circ)'] = A\Omega Q' \\ = (C'\Omega^{-1}C)^{-1}C'\Omega^{-1}\Omega B'[(\Sigma^\circ)^{-1} \otimes (\Sigma^\circ)^{-1}]BC \\ (C'B'[(\Sigma^\circ)^{-1} \otimes (\Sigma^\circ)^{-1}]BC)^{-1} \\ = (C'\Omega^{-1}C)^{-1}. \quad \square$$

Proposition 1 does not guarantee that $\hat{\theta}$ is less efficient that $\tilde{\theta}$. Since under its own distribution the maximum-likelihood estimator is asymptotically efficient, the two are equally efficient asymptotically when the f_t and ε_t are normally distributed. Then (see Anderson and Rubin, 1956) $\Omega^{-1} = B'[(\Sigma^\circ)^{-1} \otimes (\Sigma^\circ)^{-1}]B$ so that $Q\Omega Q' = (C'\Omega^{-1}C)^{-1}$. A second instance of equal efficiency is given by

Corollary 1.1. Suppose that $J = G(G - 1)/2$. Then $\hat{\theta}$ and $\tilde{\theta}$ are equally efficient asymptotically.[4]

Proof. When $J = G(G - 1)/2$, C is square and of full rank so that using the expression in the proof of proposition 1, $Q = V^{-1}F = C^{-1}$ from which $Q\Omega Q' = C^{-1}\Omega C'^{-1} = (C'\Omega^{-1}C)^{-1}$. $\square$

Against the gain in efficiency from GLS pointed out in proposition 1, a consistent estimate of Ω is needed for calculating $\tilde{\theta}$ while it is not required for $\hat{\theta}$. However, $\hat{\theta}$ is not the only way to estimate the parameters consistently without knowledge of Ω. For example the ordinary least-squares estimator

$$\check{\theta}_L = \underset{\theta}{\operatorname{argmin}}(\hat{\sigma}(T) - \sigma(\theta(T))'(\hat{\sigma}(T) - \sigma(\theta(T)) \qquad (2.3)$$

has, using exactly the same types of arguments used for $\hat{\theta}$ and $\tilde{\theta}$, the properties that $\operatorname{plim} \check{\theta}_L = \theta^\circ$ and $\sqrt{T}(\check{\theta}_L - \theta^\circ) \xrightarrow{d} N(0, P)$. Only if P needs to be calculated is a consistent estimate of Ω required since

$$P = (C'C)^{-1}C'\Omega C(C'C)^{-1}.$$

One advantage of using $\tilde{\theta}$ is that the same framework can be used to test whether in fact the number of factors is K and to estimate the value of K when it is not known. This is because the analysis of Cragg and Donald (1992a) applies directly to the minimization problem defining $\tilde{\theta}$ in (2.1). An equally straightforward procedure does not seem to be available for $\hat{\theta}$ when we leave the i.i.n.d. case.

One major feature of the model is that consistent estimates of ψ may be obtained using only part of $\hat{\Sigma}$ and its asymptotic distribution depends[5] only on the corresponding portion of Ω. Partition Ω, C and Q':

$$\Omega = \begin{bmatrix} \Omega_{11} & \Omega_{12} \\ \Omega_{21} & \Omega_{22} \end{bmatrix} \quad C = \begin{bmatrix} C_{11} & C_{12} \\ C_{21} & C_{22} \end{bmatrix} \quad Q' = \begin{bmatrix} Q'_{11} & Q'_{21} \\ Q'_{12} & Q'_{22} \end{bmatrix}$$
$$\qquad G \quad G(G-1)/2 \qquad\qquad G \quad J \qquad\qquad G \quad J$$

where the partitionings are into G and $G(G - 1)/2$ rows and the indicated numbers of columns. Partition Ω^{-1}, σ and $\hat{\sigma}$ conformably:

$$\Omega^{-1} = \begin{bmatrix} \Omega^{11} & \Omega^{12} \\ \Omega^{21} & \Omega^{22} \end{bmatrix} \quad \sigma = \begin{pmatrix} \sigma_1 \\ \sigma^* \end{pmatrix} \quad \hat{\sigma} = \begin{pmatrix} \hat{\sigma}_1 \\ \hat{\sigma}^* \end{pmatrix}$$

(so that $\sigma^* = \operatorname{vecl}(\Sigma)$ and $\hat{\sigma}^* = \operatorname{vecl}(\hat{\Sigma})$). Assume that $C_{21} = 0$, which is equivalent to assuming that $\sigma^{*\circ} = \sigma^*(\psi^\circ)$ without dependence[6] on ξ where $\sigma^{*\circ} = \operatorname{vecl}(\Sigma^\circ)$. Then with these preliminaries

Proposition 2. (a) $\sqrt{T}(\tilde{\psi} - \psi^\circ) \xrightarrow{d} N(0, (C'_{22}\Omega_{22}^{-1}C_{22})^{-1})$;
(b) $\operatorname{plim}[\sqrt{T}(\tilde{\psi} - \psi^\circ) - [C'_{22}\Omega_{22}^{-1}C_{22}]^{-1}C'_{22}\Omega_{22}^{-1}\sqrt{T}(\hat{\sigma}^* - E(\hat{\sigma}^*))] = 0$.

Proof. The structure of $\tilde{\psi}$ is more easily revealed if we reparameterize the model by defining the G-vector

$$v = \{v_i\} = \{\xi_i + \lambda_i'\Phi\lambda_i\}. \qquad (2.4)$$

where λ_t' is the ith row of Λ, and use v instead of ξ and let $\theta_a' = \{v' \quad \psi'\}$.

(a) Let $C_a = \partial\sigma/\partial\theta_{a|\theta_a=\theta_a^\circ}$. Note that

$$C_a = \begin{bmatrix} I_G & 0 \\ 0 & C_{22} \end{bmatrix}.$$

Minimizing (2.1) w.r.t θ_a gives the values of $\tilde{\psi}$ obtained earlier and $\tilde{\nu}_i = \tilde{\xi}_i + \tilde{\lambda}_i'\tilde{\Phi}\tilde{\lambda}_i$. It follows from lemma 1 that

$$\sqrt{T}(\tilde{\theta}_a - \theta_a^\circ) \xrightarrow{d} N(0, (C_a'\Omega^{-1}C_a)^{-1})$$

and

$$\sqrt{T}(\tilde{\psi} - \psi^\circ) \xrightarrow{d} N(0, (C_a'\Omega^{-1}C_a)_{22}^{-1})$$

where the partitioning of $(C'\Omega^{-1}C)^{-1}$ is into G and J rows and columns. Now

$$C_a'\Omega^{-1}C_a = \begin{bmatrix} \Omega^{11} & \Omega^{12}C_{22} \\ C_{22}'\Omega^{21} & C_{22}'\Omega^{22}C_{22} \end{bmatrix}$$

so that

$$\begin{aligned}(C_a'\Omega^{-1}C_a)_{22}^{-1} &= (C_{22}'\Omega^{22}C_{22} - C_{22}'\Omega^{21}(\Omega^{11})^{-1}\Omega^{12}C_{22})^{-1} \\ &= (C_{22}'(\Omega^{22} - \Omega^{21}(\Omega^{11})^{-1}\Omega^{12})C_{22})^{-1} \\ &= (C_{22}'\Omega_{22}^{-1}C_{22})^{-1}.\end{aligned}$$

(b) Let $\eta' = \{\Sigma_{11} \ldots \Sigma_{GG}\}$ so that $\sigma' = \{\eta' \quad \sigma^{*\prime}\}$. Then

$$\begin{aligned}&\begin{bmatrix} \sqrt{T}(\tilde{\nu} - \nu^\circ) \\ \sqrt{T}(\tilde{\psi} - \psi^\circ) \end{bmatrix} \\ &= \begin{bmatrix} \Omega^{11} & \Omega^{12}C_{22} \\ C_{22}'\Omega^{21} & C_{22}'\Omega^{22}C_{22} \end{bmatrix}^{-1} \begin{bmatrix} \Omega^{11} & \Omega^{12} \\ C_{22}'\Omega^{21} & C_{22}'\Omega^{22} \end{bmatrix} \\ &\quad \begin{bmatrix} \sqrt{T}(\hat{\eta} - E(\hat{\eta})) \\ \sqrt{T}(\hat{\sigma}^* - E(\hat{\sigma}^*)) \end{bmatrix} + o_p(1) \\ &= \begin{bmatrix} I & \gamma \\ 0 & (C_{22}'\Omega_{22}^{-1}C_{22})^{-1}C_{22}'(\Omega^{22} - \Omega^{21}(\Omega^{11})^{-1}\Omega^{12}) \end{bmatrix} \\ &\quad \begin{bmatrix} \sqrt{T}(\hat{\eta} - E(\hat{\eta})) \\ \sqrt{T}(\hat{\sigma}^* - E(\hat{\sigma}^*)) \end{bmatrix} + o_p(1) \\ &= \begin{bmatrix} I & \gamma \\ 0 & (C_{22}'\Omega_{22}^{-1}C_{22})^{-1}C_{22}'\Omega_{22}^{-1} \end{bmatrix} \begin{bmatrix} \sqrt{T}(\hat{\eta} - E(\hat{\eta})) \\ \sqrt{T}(\hat{\sigma}^* - E(\hat{\sigma}^*)) \end{bmatrix} + o_p(1). \quad \square\end{aligned}$$

While the estimator $\tilde{\psi}$ still requires $\hat{\sigma}$ rather than $\hat{\sigma}^*$ *and* $\check{\Omega}$ rather than $\check{\Omega}_{22}$ for its calculation, lemma 1 and proposition 2 have an immediate implication establishing the asymptotic equivalence to $\tilde{\psi}$ of an estimator which does use only $\hat{\sigma}^*$ *and* $\check{\Omega}_{22}$:

Corollary 2.1. Let

$$\tilde{\psi}_p = \underset{\psi}{\operatorname{argmin}}((\hat{\sigma}^* - \sigma^*(\psi))'\check{\Omega}_{22}^{-1}(\hat{\sigma}^* - \sigma^*(\psi))). \tag{2.5}$$

Then $\operatorname{plim}[\sqrt{T}(\tilde{\psi}_p - \psi^\circ) - \sqrt{T}(\tilde{\psi} - \psi^\circ)] = 0$ and

$$\sqrt{T}(\tilde{\psi}_p - \psi^\circ) \xrightarrow{d} N(0, [C_{22}'\Omega_{22}^{-1}C_{22}]^{-1})$$

Proof. Except for notation, the proof of lemma 1 holds directly, so that

$$\operatorname{plim}\sqrt{T}(\tilde{\psi}_p - \psi^\circ) = (C_{22}'\Omega_{22}^{-1}C_{22})^{-1}C_{22}'\Omega_{22}^{-1}\operatorname{plim}\sqrt{T}(\hat{\sigma}^* - E(\hat{\sigma}^*)). \tag{2.6}$$

But this is also the random vector to which $\sqrt{T}(\tilde{\psi} - \psi^\circ)$ converges in probability. The distribution statement follows directly either from this fact or else from (2.6) and assumption 2 as in lemma 1. □

Corollary 2.1 is simply an explicit example of a much wider proposition on minimum-distance estimators applied to summary statistics when some parameters are exactly identified from the information used (see Rothenberg, 1973; Rothenberg and Ruud, 1990).

Possibly contrary to intuition, however, the same property does not hold for estimating ν and so for ξ. In particular

Corollary 2.2. (a) $\tilde{\nu} \neq \hat{\nu}$ and (b) $\operatorname{plim}[\sqrt{T}(\tilde{\nu} - E(\tilde{\nu})) - \sqrt{T}(\hat{\nu} - E(\hat{\nu}))]$
$\neq 0$.

Proof. Part (b) follows from the fact that γ in the proof of proposition 2 is

$$\gamma = R\Omega^{12}[I - C_{22}(C_{22}'\Omega_{22}^{-1}C_{22})^{-1}C_{22}'\Omega^{22}] \neq 0$$

where $R = [\Omega^{11} - \Omega^{12}C_{22}(C'_{22}\Omega_{22}^{-1}C_{22})^{-1}C_{22}'\Omega^{21}]^{-1}$. (a) Note that for $\psi = \tilde{\psi}$ the first order condition defining $\tilde{\nu}$ is given by

$$0 = -2\check{\Omega}^{11}(\hat{\upsilon} - \tilde{\nu}) - 2\check{\Omega}^{12}(\hat{\sigma}^* - \sigma^*(\tilde{\psi}))$$

from which $\tilde{\nu} = \hat{\upsilon} + (\check{\Omega}^{11})^{-1}\check{\Omega}^{12}((\hat{\sigma}^* - \sigma^*(\tilde{\psi}))$. □

3 Consistent Estimation of the Covariance Matrix

The major problem that arises in using either the ML or the GLS approach is obtaining a consistent estimate of Ω, the covariance matrix of $\hat{\sigma}$, or, in the event that we do not require inference about ξ, of Ω_{22}, the covariance matrix of σ^*. The most straightforward case arises with homoskedastic f_t and ε_t.

Assumption 3. Suppose that f_t and ε_t are independent across observations, with $E(f_t f_t') = \Phi^\circ$ and $E(\varepsilon_t\varepsilon_t') = \text{diag}\{\xi^\circ\}$, that $E(|f_{it}|^{(4+\delta)}) \leqslant \Delta < \infty$, and that $E(|\varepsilon_{it}|^{(4+\delta)}) \leqslant \Delta < \infty$.

For ease of notation define $z_t = x_t - \mu$ and $\hat{z}_t = x_t - \bar{x}$. Now consider $\hat{\sigma}_t = \text{vecd}(\hat{z}_t\hat{z}_t')$ and $\hat{\sigma} = \Sigma_{t=1}^T \hat{\sigma}_t/T$. Let $\hat{\Omega} = \Sigma_{t=1}^T(\hat{\sigma}_t - \hat{\sigma})(\hat{\sigma}_t - \hat{\sigma})'/T$. Then

Proposition 3. Under assumptions 1 and 3, $\hat{\sigma}$ and $\hat{\Omega}$ fulfill the conditions of assumption 2.

Proof. $\hat{\sigma} = \Sigma_{t=1}^T \text{vecd}[(x_t - \mu)(x_t - \mu)']/T - \text{vecd}[(\mu - \bar{x})(\mu - \bar{x})']$. Using Markov's LLN and assumption 3, $\text{plim}\,\bar{x} = \mu$ and

$$\text{plim}\sum_{t=1}^{T} \text{vecd}[(x_t - \mu)(x_t - \mu)']/T = \sigma^\circ$$

from which the condition in assumption 2(a) follows. To show that assumption 2(b) is met, note that by assumption 3 and the Liapounov CLT $\sqrt{T}(\bar{x} - \mu) = O_p(1)$. Furthermore,

$$\sqrt{T}(\hat{\sigma} - \sigma^\circ) = \sum_{t=1}^{T}\{\text{vecd}[(x_t - \mu)(x_t - \mu)'] - \sigma^\circ\}/\sqrt{T} - \sqrt{T}\,\text{vecd}[(\bar{x} - \mu)(\bar{x} - \mu)']$$

so that

$$\sqrt{T}(\hat{\sigma} - \sigma^\circ) = \sum_{t=1}^{T}\{\text{vecd}[(x_t - \mu)(x_t - \mu)'] - \sigma^\circ\}/\sqrt{T} + O_p(T^{-1/2}). \tag{3.1}$$

The condition in assumption 2(b) then follows from applying the Liapounov CLT to the first term of the RHS of (3.1) to which the LHS converges in probability. Finally, the same argument used for the consistency of $\hat{\sigma}$ applies to $\hat{\Omega}$. Since as noted above $\sqrt{T}(\hat{\sigma} - \sigma^\circ) = O_p(1)$ and $\sqrt{T}(\bar{x} - \mu) = O_p(1)$

$$\hat{\Omega} = \sum_{t=1}^{T}(\hat{\sigma}_t - \sigma^\circ)(\hat{\sigma}_t - \sigma^\circ)'/T + o_p(1)$$

while, by assumption 3, the Markov LLN applies to the first term on the RHS. □

Proposition 3 is routine. However, it does not seem to have been suggested previously that $\hat{\Omega}$ be used to form estimates of the covariance matrix of $\hat{\theta}$ or especially that it be used to produce GLS estimates of θ. The import of proposition 3 is that lemmas 1 and 2 as well as proposition 2 apply to inference based on $\hat{\sigma}$ and especially $\hat{\Omega}$. Note that if instead we confine ourselves to σ^* and Ω_{22}, we can weaken assumption 3 by only requiring $(2 + \delta)$th moments of ε_t while the argument of proposition 3 still applies to $\hat{\sigma}^*$ and $\hat{\Omega}_{22}$ so that proposition 2 and corollary 2.1 apply to $\hat{\psi}$ and $\tilde{\psi}_p$.

In the presence of heteroskedasticity, the argument of proposition 3 does not apply immediately to $\hat{\sigma}$. A number of other possibilities present themselves for fulfilling the conditions of assumption 2, at least with respect to estimates of σ^* and Ω_{22}.

Suppose that any heteroskedasticity only applies to ε_t. Specifically

Assumption 4. Assume that: (a) $E(f_t f_t') = \Phi°$; (b) f_t and ε_t are independent across t and have finite $(4 + \delta)$th and $(2 + \delta)$th moments respectively.

Let $\hat{\sigma}_t^* = \text{vecl}(\hat{z}_t \hat{z}_t')$. Note that $E(\hat{\sigma}_t^*) = \text{vecl}(\Lambda\Phi°\Lambda') + O(N^{-1}) = \sigma^{*\circ} + O(N^{-1})$ where the approximation term arises from subtracting their means from the x_t to obtain $\hat{z}_t$. Furthermore, let $\hat{\Omega}_{22} = \Sigma_{t=1}^T (\hat{\sigma}_t{}^* - \hat{\sigma}^*)(\hat{\sigma}_t{}^* - \hat{\sigma}^*)/T$. Then

Proposition 4. Under assumptions 1 and 4: (a) $\sqrt{T}(\hat{\sigma}^* - E(\hat{\sigma}^*)) \xrightarrow{d} N(0, \Omega_{22})$; (b) $\text{plim}\, \hat{\Omega}_{22} = \Omega_{22}$.

Proof. Exactly the same arguments apply as were used in proving proposition 3, the only difference being that now only the off-diagonal elements of $(x_t - \mu)(x_t - \mu)'$ are involved. □

Proposition 4 means that proposition 2 applies so that we can use $\hat{\Omega}_{22}$ to make inferences about $\hat{\psi}$ and can use it both in estimating $\hat{\psi}_p$ and in making inferences about it. However, proposition 4 does not provide a way of making inferences about the distribution of $\hat{\xi}$, though $\hat{\xi}$ remains consistent and asymptotically normally distributed, or of calculating $\tilde{\xi}$, though $(\hat{\Sigma}_{ii} - \tilde{\lambda}_i'\tilde{\Phi}\tilde{\lambda}_i)$ is a consistent estimator of ξ_i.

By contrast, direct inference when $E(f_t f_t') = \Phi_t \neq \Phi°$ does not seem to be possible, even when $\xi_t = \xi°$. Even if we observed f_t, we could not directly estimate $\Sigma_{t=1}^T E[(\text{vecd}(f_t f_t') - \text{vecd}(\Phi_t))(\text{vecd}(f_t f_t') - \text{vecd}(\Phi_t))']/T$ and *a fortiori* we cannot directly obtain consistent estimates of Ω. Instead, we may take the standard approach (see Anderson and Rubin, 1956; Anderson and Amemiya, 1988) of treating the f_t as mathematical variables or incidental nuisance parameters. The major difference in procedures produced by this is that consistent estimates of θ will be needed in order to calculate the covariance matrix of $\hat{\psi}$ consistently and to calculate $\tilde{\psi}_p$ consistently. Specifically,

Assumption 5. Assume (a) that the f_t are fixed, finite mathematical variables; (b) that the f_t are such that $\lim_{T\to\infty} \Sigma_{t=1}^{T} f_t/T = 0$, and that $\lim_{T\to\infty} \Sigma_{t=1}^{T} f_t f_t'/T = \Phi^\circ$; (c) that the ε_τ are i.i.d. or else that the ε_t are independent across t and $E(|\varepsilon_{it}|^{2+\delta}) \leqslant \Delta < \infty$, $t = 1, \ldots, T$, and $i = 1, \ldots, G$; (d) that the ε_t are homoskedastic with

$$
\begin{aligned}
E(\varepsilon_t) &= 0; \\
E(\text{vecd}(\varepsilon_t\varepsilon_t')') &= \{\xi' \quad 0\}; \\
E(\varepsilon_{it}\varepsilon_{jt}\varepsilon_{kt}) &= 0; && \text{unless } i = j = k; \\
E((\varepsilon_{ht}\varepsilon_{it})(\varepsilon_{jt}\varepsilon_{kt})) &= \xi_h\xi_j, && h = i, j = k, h \neq j, \\
&= \xi_h\xi_i, && h = j, i = k, h \neq i, \\
&= \xi_h\xi_i, && h = k, i = j, h \neq i, \\
&= 0, && \text{otherwise,} \\
& && \text{excluding } h = i = j = k.
\end{aligned}
$$

Part (d) would be the case if the ε_{it} were independent of each other. It has the effect that we can express Ω_{22} in terms of the parameters θ of the model.

The nature of some of the parameters has changed with the change in the treatment of the f_t. For example, the relevant mean of the x_t ceases to be μ, but instead becomes $\mu^\circ(T) = \mu + \Lambda \Sigma_{t=1}^{T} f_t/T$. To accommodate this, let $f_t^\dagger = f_t - \Sigma_{t=1}^{T} f_t/T$ and similarly let $z_t^\dagger = z_t - \mu^\circ(T)$. With these changes we obtain by assumptions 5(a) and 5(d) for $i \neq j$, $E(z_{it}^\dagger z_{jt}^\dagger) = \lambda_i' f_t^\dagger f_t^{\dagger\prime} \lambda_j$. Therefore

$$z_{it}^\dagger z_{jt}^\dagger - E(z_{it}^\dagger z_{jt}^\dagger) = \varepsilon_{it}\varepsilon_{jt} + \varepsilon_{it} f_t^{\dagger\prime}\lambda_j + \varepsilon_{jt} f_t^{\dagger\prime}\lambda_i$$

so that for $h > i$ and $j > k$,

$$
\begin{aligned}
&E(z_{ht}^\dagger z_{it}^\dagger - E(z_{ht}^\dagger z_{it}^\dagger))(z_{jt}^\dagger z_{kt}^\dagger - E(z_{jt}^\dagger z_{\text{kt}}^\dagger)) \\
&\quad = E(\varepsilon_{ht}\varepsilon_{it}\varepsilon_{jt}\varepsilon_{kt}) + E(\varepsilon_{ht}\varepsilon_{jt}\lambda_i' f_t^\dagger f_t^{\dagger\prime}\lambda_k) + E(\varepsilon_{it}\varepsilon_{jt}\lambda_h' f_t^\dagger f_t^{\dagger\prime}\lambda_k) \\
&\qquad + E(\varepsilon_{it}\varepsilon_{kt}\lambda_h' f_t^\dagger f_t^{\dagger\prime}\lambda_j).
\end{aligned}
$$

Then by assumption 5(d), recalling that $\hat{\sigma}^*$ involves only the sub-diagonal elements of $\Sigma_{t=1}^{T} \hat{z}_t \hat{z}_t'$ and supposing that σ_a^* corresponds to $\{\Sigma_{hi}\}$ and that σ_b^* corresponds to $\{\Sigma_{jk}\}$,

$$
\begin{aligned}
\{\Omega_{22}\}_{ab} &= \lim E[\sqrt{T}(\hat{\sigma}_a^* - E(\hat{\sigma}_a^*))\sqrt{T}(\sigma_b^* - E(\hat{\sigma}_b^*))] \\
&= \xi_h\xi_i + \xi_h\lambda_i'\Phi^\circ\lambda_i + \xi_i\lambda_h'\Phi^\circ\lambda_h \quad a = b,
\end{aligned}
$$

$$= \xi_h \lambda_i' \Phi^\circ \lambda_k \qquad a \neq b,\ h = j;$$
$$= \xi_i \lambda_h' \Phi^\circ \lambda_k \qquad a \neq b,\ i = j;$$
$$= \xi_i \lambda_h' \Phi^\circ \lambda_j \qquad a \neq b,\ i = k;$$
$$= 0 \qquad a \neq b, \text{ otherwise} \quad (3.2)$$

where $E(\hat{\sigma}^*) = \Sigma_{t=1}^T E\{\text{vecl}[z_t^\dagger z_t^{\dagger\prime}]\}/T$. Only $(2 + \delta)$th moments are needed for the ε_t because we shall only be using the asymptotic distributions of the cross-products of different elements of ε_t. Then, letting, $\sigma^{*\circ} = \lim_{T\to\infty} E(\hat{\sigma}^*)$,

Proposition 5. Under assumptions 1 and 5,

(a) $\text{plim}\,\hat{\sigma}^* = \sigma^{*\circ}$ and $\sqrt{T}(\hat{\sigma}^* - E(\hat{\sigma}^*)) \xrightarrow{d} N(0, \Omega_{22})$
(b) $\text{plim}\,\hat{\theta} = \theta^\circ$.
(c) Let $\hat{\Omega}_{22}$ be formed from $\hat{\theta}$ as Ω_{22} is formed from θ in (3.2). Then

$$\text{plim}\,\hat{\Omega}_{22} = \lim E(T)(\hat{\sigma}^* - E(\hat{\sigma}^*))(\hat{\sigma}^* - E(\hat{\sigma}^*))' = \Omega_{22}.$$

Proof. (a) With the change in the values about which quantities are centered, the steps proving proposition 3 lead *mutatis mutandis* under assumptions 1 and 5 to part (a). (b) Follows directly the corresponding proof for lemma 2 given (a) since the objective function (2.2) continues to have the properties that led to consistency. (c) From part (b) $\text{plim}\,\hat{\xi}_i\hat{\xi}_j = \xi_i^\circ \xi_j^\circ$ and $\text{plim}\,\hat{\xi}_i \hat{\lambda}_j' \hat{\Phi} \hat{\lambda}_k = \xi_i^\circ \lambda_j^{\circ\prime} \Phi^\circ \lambda_k^\circ$. □

This way of estimating the model and performing inference in it with mathematical f_t and homoskedastic ε_t can be extended to heteroskedastic ε_t. The reason is that we can estimate $\text{vecl}(\Sigma_{t=1}^T E[(\hat{\sigma}_t^* - E(\hat{\sigma}_t^*))(\hat{\sigma}_t^* - E(\sigma_t^*))']/T)$ consistently using a structure similar to that in assumption 5. To do this we need to extend the assumption about the f_t and alter the assumptions about the ε_t:

Assumption 6.

(a) the f_t are fixed, mathematical variables;
(b) the f_t are such that $\lim_{T\to\infty} \Sigma_{t=1}^T f_t/T = 0$, $\lim_{T\to\infty} \Sigma_{t=1}^T f_t f_t'/T = \Phi^\circ$ and $\lim \Sigma_{t=1}^T \text{vecd}[\text{vecd}(f_t f_t')\ \text{vecd}(f_t f_t')']/T = \chi^\circ$;
(c) the ε_t are independent across t and $E(|\varepsilon_{it}|^{2+\delta}) \leqslant \Delta < \infty$, $t = 1, \ldots,$
T, and $i = 1, \ldots, G$.
(d) the ε_t are heteroskedastic with

$$E(\varepsilon_i) = 0$$

$$\text{vecd}(E\varepsilon_t\varepsilon_t')' = \{\xi_t' \quad 0'_{G(G-1)/2}\}$$

$$E(\varepsilon_{it}\varepsilon_{jt}\varepsilon_{kt}) = 0, \quad \text{unless} \quad i = j = k$$

$$\text{vecl}(E(\text{vecl}[\varepsilon_t\varepsilon_t']\,\text{vecl}[\varepsilon_t\varepsilon_t']')) = 0_{H(H-1)/2}$$

where $H = G(G-1)/2$.

(e) $\Sigma_{t=1}^{T} E(\varepsilon_{ht}\varepsilon_{it}) f_{jt} f_{kt}/T$ converges to a constant.

There are $\Sigma_{i=1}^{K}\Sigma_{j=i}^{K}\Sigma_{k=j}^{K}(K-k+1) = K(K+1)(K+2)(K+3)/24$ elements of χ°. We shall use the notation $\chi^\circ(hijk)$ to indicate the (single) element of χ° which involves the four arguments (in any order) corresponding to the indices of the elements of f involved in each. Part (e) is needed only to guarantee that Ω_{22}° is well defined.

The worthwhile aspect of assumption 6 comes when we consider the elements of $\text{vecl}(E\hat{\sigma}_t^*\hat{\sigma}_t^{*\prime})$ of the form $\hat{z}_{ht}\hat{z}_{it}\hat{z}_{jt}\hat{z}_{kt}$ with $h < i < j < k$. Under assumption 6 for such elements

$$\begin{aligned} E(z_{ht}^\dagger z_{it}^\dagger z_{jt}^\dagger z_{kt}^\dagger) &= \{\lambda_h' f_t^\dagger f_t^{\dagger\prime}\lambda_i\lambda_j' f_t^\dagger f_t^{\dagger\prime}\lambda_k\} \\ &= \sum_{m_1=1}^{K}\sum_{m_2=1}^{K}\sum_{m_3=1}^{K}\sum_{m_4=1}^{K} \Lambda_{hm_1}\Lambda_{im_2}\Lambda_{jm_2}\Lambda_{km_4} f_{m_1t}^\dagger f_{m_2t}^\dagger f_{m_3t}^\dagger f_{m_4t}^\dagger \end{aligned}$$

so that for those elements

$$\begin{aligned} \lim \sum_{t=1}^{T} E(\hat{z}_{ht}\hat{z}_{it}\hat{z}_{jt}\hat{z}_{kt})/T &= \lim \sum_{t=1}^{T} \lambda_h' f_t^\dagger f_t^{\dagger\prime}\lambda_i\lambda_j' f_t^\dagger f_t^{\dagger\prime}\lambda_k/T \\ &= \sum_{m_1=1}^{K}\sum_{m_2=1}^{K}\sum_{m_3=1}^{K}\sum_{m_4=1}^{K} \Lambda_{hm_1}\Lambda_{im_2}\Lambda_{jm_2}\Lambda_{km_4}\chi^\circ(m_1m_2m_3m_4). \end{aligned} \quad (3.3)$$

Now let D be an $H \times H$ permutation matrix which when applied to $\text{vecd}(\sigma^*\sigma^{*\prime})$ brings the elements involving $z_{ht}z_{it}z_{jt}z_{kt}$ with $h < i < j < k$ into the leading positions (this is feasible only if $G \geqslant 4$). There are

$$L = \sum_{m_1=1}^{G-3}\sum_{m_2=m_1+1}^{G-2}\sum_{m_3=m_2+1}^{G-1}(G-m_3) = G(G-1)(G-2)(G-3)/24$$

such elements. Let

$$\gamma^\circ = D\{\lim \text{vecd}[(E\hat{\sigma}^*)(E\hat{\sigma}^*)']\} \quad (3.4)$$

and partition γ into L and $H(H+1)/2 - L$ elements: $\gamma' = \{\gamma_1' \;\; \gamma_2'\}$. Define

$$\zeta^\circ = \text{vecd}(\sigma^{*\circ}\sigma^{*\circ\prime}) \quad (3.5)$$

and partition it conformably. Note that $\zeta_1^\circ = \gamma_1^\circ$ and that

$$D^{-1}(\zeta^\circ - \gamma^\circ) = \text{vecd}(\Omega_{22}^\circ). \quad (3.6)$$

Furthermore, we can write on the basis of equation (3.3)

$$\begin{bmatrix} \gamma_1 \\ \gamma_2 \end{bmatrix} = \begin{bmatrix} \Pi_1 \\ \Pi_2 \end{bmatrix} \chi \tag{3.7}$$

where from equation (3.3) the elements of Π are the sums of the products of four elements of Λ with indices corresponding to those producing the corresponding elements of χ° and of γ°. Putting these considerations together we obtain

Proposition 6. Under assumptions 1 and 6, and assuming that $G \geqslant K + 3$

(a) $\operatorname{plim} \hat{\sigma}^* = \sigma^{*\circ}$ and $\sqrt{T}(\hat{\sigma}^* - E(\hat{\sigma}^*)) \xrightarrow{d} N(0, \Omega_{22})$, where $\operatorname{vecd}(\Omega_{22}) = D^{-1}(\zeta^\circ - \gamma^\circ)$.
(b) $\operatorname{plim} \hat{\psi} = \psi^\circ$.
(c) $\operatorname{plim} \hat{\zeta} = \zeta^\circ$ where $\hat{\zeta} = D \, \Sigma_{t=1}^{T} \operatorname{vecd}(\operatorname{vecl}[\hat{z}_t \hat{z}_t'] \operatorname{vecl}[\hat{z}_t \hat{z}_t']')/T$.
(d) Defining $\hat{\chi} = (\hat{\Pi}_1' \hat{\Pi}_1)^{-1} \hat{\Pi}_1' \hat{\zeta}_1$, where $\hat{\Pi}_1$ is formed from $\hat{\Lambda}$ in the same way that Π_1 is formed from Λ using (3.3) and (3.7), $\operatorname{plim} \hat{\chi} = \chi^\circ$.
(e) Letting $\hat{\gamma}_2 = \hat{\Pi}_2 \hat{\chi}$ where $\hat{\Pi}_2$ is formed from $\hat{\Lambda}$ in the same way that Π_2 is formed from λ° and $\hat{\gamma}_1 = \hat{\zeta}_1$, plim $\hat{\gamma} = \gamma^\circ$ so that $\operatorname{plim}(\hat{\zeta} - \hat{\gamma}) = (\zeta^\circ - \gamma^\circ)$.

Proof. Part (a) follows the proof of proposition 3, using expressions (3.4) to (3.6). Part (b) then follows from lemma 1. Part (c) arises by noting that the elements of $\hat{\zeta}$ are of the form, with $i > h$ and $j > k$,

$$\begin{aligned} \hat{z}_{ht}\hat{z}_{it}\hat{z}_{jt}\hat{z}_{kt} &= [z_{ht}^\dagger - (\bar{x}_{ht} - \mu_{ht}^\circ(T))][z_{it}^\dagger - (\bar{x}_{it} - \mu_{it}^\circ(T))] \\ &\quad [z_{jt}^\dagger - (\bar{x}_{jt} - \mu_{jt}^\circ(T))][z_{kt}^\dagger - (\bar{x}_{kt} - \mu_{kt}^\circ(T))] \\ &= z_{ht}^\dagger z_{it}^\dagger z_{jt}^\dagger z_{kt}^\dagger + O_p(T^{-1/2}) \end{aligned}$$

since from assumptions 6(a) to (d), $\sqrt{T}(\bar{x} - \mu^\circ(T))$ meets the conditions of the Liapounov CLT. Part (c) then follows from assumption 6(c) and Markov's LLN using the definitions in (3.4) and (3.5). Parts (d) and (e) follow directly from the consistency of the various elements established in parts (b) and (c). □

The practical implication of proposition 6 is again that we can use the results of section 2 to make inferences with $\hat{\psi}$ and to form the more efficient estimates, $\tilde{\psi}_p$, in the fixed f_t case. Importantly, many forms of hypothesis testing using $\tilde{\psi}_p$ and $\hat{\Omega}_{22}$, for example testing hypotheses of the form $B\psi = b$ where B and b are a prespecified matrix and vector respectively, involve statistics which have under the null a χ^2 distribution asymptotically. Since this distribution does not involve f_t, we can instead treat the fixed f_t situation as applying to the situation where the f_t are random, but we initially condition on them and then obtain marginal distributions by noting that the null distribution does not depend on the conditioning.

4 Conclusion

This chapter has established a number of points about estimating the factor-analysis or multivariate errors-in-variables model when we consider heteroskedastic models. First we showed that GLS estimates, which have the same information requirement for inference as maximum likelihood, are more efficient asymptotically in situations which are not i.i.n.d. Second, we showed how to adapt the procedures for homoskedastic models to ones where the common factors are homoskedastic but the idiosyncratic errors are heteroskedastic. Next we noted that it does not seem possible to proceed with random, heteroskedastic common factors, but that we can still proceed under the assumption that the factors should be treated as unobserved mathematical variables or incidental parameters. With homoskedastic idiosyncratic errors this involved using the consistent estimates of their variances to estimate consistently the covariance matrix of the off-diagonal elements of the sample covariance matrix of the observations. When the errors are also heteroskedastic, we showed that the fourth cross-moments of the observations can be combined with consistent estimates of the factor loadings to obtain the covariance matrix of these estimates and to perform GLS estimation.

These results are entirely asymptotic. Since the starting point is the sample covariance matrix, itself a form using heteroskedastic residuals, one may wonder whether adjustments such as Rao's (1970) MINQUE would be beneficial in practice. Similarly, we can conjecture that using jack-knife techniques in the estimation of the factor loadings and other quantities needed in the course of calculating estimates may improve their finite sample performance just as they do (see MacKinnon and White, 1985; Cragg, 1992) in the case of using the Eicker (1967) and White (1980) approach to heteroskedasticity in regression. Indeed, the use of the jack-knife for the procedures might well be desirable for all aspects of the inferences. These conjectures and indeed all aspects of the finite-sample performance of the estimators remain matters for further research.

Notes

The first author's research was supported by the Social Sciences and Humanities Research Council of Canada under grant 90-0627. We are indebted to Tom Rothenberg for helpful comments.

1 The principal exception to this is the literature showing the relationship of factor analysis to principal-component analysis. It has also been suggested by Jöreskog and Goldberger (1972) and by Dahm and Fuller (1986) that the model might be estimated by generalized least squares.
2 This is not necessarily the case. For an important exception, see the model considered by Christensen (1992).
3 If there are no further restrictions beyond those needed for identification, $J = K(K + 1)/2 + K(G - K)$.
4 $\hat{\theta}$ and $\tilde{\theta}$ are numerically identical both asymptotically and, if we strengthen assumption 1(f) slightly to assume that $\sigma(\theta(T))$ is continuously differentiable with Jacobian of full rank for all values of $\theta(T)$, in small samples. The reason is that then there is an inverse function, σ^{-1}, and $\hat{\theta} = \sigma^{-1}(s)$ minimizes either of the two objective functions.
5 A similar property holds for $\hat{\psi}$ (Anderson and Amemiya, 1988).
6 Our assumptions about the form of identification ensure that this is the case unless there are additional restrictions on the model that link ξ to the other parameters.

References

Amemiya, T. (1985) *Advanced Econometrics*. Cambridge, MA: Harvard University Press.

Amemiya, Y., Fuller, W. and Pantula, S. G. (1987) The asymptotic distributions of some estimators for a factor analysis model. *Journal of Multivariate Analysis*, 22, 51–64.

Anderson, T. W. and Amemiya, Y. (1988) The asymptotic normal distribution of estimators in factor analysis under general conditions. *Annals of Statistics*, 16, 759–71.

Anderson, T. W. and Rubin, H. (1956) Statistical inference in factor analysis. In *Proceedings of the Third Berkeley Symposium on Mathematical Statistics and Probability, volume 5*. Berkeley: University of California Press, pp. 111–50.

Christensen, B. J. (1992) The likelihood ratio test of the APT with unobservable factors against the unrestricted factor model. New York University, Finance Department, xerox.

Cragg, J. G. (1992) Quasi-Aitken estimation for heteroskedasticity of unknown form. *Journal of Econometrics*, 54, 179–201.

Cragg, J. G. and Donald, S. G. (1992a) Inferring the rank of a matrix. Discussion paper 91-92-12, Department of Economics, University of Florida.

Cragg, J. G. and Donald, S. G. (1992b) Testing and determining arbitrage pricing structure from regressions on macro variables. Discussion paper 92-14, Department of Economics, University of British Columbia.

Dahm, P. F. and Fuller, W. A. (1986) Generalized least squares estimation of the functional multivariate linear errors-in-variables model. *Journal of Multivariate Analysis*, 19, 132–41.

Eicker, F. (1967) Limit theorems for regression with unequal and dependent errors. In *Proceedings of the Fifth Berkeley Symposium on Probability and Statistics*. Berkeley: University of California Press, pp. 59–82.

Henderson, H. V. and Searle, S. R. (1979) Vec and Vech operators for matrices with some uses in Jacobians and multivariate statistics. *Canandian Journal of Statistics*, 7, 65–81.

Jöreskog, K. G. and Goldberger, A. S. (1972) Factor analysis by generalized least squares. *Psychometrika*, 37, 243–60.

Lawley, D. N. (1940) The estimation of factor loadings by the method of maximum likelihood. *Proceedings of the Royal Society of Edinburgh A*, 60, 64–82.

MacKinnon, J. G. and White, H. (1985) Some heteroskedasticity consistent covariance matrix estimators with improved finite sample properties. *Journal of Econometrics*, 29, 305–25.

Rao, C. R. (1955) Estimation and tests of significance in factor analysis. *Psychometrika*, 20, 93–111.

Rao, C. R. (1970) Estimation of heteroskedastic variances in linear models. *Journal of the American Statistical Association*, 65, 161–72.

Rothenberg, T. J. (1973) *Efficient Estimation with A Priori Information*. New Haven, CT and London: Yale University Press.

Rothenberg, T. J. and Ruud, P. A. (1990) Simultaneous equations with covariance restrictions. *Journal of Econometrics*, 44, 25–39.

White, H. (1980) A heteroskedasticity-consistent covariance estimator and a direct test for heteroskedasticity. *Econometrica*, 48, 817–38.

13 Inference in Factor Models

Christian Gouriéroux, Alain Monfort, and Eric Renault

1 Introduction

In a seminal paper, Rao (1948) provided an extension of the usual Fisher's significance tests to a multivariate linear model

$$Y_t = BX_t + CZ_t + u_t, \quad t = 1, \ldots, T, \tag{1.1}$$

where Y_t is an n-vector of endogeneous variables, X_t (resp. Z_t) is a k-vector (resp. an l-vector) of exogeneous variables and B (resp. C) an $n \times k$ matrix (resp. $n \times l$ matrix) of unknown coefficients. The error terms u_t are assumed to be independently and identically distributed and such that $E(u_t) = 0$, $V(u_t) = \Omega$ invertible.

In the standard linear model framework considered by Rao (1948), the probability distribution of the error terms is defined conditionally to the whole set of exogenous variables and assumed to be Gaussian. In the present chapter, we shall relax the normality assumption and consider dynamic models where the assumptions about the error terms are made on their marginal moments. Besides these assumptions, we only assume here that u_t is independent of $X_t, Z_t, X_{t-1}, Z_{t-1}, \ldots$.

Under his more restrictive assumptions, Rao (1948) provided a significance test for B (the null hypothesis is defined by $B = 0$); it is based on the statistic

$$U = \frac{\det \hat{\Omega}_T}{\det \hat{\Omega}_{0T}} \tag{1.2}$$

where $\hat{\Omega}_{0T}$ and $\hat{\Omega}_T$ are the ML estimators of Ω, under the null and the maintained hypothesis respectively. The hypothesis $B = 0$ is rejected when the value U is less than the critical $U^{(\varepsilon)}_{n,k,T-k-l}$ value associated with level ε. Rao (1948) gave an approximation to $U^{(\varepsilon)}_{n,k,T-k-l}$, based on an asymptotic expansion of the distribution of $\log U$.

But, as noted by Anderson (1951), if $B \neq 0$, "there enters into the multivariate case a new feature which does not appear in the univariate case . . . all the elements of B may be different from zero, but the rank of B may be less than the maximum possible rank. That implies that it is possible to take a linear combination of components of Y_t such that the expected value of this linear combination is independent of X_t." Then we are led to consider some generalized tests concerning these combinations and more precisely the range and/or the kernel of B.

A hypothesis on the range of B can be put in an explicit or an implicit form. Let us denote by r the dimension of the range of B, equal to the rank of B, and by β_0 a given $(n \times r)$ matrix, whose rank is r and whose columns span the range. We may be interested in the following null hypothesis H_0^R given in an explicit form:

$$H_0^R = \left\{ \begin{matrix} \text{there exits a } (k \times r) \text{ matrix } \alpha \\ \text{such that } B = \beta_0 \alpha' \end{matrix} \right\}. \tag{1.3}$$

H_0^R, which exactly means that the r given columns of the matrix β_0 provide a basis of the range of B, can be equivalently expressed in an implicit form. Introducing an $n \times (n - r)$ matrix δ_0, whose rank is $n - r$ and whose columns are orthogonal to those of β_0, we see that H_0^R has the following equivalent implicit form:

$$H_0^R = \{\delta_0' B = 0\}. \tag{1.4}$$

Then, the $(n - r)$ variables $\delta_0' Y_t$ do not depend on X_t. Anderson (1951) is primarily interested in estimating a full rank matrix δ_0 satisfying (1.4), since the main econometric application he has in mind is "testing structural specification using the unrestricted reduced form" (see also Byron, 1974). Following this interpretation, (1.1) is considered as the reduced form of a simultaneous equation model, where the exogenous variables X_t are excluded from a given set of structural equations:

$$\delta_0' Y_t - DZ_t = v_t, \quad Ev_t = 0. \tag{1.5}$$

Anderson's remark about the "new feature" of the multivariate framework, i.e. the fact that "all of the elements of B may be different from zero, but the rank of B may be less than the maximum possible rank," has been taken into account much more recently in a pure time series framework. For instance, the fact that a VAR process Y_t defined by

$$\phi(L)Y_t = \varepsilon, \quad \varepsilon_t \text{ white noise,} \tag{1.6}$$

may be nonstationary because det $\phi(1) = 0$ but does not admit a VAR representation after differencing, because $\phi(1) \neq 0$, has only been noticed in the literature since the seminal paper by Engle and Granger (1987) about cointegration. In the same spirit, the notion of co-dependence has been introduced by Gouriéroux and Peaucelle (1994) in order to adapt the idea of cointegration to the case of stationary series. This notion can be defined through the rank of the multivariate correlogram and has been applied to the hypotheses of relative purchasing power parity (Gouriéroux and Peaucelle, 1988) and of relative interest rate parity (Kugler and Neusser, 1990).

The same type of idea exactly fits our dynamic setting (1.1) (with u_t assumed to be independent of X_t, Z_t, X_{t-1}, $Z_{t-1}, \ldots$) as soon as we are interested in the partial multivariate correlogram or, more generally, in the matricial coefficients ϕ_h; $h = 1, \ldots, H$, of a VAR(H) representation:

$$Y_t = \mu + \phi_1 Y_{t-1} + \ \ldots \ + \phi_H Y_{t-H} + u_t. \tag{1.7}$$

Such a representation is clearly a particular case of our dynamic setting (1.1) with $Z_t = 1$ and $X_t = (Y_{t-1}, Y_{t-2}, \ldots, Y_{t-H})$.

Moreover, the "white noise directions" δ_0 which have been defined by Tsay and Tiao (1985) by:

$$\delta_0'\phi_1 = \delta_0'\phi_2 = \ \ldots \ = \delta_0'\phi_H = 0,$$

clearly corresponds to all assumption on the form (1.4). Ahn and Reinsel (1988) have also outlined the interest of a rank condition of the form:

$$\text{rank } \phi_1 \geqslant \text{rank } \phi_2 \geqslant \ldots \geqslant \text{rank } \phi_H.$$

A methodology of finite sample inference is not available for such dynamic models and result (1.2) in Rao (1948) can only be extended by using an asymptotic viewpoint, when the number T of observations converges to infinity. Asymptotic inference is one of the two main purposes of this chapter.

The other purpose is to emphasize the usefulness of the canonical correlation analysis for econometric modelling. Models with factors are more and more used in econometrics, particularly for financial or macroeconomic applications; however, a careful study of the literature shows that there exist different notions of factors and various terminologies (factor, factor loading, beta, index variables, state variables, cointegration or codependence directions, stable relationships, common trend, etc.). Surprisingly, multivariate analysis in the sense of Rao (1965) is relatively unknown to econometricians and it is a pity that canonical correlation analysis is not sufficiently used in order to unify these terminologies.

The starting point for introducing the concept of factor is a dual characterization of a set of matrices B whose rank r is "less than the maximum possible" rank. Instead of the explicit or implicit characterizations (1.3) or (1.4) through the range of B, it may be interesting to consider some characterizations through the kernel of B, i.e. through the range of the transpose B' of matrix B. Let us consider for instance a known $k \times (k - r)$ matrix γ_0 whose rank is $k - r$. We may be interested in the following null hypothesis H_0^K about the kernel of B:

$$H_0^K = \{B\gamma_0 = 0\}. \tag{1.8}$$

This null hypothesis is given by (1.8) in an implicit form and uses a basis (the columns of γ_0) for the kernel of B. However, H_0^K also admits an explicit form. For instance, let us consider a $k \times r$ matrix α_0, whose rank is r and whose columns vectors are orthogonal to those of γ_0. The null hypothesis H_0^K may be written:

$$H_0^K = \left\{\begin{matrix}\text{there exists an } n \times r \text{ matrix} \\ \beta \text{ such that } B = \beta\alpha_0'\end{matrix}\right\}. \tag{1.9}$$

In this form, H_0^K points out the linear combinations of the X_t variables which have a real influence on the Y_t, conditionally to Z_t. These linear combinations $\alpha_0'X_t$ are naturally called "factors." The column vectors of β associated with these factors measure the sensitivities of the Y variables with respect to the factors and will be called "factor loadings." Such factorial representations are very popular in econometrics of finance, more precisely in the arbitrage pricing theory or in the efficient portfolios theory (see Chamberlain and Rothschild, 1983; Brown, 1989); in these frameworks the factor loadings are usually named "beta coefficients." Similar models may also be found (with another terminology) in descriptive approaches of macroeconomic phenomena (Sargent and Sims, 1977, in multivariate panel data problems (Bhargava, 1991) or in the pure time series framework (Box and Tiao, 1977; Tsay and Tiao, 1985; Velu et al., 1986; Tiao and Tsay, 1989). See also Gouriéroux et al. (1994) for various applications.

The main aims of this chapter are the following:

- First, we want to unify the relevant asymptotic inference for multivariate linear models without the normality assumption. As far as testing is concerned, we shall consider all the classical test procedures: pseudo-likelihood ratio tests, generalized Wald tests and Rao's score tests for various forms of the null hypotheses: explicit or implicit form about the range or the kernel or B.
- Second, we shall systematically provide an interpretation of the inference procedures in term of canonical correlations in order to propose a link with this classical literature, from both a theoretical and a computational point of view.

Inference problems in these models have already been considered by various authors since Anderson (1951) and Rao (1965); the recent work by Anderson and Kunitomo (1992) provides a very comprehensive synthesis of these previous works in the particular case of simultaneous equation models. In the present chapter, besides the emphasis on the relationships among a wide variety of asymptotic tests through their interpretation in terms of canonical correlations, we want to underline that their asymptotic properties do not depend on specific distributional assumptions. It is often claimed (e.g. Anderson and Kunitomo, 1992) that "the tests are derived on the basis of normality but are asymptotically valid under very general conditions." However, the reasons for this validity are rarely explained and, in particular, it is often argued that the asymptotic normality of least squares estimators ensures the asymptotic validity of the usual test procedures based on a Gaussian likelihood. Such arguments are not correct. Of course, asymptotic normality of estimators allows us to build some asymptotic tests based on χ^2 statistics (see, for instance, Gill and Lewbel, 1992, for such a work on testing the rank of estimated matrices) but these tests generally do not coincide with usual asymptotic tests based on a Gaussian likelihood function. This is the reason why we propose a careful study of statistical inference for misspecified models, based on the pseudo maximum likelihood theory (in the sense of Gouriéroux et al., 1984), in order to check that the usual tools can be applied for our hypotheses of interest.

The chapter is organized as follows. In section 2, we briefly recall the theory of canonical correlation analysis and explain how it is related to our framework. In section 3, we describe the tests on the kernel and on the range of matrix B by systematically studying the impact of a particular choice of a test procedure and/or of a characterization of the null hypothesis. In section 4, we consider the test about the rank of matrix B. Section 5 concludes and various proofs are gathered in five appendices.

2 Canonical Correlation Analysis and Dynamic Factor Models

The general framework

Throughout the chapter, we assume that Y_t has a "linear factorial representation" with respect to $X_t, Z_t, X_{t-1}, Z_{t-1}, \ldots$, that is to say that:

$$\left\{\begin{array}{l} Y_t = BX_t + CZ_t + u_t, \\ E(u_t) = 0,\ V(u_t) = \Omega, \\ u_t \text{ independent of } X_t, Z_t, X_{t-1}, Z_{t-1}, \ldots \end{array}\right\} \tag{2.1}$$

and we are essentially concerned with stationary observations, even though some analogous procedures might be defined for integrated series (e.g. Johansen, 1988).

Such a linear factorial representation is a seemingly unrelated regression model defined conditionally to a dynamic information set $J_t = (X_t, Z_t, X_{t-1}, Z_{t-1}, \ldots)$ with regression coefficients B, C and error term u_t independent of J_t, and with the same explanatory variables in all the equations.

These explanatory variables $X_{1t}, \ldots, X_{kt}, Z_{1t}, \ldots, Z_{lt}$ summarize the effect of J_t on Y_t up to the second order moment; they will always be considered as *a priori* given, observable, and linearly independent. Thus our purpose is not really the same as in the classical factor analysis. First, our model is more general than the usual one since it is dynamic and allows for some cross-correlations between the error terms ($V(u_t) = \Omega$ is not assumed to be diagonal). We never refer to something like an "approximate factor model" which allows us to neglect the cross-correlation when n is large (see Chamberlain, 1983) because the aim of our factorial representation is to summarize the dynamics of the variable Y_t and not the instantaneous cross-correlations; in other words, the parsimonious representations we are interested in are for longitudinal rather than for transversal phenomena. Second, even though the usual factor analysis has been extended to dynamic settings (see Geweke, 1977), our framework is different since the latent factors we are looking for are *a priori* assumed to be linear combination of observable explanatory variables $X_{1t}, \ldots, X_{kt}$.

As already mentioned, these latent factors are given by some linear combinations $\alpha' X_t$ associated with a decomposition of the B matrix $B = \beta\alpha'$, since this decomposition ensures that the influence of the X_t variable on the dynamics of Y_t, given Z_t, is summarized by the variables $\alpha' X_t$. In such a framework, testing an hypothesis like (1.9) about the kernel of B is of interest if an economic theory suggests some *a priori* given factors $\alpha_0' X_t$. This is the case, for instance, in financial econometrics, where asset pricing theories may suggest some factors: e.g. market portfolio return, interests rates for given maturities, exchange rates with respect to a given leading currency.

Symmetrically, we may be interested in some given "cofactors," that is to say some directions δ_0 such that $\delta_0' B = 0$ (see 1.4). Such cofactors are, for instance, the identifying restrictions for simultaneous equations system, the directions of white noise, codependence, and cointegration. In finance we have the well-known concept of "zero-beta portfolio," which is precisely a return $\delta' Y_t$ (where Y_t is a vector of returns on n individual assets) such that $\delta' B = 0$. An *a priori* given direction never exactly provides a factor or a cofactor for a real data set. But canonical correlation analysis can precisely be interpreted as an exploratory statistical technique to detect the best factors and/or cofactors, thanks to the definition of "canonical variables."

Factors and canonical variables

First developed by Hotelling (1936), the canonical correlation analysis is usually concerned with reducing the correlation structure between two sets of variables X_t and Y_t to the simplest possible form by means of linear transformations on X_t and Y_t. It is easy to extend this technique to a framework like (2.1), where we are interested in the relationships between Y_t (n variables) and X_t (k variables) given Z_t (l variables). The matrices of interest are the following moments where the subscript t is dropped thanks to stationarity:

$$\left\{\begin{array}{l} \Sigma_{11} = E[X_t - EL(X_t|Z_t)][X_t - EL(X_t|Z_t)]' \\ \left.\begin{array}{l}\Sigma_{12} = E[X_t - EL(X_t|Z_t)][Y_t - EL(Y_t|Z_t)]' \\ \Sigma_{21} = E[Y_t - EL(Y_t|Z_t)][X_t - EL(X_t|Z_t)]'\end{array}\right. = \Sigma_{21}' \\ \Sigma_{22} = E[Y_t - EL(Y_t|Z_t)][Y_t - EL(Y_t|Z_t)]' \end{array}\right\}. \tag{2.2}$$

As usual, we denote by $EL(Y_t|Z_t)$ (resp. $EL(X_t|Z_t)$) the theoretical linear regression of Y_t (resp. X_t) on Z_t. It coincides with usual affine regressions if X_t, Y_t, Z_t are centered or if one of the Z_t variables is a constant one; if, moreover, the random vector $(X_t', Y_t', Z_t')'$ is Gaussian, it coincides with conditional expectations and the Σ_{ij} matrices are the corresponding conditional covariance matrices. The terminology "conditional" and "correlation" will be used in the rest of the paper without explicit distinction between linear regression, affine regression, and conditional expectation. Even though the matrices Σ_{11}, Σ_{12}, Σ_{21}, Σ_{22} are not necessarily genuine conditional covariance matrices, the algebraic methodology of the canonical correlation analysis can be employed in this extended framework; the only thing to change according to the context is its statistical interpretation.

The starting point of the canonical correlation analysis is a factorization of the following $k \times n$ matrix:

$$M = \Sigma_{11}^{-1/2}\Sigma_{12}\Sigma_{22}^{-1/2}.$$

More precisely, if we denote by r the rank of B (which is also the rank of M since $B = \Sigma_{21}\Sigma_{11}^{-1} = \Sigma_{22}^{1/2}M'\Sigma_{11}^{-1/2}$) and by $\rho_1^2, \rho_2^2, \ldots, \rho_r^2$ the non-zero eigenvalues of the symmetric positive matrices:

$$MM' = \Sigma_{11}^{-1/2}\Sigma_{12}\Sigma_{22}^{-1}\Sigma_{21}\Sigma_{11}^{-1/2},$$

and

$$M'M = \Sigma_{22}^{-1/2}\Sigma_{21}\Sigma_{11}^{-1}\Sigma_{12}\Sigma_{22}^{-1/2},$$

we know (see Muirhead, 1982, theorem A9.10, p. 593) that there exist orthogonal matrices H and Q such that:

$$M = H'\Delta Q,$$

where Δ is the $k \times n$ matrix whose north-west block of size $r \times r$ is the diagonal matrix with diagonal coefficients $\rho_1, \rho_2, \ldots, \rho_r$ and whose other coefficients are zero. Moreover, it is clear that the orthogonal matrices H and Q may always be chosen such that:

$$\rho_1 \geqslant \rho_2 \geqslant \ldots \geqslant \rho_r > 0.$$

Now, since:

$$MM' = H'\Delta^2 H,$$

and

$$M'M = Q'\Delta^2 Q,$$

the columns of H' (resp. Q') provide an orthonormal basis of eigenvectors for MM' (resp. $M'M$), the ith column of H' (resp. Q') being associated for $i \leqslant r$ to the eigenvalue ρ_i^2.

Let us denote by h_j, $j = 1, 2, \ldots, k$ (resp. q_i, $i = 1, 2, \ldots, n$) the columns of H' (resp. Q') and define:

$$\left.\begin{cases} e_j = \Sigma_{11}^{-1/2} h_j & \text{for } j = 1, 2, \ldots, k \\ f_i = \Sigma_{22}^{-1/2} q_i & \text{for } i = 1, 2, \ldots, n \end{cases}\right\}. \tag{2.3}$$

Since:

$$\Delta = HMQ' = H\Sigma_{11}^{-1/2}\Sigma_{12}\Sigma_{22}^{-1/2}Q',$$

we see that:

$$e_j'\Sigma_{12}f_i = \begin{cases} \rho_i & \text{if } i = j \leqslant r \\ 0 & \text{otherwise.} \end{cases} \tag{2.4}$$

In other words, the scalar ρ_i can be interpreted, for $i = 1, 2, \ldots, r$, as:

$$\rho_i = E[f_i'Y_t - EL(f_i'Y_t|Z_t)][e_i'X_t - EL(e_i'X_t|Z_t)]. \tag{2.5}$$

Moreover, since H and Q are orthogonal matrices we have:

$$\begin{cases} e_i'\Sigma_{11}e_j = \delta_{ij} & \text{for } i, j = 1, 2, \ldots, k, \\ f_i'\Sigma_{22}f_j = \delta_{ij} & \text{for } i, j = 1, 2, \ldots, n, \end{cases} \tag{2.6}$$

(where $\delta_{ij} = 1$ if $i = j$ and 0 otherwise), which implies in particular that:

$$E[f_i'Y_t - EL(f_i'Y_t|Z_t)]^2 = 1 \quad \text{for } i = 1, 2, \ldots, n. \tag{2.7}$$

and

$$E[e_j'X_t - EL(e_j'X_t|Z_t)]^2 = 1 \quad \text{for } j = 1, 2, \ldots, k. \tag{2.8}$$

Because of Schwartz inequality,

$$0 < \rho_i \leqslant 1 \quad \text{for } i = 1, 2, \ldots, r. \tag{2.9}$$

In particular, when the matrices Σ_{ij} are genuine covariance matrices (if the variables are centered or one of the Z_t-variable is the constant 1), we see that ρ_i is the partial correlation coefficient, given Z_t between $f_i'Y_t$ and $e_i'X_t$. By extending the usual terminology, we call *canonical variables* the variables $f_i'Y_t$, $e_i'X_t$ for $i = 1, 2, \ldots, r$ and *canonical correlations* the associated coefficients ρ_i. For notational convenience, we use also the notation ρ_i for $i = 1, 2, \ldots, \max(k, n)$ by taking $\rho_i = 0$ for $i > r$.

We shall not give here more details about the usual interpretation of the canonical variables: the first canonical variables $e_1'X_t$, $f_1'Y_t$ are the two linear functions of X_t and Y_t having the maximum correlation subject to the unit variance condition; the second canonical variables $e_2'X_t$, $f_2'Y_t$ are the two linear functions having maximum correlation subject to the condition of zero correlation with the first canonical variables and of unit variance; and so on. It is clear that in our framework such interpretations in term of correlations have to be considered *given* Z_t, and possibly without centering.

Nevertheless, it is straightforward to check that this canonical correlation analysis directly provides the matrices α, β, γ, δ we are interested in. The following proposition is proved in appendix 1.

Proposition 2.1

(i) A basis α of the space orthogonal to the kernel of B can be defined as: $\alpha_i = e_i$ for $i = 1, 2, \ldots, r$.
(ii) A basis δ of the space orthogonal to the range of B can be defined as: $\delta_i = f_i$ for $i = r + 1, r + 2, \ldots, n$.
(iii) A basis γ of the kernel of B can be defined as: $\gamma_i = \Sigma_{11}e_i$ for $i = r + 1, r + 2, \ldots, k$.
(iv) A basis β of the range of B can be defined as: $\beta_i = \Sigma_{22}f_i$ for $i = 1, 2, \ldots, r$.

Then we have: $B = \beta\Delta_r\alpha'$, where Δ_r is the $r \times r$ diagonal matrix with diagonal coefficients ρ_i, $i = 1, 2, \ldots, r$.

The canonical directions e_j, $j = 1, 2, \ldots, k$ and f_i, $i = 1, 2, \ldots, n$ can easily be characterized as eigenvectors of the *noncentered canonical correlation matrices* between Y_t and X_t, conditionally to Z_t. These matrices are usually defined as natural multivariate extensions of R^2 coefficients, where the subscript t is dropped thanks to stationarity:

$$\begin{cases} R^2(X_t, Y_t|Z_t) = \Sigma_{11}^{-1}\Sigma_{12}\Sigma_{22}^{-1}\Sigma_{21} \\ R^2(Y_t, X_t|Z_t) = \Sigma_{22}^{-1}\Sigma_{21}\Sigma_{11}^{-1}\Sigma_{12}. \end{cases} \tag{2.10}$$

Now, we see that:

$$\begin{cases} R^2(X_t, Y_t|Z_t) = \Sigma_{11}^{-1/2}MM'\Sigma_{11}^{1/2} \\ R^2(Y_t, X_t|Z_t) = \Sigma_{22}^{-1/2}M'M\Sigma_{22}^{1/2}. \end{cases}$$

Since h_j, $j = 1, 2, \ldots, k$ (resp. q_i, $i = 1, 2, \ldots, n$) are orthonormal bases such that:

$$\begin{cases} MM'h_j = \rho_j^2 h_j \\ M'Mq_i = \rho_i^2 q_i \end{cases}$$

we deduce from (2.3) that:

$$\begin{cases} R^2(X_t, Y_t|Z_t)e_j = \rho_j^2 e_j & \text{for } j = 1, 2, \ldots, k \\ R^2(Y_t, X_t|Z_t)f_i = \rho_i^2 f_i & \text{for } i = 1, 2, \ldots, n. \end{cases} \tag{2.11}$$

In other words e_j, $j = 1, 2, \ldots, k$ (resp. f_i, $i = 1, 2, \ldots, n$) is a basis of eigenvectors of $R^2(X_t, Y_t|Z_t)$ (resp. $R^2(Y_t, X_t|Z_t)$), the characterization being completed by the normalizing rule (2.6). The corresponding eigenvalues are the square of (noncentered, theoretical) canonical correlations.

So (2.11) provides a natural way to estimate canonical directions and canonical correlations by their empirical counterparts. Let us finally note that the squared canonical correlations are the eigenvalues of the matrices $R^2(X_t, Y_t|Z_t)$ and $R^2(Y_t, X_t|Z_t)$ (associated to canonical direction); this justifies the terminology "canonical correlation matrices."

3 Tests on the Kernel and on the Range

The general framework

We consider a multivariate linear model:

$$Y_t = BX_t + u_t, \quad t = 1, \ldots, T,$$

where Y_t is an n-vector, X_t a k-vector an B an $n \times k$ matrix of unknown coefficients. The errors terms u_t are assumed to be independently and identically distributed and such that $E(u_t) = 0$, $V(u_t) = \Omega$ invertible. Moreover, u_t is assumed to be independent of X_t, $X_{t-1} \ldots$ The inference problems we are interested in are related with the kernel and the range of the matrix B. The extension of these issues of the case where there are other explanatory variables Z will be considered below under the heading "Extension to a conditional analysis." We want to derive statistical procedures whose asymptotic properties do not depend on specific distributional assumptions; in particular, we never assume that the probability distribution of the error term u_t is Gaussian. But we consider the pseudo loglikelihood function (in the sense of Gouriéroux et al., 1984) based on a pseudo normality of the errors u_t:

$$L_T = \sum_{t=1}^{T} l_t$$

with

$$l_t = -\frac{n}{2}\log 2\pi - \frac{1}{2}\log\det\Omega - \frac{1}{2}(Y_t - BX_t)'\Omega^{-1}(Y_t - BX_t)$$
$$= -\frac{n}{2}\log 2\pi - \frac{1}{2}\log\det\Omega$$
$$-\frac{1}{2}[Y_t - (Id_n \otimes X_t')b]'\hat{\Omega}^{-1}[Y_t - (Id_n \otimes X_t')b],$$

and $b = \text{vec}(B')$.

The model may also be written:

$$y = (Id_n \otimes X)b + u$$

with $y = \text{vec}\,Y$, Y being the $T \times n$ matrix whose rows are the Y_t', $t = 1, \ldots, T$, $u = \text{vec}\,U$, U being the $T \times n$ matrix whose rows are the u_t', X is the $T \times k$ matrix whose rows are the X_t', $t = 1, \ldots, T$.

We have $V(u) = \Omega \otimes Id_T$ and the pseudo loglikelihood function L_T can be written:

$$L_T = -\frac{nT}{2}\log 2\pi - \frac{T}{2}\log\det\Omega$$
$$-\frac{1}{2}\{[y - (Id_n \otimes X)b]'(\Omega^{-1} \otimes Id_T)[y - (Id_n \otimes X)b]\}. \tag{3.1}$$

Let us denote $\theta_1 = b$, $\theta_2 = \text{vec}\Omega^{-1}$ and $\theta = (\theta_1', \theta_2')'$. The pseudo maximum likelihood (PML) methodology allows us to adress some inference issues about the vector θ of unknown parameters by maximizing L_T with respect to θ.

But, due to the possible non-normality of the error terms u_t, we have generally to distinguish the two usual forms of the information matrix:

$$I = \text{plim}\frac{1}{T}\sum_{t=1}^{T}\frac{\delta l_t}{\delta\theta}\frac{\delta l_t}{\delta\theta'} = E\frac{\delta l_t}{\delta\theta}\frac{\delta l_t}{\delta\theta'},$$

and

$$J = -\text{plim}\frac{1}{T}\frac{\delta^2 L_t}{\delta\theta\delta\theta'} = -E\frac{\delta^2 l_t}{\delta\theta\delta\theta'}.$$

Considering the test of a null hypothesis H_0 and denoting by $\hat{\theta}_T$ (resp. $\hat{\theta}_{0T}$) the unconstrained (resp. constrained) PML estimator of θ, it is, for instance, known (see Gouriéroux and Monfort, 1989a) that the "pseudo likelihood ratio" statistic:

$$\xi_{LR} = 2[L_T(\hat{\theta}_T) - L_T(\hat{\theta}_{0T})],$$

is not, in general (i.e. when $I \neq J$) asymptotically distributed as a chi-square but as a mixture of chi-squares.

On the other hand, Gouriéroux and Monfort (1989a) have shown that pseudo Rao's score test and Wald test statistics can still be defined, that they are generally asymptotically equivalent under H_0, and that their common asymptotic probability distribution is a chi-square distribution (whose number of degrees of freedom is equal to the number of constraints) as usual. Since Rao's score test statistic is independent of the form of H_0 (implicit or explicit), which is not the case for the Wald-type tests, we shall first characterize Rao's pseudo score test and then address the issue of its comparison with various other test procedures: Wald type tests for a null hypothesis in a implicit or explicit form, and pseudo likelihood ratio test.

Let us first note that the pseudo maximum likelihood estimation based on a pseudo normality of the error u_t is directly related to OLS estimation, not only for unconstrained estimation but also for constrained one, since the null hypotheses we are interested in (hypotheses on the kernel and on the range of B) can be defined by linear constraints with respect to the subvectors of parameters $\theta_1 = b$. In fact, the methodology which is set in the following could be more generally applied to the issue of testing a null hypothesis H_0 which admits an implicit form:

$$H_0 = \{g(\theta) = 0\}, \tag{3.2}$$

where $g(\theta)$ is a p-vector of (linear or nonlinear) differentiable functions of θ which depend on θ only through $\theta_1 = b$ and such that:

$$\frac{\delta g'}{\delta \theta}(\theta) = \left[\frac{\delta g}{\delta \theta_1'}(\theta), 0\right]'$$

is of full column ranks p ($p < nk$).

The constrained and unconstrained PML estimators $(\hat{B}_{0T}, \hat{\Omega}_{0T})$ and $(\hat{B}_T, \hat{\Omega}_T)$ satisfy:

$$\frac{\delta L_T}{\delta \theta_2}(\theta) = \frac{1}{2}\left[T\Omega - \sum_{t=1}^{T}(Y_t - BX_t)(Y_t - BX_t)'\right] = 0,$$

and thus:

$$\hat{\Omega}_T = \frac{1}{T}\sum_{t=1}^{T}(Y_t - \hat{B}_T X_t)(Y_t - \hat{B}_T X_t)' = \frac{1}{T}\hat{U}_T'\hat{U}_T,$$
$$\text{with } \hat{U}_T' = Y' - \hat{B}_T'X'. \tag{3.3}$$

and

$$\hat{\Omega}_{0T} = \frac{1}{T}\sum_{t=1}^{T}(Y_t - \hat{B}_{0T} X_t)(Y_t - \hat{B}_{0T} X_t)' = \frac{1}{T}\hat{U}_{0T}'\hat{U}_{0T},$$
$$\text{with } \hat{U}_{0T}' = Y' - \hat{B}_{0T}X'. \tag{3.3'}$$

So $\hat{\Omega}_T$ and $\hat{\Omega}_{0T}$ are the empirical covariance matrices associated with the estimated residuals:

$$\hat{U}_T = Y' - \hat{B}_T X' \quad \text{and} \quad \hat{U}_{0T} = Y' - \hat{B}_{0T}X'.$$

Moreover, it is well known, thanks to (3.1) and to Zellner's theorem, that $\hat{b}_T = \operatorname{vec}\hat{B}_T'$ is identical to the OLS estimator equation by equation:

$$\hat{b}_T = [Id_n \otimes (X'X)^{-1}X']y,$$
$$\hat{B}_T' = (X'X)^{-1}X'Y,$$
$$\hat{\Omega}_T = \frac{1}{T}Y'(Id - P_X)Y,$$

where $P_X = X(X'X)^{-1}X'$ is the matrix of the orthogonal projector on the subspace spanned by the columns of X.

Rao's pseudo score tests

The general expression

Since the constraints of interest depend on θ only through $\theta_1 = b$, we are interested in the (pseudo) score:

$$\frac{\delta L_T}{\delta b}(\hat{\theta}_{0T}) = (Id_n \otimes X')(\hat{\Omega}_{0T}^{-1} \otimes Id_T)(y - (Id_n \otimes X)\hat{b}_{0T}).$$

Since $(\delta^2 L_T/\delta b \delta b')(\hat{\theta}_{0T})$ has the following simple form:

$$\frac{\delta^2 L_T}{\delta b \delta b'}(\hat{\theta}_{0T}) = -(Id_n \otimes X')(\hat{\Omega}_{0T}^{-1} \otimes Id_T)(Id_n \otimes X) = -(\hat{\Omega}_{0T}^{-1} \otimes X'X),$$

it would be convenient to get Rao's pseudo score test statistic ξ_S with the following usual expression:

$$\xi_S = -\left[\frac{\delta L_T}{\delta b'}(\hat{\theta}_{0T})\right]\left[\frac{\delta^2 L_T}{\delta b \delta b'}(\hat{\theta}_{0T})\right]^{-1}\left[\frac{\delta L_T}{\delta b}(\hat{\theta}_{0T})\right]. \tag{3.4}$$

It is proved in appendix 2 that (3.4) does provide a pseudo score test statistic; in particular ξ_S is, as usual, asymptotically distributed under H_0 as a chi-square with p degrees of freedom. This result (which was not *a priori* straightforward since $I \neq J$ and I is not block-diagonal) is shown to be a consequence of two pleasant features of our problem:

First, the block-decompositions of I and J with respect to θ_1 and θ_2 satisfy

$$I_{11} = J_{11} \quad \text{and} \quad J_{12} = 0; \tag{3.5}$$

Second, since $g(\theta)$ depends on θ only through θ_1:

$$\begin{aligned} \frac{\delta g}{\delta \theta'} J^{-1} &= \left[\frac{\delta g}{\delta \theta_1'}, 0\right]\begin{bmatrix} J_{11}^{-1} & 0 \\ 0 & J_{22}^{-1} \end{bmatrix} \\ &= \left[\frac{\delta g}{\delta \theta_1'} J_{11}^{-1}, 0\right] = \left[\frac{\delta g}{\delta \theta_1'} I_{11}^{-1}, 0\right], \end{aligned} \tag{3.6}$$

so that, for asymptotic expansions which are similar to those standarly used in the likelihood theory, the difference between I and J (namely, the fact that I is generally not block-diagonal) is irrelevant for our problem.

Therefore, we have a genuine pseudo score test statistic given by:

$$\xi_S = [y - (Id_n \otimes X)\hat{b}_{0T}]'[\hat{\Omega}_{0T}^{-1} \otimes P_X][y - (Id_n \otimes X)\hat{b}_{0T}],$$

or, in a more compact form:

$$\xi_S = \text{trace}\,[\hat{\Omega}_{0T}^{-1}\hat{U}_{0T}'P_X\hat{U}_{0T}].$$

Note that $\hat{U}_{0T}'P_X\hat{U}_{0T}$ can also be written:

$$\begin{aligned} \hat{U}_{0T}'P_X\hat{U}_{0T} &= \hat{U}_{0T}'\hat{U}_{0T} - \hat{U}_{0T}'(Id_T - P_X)\hat{U}_{0T} \\ &= \hat{U}_{0T}'\hat{U}_{0T} - \hat{U}_T'\hat{U}_T = T(\hat{\Omega}_{0T} - \hat{\Omega}_T), \end{aligned}$$

since the columns of $\hat{U}_T - \hat{U}_{0T}$ are in the subspace spanned by the columns of X.

Proposition 3.1

A pseudo score test statistic for the null hypothesis H_0 defined by (3.2) is given by:

$$\xi_S = T\,\text{Trace}\,[\hat{\Omega}_{0T}^{-1}(\hat{\Omega}_{0T} - \hat{\Omega}_T)].$$

The asymptotic probability distribution of ξ_S under the null is a chi-square with p degrees of freedom.

Tests on the kernel of B

Following section 1 (see (1.8) and (1.9)), the null hypothesis of interest is:

$$H_0^K = \{B\gamma_0 = 0\} = \begin{Bmatrix}\text{There exists an } n \times r \\ \text{matrix } \beta \text{ such that } B = \beta\alpha_0'\end{Bmatrix}$$

where H_0^K is defined: either in an implicit form through a known $k \times (k - r)$ matrix γ_0 whose columns provide a basis of the kernel of B; or in an explicit form through a known $k \times r$ matrix α_0 whose columns provide the factors $\alpha_0'X_t$.

Rao's pseudo score test statistic:

$$\xi_S = T\,\mathrm{Trace}\,[\hat{\Omega}_{0T}^{-1}(\hat{\Omega}_{0T} - \hat{\Omega}_T)],$$

depends neither on the form of the null hypothesis, nor on the choice of γ_0 or α_0, for a given subspace spanned by the columns of γ_0 (whose orthogonal complement is spanned by the columns of α_0). Using the explicit form, the model under H_0^K can be written:

$$Y_t = \beta\alpha_0'X_t + u_t, \quad t = 1, \ldots, T. \tag{3.7}$$

This is another multivariate linear model in which the explanatory variables are the components of $\alpha_0'X_t$. In this model, the PML estimator of $\mathrm{vec}\,\beta'$ is identical to the OLS estimator equation by equation, so that:

$$\hat{\Omega}_{0T} = \frac{1}{T}Y'(Id - P_{X\alpha_0})Y,$$

where $P_{X\alpha_0}$ is the matrix of the orthogonal projector on the subspace spanned by the columns of $X\alpha_0$. Since $\alpha_0'\gamma_0 = 0$, we also have $(X\alpha_0)'X(X'X)^{-1}\gamma_0 = 0$, which implies:

$$P_X = P_{X\alpha_0} + P_{X(X'X)^{-1}\gamma_0}. \tag{3.8}$$

Thus:

$$\begin{aligned}\hat{\Omega}_{0T} - \hat{\Omega}_T &= \frac{1}{T}Y'(Id - P_{X\alpha_0})Y - \frac{1}{T}Y'(Id - P_X)Y \\ &= \frac{1}{T}Y'(P_X - P_{X\alpha_0})Y = \frac{1}{T}Y'P_{X(X'X)^{-1}\gamma_0}Y.\end{aligned}$$

So the matrix:

$$
\begin{aligned}
&\hat{\Omega}_{0T}^{-1}(\hat{\Omega}_{0T} - \hat{\Omega}_T) \\
&= [Y'(Id - P_{X\alpha_0})Y]^{-1} Y' P_{X(X'X)^{-1}\gamma_0} Y \\
&= \left[\frac{1}{T} Y'(Id - P_{X\alpha_0})Y\right]^{-1} \frac{1}{T} Y'(Id - P_{X\alpha_0}) X(X'X)^{-1}\gamma_0 \\
&\left[\frac{1}{T}(X(X'X)^{-1}\gamma_0)'(Id - P_{X\alpha_0})(X(X'X)^{-1}\gamma_0)\right]^{-1} \\
&\left[\frac{1}{T}(X(X'X)^{-1}\gamma_0)'(Id - P_{X\alpha_0})Y\right],
\end{aligned}
$$

is the empirical noncentered canonical correlation matrix between Y and $X(X'X)^{-1}\gamma_0$ conditionally to $X\alpha_0$; note that this matrix reduces to the usual conditional canonical correlation matrix if the variables X and Y are centered or if the variables $X\alpha_0$ contain a constant. Let us denote by $R^2(Y, X(X'X)^{-1}\gamma_0 | X\alpha_0)$ this $n \times n$ matrix and by $\hat{\lambda}_{1T} \geqslant \hat{\lambda}_{2T} \geqslant \ldots \geqslant \hat{\lambda}_{nT} \geqslant 0$ its eigenvalues; in other words $\hat{\lambda}_{iT}$, $i = 1, \ldots, n$ are the empirircal squared canonical correlations between Y and $X(X'X)^{-1}\gamma_0$ conditionally to $X\alpha_0$ and we have shown that:

$$\xi_S = T \sum_{i=1}^{n} \hat{\lambda}_{iT}.$$

Proposition 3.2

The Rao's pseudo score test statistic for the test of H_0^K is

$$\xi_S = T \sum_{i=1}^{n} \hat{\lambda}_{iT},$$

where $\hat{\lambda}_{1T} \geqslant \hat{\lambda}_{2T} \geqslant \ldots \geqslant \hat{\lambda}_{nT}$ are the empirical squared canonical correlatiosn between Y and $X(X'X)^{-1}\gamma_0$ conditionally to $X\alpha_0$. The asymptotic probability distribution of ξ_S under the null H_0^K is $\chi^2[n(k - r)]$.

There are $n(k - r)$ restrictions to test since $B\gamma_0$ is an $n \times (k - r)$ matrix. The Rao's pseudo score test of H_0^K with asymptotic size ε leads us to reject H_0^K if the canonical correlations between the endogeneous variables Y and the "omitted" explanatory variables $X(X'X)^{-1}\gamma_0$ conditionally to the selected factors $X\alpha_0$ are significative in the sense that

$$\xi_S = T \sum_{i=1}^{n} \hat{\lambda}_{iT} = T \sum_{i=1}^{\min(n,k-r)} \hat{\lambda}_{iT} > \chi^2_{1-\varepsilon}[n(k - r)],$$

where $\chi^2_{1-\varepsilon}$ is the $(1 - \varepsilon)$ quantile.

In the extreme case where we have no a priori factors $X\alpha_0$ in mind, we can consider the model

$$Y_t = b.1 + B^* X_t^* + u_t = (b, B^*)\begin{bmatrix} 1 \\ X_t^* \end{bmatrix} + u_t,$$

and the null hypothesis

$$H_0^K = \{B^* = 0\}.$$

It is clear that, in such a case, the Rao's pseudo score test statistic is

$$\xi_S = T \operatorname{Trace}(R^2).$$

where

$$R^2 = (V_{\text{emp}} Y)^{-1} \text{Cov}_{\text{emp}}(Y, X)(V_{\text{emp}} X)^{-1} \text{Cov}_{\text{emp}}(X, Y),$$

is the empirical canonical correlation matrix between the two sets of variables Y and X. Matrix R^2 is thus the analogue, for the multivariate case, of the usual determination coefficient; the eigenvalues and the eigenvectors of this matrix allows us to derive the linear combinations of the endogenous variables which are the more "explained" by X (the ones associated with the largest eigenvalues) and the less "explained" (the ones associated with the smallest eigenvalues).

Test on the range of B

Following section 1 (see (1.3) and (1.4)) the null hypothesis of interest is:

$$H_0^R = \{\delta_0' B = 0\} = \begin{Bmatrix} \text{there exists a } k \times r \\ \text{matrix } \alpha \text{ such that } B = \beta_0 \alpha' \end{Bmatrix},$$

where H_0^R is defined: either in an explicit form through a known $n \times r$ matrix β_0 whose columns provide a basis of the range of B or in an implicit form through a known $n \times (n - r)$ matrix δ_0 whose columns provide the cofactors. Since the Rao's pseudo score test statistic does not depend on the form of the null hypothesis, it can be derived from any equivalent parameterization of the model.

Let us consider for instance the following new parameterization by the coefficients of matrices B_1, B_2, C, Λ_{11} and Λ_{22}:

$$B_1 = \delta_0' B,$$

$$\Lambda_{11} = \delta_0' \Omega \delta_0,$$

$$B_2 = \beta_0' B - (\beta_0' \Omega \delta_0) \Lambda_{11}^{-1} B_1,$$
$$C = (\beta_0' \Omega \delta_0) \Lambda_{11}^{-1},$$
$$\Lambda_{22} = \beta_0' \Omega \beta_0 - (\beta_0' \Omega \delta_0) \Lambda_{11}^{-1} (\delta_0' \Omega \beta_0). \tag{3.9}$$

When we consider this new parameterization, we have in mind the following recursive form of the initial model:

$$\begin{cases} \delta_0' Y_t = B_1 X_t + v_{1t} \\ \beta_0' Y_t = B_2 X_t + C \delta_0' Y_t + v_{2t}, \end{cases} \tag{3.10}$$

where v_{1t} and v_{2t} are two uncorrelated error vectors whose covariance matrices are denoted by Λ_{11} and Λ_{22}. Since we do not assume that the error terms u_t are normally distributed, we do not known if v_{1t} and v_{2t} are independent and if $B_2 X_t + C \delta_0' Y_t$ is the conditional expectation of $\beta_0' Y_t$ given X_t and $\delta_0' Y_t$. However, as far as the pseudo loglikelihood function based on a pseudo normality of the errors is concerned, we can claim that it admits the usual additive decomposition:

$$L_T = L_T^1 + L_T^2$$

where:

$$L_T^1 = -\frac{(n-r)T}{2} \log 2\pi - \frac{T}{2} \log \det \Lambda_{11}$$
$$- \frac{1}{2} \sum_{t=1}^{T} (\delta_0' Y_t - B_1 X_t)' \Lambda_{11}^{-1} (\delta_0' Y_t - B_1 X_t)$$

and

$$L_T^2 = -\frac{rT}{2} \log 2\pi - \frac{T}{2} \log \det \Lambda_{22}$$
$$- \frac{1}{2} \sum_{t=1}^{T} (\beta_0' Y_t - B_2 X_t - C \delta_0' Y_t)' \Lambda_{22}^{-1} (\beta_0' Y_t - B_2 X_t - C \delta_0' Y_t).$$

With this new parameterization the null hypothesis is $H_0^R = \{B_1 = 0\}$. Thus, we know thanks to (3.4) that the Rao's pseudo score test statistic is obtained (with the usual asymptotic probability distribution under the null) by considering:

$$\xi_S^* = -\left[\frac{\delta L_T}{\delta b_1'} (\hat{\theta}_{0T})\right] \left[\frac{\delta^2 L_T}{\delta b_1 \delta b_1'} (\hat{\theta}_{0T})\right]^{-1} \left[\frac{\delta L_T}{\delta b_1} (\hat{\theta}_{0T})\right], \tag{3.11}$$

where $b_1 = \text{vec} B_1'$ and $\hat{\theta}_{0T}$ is the constrained PML estimator of the new vector θ of parameters (associated with the coefficients of B_1, Λ_{11}, B_2,

C, and Λ_{22}). Constrained estimators $\hat{B}_{10T}$, $\hat{\Lambda}_{110T}$, $\hat{B}_{20T}$, $\hat{C}_{0T}$, and $\hat{\Lambda}_{220T}$ are associated with $\hat{\theta}_{0T}$.

With some straightforward arguments and notations, we see that:

$$\frac{\delta L_T}{\delta b_1}(\hat{\theta}_{0T}) = \frac{\delta L_T^1}{\delta b_1}(\hat{B}_{10T}, \hat{\Lambda}_{110T}),$$

$$\frac{\delta^2 L_T}{\delta b_1 \delta b_1'}(\hat{\theta}_{0T}) = \frac{\delta^2 L_T^1}{\delta b_1 \delta b_1'}(\hat{B}_{10T}, \hat{\Lambda}_{110T}),$$

and $(\hat{B}_{10T}, \hat{\Lambda}_{110T})$ corresponds to the constrained PML estimator based on the submodel:

$$\delta_0' Y_t = B_1 X_t + v_{1t}, \quad V(v_{1t}) = \Lambda_{11}, \tag{3.12}$$

associated with the pseudo loglikelihood function L_T^1. The constraint $H_0^R = \{B_1 = 0\}$ leads to:

$$\hat{B}_{10T} = 0, \quad \hat{\Lambda}_{110T} = \frac{1}{T}\delta_0' Y' Y \delta_0,$$

while the unconstrained PML estimation provides:

$$\hat{\Lambda}_{11T} = \frac{1}{T}\delta_0' Y'(Id - P_X) Y \delta_0.$$

The Rao's pseudo score test statistic (3.11) can then be directly computed from the submodel (3.12) by applying the general results in propositions 3.1 and 3.2 in an extreme case where the "omitted" explanatory variables (under the null) are the whole set of X variables and where the endogenous variables are now defined by $Y\delta_0$:

$$\begin{aligned}\xi_S^* &= T\,\mathrm{Trace}\,[\hat{\Lambda}_{110T}^{-1}(\hat{\Lambda}_{110T} - \hat{\Lambda}_{11T})] \\ &= T\,\mathrm{Trace}\,R^2(Y\delta_0, X).\end{aligned}$$

Proposition 3.3

The Rao's pseudo score test statistic for the null hypothesis H_0^R is

$$\xi_S^* = T \sum_{i=1}^{n-r} \hat{\lambda}_{iT}^*$$

where $\hat{\lambda}_{1T}^* \geqslant \hat{\lambda}_{2T}^* \geqslant \ldots \geqslant \hat{\lambda}_{n-r,T}^*$ are the empirical squared canonical correlations between $Y\delta_0$ and X. The asymptotic probability distribution of ξ_2 under the null H_0^R is $\chi^2[k(n-r)]$.

There are $k(n-r)$ restrictions to test since $\delta_0' B$ is a matrix $(n-r) \times$

k. The Rao's pseudo score test of H_0^R with asymptotic size ε leads us to reject H_0^R if the canonical correlations between the explanatory variables X and the proposed cofactors $Y\delta_0$ are significative in the sense that:

$$\xi_S^* = T\sum_{i=1}^{n-r}\hat{\lambda}_{iT}^* = T\sum_{i=1}^{\min(n-r,k)}\hat{\lambda}_{iT}^* > \chi^2_{1-\varepsilon}[k(n-r)].$$

Comparison of the various test procedures

The pseudo likelihood ratio statistic

This statistic, defined by

$$\xi_{LR} = 2[L_T(\hat{\theta}_T) - L_T(\hat{\theta}_{0T})],$$

does not depend on the form (implicit or explicit) of the null hypothesis.

Since we are interested in a null hypothesis of the type (3.2) which entails some restrictions on θ only through $\theta_1 = b$, it is well known that the usual concentration of the Gaussian pseudo loglikelihood function leads to:

$$\xi_{\mathrm{LR}} = T\log\frac{\det\hat{\Omega}_{0T}}{\det\hat{\Omega}_T}. \tag{3.13}$$

So:

$$\begin{aligned}\xi_{LR} &= -T\log\frac{\det\hat{\Omega}_T}{\det\hat{\Omega}_{0T}} = -T\log\det(\hat{\Omega}_{0T}^{-1}\hat{\Omega}_T)\\ &= -T\log\det[Id - \hat{\Omega}_{0T}^{-1}(\hat{\Omega}_{0T} - \hat{\Omega}_T)].\end{aligned}$$

We recognize the matrix $\hat{\Omega}_{0T}^{-1}(\hat{\Omega}_{0T} - \hat{\Omega}_T)$ whose (T times) trace defines the pseudo score test statistic. So, if we denote by $\hat{\lambda}_{1T} \geqslant \hat{\lambda}_{2T} \geqslant \ldots \geqslant \hat{\lambda}_{nT} \geqslant 0$ its eigenvalues, we have:

$$\begin{aligned}\xi_{LR} &= -T\log\prod_{i=1}^{n}(1 - \hat{\lambda}_{iT})\\ &= -T\sum_{i=1}^{n}\log(1 - \hat{\lambda}_{iT})\end{aligned}$$

while

$$\xi_S = \sum_{i=1}^{n}\hat{\lambda}_{iT}.$$

Due to the convergence of $\hat{\lambda}_{iT}$ to zero under the null, we have some asymptotic equivalences under the null:

$$-\log(1 - \hat{\lambda}_{iT}) \sim \hat{\lambda}_{iT} \sim \log(1 + \hat{\lambda}_{iT}).$$

We are then led to consider three tests statistics which are asymptotically equivalent under the null.

The Rao's pseudo score test statistic:

$$\xi_S = T \sum_{i=1}^{n} \hat{\lambda}_{iT}, \tag{3.14}$$

The pseudo likelihood ratio test statistic:

$$\xi_{LR} = -T \sum_{i=1}^{n} \log(1 - \hat{\lambda}_{iT}), \tag{3.15}$$

A modified pseudo likelihood ratio test statistic:

$$\tilde{\xi}_{LR} = T \sum_{i=1}^{n} \log(1 + \hat{\lambda}_{iT}), \tag{3.16}$$

Let us note that the asymptotic equivalence under the null between ξ_{LR} and ξ_S was not *a priori* ensured since $I \neq J$. Gouriéroux and Monfort (1989a) have proved in a general framework that this asymptotic equivalence is more generally ensured as soon as J is a generalized inverse of the asymptotic covariance matrix of $\sqrt{T}(\hat{\theta}_T - \hat{\theta}_{0T})$. This property could be checked here thanks to (3.5) and (3.6), as is shown in appendix 3. The asymptotic equivalence which we have directly deduced from the comparison of (3.14) and (3.15) is an illustration of this general result.

Moreover, the expression (3.13) and asymptotically equivalent statistic of the type (3.14), (3.15), and (3.16) can be computed, for testing H_0^R, from the additive decomposition of the pseudo loglikelihood $L_T = L_T^1 + L_T^2$ which is associated with the recursive form (3.10). In this case:

$$\xi_{LR} = T \log \frac{\det \hat{\Lambda}_{110T}}{\det \hat{\Lambda}_{11T}} = -T \sum_{i=1}^{n-\lambda} \log(1 - \hat{\lambda}_{iT}^{*})$$

and $\hat{\lambda}_{1T}^{*} \geqslant \hat{\lambda}_{2T}^{*} \geqslant \ldots \geqslant \hat{\lambda}_{n-r,T}^{*}$ are also the eigenvalues of the matrix $\hat{\Lambda}_{110T}^{-1}(\hat{\Lambda}_{110T} - \hat{\Lambda}_{11T})$.

The generalized Wald test statistic

The generalized Wald test statistic is, for any null hypothesis on b, defined as (see Szroeter, 1983; Gouriéroux and Monfort, 1989a)

$$\xi_W = \min_{b \in H_0} (\hat{b}_T - b)'[\hat{\Omega}_T \otimes (X'X)^{-1}]^{-1}(\hat{b}_T - b), \qquad (3.17)$$

since $T(\hat{\Omega}_T \otimes X'X^{-1})$ is clearly the asymptotic covariance matrix of the OLS estimator $\sqrt{T}(\hat{b}_T - b)$. Let $\tilde{b}_{0T}$ be the estimator deduced from this minimization.

We have, with obvious notations:

$$\begin{aligned} \xi_W &= (\hat{b}_T - \tilde{b}_{0T})'[\hat{\Omega}_T^{-1} \otimes (X'X)](\hat{b}_T - \tilde{b}_{0T}) \\ &= \mathrm{tr}[\hat{\Omega}_T^{-1}(\hat{B}_T - (\tilde{B}_{0T})X'X(\hat{B}'_T - (\tilde{B}'_{0T})] \\ &= \mathrm{tr}[\hat{\Omega}_T^{-1}(\tilde{U}_0 - (\hat{U})'(\tilde{U}_0 - (\hat{U})] \\ &= \mathrm{tr}[\hat{\Omega}_T^{-1}(\tilde{U}'_0\tilde{U}_0 - (\hat{U}'_0\hat{U})], \end{aligned}$$

since

$$\begin{aligned} \hat{U}'\tilde{U}_0 &= \hat{U}'(\hat{U} + \hat{U}_0 - \hat{U}) \\ &= \hat{U}'[\hat{U} + X(\tilde{B}'_{0T} - \hat{B}'_T)] \\ &= \hat{U}'\hat{U}. \end{aligned}$$

Therefore:

$$\xi_W = T \,\mathrm{trace}\,[\hat{\Omega}_T^{-1}(\hat{\Omega}_{0T} - \hat{\Omega}_T)] \quad \text{with } \hat{\Omega}_{0T} = \frac{1}{T}\tilde{U}'_0\tilde{U}_0. \qquad (3.18)$$

It is easy to prove the asymptotic equivalence between the generalized Wald test statistic ξ_W and the Rao's pseudo score test statistic ξ_S defined in proposition 3.1 if we check that $\tilde{b}_{0T}$ and $\hat{b}_{0T}$ (and then $\tilde{\Omega}_{0T}$ and $\hat{\Omega}_{0T}$) are asymptotically equivalent under the null. Thanks to (3.5), this could be deduced from a general result of Gouriéroux and Monfort (1989a).

Moreover, as far as we are interested in solving the program (3.17) for the hypotheses of interest H_0^K or H_0^R defined in an explicit form (1.9) or (1.3), it is possible to perform a numerical comparison between $\tilde{b}_{0T}$ and the constrained PML estimator.

First, under the null H_0^K defined by (1.9), we consider the model:

$$Y_t = \beta(\alpha'_0 X_t) + u_t.$$

In this multivariate linear model, the PML estimator of $\mathrm{vec}\,\beta'$ is identical to the OLS estimator equation by equation $\mathrm{vec}\,\hat{\beta}_{0T}$, so that

$$\hat{B}_{0T} = \hat{\beta}_{0T}\alpha'_0.$$

That is to say that $\hat{\beta}_{0T}$ can be obtained by maximization of the pseudo loglikelihood function based on a pseudo normality of the errors u_t:

$$L_T^0 = \sum_{t=1}^{T} l_T^0$$

with

$$l_t^0 = -\frac{n}{2}\log 2\pi - \frac{1}{2}\log\det\Omega$$
$$-\frac{1}{2}[Y_t - (Id_n \otimes X_t'\alpha_0)\beta]'\Omega^{-1}[Y_t - (Id_n \otimes X_t'\alpha_0)\beta].$$

But, since $\hat{\beta}_{0T}$ is also the OLS estimator, we know (from Zellner's result) that the maximization of L_T^0 with respect to β can be performed for any given Ω. For instance $\hat{\beta}_{0T}$ is the solution of

$$\min_\beta \sum_{t=1}^{T} [Y_t - (Id_n \otimes X_t'\alpha_0)\beta]'\hat{\Omega}_T^{-1}[Y_t - (Id_n \otimes X_t'\alpha_0)\beta]. \quad (3.19)$$

Then, by a straightforward argument of orthogonality, we notice that Y_t can be replaced in (3.19) by $\hat{B}_T X_t$ without modifying the value of the function to minimize, up to an additive constant (independent of β). Thus, $\hat{\beta}_{0T}$ is also the solution of:

$$\min_\beta \sum_{t=1}^{T} [\hat{B}_T X_t - (Id_n \otimes X_t'\alpha_0)\beta]'\hat{\Omega}_T^{-1}[\hat{B}_T X_t - (Id_n \otimes X_t'\alpha_0)\beta]. \quad (3.20)$$

This is precisely program (3.17) in the case of H_0^K defined by (1.9), which proves that $\tilde{b}_{0T}$ and the constrained PML estimator $\hat{b}_{0T}$ are numerically equal in this case:

$$\hat{b}_{0T} = \tilde{b}_{0T}.$$

Second, under the null H_0^R defined by (1.3), we consider the model:

$$Y_t = \beta_0(\alpha' X_t) + u_t. \quad (3.21)$$

With an argument similar to the one previously used about (3.19) and (3.20), we can claim that the minimum distance estimator $\tilde{b}_{0T}$ defined by

$$\min_b (\hat{b}_T - b)'[\hat{\Omega}_T \otimes (X'X)^{-1}]^{-1}(\hat{b}_T - b)$$
$$\text{subject to } b = \text{vec}(\beta_0\alpha')'$$

is also $b = \text{vec}\,(\tilde{\alpha}_{0T}\beta_0')$, where $\tilde{\alpha}_{0T}$ is solution of

$$\min_\alpha L_T(B, \hat{\Omega}_T)$$

$$\text{subject to } B = \beta_0\alpha'.$$

In other words, $\tilde{\alpha}_{0T}$ is the GLS estimator of α in the linear model

$$\begin{cases} Y_{it} = X_t'(\alpha\beta_{0i}) + u_t, \\ t = 1, \ldots \quad \text{and } i = 1, 2, \ldots n, \end{cases} \tag{3.22}$$

associated with the covariance matrix $\hat{\Omega}_T \otimes Id_T$, where we denote by β_{0i} the ith column of β_0'. The main difference with the previous case is that, due to the linear restriction $b_i = \alpha\beta_{0i}$, Zellner's theorem can no longer be applied and the GLS estimator does not coincide in general with OLS estimator equation by equation. In particular, the GLS estimator depends in general on the covariance matrix which is used.

On the other hand, the constrained PML estimator $\hat{B}_{0T} = \beta_0\hat{\alpha}_{0T}'$ is by definition such that $\hat{\alpha}_{0T}$ is solution of

$$\min_{\alpha} L_T(B, \hat{\Omega}_{0T})$$

$$\text{subject to } B = \beta_0\alpha'.$$

$\hat{\alpha}_{0T}$ is the GLS estimator of α in the linear model (3.22) associated with the covariance matrix $\hat{\Omega}_{0T} \otimes Id_T$. This estimator will be in general different from $\tilde{\alpha}_{0T}$ since $\hat{\Omega}_{0T} \neq \hat{\Omega}_T$; nevertheless they are asymptotically equivalent under the null since it is well known that quasigeneralized least squares associated with consistent estimators of the covariance matrix are asymptotically equivalent to the unfeasible GLS estimator. Therefore, $\hat{b}_{0T}$ and $\tilde{b}_{0T}$ are numerically different in general, but asymptotically equivalent under the null.

In summary, the generalized Wald test statistic $\xi_W = T \operatorname{trace}[\hat{\Omega}_T^{-1}(\tilde{\Omega}_{0T} - \hat{\Omega}_T)]$ and the test statistic $\xi_W^* = T \operatorname{trace}[\hat{\Omega}_T^{-1}(\hat{\Omega}_{0T} - \hat{\Omega}_T)]$ are such that: $\xi_W = \xi_W^*$ when the null hypothesis of interest is H_0^K in the explicit form; ξ_W and ξ_W^* are asymptotically equivalent under the null but in general numerically different when the null hypothesis of interest is H_0^R in the explicit form.

The Wald statistic based on the implicit form

ξ_W^* is the usual Wald test statistic for testing a null hypothesis H_0 in an implicit form (3.2): $H_0 = \{g(\theta) = 0\}$ where $g(\theta)$ depends on θ only through $\theta_1 = b$. Moreover, the possible nonnormality of the errors u_t does not change the usual expression of this Wald test statistic since the asymptotic covariance matrix under the null of $\sqrt{T}g(\hat{\theta}_T)$ is (see appendix 2)

$$\frac{\delta g}{\delta \theta_1'} I_{11}^{-1} \frac{\delta g'}{\delta \theta_1} = \frac{\delta g}{\delta \theta_1'} J_{11}^{-1} \frac{\delta g'}{\delta \theta_1},$$

and we do not have to take into account the difference between I and J in order to compute

$$\xi_W^* = Tg(\hat{\theta}_T)' \left[\frac{\delta g}{\delta \theta_1'}(\hat{\theta}_T) \hat{I}_{11}^{-1} \frac{\delta g'}{\delta \theta_1}(\hat{\theta}_T) \right]^{-1} g(\hat{\theta}_T).$$

The (pseudo) Wald test statistic associated with a null hypothesis H_0^K or H_0^R in a implicit form is then

$$\xi_W^* = T \sum_{i=1}^{n} \hat{\mu}_{iT},$$

where $\hat{\mu}_{1T} \geqslant \hat{\mu}_{2T} \geqslant \ldots \geqslant \hat{\mu}_{nT} \geqslant 0$ are the eigenvalues of the matrix $\hat{\Omega}_T^{-1}(\hat{\Omega}_{0T} - \hat{\Omega}_T)$.

Finally it is clear, from straightforward algebraic manipulations that the three following properties are equivalent:

$\hat{\mu}_{1T} \geqslant \hat{\mu}_{2T} \geqslant \ldots \hat{\mu}_{nT}$ are the eigenvalues of $\hat{\Omega}_T^{-1}(\hat{\Omega}_{0T} - \hat{\Omega}_T)$;

$(1 + \hat{\mu}_{1T})^{-1} \leqslant (1 + \hat{\mu}_{2T})^{-1} \leqslant \ldots \leqslant (1 + \hat{\mu}_{nT})^{-1}$ are the eigenvalues of $\hat{\Omega}_{0T}^{-1}\hat{\Omega}_T$; $\dfrac{\hat{\mu}_{1T}}{1 + \hat{\mu}_{1T}} \geqslant \dfrac{\hat{\mu}_{2T}}{1 + \mu_{2T}} \geqslant \ldots \geqslant \dfrac{\hat{\mu}_{nT}}{1 + \mu_{nT}}$ are the eigenvalues of $\hat{\Omega}_T^{-1}(\hat{\Omega}_{0T} - \hat{\Omega}_T)$.

Therefore, the eigenvalues $\hat{\mu}_{it}$ of $\hat{\Omega}_T^{-1}(\hat{\Omega}_{0T} - \hat{\Omega}_T)$ are one-to-one related (in an increasing order) to the eigenvalues $\hat{\lambda}_{iT}$ of $\hat{\Omega}_{0T}^{-1}(\hat{\Omega}_{0T} - \hat{\Omega}_T)$:

$$\hat{\lambda}_{iT} = \frac{\hat{\mu}_{iT}}{1 + \hat{\mu}_{iT}}, \quad \hat{\mu}_{iT} = \frac{\hat{\lambda}_{iT}}{1 - \hat{\lambda}_{iT}},$$

and the Wald test statistic ξ_W^* can also be written

$$\xi_W^* = T \sum_{i=1}^{n} \frac{\hat{\lambda}_{iT}}{1 - \hat{\lambda}_{iT}}.$$

Synthesis

In the previous sections we have proposed various test statistics which are all asymptotically equivalent under the null. In many cases, the admit simple expressions in terms of the same eigenvalues $\hat{\lambda}_{iT}$. The only difference between these test procedures are their finite sample properties. As in the classical univariate linear model with normal errors, various inequalities can be established by using standard convexity inequality:

$$x \geqslant \log(1 + x), \quad x \leqslant -\log(1 - x),$$

$$x = \frac{\lambda}{1 - \lambda} \quad \text{we get} \quad \frac{\lambda}{1 - \lambda} \geqslant -\log(1 - \lambda).$$

Proposition 3.4

Let $\hat{\lambda}_{1T} \geqslant \hat{\lambda}_{2T} \geqslant \ldots \geqslant \hat{\lambda}_{n,T}$ be the squared empirical canonical correlations between Y and $X(X'X)^{-1}\gamma_0$ conditionally to $X\alpha_0$.

(i) The Rao's pseudo score test statistic for the test of H_0^K is:

$$\xi_S = T \sum_{i=1}^{n} \hat{\lambda}_{iT}.$$

(ii) The pseudo likelihood ratio statistic is:

$$\xi_{LR} = -T \sum_{i=1}^{n} \log(1 - \hat{\lambda}_{iT});$$

the modified pseudo likelihood ratio statistic is:

$$\tilde{\xi}_{LR} = T \sum_{i=1}^{n} \log(1 + \hat{\lambda}_{iT}).$$

(iii) The Wald statistic does not depend on the form of H_0^K retained (implicit or explicit) and it is equal to:

$$\xi_W = T \sum_{i=1}^{n} \frac{\hat{\lambda}_{iT}}{1 - \hat{\lambda}_{iT}}.$$

(iv) These statistics are asymptotically equivalent under H_0^K and their asymptotic distribution is: $\chi^2[n(k - r)]$.

(v) The following inequalities hold:

$$\xi_W \geqslant \xi_{LR} \geqslant \xi_S \geqslant \tilde{\xi}_{LR}.$$

Proposition 3.5

Let $\hat{\lambda}_{1T}^* \geqslant \hat{\lambda}_{2T}^* \geqslant \ldots \geqslant \hat{\lambda}_{n-r,T}^*$ be the squared empirical canonical correlations between $Y\delta_0$ and X.

(i) The Rao's pseudo score test statistics for the test of H_0^R is

$$\xi_S^* = T \sum_{i=1}^{n-r} \hat{\lambda}_{iT}^*$$

(ii) The pseudo likelihood ratio statistic is

$$\xi_{LR}^* = -T\sum_{i=1}^{n-r}\log(1 - \hat{\lambda}_{iT}^*)$$

The modified statistic is

$$\tilde{\xi}_{LR}^* = T\sum_{i=1}^{n-r}\log(1 + \hat{\lambda}_{iT}^*)$$

(iii) The Wald statistic for the test of H_0^R in the implicit for $\{B'\delta_0 = 0\}$ does not depend on the choice of δ_0 (for a given range) and it is equal to

$$\xi_W^* = T\sum_{i=1}^{n}\frac{\hat{\lambda}_{iT}^*}{1 - \hat{\lambda}_{iT}^*}$$

On the other hand, the generalized Wald statistic ξ_W for the test of H_0^R in an explicit form is generally different.

(iv) These statistics are asymptotically equivalent under H_0^R and their asymptotic distribution is $\chi^2[k(n - r)]$.

(v) The following inequalities hold

$$\xi_W^* \geqslant \xi_{LR}^* \geqslant \xi_S^* \geqslant \tilde{\xi}_{LR}^*.$$

Extension to a conditional analysis

Until now, we have considered inference problems on the kernel and on the range of a matrix B appearing in a linear model $Y_t = BX_t + u_t$. The results can easily be extended to the case where other explanatory variables Z_t exist. The model becomes

$$Y_t = BX_t + CZ_t + u_t.$$

We are still interested in matrix B. The various test statistics of hypotheses on the kernel of B can be expressed in the same way as above in terms of the OLS residuals in the models:

$$\tilde{y}_i = Xb_i + Zc_i + \tilde{u}_i$$
$$\tilde{y}_i = X\alpha_0\beta_i + Zc_i + \tilde{u}_i \quad i = 1, \ldots, n.$$

where $\tilde{y}_i$ and $\tilde{u}_i$ are the T-vectors whose components are the ith components of Y_t and u_t whereas b_i', c_i', β_i' and the ith rows of B, C, β.

Similarly, the test statistics of hypotheses on the range of B are based on the OLS residuals in the models:

$$Y\delta_{0j} = Xd_j + Zc_j + v_j$$

and

$$Y\delta_{0j} = Zc_j + v_j$$

where δ_{0j} is the jth column of δ_0, $j = 1, \ldots, n - r$ and d_j the jth row of B_1 (see (3.10)).

These residuals can also be obtained from the previous regressions in which the Z terms are cancelled and the matrices X and Y replaced by $(Id - P_Z)X$ and $(I - P_Z)Y$ respectively (which implies that the columns of Y, i.e. the $\tilde{y}_i$, are replaced by $(Id - P_Z)\tilde{y}_i$). This is a consequence of the following result: if W and Z are $T \times k_1$ and $T \times k_2$ matrices and if P_L is the orthogonal projector on the subspace spanned by the columns of L we have:

$$\begin{aligned}(Id - P_{W,Z})Y &= (Id - P_{(Id-P_Z)W} - P_Z)Y \\ &= (Id - P_Z)Y - P_{(Id-P_Z)W}(Id - P_Z)Y \\ &= (Id - P_{(Id-P_Z)W})(Id - P_Z)Y.\end{aligned}$$

In other words, all the formulae of section 3 remain valid if Y is replaced by $(Id - P_Z)Y$ and X by $(Id - P_Z)X$. All the canonical correlations considered have now to be understood conditionally to Z. In the same way, the results of section 4, which are based on those of section 3, could be extended to this conditional analysis.

4 Tests on the Rank

Hypotheses and parameters

In this section we focus on the determination of the rank of B and we shall obtain, as a byproduct, an estimation of the range and of the kernel of B. Since the rank is an integer, the determination of this parameter leads to sequential procedures which are similar to those used in the identification of the orders in an ARMA process. The sequences of hypotheses are defined by:

$$H_{0r} = \{\text{rank } B = r\}, \tag{4.1}$$

and

$$H_r = \{\text{rank } B \geqslant r\}, \tag{4.2}$$

We want to test H_{0r} against $H_{r+1} = H_r - H_{0r}$ and we consider the following sequences of tests:

- Test of $H_{00} = \{\text{rank } B = 0\}$ against $H_1 = \{\text{rank } B \geqslant 1\}$. If H_{00} is accepted, the procedures stops and we accept the hypothesis: rank $B = 0$.
- Otherwise, H_{01} is tested against H_2; if H_{01} is accepted the procedure stops and we accept the hypothesis: rank $B = 1$. And so on.

A hypothesis on the rank can be seen as an assumption about the range, since the dimension of the range is rank B, or as an assumption on the kernel, since the dimension of the kernel is k − rank B. Moreover, the forms of these hypotheses may be explicit or mixed. Let us now consider various forms characterizing H_{0r} within the maintained hypothesis H_r.

Explicit form

$$H_{0r} = \left\{ \begin{matrix} \text{there exists a } (k \times r) \text{ matrix } \alpha \text{ and} \\ \text{an } (n \times r) \text{ matrix } \beta \text{ such that } B = \beta\alpha' \end{matrix} \right\}. \tag{4.3}$$

Within H_r we know that the rank of α and β is necessarily r.

Mixed form based on the kernel

$$H_{0r} = \left\{ \begin{matrix} \text{there exists a } k \times (k - r) \text{ matrix } \gamma, \\ \text{whose rank is } (k - r), \text{ such that } B\gamma = 0 \end{matrix} \right\} \tag{4.4}$$

Within H_r it is not possible to find a $(k \times k - \tilde{r})$ matrix $\tilde{\gamma}$, whose rank is $k - \tilde{r}$, such that $B\tilde{\gamma} = 0$, and $\tilde{r} < r$.

Mixed form based on the range

$$H_{0r} = \left\{ \begin{matrix} \text{there exists an } n \times (n - r) \text{ matrix } \delta, \\ \text{whose rank is } (n - r), \text{ such that } \delta' B = 0 \end{matrix} \right\} \tag{4.5}$$

At this stage it is important to note that the test procedures will imply (constrained) estimation of various parameters: α (i.e. the range of B' or the orthogonal of the kernel of B), β (i.e. the range of B), γ (i.e. the kernel of B), and δ (i.e. the kernel of B' or the orthogonal of the range of B). As a consequence, constrained estimation procedures will be developed along with the tests procedures: (pseudo) maximum likelihood methods with the (pseudo) likelihood ratio tests, and asymptotic least squares with the generalized Wald tests.

H_{0r} is defined from the hypotheses of interest in the previous section (H_0^K or H_0^R) by introducing some degrees of freedom α, β, γ, or δ. Therefore, the likelihood ratio and generalized Wald test statistics for H_0^r are the minimum values (over these free parameters α, β, γ, or δ) of the previous test statistics (where the corresponding matrix was fixed, by considering a given kernel or a given range). Such a natural correspondence does not exist for Rao's score test statistic and this is the reason why it will not be considered here.

Estimation and test based on the maximization of the (pseudo) likelihood function

The test procedure

The (pseudo) likelihood ratio test statistic does not depend on the form of the null hypothesis. This statistic is

$$\xi^r_{LR} = T \log \frac{\det \hat{\Omega}^r_{0T}}{\det \hat{\Omega}^r_T}, \tag{4.6}$$

where $\hat{\Omega}^r_{0T}$ is the empirical variance–covariance matrix of the residuals obtained under H_{0r}. This statistic can be derived from the similar statistics previously derived for the tests on the kernel or on the range.

We proved in the previous section that

$$\hat{\Omega}_T = \frac{1}{T} Y'(Id - P_X)Y, \tag{4.7}$$

$$\hat{\Omega}_{0T} = \frac{1}{T} Y'(Id - P_{X\alpha_0})Y, \tag{4.8}$$

when $H_0^K = \{B\gamma_0 = 0\}$ and α_0 is a $(k \times r)$ matrix whose rank is r and whose column vectors are orthogonal to those of γ_0. In other words, the likelihood ratio test statistic for H_0^K is

$$\xi_{LR}(\gamma_0) = T \log \frac{Y'(Id - P_{X\alpha_0})Y}{Y'(Id - P_X)Y} \tag{4.9}$$

In the same way, for testing $H_0^R = \{\delta_0' B = 0\}$ the likelihood ratio test statistic is

$$\xi^*_{LR}(\delta_0) = T \log \frac{\det \hat{\Lambda}_{110T}}{\det \hat{\Lambda}_{11T}} = T \log \frac{\det[\delta_0' Y' Y \delta_0]}{\det[\delta_0' Y'(Id - P_X) Y \delta_0]}. \tag{4.10}$$

From the definition of the (pseudo) likelihood ratio statistic, we deduce the following proposition.

Proposition 4.1

(i) $\xi^r_{LR} = \min_\delta \xi_{LR}(\gamma) = \min_r \xi^*_{LR}(\delta)$, where the first minimization is with respect to the $k \times (k - r)$ matrices γ whose rank is $(k - r)$, and the second one is with respect to the $n \times (n - r)$ matrices δ, whose rank is $n - r$.

(ii) Any solution $\hat{\gamma}_0$ (resp. $\hat{\delta}_0$) of the first (resp. second) minimization problem is a constrained (pseudo) maximum likelihood estimator of a basis of the kernel of B (resp. the orthogonal of the range of B).

The test statistic and the estimators

Therefore we have to solve the minimization problem described above; it is done in appendix 4. These minimizations rest on the canonical correlations between X and Y, so we shall first consider this canonical analysis.

Let us consider the $(k \times k)$ and $(n \times n)$ matrices

$$R^2(X, Y) = (X'X)^{-1}X'Y(Y'Y)^{-1}Y'X,$$

and

$$R^2(Y, X) = (Y'Y)^{-1}Y'X(X'X)^{-1}X'Y.$$

These matrices are the empirical counterparts of the theoretical correlation matrices defined by (2.10). These matrices have the same eigenvalues and these eigenvalues are positive and smaller than one (the zero eigenvalue having, in general, different multiplicity orders). These eigenvalues are denoted by

$$\hat{\eta}_{1T} \geqslant \hat{\eta}_{2T} \geqslant \ldots$$

They are the squared (noncentered, empirical) canonical correlations between Y and X. Moreover, we can derive bases of eigenvectors which are the empirical counterparts of the bases defined in proposition 2.1. We denote by $\hat{e}_{1T}, \ldots, \hat{e}_{kT}$ a basis corresponding to $R^2(X, Y)$, normalized by

$$\hat{e}'_{iT}X'X\hat{e}_{jT} = \delta_{ij} \quad i, j = 1, \ldots, k.$$

(where $\delta_{ij} = 1$ if $i = j$ and 0 otherwise).

Similarly, we denote by $\hat{f}_{1T}, \ldots, \hat{f}_{nT}$ a basis corresponding to $R^2(Y, X)$ normalized by

$$\hat{f}'_{iT}Y'Y\hat{f}_{jT} = \delta_{ij}, \quad i, j = 1, \ldots, n.$$

From appendix 4, we get the following proposition:

Proposition 4.2

(i)
$$\xi^r_{LR} = -T \sum_{i=r+1}^{n} \log(1 - \hat{\eta}_{iT})$$

$$= -T \sum_{i=r+1}^{k} \log(1 - \hat{\eta}_{iT}).$$

(ii) A basis α of the orthogonal of the kernel of B can be consistently estimated by

$$\hat{a}_{1T} = \hat{e}_{1T}, \ldots, \hat{a}_{rT} = \hat{e}_{rT}.$$

(iii) A basis δ of the orthogonal of the range of B can be consistently estimated by

$$\hat{f}_{r+1,T}, \ldots, \hat{f}_{n,T}.$$

(iv) A basis γ of the kernel of B can be consistently estimated by

$$(X'X)\hat{e}_{r+1,T}, \ldots, (X'X)\hat{e}_{k,T}.$$

(v) A basis β of the range of B can be consistently estimated by

$$(Y'Y)\hat{f}_{1,T}, \ldots, (Y'Y)\hat{f}_{r,T}.$$

Symmetry of the procedure

The previous proposition shows some symmetry between X and Y. Indeed it is equivalent to test $H_0 = \{\text{rank } B = r\}$ in the model $Y_t = BX_t + u_t$, $t = 1, \ldots, T$, or to test $\tilde{H}_{0r} = \{\text{rank } D = r\}$, in the model

$$X_t = DY_t + w_t \quad t = 1, \ldots, T.$$

This is easily understood since, if (X_t, Y_t) is stationary, we have

$$\begin{aligned} D &= E(XY')(E(YY'))^{-1} = E(XX')(E(XX'))^{-1}E(XY')(E(YY')^{-1} \\ &= E(XX')B'(E(YY'))^{-1}, \end{aligned}$$

and, therefore rank D = rank B'.

Generalized Wald test and asymptotic least squares estimation

Expression of the test statistic and of the estimators

Using similar notations to those in section 3, the generalized Wald statistic based on the mixed form of H_{0r} (see Szroeter, 1983; Gouriéroux and Monfort, 1989a, b) is

$$\begin{aligned} \xi_W^r = \min_{\alpha,\beta} & (\hat{b}_T - (Id_n \otimes \alpha)\,\text{vec}\,\beta')'[\hat{\Omega}_T \otimes (X'X)^{-1}]^{-1} \\ & (\hat{b}_T - (Id_n \otimes \alpha)\,\text{vec}\,\beta'). \end{aligned}$$

The minimization is different from that of section 3, since it is with respect to α and β and not only with respect to α. A solution $\tilde{\alpha}_0$, $\hat{\beta}_0$ of this problem provides an asymptotic least squares estimator of the bases α and β.

The minimization with respect to β has already been performed in section 3, so using (3.18) (3.20), (4.7), and (4.8), and denoting by $\xi_W(\alpha)$ the statistic concentrated with respect to β, we get

$$\begin{aligned}\xi_W^r = \min_\alpha \xi_W(\alpha) &= \min_\alpha T \operatorname{tr}[\hat{\Omega}_T^{-1}(\hat{\Omega}_{0T}(\alpha) - \hat{\Omega}_T)] \\ &= \min_\alpha \{\operatorname{tr}(\hat{\Omega}_T^{-1} Y' P_X Y) - \operatorname{tr}(\hat{\Omega}_T^{-1} Y' P_{X\alpha} Y\} \\ &= \operatorname{tr}\{\hat{\Omega}_T^{-1} Y' P_X Y\} - \max_\alpha \operatorname{tr}\{\hat{\Omega}_T^{-1} Y' P_{X\alpha} Y\}.\end{aligned}$$

This optimization problem is solved in appendix 5 and we obtain:

Proposition 4.3

(i) The generalized Wald statistic is

$$\xi_W^r = T \sum_{i=r+1}^{k} \frac{\hat{\eta}_{iT}}{1 - \hat{\eta}_{iT}}.$$

(ii) The asymptotic least squares estimators of α and β are identical to the (pseudo) maximum likelihood estimators.

Comparison of the generalized Wald statistic and of the pseudo likelihood ratio statistic

Proposition 4.4

(i) The generalized Wald statistic is larger than the pseudo likelihood ratio statistic:

$$\xi_W^r \geqslant \xi_{LR}^r.$$

(ii) The statistics are asymptotically equivalent under the null hypothesis and their asymptotic distribution is

$$\chi^2[(n - r)(k - r)].$$

Proof. (i) The inequality is a consequence of

$$-\log(1 - x) = \log\left(1 + \frac{x}{1 - x}\right) < \frac{x}{1 - x}$$

(ii) Under the null hypothesis, $\hat{\eta}_{iT}$ converges to zero at the rate $1/T$, for $i = r + 1, \dots, k$ (see Anderson, 1984). Therefore we have the following expansions:

$$\xi_W^r = T \sum_{i=r+1}^{k} \hat{\eta}_{iT} + o_P(1),$$

and

$$\xi_{LR}^r = T \sum_{i=r+1}^{k} \hat{\eta}_{iT} + o_P(1).$$

The asymptotic distribution can be derived from the results of appendix 4; in particular, it is important to stress that the normality of the error terms is not required. The number of degrees of freedom can be, for instance, computed by a formula based on the explicit form: {number of initial parameters in B} − {number of parameters under H_{0r}: α and β} + {number of identifying restrictions: α and β are defined up to a multiplication by a $(r \times r)$ invertible matrix}. This leads to $nk - kr - nr + r^2 = (n - r)(k - r)$. □

5 Conclusion

In this chapter, we have shown that, without any normality assumption, various inference procedures can be completely worked out. Moreover, the links with canonical correlation theory can be given for all the inference procedures considered, and this allows the use of canonical correlation packages for their implementation. Finally, the various classical asymptotic approaches have been considered and their properties compared. These statistical tools should be useful in the numerous economic domains where the factor models have been shown to be relevant.

Appendix 1: factors and canonical variables

From (2.3):

$$H' = [h_1\, h_2 \ldots h_k] \Rightarrow \Sigma_{11}^{-1/2} \quad H' = [e_1, \ldots, e_k],$$

$$Q' = [q_1\, q_2 \ldots q_n] \Rightarrow \Sigma_{22}^{-1/2} \quad Q' = [f_1, \ldots, f_r].$$

Thus:

$$B = \Sigma_{22}^{1/2} M' \Sigma_{11}^{-1/2} = \Sigma_{22}^{1/2} Q' \Delta' H \Sigma_{11}^{-1/2}$$

$$= \Sigma_{22}[f_1, \ldots, f_n]\Delta' \begin{bmatrix} e_1' \\ \vdots \\ e_k' \end{bmatrix},$$

$$\Rightarrow B = \Sigma_{22}[f_1, \ldots, f_r]\Delta_r \begin{bmatrix} \varepsilon_1' \\ \vdots \\ \varepsilon'_r \end{bmatrix} = \beta\Delta_r\alpha'.$$

This proves that the r columns of the matrix β (resp. α) provide a basis of the range (resp. of the orthogonal of the kernel) of B.

From (2.6):

$$e_i'\Sigma_{11}e_j = \alpha_j'\gamma_j = 0 \quad \text{for} \quad \begin{cases} i = 1, 2, \ldots, r \\ j = r+1, \ldots, k, \end{cases}$$

and

$$f_i'\Sigma_{22}f_j = \delta_i'\beta_j = 0 \quad \text{for} \quad \begin{cases} i = r+1, \ldots, n \\ j = 1, 2, \ldots, r. \end{cases}$$

Thus, the $(k - r)$ (resp. $(n - r)$) columns of the matrix γ (resp. δ) provide a basis of the kernel (resp. of the orthogonal of the range) of B.

Appendix 2: Rao's pseudo score test

The constrained PML estimator $\hat{\theta}_{0T}$ is solution of the first order conditions:

$$\frac{\delta L_T}{\delta\theta}(\hat{\theta}_{0T}) = \frac{\delta g'}{\delta\theta}(\hat{\theta}_{0T})\hat{\lambda}_{0T}, \tag{A.1}$$

where $\hat{\lambda}_{0T}$ is the p-vector of Lagrange multipliers associated with the constraint $g(\theta) = 0$.

From expansions around the true unknown value θ^0, we know that under H_0

$$\sqrt{T}g(\hat{\theta}_T) = \frac{\delta g}{\delta\theta'}(\theta^0)\sqrt{T}(\hat{\theta}_T - \hat{\theta}_{0T}) + o_P(1), \tag{A.2}$$

$$\frac{1}{\sqrt{T}}\frac{\delta L_T}{\delta\theta}(\hat{\theta}_{0T}) = \frac{1}{\sqrt{T}}\frac{\delta L_T}{\delta\theta}(\theta^0) - J\sqrt{T}(\hat{\theta}_{0T} - \theta^0) + o_P(1), \tag{A.3}$$

$$0 = \frac{1}{\sqrt{T}}\frac{\delta L_T}{\delta\theta}(\hat{\theta}_T) = \frac{1}{\sqrt{T}}\frac{\delta L_T}{\delta\theta}(\theta^0) - J\sqrt{T}(\hat{\theta}_T - \theta^0) + o_P(1), \tag{A.4}$$

and, from (A.3) and (A.4),

$$\frac{1}{\sqrt{T}}\frac{\delta L_T}{\delta\theta}(\hat{\theta}_{0T}) = J\sqrt{T}(\hat{\theta}_T - \hat{\theta}_{0T}) + o_P(1). \tag{A.5}$$

Thus, from (A.2), (A.5), and (3.6):

$$\begin{aligned}\sqrt{T}g(\hat{\theta}_T) &= \frac{\delta g}{\delta\theta'}(\theta^0)J^{-1}\frac{1}{\sqrt{T}}\frac{\delta L_T}{\delta\theta}(\theta_{0T}) + o_P(1) \\ &= \left[\frac{\delta g}{\delta\theta_1'}(\theta^0)I_{11}^{-1}, 0\right]\frac{1}{\sqrt{T}}\frac{\delta L_T}{\delta\theta}(\hat{\theta}_{0T}) + o_P(1)\end{aligned}$$

$$= \frac{\delta g}{\delta \theta_1'}(\theta^0) I_{11}^{-1} \frac{1}{\sqrt{T}} \frac{\delta L_T}{\delta \theta_1}(\hat{\theta}_{0T}) + o_P(1).$$

So, from (A.1):

$$\sqrt{T} g(\hat{\theta}_T) = \frac{\delta g}{\delta \theta_1'} I_{11}^{-1} \frac{\delta g'}{\delta \theta_1} \frac{\hat{\lambda}_{0T}}{\sqrt{T}} + o_P(1).$$

$$\frac{\hat{\lambda}_{0T}}{\sqrt{T}} = \left[\frac{\delta g}{\delta \theta_1'} I_{11}^{-1} \frac{\delta g'}{\delta \theta_1}\right]^{-1} \sqrt{T} g(\hat{\theta}_T) + o_P(1) \tag{A.6}$$

where $\delta g / \delta \theta_1'$ and I_{11} are evaluated at the true unknown value θ^0. But we know that

$$\sqrt{T} g(\hat{\theta}_T) = \frac{\delta g}{\delta \theta'}(\theta^0) \sqrt{T}(\hat{\theta}_T - \theta^0) + o_P(1)$$

$$= \frac{\delta g}{\delta \theta'}(\theta^0) J^{-1} \frac{1}{\sqrt{T}} \frac{\delta L_T}{\delta \theta}(\theta^0) + o_P(1)$$

$$= \frac{\delta g}{\delta \theta_1'} I_{11}^{-1} \frac{1}{\sqrt{T}} \frac{\delta L_T}{\delta \theta_1}(\theta^0) + o_P(1),$$

thanks to an expansion of $\sqrt{T} g(\hat{\theta}_T)$ around θ^0 and to (A.4) and (3.6).

So:

$$\frac{\hat{\lambda}_{0T}}{\sqrt{T}} = \left[\frac{\delta g}{\delta \theta_1'} I_{11}^{-1} \frac{\delta g'}{\delta \theta_1}\right]^{-1} \frac{\delta g}{\delta \theta_1'} I_{11}^{-1} \frac{1}{\sqrt{T}} \frac{\delta L_T}{\delta \theta_1}(\theta^0) + o_P(1). \tag{A.7}$$

We deduce that the asymptotic covariance matrix of $\hat{\lambda}_{0T}/\sqrt{T}$ under H_0 is the usual one:

$$\left[\frac{\delta g}{\delta \theta_1'} I_{11}^{-1} \frac{\delta g'}{\delta \theta_1}\right]^{-1},$$

and a Lagrange mutiplier test can be defined as usual:

$$\xi_S = \frac{1}{T} \hat{\lambda}_{0T}' \frac{\delta g}{\delta \theta_1'}(\hat{\theta}_{0T}) \hat{I}_{11}^{-1} \frac{\delta g'}{\delta \theta_1}(\hat{\theta}_{0T}) \hat{\lambda}_{0T}.$$

The asymptotic probability distribution of ξ_S under H_0 is a chi-square with p degrees of freedom as soon as $\hat{I}_{11}$ is a consistent estimator of I_{11} under H_0.

Since $I_{11} = J_{11}$, we can choose

$$\hat{I}_{11} = -\frac{1}{T} \frac{\delta^2 L_T}{\delta b \delta b'}(\hat{\theta}_{0T}) = \frac{1}{T}(\hat{\Omega}_{0T}^{-1} \otimes X'X),$$

which provides, thanks to (A.1) the usual interpretation of ξ_S as Rao's score test statistic:

$$\xi_S = -\frac{\delta L_T}{\delta b'}(\hat{\theta}_{0T}) \left[\frac{\delta^2 L_T}{\delta b \delta b'}(\hat{\theta}_{0T})\right]^{-1} \frac{\delta L_T}{\delta b}(\hat{\theta}_{0T}).$$

Appendix 3

From expansions under the null, we have

$$\sqrt{T}(\hat{\theta}_T - \hat{\theta}_{0T}) = J^{-1}\frac{1}{\sqrt{T}}\frac{\delta L_T}{\delta\theta}(\hat{\theta}_{0T}) + o_P(1) \qquad \text{(see A.5)}$$

$$= J^{-1}\frac{\delta g'}{\delta\theta}(\hat{\theta}_{0T})\frac{\hat{\lambda}_{0T}}{\sqrt{T}} + o_P(1) \qquad \text{(see A.1)}$$

Thus, we deduce from (A.7) that the asymptotic covariance matrix of $\sqrt{T}(\hat{\theta}_T - \hat{\theta}_{0T})$ is, under the null,

$$V = J^{-1}\frac{\delta g'}{\delta\theta}(\theta^0)\left[\frac{\delta g}{\delta\theta_1'}I_{11}^{-1}\frac{\delta g'}{\delta\theta_1}\right]^{-1}\frac{\delta g}{\delta\theta'}(\theta^0)J^{-1}$$

By taking into account (3.5) and (3.6), we conclude that

$$VJV = V,$$

which means that J is a generalized inverse of V, as defined by Rao (1965, p. 24).

Appendix 4: solutions of the maximum likelihood problems

Two preliminary lemmas

We shall consider two lemmas already used in similar situations by Anderson (1984) and Johansen (1988). Let us consider a symmetric positive definite matrix admitting the following block decomposition:

$$\begin{pmatrix} S_{00} & S_{01} \\ S_{10} & S_{11} \end{pmatrix},$$

where S_{00}, S_{01}, S_{11} are respectively $n \times n$, $n \times k$, $k \times k$ matrices. Let us consider the eigenvalues of $S_{11}^{-1}\ S_{10}\ S_{00}^{-1}\ S_{01}$, which are real positive, smaller than 1 and can be ordered in a decreasing order; they are denoted by

$$1 \geqslant \eta_1 \geqslant \ldots \geqslant \eta_k \geqslant 0.$$

Let us also introduce a basis of corresponding eigenvectors $e_1, \ldots, e_k$, normalized by

$$e_i' S_{11} e_j = \delta_{ij} \quad i, j = 1 \ldots, k.$$

We are interested in the problem

$$\min_{\alpha}\frac{\det(S_{00} - S_{01}\alpha(\alpha' S_{11}\alpha)^{-1}\alpha' S_{10})}{\det S_{00}},$$

with respect to $(k \times r)$ matrices α. Note that the objective function is not modified if α is replaced by αQ where Q is an $(r \times r)$ invertible matrix.

Lemma A.1

$$\frac{\det(S_{00} - S_{01}\alpha(\alpha' S_{11}\alpha)^{-1}\alpha' S_{10})}{\det S_{00}},$$

$$= \frac{\det(\alpha' S_{11}\alpha - \alpha' S_{10} S_{00}^{-1} S_{01}\alpha)}{\det(\alpha' S_{11}\alpha)}$$

Lemma 4.2

(i) A solution in α of the optimization problem is

$$\alpha_1 = e_1, \ldots, a_r = e_r$$

(ii) The optimal value of the objective function is

$$\prod_{i=1}^{r}(1 - \eta_i)$$

The problem can be symmetrically solved if we are interested in a maximization in α of the objective function.

Solution of the problem $\xi_{LR}^r = \min_\gamma \xi_{LR}(\gamma)$.

We have to minimize

$$\begin{aligned}\xi_{LR}(\gamma) &= T \log \frac{\det \frac{1}{T} Y'(Id - P_{X\alpha})Y}{\det \frac{1}{T} Y'(Id - P_X)Y} \\ &= T \log \frac{\det \frac{1}{T} Y'Y}{\det \frac{1}{T} Y'(Id - P_X)Y} + T \log \frac{\det \frac{1}{T} Y'(Id - P_{X\alpha})Y}{\det \frac{1}{T} Y'Y} \\ &= -T \log \det(Id - (Y'Y)^{-1}Y'P_X Y) + T \log \det(Id - (Y'Y)^{-1}Y'P_{X\alpha}Y) \\ &= -T \log \det(Id - R^2[Y, X]) \qquad + T \log \det(Id - R^2(Y, X\alpha)).\end{aligned}$$

Therefore, we are led to the optimization with respect to a matrix α such that the knowledge of its range is equivalent to that of γ.

We have to minimize

$$\det[Id - R^2(Y, X\alpha)] = \det[Id - (Y'Y)^{-1}Y'X\alpha(\alpha'X'X\alpha)^{-1}\alpha'X'Y].$$

Using lemma A.2, we have to introduce the matrix:

$$R^2(X, Y) = (X'X)^{-1}X'Y(Y'Y)^{-1}Y'X,$$

and to find its eigenvalues $\hat{\eta}_{1T} \geqslant \hat{\eta}_{2T} \geqslant \ldots \geqslant \hat{\eta}_{kT}$ as well as the corresponding eigenvectors $\hat{e}_{1T} \ldots \hat{e}_{kT}$ normalized by

$$\hat{e}_{iT}' X' X \hat{e}_{jT} = \delta_{ij}.$$

A solution of the minimization problem is

$$\hat{\alpha}_{1T} = \hat{e}_{1T}, \ldots, \hat{\alpha}_{rT} = \hat{e}_{rT}.$$

This solution is thus obtained by taking the r eigenvectors associated with the r greatest eigenvalues. The test statistic is

$$\begin{aligned} \xi^r_{LR} &= -T\sum_{i=1}^{k} \log(1 - \hat{\eta}_{iT}) + T\sum_{i=1}^{r} \log(1 - \hat{\eta}_{iT}) \\ &= -T \sum_{i=r+1}^{k} \log(1 - \hat{\eta}_{iT}). \end{aligned}$$

Solution of the problem $\xi^r_{LR} = \min_{\delta} \xi^*_{LR}(\delta)$.

We have to minimize:

$$\begin{aligned} \xi^*_{LR}(\delta) &= T \log \frac{\det(\delta' Y' Y\delta)}{\det[\delta' Y'(Id - P_X)Y\delta]} \\ &= T\log \frac{\det(\delta' Y' Y\delta)}{\det[\delta' Y' Y\delta - \delta' Y' X(X'X)^{-1}X' Y\delta]}. \end{aligned}$$

Using lemmas A.1 and A.2, we are led to introduce the matrix

$$R^2(Y, X) = (Y'Y)^{-1}Y'X(X'X)^{-1}X'Y,$$

and to choose as the estimators of δ_1 $i = 1, \ldots, n - r$, for instance, the vectors $\hat{f}_{r+1,T}, \ldots, \hat{f}_{n,T}$ associated with the $n - r$ smallest eigenvalues. The corresponding value of the objective function is the same as before:

$$\begin{aligned} \xi^r_{LR} &= T \log \frac{1}{\sum_{i=r+1}^{n} (1 - \hat{\eta}_{iT})} = -T \sum_{i=r+1}^{n} \log(1 - \hat{\eta}_{iT}) \\ &= -T \sum_{i=r+1}^{k} \log(1 - \hat{\eta}_{iT}). \end{aligned}$$

Appendix 5: determination of the generalized Wald statistic of the asymptotic least squares estimators

We have to solve the problem:

$$\begin{aligned} &\max_{\alpha} \operatorname{tr}(\hat{\Omega}_T^{-1} Y' P_{X\alpha} Y) \\ \Leftrightarrow &\max_{\alpha} \operatorname{tr}[\hat{\Omega}_T^{-1} Y' X_\alpha (\alpha' X' X\alpha)^{-1} \alpha' X' Y] \\ \Leftrightarrow &\max_{\alpha} \operatorname{tr}[\alpha' X' Y \hat{\Omega}_T^{-1} Y' X_\alpha (\alpha' X' X\alpha)^{-1}]. \end{aligned}$$

The column vectors of α being defined up to a change of basis, we always can impose the normalization constraint:

$$\alpha' X' X_\alpha = Id_r$$

The problem thus becomes

$$\begin{cases} \max_{\alpha} \operatorname{tr}(\alpha' X' Y \hat{\Omega}_T^{-1} Y' X \hat{\alpha}) \\ \text{s.t. } \alpha' X' X \alpha = Id_r. \end{cases}$$

It is a problem whose solution is obtained by taking the eigenvalues $\hat{\mu}_{1T} \geqslant \ldots \geqslant \hat{\mu}_{kT}$ of $Q = (1/T)(X'X)^{-1}X'Y\hat{\Omega}_T^{-1}Y'X$ and by considering a basis of corresponding eigenvectors $\tilde{e}_{1T}, \ldots, \tilde{e}_{kT}$, which may be normalized by

$$\tilde{e}'_{iT} X' X \tilde{e}_{jT} = \delta_{ij}, \quad i, j = 1, \ldots, k.$$

Then, the solution is

$$\hat{\alpha}_{1T} = \tilde{e}_{1T}, \ldots, \hat{\alpha}_{rT} = \tilde{e}_{rT}.$$

and the optimal value of the objective function is

$$T \sum_{j=1}^{r} \hat{\mu}_{jT}.$$

Consequently the statistic ξ_W^r is equal to

$$T \sum_{j=r+1}^{k} \hat{\mu}_{jT}.$$

It remains to link the previous result to the canonical analysis procedure. For this purpose we can note that Q has the same eigenvalues as $Q^* = (1/T)\hat{\Omega}_T^{-1}Y'X(X'X)^{-1}X'Y$, and, if we note e_{jT}^* eigenvectors of Q^*, corresponding to the eigenvalues $\hat{\mu}_{jT} > 0$ and normalized by

$$e_{iT}^{*\prime} Y' X (X'X)^{-1} X' Y e_{jT}^* = \delta_{ij},$$

we can take $\tilde{e}_{jT} = (X'X)^{-1}X'Ye_{jT}^*$. It is then clear that the eigenvalues $\hat{\mu}_{jT}$ are equal to $\hat{\eta}_{jT}/(1 - \hat{\eta}_{jT})$, where the $\hat{\eta}_{jT}$ are the squared canonical correlations between Y and X. Moreover, the e_{jT}^* are the eigenvectors of $R^2(Y, X)$; this implies that the $\tilde{e}_{jT}$ are eigenvectors of $R^2(X, Y)$. Therefore, ξ_W^r is equal to

$$T \sum_{j=r+1}^{k} \hat{\eta}_{jT}/(1 - \hat{\eta}_{jT}),$$

whereas the columns of α are estimated by the eigenvectors $\tilde{e}_{1T}, \ldots, \tilde{e}_{rT}$ of $R^2(X, Y)$, satisfying the normalization conditions $\tilde{e}_{iT}X'X\tilde{e}_{jT} = \delta_{ij}$.

Let us now consider the asymptotic least squares estimator of β. We know that

$$\begin{aligned} \widehat{\operatorname{vec}} \beta' &= \{Id_n \otimes (\hat{\alpha}' X' X \hat{\alpha})^{-1} \hat{\alpha}' X'\} y \\ &= \{Id_n \otimes (\hat{\alpha}' X')\} y \quad \text{(because of the normalization condition)} \\ &\Leftrightarrow \hat{\beta} = Y' X \hat{\alpha}. \\ &\quad (Y'Y)^{-1} \hat{\beta} = (Y'Y)^{-1} Y' X \hat{\alpha}. \end{aligned}$$

Since $\hat{\alpha}_{jT}$ is an eigenvector of $R^2(X, Y)$, $(Y'Y)^{-1}Y'X\hat{\alpha}_{jT}$ is an eigenvector of $R^2(Y, X)$ associated with the same eigenvalues. Since, moreover, the normalization condition is satisfied, we have

$$(Y'Y)^{-1}\hat{\beta}_{jT} = \hat{f}_{jT} \Leftrightarrow \hat{\beta}_{jT} = Y'Y\hat{f}_{jT}$$

References

Ahn, S. and Reinsel, G. (1988) Nested reduced rank autoregressive models for multiple time series. *Journal of the American Statistical Association*, 83, 849–56.

Anderson, T. W. (1951) Estimating linear restrictions on regression coefficients for multivariate normal distributions. *Annals of Mathematical Statistics*, 22, 327–51.

Anderson, T. W. (1984) *An Introduction to Multivariate Statistical Analysis*, 2nd edn. New York: Wiley.

Anderson, T. W. and Kunitomo, N. (1992) Tests of overidentification and predeterminedness in simultaneous equation models. *Journal of Econometrics*, 54, 49–78.

Bhargava, A. (1991) Identification and panel data models with endogenous regressors. *Review of Economic Studies*, 58, 129–40.

Box, G. and Tiao, G. (1977) A canonical analysis of multiple time series. *Biometrika*, 64, 355–65.

Brown, S. (1989) The number of factors in security returns. *Journal of Finance*, 44, 1247–62.

Byron, R. P. (1974) Testing structural specification using the unrestricted reduced form. *Econometrica*, 42, 869–83.

Chamberlain, G. (1983) Funds, factors, and diversification in arbitrage pricing models. *Econometrica*, 51, 1305–23.

Chamberlain, G. and Rothschild, M. (1983) Arbitrage and mean variance analysis in large asset markets. *Econometrica*, 51, 1281–304.

Engle, R. F. and Granger, C. W. J. (1987) Co-integration and error correction: representation, estimation and testing. *Econometrica*, 55, 251–76.

Geweke, J. (1977) The dynamic factor analysis of economic time series. In D. J. Aigner and A. S. Golberger (eds), *Latent Variables in Socioeconomic Models*. Amsterdam: North-Holland.

Gill, L. and Lewbel, A. (1992) Testing the rank and definiteness of estimated matrices with applications to factor state-space and ARMA models. *Journal of the American Statistical Association*, 87, 766–76.

Gouriéroux, C., Monfort, A. and Trognon, A. (1984) Pseudo maximum likelihood methods: theory. *Econometrica*, 52, 681–700.

Gouriéroux, C. and Monfort, A. (1989a) A general framework for testing a null hypothesis in a mixed form. *Econometric Theory*, 5, 63–82.

Gouriéroux, C. and Monfort, A. (1989b) *Statistique et modèles économetriques*. Paris: Economica, 2 volumes.

Gouriéroux, C., Monfort, A. and Renault, E. (1993) Dynamic factor models. Discussion Paper, GREMAQ.

Gouriéroux, C. and Peaucelle, J. (1988) Detecting a long run relationships. Discussion paper, CEPREMAP.

Gouriéroux, C. and Peaucelle, J. (1994) Séries codépendantes: application à l'hypothèse de parité de pouvoir d'achat. *Actualités Economiques*, in the press.

Hotelling, H. (1936) Relations between two sets of variates. *Biometrika*, 28, 321–77.

Johansen, S. (1988) Statistical analysis of cointegration vectors. *Journal of Economic Dynamics and Control*, 12, 231–54.

Kugler, P. and Neusser, K. (1990) International real interest rate equalization. Discussion paper, University of Vienna.

Muirhead, R. J. (1982) *Aspects of Multivariate Statistical Theory*. New York: Wiley.

Rao, C. R. (1948) Tests of significance in multivariate analysis. *Biometrika*, 35, 58–79.

Rao, C. R. (1965) *Linear Statistical Inference and Its Applications*. New York: Wiley.

Sargent, T. and Sims, C. (1977) *Business Cycle Modeling without Pretending to Have Too Much* a priori *Economic Theory. New Methods in Business Cycle Research*. Minneapolis: Federal Reserve Bank of Minneapolis.

Szroeter, J. (1983) Generalized Wald methods for testing nonlinear implicit and overidentifying restrictions. *Econometrica*, 51, 335–53.

Tiao, G. and Tsay, R. (1989) Model specification in multivariate time series. *Journal of the Royal Statistical Society B*, 51, 157–213.

Tsay, R. and Tiao, G. (1985) Use of canonical analysis in time series model identification. *Biometrika*, 72, 299–315.

Velu, R., Reinsel, G. and Wichern, D. (1986) Reduced rank models for multiple time series. *Biometrika*, 73, 105–18.

14 Expectations: Are They Rational, Adaptive, or Naive? *An Essay in Simulation-based Inference*

Marc Nerlove and Til Schuermann

1 Introduction

There is an extensive empirical literature on how economic agents form their expectations, three popular hypotheses being adaptive, rational and naive expectations. Agents who revise their expectations by considering their past mistakes have adaptive expectations, whereas rationality implies that agents purposefully acquire and use all available information when forming their expectations. If agents look only at current realizations, they are called naive. It is usual to test these hypotheses in a time-series context, and it is common to reject all three. Instead of inferring indirectly the effects of changing expectations through observations of the aggregated outcomes of individual decisions, as is common in a time-series analysis, we have cross-sections of microlevel data on both expectations and realizations and thus test the hypotheses directly. None of the usual intuition for time series, therefore, applies. Bear in mind throughout this chapter that we are dealing with two cross-sections, and that the estimation framework is a cross-sectional one.

The monthly and quarterly business test survey (BTS) conducted by the Konjunkturforschungstelle (KOF) of Switzerland and the quarterly surveys conducted by the Confederation of British Industries (CBI) ask manufacturing firms questions concerning those firms' changes in demand, production, and prices, their expectations of future changes in these variables, and other aspects of firm behavior. Their responses are primarily ordered and categorical; that is, they answer "increase," "remains the same," or "decrease" in comparison with the previous month or quarter. As a result, standard time-series techniques for testing expectations hypotheses are not appropriate when applied directly to the categorical data.

A more appropriate approach treats the categorical responses as being triggered by latent structural variables as they move across certain thresholds (Nerlove, 1988). Traditionally, these data have been analyzed by means of conditional log-linear probability (CLLP) models which permit reduction of the parameter space to manageable size but essentially treat the data as truly discrete and unordered.

The data are arranged in a J^Q contingency table, where J is the number of categories (for the BTS model, $J = 3$) and Q the number of variables under consideration. A standard tool in the econometrician's kit for contingency table analysis is the method of minimum chi-square (see Rao, 1955). While this method may be appealing on grounds of familiarity, maximum likelihood is preferable for our application.[1] The relationships between the latent variables can be summarized in a covariance matrix that can theoretically be estimated by maximum likelihood. However, standard ML procedures are not feasible even in small models due to problems involving the computation of multidimensional integrals. This is not to say that such models have not been estimated. However, conventional econometric techniques, either the pairwise calculation of polychoric correlations (Pearson and Pearson, 1922; Olsson, 1979) by maximum likelihood (Poon and Lee, 1987) or the two-step method (Martinson and Hamdan, 1971), ignore the true multivariate nature of the data and thus bias the usual tests.

In this chapter we formulate a method for testing jointly the rational, adaptive, and naive expectations hypotheses using business survey data from two countries: Switzerland and the United Kingdom. Our work is an extension of that of Horvath et al. (1992), who test (and reject) only rationality of British manufacturing firms for several periods using numerical (*not* simulation) full-information maximum-likelihood (FIML) methods and builds on Nerlove and Schuermann (1992). In our earlier work, we rejected both the rational and adaptive expectations hypotheses using only British data. To what degree were those rejections, both in our paper and in the study by Horvath et al., particular to the British survey data? In an attempt to answer that question, we add another country, namely Switzerland, to the exercise. Nerlove and Willson did not provide a specific alternative to rational expectations. In our work, we further embed a third hypothesis, naive expectations, into the framework to give a fuller range of alternative ways in which economic agents may form their expectations.

Simulation techniques developed by McFadden (1989), Pakes and Pollard (1989), and Hajivassiliou et al. (1990) lend themselves naturally to the estimation of latent-variable models. In these papers, it is shown how various simulators can be used to calculate multivariate integrals in the context of limited dependent variable (LDV) models. In this chapter we employ the smooth recursive conditioning (SRC) simulator to obtain simulated maximum likelihood (SML) as a way of testing the joint hypothesis. The SRC has low variance, which is crucial when maximizing the likelihood function directly.

The latent variable framework as proposed originally by Nerlove (1988) is introduced in section 2. The rational, adaptive and naive expectations hypotheses are formulated in this framework. We then present formulation for joint testing.

In section 3, we discuss maximum likelihood estimation in the BTS context, where we will demonstrate the infeasibility of numerical FIML procedures and show how simulation methods may be used. In section 4, we test the joint hypothesis formulation with Swiss monthly and UK quarterly surveys of manufacturing firms. Section 5 concludes.

2 Econometric Model Formulation for Categorical Business Survey Data

Latent variable model

The categorical nature of the data requires careful construction of the econometric framework. The idea that these data are really partial information about firms' beliefs is conveniently modelled with latent variables.

Let $z_{it}^* = (y_{it}^*, x_{1it}^*, x_{2it}^*, \ldots, x_{kit}^*)'$ be a $((k + 1) \times 1)$ vector of latent dependent and independent variables that satisfies the following linear relationship:

$$y_{it}^* = x_{it}^* \beta + \varepsilon_{it} \tag{2.1}$$

where β is a $(k \times 1)$ vector of coefficients and ε_{it} is a disturbance term. We assume that $E(\varepsilon_{it}) = 0$ and that ε_{it} and x_{it}^* are uncorrelated. For firm i we observe categorical indicators $z_{it} = (y_{it}, x_{it})'$ of the unobservable latent variables $z_{it}^* = (y_{it}^*, x_{it}^*)$ such that

$$\begin{aligned} z_{ijt} &= 1 \quad \text{if } z_{jt}^* \leqslant a_{1jt} \\ &= 2 \quad \text{if } a_{1jt} < z_{jt}^* \leqslant a_{2jt} \\ &= 3 \quad \text{if } a_{2jt} < z_{jt}^*, \end{aligned} \tag{2.2}$$

where $j = 1, \ldots, k$, $k + 1$ is the total number of variables in the model.[2]

We assume further that y_t^* and x_t^* are jointly normally distributed with covariance matrix Σ.[3] Since the joint distribution of y_t^* and x_t^*, $f(y_t^*, x_t^*)$, is normal, so is the conditional distribution of y_t^* given x_t^*, $f(y_t^*|x_t^*)$. The parameter vector β in (2.1) can be inferred from $\hat{\Sigma}$ using

$$E(y_t^*|x_t^*) = \beta x_t^* \tag{2.3}$$

$$\varepsilon_t = y_t^* - E(y_t^*|x_t^*) \tag{2.4}$$

The estimated parameter $\hat{\beta}$ has the form

$$B = \Sigma_{y_t^* x_t^*} \Sigma_{x_t^* x_t^*}^{-1}. \tag{2.5}$$

It is in general not possible to identify all elements of $\theta = (\Sigma; a_{ijt}, i = 1, 2, j = 1, \ldots, k, k + 1)'$ separately from a single cross-section of data.[4] In particular, consider the contingency table obtained from the bivariate latent variable distribution $h(y^*, x^*)$ with thresholds $\{a_{y1}, a_{y2}, a_{x1}, a_{x2}\}$. This table will be identical to the one generated by the distribution $h(y^*/c_1, x^*/c_2)$ and thresholds $\{a_{y1}/c_1, a_{y2}/c_1, a_{x1}/c_2, a_{x2}/c_2\}$, where c_1 and c_2 are arbitrary constants.[5] Therefore, we may normalize each z^* to have arbitrary location and variance.[6] If all z_t^* have unit variances, then Σ is really just a matrix of $\frac{1}{2}[(k)(k + 1)]$ correlations. Maximum-likelihood estimates of θ may be obtained using theory for the estimation of polychoric correlation coefficients (Olsson, 1979), and estimates for B follow directly from (2.5) after replacing population with sample correlations. As we shall see shortly, numerical FIML estimates of θ are not feasible for $(k + 1) > 3$ latent variables due to problems associated with the calculation of multidimensional integrals; specifically, the dimension of integration is $(k + 1)$. Because the joint testing of the rational and adaptive expectations hypotheses involves *four* dimensions, alternative procedures are required. Simulation-based techniques as adapted to our data environment are outlined in section 3.

One solution to the integration problem is the so-called two-step estimator, developed by Martinson and Hamdan (1979). It estimates the thresholds, first, from the marginal frequencies by simply inverting the univariate standard normal c.d.f. The second step calculates the correlations pairwise by iterating to a root of the sample score, conditional on the first stage estimated thresholds.[7] In achieving computational feasibility, however, this method ignores the true multivariate nature of the data-generating process.

Models of expectation formation

Rational expectations

We present a brief review of the rational, adaptive, and naive expectations hypotheses and some notation before formulating the joint testing procedure. Let $y_{it}^{t} \equiv E(y_{it}|\Omega_{it-1})$ be the expectation formed by firm i at time $t - 1$ of variable y at time t conditional on their information set Ω_{it-1}.[8]

Standard rationality test usually consider one particular agent's expectations using a time series of observations $\{y_{it}, y_{it}^{e}, t = 1, \ldots, T\}$. These tests can be suitably modified for a time series of cross-sections, or, as the limitations of the data dictate, to handle serial tests based on an aggregate across firms at each particular time. We test the different hypotheses directly using cross-section techniques. Unless otherwise specified, we will write the expectations relationships in terms of the continuous latent variables, not their discrete realizations.

The essential assumption for rational expectations is that prediction errors are uncorrelated with anything in the information set Ω_{t-1}. The regression equation commonly estimated is of the form[9]

$$y_t = \alpha_0 + \alpha_1 y_t^e + \alpha_2 z_{t-1} + \varepsilon_t, \tag{2.6}$$

where z_{t-1} is usually taken to be the lagged realization, y_{t-1}, or anything else in the information set Ω_{t-1}. If the prediction error is indeed correlated with any variables in the information set, it implies that the forecaster has not used all available information. The expectations variable y_t^e depends on Ω_{t-1} and is thus uncorrelated with ε_t. Equation (2.6), with the following parameter restrictions, is well known as a test for efficiency:

$$H_0\colon \alpha_0 = \alpha_2 = 0,\ \alpha_1 = 1.$$

Alternatively, one may test only the simpler hypothesis of unbiasedness:

$$y_t = \alpha_0 + \alpha_1 y_t^e + \varepsilon_t \tag{2.7}$$

$$H_0\colon \alpha_0 = 0,\ \alpha_1 = 1.$$

By unbiasedness we simply mean that agents do not make systematic errors, which implies that forecast errors should have zero mean.

Under the null of rational expectations, one implication of (2.6) and (2.7) is that $\mathrm{Var}(y_t) = \mathrm{Var}(y_t^e) + \mathrm{Var}(\varepsilon_t)$ and hence $\mathrm{Var}(y_t) \geqslant \mathrm{Var}(y_t^e)$. In general for business surveys, the variance of realizations has been observed to be greater than for expectations. Our findings confirm this pattern.

Adaptive expectations

If an agent considers his forecasting mistakes from the past and revises his expectations about the future accordingly, then we say that he has adaptive expectations. More precisely, there is an upward or downward revision described by

$$y_{t+1}^e - y_t^e = \gamma[y_t - y_t^e] + u_t, \tag{2.8}$$

where $0 < \gamma < 1$ is the adjustment factor. As $\gamma \rightarrow 1$, the agent looks at today's realization to form tomorrow's expectation with less and less consideration of past mistakes. The hypothesis $\gamma = 1$ is often called naive expectations and is discussed below. As $\gamma \rightarrow 0$, past mistakes are increasingly ignored; there is no learning. Expression (2.8) degenerates to

$$y_{t+1}^e = y_t^e + u_t.$$

We include a residual u_t since we directly observe expectations as well as realizations. The residual may include factors that affect short-term expectations. This is consistent with the early formulation of the adaptive expectations hypothesis where the agent is presumed to be interested in expectations of long-term "normal" levels of certain variables (such as prices, for example).

Estimation of the adaptive expectations hypothesis is often done by manipulating equation (2.8) such that one arrives at an expression which contains only directly observable realizations. The parameter γ then depends on changes in realizations; it is the coefficient of past realizations in an equation explaining current realizations.

As shown in Muth (1961), the adaptive expectations in (2.8) are in fact fully rational if

$$y_t = \varepsilon_t + \gamma \sum_{i=1}^{\infty} \varepsilon_{t-i}$$

so that

$$\Delta y_t = \varepsilon_t + (\gamma - 1)\varepsilon_{t-1}.$$

That is, if y_t is generated by a moving average of i.i.d. random variables, then the agent's best forecast for y_{t+1} depends only on y_t.

Naive expectations

As we observed above, naive expectations can be considered a boundary case of adaptive expectations. Agents essentially form their expectations by looking only at current realizations. This is achieved by setting $\gamma = 1$ in (2.8):

$$y^e_{t+1} = y_t + u_t. \tag{2.9}$$

Firms believe that tomorrow's production, demand or prices will be the same as today's. While the naive expectations hypothesis may be indeed too simple to be of much use, it is often used as a benchmark against which other hypotheses are measured.

A joint formulation

Can we find a way to nest all three of these hypotheses in a larger model and test them jointly? Before explicitly formulating such a model, it is important to keep in mind exactly how the data is presented to us. All we have is a $3^{(k+1)}$ contingency table filled with observed frequencies.[10] If one casts the model into a latent variable framework as was done in the latent variable model, one can recover estimates of model parameters by assuming that all variables are jointly normally distributed and then use properties of the multivariate normal distribution to find conditional means. All that is necessary in order to construct these model parameters is an estimate of the covariance matrix. This matrix is then partitioned to recover the model parameters (see equation (2.5)). In section 3 we show how maximum likelihood can be used to estimate this covariance matrix. If we are to construct any tests of hypotheses about expectation formation, we must write them in terms of these variances and covariances, the elements of the covariance matrix Σ. What are the implied moment restrictions of the rational, adaptive and naive expectations hypotheses?

The four variables are jointly normally distributed with mean zero and covariance matrix Σ

$$\begin{bmatrix} y^1 \\ y^2 \\ y^3 \\ y^4 \end{bmatrix} \equiv \begin{bmatrix} y_t \\ y_{t-1} \\ y^e_{t+1} \\ y^e_t \end{bmatrix} \sim N\left([0], \begin{bmatrix} \sigma_{11} & \sigma_{12} & \sigma_{13} & \sigma_{14} \\ & \sigma_{22} & \sigma_{23} & \sigma_{24} \\ & & \sigma_{33} & \sigma_{34} \\ & & & \sigma_{44} \end{bmatrix} \right) \equiv N(0, \Sigma). \tag{2.10}$$

Recall the problems of identification described in for the latent variable model. For a particular variable in a multivariate latent variable model, one cannot separately identify both the thresholds and the variance. Either one restricts both the thresholds to be the same (in absolute value) and therefore identifies the variance, or the variance is restricted (to unity) and the thresholds are free parameters.

Our identifying restrictions are very similar to those made in Horvath et al. (1992), although our problem is more complex. Expectations and realizations (y_t^e and y_t respectively) of a variable are assumed to have the same threshold but different variances. Otherwise we restrict the variance to be one and allow the thresholds to vary. At the individual firm level, equivalence of thresholds for expectations and realizations means that firms use the same "yardstick" when evaluating expected future movements in y_t as well as past realizations.[11] The covariance matrix Σ is somewhat simplified to

$$\Sigma = \begin{bmatrix} \sigma_{11} & \sigma_{12} & \sigma_{13} & \sigma_{14} \\ & 1 & \sigma_{23} & \sigma_{24} \\ & & 1 & \sigma_{34} \\ & & & \sigma_{44} \end{bmatrix}. \tag{2.11}$$

The test of the rational expectations hypothesis (REH) is straightforward. Since the joint distribution of the four variables is normal, so is their conditional distribution. We are interested in the following conditional mean

$$E(y_t|y_t^e, y_{t-1}) = \alpha_1 y_t^e + \alpha_2 y_{t-1} \tag{2.12}$$

and the null hypothesis to test is

$$H_0\colon \alpha_1 = 1, \alpha_2 = 0,$$

and there is a maintained hypothesis that α_0, the intercept term, is equal to zero, required for identification of the model in latent variable form. However, note that the completely unrestricted formulation as expressed by (2.11) contains an additional variable, namely y_{t+1}^e. Implicitly, the REH assumes that y_{t+1}^e does not affect y_t. In other words, in the following conditional mean expression,

$$E(y_t|y_t^e, y_{t-1}, y_{t+1}^e) = \alpha_1 y_t^e + \alpha_2 y_{t-1} + \alpha_3 y_{t+1}^e, \tag{2.13}$$

the coefficient $\alpha_3 = 0$. This merely states that future expectations do not affect current realizations. It is indeed not appropriate to include future expectations in a test of the REH. Restricting $\alpha_3 = 0$ in (2.13) is our way of excluding y_{t+1}^e in the conditional expectation of the current value y_t. Of course, in the completely unrestricted alternative (2.11), which is more general than rational expectations, future expectations *are* allowed to affect current realizations although not necessarily in simple linear fashion. But clearly this is different.

What would it mean if $\alpha_3 \neq 0$? A nonzero α_3 could be the consequence of an incomplete model, in which some unmeasured variables that affect both y^e_{t+1} and y_t are left out. Since it would be unfair to burden the REH test with the inclusion of future expectations and this form of model misspecification, an alternative to the REH test as described by (2.12) sets $\alpha_3 = 0$ in (2.13) and estimates α_1 and α_2 freely. Furthermore, we will test this modified alternative against the completely unrestricted model described by (2.11). Our finding that this and, indeed, all restricted models are rejected in favor of the completely unrestricted model simply means that all simple models of expectation formation are misspecified.

The test of the adaptive expectations hypothesis (AEH) is almost as simple. Recall that we are interested in

$$y^e_{t+1} - y^e_t = \gamma[y_t - y^e_t] + u_t,$$

which is equation (2.8). We need to assume that u_t is uncorrelated with y_t and y^e_t. Again, taking into account the multivariate setup, the conditional expectation of interest is

$$E(y^e_{t+1}|y^e_t, y_t) = \beta_1 y^e_t + \beta_2 y_t. \tag{2.14}$$

We test the restriction:

$$\beta_1 + \beta_2 = 1,$$

where $\beta_1 = (1 - \gamma)$ and $\beta_2 = \gamma$, presuming $0 < \gamma < 1$. We call this the strong form of the AEH. Again, the completely unrestricted model contains an additional variable: y_{t-1}. The appropriate alternative against which to test the AEH is given by

$$E(y^e_{t+1}|y^e_t, y_t, y_{t-1}) = \beta_1 y^e_t + \beta_2 y_t + \beta_3 y_{t-1}, \tag{2.15}$$

where the restriction $\beta_3 = 0$ is imposed. We call this the weak form of AEH where future expectations are related to past expectations and current realizations (but *not* lagged realizations). The strong form puts a particular restriction on this relation, namely that $\beta_1 + \beta_2 = 1$. In section 4 we first test the weak form against the completely unrestricted model and then proceed to the test of the strong against the weak form.

Finally, recall that we obtain naive expectations by setting $\gamma = 1$ in (2.8). Thus, we test the null of NEH by looking at the conditional expectations

$$E(y^e_{t+1}|y_t) = \delta y_t \qquad (2.16)$$

and testing for $\delta = 1$. As with the other two hypotheses of expectation formation, we need to consider an appropriate alternative given that there are two other variables in the model: y_{t-1} and y^e_t. We write the appropriate alternative as

$$E(y^e_{t+1}|y^e_t, y_t, y_{t-1}) = \delta_1 y^e_t + \delta_2 y_t + \delta_3 y_{t-1}, \qquad (2.17)$$

where the restriction $\delta_1 = \delta_2 = 0$ is imposed and δ_3 is estimated freely.

We need to ask what the unrestricted model means and what it implies about the alternative hypothesis. Although the rational and adaptive expectations hypotheses are not nested one inside the other, in our representation they are both nested in a more general expectations formation framework. This general formulation simply says that realizations (y_t), lagged realizations (y_{t-1}), future expectation (y^e_{t+1}), and expectations (y^e_t) are jointly related, whereas the rational and adaptive expectations hypotheses state that realizations and expectations are related in a particular way. By contrast, in more conventional analyses the alternative to the rational expectations hypothesis in isolation simply states that expectations are *not* rational; one has, in fact, no idea what they may be if the null of rational expectations is rejected. In our case, the alternative is estimated. The alternative is that *all* three expectations models, RE, AE, and NE, are misspecified.

A given variable of this set of four variables, y_t, y_{t-1}, y^e_{t+1}, and y^e_t, may contain information about the others. Unobserved information reflected in future expectations may affect current realizations. What does one expect this information to be for the case of the rational or adaptive expectations hypothesis? Do expectations (and only expectations) influence realizations? Do expectations and realizations (but not lagged realizations) influence future expectations? Our formulations allows us to answer such questions within one structure: the covariance matrix of the four variables of interest. The most general hypothesis is that all four variables depend on some information in common but not directly observed.

Covariance restrictions

Recall that any model parameter restriction must be written in terms of a set of covariance restrictions on Σ. The assumption of multivariate normality allows us to write the conditional expectations of interest, in other words precisely the expectations hypotheses, in terms of submatrices of the covariance matrix Σ. Of course, the identifying restrictions made above are incorporated.

Rational expectations We proceed from the less to the more restrictive model. The least restrictive alternative is described by (2.13). It is

$$E(y_t|y_t^e, y_{t-1}, y_{t+1}^e) = \alpha_1 y_t^e + \alpha_2 y_{t-1} + \alpha_3 y_{t+1}^e,$$

with the only restriction being $\alpha_3 = 0$. Following the notation of (2.9), we write the conditioning variables in slightly different order

$$E(y_t|y_{t-1}, y_{t+1}^e, y_t^e) = \begin{bmatrix} 1 & \sigma_{23} & \sigma_{24} \\ & 1 & \sigma_{34} \\ & & \sigma_{44} \end{bmatrix}^{-1} \begin{bmatrix} \sigma_{12} \\ \sigma_{13} \\ \sigma_{14} \end{bmatrix} = \begin{bmatrix} \alpha_2 \\ \alpha_3 \\ \alpha_1 \end{bmatrix}.$$

The implied covariance restrictions are

$$\sigma_{13} = \sigma_{23} = \sigma_{24} = \sigma_{34} = 0.$$

Thus we estimate the following covariance matrix

$$\begin{bmatrix} \sigma_{11} & \sigma_{12} & 0 & \sigma_{14} \\ & 1 & 0 & 0 \\ & & 1 & 0 \\ & & & \sigma_{44} \end{bmatrix}$$

For the null of rational expectations, we consider the conditional expectation (2.12),

$$E(y_t|y_t^e, y_{t-1}) = \alpha_1 y_t^e + \alpha_2 y_{t-1},$$

with the restrictions that $\alpha_1 = 1$ and $\alpha_2 = 0$. This yields the following additional covariance restrictions

$$\sigma_{12} = 0, \quad \sigma_{14} = \sigma_{44} \equiv \bar{\sigma}.$$

Thus, the covariance matrix that is estimated is of the form

$$\begin{bmatrix} \sigma_{11} & 0 & 0 & \bar{\sigma} \\ & 1 & 0 & 0 \\ & & 1 & 0 \\ & & & \bar{\sigma} \end{bmatrix}$$

Adaptive expectations Again, we proceed from the less to the more restrictive model. The AEH alternative, or its weak form, as described by (2.15), is

$$E(y_{t+1}^e|y_t^e, y_t, y_{t-1}) = \beta_1 y_t^e + \beta_2 y_t + \beta_3 y_{t-1},$$

with $\beta_3 = 0$ being the only restriction. To follow the notation of (2.10), we write the conditioning variables in slightly different order

$$E(y^e_{t+1}|y_t, y_{t-1}, y^e_t) = \begin{bmatrix} \sigma_{11} & \sigma_{12} & \sigma_{14} \\ & 1 & \sigma_{24} \\ & & \sigma_{44} \end{bmatrix}^{-1} \begin{bmatrix} \sigma_{13} \\ \sigma_{23} \\ \sigma_{43} \end{bmatrix} = \begin{bmatrix} \beta_2 \\ \beta_3 \\ \beta_1 \end{bmatrix}.$$

The implied covariance restrictions are

$$\sigma_{12} = \sigma_{23} = \sigma_{24} = 0.$$

Thus, we estimate the following covariance matrix

$$\begin{bmatrix} \sigma_{11} & 0 & \sigma_{13} & \sigma_{14} \\ & 1 & 0 & 0 \\ & & 1 & \sigma_{34} \\ & & & \sigma_{44} \end{bmatrix}.$$

For the null of the strong form of adaptive expectations, we consider the conditional expectation given by (2.14)

$$E(y^e_{t+1}|y^e_t, y_t) = \beta_1 y^e_t + \beta_2 y_t,$$

with the restriction $\beta_1 + \beta_2 = 1$. The implied additional covariance restrictions are

$$\sigma_{14} = 0, \quad \sigma_{13} = 1 - \sigma_{34}.$$

The covariance matrix that is estimated is of the form

$$\begin{bmatrix} \sigma_{11} & 0 & (1 - \sigma_{34}) & 0 \\ & 1 & 0 & 0 \\ & & 1 & \sigma_{34} \\ & & & \sigma_{44} \end{bmatrix}.$$

Naive expectations The NEH alternative, as described by (2.17), is

$$E(y^e_{t+1}|y_t, y_{t-1}, y^e_t) = \delta_1 y_t + \delta_2 y_{t-1} + \delta_3 y^e_t$$

with the restriction $\delta_1 = \delta_2 = 0$ and δ_3 being estimated freely. To follow again the notation of (2.10), we write the conditioning variables in slightly different order than (2.17)

$$E(y^e_{t+1}|y_t, y_{t-1}, y^e_t) = \begin{bmatrix} \sigma_{11} & \sigma_{12} & \sigma_{14} \\ & 1 & \sigma_{24} \\ & & \sigma_{44} \end{bmatrix}^{-1} \begin{bmatrix} \sigma_{13} \\ \sigma_{23} \\ \sigma_{43} \end{bmatrix} = \begin{bmatrix} \delta_2 \\ \delta_3 \\ \delta_1 \end{bmatrix}.$$

The implied covariance restrictions are

$$\sigma_{12} = \sigma_{14} = \sigma_{23} = \sigma_{34} = 0.$$

So the covariance matrix we estimate is

$$\begin{bmatrix} \sigma_{11} & 0 & \sigma_{13} & 0 \\ & 1 & 0 & \sigma_{24} \\ & & 1 & 0 \\ & & & \sigma_{44} \end{bmatrix}.$$

For the null of naive expectations, consider the conditional expectation given by (2.16)

$$E(y^e_{t+1}|y_t) = \delta_3 y_t,$$

with the restriction that $\delta_3 = 1$. The implied additional covariance restrictions are

$$\sigma_{11} = \sigma_{13} = \bar{\sigma}.$$

The covariance matrix which we estimate for the null of naive expectations is

$$\begin{bmatrix} \bar{\sigma} & 0 & \bar{\sigma} & 0 \\ & 1 & 0 & \sigma_{24} \\ & & 1 & 0 \\ & & & \sigma_{44} \end{bmatrix}.$$

3 Maximum Likelihood Estimation

The sample likelihood

In section 2 we outlined a structural latent variable model which is useful for estimation with business survey data. Following equation (2.1), the data can be arranged into a $3^{(k+1)}$ contingency table, where $(k + 1)$ is the total number of variables in the model. A useful way of writing down the likelihood is to consider that there are $M = 3^{(k+1)}$ different regimes. Any given observation can fall into only one cell in the M-cell contingency table. Thus, if we let n_j be the frequency (or the number of observations) in the jth cell (or the jth regime), then the model likelihood is

$$\ln l(\theta) = \mathrm{C} + \sum_{j=1}^{M} n_j \ln \pi_j(\theta),$$

where C is a constant of proportionality, and the parameter vector θ contains all thresholds and covariances. For the purpose of this chapter, $(k + 1) = 4$, and therefore we have $M = 81$ regimes.

Let us consider the form of the log-likelihood for the simple bivariate case. The data will fall into a *3* × *3* contingency table. Let n_{rs} be the frequency associated with the *rs*th cell, and let π_{rs} be the probability that an observation falls into the cell *rs*.[12] The log-likelihood is

$$\begin{aligned} \ln l(\theta) \propto\ & n_{11} \ln \pi_{11} + n_{12} \ln \pi_{12} + n_{13} \ln \pi_{13} \\ & + n_{21} \ln \pi_{21} + \ln \pi_{22} + n_{23} \ln \pi_{23} \\ & + n_{31} \ln \pi_{31} + n_{32} \ln \pi_{32} + n_{33} \ln \pi_{33}. \end{aligned} \tag{3.1}$$

The associated score can be written as

$$\partial \ln l(\theta)/\partial\theta = \sum_{i=1}^{3} \sum_{s=1}^{3} [W_{rs}(n_{rs} - \pi_{rs})] \tag{3.2}$$

where

$$W_{rs} = \partial \ln \pi_{rs}/\partial\theta = 1/\pi_{rs}\partial\pi_{rs}/\partial\theta. \tag{3.3}$$

We can think of (3.3) as a weighted residual, the residual $[n_{rs} - \pi_{rs}(\theta)]$ being the deviation of the sample frequency from its expectation.

As Hajivassiliou and McFadden (1990) and others have pointed out, the primary obstacle to computing the ML estimates for θ is the calculation of the probabilities π_{rs} which appear both linearly and nonlinearly in the likelihood and score expressions. Each of these probabilities involves integration over a $(k + 1)$-dimensional space. It will be instructive to consider this integration more carefully.

The computational barrier

The computational barrier for latent variable and multinomial probit (MNP) models is reached when the degree of integration is greater than three. However, even in the case of a trivariate latent variable or a four-alternative MNP model, the computational burden is considered to be exceptionally high. To illustrate the problem of integration, let us look at a particular probability expression of the bivariate latent variable BTS model more closely.

$$E(n_{23}) = \pi_{23} = \Pr(y = 2, x = 3) = \Pr(a_{y1} < y^* \leqslant a_{y2}, a_{x2} < x^*) \tag{3.4}$$

Rewrite this probability as

$$\begin{aligned} \pi_{23} &= \int_{a_{x2}}^{\infty} \int_{a_{y2}}^{a_{y2}} f(y^*, x^*) dy^* dx^* \\ &= \iint I(a_{y1} < y^* \leqslant a_{y2}, a_{x2} < x^*) f(y^*, x^*) dy^* dx^*, \end{aligned} \tag{3.5}$$

where $I(.)$ is the indicator function, $f(x^*, y^*)$ is the bivariate normal density, and the range of integration for the second part of (3.5) is the entire real plane. This can be rewritten in a more general form as

$$\Pr(D(z); \mu, \Sigma) = \int_{D(z)} N(z - \mu, \Sigma)dz \equiv E_z[I(z \in D(z))], \quad (3.6)$$

where z is a normal $(k + 1)$-dimensional vector with mean μ and covariance matrix Σ, and $N(.)$ is the multivariate normal density. $I(z \in D)$ is the indicator function defined for the event $D(z) = \{z|a_1 < z < a_2\}$. A leading case is the negative orthant probability which is particular to the MNP model, where the conditioning region $D(z) = \{z|z < 0\}$. Hajivassiliou et al. (1991) outline and compare several simulators designed to estimate the probabilities π and their derivatives.

Simulated maximum likelihood (SML)

The idea of using simulations for estimation in a maximum-likelihood context is not new. Lerman and Manski (1981), in the case of the MNP model, attempted to maximize the likelihood function directly by simulating the probability expressions which appeared in the likelihood function. The simulated maximum likelihood (SML) approach does not yield unbiased estimates of the parameters of interest for a fixed number of replications. The reason for this is that, because of the concavity of the logarithm transformation, the probabilities do not enter the likelihood function expression linearly, so neither do the simulation errors of those probabilities.[13] If we denote $\tilde{l}$ as a simulator for the likelihood $\tilde{l}$, then $E\tilde{l} = l$. However, $B(\tilde{l}) \equiv E(\log \tilde{l}) - \log(E\tilde{l}) = -(\mathrm{Var}(\tilde{l}))/2l^2 < 0$ (see Börsch-Supan and Hajivassiliou, 1990). The bias depends on the variance of $\tilde{l}$ (the simulation noise), which will be positive for any finite number of replications.[14]

As we will estimate a four-dimensional model with fourteen parameters (six free thresholds, six covariances and two free variances), the complexity and number of first-order conditions is rather high. To make efficient use of MSM for the estimation of moment conditions such as (3.2) for a general weight matrix would require the simulation of good instruments. McFadden (1989) stresses that this weight matrix be constructed using simulations that are independent of $\pi(\theta)$. In the MNP case, he suggests using a polynomial of the regressors for an initial W and constructing the ideal W only in the final iteration. We cannot do this, for we do not have regressors in the conventional sense. The computational burden for the construction of the ideal W at each iteration across θ would be very high indeed.

Hajivassiliou and McFadden (1990) have devised a method for simulating directly the score of the likelihood contribution (this is called the method of simulated scores – MSS). It was developed for the estimation of LDV models and is based on a suggestion by Ruud (1986) that the score for the general linear exponential model can be written as conditional expectations which can be simulated directly. Since the BTS model has no regressors in the conventional sense, the score expression *cannot* be written in terms of conditional expectations. We thus settle for SML despite its poorer asymptotic properties.[15]

To employ conventional optimization routines which maximize the likelihood function directly. we needed a simulator with very low variance to minimize $B(\tilde{l})$. The SRC turns out to fit the bill and is described below.

Some simulation procedures

The crude frequency simulator (CFS)

To illustrate the basic simulation procedure, consider the simplest of the simulators, the crude frequency simulator (CFS), outlined by McFadden (1989). Write the random vector z as

$$z = \mu + \Gamma\eta, \tag{3.7}$$

where μ is an M-dimensional vector of means, η is an i.i.d. standard normal vector of dimension M, and Γ is a lower triangular Cholesky factor of Σ such that $\Sigma = \Gamma\Gamma'$. A simple approach for approximating the probability in (3.5) or in (3.6) is to make repeated Monte Carlo draws for η, use (3.7) to calculate z for each parameter vector, and then retain that fraction which satisfies the indicator function $I(D(z))$, in other words that which falls into the conditioning region $D(z)$. The expression for the CFS for a given probability is simply

$$\hat{\pi} = \frac{1}{R}\sum_{r=1}^{R} I(z \in D(Z)). \tag{3.8}$$

The CFS has several shortcomings. One significant limitation is that, for small π which appear in the denominator of the matrix W_{rs} in (3.3), the simulator may not be stochastically bounded. Moreover, although the CFS is unbiased, it can be very inefficient. Hajivassiliou discusses alternative methods, such as antithetic and control variates, which can greatly improve the performance of this and other simulators.[16]

A second problem is that minor perturbations of the parameter θ will not effect $\hat{\pi}(\theta)$ smoothly. Instead we may get discrete jumps in the simulated probabilities $\hat{\pi}$. These jumps are due to the inherently discontinuous nature of the indicator function. This can also be seen from expression (3.5), which is an expectation of an indicator function; this is *not* a smooth object. A more practical consequence is that the lack of smoothness will prevent us from implementing the usual gradient methods to compute an estimate for θ. A large number of draws may serve to smooth the discontinuity of a single draw. However, that number may indeed be impractically large, particularly for small π.

The smooth recursive conditioning (SRC) simulator

Geweke (1989) and Keane (1990) independently proposed algorithms to compute random variates from a multivariate truncated normal distribution by reducing the multidimensional frequency simulator to a recursive sequence of multivariate acceptance/rejection draws. Hajivassiliou and McFadden (1990) modified this procedure to allow for smooth simulation of the score of a likelihood contribution.

The essence and tractability of this approach relates the manner in which it exploits the fundamental relationship between the joint, conditional, and marginal probability distributions. It is a straightforward application of Bayes' rule.

Suppose one were interested in drawing a series $\{y_i^*\}$ from the truncated M-dimensional multivariate normal distribution

$$Y^* \sim N(0, \Omega) \text{ s.t. } a \leqslant Y^* \leqslant b \equiv D(Y^*),$$

where Ω is a positive definite matrix.[17] Let L be the lower Cholesky factor of Ω such that $LL' = \Omega$.

We will construct a draw from this M-dimensional variable and its associated probability one dimension at a time. In the end we will have

$$e_{(M\times 1)} \sim N(0, I) \text{ s.t. } a \leqslant Le \leqslant b.$$

We will draw these e_is sequentially using an application by Hajivassiliou and McFadden (1990) of the integral-transform theorem. The main difficulty will be in the construction of the thresholds.

Let us consider the first draw, e_1. We need

$$\begin{aligned} e_1 \sim N(0, 1) \text{ s.t. } a_1 &\leqslant l_{11}e_1 \leqslant b_1 \\ a_1/l_{11} &\leqslant e_1 \leqslant b_1/l_{11} \\ \tilde{a}_1 &< e_1 < \tilde{b}_1, \end{aligned}$$

where l_{ii} is the ith diagonal of L, and a_i and b_i are the ith row of the threshold vector a and b respectively. How do we obtain this initial e_1? Here we appeal to a proposition in Hajivassiliou and McFadden (1990). Let u be uniformly distributed on the unit interval. Then

$$z \equiv G(u)^{-1} = \Phi^{-1}[(\Phi(b) - \Phi(a)) \cdot u + \Phi(a)]$$

is distributed $N(0, 1)$ s.t. $a \leqslant z \leqslant b$ since the corresponding c.d.f. is

$$G(z) = \frac{\Phi(z) - \Phi(a)}{\Phi(b) - \Phi(a)}.$$

It is important to note that z is a continuous and differentiable function of the thresholds a and b.[18]

The first draw, e_1, is found by

$$e_1 = \Phi^{-1}[\Phi(\tilde{b}_1) - \Phi(\tilde{a}_1)) \cdot u + \Phi(\tilde{a}_1)]. \tag{3.9}$$

e_1 will be used to construct e_2:

$$e_2 \sim N(0, 1) \text{ s.t. } a_2 \leqslant l_{21}e_1 + l_{22}e_2 \leqslant b_2$$
$$(a_2 - l_{21}e_1)/l_{22} \leqslant e_2 \leqslant b_2 - l_{21}e_1/l_{22}$$
$$\tilde{a}_2 \leqslant e_2 \leqslant \tilde{b}_{21}.$$

Having defined the appropriate thresholds, we apply Hajivassiliou and McFadden's proposition again to find e_2. This is repeated M times until we have filled the entire e vector. In general we have

$$e_j \sim N(0, 1) \text{ s.t. } a_j \leqslant l_{j1}e_1 + \ldots + l_{jj-1}e_{j-1} + l_{jj}e_j \leqslant b_j.$$

The joint p.d.f. of e is

$$\prod_{j=1}^{M}\left[\frac{\phi(e_j)}{Q_j(e_1, \ldots, e_{j-1})}\right],$$

where $\phi(.)$ is the standard normal p.d.f. and Q_j is the probability content of the jth interval of e_j over an $N(0, 1)$. More precisely,

$$Q_j = \Pr(\tilde{a}_j \leqslant e_j \leqslant \tilde{b}_j | e_1 e_2, \ldots, e_{j-1})$$
$$= \Phi(\tilde{b}_j) - \Phi(\tilde{a}_j).$$

Why is this true? First, note that the e_js are *not* independent by construction. Thus,

$$f(e_1, e_2, \ldots, e_M) = f(e_1) \cdot f(e_2|e_1) \cdot \ldots \cdot f(e_M|e_{M-1}\, e_{M-2}, \ldots, e_1)$$
$$= f(e_M|e_{M-1}\, e_{M-2}, \ldots, e_1) \cdot f(e_1, \ldots, e_{M-1})$$

which follows directly from Bayes' rule. By design, all densities are truncated standard normals over different ranges. It follows

$$f(e_1) = \phi(e_1)/Q_1, f(e_2|e_1) = \phi(e_m|e_2)/Q_2, \ldots, f(e_{M-1}, \ldots, e_1) \\ = \phi(e_M)/Q_M.$$

Finally, the simulator for a given observation is denoted by

$$\tilde{l}_i \equiv \frac{1}{R}\sum_{r=1}^{R}\prod_{j=1}^{M} Q_j[e_{1r}, \ldots, e_{j-1r}], \tag{3.10}$$

where R is the number of replications. Börsch-Supan and Hajivassiliou (1990) show that this simulator is unbiased for $R = 1$.

McFadden stresses the importance of recycling random numbers to reduce "chatter," in other words to use the same string of uniform random variates in (3.10) for each iteration.[19] This turns out to be particularly important when using a numerical optimization routine (such as Newton–Raphson, for instance) to maximize a likelihood function which contains simulated probabilities. If the (pseudo) random variates u change across iterations over the parameter vector θ, the optimization routine cannot distinguish between changes in the objective function induced by changes in θ and those induced by a different set of draws of u.

4 Testing the Expectations Hypotheses with Swiss and British Survey Data

The data

Do Swiss and British manufacturing firms form their expectations adaptively, rationally, naively, or in some other way? We attempt to answer that question here. Horvath et al. (1992) use price realizations and expectations with data from the UK survey to test forecast rationality. In this chapter, we use demand in the form of incoming orders instead. The reasoning is simple: since the vast majority of firms surveyed are in manufacturing, it is unlikely that they operate in anything near to a perfectly competitive market. These firms are therefore quite likely to be price setters rather than price takers. Demand may be less under their direct control and therefore less endogenous to their own actions. We would like to point out that the notion of whether the firm has control over prices and demand is a question of degree, and, from this standpoint, demand seems more attractive. If a test is based on prices, in effect it tests whether expectations, *on the basis of which prices are set*, are rational, adaptive, or neither.

The Swiss survey is conducted monthly whereas the British one is quarterly.[20] In addition, the horizon over which expectations are taken are different for the two surveys. The KOF asks firms what their expectations are for the following *three* months while the CBI asks firms to consider a *four*-month horizon. To adjust for the different surveying frequencies, we used the October survey for the fourth quarter equivalent and January for the first quarter equivalent, etc. The UK sample consists of 1008 manufacturing firms for the fourth quarter of 1986 ($t - 1$) and the first quarter of 1987 (t). The Swiss sample contains 942 firms.

Some Monte Carlo experimentation suggests that $R = 20–30$ replications for the simulator are sufficient, and the marginal gain from raising R to 100 is negligible. We thus settle for $R = 50$. The appendix gives parameter estimates for the completely unconstrained model. Of principal interest to us, however, are not the point estimates themselves but rather the value of the log-likelihood at the respective constrained and unconstrained optima.

The tests for the REH, AEH, and NEH are performed sequentially. In section 2 we discussed the implications of the completely unconstrained model (2.10) and the respective alternatives to the two null hypotheses. It is important to keep in mind that each expectations hypothesis's alternative is nested in the completely unconstrained model, and that, of course, each null is in turn contained in its alternative. We find that *all* null hypotheses can be rejected.

The tests

Tables 14.1 and 14.2 contain a summary of the results. For both Switzerland and the UK, we reject the adaptive, rational, and naive expectations hypotheses. Furthermore, we reject their respective alternatives against the completely unrestricted model. For both countries, the rejection of the AEH is the weakest of the three, but whether this is meaningful or not is not clear since all hypotheses are rejected with *p*-values of less than 0.001. The British data lead to stronger rejections of the hypotheses than do the Swiss data. These findings are in accord with the work of Horvath et al. (1992), who reject rationality consistently for 18 quarters of UK surveys, as well as the findings in our earlier work where we reject both rational and adaptive expectations for the British data alone.

Table 14.1 Log-likelihoods

	Switzerland	*United Kingdom*
$l(\Sigma_1)$	−3624.64	−3849.69
$l(\Sigma_1^{REH})$	−3658.49	−3908.84
$l(\Sigma_0^{REH})$	−3698.32	−4012.02
$l(\Sigma_1^{AEH})$	−3632.46	−3928.19
$l(\Sigma_0^{AEH})$	−3674.92	−4001.33
$l(\Sigma_1^{NEH})$	−3654.33	−3982.73
$l(\Sigma_0^{NEH})$	−3688.47	−4009.17

The notation of the log-likelihood values is:
$l(\Sigma_1)$: completely unrestricted model (equation 2.11)
$l(\Sigma_1^{REH})$: REH alternative (equation 2.13)
$l(\Sigma_0^{REH})$: REH null (equation 2.12)
$l(\Sigma_1^{AEH})$: AEH alternative (equation 2.15)
$l(\Sigma_0^{AEH})$: AEH null (equation 2.14)
$l(\Sigma_1^{NEH})$: NEH alternative (equation 2.17)
$l(\Sigma_0^{NEH})$: NEH null (equation 2.16).

Table 14.2 LR statistics

$\lambda(r)$	*Switzerland*	*United Kingdom*
$\bar{\lambda}^{REH}$ (4)	67.6	118.3
λ^{REH} (2)	79.66	206.36
$\bar{\lambda}^{AEH}$ (3)	15.54	157.0
λ^{AEH} (2)	84.92	146.28
$\bar{\lambda}^{NEH}$ (4)	59.38	266.08
λ^{NEH} (1)	68.28	52.88

$\lambda(r)$ is the likelihood ratio statistic distributed asymptotically $\chi^2(r)$, where r is the number of restrictions (here, the number of covariance restrictions).

$\bar{\lambda}^{REH}$: test of unconstrained model against REH alternative

λ^{REH}: test of the REH alternative against the REH null
The notation is similar for the AEH and NEH cases. In all cases the p-value is less than 0.001.

5 Summary and Conclusion

Business test surveys provide us with microlevel data on firms' realizations *and* expectations about such variables as prices, demand and production. The data are in the form of a J^Q contingency table, where J is the number of categories and $Q = (k + 1)$ the number of variables in the model under investigation (for us, $J = 3$ and $Q = 4$). It is useful and convenient to cast the model into a latent variable framework, in which the relationship between the latent variables can be summarized in a covariance matrix that can theoretically be estimated by maximum likelihood. When the number of variables in the model $(k + 1)$ exceeds three, conventional numerical methods are no longer feasible due to $(k + 1)$-dimensional probability expressions which appear in the likelihood. We employ the smooth recursive conditioning simulator to conduct simulated maximum likelihood. This technique is used to test the rational, adaptive, and naive expectations hypotheses against an estimable alternative using two microlevel cross-sections of adjacent quarterly surveys of British and monthly surveys three months apart of Swiss manufacturing firms. We find that we can strongly reject all three hypotheses in favor of a specific alternative which describes a joint relation of current and future expectations and current and lagged realizations. This means that *all* three expectations hypotheses, REH, AEH, and NEH, are misspecified.

All our conclusions rest on the assumption of multivariate normality. To what extent is this assumption too strong? Horvath et al. (1992) perform goodness of fit (GFI) tests and reject the null of normality for the case of three dimensions. It is therefore quite likely that we too would fail GFI tests for joint normality. This begs the question: is the rejection of all three expectations hypotheses a result of a general model misspecification, or rather of a simple violation of the underlying distributional assumptions? Moreover, the survey responses are, as is commonly the case, lumped in the "no change" category, which may cause normality to fail. We are currently exploring seminonparametric procedures which allow for a richer distributional class than normality. For the present our rejection of the rational, adaptive, as well as naive, expectations hypotheses is conditional on normality. As is, of course, always the case when modelling or doing hypothesis testing, until we can be more certain of the validity of our distributional assumption, we cannot be sure of the rejection of the stated expectations hypotheses.

We have demonstrated that simulation procedures are readily applied to models and problems employing business surveys. Because the survey data are categorical, inference is a difficult task. With simulation techniques such as those used here, larger and more complex models can be estimated with relative ease. In fact, simulation methods applied to large MNP models have demonstrated the feasibility of 20 or higher dimensional integration. This four-dimensional example should encourage other researchers using business survey data to estimate more complex models.

Appendix

We present here the point estimates for the unrestricted model. In addition to the variance and covariance terms given in (2.10), there are also the relevant thresholds for the latent variables. These thresholds are estimated for *all* models. Recall

$$\begin{bmatrix} y^1 \\ y^2 \\ y^3 \\ y^4 \end{bmatrix} \equiv \begin{bmatrix} y_t \\ y_{t-1} \\ y_{t+1}^e \\ y_t^e \end{bmatrix} \sim N\left([0], \begin{bmatrix} \sigma_{11} & \sigma_{12} & \sigma_{13} & \sigma_{14} \\ & 1 & \sigma_{23} & \sigma_{24} \\ & & 1 & \sigma_{34} \\ & & & \sigma_{44} \end{bmatrix}\right).$$

The identifying restrictions yield the following thresholds to estimated:

$$y_t\colon\ -a_1,\ a_4$$

$$y_{t-1}\colon\ a_{21},\ a_{22}$$

Table 14.3 Point estimates of unrestricted model

	Switzerland	*United Kingdom*
a_1	0.829	0.513
a_4	0.641	0.895
a_{21}	−0.536	−0.739
a_{22}	0.558	0.429
a_{31}	−0.819	−0.496
a_{32}	1.101	1.371
σ_{11}	1.934	1.418
σ_{44}	0.549	0.779
σ_{12}	−0.037	0.532
σ_{13}	0.104	0.104
σ_{14}	0.114	0.331
σ_{23}	0.083	0.045
σ_{24}	0.112	0.202
σ_{34}	0.227	0.327

$$y^e_{t-1}: a_{31}, a_{32}$$

$$y^e_t: -a_1, a_4.$$

The results are summarized in table 14.3.

Standard errors are not given in table 14.3 because the estimated Hessian of the log-likelihood was not positive definite. We believe this to be due to the small number of observations for such a large contingency table (81 cells). We have done some experiments with 50 000 artificially generated data points where the likelihood was very well behaved and standard errors were very small (asymptotic t-ratios in excess of 20). The reader should bear in mind that it is not the point estimates, after all, that are of interest for the hypothesis testing but rather the values of the log-likelihoods.[21]

Notes

We would like to thank Vassilis Hajivassiliou, Roberto Mariano, Melvyn Weeks, Douglas Willson, Frank de Jong, Viktoria Dalko, an anonymous referee, and, particularly, Jon Breslaw for helpful comments. We would also like to thank the Konjunkturforschungstelle (KOF) of Switzerland and the Confederation of British Industry (CBI) of the UK for providing access to their survey data for 1986–7. All remaining errors are ours. This chapter extends our earlier work in Nerlove and Schuermann (1992).

1 For a discussion of first-order asymptotic equivalence of minimum chi-square and maximum likelihood, see Rao (1961, 1963). For a direct comparison of these two methods in a simulation context, see Schuermann (1993).

2 The conditions under which the categorical survey responses for expectations and realizations can be considered as independent draws from an aggregate distribution are developed in Theil (1952). In addition to cross-sectional independence, the major requirement is that individual firm's reporting thresholds are identical.

3 The notation y_t^* and x_t^* indicates that we stack over firms.

4 Our discussion of identification ignores the issue of sampling zeroes in the contingency table. While there are some empty cells, our samples are sufficiently large to ensure that their number is relatively small (always fewer than 10 out of 81).

5 The same logic holds with respect to a nonzero mean of the latent variables. The contingency table obtained from $h(y^*, x^*)$ and thresholds $\{a\}$ will be identical to that obtained from $h(y^* - \mu_y, x^* - \mu_x)$ and thresholds $\{a - \mu\}$ (see also Horvath et al., 1992).

6 Specific assumptions of thresholds and variances are treated later. In some instances we can relax the unit variance assumption if we then restrict the thresholds to be equal.

7 Nerlove et al. (1993) point out that the information matrix, evaluated at $\hat{\Sigma}$, provides a biased estimate of the variance–covariance matrix of the

estimator because it ignores the fact that the thresholds are estimated in the first stage. Olsson (1979) presents Monte Carlo evidence suggesting that the bias is not substantial.

8 Given cross-sectional independence, $E(y_{it}|\Omega_{it-1}) = E(y_{it}|\Omega_{t-1})$, where $\Omega_{t-1} = \cup_{i=1}^{N}\Omega_{it-1}$.

9 For a survey of empirical tests of the rational expectations hypothesis, see Lovell (1986).

10 For the four variable case, that means that we have 81 numbers to work with, 80 of which are independent. The frequency count in the 81st cell is simply the total number of firm responses minus the total count in the first 80 cells.

11 The variance of the latent variable underlying the conditional expectations will be less than or equal to that of the realization under rational expectations since $\text{Var}(y_t) = \text{Var}(y_t^e) + \text{Var}(\varepsilon_t)$. It is therefore desirable to allow those variances be free parameters in the estimation.

12 Thus, $\pi_{rs} = \Pr(y = r, x = s) = E(n_{rs})$.

13 This result is a straightforward application of Jensen's inequality.

14 When we say that consistency and asymptotic unbiasedness is achieved for a finite number of replications R, we mean

$$\hat{\theta}_R - \theta_0 = 0(1/\sqrt{n}),$$

whereas in the SML case we need R and n to go to infinity, but at rate $\sqrt{n}/R$;

$$\hat{\theta}_R - \theta_0 = 0(\sqrt{n}/R).$$

See also Gouriéroux and Monfort (1991) for a special case of the simulated pseudo ML estimator which is consistent for finite R.

15 One may reduce the (small sample) bias of the SML estimator by incorporating a bias correction factor which will be a function of the variance of the simulator itself. Recall that $B(\tilde{l}) = -\text{Var}(\tilde{l})/2l^2$. Rewrite this as $\lambda\,\text{Var}(\tilde{l})$, where $\lambda = (2l^2)^{-1}$. We know $\text{Var}(\tilde{l})$; it is simply the variance of the simulated probability across R replications, and $\lambda \in (\frac{1}{2}, \infty)$. We have found the gain to be minimal for various (small) values of λ. For alternative bias corrections procedures, see Brown (1992).

16 Lerman and Manski used the CFS to maximize a likelihood function directly in the case of the MNP model. They found the CFS to perform very poorly because consistency of the estimator is achieved only as *both* R (the number of replications) and N (the sample size) increase without bound.

17 Börsch-Supan and Hajivassiliou (1990) outline the notationally more complex case of a nontrivial mean.

18 Note that for $a = -\infty$ and $b = +\infty$, $G(z)$ collapses to $\Phi(z)$.

19 This is to satisfy certain regularity conditions such as bounded simulation bias and equicontinuity in the parameter of interest θ (McFadden, 1989, pp. 998–9).

20 The KOF also conducts a quarterly survey which asks, among other things, questions on price expectations and realizations.

21 A program written in GAUSSX is available from the authors.

References

Börsch-Supan, A. and Hajivassiiou, V. (1990) Smooth unbiased multivariate probability simulators for maximum likelihood estimation of limited dependent variable models. Cowles Foundation discussion paper no. 960.

Breslaw, J. A. and McIntosh, J. (1991) Multivariate analysis of ordered categorical data. Mimeo, Concordia University.

Brown, B. W. (1992) Simulation-based inference in nonlinear systems with errors-in-variables. Mimeo, Rice University.

Brown, B. W. and Mariano, R. S. (1990) Stochastic simulations for inference in nonlinear errors-in-variables models. Mimeo, University of Pennsylvania.

Geweke, J. (1990) Efficient simulation from the multivariate normal and student distributions subject to linear constraints. Mimeo, University of Minnesota.

Gouriéroux, C. and Monfort, A. (1991) Simulation-based inference. INSEE working paper no. 37/G301.

Hajivassiliou, V. and McFadden, D. L. (1990) The method of simulated scores for the estimation of LDV models with an application to external debt crisis. Cowles Foundation discussion paper no. 967.

Hajivassiliou, V. and McFadden, D. L. and Ruud, P. (1990) Simulation of multivariate normal orthant probabilities: methods and programs. Mimeo, Yale University.

Horvath, B., Nerlove, M. and Willson, D. (1992) A reinterpretation of direct tests of forecast rationality using business survey data. Mimeo, University of Pennsylvania.

Ivaldi, M. (1990) Statistical methods and business surveys. In J. P. Florens, M. Ivaldi, J.-J. Laffont and F. Laisney (eds), *Microeconometrics: Surveys and Applications*. Oxford: Basil Blackwell, pp. 85–122.

Keane, M. P. (1990) A computationally practical simulation estimator for panel data, with applications to estimating temporal dependence in employment and wages. Mimeo, University of Minnesota.

Lerman, S. R. and Manski, C. F. (1981) On the use of simulated frequencies to approximate choice probabilities. In C. F. Manski and D. L. McFadden (eds), *Structural Analysis of Discrete Data with Econometric Applications*. Cambridge, MA: MIT Press, pp. 305–19.

Lovell, M. C. (1986) Test of the rational expectations hypothesis. *American Economic Review*, 76, 110–24.

McFadden, D. L. (1989) A method of simulated moments for estimation of discrete response models without numerical integration. *Econometrica*, 57, 995–1026.

Martinson, E. O. and Hamden, M. A. (1971) Maximum likelihod and some other asymptotically efficient estimators of correlation in two-way contingency. *Journal of Statistical Computation and Simulation*, 1, 544–65.

Muth, J. F. (1961) Rational expectations and the theory of price movements. *Econometrica*, 29, 315–35.

Nerlove, M. (1983) Expectations, plans and realizations in theory and practice. *Econometrica*, 51, 1251–79.

Nerlove, M. (1988) Analysis of business-test survey data by means of latent variable models. In W. Franz, W. Gaab and J. Walters (eds), *Theoretische und Angewandte Wirtschaftsforschung, Heinz König zum 60*. Heidelberg: Springer-Verlag.

Nerlove, M., Ross, D. and Willson, D. (1993) The importance of seasonality in inventory models: evidence from survey data. *Journal of Econometrics*, 55, 105–28.

Nerlove, M. and Schuermann, T. (1992) Testing a simple joint hypothesis of rational and adaptive expactations with business surveys: an exercise in simulation-based inference. Presented at Conference on Econometric Inference Using Simulation Techniques, Erasmus University, Rotterdam, June.

Nerlove, M. and Weeks, M. (1992) The construction of multivariate probability simulators with an application to the multinomial probit model. Mimeo, University of Pennsylvania.

Olsson, U. (1979) Maximum likelihood estimation of the polychoric correlation coefficient. *Psychometrica*, 44, 443–60.

Pakes, A. (1986) Patents as options: some estimates of the value of holding European patent stocks. *Econometrica*, 54, 755–84.

Pakes, A. and Pollard, D. (1989) Simulation and the asymptotics of optimization estimators. *Econometrica*, 57, 1027–57.

Pearson, K. and Pearson, E. S. (1922) On polychoric coefficients of correlation. *Biometrika*, 14, 127–56.

Poon, W. Y. and Lee, S. Y. (1987) Maximum likelihood estimation of multivariate polyserial and polychoric correlation coefficients. *Psychometrica*, 52, 409–30.

Rao, C. R. (1955) Theory of the method of estimation by minimum chi-square. *Bulletin de l'Institut Statistique International*, 35, 25–32.

Rao, C. R. (1961) A study of large sample test criteria through properties of efficient estimators. *Sankhya*, 23, 25–40.

Rao, C. R. (1963) Criteria of estimation in large samples. *Sankhya*, 25, 189–206.

Ruud, P. A. (1986) On the method of simulated moments for the estimation of limited dependent variable models. Mimeo, University of California at Berkeley.

Schuermann, T. (1993) Three essays in simulation-based econometrics: methods, expectations and ARCH. PhD dissertation, University of Pennsylvania.

Theil, H. (1952) On the time shape of economic micro-variables and the munich business test. *Revue de l'Institute Internationale de Statistique*, 20, 105–20.

Willson, D. (1991) Inventory investment: international evidence from business survey data. Mimeo, Concordia University.

15 Tests of Some Hypotheses about the Time Series Behavior of Commodity Prices

Pravin K. Trivedi

1 Introduction

The important topic of commodity prices attracts attention in economics from macro- and microeconomists, development economists, and finance specialists. Markets for primary commodities are often regarded as a close first approximation to rapidly equilibrating "auction markets," and hence are studied in depth by theoretical and empirical microeconomists. Since many less-developed countries rely heavily on the revenues generated by commodity exports, and since the extreme volatility of commodity prices generates corresponding volatility to export revenues, commodity price behavior is of great interest to development economists and policymakers. From a long-run viewpoint, the movements in the prices of commodities relative to those of industrial goods is also a topic of importance. Finance specialists tend to view primary commodities as tradeable assets. This viewpoint is relevant when one considers the possible role of futures markets in commodity price stabilization. This raises issues such as the role of speculation on financial markets in reducing or amplifying price volatility. These issues illustrate the diverse motivations for studying commodity markets from alternative viewpoints.

This chapter examines certain hypotheses about the time series behavior of commodity prices. These hypotheses do not derive from one single economic model reflecting a coherent perspective of how commodity markets function. Rather, each hypothesis emphasizes different facets of commodity markets. A common element in these themes is that they pose challenging problems of econometric estimation and testing, which is the main emphasis of this chapter. The main part of the chapter consists of three distinct and loosely related sections; each deals with certain hypotheses from a specific perspective. I shall begin by sketching the literature context within which these hypotheses arise and mention some of the leading contributions in each area.

An important approach to the study of commodity markets is based on the so-called *competitive* (or *speculative*) *storage model* developed by Gustafson (1958) and Samuelson (1971). The basic model of this literature is a supply–demand model in which commodity speculators with rational price expectations have a demand for inventories. A key feature of this model, the nonnegativity constraint applying to commodity inventories, which precludes the possibility of carrying forward negative inventories, generates highly nonlinear behavior of commodity prices. Samuelson showed that the model generates a nonlinear first order autoregressive process for prices. Important later contributions to this literature include Wright and Williams (1982) and Williams and Wright (1991). In an important recent contribution, Deaton and Laroque (1992) attempt to test the adequacy of this theory to explain the actual behavior of 13 commodity prices using annual data from 1900 through 1988. The centerpiece of their empirical investigation is also a nonlinear first order autoregression in prices, which they estimate and whose empirical adequacy they evaluate. In this chapter I shall also examine the behavior of commodity prices, but from a rather statistical viewpoint, by focusing on the nature of *nonlinear dependence* in the annual commodity price series, with specific reference to the autoregressive model examined by Deaton and Laroque. My objective is to model the nonlinearities in the conditional variance function and to compare this approach with that which concentrates on the nonlinearity in the conditional mean function.

My second focus is concerned with the hypothesis of *excess co-movement* of commodity prices. This hypothesis arises in the literature which treats primary storable commodities as financial assets because they are frequently traded on futures exchanges. The returns on these assets are expected to exhibit co-movements which reflect the common impact of macroeconomic variables on all commodity prices. In addition to their dependence on market fundamentals, these returns can also be influenced by an irrational "herd" or "fad" mentality of traders in the financial markets. Is there any evidence that such irrational trading behavior is an important explanation of actual commodity price movements?

The third and final focus of this chapter is an empirical reexamination of the *Prebisch–Singer hypothesis*. Secular trends in commodity prices have attracted considerable attention from economists since Prebisch (1950) and Singer (1950) proposed that the net barter terms-of-trade (NBTT) between primary commodity producers and manufactures have deteriorated over the long run. The issue, which ultimately relates to considerations of the distribution of world income and welfare, is of obvious importance in the context of North–South economic relations. There have been several previous statistical investigations (e.g. Spraos, 1980; Sapsford, 1985; Grilli and Yang, 1988; Cuddington and Urzua, 1989; Perron, 1990), but they have not led to a satisfactory resolution of the debate. Both fixed and stochastic trends have been tried, and the conclusion has not been found robust with respect to these formulations. I shall reexamine the issue using the newer econometric techniques of Perron (1989, 1990) and Zivot and Andrews (1992), to see whether these can narrow the range of disagreement.

Despite the attention received from empirical economists, all three issues remain open. My reexamination of these issues uses techniques of inference which have not been tried before. The detailed examination of the three hypotheses is in sections 3, 4 and 5; this is preceded by a brief section on the descriptive characteristics of the commodity price data, which provides a useful background for sections 3 and 4.

2 A Preliminary Look at the Data

Figure 15.1 displays annual time series of 12 commodities to illustrate some salient features of commodity prices. Three notable features of these time series are nonlinearity, non-Gaussianity, and asymmetry. Nonlinearity here refers to the phenomenon which causes periods of quiescent movements, akin to those of serially correlated but stationary processes, to be puntuated by periods of high volatility, characterized by occasional sharp spikes that break the preexisting serial correlation pattern and are strongly suggestive of a nonlinearity of the underlying data generating process (d.g.p.). Sudden sharp increases in commodity prices, easily of the order of 20 to 30 percent within a month, are at odds with the assumption of an underlying linear Gaussian d.g.p. The asymmetry feature of the time series refers to the fact that the increases above the long run average are typically much larger than the decreases, and the price spikes are relatively infrequent, which might lead one to anticipate problems in modelling this feature of the data. There is substantial empirical evidence that nonlinearity and non-Gaussianity are pervasive in commodity price models (see von Hagen, 1989; Williams and Wright, 1991; Deaton and Laroque, 1992). An econometric challenge is to model such a process using the insights provided by the relevant economic theory.

Well established *a priori* reasons for expecting the time series of some argicultural commodity prices to exhibit strong nonlinearity and non-Gaussianity come from the *competitive storage model* with speculators holding rational expectations. The model, which is further explained in the next section, can explain the presence of occasional spikes in the spot price observed when it jumps to a level much higher than the long-run average. Such occasional sharp upward movements are not always matched by similar downward movements, the typical increase in price being larger than the typical decrease. Consequently, the distribution of prices for storable commodities is skewed. As Williams and Wright (1991, p. 159) observe: "because storage is asymmetric – able to support a glut but not alleviate every shortage – changes in spot prices are asymmetric. Once that nonlinearity and that nonnormality are admitted, it follows that standard ARMA procedures and standard *t*-tests and *F*-tests are inappropriate, at least to some extent. Thus there is a tension from the outset when discussing commodity prices as linear, gaussian stochastic processes." These observations motivate investigations of nonlinear dependence in commodity prices.

In this section we take a preliminary descriptive look at the data set used in section 3 of this chapter. This is the set of annual observations for the period 1900–88 for 13 primary commodities whose nominal US dollar prices were deflated by the US CPI. I use annual data to overcome the complications of seasonally varying supplies of agricultural commodities that would affect higher frequency data. The main features of the annual commodity price data, summarized in table 15.1, are high serial correlation (reflected in the first order autocorrelation coefficient given in column 1 of table 15.1), predominantly positive skewness (as reflected in the skewness coefficient of column 3), and large nonnormal kurtosis for nearly half of the 13 commodities (reflected in the excess kurtosis column). The last two features together lead to unconditional nonnormality of the observations. The high price volatility of several commodities, especially cocoa, palm oil, and sugar,

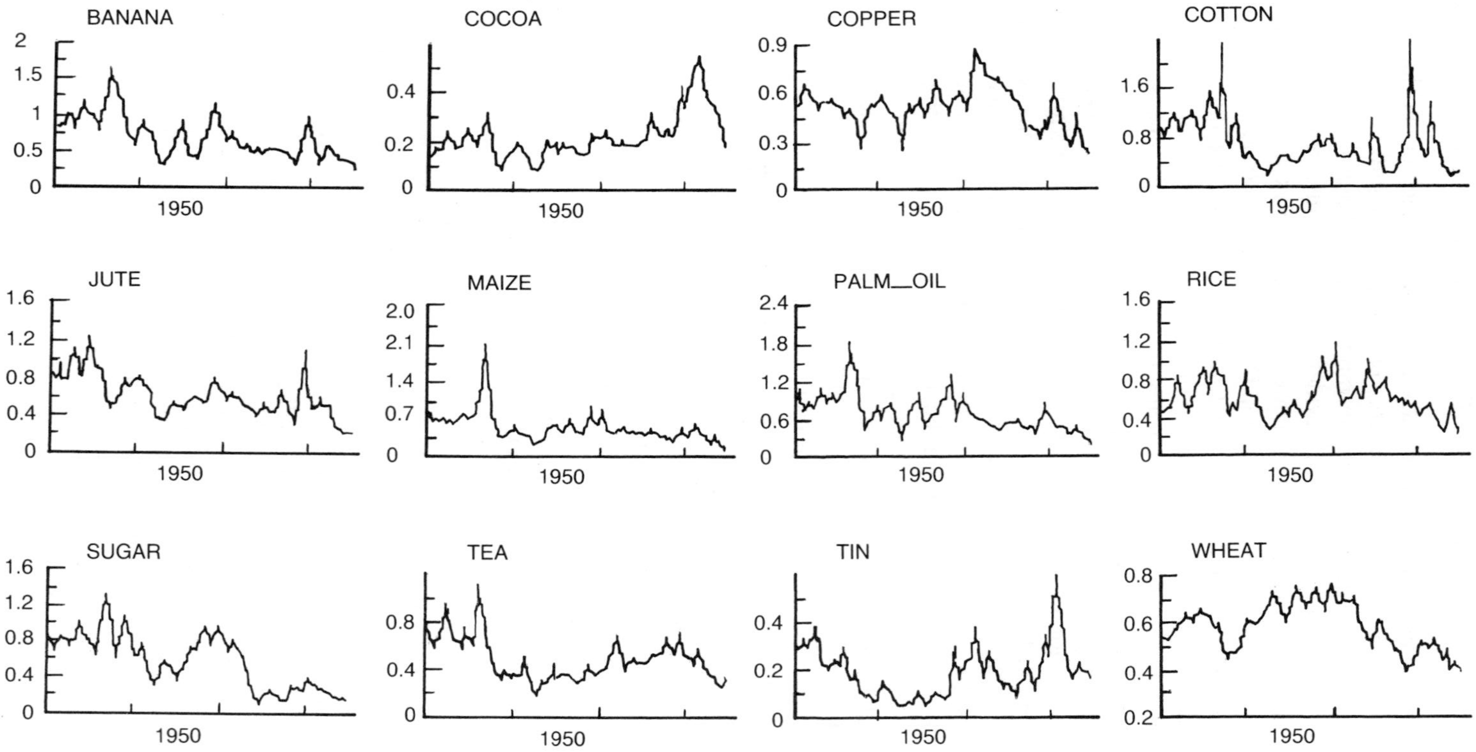

Figure 15.1 Index of real commodity prices, 1900–88.

is further reflected in the coefficient of variation close to, or in excess of, 0.5. The autocorrelation coefficients of order 2, 3, and 4 are also given. If the underlying d.g.p. were a random walk these coefficients should decline very slowly, reflecting the high degree of persistence of the process. But, it fact, with a possible exception of bananas, they decline rather rapidly, casting doubt that the underlying process is a random walk. On the other hand, as noted by Williams and Wright (1991), these "stylized facts" are consistent with the predictions of a time stationary competitive storage model of commodity prices.

The summary statistics in table 15.1 cannot provide insights into the source of nonlinear dependence in commodity prices, which is the topic of section 3. For econometric modelling, an immediate issue is whether to model nonlinearities through the conditional mean of the price regression, or through its conditional variance, or both. Nonlinear time series models in which the focus is on modelling "volatility" in terms of the past history of the process, such as the so-called GARCH

Table 15.1 Commodity prices, descriptive statistics, annual data 1900–88

	a–c coefficients (1–4) (1)	*c.v.* (2)	*Skewness* (3)	*Excess kurtosis* (4)
Bananas	0.93; 0.80; 0.72; 0.62	0.17	−0.13	−1.03
Cocoa	0.83; 0.65; 0.57; 0.49	0.54	1.00	1.18
Coffee	0.79; 0.60; 0.49; 0.35	0.45	1.65	3.72
Copper	0.83; 0.62; 0.53; 0.47	0.38	1.03	0.86
Cotton	0.90; 0.66; 0.54; 0.51	0.35	0.35	−0.00
Jute	0.72; 0.44; 0.42; 0.28	0.32	0.63	0.22
Maize	0.78; 0.52; 0.38; 0.26	0.38	1.14	2.33
Palm oil	0.74; 0.47; 0.30; 0.23	0.48	3.16	16.33
Rice	0.83; 0.60; 0.49; 0.43	0.37	0.53	−0.03
Sugar	0.62; 0.38; 0.36; 0.06	0.60	1.49	3.03
Tea	0.83; 0.58; 0.46; 0.42	0.26	−0.01	−0.02
Tin	0.86; 0.74; 0.64; 0.50	0.41	1.63	3.01
Wheat	0.88; 0.66; 0.51; 0.37	0.39	0.86	0.56

Notes: (1) first four autocorrelation coefficients; (2) coefficient of variation; (3) skewness coefficient, defined as $\mu_3/\mu_2^{1.5}$, where μ_j denotes the jth central moment; (4) measure of excess kurtosis, $(\mu_4/\mu_2^2) - 3$.

model ("generalized autoregressive conditional heteroskedasticity"), is currently very popular in economics and finance. By contrast, time series models with nonlinear conditional mean function, as, for example, in the bilinear class of models (Granger and Andersen, 1978; Tong, 1990), are much less used, partly due to the difficulties associated with identification and estimation of these models.

For preliminary guidance into the inadequacy of the linear model, I begin by conducting diagnostic tests on the simple first order regression for the commodity price variables listed in table 15.1. Using Rao's (1947) well-known score test principle, widely known in econometrics as the Lagrange multiplier test, we can easily test for the presence of ARCH(1) dependence in the errors (Engle, 1982) and for bilinearity (Weiss, 1986).[1] These test statistics are given in table 15.2. For five of the 13 commodities (coffee, cotton, jute, palm oil, and rice) the ARCH(1) test is highly significant; for five commodities (copper, cotton, palm oil, rice, and sugar) the bilinearity test indicates de-

Table 15.2 LM tests of nonlinear dependence, AR(1) specification

	ARCH	*Bilinarity*
Bananas	0.50	0.79
Cocoa	0.88	1.83
Coffee	21.43	0.60
Copper	1.50	3.57
Cotton	7.29	19.02
Jute	4.12	2.19
Maize	0.00	0.62
Palm oil	24.14	42.06
Rice	20.06	5.83
Sugar	1.65	13.49
Tea	1.11	0.31
Tin	2.97	2.34
Wheat	0.08	8.70

Notes: Each reported test statistic is distributed as $\chi^2(1)$ on the null hypothesis of independence against the alternative of dependence of the type specified under each column. The score version of ARCH(1)) test is due to Engle (1982) and that for bilinearity is due to Weiss (1986).

partures from linearity. Since these tests are known to have power in directions other than those tested, and are likely to be correlated, it seems reasonable to conclude that there is a basis for considering more general alternatives that incorporate nonlinearities in the conditional mean and variance.

3 Nonlinear Dependence in Commodity Prices

The model of Deaton and Laroque

I shall use Deaton and Laroque (1992) as a starting point. This model is in the market clearing supply–demand tradition. Each period prices, denoted by P_t, adjust to equate demand with supply, which consists of current harvests, denoted by z_t, and inventories carried over from the past, denoted by I_{t-1}; $I_{t-1} \geqslant 0$ is the nonnegativity constraint. Inventories are held by competitive speculators in the expectation of making profits. The model assumes that harvests (z) are i.i.d. over time. Carrying inventories is costly, and inventories have a per period "depreciation" rate of δ. Hence the per period cost of inventory is $\theta \equiv (1 - \delta)/(1 + r)$, $\theta < 1$ if $\delta > 0$, where r is constant real market interest rate. Zero inventories are carried if the expected profit from a unit of inventories is less than the price; inventories are nonnegative if the expected profit from carrying them is positive.

The authors prove a theorem on the existence of a unique stationary rational expectations equilibrium. They also show the existence of two regimes for the price process. In the first of these, which corresponds to a "stockout," $p_t \geqslant p^*$, $I_t = 0$, and p_{t+1} will be independent of p_t and will depend only on the harvest, z_{t+1}, through the function $f(z_{t+1})$. Thus p^* is interpreted as the time-invariant price level above which the price process ceases to display any autoregressive dependence. In the second regime, which corresponds to commodity "glut," $p_t \leqslant p^*$, $I_t > 0$, and the price process is a first order autoregression. The cut-off between the two regimes is defined by the price level p^*, assumed constant, at which the unit of inventory carried forward yield zero expected profit. That is, the price equation is as follows:

$$p_{t+1} = f(z_{t+1}) \quad \text{if } p_t \geqslant p^*, \tag{3.1}$$

$$p_{t+1} = \theta^{-1} p_t + \varepsilon_{t+1} \quad \text{if } p_t < p^*, \tag{3.2}$$

$$p^* = \theta \cdot \mathbb{E}[f(z)]. \tag{3.3}$$

where ε_{t+1} denotes an innovation (not necessarily i.i.d.). Deaton and Laroque estimate the parameters (θ, p^*) of a "switching" first order autoregression,

$$p_{t+1} = \theta^{-1}\min(p_t, p^*) + \varepsilon_{t+1}, \tag{3.4}$$

by the generalized method of moments.

The above model leads to a price equation with a nonlinear conditional mean. The nonlinearity can potentially account for the price spikes that are a conspicuous feature of the data. However, the empirical success of the model is dependent upon one's ability to identify the parameter p^* in the data, and this is difficult whenever there are only a few data points above the cut-off p^*. That is, if the stockout phenomenon is relatively rare, then the nonlinearity is harder to identify. The empirical results of Deaton and Laroque show that they are able to replicate important features of the data. Their estimated θ is close to 1 in most cases, and p^* has a relatively large standard error. However, the model also has some predictable deficiencies acknowledged by the authors. For example, there is more first order serial correlation in p_t than is explained by the model, which suggests possible misspecification of the model. The assumed constancy of p^*, derived from the assumption of i.i.d. harvests and a completely inelastic supply curve, may be too strong an assumption. The assumption that speculators have no advance information about the harvests is also not plausible for tree crops like cocoa, coffee, palm oil, and tea. Further, though the model assumes perfect competition, it is known that there were periods of policy intervention, in the form of international price agreements, marketing monopolies, and buffer stock schemes, that affected the price movements; examples include cocoa, coffee, wheat, and copper. Having said this, it is less easy to predict the direction of failure of the estimated model resulting from the failure of these assumptions.

An alternative specification for the price process

Note that according to the Deaton–Laroque specification the term ε_{t+1} in (3.4) is *not* assumed to be i.i.d. Hence one may consider alternative error specifications that also might account for heteroskedasticity, nonnormal kurtosis and patterns of nonlinear dependence in the price process. I propose to evaluate the adequacy of the following alternative time series model for prices, subsequently referred to as AR(1)–ARCH(1) specification:

$$p_t = \phi_0 + \phi_1 p_{t-1} + u_t, \quad (3.5)$$

$$u_t = \eta_t \sqrt{h_t}, \quad (3.6)$$

$$\eta_t \sim t(v), \quad (3.7)$$

$$h_t = \alpha_0 + \alpha_1 u_{t-1}^2. \quad (3.8)$$

The assumptions are $\mathbb{E}(u_t|\Phi_{t-1}) = \sqrt{h_t}\,\mathbb{E}(\eta_t|\Phi_{t-1}) = 0$, and $\text{var}(u_t|\Phi_{t-1}) = h_t \text{var}(\eta_t|\Phi_{t-1}) = h_t(v/(v-2))$ for $v > 2$, and $\Phi_{t-1} = \{p_{t-1}, p_{t-2}, \ldots\}$. That is, I specify a linear first order autoregression with ARCH(1) (first order autoregressive conditional heteroskedastic) errors in which the innovations follow, conditional on the information set Φ_{t-1}, a Student's $t(v)$ distribution with the degrees of freedom parameter v; $v > 2$ for the variance to exist and $v > 4$ for the fourth moment to exist. I choose the conditional $t(v)$ error distribution in preference to the normal distribution because, in line with prior expectations, the price distributions display considerable excess kurtosis.

The above specification is simply the well-known ARCH(1) regression model commonly used in studies of volatility. Its appeal is based in part on its ability to capture persistence in volatility, a feature absent in Deaton and Laroque's empirical treatment though consistent with their model. In contrast to Deaton and Laroque, the model assumes a time-invariant conditional mean function, but time-varying conditional variance. This specification may appear to be rather *ad hoc* and atheoretic. On the other hand, an ARCH process has a number of plausible alternative interpretations. An AR(1) price process in which the autoregressive parameter is random will have an algebraic structure similar to that given by (3.5) to (3.8). The price model (3.4) implies a discrete shift between two regimes; by contrast, the assumption that the autoregressive parameter varies randomly may lead to a model with a less sharp nonlinearity, but which may be an improved approximation if the assumptions of the competitive storage model are too stringent.

The random coefficient interpretation of the AR(1)–ARCH(1) specification is not unique. Bera and Higgins (1993) summarize other interpretations, including the one based on a close affinity between the bilinear and ARCH models. Bilinear models provide a more natural alternative to the Deaton–Laroque model. Unfortunately, however, they are difficult to identify and estimate, so I shall maintain the focus on the AR(1)–ARCH(1) formulation.

Table 15.3 provides maximum likelihood estimates of the parameters $(\phi_0, \phi_1, \alpha_0, \alpha_1, v)$ for the 13 commdities. The AR(1) parameter varies

Table 15.3 Estimates of AR(1)–ARCH(1) model based on $t(v)$ errors

	ϕ_0	ϕ_1	α_0	α_1	v	NR^2
Bananas	0.0289	0.949	0.0016	0.000	3.72	
	(0.004)	(0.072)	(0.0003)	(0.000)	(3.45)	–
Cocoa	0.0129	0.901	0.0014	0.773	3.24	
	(1.423)	(15.382)	(1.963)	(2.853)	(4.31)	0.32
Coffee	0.0887	0.755	0.0112	0.632	2.69	
	(3.652)	(12.651)	(1.472)	(1.404)	(3.72)	0.90
Copper	0.0917	0.774	0.0046	0.771	4.09	
	(3.317)	(11.663)	(2.444)	(2.410)	(1.88)	4.72
Cotton	0.0137	0.959	0.0086	0.550	2.95	
	(0.858)	(30.608)	(1.919)	(1.577)	(3.36)	6.58
Jute	0.1505	0.726	0.0142	0.271	6.22	
	(3.418)	(9.910)	(3.662)	(1.268)	(1.44)	0.87
Maize	0.1555	0.776	–	–	–	
	(2.826)	(10.842)				
Palm oil	0.0562	0.878	0.0056	0.795	3.50	
	(1.547)	(12.452)	(2.287)	(3.446)	(3.42)	0.27
Rice	0.0576	0.876	0.0102	0.532	3.05	
	(1.810)	(16.493)	(1.966)	(1.552)	(3.13)	2.65
Sugar	0.0881	0.818	0.0562	0.765	2.52	
	(2.473)	(12.297)	(1.629)	(2.653)	(7.04)	0.04
Tea	0.0509	0.880	0.0033	0.590	4.03	
	(1.552)	(15.183)	(2.604)	(2.054)	(2.21)	0.06
Tin	0.0438	0.785	0.0010	0.954	2.99	
	(4.391)	(17.106)	(2.091)	(12.289)	(4.38)	4.55
Wheat	0.0703	0.848	0.0124	0.715	2.83	
	(2.594)	(19.987)	(1.586)	(2.129)	(4.44)	2.63

Note: Asymptotic "t-ratio" is given in parenthesis. The NR^2 column gives the $\chi^2(1)$ test tatistic for the null of zero serial correlation of residuals.

between 0.7 and 0.96; the ARCH(1) parameter is always positive and varies between the low value close to zero and the high value of about 0.8. In general the AR(1) parameter is smaller than in Deaton and Laroque. However, if, like Deaton and Laroque, I were to exclude the intercept in the regression the AR(1) parameter would be larger and almost always much closer to 1. The other qualitative features of the model would not change much. In most cases the ARCH effect is quite pronounced and significant at conventional significance levels. The degrees of freedom parameter ν is estimated to be around 3 or 4, which confirms the prior expectations of non-Gaussianity, but which is also consistent with the nonexistence of the fourth moment of the error distribution, a result somewhat similar to that found in several empirical finance studies.

As a model diagnostic test, I tested for the presence of first order serial correlation in the residuals. The test procedure used here is the Rao-type LM procedure due to Bera et al. (1992); assuming correctly specified ARCH process, the test statistic is the $\tau_1 = NR^2$ from the regression of standardized residuals $\hat{\eta}_t$ on $\hat{\eta}_{t-1}$, which has a $\chi^2(1)$ distribution under the null of zero serial correlation. The test statistic is also given in table 15.2. In three cases, copper, cotton and tin, the test shows significant serial correlation. Interestingly, table 4 in Deaton and Laroque, which presents Durbin–Watson statistics for their estimated models, also suggests a presence of serially correlated errors in several cases, i.e. cotton, wheat, rice, and coffee. Thus, the AR(1)–ARCH(1) model does not seem to be an unreasonable model for these data.

Testing for asymmetry

Section 2 quoted Williams and Wright (1991), who emphasized asymmetry in the response of price to shocks; in times of stockouts the response is sharp, but in times of glut it is weak. Following Nelson (1991), who proposed the exponential GARCH (EGARCH) model, it is possible to formulate the asymmetry hypothesis for the conditional variance. Equation (3.8) is replaced by the following EARCH(1) specification:

$$\log(h_t) = \alpha_0 + \omega\eta_{t-1} + \varphi[|\eta_{t-1}| - \mathbb{E}|\eta_{t-1}|]. \qquad (3.8a)$$

This specification ensures nonnegativity of h_t. The asymmetry in the response of h_t arises because the innovation in $\log(h_t)$, which is piecewise linear in η_{t-1}, is $(\omega + \varphi)\eta_{t-1}$ when $\eta_{t-1} > 0$, and is $(\omega - \varphi)\eta_{t-1}$ when $\eta_{t-1} < 0$. The ω parameter is the asymmetry parameter and the

φ parameter is the ARCH parameter. If $\omega < \varphi$, then a positive η_{t-1} increases volatility, and a negative η_{t-1} decreases volatility. If one associates a positive η_{t-1} with a stockout, and a negative η_{t-1} with a glut, then the implication of $\omega < \varphi$ would be that the response of price volatility to a positive price shock would be greater in times of stockouts and much less in times of glut. This is consistent with the prediction of the competitive storage model.

The AR(1)–EARCH(1) model may be estimated under the normality assumption $\eta_t \sim N(0, 1)$, but a more fat-tailed distribution is *a priori* preferred. Nelson (1991) suggested the generalized error distribution (g.e.d.) with an additional parameter $(1/\kappa)$, $\kappa < 1$, as a possibility, but this may not be satisfactory if, as is the case here, the data display very high kurtosis. The model was estimated by maximum likelihood under normality and g.e.d. assumptions, but the constraint $\kappa < 1$ was violated for a number of commodities, so meaningful estimates were not obtained. Therefore I shall only emphasize the results obtained for the former case.

Table 15.4 gives the estimates of the AR(1)–EARCH(1) model. Only the estimates of the asymmetry and the ARCH parameters are reported as the AR(1) parameter estimates are similar to those in table 15.3; log-likelihood values for AR(1)–EARCH(1) and AR(1)–ARCH(1) are given to facilitate crude comparisons. Note that only in the case of copper, maize, jute, and tin is the log-likelihood higher for the EGARCH model. The asymmetry parameter is significant and positive in six cases (cocoa, copper, maize, sugar, tin, wheat) whereas the ARCH parameter is significant in five cases (copper, maize, sugar, tea, tin). These results are less clear-cut than for the AR(1)–ARCH(1) specification because of the relative large standard errors. The ARCH parameter is larger than the asymmetry parameter in the case of copper, cotton, maize, palm oil, sugar, tea, and tin, and this may be interpreted as evidence in favor of an asymmetric ARCH effect.

Two remarks will conclude this section. Several predictions of the competitive storage model get broad support from the models in this section. The models considered here only use data on the commodity price history, which may be the reason why a model with a time-varying conditional variance rather than the mean seems to do just as well in explaining the historical data. If that model were to incorporate the time-varying conditional variance feature, this aspect could be better investigated. Further, since the identification of nonlinearity depends in some cases on only a few data points, caution is advised in interpreting the results.

Table 15.4 Estimates of AR(1)–EARCH(1) model based on normal errors

	ω *(asymmetry parameter)*	φ *(ARCH parameter)*	*Log-likelihood AR(1)–EARCH(1)/ AR(1)–ARCH(1)*
Bananas	−0.012	−0.115	160.08/164.03
	(0.076)	(0.399)	
Cocoa	0.616	0.094	130.25/140.37
	(4.424)	(0.459)	
Copper	0.345	0.686	83.85/81.11
	(1.623)	(2.560)	
Cotton	0.197	0.416	75.55/82.69
	(0.922)	(1.569)	
Jute	0.477	0.122	55.42/52.98
	(0.171)	(0.395)	
Maize	0.700	1.533	38.88/27.04
	(2.728)	(8.171)	
Palm oil	0.219	0.516	54.63/75.30
	(1.388)	(1.390)	
Rice	0.381	0.038	64.48/73.78
	(2.003)	(0.197)	
Sugar	1.709	−0.776	−9.08/4.92
	(9.901)	(3.600)	
Tea	0.189	0.677	101.09/109.37
	(1.163)	(2.066)	
Tin	0.491	0.773	160.43/150.91
	(2.447)	(3.313)	
Wheat	0.636	−0.046	55.74/62.32
	(3.586)	(0.017)	

4 The Hypothesis of Excess Co-movement of Commodity Prices

In this section I shall examine the hypothesis of excess co-movement of commodity prices. Though it has occasionally surfaced in informal discussions, it was only recently given a formal expression by Pindyck and Rotemberg (1990), subsequently referred to as PR. They argued that a broad range of prices of largely unrelated commodities display excess co-movement (EC) in the sense that they show a persistent tendency to move together, even after accounting for the linear effects of macroeconomic shocks. PR characterize the EC hypothesis as irrational behavior on the part of dealers in commodity markets, in the sense that "traders are alternatively bullish or bearish on all commodities for no plausible reason" (PR, p. 1173). In short, traders exhibit a "herd" mentality. PR test the EC hypothesis in several ways but their principal method consists of estimating regression equations for monthly price changes of seven commodities and then testing the null hypothesis that the regression residuals are contemporaneously independent across commodities. They interpret their null hypothesis as a test of zero excess co-movement and also of the standard competitive storage model of price formation referred to earlier. Their tests lead to the rejection of the null. The consequences of their unambiguous rejection of the null hypothesis have important implications for any attempt to understand, model or forecast the behavior of commodity prices (see Maddala, 1990). The methodology employed by PR and the specific details of the application raise interesting and important issues that need further attention.

In PR's approach one first selects a group of commodities for which "the cross-price elasticities of demand and supply are close to zero" (PR, p. 1173). This is important because the EC hypothesis applies to essentially unrelated commodities. PR work with monthly data, 308 monthly observations from April 1960 to November 1985 for seven commodities: wheat, cotton, copper, gold, crude oil, lumber, and cocoa. They state: "None of the commodities are substitutes or complements, none are co-produced, and none is used as a major input into the production of another" (PR, p. 1174). They model the price changes in terms of a reduced form regression with a common set of macro variables to remove the linear influence of macro shocks. The macro variables, denoted x, are inflation, industrial production, interest rate, and exchange rate, and the exogenous variables that might be used to predict future values of macro variables, denoted z, are index of share prices and money stock. The specified regression equation for percentage change in the price of each commodity, estimated from monthly data, includes current and one-period lagged changes of the six macro variables, and one-period lagged dependent variable; that is,

$$\Delta p_{i,t} = \sum_{k=0}^{k} \alpha_{ik}\Delta x_{t-k} + \sum_{k=0}^{k} \alpha_{ik}\Delta z_{t-k} + \rho_i \Delta p_{i,t-1} + \varepsilon_{i,t} \tag{4.1}$$

where i is the commodity subscript, k is the lag subscript, and Δ is the first difference operator. In a Gaussian model, independence of the regression residuals from different equations implies that the contemporaneous covariance matrix of regression residuals would be diagonal, i.e. the cross-covariances would be zero, $\mathbb{E}[\varepsilon_{i,t}\varepsilon_{j,t}] = 0$, all i, j. This is tested using a likelihood ratio test under the assumption that the regression residuals are homoskedastic, independent, and normally distributed. PR use a generalized correlation test between regression residuals supplemented by mention of significant pairs of correlations among residuals. A joint test of the null leads to its rejection.

Given the importance of the conclusion, one should consider whether it is based on adequately specified models and whether that conclusion is robust to the failure of the maintained assumption of multivariate normality, independence, and homoskedasticity of regression disturbances. These assumptions seem strong both in relation to the observed properties of commodity prices reviewed in the previous section, and also contrary to the explicit theoretical predictions of some nonlinear commodity price models which imply nonnormality and heteroskedasticity. In the remainder of this section I reexamine the EC hypothesis, subject the PR model to a battery of specification tests, and discuss the problems of inference arising from strong and data-inconsistent assumptions maintained under the null.

As a part of a reexamination of the issues the PR regressions were reestimated using their sample period and also with the extended period April 1960 to November 1989, using data for both monthly and annual frequency, and for two subperiods, January 1974 to June 1990, and January 1978 to June 1990. Split sample tests permit an examination of the parameter stability of the PR regression specification which is essential for consistent estimation of the residual correlations on which PR's test of excess co-movement is based. Yet it is unlikely to be realized for several commodities during 1960–85. For example, for well-known reasons the behavior of gold and petroleum prices before and after 1973 (pre- and post-OPEC) was very different.

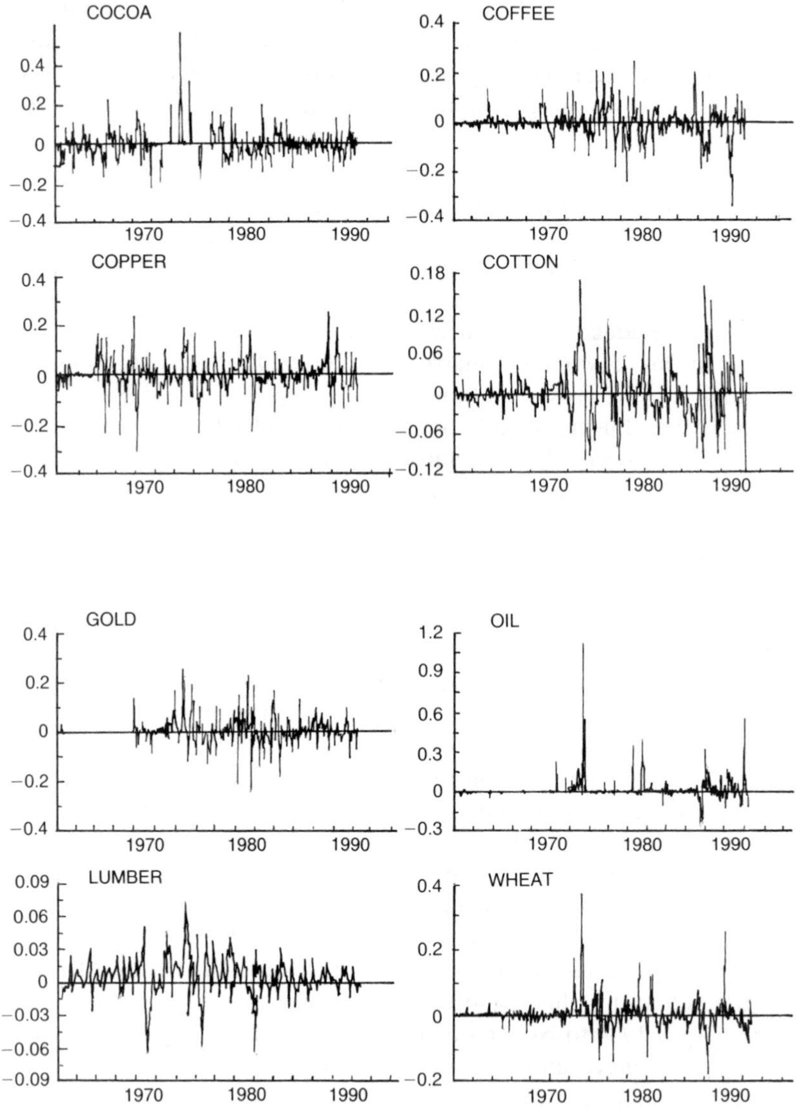

Figure 15.2 Monthly percentage changes in prices of eight commodities, 1960–90.

Figure 15.2 shows the graphs of mothly price changes for the eight commodities from 1960 to 1990. The graphs for gold, oil, and wheat especially stand out as having rather different patterns of variation pre- and post-1973. Nonhomogeneities in sample data for cocoa, coffee, and copper are also obvious, possibly due to commodity price agreements. If the data are used for modelling, but their special features are ignored, then the conditional mean function will be misspecified. Such misspecifications affect the size as well as the power of the test of the EC based on the assumption of correct specification. The rejection of the null of zero excess co-movement may stem from the failure of other false and untested statistical assumptions. Of course, the issue of the sensitivity of inference to ignored misspecifications is generic and here one is simply dealing with a particular manifestation of it.

I begin with an account of a battery of standard specification tests. Table 15.5 presents the results for the RESET functional form (FF-test) test; a test of the null of homoskedasticity (H-test) against the alternative that variances are proportional to the squared expected value of the dependent variable; a test of normality (N-test) comprising the joint test of symmetry and nonnormal kurtosis; the Box–Pierce test of serial correlation (AC-test) based on the first 12 estimated autocorrelation coefficients; and a Chow-test of parameter stability (S-test) based on the predictions of the regression for either the period 1985(12)–1990(6), or the period 1990(1)–1990(6), whichever is appropriate.

The results in table 15.5 overwhelmingly reject the null hypotheses of normality, homoskedasticity, and serial independence of disturbances in monthly models based on either PR's original 1960–85 period or the extended 1960–90 period. Violations of homoskedasticity and normality are spectacular, but also predictable. The choice of the original PR sample period of 1960(4)–1985(11), or the extended period 1960(4)–1990(12), in conjunction with their linear specification, provides an unsatisfactory basis for testing the EC hypothesis. The test outcomes yield fewer rejections of the null when shorter, more homogeneous, sample periods are used and when annual rather than monthly data are employed, but for seven out of eight commodities there is still evidence of specification problems that are likely to affect the test of the EC hypothesis.

As a special case of the approach developed in Cameron and Trivedi (1993), consider a test of independence based on regression errors from (say) r regressions, i.e. a test based on covariances between u_i and u_j, when there are potentially $r(r-1)/2$ pairs to test, each a $\chi^2(1)$

Table 15.5 Diagnostic tests of the basic PR specification

Commodity		*FF-test*	*H-test*	*N-test*	*AC-test*	*S-test*
Wheat	(1)	7.97	45.63	2 322.0	28.41	25.35
	(2)	5.53	37.00	2 454.0	16.99	–
	(3)	0.01	0.10	216.6	7.04	–
	(4)	3.29	1.86	389.0	6.33	–
Cotton	(1)	7.38	39.21	77.21	21.91	21.70
	(2)	0.28	21.40	106.4	34.60	–
	(3)	1.39	3.39	25.06	23.28	–
	(4)	0.81	0.80	39.95	22.34	–
Copper	(1)	1.04	5.31	144.3	17.98	19.18
	(2)	0.85	4.56	115.91	20.33	–
	(3)	0.19	3.26	9.68	17.21	–
	(4)	0.00	1.48	12.49	19.38	–
Gold	(1)	2.29	25.25	157.14	35.63	14.19
	(2)	1.65	20.52	323.13	34.53	–
	(3)	0.93	4.24	19.45	10.25	–
	(4)	2.22	0.99	25.81	10.13	–
Crude oil	(1)	33.25	44.48	261 174.0	16.39	51.99
	(2)	8.26	44.17	132 674.0	34.53	–
	(3)	23.75	60.59	21 443.0	9.26	–
	(4)	1.23	11.66	384.84	6.08	–
Lumber	(1)	0.61	14.41	78.34	30.09	6.43
	(2)	0.55	18.40	121.77	31.87	–
	(3)	5.36	16.01	5.37	24.06	–
	(4)	0.79	24.97	2.72	30.22	–
Cocoa	(1)	0.22	0.14	2 207.8	7.69	11.85
	(2)	0.13	0.12	2 624.0	9.64	–
	(3)	0.01	0.08	138.00	16.89	–
	(4)	0.01	0.02	6.13	24.66	–
95% critical chi-square		5.99	3.84	5.99	21.03	

Notes: FF-test: functional form (RESET) test; d.f. = 2. H-test: heteroskedasticity test; d.f. = 1. N-test: joint test of normality (symmetry and excess kurtosis); d.f. = 2. AC-test: joint test of serial independence based on 12 autocorrelation coefficients. S-test: Chow test of parameter stability.

Sample periods: (1) April 1960 to November 1985, (2) April 1960 to December 1989, (3) January 1974 to June 1990, (4) January 1978 to June 1990.

test. The joint test will be a $\chi^2(r(r-1)/2)$ test. A simpler problem is that of testing for zero correlation between two subsets of random variables, denoted by U_1 and U_2 with the covariance matrix $\Sigma = [\Sigma_{ij}]$, $i, j = 1, 2$, where rank $(\Sigma_{11}) = r_1$ and rank $(\Sigma_{22}) = r_2$. Then the squared canonical correlation coefficient $\rho_c^2 = (\text{vec}\,\Sigma_{21})'(\Sigma_{11}^{-1} \otimes \Sigma_{22}^{-1})(\text{vec}\,\Sigma_{21}) = \text{tr}(\Sigma_{11}^{-1}\Sigma_{12}\Sigma_{22}^{-1}\Sigma_{21})$ is zero under the null hypothesis of independence of U_1 and U_2. If r_c^2 denotes the sample squared canonical correlation coefficient, then it can be shown that under the null hypothesis of independence, $T \cdot r_c^2 \sim \chi^2(r_1 r_2)$. The simplest case is that of two random vectors, which yields a $\chi^2(1)$-test based on the Tr^2 statistic under the null of zero correlation. The pairwise correlations are useful in evaluating the impact of model misspecifications.

Table 15.6 shows the significant pairs of correlations in monthly data. Ignoring the issue of misspecification, we see that there are many pairs of significant correlations, and hence many sources of rejections of the null hypothesis of zero EC. Unfortunately, a large proportion of these are based on residuals from misspecified regression equations. If pairs involving wheat, cotton, gold, oil, and lumber were ignored on grounds of misspecification, only the copper–cocoa correlation would survive and even the copper equation is less than satisfactory. Since Monte Carlo evidence given in Cameron and Trivedi (1993) shows that the Tr^2 test tends to overreject the null of independence when the underlying models are misspecified, one might strongly discount this evidence against the null hypothesis. Alternatively, one should robustify the Tr^2 test.

An informal method of robustification was tried as follows. The residuals were estimated from a multivariate nonparametric kernel (NK) regression. This avoids strong distributional assumptions about the regression errors or functional form assumptions about the conditional mean function by allowing the partial derivatives of the regression function to vary over sample points. To implement NK regression I used the McQueen program (see Delgado and Stengos 1991) in which it is necessary to choose the smoothing parameter ("group radius"). If this parameter is chosen to be too large, then one replicates the least squares results, and if it is chosen to be too small estimation is not feasible at all, because an insufficient number of observations would be available to apply the procedure. By trial and error I selected the smallest group radius for which estimation was feasible (this is one but not the best way of choosing that parameter). The results showed that at 5 percent significance level only three pairs out of the 21 tested – gold–copper, copper–cotton, and copper–cocoa – are clearly

Table 15.6 "Significant" pairs of correlations between regression residuals

Commodity pair	*Period*	*Correlation*	TR^2	$NK-TR^2$
Copper, cocoa	60–85	0.1136	3.97	4.65
	60–90	0.1231	5.60	
Cotton, cocoa	60–85	0.1061	3.46	
	60–90	0.1073	4.25	
	74–90	0.1480	4.33	
Gold, copper*	60–85	0.1167	4.19	
	60–90	0.1308	6.33	
	74–90	0.2528	12.65	12.26
	78–90	0.3213	14.86	
Wheat, cotton*	60–85	0.2079	13.31	
	60–90	0.1777	11.68	
	74–90	0.1613	5.15	
Oil, cocoa	60–85	0.2155	14.30	
	60–90	0.1623	9.74	
	74–90	0.3150	19.64	
Oil, cotton	60–85	0.1551	7.40	
	60–90	0.1154	4.92	
	74–90	0.2321	10.66	3.80
Oil, gold*	60–85	0.2111	13.72	
	60–90	0.1644	10.00	
	74–90	0.2270	10.20	3.21
	78–90	0.1654	3.94	
Wheat, copper	74–90	0.1703	5.74	
Copper, cotton	74–90	0.1498	4.44	5.74
Copper, cotton	78–90	0.2133	6.55	
95% critical chi-square (1)			3.84	

Note: The asterisk indicates that PR also reported a similar result.

significant and the cotton–oil and gold–oil correlations have now become somewhat marginal. These results underscore the fragility of the evidence in favor of the EC hypothesis.

The second method of robustifying inferences is to apply the Tr^2

test to monthly subsamples for 1974–90 and 1978–90 since the subsamples appear to show fewer indications of extreme mispecifications. Table 15.6 also shows the "significant" pairs of correlations for the monthly subsamples. Note that when using the pairwise test seven "significant" pairs of correlations were found for each of the three sample periods 1960–85, 1960–90, and 1974–90, but only three such "significant" pairs were found for the period 1978–90.

As a postscript to this section, I refer the reader to Deb et al. (1993), which was written before the final revisions were made to the present chapter. This paper contains tests of the excess co-movement hypothesis in the same spirit as Pindyck and Rotemberg, but using, as the benchmark model, univariate and multivariate GARCH(1, 1) models based on (conditionally) Gaussian or Student $t(\upsilon)$ errors. That is, in this formulation, the regression error in (4.1) is assumed to be of the form $\varepsilon_{it} = \eta_{it}\sqrt{h_{it}}$, and $\eta_{it} \sim D(0, 1)$, and

$$h_{it} = \gamma + \alpha\varepsilon_{i,t-1}^2 + \beta h_{i,t-1}, \tag{4.2}$$

where i denotes the commodity subscript. The advantage of this formulation is that the specification incorporates heavy-tailed autoregressive conditionally heteroskedastic errors which seem to be a prominent feature of many commodity prices. If univariate models are estimated, then it is easy to show that a Rao (1948) type score (LM) test of zero correlation between the (i, j) pair can be carried out using the Tr_{ij}^2 statistic, where r_{ij}^2 denotes the squared correlation between the standardized residuals $\varepsilon_{it}/\sqrt{h_{it}}$ Alternatively, multivariate GARCH (1, 1) models may be estimated and likelihood ratio tests of zero contemporaneous correlation may be carried out. Such tests are applied in Deb et al. to a number of data sets and time periods, including the Pindyck–Rotemberg samples, and they produce very weak evidence of excess co-movement. These results confirm that the Pindyck–Rotemberg tests are not robust to the misspecifications highlighted in this section and that the neglect of such misspecification may well lead to overrejection of the null hypothesis of zero excess co-movement.

5 Long-term Movements in Net Barter Terms-of-trade for Primary Producers

Secular trends in commodity prices have attracted considerable attention from economists since Prebisch (1950) and Singer (1950) proposed the hypothesis that the net barter terms-of-trade (NBTT) between primary commodity producers and manufactures have deteriorated over the long run. The issue is of obvious importance in the context of North–South economic relations. Following the publication of Grilli and Yang (1988), who provided a number of relevant time series and estimated exponential trend regression models, econometricians have used modern time series decomposition techniques to test the null hypothesis that the terms of trade may be modelled as a trend-stationary process against the alternative that the process is difference-stationary. Cuddington and Urzua (1989) compared trend-stationary and difference-stationary specifications for the Grilli–Yang aggregate index of real commodity prices and were unable to reject the hypothesis that the series has a unit root. They concluded, contrary to Grilli and Yang (1988), that apart from an abrupt one-time drop in 1920, there was no evidence of an ongoing continuous decline in commodity prices. The abrupt price drop in 1920, evident in the graph of the series in figure 15.3, and also noted by Grilli and Yang, prompted Perron (1990) to carry out the tests of unit root in this series against the alternative of trend stationarity after allowing for a single one-time break in the mean level of the series at an exogenously determined time, i.e. 1920, using the methods in Perron (1989, 1990) and Perron and Vogelsang (1992). His postulated null model was

$$y_t = \mu + y_{t-1} + \varepsilon_t, \tag{5.1}$$

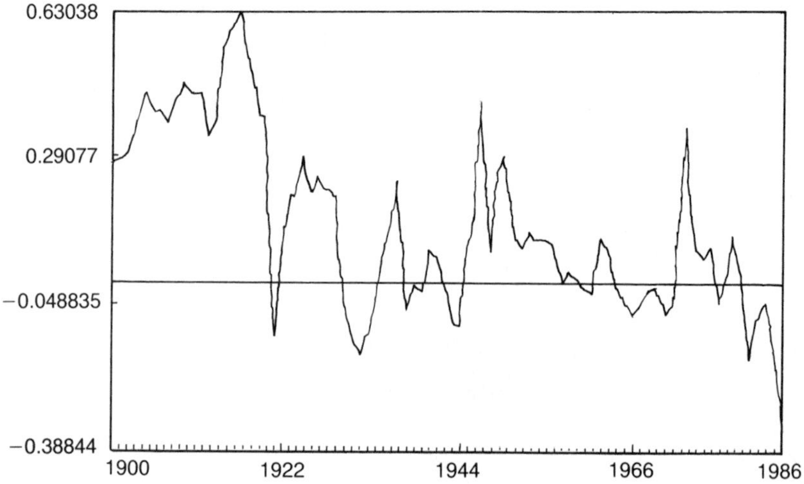

Figure 15.3 Grilli–Yang index (log) of relative price of primary commodities.

against two alternative models, an additive outlier model and an innovational outlier model, defined below. The tests based on the first model led to the rejection of the unit root hypothesis, but those based on the second did not. However, Perron argued that the results based on the first were more robust and concluded that Cuddington and Urzua's rejection of trend stationarity was incorrect, at least once the change in the mean of the process had been allowed for. However, the study did not go on to consider whether the preferred model was consistent with the Prebisch–Singer hypothesis.

Perron (1989, 1990) has considered the test of the null hypothesis of a unit root with a drift, given a one-time shift in the mean of the series at a known date T_B, $1 < T_B < T$. If λ is defined as $\lambda = T_B/T$, then Perron assumes λ known. For the NBTT series, he followed the augmented Dickey–Fuller (ADF) regression strategy by including in the model k lagged first differences of y_t (which controls for possibly serially correlated errors in the null model). Perron's alternatives to the null are the following *additive outlier model* and *innovational outlier model*:

$$\tilde{y}_t = \sum_{j=1}^{k} \omega_j D(TB)_{t-j} + \alpha \tilde{y}_{t-1} + \sum_{j=1}^{k} c_j \Delta \tilde{y}_{t-j} + v_t, \quad t = k+1, \ldots, T \tag{5.2}$$

$$\tilde{y}_t = \mu + \gamma DU_t + dD(TB)_t + \alpha \tilde{y}_{t-1} + \sum_{j=1}^{k} c_j \Delta \tilde{y}_{t-j} + v_t, \quad t = k+1, \ldots, T, \tag{5.3}$$

where $\tilde{y}_t$ denotes the residuals from the regression of y_t on a constant and DU_t, $DU_t = 0$ if $t \leqslant T_B$ and 1 otherwise, $D(TB)_t = 1$ if $t = T_B + 1$ and 0 otherwise. Perron (1990) uses the Phillips–Perron (Perron, 1989) statistics to test the H_0: $\alpha = 1$ using (5.2). He also uses the t-statistic, $t(\hat{\alpha})$, from the OLS estimate of (5.3) to test the same null, the asymptotic distribution of this test being the same as for the t-statistic for the OLS estimate $\hat{\alpha}$ in (5.2). The specification of the second model implies that the mean-shift in the series is not instantaneous and that its effect on the level of y depends upon the dynamics of the process.

When Perron's methodology was applied with $T_B = 1920$, the t_α-statistics against the alternative of additive outlier model (5.2) were as follows:

k	1	2	3	4	5	6
t_α	−3.78	−3.90	−3.37	−2.97	−2.81	−2.50

The 5 and 10 percent critical values of −3.68 and −3.40, respectively. Again, therefore, the unit root null is rejected at the 5 percent level for $k = 1, 2$ but not for larger values of k. Against the alternative of innovation outlier model (5.3) the null is not rejected as the t_α statistic in this case was −2.53 compared with 5 and 10 percent level critical values of −3.65 and −3.36, respectively. For a slightly different sample and $k = 6$, Perron and Vogelsang (1992) easily rejected the null hypothesis of unit root; see the third row in their table 1.

I shall reexamine the conclusions of Perron and Vogelsang (1992) using the Grilli–Yang data for the period 1900–86. The motivation for this reexamination comes from the criticism of Perron's methodology by Zivot and Andrews (1992), who have proposed a new variant of the Perron test in which the break-point is estimated rather than fixed, thereby taking account of the possibility of bias due to pretesting. In the Zivot–Andrews (ZA) formulation, the problem is one of testing for a unit root against one or more plausible alternatives of stationarity with structural change at some unknown date, using specifications of d.g.p.s which allow for a change in the mean or a change in the mean and the slope of the trend function. The issues are discussed in Zivot and Andrews (1992). In the remainder of this section this methodology is applied to the NBTT series.

Two alternatives, A and B, to the unit root null considered by ZA are as follows:

$$y_t = \mu^A + \gamma^A DU(\hat{\lambda})_t + \theta^A t + \alpha^A y_{t-1} + \sum_{j=1}^{k} c_j^A \Delta y_{t-j} + v_t, \quad (5.4)$$

$$\begin{aligned} y_t = \mu^B + \gamma^B DU(\hat{\lambda})_t + \theta^B t + \beta^B D(TB(\hat{\lambda}))_t \\ + \alpha^B y_{t-1} + \sum_{j=1}^{k} c_j^B \Delta y_{t-j} + v_t, \end{aligned} \quad (5.5)$$

where $DU(\hat{\lambda}) = 1$ if $t > \lambda T$ and 0 otherwise, and $D(TB(\hat{\lambda}))_t = t - T\hat{\lambda}$ if $t > T\hat{\lambda}$ and 0 otherwise. This specification generalizes Perron's innovational outlier model by allowing λ to be an unknown parameter estimated from the data, and by including a trend. The ZA criterion for selecting the break point $T_B = T\lambda$ is the value for which the one-sided t-statistic is minimized for the null hypothesis $\alpha = 1$ against the alternative that $\alpha < 1$. For the set of models corresponding to alternative i, the ZA criterion for selecting $\hat{\lambda}$ is $\inf_{\lambda \in \Lambda} t_\alpha(\hat{\lambda})$. The null hypothesis of a unit root is rejected if $t_\alpha(\hat{\lambda})$ is smaller than the α per cent critical value. The critical values for $\inf_{\lambda \in \Lambda} t_\alpha(\hat{\lambda})$ have been given by ZA for both fixed and estimated λ.

To implement the test specifications (5.4) and (5.5) were estimated with the break point T_B ranging from $t = 2$ to $t = 87$, with the lag truncation parameter fixed at 6.[2] For (5.5) the smallest value of t_α was found to be -3.90 corresponding to $T_B = 1920$; $\lambda = 21/87 = 0.24$. The next smallest value was -3.84 corresponding to $T_B = 1946$. The percentage points for the asymptotic distribution of $\inf_{\lambda \in \Lambda} t_\alpha(\lambda)$ for the unit root null against the alternative (3.5) above are given in ZA for selected values of λ. The 1, 2.5, and 5.0 percent critical values are, respectively, -5.57, -5.30, and -5.08. The corresponding values for the case of fixed $\lambda = 0.2$ are -4.65, -4.32, and -3.99; for $\lambda = 0.3$ they are -4.78, -4.46, and -4.17. Thus, for the case λ unknown, the null hypothesis is not rejected. Assuming $T_B = 1920$, the null is still not rejected against the alternative (5.5) at the 5 percent significance level, but it is at the 10 percent level. Thus the test outcome is marginal.

It might be argued that in view of the low power of several unit root tests, the marginal nature of the rejection of the unit root hypothesis should be interpreted as a rejection. This was the conclusion of Perron and Vogelsang. If one treats the breakpoint as known, and if the test is conducted at a higher significance level, the unit root null is rejected; hence it seems important to scrutinize further the reasons why 1920 might be regarded as a plausible breakpoint.

There has been little discussion of this in the literature relative to the space devoted to the hypothesis of the "great crash of 1973." Even Grilli and Yang (1988), who pointed out the abrupt shift in the terms-of-trade series in 1920, did not discuss its possible causes. Cuddington and Urzua (1989, pp. 429–30) argue thus: "Presumably it reflects adjustments in commodity supplies and demands following the First World War. According to the NBER's dating of US business cycles, the prolonged economic expansion associated with the war peaked in January 1920." They also note, by appeal to the historical evidence in Friedman and Schwartz (1963), that a sharp monetary contraction which followed the First World War caused industrial production and employment in US manufacturing to drop sharply. Similar conditions were experienced worldwide in the aftermath of the First World War. They conclude by observing that "it is well-known that in such downturns the relative price of manufactures tends to move procyclically."

The historical facts described above support the treatment of 1920 as a structural break. However, there is one important problem obscured by the data. When data relate to long historical spans, consistency of the series may be compromised. If interpolation is used to fill in missing observations, there is a potential for introducing spurious discontinuities. Grilli and Yang faced such a situation. Their terms-of-trade series was obtained by deflating the nominal commodity price index by an annual index of manufactured good unit value. For the index of manufacturing unit value, Grilli and Yang used the United Nations data except for two gaps, 1914–20 and 1939–47. These observations were obtained by interpolation (see Grilli and Yang, 1988, footnote 3, pp. 3–4). Thus it seems significant that the ZA procedure threw up the two smallest t_{α}-statistics for periods 1920 and 1946. Given the method of data construction which was used, one might discount the importance of apparently "abrupt" changes in the mean level of the series unless one obtains independent corroboration of the possibility of exogenous shifts.[3] While Grilli and Yang (p. 10) refer to "prior knowledge of exogenous events" suggestive of structural breaks in 1920, 1932, and 1945, they do not document this point any further. Others have suggested other possible dates for structural breaks; Sapsford (1985) has argued that 1950 is a date for a structural break. In view of the absence of consensus on the number and timing of structural breaks, the problem of testing whether there has been a secular decline in NBTT becomes even more delicate.

Suppose one accepts or assumes that the terms-of-trade can be characterized as a time stationary series with a changing mean. Is there evidence of a secular decline of NBTT in this model? The answer is less than straightforward. If we estimate the linear regression of y_t on an intercept, a linear time trend and a dummy variable for 1920, the trend variable has a significant negative sign; but the regression residuals exhibit strong serial correlation. If we add a lagged dependent variable, or reestimate the model subject to a first order autoregressive error, the previous conclusion remains unchanged. If, in recognition of a structural break in 1950, the model is estimated for the period 1951–86, thereby allowing for the possibility that the slope of the trend function may have also changed, then there is no longer support for the Prebisch–Singer hypothesis. Only in this last case do our conclusions agree with those of Cuddington and Urzua, who reported that, in their preferred regression models, there was no evidence of a long-run decline of relative commodity prices. The conclusion from my own investigation is less clear-cut. First, it is difficult to identify a post Second World War structural break; second, not assuming that such a break did in fact occur leads to some evidence suggesting a long-run decline. Future work in this area will need to devise considerably more robust tests than have been applied to date.

Appendix: data description

Sections 2 and 3

The annual time series data came from the World Bank Commodities Division. The data are based on index numbers of average prices for each year, deflated by the US consumer price index.

Section 4

1 *Macro variables* The data used for the US macroeconomic variables are as follows. For the rate of interest I used the nominal three-month Treasury bill, for money supply I used the M1 seasonally adjusted; for the exchange rate I used the equally weighted average of the yen, Deutsch mark and pound sterling *vis-à-vis* the US dollar; for inflation I used the US Consumer Price Index. The total index of industrial production, seasonally adjusted, was used and, finally, the Standard and Poor's combined index of 500 stock was used as an indicator of stock prices. All data, except exchange rates, were obtained from the *Survey of Current Business* (current business statistics) of the Department of Commerce, various issues. Exchange rate data were obtained by the IMF/IFS statistics, various issues. All these data conform to the data description in Pindyck and Rotemberg (1990, p. 1178). However, they do not mention the sources for their macro data, but these data are standard and do not vary according to the source.

2 *Commodity prices* Monthly data are from the following sources. Lumber: Aggregate Price Index for Lumber and Wood Products, from US Department of Labor. Copper: Producers' Prices of Electrolytic (wirebar) Copper, f.o.b. refinery, from *Metals Week*. Wheat: US No. 2, soft red winter, for prompt shipment, from *Grain and Feed Market News* (USDA). Cocoa: ICCO, daily price, average of the first three positions on the terminal markets of New York and London, nearest three future trading months, from the *Financial Times* (daily). Cotton: US middling 1-1/32 inch, Orleans/Texas, from *Cotton Outlook*, Cotlook Limited. Oil: Average spot price of OPEC crude oils, from *Platts Oilgram*. Gold: Average of daily spot prices, from Handy and Harman.

There are some differences in the data definitions from those used by Pindyck and Rotemberg (PR). The data used for wheat and cotton are quite similar, but not identical, to the series used by PR, though the differences should not significantly alter the results. More significant differences exist in the definitions of cocoa and oil price. Either price is not explicitly for the US market, although prices in the US for those products are highly correlated with the prices used in this study. For cocoa, however, the price I use is not a spot price, strictly speaking. However, spot cocoa prices closely reflect changes in the ICCO daily price. Furthermore, a large number of transactions for cocoa are priced on the nearby futures prices in New York or London plus a fixed premium. The cocoa price, though, may have made a difference to my results since, unlike PR, I find cases in which cocoa prices show "excess co-movement" in the sense of PR. Finally, the price series for lumber, copper, and gold are the same as PR's. To conclude, the data differences between this study and PR are not large enough to have resulted in the specification problems reported in this chapter.

Section 5

The series used come from Grilli and Yang (1988).

Notes

Panos Varangis, Taka Akiyama, Angus Deaton, Partha Deb, Ron Duncan, and T. N. Srinivasan provided guidance with respect to data used, and/or comments and suggestions for improvements. I thank them for their help but retain responsibility for the contents of the present version. Section 4 of this chapter draws on parts of an unpublished discussion paper written during the author's tenure as Visiting Research Fellow at the World Bank, on leave from my department in 1991.

1 In annual data it seems enough to restrict oneself to first order lags.
2 Perron has provided a procedure for selecting the lag truncation parameter but this was not used; for evidence on the sensitivity of the test outcome to the choice of the truncation lag, see Ng and Perron (1993).
3 Another important data problem relates to the absence of quality adjustments, which affects both the primary commodities and the manufactured good price indices (Spraos, 1980; Grilli and Yang, 1988, p. 7).

References

Bera, A. K. and Higgins, M. L. (1993) A survey of ARCH models: properties, estimation and testing. *Journal of Economic Surveys*, 7, 305–66.

Bera, A. K., Higgins, M. L. and Lee, S. (1992) Interaction between autocorrelation and conditional heteroskedasticity: a random coefficient approach. *Journal of Business and Economic Statistics*, 10, 133–42.

Cameron, A. C. and Trivedi, P. K. (1993) Tests of independence in parametric models: with applications and illustrations. *Journal of Business and Economic Statistics*, 11, 29–43.

Cuddington, J. T. and Urzua, C. M. (1989) Trends and cycles in the net barter terms of trade. *Economic Journal*, 99, 426–42.

Deaton, A. and Laroque, G. (1992) On the behavior of commodity prices. *Review of Economic Studies*, 59, 1–23.

Deb, P., Trivedi, P. K. and Varangis, P. (1993) The excess co-movement of commodity prices reconsidered. Unpublished paper, Indiana University.

Delgado, M. and Stengos, T. (1991) N-Kernel: a review. *Journal of Applied Econometrics*, 5, 209–304.

Engle, R. F. (1982) Autoregressive conditional heteroskedasticity with estimates of the variance of inflationary expectations. *Econometrica*, 50, 987–1007.

Friedman, M. and Schwartz, A. (1963) *A Monetary History of the United States: 1867–1960*. Princeton, NJ: Princeton University Press.

Granger, C. J. W. and Andersen, A. P. (1978) *An Introduction to Bilinear Time Series Models*. Göttingen: Vandenhoeck & Ruprecht.

Grilli, E. and Yang, M. C. (1988) Primary commodity prices, manufactured goods prices, and the terms of trade of developing countries: what the long-run shows. *World Bank Economic Review*, 2, 1–48.

Gustafson, R. L. (1958) Carryover levels for grains. US Department of Agriculture, Technical Bulletin 1178.

McQueen, D. (1989) *N-Kernel User's Manual*. Santa Monica: N-SSS.

Maddala, G. S. (1990) Estimation of dynamic disequilibrium models with rational expectations: the case of commodity markets. In L. A. Winters and D. Sapsford (eds), *Primary Commodity Prices: Economic Models and Policy*. Cambridge: Cambridge University Press, pp. 21–43.

Nelson, D. B. (1991) Conditional heteroskedasticity in asset returns: a new approach. *Econometrica*, 59, 347–70.

Ng, S. and Perron, P. (1993) Unit root tests in ARMA models with data dependent methods for the selection of the truncation lag. Unpublished paper, University of Montreal.

Perron, P. (1989) The great crash, the oil price shock and the unit root hypothesis. *Econometrica*, 57, 1361–401.

Perron, P. (1990) Testing for a unit root in a time series with a changing mean. *Journal of Business and Economic Statistics*, 8, 153–62.

Perron, P. and Vogelsang, T. J. (1992) Testing for a unit root in a time series with a changing mean: corrections and extensions. *Journal of Business and Economic Statistics*, 10, 467–9.

Pindyck, R. S. and Rotemberg, J. J. (1990) The excess co-movement of commodity prices. *Economic Journal*, 100, 1173–89.

Prebisch, R. (1950) *The Economic Development of Latin America and Its Principal Problems*. Lake Success: United Nations.

Rao, C. R. (1947) Large sample tests of statistical hypotheses concerning several parameters with applications to problems of estimation. *Proceedings of the Cambridge Philosophical Society*, 44, 50–7.

Samuelson, P. A. (1971) Stochastic speculative price. *Proceedings of the National Academy of Science*, 68, 335–7.

Sapsford, D. (1985) The statistical debate on the net barter terms of trade between primary commodities and manufactures: a comment and some additional evidence. *Economic Journal*, 95, 781–8.

Singer, H. (1950) The distribution of gains between investing and borrowing countries. *American Economics Review, Papers and Proceedings*, 40, 473–85.

Spraos, J. (1980) The statistical debate on the net barter terms of trade between primary commodities and manufacturers. *Economic Journal*, 90, 107–28.

Tong, H. (1990) *Non-linear Time Series*. Oxford: Oxford University Press.

Trivedi, P. K. (1990) The prices of perennial crops: the role of rational expectations and commodity stocks. In L. A. Winters and D. Sapsford (eds), *Primary Commodity Prices: Economic Models and Policy*. Cambridge: Cambridge University Press, pp. 72–97.

Trivedi, P. K. and Varangis, P. (1991) Excess co-movement of commodity prices: a statistical illusion? Unpublished discussion paper.

von Hagen, J. (1989) Relative commodity prices and cointegration. *Journal of Business and Economic Statistics*, 7, 497–503.

Weiss, A. A. (1986) ARCH and bilinear time series models: comparison and combination. *Journal of Business and Economic Statistics*, 4, 59–70.

Williams, J. C. and Wright, B. D. (1991) *Storage and Commodity Markets*, Cambridge: Cambridge University Press.

Wright, B. D. and Williams, J. C. (1982) The economic role of commodity storage. *Economic Journal*, 92, 596–614.

Zivot, E. and Andrews, D. W. K. (1992) Further evidence on the great crash, the oil-price shock, and the unit-root hypothesis. *Journal of Business and Economic Statistics*, 10(3), 251–70.

16 A Review of the Derivation and Calculation of Rao Distances with an Application to Portfolio Theory

Uwe Jensen

1 Introduction

Since the fundamental paper by Efron (1975), differential-geometrical methods are of increasing importance in theoretical statistics, e.g. in nonlinear regression analysis or in the asymptotic theory of estimation and tests. Distances (divergences) between statistical distributions play an important role in this interplay, but they are also of interest in many practical applications. Rao (1945) presented a "geodesic distance" (or "Rao distance") which has outstanding theoretical properties but is based on a demanding differential-geometrical approach. These mathematical requirements are responsible for the fact that this distance concept, a generalization of the well-known Mahalanobis distance, had to wait until Efron raised the interest of statisticians in differential geometry.

Statisticians or econometricians need some knowledge of Riemannian (or even non-Riemannian) geometry for understanding the work of Rao, Mitchell, Burbea, Oller, and others on Rao distances. Because that knowledge is not part of mathematical propaedeutics, this chapter intends to give an introduction to this theory. It aims to enlarge the interest in this profound distance concept and to make it known to many statisticians and econometricians. This seems necessary because, according to Murray and Rice (1993, p. 157), "it does not seem that this particular concept of distance between points is of any real statistical significance."

The next section demonstrates the practical benefit of a good distance measure by describing some simple problems in portfolio theory. Section 3 reviews some advantages and disadvantages of Rao distance compared with some standard distance (divergence) measures. Section 4 presents the differential-geometrical and statistical theory necessary for the derivation of the general Rao distance formula. Section 5 deals with the calculation of Rao distances in specific statistical distributions. The results on Rao distances, sectional curvatures and isocircles scattered throughout the literature are summarized. In section 6, the few available results on estimated Rao distances and Rao distance tests are reported. Section 7 shows the application of the theoretical concepts to a practical problem in portfolio theory. Some concluding remarks are given in the last section.

2 Econometric Motivation

This section aims to motivate interest in the mathematical concepts of the next section using a simple econometric problem and some questions arising from it.

Let A be a stock represented by its yield $Y \sim N(\mu, \sigma_0^2)$ with the unknown expected yield μ and the known risk σ_0^2. Assume for a few seconds that

$$H_0\colon \mu = \mu_0 \quad \text{versus} \quad H_1\colon \mu \neq \mu_0 \tag{2.1}$$

will be tested with a sample of size $m = 1$. The optimal test in this situation with the critical region

$$K = \{\bar{x}\colon |\bar{x} - \mu_0| > \lambda_{1-\alpha/2}\sigma_0\} \tag{2.2}$$

answers the question "Is the distance between $N(\mu_0, \sigma_0^2)$ and $N(\bar{x}, \sigma_0^2)$ big enough for rejecting H_0?"

This distance can be seen in figure 16.1, where the upper real half-plane of all (μ, σ)-points with $\sigma > 0$ is identified with the family of all normal distributions. The distance quantifies how difficult it is to discriminate between the two distributions. It depends on σ and on the distributional assumption. The distance between $N(\mu_0, \sigma_1^2)$ and $N(\bar{x}, \sigma_1^2)$ (see figure 16.1) should be bigger than the distance mentioned before. For $\sigma \to \infty$, the distances between $N(\mu_0, \sigma^2)$ and $N(\bar{x}, \sigma^2)$

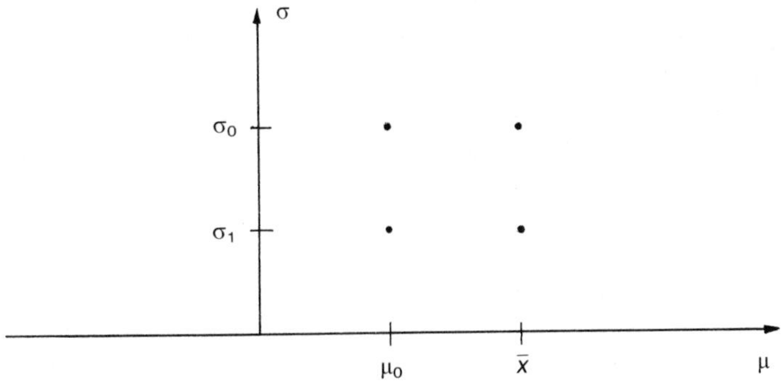

Figure 16.1 $N(\mu_0, \sigma_i^2)$ and $N(\bar{x}, \sigma_i^2)$ for $i = 0, 1$.

should converge to zero; for $\sigma \to 0$ they should become infinitely large. For that reason, the family of normal distributions should not be identified with a flat plane but with a curved surface. How can this curvature be determined? How does it depend on the distributional assumption?

Assume now that there are two stocks A_1 and A_2 with yields $Y_i \sim N(\mu_i, \sigma_0^2)$, unknown expected yields μ_i and known risk σ_0^2. The μ_i have been estimated with a sample of size $m_1 = m_2 = 100$ as $\hat{\mu}_1 = 1$ and $\hat{\mu}_2 = 2$. Is it also possible to estimate distances? Which properties do these estimates have?

Distance measures can illustrate test decisions, but they can also be applied for the construction of distance tests. Are these distance tests a reasonable alternative to standard tests? Their properties have to be discussed later, but a special feature shall be mentioned now. If it is intended to test

$$H_0\colon \mu_1 = \mu_2 \quad \text{versus} \quad H_1\colon \mu_1 \neq \mu_2, \tag{2.3}$$

a standard test would combine the information on the sample sizes and on the (μ, σ)-values to a "0–1 decision." A distance measure converts the information on the (μ, σ)-values to a measure of (dis-)similarity of $N(1, \sigma_0^2)$ and $N(2, \sigma_0^2)$. This positive real number is independent of the sample size and it is very interesting for investors. Subsequently, the distance can be combined with the sample size to a distance test for (2.3).

In general, one unit expected yield should be different from one unit risk. Hence, the distance between, e.g., $N(1, 1)$ and $N(1, 2)$ should be different from the distance between $N(1, 1)$ and $N(2, 1)$ –

another argument for a curved surface instead of a flat plane. Are these non-Euclidean concepts compatible with utility theory?

The distances between arbitrary stocks with yields following arbitrary normal or nonnormal distributions are of interest to investors. Are these distances invariant with regard to reparametrization, so that it is possible to change into the yield-risk space for distributions different from the normal distribution? Does the interpretation of the distances depend on the distributional assumption? Do we speak of distances in the mathematical sense?

All questions will be answered in the following sections. A first survey of the capabilities and limits of Rao distance will be given in the next section.

3 Distance Measures

In the following, we will examine only those measures developed for the measurement of dissimilarity between (continuous or discrete) distributions. There is an extensive literature on distance measures, measures of information, measures of divergence, and several different keywords (see the surveys in Burbea and Rao, 1982; Burbea, 1983; Papaioannou, 1985; Jensen, 1993; Maasoumi, 1993). The names of these measures are so different, because some of them are not distances in the mathematical sense (see below) and because others have their root in information theory. The most popular ones are probably Mahalanobis distance (Mahalanobis, 1936), Kullback–Leibler information (Kullback and Leibler, 1951), Matusita distance (Matusita, 1955), and Cziszár divergence (or f divergence) (Cziszár, 1963; Ali and Silvey, 1966).

Since there is no generally optimal "distance" measure, we must have a closer book at some desirable properties.

1 The "distance" measure $d(.,.)$ is called a distance in the mathematical sense, if the following conditions hold for distribution functions F_1, F_2, and F_3:

$$\begin{aligned}
&\text{(i)} \quad d(F_1, F_1) = 0,\\
&\text{(ii)} \quad d(F_1, F_2) \geqslant 0,\\
&\text{(iii)} \quad d(F_1, F_2) = d(F_2, F_1),\\
&\text{(iv)} \quad d(F_1, F_2) \leqslant d(F_1, F_3) + d(F_3, F_2).
\end{aligned} \tag{3.1}$$

The Rao distance meets these conditions by definition (see below). The Mahalanobis distance (e.g. because it is a special case of the Rao distance) and the Matusita distance (see Matusita, 1955) do as well. In contrast to this, the KL information does not meet conditions (iii + iv) (see Kullback, 1959, p. 6f) and the Cziszár divergence even violates (ii–iv) in general.

2 The distance measure should be parametrization invariant (see Barndorff-Nielsen, 1988) for a large group of transformations. Rao distance is invariant for all nonsingular differentiable transformations of the parameter space and the sample space. The Mahalanobis distance is invariant for all nonsingular affine transformations. The other measures mentioned above have only much weaker invariance properties (see Papaioannou, 1985).

3 The distance measure should provide statistically sensible results: the distance between two distributions should quantify how difficult it is to discriminate between them with a good test (see Kullback and Leibler, 1951, p. 79). This condition is designed to eliminate statistically senseless mathematical distances and it is met by all measures mentioned above (the Rao distance is based on the Fisher information).

4 It should be possible to estimate distances and to construct distance tests. The properties of estimates and tests should be sufficiently known and good. The necessary results for the Mahalanobis distance and the KL information are well known: estimation and testing can be done in the usual way. For the Matusita distance, there are some results for the application to discrete distributions, but only very few for continuous distributions (see Ahmad, 1985, p. 335). The necessary theory for the Rao distance has just begun to be created. The first results will be mentioned in this chapter.

5 The distance measure should be applicable in a large class of distributions. Rao distances can only be calculated if the particular distribution family meets several regularity conditions. As a result, most distributions outside the exponential family cannot be analysed with this concept. Application of the KL information and the Matusita distance is not limited in a comparable way.

6 Finally, the effort involved in calculation of the distances should be reasonable. Application of the KL information often leads to relatively easy formulae. In the case of the Rao distance, the derivation of the necessary formulae is lengthy, and sometimes these formulae are as yet unknown. Matusita distances have to be calculated by numerical integration in most cases.

We have seen that the Rao distance is a distance in the mathematical sense, with far-reaching invariance properties but shortcomings in its applications. The well-known KL information is just the opposite, with broad applicability but theoretical drawbacks. The Matusita distance lies between these extremes. Therefore, it seems reasonable to take a closer look at the Rao distance.

4 Derivation of the Rao Distance

The nonmathematical reader of literature on differential geometry in statistics has to cope with several difficulties. Mathematicians like Gallot et al. (1990) prefer the new coordinate-free notation, whereas most statisticians – Lauritzen (1987) is an exception – give preference to the old index notation, which, therefore, is used in this chapter too. But the latter becomes hardly readable if the Einstein summation convention (see Kay, 1988, for a good introduction) is applied (which is avoided in this chapter). Finally, most of the literature on differential geometry in statistics deals with non-Riemannian geometry (see below), which is not necessary for the calculation of Rao distances based on Riemannian geometry. That is why many notions in those papers with an α-prefix (e.g. α-connection) have to be considered simply for $\alpha = 0$. This is done in the following without remark.

In this section, we will give a short summary of the differential-geometrical and statistical theory necessary for the derivation of the Rao distance. Atkinson and Mitchell (1981), Burbea (1986b), Rao (1987), and Jensen (1993) are sources of literature on this special topic. Amari (1985), Barndorff-Nielsen et al. (1986), Burbea (1986a), Amari et al. (1987), Kass (1989), and Murray and Rice (1993) are introductions to or reviews of differential geometry in statistics. Kobayashi and Nomizu (1963 and 1969), Spivak (1970–5), Berger and Gostiaux (1988), Kay (1988), and Gallot et al. (1990) are mathematical introductions to differential geometry.

Statistical models and manifolds

Let Ω be a sample space, $\mathcal{A}$ a σ-algebra of subsets of Ω and P: $\mathcal{A} \to [0, 1]$ a probability measure. The random variable X has a density function $p(x, \theta)$ with an n-dimensional parameter $\theta = (\theta_1, \theta_2, \ldots, \theta_n)$ and $\theta \in \Theta$. The parameter space Θ is an open subset of $\mathbf{R}^n$. Then,

$$S = \{p(x, \theta) | \theta \in \Theta\} \tag{4.1}$$

is a statistical model.

Example 4.1. If X follows a normal distribution with

$$(\theta_1, \theta_2) = (\mu, \sigma), \quad \Theta = \{(\mu, \sigma) | \mu \in \mathbf{R}, \sigma > 0\}, \tag{4.2}$$

we identify the family of all normal distributions and the set of all points p on the upper real half-plane. But this identification, does not mean that the family of normal distributions is geometrically flat. Because, for example, $N(\mu_1, 0.1)$ and $N(\mu_2, 0.1)$ can be discriminated more easily than $N(\mu_1, 10)$ and $N(\mu_2, 10)$, this surface should be curved. □

It is assumed therefore that an n-parametric family of distributions only behaves locally (in open neighborhoods of its points (distributions) $p \in S$) like $\mathbf{R}^n$, so that its potential curvature can be analysed later. Such a generalization of a real space is called n-dimensional manifold (see the literature on differential geometry for an exact definition).

Then, local coordinates are transferred from $\Theta \subseteq \mathbf{R}^n$ to open neighborhoods of the points on the n-manifold. In the example of the 2-parameter normal distribution, we could take (μ, σ) for this purpose. These coordinates can be changed by admissible (smooth) transformations being three times continuously differentiable and having a nonsingular functional determinant. By this means, S is equiped with a differentiable structure and S is called a differentiable n-manifold.

Regularity conditions

A statistical model is called regular if the following regularity conditions (known from the Cramér–Rao inequality) hold:

1 For all $\theta \in \Theta$, $p(x, \theta)$ has a common support so that $p(x, \theta) > 0$ holds for all x.

2 Let $l(x, \theta) = \ln p(x, \theta)$. For all $\theta \in \Theta$, n functions

$$\frac{\partial}{\partial \theta_i} l(x, \theta), \quad i = 1, 2, \ldots, n \tag{4.3}$$

are linearly independent.

3 For $r = 3$, $i = 1, 2, \ldots, n$ and for all $\theta \in \Theta$,

$$\mathrm{E}\left[\frac{\partial}{\partial \theta_i} l(x, \theta)\right]^r < \infty \tag{4.4}$$

4 For any functions $f(x, \theta)$ treated in this chapter,

$$\frac{\partial}{\partial\theta_i}\int f(x, \theta)dP = \int \frac{\partial}{\partial\theta_i} f(x, \theta)dP \tag{4.5}$$

Condition 1 is necessary for taking logarithms. Condition 2 ensures the existence of a tangent space in each point of the manifold, because the components of the score function

$$\left(\frac{\partial}{\partial\theta_1}l(x, \theta), \frac{\partial}{\partial\theta_2}l(x, \theta), \ldots, \frac{\partial}{\partial\theta_n}l(x, \theta)\right) \tag{4.6}$$

will be its base. Condition 3 is a first example for the double meaning (geometrical and statistical) of many notions in the theory presented here.

In the following, we will only inspect regular statistical models which are differentiable n-dimensional manifolds and which will be called statistical models or n-manifolds for short. It is well known from classical statistical theory that some standard distributions are ruled out by the regularity conditions: the discrete uniform, the hypergeometric and the rectangular distribution are eliminated completely; the binomial, the Pareto and the double exponential distribution can only be analysed as 1-manifolds.

Tangent spaces

The tangent space to a point on a manifold must be constructed abstractly because the manifold is not yet embedded in a surrounding space. This can be done in the following two ways.

A curve c lying completely in S is the image of a smooth map from a closed interval $I \subset \mathbf{R}$ into S, and it has the coordinate representation

$$c: I \to S, \quad c(t) = \theta(t) = (\theta_1(t), \ldots, \theta_n(t)), \tag{4.7}$$

where t is a curve parameter. A tangent vector of a point $p \in S$ can now be defined as an equivalence class of curves having the same directional derivative in p. Then, the tangent space T_p is the set of all tangent vectors in p. It is a vector space with dimension n.

Taking the n linearly independent vectors (see the last subsection)

$$\frac{\frac{\partial}{\partial\theta_i}p(x, \theta)}{p(x, \theta)} = \frac{\partial}{\partial\theta_i}l(x, \theta) = \partial_i l(x, \theta) \tag{4.8}$$

(called self-information) as a base for the n-dimensional vector space

$$T_\theta^{(1)} = \left\{ A(x) \middle| A(x) = \sum_{i=1}^{n} A_i \frac{\partial}{\partial \theta_i} l(x, \theta),\ A_i \in \mathbf{R} \right\}, \tag{4.9}$$

we get the so-called 1-representation of the tangent space, which is isomorphic to T_p in a natural way and which will be employed in the following because the self-information measures relative density changes.

Example 4.2. The base of $T_\theta^{(1)}$ for the 2-manifold of normal distributions with $(\theta_1, \theta_2) = (\mu, \sigma)$ is

$$\frac{\partial}{\partial \theta_1} l(x, \theta) = \frac{x - \mu}{\sigma^2} \quad \text{and} \quad \frac{\partial}{\partial \theta_2} l(x, \theta) = \frac{(x - \mu)^2}{\sigma^3} - \frac{1}{\sigma} \quad . \quad \square \tag{4.10}$$

Fisher information

In order to measure distances on S, the inner product

$$g_{ij}(\theta) = \langle \partial_i l(x, \theta), \partial_j l(x, \theta) \rangle = E[\partial_i l(x, \theta) \partial_j l(x, \theta)] \tag{4.11}$$

is formed of the base of $T_\theta^{(1)}$ by averaging out x. Because of the well-known property

$$E[\partial_i l(x, \theta)] = 0 \quad \text{for } i = 1, 2, \ldots, n, \tag{4.12}$$

we have

$$g_{ij}(\theta) = \operatorname{cov}[\partial_i l(x, \theta), \partial_j l(x, \theta)]. \tag{4.13}$$

Of course, $g_{ij}(\theta)$ is the Fisher information.

Since this $(n \times n)$-matrix is defined for every point $p \in S$, it is a matrix field $(g_{ij}(\theta))$. This matrix field is a Riemannian metric tensor, i.e. a tensor of order two with positive definite matrices and the property that the arc-length defined in the next subsection is an invariant. It is not the intention to deal with tensor calculus in this chapter (see the introduction in Kay, 1988), but only to explain its main ideas: if an expression is known to be a tensor, it is known how this expression changes under any admissible coordinate transformation. And tensorial properties and equations hold – although defined pointwise – in any admissible coordinate system and for all $p \in S$. Vector fields $V(S)$ can be tensors of order one, matrix fields can be tensors of order two, etc. An invariant is a tensor of order zero. If a Riemannian metric tensor is introduced on a manifold (allowing the measurement of distances and angles), this manifold is called a Riemannian manifold.

Besides the statistical and tensorial interpretation, the Fisher information can also be interpreted geometrically. The main diagonal provides the lengths of the base vectors (identical to the standard deviation of the self-information):

$$|\partial_i l(x,\theta)|^2 = \langle \partial_i l(x,\theta), \partial_i l(x,\theta)\rangle = g_{ii}(\theta) = \mathrm{var}(\partial_i l(x,\theta)) \tag{4.14}$$

Beside the main diagonal, we find the necessary information on the angles α_{ij} of the base vectors:

$$\cos\alpha_{ij} = \frac{\langle \partial_i l(x,\theta), \partial_j l(x,\theta)\rangle}{|\partial_i l(x,\theta)\|\partial_j l(x,\theta)|} = \frac{g_{ij}}{\sqrt{g_{ii}g_{jj}}} = \mathrm{corr}(\partial_i l(x,\theta), \partial_j l(x,\theta)) \tag{4.15}$$

Example 4.3. With the help of

$$g_{ij}(\theta) = -E[\partial_i\partial_j l(x,\theta)], \tag{4.16}$$

the Fisher information of the 2-manifold of normal distributions is found to be

$$(g_{ij}(\theta)) = \frac{1}{\sigma^2}\begin{pmatrix}1 & 0\\ 0 & 2\end{pmatrix} \tag{4.17}$$

Since $g_{12}(\theta) = 0$, the coordinate vectors of the coordinate system $\theta = (\mu, \sigma)$ are orthogonal for all $p \in S$. But the lengths of the coordinate vectors

$$|\partial_1 l(x,\theta)| = \sqrt{g_{11}(\theta)} = 1/\sigma \tag{4.18}$$

$$|\partial_2 l(x,\theta)| = \sqrt{g_{22}(\theta)} = \sqrt{2}/\sigma \tag{4.19}$$

depend on σ. Therefore, (μ, σ) is not a cartesian coordinate system. □

Rao distance

Having defined the metric tensor, the last step towards the distance between two distributions F_1 and F_2 represented by parameter values θ_1 and θ_2 is straightforward. Let $C_\lambda = \{c_\lambda | \lambda \in \Lambda\}$ be the set of all curves connecting F_1 and F_2 and lying completely in S. With $t_1 < t_2$, $c_\lambda(t_1) = \theta_1$ and $c_\lambda(t_2) = \theta_2$, the Rao distance (or geodesic distance or Riemannian distance) is the minimum arc-length of all these curves:

$$d(F_1, F_2) = \min_{c_\lambda \in C_\Lambda} \int_{t_1}^{t_2} \sqrt{\sum_{i=1}^{n}\sum_{j=1}^{n} g_{ij}(\theta(t)) \frac{d\theta_i(t)}{dt}\frac{d\theta_j(t)}{dt}}\, dt \tag{4.20}$$

$d(F_1, F_2)$ is a distance and – since the Fisher information is a Riemannian metric tensor – it is an invariant. This means that reparametrizing the original model and then calculating the Rao distance yields the same result as first calculating the distance and then translating this distance into the new parametrization (Barndorff-Nielsen, 1988, p. 13). The argument of the square root is called first fundamental form. All quantities depending only on this quadratic form are called intrinsic.

5 Calculation of Rao Distances

Following the derivation of the Rao distance in section 4, this section is concerned with the calculation of Rao distances for specific statistical distribution families. The literature mentioned at the beginning of section 4 applies to this section as well.

Affine connections and geodesics

In order to determine the curves with minimum length between two points on S, we first have to define how to go from one tangent space to another, i.e. we have to "connect" the tangent spaces. An affine connection is a bilinear map on a cartesian product of vector fields $V(S) \times V(S) \to V(S)$ providing the directional derivation of vector fields. By definition of an affine connection, a particular way is fixed for how one can move vectors from one tangent space to another. This movement is called parallel transport, and is an isomorphism between tangent spaces.

There is an infinite number of possible affine connections, but there is only one for which the parallel transport is an isometry (preserving all distances and angles) and the Christoffel symbols (see below) are symmetric. This connection is called the Levi–Civita connection. By choice of a specific connection on a manifold, specific curves – called geodesics – are distinguished to be generalizations of the straight lines in $\mathbf{R}^n$. If the Levi–Civita connection has been chosen, these geodesics locally show the shortest way (in S) between any two points on S. In $\mathbf{R}^n$, the geodesics are the straight lines. On the sphere, they are given by the "great circles," i.e. by the circles of intersection of the surface of the sphere and all planes through the center of the sphere (explaining the name "geodesic," meaning "dividing the earth").

The Levi–Civita connection is said to be compatible with the metric tensor. If a different connection is selected (e.g. the exponential connection distinguishing 1-parametric exponential families as geodesics: see Efron, 1975; Amari, 1985), this leads in general to non-Riemannian geometry and the geodesics are no longer minimizing distance.

An affine connection can be defined with the help of the n^3 Christoffel symbols of the first kind

$$\Gamma_{ijk} = \frac{1}{2}\left(\frac{\partial}{\partial\theta_i} g_{jk}(\theta) + \frac{\partial}{\partial\theta_j} g_{ki}(\theta) - \frac{\partial}{\partial\theta_k} g_{ij}(\theta)\right). \tag{5.1}$$

The Γ_{ijk} are not tensors, but they permit the definition of a so-called covariant derivative which has this property. The Christoffel symbols are symmetric in the first two indices (analogous to the commutativity of partial derivatives in $\mathbf{R}^n$):

$$\Gamma_{ijk} = \Gamma_{jik} \quad \text{forf } i, j, k = 1, 2, \ldots, n \tag{5.2}$$

And in all admissible coordinate systems, $\Gamma_{ijk} = 0$ holds iff all g_{ij} are constant.

Example 5.1. For the normal distribution and the coordinate system $\theta = (\mu, \sigma)$, the Christoffel symbols are:

$$\Gamma_{111} = \Gamma_{122} = \Gamma_{212} = \Gamma_{221} = 0 \tag{5.3}$$

$$\Gamma_{112} = \frac{1}{\sigma^3}, \quad \Gamma_{121} = \Gamma_{211} = -\frac{1}{\sigma^3}, \quad \Gamma_{222} = -\frac{2}{\sigma^3} \quad \square \tag{5.4}$$

The geodesics can be determined as solutions of the n Euler–Lagrange equations

$$\sum_{i=1}^{n} g_{ik}(\theta)\frac{d^2\theta_i}{dt^2} + \sum_{i=1}^{n}\sum_{j=1}^{n} \Gamma_{ijk}\frac{d\theta_i}{dt}\frac{d\theta_j}{dt} = 0 \tag{5.5}$$

ensuring that the "acceleration" (because of the second derivatives) on the geodesics is zero. The solution of this system of ordinary differential equations can be very difficult. The calculation of the integral in (4.20) is not any easier. But we will see more straightforward ways to calculate Rao distances in the next sections.

Rao distances in one-manifolds

If the distribution is one-parametric, the manifold simply is a curve and all calculations turn out to be rather easy. Any two Riemannian one-manifolds are locally isometric. Hence, any curve can be transformed to a straight line without changing the distances on it. The metric tensor $g(\theta)$ is a (1×1)-matrix which can be transformed to 1, the Christoffel symbol $\Gamma_{111} = g'(\theta)$ vanishes in this case, the minimization in (4.20) is unnecessary and the Rao distance of two distributions F_1 and F_2 represented by θ_1 and θ_2 reduces to

$$d(F_1, F_2) = \left| \int_{\theta_1}^{\theta_2} \sqrt{g(\theta)}\, d\theta \right| \tag{5.6}$$

(see Atkinson and Mitchell, 1981, p. 350f).

Example 5.2. For the normal distribution with known σ, it follows that $\theta = \mu$ and $g(\mu) = 1/\sigma^2$. The Rao distance of $N(\mu_1, \sigma^2)$ and $N(\mu_2, \sigma^2)$ is

$$d(F_1, F_2) = \left| \int_{\mu_1}^{\mu_2} \frac{1}{\sigma} d\mu \right| = \frac{|\mu_1 - \mu_2|}{\sigma} \tag{5.7}$$

If μ is fixed, $\theta = \sigma$ and $g(\sigma) = 2/\sigma^2$. Hence, the Rao distance of $N(\mu, \sigma_1^2)$ and $N(\mu, \sigma_2^2)$ is

$$d(F_1, F_2) = \left| \int_{\sigma_1}^{\sigma_2} \frac{\sqrt{2}}{\sigma} d\sigma \right| = \sqrt{2} \left| \ln\left(\frac{\sigma_1}{\sigma_2}\right) \right| \tag{5.8}$$

(see Rao, 1945). □

Example 5.3. The Poisson distribution with $E(X) = \theta = \lambda > 0$ is analysed by Atkinson and Mitchell (1981). They derive the Rao distance of poi(λ_1) and poi(λ_2):

$$d(F_1, F_2) = 2|\sqrt{\lambda_1} - \sqrt{\lambda_2}| \tag{5.9}$$

For the binomial distribution with $m \in \mathbf{N}$ fixed, $\theta = p \in [0, 1]$ and $E(X) = mp$, they calculate the Rao distance of bin(m, p_1) and bin(m, p_2)

$$d(F_1, F_2) = 2\sqrt{m} \arccos\left(\sqrt{p_1 p_2} + \sqrt{(1 - p_1)(1 - p_2)}\right) \tag{5.10}$$

(including the Bernoulli distribution for $m = 1$). Finally, in the case of the gamma distribution with $r > 0$ fixed, $\theta = \lambda > 0$ and $E(X) = r/\lambda$, they obtain for gam(r, λ_1) and gam(r, λ_2)

$$d(F_1, F_2) = \sqrt{r} \left| \ln\left(\frac{\lambda_1}{\lambda_2}\right) \right| \tag{5.11}$$

(with the exponential distribution for $r = 1$). □

Example 5.4. Oller and Cuadras (1985) derive the Rao distance for the negative binomial distribution with $r > 0$ fixed, $\theta = p \in [0, 1]$ and $E(X) = r(1 - p)/p$. The distance of negbin(r, p_1) and negbin(r, p_2) is

$$d(F_1, F_2) = 2\sqrt{r}\cosh^{-1}\left(\frac{1 - \sqrt{(1 - p_1)(1 - p_2)}}{\sqrt{p_1 p_2}}\right) \tag{5.12}$$

(including the geometric distribution for $r = 1$). □

Example 5.5. Burbea (1986b) adds the Pareto distribution with $x_0 > 0$ fixed, $\theta = \lambda > 0$ and $E(X) = \lambda x_0/(\lambda - 1)$ (for $\lambda > 1$). The distance between par(x_0, λ_1) and par(x_0, λ_2) turns out to be

$$d(F_1, F_2) = \left|\ln\left(\frac{\lambda_1}{\lambda_2}\right)\right| \tag{5.13}$$

For the Weibull distribution with fixed $b > 0$, $\theta = a > 0$ and $E(X) = a^{-1/b}\Gamma(1 + b^{-1})$, Burbea obtains as Rao distance of wei(a_1, b) and wei(a_2, b):

$$d(F_1, F_2) = \left|\ln\left(\frac{a_1}{a_2}\right)\right| \tag{5.14}$$

For the density functions of all preceding examples see Mood et al. (1974). Burbea (1986b) also analyses the power function distribution with density function

$$p(x; a, \lambda) = \lambda a^{-\lambda} x^{\lambda - 1} I_{(0,a]}(x) \tag{5.15}$$

where $a > 0$ and $\lambda > 0$. If a is fixed and $\theta = \lambda$, the distance of $pd(a, \lambda_1)$ and $pd(a, \lambda_2)$ is

$$d(F_1, F_2) = \left|\ln\left(\frac{\lambda_1}{\lambda_2}\right)\right| \quad \square \tag{5.16}$$

Example 5.6. Villarroya and Oller (1991) calculate the Rao distances for the inverse Gaussian distribution with density function

$$p(x; \lambda, \mu) = \sqrt{\frac{\lambda}{2\pi x^3}}\exp\left(\frac{-\lambda(x - \mu)^2}{2\mu^2 x}\right) I_{(0,\infty)}(x), \tag{5.17}$$

$\lambda > 0$ and $\mu > 0$. For fixed μ and $\theta = \lambda$, the Rao distance of $iG(\lambda_1, \mu)$ and $iG(\lambda_2, \mu)$ is

$$d(F_1, F_2) = \frac{1}{\sqrt{2}}\left|\ln\left(\frac{\lambda_1}{\lambda_2}\right)\right|. \tag{5.18}$$

If λ is fixed and $\theta = \mu$, we have for $iG(\lambda, \mu_1)$ and $iG(\lambda, \mu_2)$:

$$d(F_1, F_2) = 2\sqrt{\lambda}\left|\frac{1}{\sqrt{\mu_1}} - \frac{1}{\sqrt{\mu_2}}\right| \quad \square \tag{5.19}$$

Example 5.7. Finally, Mitchell (1992) carries out the computations for the distribution ("deviation from uniform") with density function

$$p(x; \lambda) = \lambda(2x)^{\lambda-1}I_{[0,1/2]}(x) + \lambda[2(1-x)]^{\lambda-1}I_{[1/2,1]}(x) \tag{5.20}$$

with $\lambda > 0$ ($\lambda = 1$ produces the uniform distribution over $[0, 1]$). For $\theta = \lambda$, the Rao distance also is

$$d(F_1, F_2) = \left|\ln\left(\frac{\lambda_1}{\lambda_2}\right)\right| \quad \square \tag{5.21}$$

The similarities between some of the distance measures in this subsection become understandable when we know some facts about curvature.

Curvature

Curvature measures are needed to get geometrical intuition (especially in the case of 2-parametric families, i.e. surfaces) and they are necessary for the classification of statistical distributions. The Christoffel symbol of the second kind

$$\Gamma_{ij}^{k} = \sum_{m=1}^{n} \Gamma_{ijm} g^{mk} \quad \text{for } i, j, k = 1, 2, \ldots, n, \tag{5.22}$$

is the first auxiliary quantity. $g^{mk}(\theta)$ is the inverse matrix of the metric tensor $g_{mk}(\theta)$. Similarly to (5.1), the Γ_{ij}^{k} are not tensors, but they serve for the definition of curvature tensors. These Christoffel symbols are also symmetric (in the lower indices):

$$\Gamma_{ij}^{k} = \Gamma_{ji}^{k} \quad \text{for } i, j, k = 1, 2, \ldots, n \tag{5.23}$$

And again, $\Gamma_{ij}^{k} = 0$ holds iff all g_{ij} are constant. The use of lower and upper indices has tensorial reasons (see the literature in section 4).

The Riemannian tensor of the second kind is a tensor of order 4 with n^4 components

$$R_{ijk}^{l} = \frac{\partial}{\partial\theta_j}\Gamma_{ik}^{l} - \frac{\partial}{\partial\theta_k}\Gamma_{ij}^{l} + \sum_{m=1}^{n}\Gamma_{ik}^{m}\Gamma_{mj}^{l} - \sum_{m=1}^{n}\Gamma_{ij}^{m}\Gamma_{mk}^{l} \tag{5.24}$$

and the Riemannian tensor of the first kind is also a tensor of order 4:

$$R_{ijkl} = \sum_{m=1}^{n} R_{jkl}^{m} g_{mi} \tag{5.25}$$

Both tensors consist of second derivatives of the metric tensor (measuring curvature). The following equations are very useful:

first skew symmetry:	$R_{ijkl} = -R_{jikl}$	(5.26)
second skew symmetry:	$R_{ijkl} = -R_{ijlk}$	(5.27)
block symmetry:	$R_{ijkl} = R_{klij}$	(5.28)
Bianchi's identity:	$R_{ijkl} + R_{iklj} + R_{\mathrm{iljk}} = 0$	(5.29)

They mean that only

$$s = \frac{n^2(n^2 - 1)}{12} \tag{5.30}$$

components of the Riemannian tensor of the first kind are independent from the rest and not identically zero. For $n = 1$ it follows that $s = 0$. For $n = 2$, 16 possible components reduce to $s = 1$ "significant" component, which is

$$R_{1212} = R_{2121} = -R_{1221} = -R_{2112} \tag{5.31}$$

The curvature measure which is most useful in the next sections is constructed as follows: in a point p of the n-manifold S, two directions $a = (a^1, \ldots, a^n)$ and $b = (b^1, \ldots, b^n)$ are selected from the infinite number of possible directions. Depending on p, a, and b, the sectional curvature (or mean Gaussian curvature) is

$$K = K(a, b) = \frac{\Sigma_{i,j,k,l=1}^{n} R_{ijkl} a^i b^j a^k b^l}{\Sigma_{p,q,r,s=1}^{n} (g_{pr} g_{qs} + g_{ps} g_{qr}) a^p b^q a^r b^s} \tag{5.32}$$

K is an invariant (a tensor of order zero), and R_{ijk}^{l} is completely determined by K. S is said to be of constant curvature, if K is constant (for all p, a, and b). S is said to be flat, if K vanishes (for all p, a, and b). Two manifolds with constant sectional curvature are locally isometric iff their sectional curvatures are identical. The curvature is called parabolic if $K = 0$, it is called elliptic if $K > 0$, and it is called hyperbolic if $K < 0$. If $K \neq 0$, there is no admissible transformation rendering the Fisher information constant.

For a 2-manifold, K is independent of the directions a and b and it reduces to

$$K = \frac{R_{1212}}{g_{11}g_{22} - g_{12}^2} \tag{5.33}$$

identical with the Gaussian curvature of surfaces in $\mathbf{R}^3$. Curves always have sectional curvature $K = 0$. In $\mathbf{R}^3$, the plane and the cylinder are standard examples for surfaces with constant $K = 0$ (the cylinder can be unwound to a plane without changing the distances locally). The sphere is the standard example for a surface with constant elliptic curvature ($K = 1/r^2 > 0$ with radius r) – in this case, tangent planes never cut the surfaces. Hyperbolic curvature can be seen on parts of the torus (the tube of a bicycle). The inner side (facing the spokes) shows hyperbolic curvature, the outer side (facing the street) is elliptically curved. In the neighborhood of hyperbolic points, tangent planes always cut the surface.

It may be appropriate to remark that the curvature measures discussed here are not identical with the "statistical curvature" introduced by Efron (1975), which is the curvature of embedding of a submanifold (known as Euler–Schouten curvature) in non-Riemannian geometry (see Amari, 1985; Lauritzen, 1987).

Example 5.8. For the normal distribution with $\theta = (\mu, \sigma)$, the inverse of the Fisher information is

$$(g_{ij}(\theta))^{-1} = (g^{ij}(\theta)) = \sigma^2\begin{pmatrix} 1 & 0 \\ 0 & 1/2 \end{pmatrix} \tag{5.34}$$

The eight Christoffel symbols of the second kind follow:

$$\Gamma^1_{11} = \Gamma^2_{12} = \Gamma^2_{21} = \Gamma^1_{22} = 0 \tag{5.35}$$

$$\Gamma^2_{11} = \frac{1}{2\sigma}, \quad \Gamma^1_{12} = \Gamma^1_{21} = \Gamma^2_{22} = -\frac{1}{\sigma} \tag{5.36}$$

The "significant" Riemannian tensors of the first and the second kind are calculated as

$$R^1_{212} = -\frac{1}{\sigma^2} \quad R_{1212} = -\frac{1}{\sigma^4} \tag{5.37}$$

Hence, the sectional curvature is

$$K = -\frac{1}{2} \tag{5.38}$$

and this two-manifold is of constant hyperbolic curvature – independent of the parametrization (see Amari, 1985, pp. 7 and 30, who derived this result in 1959). □

Example 5.9. A random variable X is said to follow a distribution of the location-scale family, if the distribution depends only on the two-dimensional parameter (μ, σ) with $\sigma > 0$ in the form

$$F(x; \mu, \sigma) = F\left(\frac{x - \mu}{\sigma}\right) \tag{5.39}$$

Yoshizawa (1971b) shows that location-scale families (like the normal distribution or the logistic distribution) always have constant hyperbolic curvature. □

Example 5.10. A p-dimensional random variable X follows an elliptic distribution – $X \sim EL_p^h(\mu, \Sigma)$ – if its density function is

$$p_h(x; \mu, \Sigma) = (\det \Sigma)^{-1/2} h\{(x - \mu)'\Sigma^{-1}(x - \mu)\} \tag{5.40}$$

with $\mu = (\mu_1, \ldots, \mu_p)$, a positive definite $(p \times p)$-matrix Σ and a function h. Mitchell (1988) examines the univariate elliptic distribution $(p = 1)$, a 2-manifold with $\theta = (\mu, \sigma)$. The t-distribution with k degrees of freedom has sectional curvature

$$K = -\frac{1}{2} - \frac{3}{2k} \tag{5.41}$$

comprising the normal distribution (for $k \to \infty$) and the Cauchy distribution for $k = 1$. Burbea and Oller (1988) analyse a more general subfamily of the univariate elliptic distribution also having constant negative curvature.

Mitchell (1989) carries out some large-scale calculations for the multivariate elliptic distribution, an n-manifold with $n = (p^2 + 3p)/2$. Then, the restriction to the subfamily with fixed matrix Σ is very simple, because this manifold with the $n = p$ parameters $\theta = (\mu_1, \ldots, \mu_p)$ is flat (see Mitchell and Krzanowski, 1985). □

Example 5.11. The most important special case of the previous distribution, the multivariate normal distribution with mean vector $\mu = (\mu_1, \ldots, \mu_p)$, positive definite covariance matrix Σ and density function

$$p(x; \mu, \Sigma) = (2\pi)^{-p/2}(\det \Sigma)^{-1/2} \exp\left\{-\frac{1}{2}(x - \mu)'\Sigma^{-1}(x - \mu)\right\} \tag{5.42}$$

also leads to an n-manifold with $n = (p^2 + 3p)/2$. Skovgaard (1984) is the fundamental paper on the differential geometry of this distribution.

Sato et al. (1979) explicitly present all results for the five-manifold of the bivariate normal distribution. In the coordinate system $\theta = (\theta_1, \ldots, \theta_5) = (\mu_1, \mu_2, \sigma_{11}, \sigma_{12}, \sigma_{22})$, the Fisher information is

$$(g_{ij}(\theta)) = \frac{1}{|\Sigma|^2}\begin{pmatrix} \sigma_{22}|\Sigma| & -\sigma_{12}|\Sigma| & 0 & 0 & 0 \\ -\sigma_{12}|\Sigma| & \sigma_{11}|\Sigma| & 0 & 0 & 0 \\ 0 & 0 & \sigma_{22}^2/2 & -\sigma_{12}\sigma_{22} & \sigma_{12}^2/2 \\ 0 & 0 & -\sigma_{12}\sigma_{22} & \sigma_{11}\sigma_{22} + \sigma_{12}^2 & -\sigma_{11}\sigma_{12} \\ 0 & 0 & \sigma_{12}^2/2 & -\sigma_{11}\sigma_{12} & \sigma_{11}^2/2 \end{pmatrix} \tag{5.43}$$

where $|\Sigma|$ is the determinant of Σ. Then, the sectional curvatures $K(i, j)$ with $i, j = 1, \ldots, 5$ and $i < j$ are calculated for all pairs of base vectors of the tangent space of this manifold (see section 4):

$$K(1, 2) = \frac{1}{4}$$

$$K(1, 3) = K(2, 5) = K(3, 4) = K(4, 5) = -\frac{1}{2}$$

$$K(1, 4) = K(2, 4) = -\frac{1 + 3\rho^2}{4(1 + \rho^2)}$$

$$K(1, 5) = K(2, 3) = -\frac{\rho^2}{2}$$

$$K(3, 5) = -\frac{\rho^2}{1 + \rho^2} \tag{5.44}$$

ρ is the correlation coefficient. $K(1, 3) = K(2, 5)$ is the univariate case.

Independence of the marginal distributions ($\sigma_{12} = 0$) leads to a 4-manifold with diagonal Fisher information and constant $K(i, j)$ (see Sato et al., 1979; Burbea, 1986b). Restriction to the subfamily with fixed matrix Σ leads to a flat two-manifold with $\theta = (\mu_1, \mu_2)$ and constant metric tensor (see the previous example). On the contrary, setting $\mu_1 = \mu_2 = 0$ reduces the dimension of the manifold to three but does not simplify the geometry. □

Example 5.12. Oller (1986) analyzes the following distributions. The Gumbel distribution with $\theta = (\alpha, \beta)$, $\beta > 0$ and $E(X) = \alpha + \beta\gamma$ (with the Euler constant $\gamma = 0.5772$) and the Weibull distribution (see example 5.5) with $\theta = (a, b)$ both have sectional curvature

$$K = -\frac{6}{\pi^2} \tag{5.45}$$

because the two-manifolds of these extreme value distributions are isometric (see Johnson and Kotz, 1970, volume I, pp. 272ff, for the transformations).

The logistic distribution with $\theta = (\alpha, \beta)$, $\beta > 0$ and $E(X) = \alpha$ also has constant negative curvature

$$K = -\frac{9}{\pi^2 + 3} \tag{5.46}$$

See Mood et al. (1974) for the density (distribution) functions. □

Example 5.13. The sectional curvature of the inverse Gaussian distribution (see example 5.6) with $\theta = (\lambda, \mu)$ is calculated by Lauritzen (1987):

$$K = -\frac{1}{2} \tag{5.47}$$

This two-manifold is isometric to the submanifold of the two-manifold of normal distributions $N(\eta, \sigma^2)$ with $\eta > 0$. The isometric transformation is

$$\eta = \frac{2}{\sqrt{\mu}} \quad \text{und} \quad \sigma = \frac{2}{\sqrt{\lambda}} \tag{5.48}$$

(see Villarroya and Oller, 1991, p. 4). □

Example 5.14. The two-manifold of gamma distributions with $\theta = (r, \lambda)$ (cf. example 5.3) possesses non-constant sectional curvature

$$K = \frac{\phi(r) + r\phi'(r)}{4r^2\phi(r)} \tag{5.49}$$

calculated by Lauritzen (1987, pp. 203ff) where

$$\phi(r) = \frac{d^2}{dr^2}\ln\Gamma(r) - \frac{1}{r} \tag{5.50}$$

The complications arise because of the derivatives of the gamma function. That is also why no results are published for the beta distribution. □

Example 5.15. If $r > 0$ is fixed, $x = (x_1, \ldots, x_n) \in \mathbf{N}^n$, $\theta = (q_1, \ldots, q_n)$, $q_{n+1} = 1 - \Sigma_{i=1}^n q_i$ with $0 < q_i < 1$ for $i = 1, \ldots, n + 1$ and the density function has the form

$$p(x; \theta, r) = \frac{\Gamma(x_1 + \ldots + x_n + r)}{x_1! \cdot \ldots \cdot x_n! \cdot \Gamma(r)} q_1^{x_1} \cdot \ldots \cdot q_n^{x_n} \cdot q_{n+1}^r \tag{5.51}$$

the random variable X is said to follow a negative multinomial distribution. Oller and Cuadras (1985) derive that, for $n \geqslant 2$, this n-manifold has constant negative curvature

$$K = -\frac{1}{4r} \tag{5.52}$$

Hence, for any n, the sectional curvature does not depend on the directions (see definition (5.32) and the example of the bivariate normal distribution). □

Example 5.16. Yoshizawa (1971a) shows that the n-manifold of multinomial distributions with $m \in \mathbf{N}$ fixed, $\theta = (p_1, \ldots, p_n)$, $p_{n+1} = 1 - \Sigma_{i=1}^n p_i$ with $0 < p_i < 1$ for $i = 1, \ldots, n + 1$ (see Mood et al., 1974, p. 137, for the density function) possesses constant positive (elliptic) curvature

$$K = \frac{1}{4m} \tag{5.53}$$

for $n \geqslant 2$ (see also Kass, 1989; Amari, 1985, pp. 12ff). Hence, the two-manifold of the trinomial distribution is isometric to the sphere with radius $2\sqrt{m}$. □

The sectional curvatures of two-parametric distribution families are collected in table 16.1. It is interesting to see that there is no distribution in this list with $K < -1$ and existing second moments.

The results of the examples above provide a hierarchy of statistical distributions with regard to the easy calculability of Rao distances. In one case – the multivariate elliptic (normal) distribution with fixed matrix Σ – the manifold is flat so that the determination of Rao distances consists of an admissible transformation and the application of the theorem of Pythagoras. In one case – the multinomial distribution – the manifold has constant positive sectional curvature which reduces the calculation of the Rao distance to an admissible transformation and the application of the results of spherical geometry.

Many standard statistical distributions lead to manifolds with constant negative sectional curvature. This calls for deeper knowledge

Table 16.1 Sectional curvatures in twoparametric families

Distribution	*Sectional curvature K*
trinomial (m fixed)	$1/4m$
biv. ellipt. (Σ fixed)	0
biv. normal (Σ fixed)	0
location-scale	<0
neg. trinomial (r fixed)	$-1/4r$
normal = $t(\infty)$	-0.5
inv. Gaussian	-0.5
$t(k)$ (k fixed)	$-1/2-3/(2k)$
Gumbel	$-6/\pi^2 = -0.6079$
Weibull	$-6/\pi^2 = -0.6079$
logistic	$-9/(\pi^2 + 3) = -0.6993$
$t(3)$	-1
Cauchy = $t(1)$	-2

of the rather unfamiliar – for most statisticians – hyperbolic geometry (see below). But this problem is solvable, whereas the distributions with nonconstant sectional curvature rarely admit the calculation of Rao distances up to now. And when the sectional curvature is unknown or when the distribution is nonregular, the Rao distances are always unknown (at present).

Rao distances in two-manifolds

Any Riemannian two-manifold with positive (not necessarily constant) sectional curvature can be embedded isometrically in $\mathbf{R}^3$. Comparable results are not available for two-manifolds with hyperbolic curvature, because no embedded complete surface in $\mathbf{R}^3$ can have constant negative curvature (a metric space is called complete if any Cauchy sequence converges). Any surface in $\mathbf{R}^3$ with constant negative curvature must have singularities (like the pseudosphere: see Berger and Gostiaux, 1988, p. 361).

That is why the Poincaré-model is used in most cases for the distorted representation of two-manifolds with constant hyperbolic curvature in $\mathbf{R}^2$. For $K = -1$ (the hyperbolic analogon of the unit sphere, statistically represented by the $t(3)$-distribution), the set of points is the upper half-plane without the abscissa and the (distorted) geodesics are all semicircles with center on the abscissa and all straight lines orthogonal to the abscissa (see Millman and Parker, 1991).

The derivation of the Rao distance for a two-manifold with constant hyperbolic curvature now consists of a transformation of its metric to the Poincaré metric

$$ds^2 = \frac{(d\mu^*)^2 + (d\sigma^*)^2}{(\sigma^*)^2}, \tag{5.54}$$

which is the first fundamental form of the two-manifold with constant $K = -1$. This manifold is known to have the so-called Möbius distance

$$d(F_1, F_2) = \ln\left(\frac{1+\delta}{1-\delta}\right) = 2\tanh^{-1}(\delta) \tag{5.55}$$

with

$$\delta = \sqrt{\frac{(\mu_1^* - \mu_2^*)^2 + (\sigma_1^* - \sigma_2^*)^2}{(\mu_1^* - \mu_2^*)^2 + (\sigma_1^* + \sigma_2^*)^2}} \tag{5.56}$$

as Rao distance (see Burbea and Rao, 1982).

Example 5.17. The metric of the two-manifold of normal distributions with $\theta = (\mu, \sigma)$ is

$$ds_{NV}^2 = \frac{(d\mu)^2 + 2(d\sigma)^2}{\sigma^2} \tag{5.57}$$

which can be transformed to the Poincaré metric by the transformation

$$\mu^* = \frac{\mu}{\sqrt{2}}, \quad \sigma^* = \sigma, \quad ds^2 = \frac{ds_{NV}^2}{2} \tag{5.58}$$

Thus, the Rao distance of $N(\mu_1, \sigma_1)$ and $N(\mu_2, \sigma_2)$ is obtained by retransforming the Möbius distance to

$$d(F_1, F_2) = 2\sqrt{2}\tanh^{-1}\left(\sqrt{\frac{(\mu_1 - \mu_2)^2 + 2(\sigma_1 - \sigma_2)^2}{(\mu_1 - \mu_2)^2 + 2(\sigma_1 + \sigma_2)^2}}\right) \tag{5.59}$$

(Atkinson and Mitchell, 1981, pp. 352ff).

For $\mu_1 = \mu_2$, (5.59) reduces to (5.8) but $\sigma_1 = \sigma_2$ does not lead to (5.7). The reason for this peculiarity is that 1-manifolds are always locally isometric to straight lines, whereas the geodesics of the hyperbolic two-manifold are only straight lines for fixed μ (and not for fixed σ). If, however,

$$|\mu_1 - \mu_2| < \sigma \tag{5.60}$$

(5.7) is a good approximation for (5.59), because the arcs of the circles are similar to straight lines in this case (Atkinson and Mitchell, 1981, p. 355).

Finally, we see that for any fixed μ_1 and μ_2

$$\lim_{\sigma\to\infty} d(N(\mu_1, \sigma), N(\mu_2, \sigma)) = 0, \quad \lim_{\sigma\to 0} d(N(\mu_1, \sigma), N(\mu_2, \sigma)) = \infty \quad \square \tag{5.61}$$

Example 5.18. For the logistic distribution (see example 5.12), Oller (1986) obtains the metric

$$ds^2_{\log} = \frac{(d\alpha)^2}{3\beta^2} + \frac{\pi^2 + 3}{9\beta^2}(d\beta)^2, \tag{5.62}$$

which can be transformed to the Poincaré metric by

$$\alpha^* = \sqrt{\frac{3}{\pi^2 + 3}}\alpha, \quad \beta^* = \beta, \quad ds^2 = ds^2_{\log}\frac{9}{\pi^2 + 3} \tag{5.63}$$

The Rao distance of $\log(\alpha_1, \beta_1)$ and $\log(\alpha_2, \beta_2)$ follows:

$$d(F_1, F_2) = 2\frac{\sqrt{\pi^2 + 3}}{3} \tanh^{-1}\left(\sqrt{\frac{[3/(\pi^2 + 3)](\alpha_1 - \alpha_2)^2 + (\beta_1 - \beta_2)^2}{[3/(\pi^2 + 3)](\alpha_1 - \alpha_2)^2 + (\beta_1 + \beta_2)^2}}\right) \tag{5.64}$$

On the same way, he obtains the Rao distance of two Gumbel distributions (see example 5.12) $\text{gum}(\alpha_1, \beta_1)$ and $\text{gum}(\alpha_2, \beta_2)$:

$$d(F_1, F_2) = 2\frac{\pi}{\sqrt{6}} \tanh^{-1}\left(\sqrt{\frac{[(\alpha_2 - \alpha_1) + (1 - \gamma)(\beta_2 - \beta_1)]^2 + [\pi/\sqrt{6}]^2(\beta_2 - \beta_1)^2}{[(\alpha_2 - \alpha_1) + (1 - \gamma)(\beta_2 - \beta_1)]^2 + [\pi/\sqrt{6}]^2(\beta_2 + \beta_1)^2}}\right) \tag{5.65}$$

The results for the Cauchy–Fréchet extreme-value family and two versions of the Weibull distribution are derived by simple transformations. $\square$

Example 5.19. Mitchell (1988) derives the Rao distance for the univariate elliptic distribution, and Burbea and Oller (1988) add the distance formula for a subfamily – see example 5.10. $\square$

Example 5.20. The Rao distance of two inverse Gaussian distributions $iG(\lambda_1, \mu_1)$ and $iG(\lambda_2, \mu_2)$ emerges from (5.59) by the isometric transformation in example 5.13:

$$d(F_1, F_2) = 2\sqrt{2}\tanh^{-1}\left(\sqrt{\frac{2(\sqrt{1/\mu_2} - \sqrt{1/\mu_2})^2 + (\sqrt{1/\lambda_2} - \sqrt{1/\lambda_2})^2}{2(\sqrt{1/\mu_2} - \sqrt{1/\mu_2})^2 + (\sqrt{1/\lambda_2} + \sqrt{1/\lambda_2})^2}}\right) \quad \square \tag{5.66}$$

Isocircles

An isocircle on a two-manifold S is the set of all points $p \in S$ having constant distance $d > 0$ from a "center" $p_0 \in S$. This generalization of the circle in Euclidean space can be very useful in two-parametric applications of Rao distances (see section 7). Isointervals on curves and isospheres on n-manifolds with $n \geqslant 3$ are defined in the same way.

Example 5.21. For the calculation of the isocircle with fixed "radius" $d > 0$ and "center" (μ_1, σ_1) for the two-parametric normal distribution, (5.59) has to be solved for μ_2 and σ_2. For improved readability, we write

$$A = \left[\tanh\left(\frac{d}{2\sqrt{2}}\right)\right]^2, \quad m = \mu_1, \quad \mu = \mu_2, \quad s = \sigma_1, \quad \sigma = \sigma_2 \tag{5.67}$$

with $0 \leqslant A < 1$ and obtain

$$\sigma_{1,2} = \frac{1 + A}{1 - A}s \pm \sqrt{\frac{4As^2}{(1 - A)^2} - \frac{(m - \mu)^2}{2}} \tag{5.68}$$

σ is maximal (minimal) for $m = \mu$ and the extreme values of μ are

$$\mu_{\max,\min} = m \pm \frac{\sqrt{8A}}{1 - A}s \tag{5.69}$$

Figure 16.2 shows the isocircle for $d = 1$ and $(m, s) = (0, 1)$.

1 A shift in μ-direction does not change the isocircle, because the metric tensor only depends on σ.

2 A shift in σ-direction does not change the form but either the Euclidean volume of the isocircle or the relative position of the "center."

   (a) The isocircle for $d = 1$ and $(m, s) = (0, 0.1)$ has the same form but is much smaller because the distances increase with decreasing σ. Division by 10 of all coordinates would restore the former Euclidean volume because the decreasing volume

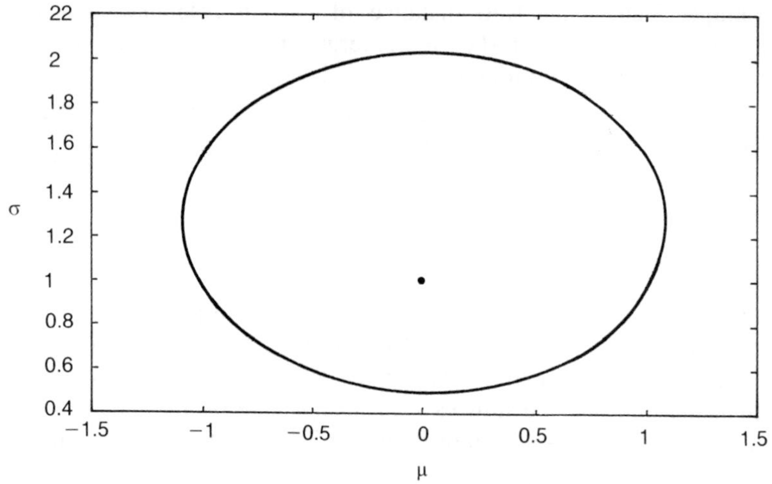

Figure 16.2 Normal distribution: isocircle for $d = 1$ and $(m, s) = (0, 1)$.

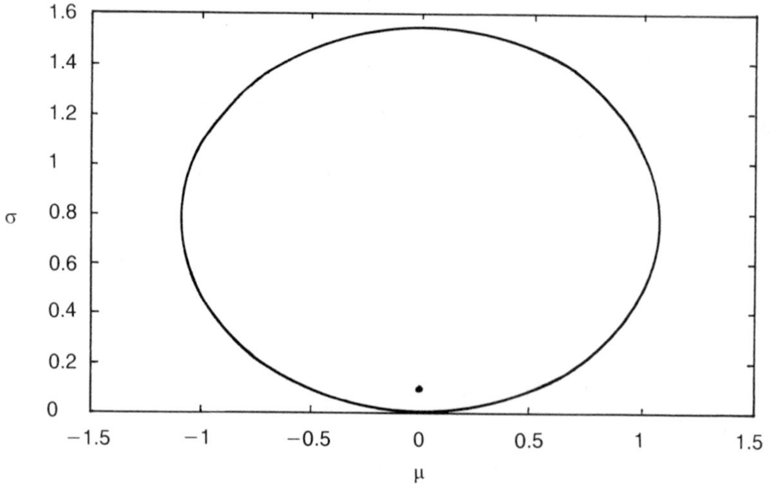

Figure 16.3 Normal distribution: isocircle for $d = 3.862$ and $(m, s) = (0, 0.1)$.

was created by the distorted representation of the hyperbolic surface in $\mathbf{R}^2$.

(b) Calculating the isocircle for $(m, s) = (0, 0.1)$ with constant Euclidean volume provides an isocircle of the same form with $d = 3.862$, where the "center" has been shifted away from the

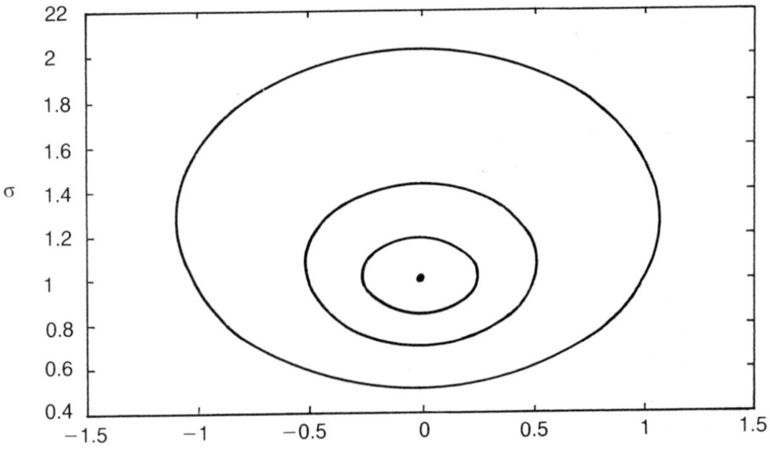

Figure 16.4 Normal distribution: isocircles for $d = 0.25$, 0.5, and 1, and $(m, s) = (0, 1)$.

Euclidean center (see figure 16.3). Note that the distance between any distribution and the μ-axis is infinity.

3 Variation of the "radius" d leads to the isocircles in figure 16.4 where $d = 0.25, 0.5, 1$ and $(m, s) = (0, 1)$: the form is identical but the size varies.

4 The form of the isocircles is always the same within the distribution family, and it depends on the transformation (5.58). Division of μ by $\sqrt{2}$ would undo the transformation producing the isocircles of the two-manifold with $K = -1$: Ordinary circles, but the "centers" remain shifted. □

Example 5.22. We also take the $(E(X), \sqrt{\text{var}(X)})$-parametrization for the logistic distribution (see example 5.18). This is easily possible because of the invariance of the Rao distance. Since

$$E[X] = \alpha \quad \text{and} \quad \text{var}[X] = \frac{\beta^2\pi^2}{3} \tag{5.70}$$

the abbreviations

$$A = \left[\tanh\left(\frac{3d}{2\sqrt{\pi^2 + 3}}\right)\right]^2, \quad \mu = \alpha_2, \quad m = \alpha_1, \quad \sigma = \frac{\beta_2\pi}{\sqrt{3}}, \quad s = \frac{\beta_1\pi}{\sqrt{3}} \tag{5.71}$$

are chosen. The isocircle with "center" (m, s) and "radius" $d > 0$ follows:

$$\sigma_{1,2} = \frac{1 + A}{1 - A}s \pm \sqrt{\frac{4As^2}{(1 - A)^2} - \frac{\pi^2}{\pi^2 + 3}(m - \mu)^2} \qquad (5.72)$$

σ is maximal (minimal) for $m = \mu$. The extreme values of μ are

$$\mu_{\max,\min} = m \pm \frac{2\sqrt{A(\pi^2 + 3)}}{\pi(1 - A)}s \qquad (5.73)$$

The sectional curvature $K = -0.6993$ of this distribution is a bit more similar to the value of the hyperbolic "unit surface" than the normal distribution is. Hence, the isocircles are a bit more "circle-like." Apart from that, the description of the previous example remains valid. □

Rao distances for multivariate distributions

The calculation of Rao distances for multivariate distributions often is still impossible without restrictions on the parameter vector leading to submanifolds with constant sectional curvature.

Example 5.23. Atkinson and Mitchell (1981) derive the Rao distance between two p-dimensional multivariate normal distributions $N_p(\mu_1, \Sigma)$ and $N_p(\mu_2, \Sigma)$ with fixed covariance matrix. Since this p-manifold is flat (cf. example 5.11), a simple transformation of the Euclidean distance leads to

$$d(F_1, F_2) = \sqrt{(\mu_1 - \mu_2)'\Sigma^{-1}(\mu_1 - \mu_2)}, \qquad (5.74)$$

the square root of the well-known Mahalanobis distance (Mahalanobis, 1936). (5.74) reduces to (5.7) for $p = 1$.

James (1973) and S. T. Jensen (1976, published in Atkinson and Mitchell, 1981) solve the problem for the multivariate normal distribution with fixed mean vector. In this n-manifold with $n = (p^2 + p)/2$ and nonconstant sectional curvatures, the Rao distance of $N_p(\mu, \Sigma_1)$ and $N_p(\mu, \Sigma_2)$ is

$$d(F_1, F_2) = \sqrt{\frac{1}{2}\sum_{i=1}^{p}(\ln \lambda_i)^2} \qquad (5.75)$$

where $0 < \lambda_1 \leqslant \lambda_2 \leqslant \ldots \leqslant \lambda_p$ are the roots of the determinantal equation

$$|\Sigma_2 - \lambda\Sigma_1| = 0 \qquad (5.76)$$

For $p = 1$, (5.75) reduces to (5.8) except for a factor 2.

Independence of the marginal distributions leads to a $(2p)$-manifold with diagonal Fisher information and constant (not identical) sectional curvatures. Since

$$I(X_1, X_2) = I(X_1) + I(X_2) \tag{5.77}$$

holds for the Fisher information $I(X_1, X_2)$ of independent random variables X_1 and X_2, the Rao distance can be derived from the univariate distance in (5.59). If

$$\Lambda = \operatorname{diag}(\sigma_1^2, \ldots, \sigma_p^2) \tag{5.78}$$

the Rao distance of $N_p(\mu_1, \Lambda_1)$ and $N_p(\mu_2, \Lambda_2)$ is

$$d(F_1, F_2) = 2\sqrt{2}\sqrt{\sum_{i=1}^{p}\left[\tanh^{-1}\left(\sqrt{\frac{(\mu_{1i} - \mu_{2i})^2 + 2(\sigma_{1i} - \sigma_{2i})^2}{(\mu_{1i} - \mu_{2i})^2 + 2(\sigma_{1i} + \sigma_{2i})^2}}\right)\right]^2} \tag{5.79}$$

reducing to (5.59) for $p = 1$ (see Burbea, 1986b).

Burbea and Oller (1988) and Oller (1989) treat the case of the univariate normal linear model. If Y is a $(t \times 1)$ random vector of dependent variables, X a constant $(t \times p)$ matrix of independent variables, β a $(p \times 1)$ parameter vector and $\sigma > 0$, the Rao distance of two linear models is

$$d(F_1, F_2) = 2\sqrt{2t}\tanh^{-1}\left(\sqrt{\frac{(\beta_1 - \beta_2)'(\beta_1 - \beta_2) + 2t(\sigma_1 - \sigma_2)^2}{(\beta_1 - \beta_2)'(\beta_1 - \beta_2) + 2t(\sigma_1 + \sigma_2)^2}}\right) \tag{5.80}$$

Unfortunately, the Rao distance for the multivariate normal distribution without restrictions on the parameter vector has not been found so far, not even for $p = 2$! Eriksen (1987) manages to derive the geodesics, but cannot prove their uniqueness in connecting any two points. That is why Calvo and Oller (1990) derive a general lower bound for the Rao distance in this manifold. This lower bound is also a distance measure with certain invariance properties. It reduces to (5.75) for fixed mean vector, and it is a monotone function of (5.74) for fixed covariance matrix. □

Example 5.24. Mitchell and Krzanowski (1985) derive the Rao distance between two p-dimensional multivariate elliptic distributions $EL_p^h(\mu_1, \Sigma)$ and $EL_p^h(\mu_2, \Sigma)$ with identical matrix Σ. This p-manifold is flat (cf. example 5.10). If the second moments exist for the family under consideration, the distance is

$$d(F_1, F_2) = \sqrt{c_h(\mu_1 - \mu_2)'\Omega^{-1}(\mu_1 - \mu_2)} \tag{5.81}$$

$\Omega = a_h\Sigma$, and the two constants a_h and c_h depend on the distribution family (i.e. on the function h). In case of the normal distribution, $a_h = c_h = 1$ and (5.81) reduces to (5.74). □

Example 5.25. Oller and Cuadras (1985) and Burbea (1986b) calculate the distance for two negative multinomial distributions negmul(r, $q_{11}, \ldots, q_{1n}$) and negmul(r, $q_{21}, \ldots, q_{2n}$) with fixed r. In this n-manifold with constant negative sectional curvature (see example 5.15), the Rao distance follows:

$$d(F_1, F_2) = 2\sqrt{r}\cosh^{-1}\left(\frac{1 - \Sigma_{i=1}^{n}\sqrt{q_{1i}q_{2i}}}{\sqrt{q_{1,n+1}q_{2,n+1}}}\right) \tag{5.82}$$

reducing to (5.12) for $n = 1$. □

Example 5.26. The family of multinomial distributions with fixed parameter m is the only known n-manifold with constant positive sectional curvature (see example 5.16). A transformation of the distance formula from spherical geometry leads to the Rao distance for mul(m, $p_{11}, \ldots, p_{1n}$) and mul(m, $p_{21}, \ldots, p_{2n}$):

$$d(F_1, F_2) = 2\sqrt{m}\arccos\left(\sum_{i=1}^{n+1}\sqrt{p_{1i}p_{2i}}\right) \tag{5.83}$$

(Rao, 1945; Atkinson and Mitchell, 1981). (5.83) reduces to (5.10) for $n = 1$. □

Example 5.27. The density function of the multivariate Poisson distribution with independent marginal distributions is defined to be

$$p(x; \lambda) = \frac{\exp(-\lambda_1 - \ldots - \lambda_n)\lambda_1^{x_1}\cdot\ldots\cdot\lambda_n^{x_n}}{x_1!\cdot\ldots\cdot x_n!} \tag{5.84}$$

where $x = (x_1, \ldots, x_n) \in \mathbf{Z}_+^n$ and $\lambda = (\lambda_1, \ldots, \lambda_n)$ with $\lambda_i > 0$ for $i = 1, \ldots, n$. This n-manifold is flat (see Burbea, 1986b). The Rao distance between poi($\lambda_{11}, \ldots, \lambda_{1n}$) and poi($\lambda_{21}, \ldots, \lambda_{2n}$) is derived as in (5.79):

$$d(F_1, F_2) = 2\sqrt{\sum_{i=1}^{n}(\sqrt{\lambda_{1i}} - \sqrt{\lambda_{2i}})^2} \tag{5.85}$$

$n = 1$ provides (5.9).

Along the same lines, Oller (1986) derives the Rao distance for the multivariate Gumbel distribution with independent marginal distributions, and Villarroya and Oller (1991) calculate the Rao distance for two versions of the multivariate inverse Gaussian distribution with independent marginal distributions. □

6 Estimation and Tests

The parameter values defining the distributions for which the Rao distance will be calculated are normally unknown. Hence, the parameter values and the Rao distances must be estimated. Distance (divergence) measures and tests are closely related. Therefore, it is not surprising to see that it is possible to construct tests from (estimated) distances. This section summarizes the few (encouraging) results on estimated Rao distances and Rao distance tests. Important papers on this topic are Skovgaard (1984), Burbea and Oller (1989), Villarroya and Oller (1991), Mitchell (1992), and Oller and Corcuera (1993).

Estimation of Rao distances

If the n-dimensional parameters θ_1 and θ_2 of an n-parametric distribution family have been estimated by maximum likelihood (ML) from independent random samples, the invariance property of ML estimators provides an ML estimation of the required Rao distance:

$$\hat{d}_{ML}(\theta_1, \theta_2) = d(\hat{\theta}_{1,ML}, \hat{\theta}_{2,ML}) \tag{6.1}$$

Mitchell (1992) calls this an estimative distance, and she compares it with a so-called predictive distance derived from a Bayesian framework. Her analysis is restricted to exponential families admitting n sufficient and continuous statistics

$$t = (t_1, \ldots, t_n) \in \mathscr{T}, \tag{6.2}$$

where $m \geqslant n$ holds for the sample size m. Let Z denote a future independent observation from $p(x|\theta)$ based on a random sample with t. t is taken as base of the n-dimensional manifold

$$\{p_Z(z|t)|t \in \mathscr{T}\} \tag{6.3}$$

where the predictive density $p_Z(z|t)$ for Z is given by

$$p_Z(z|t) = \int_\Theta p(z|\theta)\pi(\theta|t)d\theta \tag{6.4}$$

$\pi(\theta|t)$ is the posterior density of θ given t, corresponding to the prior density $\pi(\theta)$. Then, the predictive distance $\hat{d}_P$ between $p_Z(z|t_1)$ and

$p_Z(z|t_2)$ can be derived, where t_1 and t_2 are now values of t based on independent random samples of size m from $p(x|\theta_1)$ and $p(x|\theta_2)$, respectively (see Mitchell, 1992, p. 108f). In the examples considered by the author, Jeffreys's (1948) invariant prior

$$\pi(\theta) \propto \sqrt{\det(g_{ij}(\theta))} \tag{6.5}$$

is chosen.

Example 6.1. Mitchell (1992) considers the gamma distribution with known $r > 0$ and $\theta = \lambda > 0$ (see example 5.3). With

$$g(\lambda) = \frac{r}{\lambda^2} \quad t = m\bar{x} \quad \hat{\lambda}_{ML} = \frac{r}{\bar{x}} \tag{6.6}$$

the estimative distance of (5.11) is

$$\hat{d}_{ML}(\lambda_1, \lambda_2) = d(\hat{\lambda}_{1,ML}, \hat{\lambda}_{2,ML}) = \sqrt{r}\left|\ln\left(\frac{t_1}{t_2}\right)\right| \tag{6.7}$$

Based on Jeffreys's prior

$$\pi(\lambda) \propto \sqrt{g(\lambda)} \propto \frac{1}{\lambda} \tag{6.8}$$

the posterior density is

$$\pi(\lambda|t) = \frac{\lambda^{mr-1} t^{mr} e^{-\lambda t}}{\Gamma(mr)} I_{(0,\infty)}(\lambda) \tag{6.9}$$

and the predictive density is

$$p_Z(z|t) = \frac{\Gamma(mr + r) t^{mr} z^{r-1}}{\Gamma(r)\Gamma(mr)(z + t)^{mr+r}} I_{(0,\infty)}(z) \tag{6.10}$$

with the associated information

$$g_Z(t) = \frac{mr}{mr + r + 1} g(t) \tag{6.11}$$

The predictive distance then follows to be

$$\hat{d}_P(\lambda_1, \lambda_2) = \sqrt{\frac{mr}{mr + r + 1}}\hat{d}_{ML}(\hat{\lambda}_1, \lambda_2) < \hat{d}_{ML}(\lambda_1, \lambda_2) \quad \square \tag{6.12}$$

Hence, the predictive distance is a simple multiple of the estimative distance with a factor less than one. If m tends to infinity, $\hat{d}_P = \hat{d}_{ML}$. The following examples give rise to the conjecture that this relation is not random.

Example 6.2. For the normal distribution (cf. example 5.2) with known $\sigma > 0$ and $\theta = \mu$, Mitchell (1992) calculates

$$\hat{d}_{ML}(\mu_1, \mu_2) = \frac{|t_1 - t_2|}{\sigma} \quad \text{with} \quad t = \bar{x} \tag{6.13}$$

and

$$\hat{d}_P(\mu_1, \mu_2) = c \cdot \hat{d}_{ML}(\mu_1, \mu_2) \quad \text{with} \quad c = \sqrt{\frac{m}{m+1}} < 1 \tag{6.14}$$

In the case of the normal distribution with fixed μ and $\theta = \sigma$, she derives

$$\hat{d}_{ML}(\sigma_1, \sigma_2) = \sqrt{2}\left|\ln\left(\frac{t_1}{t_2}\right)\right| \quad \text{with} \quad t = \frac{1}{m}\sum_{i=1}^{m}(x_i - \mu)^2 \tag{6.15}$$

and

$$\hat{d}_P(\sigma_1, \sigma_2) = c \cdot \hat{d}_{ML}(\sigma_1, \sigma_2) \quad \text{with} \quad c = \sqrt{\frac{m}{m+1}} < 1 \tag{6.16}$$

For the "deviation from uniform" distribution (cf. example 5.7) with $\theta = \lambda > 0$, her results are

$$\hat{d}_{ML}(\lambda_1, \lambda_2) = \left|\ln\left(\frac{t_1}{t_2}\right)\right|$$

$$t = -\sum_{i=1}^{m}[\ln(2x_i)I_{[0,1/2]}(x_i) + \ln(2(1 - x_i))I_{(1/2,1]}(x_i)] \tag{6.17}$$

$$\hat{d}_P(\lambda_1, \lambda_2) = c \cdot \hat{d}_{ML}(\lambda_1, \lambda_2) \quad c = \sqrt{\frac{m}{m+2}} \tag{6.18}$$

Finally, the estimative distance $\hat{d}_{ML}((\mu_1, \sigma_1), (\mu_2, \sigma_2))$ for the 2-parametric normal distribution with $\theta = (\mu, \sigma)$ is also obtained by the substitution of

$$t = \left(\bar{x}, \frac{1}{m}\sum_{i=1}^{m}(x_i - \bar{x})^2\right) \tag{6.19}$$

into (5.59), leading to

$$\hat{d}_P((\mu_1, \sigma_1), (\mu_2, \sigma_2)) = c \cdot \hat{d}_{ML}((\mu_1, \sigma_1), (\mu_2, \sigma_2))$$
$$\text{with} \quad c = \sqrt{\frac{m}{m+3}} < 1 \tag{6.20}$$

(Mitchell, 1992). □

Burbea and Oller (1989) present several general results, such as the following theorem, dealing with the convergence of estimated Rao distances to the true Rao distance in a standard situation. A topological space is called simply connected if any closed path in this space can be contracted to a point (there are no "holes" in the space).

Theorem 6.1 (Burbea and Oller, 1989, p. 20). Let S be a regular n-parametric family of density functions and a simply connected complete Riemannian manifold with the Riemannian manifold structure induced by the Fisher information. Assume that all sectional curvatures are nonpositive. Let $X_1, \ldots, X_m$ and $Y_1, \ldots, Y_l$ be two independent samples of size m and l respectively, obtained from $p_1 \in S$ and $p_2 \in S$, $p_1 \neq p_2$. Let $\tilde{p}_m$ and $\tilde{p}_l$ be two consistent sequences of critical points of the log-likelihood functions of the samples $X_1, \ldots, X_m$ and $Y_1, \ldots, Y_l$, respectively. Then,

$$\sqrt{\frac{ml}{m+l}}[d(\tilde{p}_m, \tilde{p}_l) - d(p_1, p_2)] \xrightarrow{L} Z \sim N(0, 1) \quad \square \qquad (6.21)$$

Finally, Oller and Corcuera (1993) develop an intrinsic estimation analysis which does not depend on the parametrization, in contrast to standard instruments of statistical theory like bias or mean square error. By means of tensorial formulation, they define an intrinsic mean value (independent of the coordinate system) which reduces to $E(X)$ in $\mathbf{R}^n$. An intrinsic bias generalizes the classical bias, which appears as a special case of the former if all sectional curvatures are zero. Finally, the mean square error generalizes to the mean square Rao distance.

Example 6.3. Oller and Corcuera (1993) analyze the univariate exponential distribution with $\theta = \lambda > 0$ and $E(X) = 1/\lambda$ (see example 5.3). The maximum likelihood estimator is $\hat{\lambda}_{ML} = 1/\bar{X}_m$ where $\bar{X}_m$ is the sample mean computed from a sample of size m. Correcting the intrinsic bias of this estimator gives the intrinsically unbiased estimator (IUE)

$$\hat{\lambda}_{IUE} = \frac{e^{\psi(m)}}{m\bar{X}_m} \quad \text{with} \quad \psi(m) = \frac{\Gamma'(m)}{\Gamma(m)} \qquad (6.22)$$

On the other hand, the univariate Poisson distribution with $E(X) = \theta = \lambda > 0$ does not possess an intrinsically unbiased estimator based on the sufficient statistic $\bar{X}_m$.

In the case of the p-dimensional multivariate elliptic distribution with fixed matrix Σ (see example 5.24), the classical unbiased estimator

$$\hat{\mu} = \bar{X}_m \tag{6.23}$$

is also intrinsically unbiased because the corresponding manifold is flat. □

Oller and Corcuera (1993) continue their study by formulating intrinsic versions of the Cramér–Rao lower bound, the Rao–Blackwell theorem and the Lehmann–Scheffé theorem. Finally, the asymptotic properties of estimators are explored. Under certain conditions, maximum likelihood estimators are always asymptotically intrinsically unbiased.

Rao distance tests

Skovgaard (1984) and Villarroya and Oller (1991) explain the construction of Rao distance tests. For a density function $p(x, \theta)$ with parameter vector θ, the general test problem

$$H_0\colon g(\theta) = 0 \quad \text{versus} \quad H_1\colon g(\theta) \neq 0 \tag{6.24}$$

is considered where g is a smooth function. By the null hypothesis, a subset of the parameter space Θ (a submanifold of the manifold S)

$$\Theta_{H_0} = \{\theta \in \Theta | g(\theta) = 0\} \tag{6.25}$$

is selected.

Given a sample $X_1, \ldots, X_m$ from $p(x, \theta)$, the Rao distance between $\hat{\theta}$ and Θ_{H_0} is defined as:

$$d(\hat{\theta}, \Theta_{H_0}) = \inf\{d(\hat{\theta}, \theta) | \theta \in \Theta_{H_0}\} \tag{6.26}$$

If $\Theta_{H_0} \neq \emptyset$, the infimum exists because $d(.,.) \geqslant 0$. Then, a critical region

$$C = \{(X_1, \ldots, X_m) | d(\hat{\theta}(X), \Theta_{H_0}) > u^*\} \tag{6.27}$$

is defined with a constant u^* depending on the significance level of the test.

The minimization in (6.26) and the derivation of the test statistic may be difficult, but the idea behind a (Rao) distance test is extremely simple. The null hypothesis is rejected if the distance (weighted with the sample size) between the estimated distribution and the distribution under H_0 is too big. In addition, when testing for two or more parameters, the following theorems can provide a useful and easy alternative to the explicit derivation of the individual test statistic.

Theorem 6.2 (Burbea and Oller, 1989, p. 13f). Let S be a regular n-parametric family of density functions. Let $X_1, \ldots, X_m$ be a random sample of size m from $p_0 \in S$. Let $\tilde{p}_m$ be a consistent sequence of critical points of the log-likelihood function. Then

$$md^2(p_0, \tilde{p}_m) \xrightarrow{L} Z \sim \chi^2(n) \quad \square \tag{6.28}$$

Theorem 6.3 (Burbea and Oller, 1989, p. 14). Let S be a regular n-parametric family of density functions. Let $X_1, \ldots, X_m$ and $Y_1, \ldots, Y_l$ be two independent random samples of size m and l respectively obtained from $p_0 \in S$. Let $\tilde{p}_m$ and $\tilde{p}_l$ be two consistent sequences of critical points of the log-likelihood functions. Then

$$\frac{ml}{m+l} d^2(\tilde{p}_m, \tilde{p}_l) \xrightarrow{L} Z \sim \chi^2(n) \quad \square \tag{6.29}$$

Example 6.4. Considering the 2-parametric normal distribution (cf. example 5.2) and the test problem

$$H_0: \mu = \mu_0 \quad \text{versus} \quad H_1: \mu \neq \mu_0 \tag{6.30}$$

the Rao distance test is equivalent to the standard t test (Skovgaard, 1984, p. 219f). In the test problem

$$H_0: \sigma = \sigma_0 \quad \text{versus} \quad H_1: \sigma \neq \sigma_0 \tag{6.31}$$

the Rao distance test is equivalent to the classical χ^2 test (Skovgaard, 1984, p. 220).

Consider two independent samples of size m_1 and m_2 from $N(\mu_1, \sigma_1^2)$ and $N(\mu_2, \sigma_2^2)$ and the test problem

$$H_0: (\mu_1, \sigma_1) = (\mu_2, \sigma_2) \quad \text{versus} \quad H_1: (\mu_1, \sigma_1) \neq (\mu_2, \sigma_2) \tag{6.32}$$

A Rao distance test is easily derived with the help of theorem 6.3. The critical region is

$$C = \left\{ U = \frac{m_1 m_2}{m_1 + m_2} d^2((\hat{\mu}_1, \hat{\sigma}_1), (\hat{\mu}_2, \hat{\sigma}_2)) \middle| U > u^* \right\}, \tag{6.33}$$

where $d(.,.)$ is taken from (5.59), $P(U > u^* | H_0) = \alpha$ and $U \sim \chi^2(2)$ asymptotically under H_0.

Burbea and Oller (1989, pp. 22ff) analyse this test in a small simulation study. For sample sizes $m_1 = m_2 = m = 15$ and 30, parameter values $\mu = 0$ and 1 and $\sigma = 0.1$, 1 and 10, they generate 10,000 $N(\mu, \sigma^2)$ samples and they compare the empirical distribution function of U with the asymptotic one. By this means, they give the recommendations for critical values u^* reproduced in table 16.2.

Table 16.2 Critical values of u^* in small samples

	α	
m	*0.05*	*0.01*
15	7.12	11.54
30	6.48	10.28
∞	5.99	9.21

Testing

$$H_0\colon (\mu, \sigma) = (\mu_0, \sigma_0) \quad \text{versus} \quad H_1\colon (\mu, \sigma) \neq (\mu_0, \sigma_0), \tag{6.34}$$

theorem 6.2 can be applied to derive easily the critical region

$$C = \{U = md^2((\hat{\mu}, \hat{\sigma}), (\mu_0, \sigma_0)) | U > u^*\}, \tag{6.35}$$

where $P(U > u^* | H_0) = \alpha$ and $U \sim \chi^2(2)$ asymptotically under H_0. □

Example 6.5. For two independent random samples of size m_1 and m_2 from two multivariate normal distributions $N_p(\mu_1, \Sigma)$ and $N_p(\mu_2, \Sigma)$ with identical covariance matrix Σ,

$$\hat{D}^2 = (\bar{x}_1 - \bar{x}_2)' S^{-1} (\bar{x}_1 - \bar{x}_2) \tag{6.36}$$

is the classical estimator of the Mahalanobis distance (the square of the Rao distance) where

$$S = \frac{(m_1 - 1)S_1 + (m_2 - 1)S_2}{m} \qquad m = m_1 + m_2 - 2 \tag{6.37}$$

and S_1 and S_2 are the empirical covariance matrices (Mahalanobis, 1936) – see example 5.23. In the test problem

$$H_0\colon \mu_1 = \mu_2 \quad \text{versus} \quad H_1\colon \mu_1 \neq \mu_2 \tag{6.38}$$

the likelihood ratio test and the Rao distance test both lead to the test statistic $\hat{D}^2$. Under H_0

$$\frac{m - p + 1}{mp} \frac{m_1 m_2}{m_1 + m_2} \hat{D}^2 \sim F(p, m - p + 1) \tag{6.39}$$

(Bose and Roy, 1938).

Considering the multivariate normal distribution with identical μ, the test problem

$$H_0: \Sigma = \Sigma_0 \quad \text{versus} \quad H_1: \Sigma \neq \Sigma_0 \tag{6.40}$$

leads to the test statistic

$$d^2 = \frac{1}{2}\sum_{i=1}^{p}(\ln \lambda_i)^2 \tag{6.41}$$

where λ_i are again the roots of the determinantal equation

$$|S - \lambda\Sigma_0| = 0 \tag{6.42}$$

(see equation (5.75). Asymptotically, $md^2 \sim \chi^2((p^2 + p)/2)$ under H_0 with the sample size m (James, 1973, p. 166f). This result can also be derived by theorem 6.2.

For the univariate normal linear model (see example 5.23) and the test problem

$$H_0: R\beta = 0 \quad \text{versus} \quad H_1: R\beta \neq 0 \tag{6.43}$$

with a constant $(r \times p)$ matrix R of rank r, the Rao distance test is again equivalent to the classical F test (Burbea and Oller, 1988, pp. 218ff; Oller, 1989, p. 53f).

Finally, Calvo and Oller (1990) construct tests with the help of their lower bound for the Rao distance in the case of the multivariate normal distribution without restrictions on the parameter vector. □

Example 6.6. Villarroya and Oller (1991) extensively analyse Rao distance tests for the inverse Gaussian distribution – see examples 5.6 and 5.20. The first test problem is

$$H_0: \lambda = \lambda_0 \quad \text{versus} \quad H_1: \lambda \neq \lambda_0 \tag{6.44}$$

with unknown parameter μ. If $X_1, \ldots, X_m$ is a random sample of size m from an $iG(\mu, \lambda)$ distribution, the ML estimators are

$$\hat{\mu} = \bar{X}, \quad \hat{\lambda} = \frac{m}{\sum_{i=1}^{m}\left(\frac{1}{X_i} - \frac{1}{\bar{X}}\right)} \tag{6.45}$$

(Villarroya and Oller, 1991, p. 9). As described in (6.27), the critical region of the Rao distance test is derived to be

$$C = \{(X_1, \ldots, X_m) | (Q < Q_1) \cup (Q > Q_2)\} \quad \text{where} \tag{6.46}$$

$$Q = \frac{m\lambda_0}{\hat{\lambda}}, \quad Q_1 = me^{-\sqrt{2u_\alpha}}, \quad Q_2 = me^{\sqrt{2u_\alpha}}, \quad Q_1 < Q_2 \quad \text{and} \tag{6.47}$$

$$F(Q_1) - F(Q_2) = 1 - \alpha, \quad Q_1 Q_2 = m^2 \tag{6.48}$$

Under H_0, $Q \sim \chi^2(m-1)$ (Villarroya and Oller, 1991, p. 10).

There is no uniformly most powerful test (UMPT) in this situation. Hence, the authors compare the Rao distance test (RDT in the following) with the likelihood ratio test (LRT) and the Rao distance test with unbiased estimators (RDTUE). The latter uses the unbiased estimator

$$\hat{\lambda}^* = \frac{m-3}{m}\hat{\lambda} \tag{6.49}$$

instead of the biased $\hat{\lambda}$ in (6.45). All three tests are biased because the power function does not reach its minimum in λ_0. That is why the authors add a fourth locally unbiased test to the comparison. The latter is constructed by setting the derivative of the power function of the RDT equal to zero for $\lambda_0 = 1$. The four tests are asymptotically identical.

Comparing the power functions of the tests in the situation $\lambda_0 = 1$, significance level $\alpha = 0.05$ and $m = 5$ and $m = 20$, the ranking depends on whether $\lambda < \lambda_0$ or not. If $\lambda < \lambda_0$, the RDTUE is the most powerful test (of these four), followed by the locally unbiased test, the LRT and the RDT. If $\lambda > \lambda_0$, the ranking is exactly reverse. Computing the mean power in intervals centered in $\lambda_0 = 1$ provides the same ranking as the case $\lambda < \lambda_0$ (Villarroya and Oller, 1991, pp. 10ff).

$$H_0\colon \lambda = \lambda_0 \quad \text{versus} \quad H_1\colon \lambda \neq \lambda_0 \tag{6.50}$$

with known μ is the second test problem. The ML estimator is

$$\hat{\lambda} = \frac{m\mu^2}{\sum_{i=1}^{m} \frac{(X_i - \mu)^2}{X_i}} \tag{6.51}$$

The critical region is still (6.46), where now $Q \sim \chi^2(m)$ under H_0 (Villarroya and Oller, 1991, p. 14f).

Again, there is no UMPT. Hence, the authors compare the power of the RDT (with ML estimator), of the RDTUE with

$$\hat{\lambda}^* = \frac{m-2}{m}\hat{\lambda} \tag{6.52}$$

and of the LRT for $\lambda_0 = 1$, $\alpha = 0.05$ and $m = 5, 20$. RDT and RDTUE are biased tests, the LRT is unbiased. Once more, the result depends on λ. $\lambda < \lambda_0$ and the mean power produce the ranking RDTUE – LRT – RDT, $\lambda > \lambda_0$ reverses it (Villarroya and Oller, 1991, p. 15f).

On the other hand, the UMPT for the one-sided test problem

$$H_0\colon \lambda \leqslant \lambda_0 \quad \text{versus} \quad H_1\colon \lambda > \lambda_0 \tag{6.53}$$

exists and it is equivalent to the RDT described above (Villarroya and Oller, 1991, p. 16f).

Deriving the RDT for the test problem

$$H_0\colon \mu = \mu_0 \quad \text{versus} \quad H_1\colon \mu \neq \mu_0 \tag{6.54}$$

with unknown λ leads to the critical region

$$C = \left\{ (X_1, \ldots, X_m) \,\middle|\, T = \frac{\sqrt{m}\,|\bar{X} - \mu_0|}{\mu_0\sqrt{\bar{X}V}} \right\} \quad \text{where} \tag{6.55}$$

$$V = \frac{1}{m-1}\sum_{i=1}^{m}\left(\frac{1}{X_i} - \frac{1}{\bar{X}}\right) \tag{6.56}$$

With the ML estimators (6.45), $T \sim t(m-1)$ under H_0 and the RDT is equivalent to the uniformly most sensitive test of Kempthorne and Folks (1971) (cf. Villarroya and Oller, 1991, p. 18f).

Testing

$$H_0\colon (\mu, \lambda) = (\mu_0, \lambda_0) \quad \text{versus} \quad H_1\colon (\mu, \lambda) \neq (\mu_0, \lambda_0) \tag{6.57}$$

theorem 6.2 can be applied to derive easily the critical region

$$C = \{U = md^2((\hat{\mu}, \hat{\lambda}), (\mu_0, \lambda_0)) | U > u^*\}, \tag{6.58}$$

where $P(U > u^*|H_0) = \alpha$ and $U \sim \chi^2(2)$ asymptotically under H_0. $d(.,.)$ is taken from (5.66). Since a UMPT does not exist, the authors conduct a simulation study to compare the power of four tests: The RDT with ML estimators (6.45), the RDTUE with estimators (6.49), the LRT and the g-LMMPU test (locally most mean powerful and unbiased) by Vermeire and Wauters (1988). RDT, RDTUE and LRT are biased tests.

Villarroya and Oller (1991, pp. 20ff) analyze several null hypotheses ($(\mu_0, \lambda_0) = (1, 1), (1, 25), (2.5, 2.5)$ and $(5, 1)$), several sample sizes (mostly $m = 10$), several significance levels α and several directions in Θ under H_1 (because Θ is now two-dimensional). The results depend heavily on these conditions. The authors conclude that the g-LMMPU test performs best (followed by RDTUE). Nevertheless, the easily applicable RDTUE is a good choice in practice "because of some numerical difficulties" of the g-LMMPU test, "since it includes an integrand which is not a reasonable well behaved function" (Villarroya and Oller, 1991, p. 23).

Considering finally two independent samples of size m_1 and m_2, the RDT(UE) for the test problem

$$H_0\colon (\mu_1, \lambda_1) = (\mu_2, \lambda_2) \quad \text{versus} \quad H_1\colon (\mu_1, \lambda_1) \neq (\mu_2, \lambda_2) \tag{6.59}$$

is derived easily by theorem 6.3. The critical region is

$$C = \left\{ U = \frac{m_1 m_2}{m_1 + m_2} d^2((\hat{\mu}_1, \hat{\lambda}_1), (\hat{\mu}_2, \hat{\lambda}_2)) \,\middle|\, U > u^* \right\}, \tag{6.60}$$

where $P(U > u^* | H_0) = \alpha$ and $U \sim \chi^2(2)$ asymptotically under H_0. □

7 Empirical Application of Rao Distances

Distance (divergence) measures and tests are closely related. Distance measures like Rao distance can also replace tests in some cases, and they provide even more information than a test alone (see Bose, 1936, p. 143; Bose and Roy, 1938, p. 19). This section shows some economic applications of Rao distances, Rao distance tests and isocircles in portfolio theory. It is not the intention to deal with portfolio theory more than necessary for the description of the following problem. See Ingersoll (1987) for the economical theory held back here.

Let A_i, $i = 1, \ldots, k$, be stocks represented by their yields $Y_i \sim N(\mu_i, \sigma_i^2)$ with unknown expected yields μ_i and unknown risks σ_i^2. It is not claimed that yields are always normally distributed. The discussion about distributions meeting the requirements of the data and economic theory and allowing the application of common statistical methods has persisted for many years. The normal distribution is chosen very often as the lesser evil. The limitations set up by the Rao distance do not alter this fact.

Assume that

$$\psi(\mu, \sigma) = \mu - \frac{a\sigma^2}{2} \tag{7.1}$$

with $a > 0$ is a suitable preference function for the search for the optimal stock A^*. This choice leads to the concave indifference curves

$$\sigma = \sqrt{\frac{2}{a}(\mu - c)} \tag{7.2}$$

for $c \leqslant \mu$ and the (Bernoulli) utility function

$$u(Y) = -e^{-aY} + c \tag{7.3}$$

Then, the decision according to the (μ, σ)-rule (7.1) is consistent with the Bernoulli principle (von Neumann and Morgenstern, 1944) because

$$\psi(p) = E_p[u(Y)] \tag{7.4}$$

The parameters μ_i and σ_i have been estimated from independent samples of sizes m_i by ML estimators. Then, the estimated normal distributions $N(\hat{\mu}_i, \hat{\sigma}_i^2)_{ML}$ can be plotted as in figure 16.5. The stock with yield Y_1^* represented by $(\hat{\mu}_1^*, \hat{\sigma}_1^*) = (9, 4)$ lying on indifference curve I^* is optimal. An artificial and small data set has been chosen for a clear presentation of the following application of Rao distances.

In this typical problem of "selecting and ordering populations" (Gibbons et al., 1977), the identification of the optimum has to be followed by a check of the optimum. It is possible that, for example, $(\hat{\mu}_2, \hat{\sigma}_2) = (8, 5)$ only seems to represent a stock with smaller preference function value than $(\hat{\mu}_1^*, \hat{\sigma}_1^*)$ because of estimation errors. An investor has to cope with two risks: the risk of uncertain expected yields contained in σ^2 and the risk caused by the estimation of the parameters μ and σ. The second risk is not represented in figure 16.5, but it can be included with the help of Rao distances.

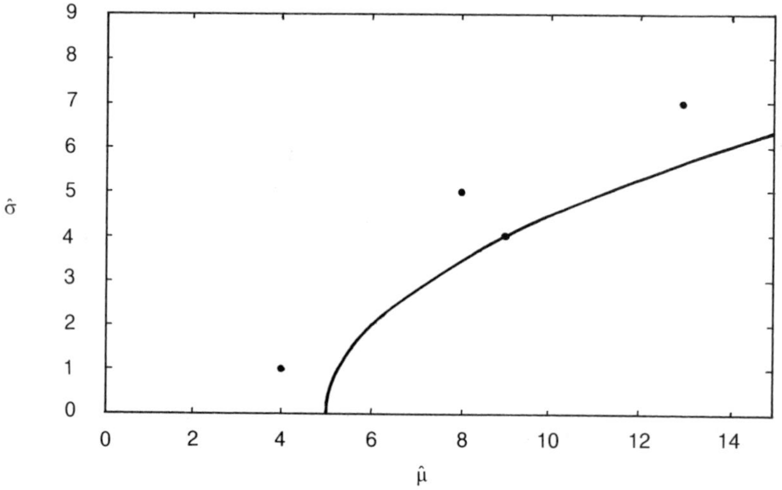

Figure 16.5 $(\hat{\mu}, \hat{\sigma})$-plane with optimal stock.

As discussed in section 6, the ML estimates of the Rao distances between the points (distributions, yields) are obtained by substituting the parameters by their ML estimates. With the knowledge of the geometry of the normal distribution from section 5, it is obvious from figure 16.5 that $(\hat{\mu}_3, \hat{\sigma}_3) = (4, 1)$ and I^* are more apart than $(\hat{\mu}_2, \hat{\sigma}_2)$ and I^*. And $(\hat{\mu}_4, \hat{\sigma}_4) = (13, 7)$ is even closer to I^*. Although the three nonoptimal stocks seem to lie on the same indifference curve parallel to I^*, it is easier to discriminate between $(\hat{\mu}_3, \hat{\sigma}_3)$ and some point on I^* than between $(\hat{\mu}_4, \hat{\sigma}_4)$ and some point on I^* (for fixed sample sizes). This makes clear that the Euclidean geometry of utility theory is different from the hyperbolic geometry of the normal distribution.

Indifference curves parallel to I^* in utility theory are obtained by a simple parallel shift of I^*, whereas the normal distributions which are equidistant to the normal distributions on I^* lie on curves deviating from I^* for growing σ. This hyperbolic analogon of a parallel line to I^* – called isoline – is plotted in figure 16.6 with the constant distance $d = 0.3$ between these curves. This isoline is constructed by moving an isocircle with radius $d = 0.3$ and center on I^* along I^* and connecting the farthest (in the Euclidean sense) points on the isocircle.

Showing similarities between points (or lines) and points (or lines) in a plane is one useful feature of Rao distances and isocircles. But,

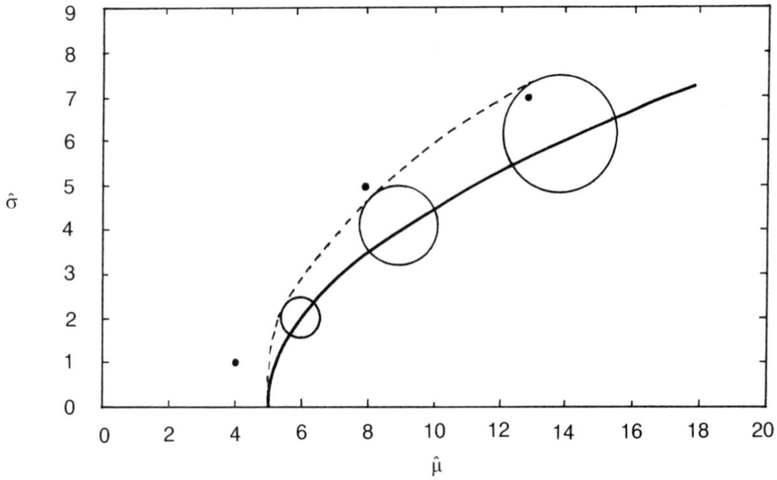

Figure 16.6 $(\hat{\mu}, \hat{\sigma})$-plane with isoline for I^* with $d = 0.3$.

combined with the information on the sample sizes, they also can serve as Rao distance tests (see section 6 and example 6.4). For the test problem

$$H_0\colon (\mu_1, \sigma_1) = (\mu_2, \sigma_2) \quad \text{versus} \quad H_1\colon (\mu_1, \sigma_2) \neq (\mu_2, \sigma_2) \tag{7.5}$$

the Rao distance test is easily derived with the help of theorem 6.3. The critical region is

$$C = \left\{ U = \frac{m_1 m_2}{m_1 + m_2} d^2((\hat{\mu}_1, \hat{\sigma}_1), (\hat{\mu}_2, \hat{\sigma}_2)) \middle| U > u^* \right\}, \tag{7.6}$$

where $P(U > u^*|H_0) = \alpha$ and $U \sim \chi^2(2)$ under H_0. In the present example, $d((9, 4), (8, 5)) = 0.3861$, $m_1 = m_2 = 100$, $u = 7.454$ and H_0 is rejected for $\alpha = 0.025$.

The previous test has demonstrated the simplicity of Rao distance tests; the following one shows further advantages of the geometric approach. It shall be tested if (μ_4, σ_4) could also be optimal. Let (μ_0, σ_0) be an unknown point on I^*. The test

$$H_0\colon (\mu_4, \sigma_4) = (\mu_0, \sigma_0) \quad \text{versus} \quad H_1\colon (\mu_4, \sigma_4) \neq (\mu_0, \sigma_0) \tag{7.7}$$

and theorem 6.2 lead to the critical region

$$C = \{U = m_4 d^2((\hat{\mu}_4, \hat{\sigma}_4), (\mu_0, \sigma_0)) | U > u^*\}, \tag{7.8}$$

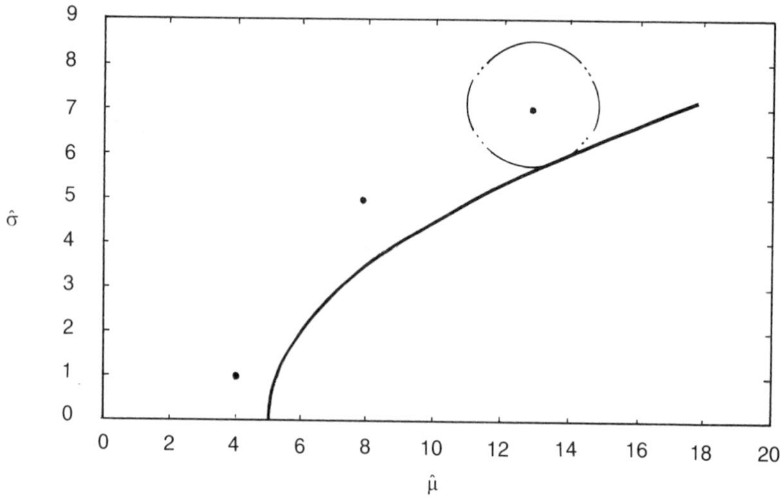

Figure 16.7 $(\hat{\mu}, \hat{\sigma})$-plane and isocircle with $d = 0.2717$.

where $P(U > u^*|H_0) = \alpha$ and $U \sim \chi^2(2)$ under H_0. If m_4 and α are known, the critical d-value can be determined and the corresponding isocircle can be plotted as in figure 16.7. If this isocircle intersects I^*, H_0 cannot be rejected. This happens in the example, where $m_4 = 100$, $\alpha = 0.025$ and $d^* = 0.2717$.

Assume finally that an investor wants to group the k stocks into g classes (with $g < k$) according to the parameter values (μ_i, σ_i). The statistical technique for this task of course is cluster analysis. But in many cases, it will be sensible to take the Rao distances (and not the Euclidean distances) between the estimated parameters $(\hat{\mu}_i, \hat{\sigma}_i)$ as input for the clustering algorithm. This can be done very easily by calculating the symmetric $(k \times k)$ distance matrix $D = (d_{ij})$ with

$$d_{ij} = \hat{d}((\mu_i, \sigma_i), (\mu_j, \sigma_j)), \quad i, j = 1, \ldots, k \tag{7.9}$$

before the classification.

8 Concluding Remarks

It has been shown in the preceding sections that Rao distance is a distance in the mathematical sense with distinguished invariance properties. Unfortunately, several problems impede its practical application. On theoretical grounds, nonregular distributions do not admit the calculation of Rao distances. Moreover, Rao distance formulae are always unknown for distributions with unknown sectional curvature, and they are rarely known if the sectional curvature is nonconstant. The multivariate normal distribution without restrictions on the parameter vector is the most glaring example of a missing Rao distance formula. Far-reaching theoretical developments are necessary to eliminate this drawback.

But the application of Rao distances is straightforward in the narrow class of distributions with known distance formula. Then, minor restrictions result from the problem that estimated Rao distances and Rao distance tests have not been investigated sufficiently until now. This is due to the fact that this distance concept is rather unknown. Increased research in this field (e.g. on small sample properties) seems promising because Rao distance tests are equivalent to classical (optimal) tests in some standard situations, and they present considerable alternatives in some nonstandard problems.

The empirical application in the previous section has demonstrated some advantages of Rao distances as well as Rao distance tests and isocircles in a two-parametric problem in portfolio theory. The Euclidean point of view expressed in the indifference curves is completed by the hyperbolic view arising from the assumption that yields are normally distributed. In this way, Rao distances and isocircles enlarge the insight in decisions based on the (μ, σ)-rule. Rao distance tests (together with isocircles) can replace standard tests in some situations because they are based on simple geometrical ideas and because a test problem like (7.7) is easily solvable with geometrical techniques.

We did not treat a multivariate problem with $n \geqslant 3$ parameters, because a two-parametric example has intuitive advantages but also because Rao distances are rarely known for multivariate distributions without restrictions on the parameter vector. This is a serious drawback of this technique. Distance (divergence) measures are applied in many areas of statistical practice, e.g. in descriptive analysis, in decision theory, in test theory, in estimation theory, or in cluster analysis. Rao distances can replace competing measures in many situations if the required formula is known for the corresponding problem. Unfortunately, Rao distances are so far only known within distribution families, not between different families, like the binomial and the normal distribution. This lack is responsible for the fact that Rao distance cannot replace the Kullback–Leibler information as the basis of a model selection criterion like AIC or the divergence measure of Read and Cressie (1988) applied for the construction of goodness-of-fit tests.

It is to be hoped that growing acquaintance of statisticians and econometricians with this demanding distance concept leads to further applied and theoretical research in this field. The results presented in this chapter have demonstrated that this should be profitable.

Note

The author would like to thank Hermann Hähl, Gerd Hansen, Thomas Holzhüter, Ingo Klein, Helmut Lütkepohl, Stefan Mittnik, Marc Paolella, Kai Tetzlaff and Wolfgang Wetzel for helpful comments. All errors and omissions remain the responsibility of the author.

References

Ahmad, I. A. (1985) Matusita's distance. In S. Kotz and N. L. Johnson (eds), *Encyclopedia of Statistical Sciences, volume V*. New York: Wiley, pp. 334–6.

Ali, S. M. and Silvey, S. D. (1966) A general class of coefficients of one distribution from another. *Journal of the Royal Statistical Society B*, 28, 131–42.

Amari, S. I. (1985) *Differential-Geometrical Methods in Statistics*. New York: Springer-Verlag.

Amari, S. I., Barndorff-Nielsen, O. E., Kass, R. E., Lauritzen, S. L. and Rao, C. R. (1987) *Differential Geometry in Statistical Inference*. Hayward, CA: Institute of Mathematical Statistics.

Atkinson, C. and Mitchell, A. F. S. (1981) Rao's distance measure. *Sankhya A*, 43, 345–65.

Barndorff-Nielsen, O. E. (1988) *Parametric Statistical Models and Likelihood*. Heidelberg: Springer-Verlag.

Barndorff-Nielsen, O. E., Cox, D. R. and Reid, N. (1986) The role of differential geometry in statistical theory. *International Statistical Review*, 54, 83–96.

Berger, M. and Gostiaux, B. (1988) *Differential Geometry: Manifolds, Curves and Surfaces*. New York: Springer-Verlag.

Bose, R. C. (1936) On the exact distribution and moment-coefficients of the D^2-statistic. Sankhya, 2, 143–54.

Bose, R. C. and Roy, S. N. (1938) The distribution of the studentised D^2-statistic. *Sankhya*, 4, 19–38.

Burbea, J. (1983) J-divergences and related concepts. In S. Kotz and N. L. Johnson (eds), *Encyclopedia of Statistical Sciences, volume IV*. New York: Wiley, pp. 290–6.

Burbea, J. (1986a) Probability spaces, metrics and distances on. In S. Kotz and N. L. Johnson (eds), *Encyclopedia of Statistical Sciences, volume VII*. New York: Wiley, pp. 241–8.

Burbea, J. (1986b) Informative geometry of probability spaces. *Expositiones Mathematicae*, 4, 347–78.

Burbea, J. (1989) Rao distance. In S. Kotz, N. L. Johnson and C. B. Read (eds), *Encyclopedia of Statistical Sciences*, supplement volume. New York: Wiley, pp. 128–30.

Burbea, J. and Oller, J. M. (1988) The information metric for univariate linear elliptic models. *Statistics and Decisions*, 6, 209–21.

Burbea, J. and Oller, J. M. (1989) *On Rao Distance Asymptotic Distribution*. Universitat de Barcelona.

Burbea, J. and Rao, C. R. (1982) Entropy differential metric, distance and divergence measures in probability spaces: a unified approach. *Journal of Multivariate Analysis*, 12, 575–96.

Calvo, M. and Oller, J. M. (1990) A distance between multivariate normal distributions based in an embedding into the Siegel group. *Journal of Multivariate Analysis*, 35, 223–42.

Cziszár, I. (1963) Eine informationstheoretische Ungleichung und ihre Andwendung auf den Beweis der Ergodizität von Markoffschen Ketten. *Publ. Math. Inst. Hung. Acad. Sci.*, 8, 85–107.

Efron, B. (1975) Defining the curvature of a statistical problem, with applications to second order efficiency. *Annals of Statistics*, 3, 1189–242.

Eriksen, P. S. (1987) Geodesics connected with the Fisher metric on the multivariate normal manifold. In C. T. J. Dodson (ed.), *Geometrization of Statistical Theory*. Lancaster: University of Lancaster, Department of Mathematics, pp. 225–9.

Gallot, S., Hulin, D. and Lafontaine, J. (1990) *Riemannian Geometry*, 2nd edn. Heidelberg: Springer-Verlag.

Gibbons, J. D., Olkin, I. and Sobel, M. (1977) *Selecting and Ordering Populations: a New Statistical Methodology*. New York: Wiley.

Ingersoll, J. E. (1987) *Theory of Financial Decision Making*. Savage: Rowman & Littlefield.

James, A. T. (1973) The variance information manifold and the functions on it. In P. K. Krishnaiah (ed.), *Multivariate Analysis III*. New York: Academic Press, pp. 157–69.

Jeffreys, H. (1948) *Theory of Probability*. Oxford: Oxford University Press.

Jensen, U. (1993) *Herleitung, Berechnung and ökonomische Anwendung von Rao-Distanzen*. Bergisch Gladbach: Verlag Josef Eul.

Johnson, N. L. and Kotz, S. (1970) *Distributions in Statistics, Continuous Univariate Distributions, volumes 1 and 2*. New York: Wiley.

Kass, R. E. (1989) The geometry of asymptotic inference. *Statistical Science*, 4, 188–234.

Kay, D. C. (1988) *Tensor Calculus*. Auckland: McGraw-Hill.

Kempthorne, O. and Folks, J. L. (1971) *Probability, Statistics and Data Analysis*. Ames: Iowa State University Press.

Kobayashi, S. and Nomizu, K. (1963 and 1969) *Foundations of Differential Geometry, volumes 1 and 2*. New York: Interscience.

Kullback, S. (1959) *Information Theory and Statistics*. New York: Whiley.

Kullback, S. and Leibler, R. A. (1951) On information and sufficiency. *Annals of Mathematical Statistics*, 22, 79–86.

Lauritzen, S. L. (1987) Statistical manifolds. In S. I. Amari, O. E. Barndorff-Nielsen, R. E. Kass, S. L. Lauritzen and C. R. Rao (eds), *Differential Geometry in Statistical Inference*. Hayward, CA: Institute of Mathematical Statistics, pp. 163–216.

Maasoumi, E. (1993) A compendium to information theory in economics and econometrics, *Econometric Reviews*, 12, 137–81.

McCullagh, P. (1987) *Tensor Methods in Statistics*. New York: Chapman & Hall.

Mahalanobis, P. C. (1930) On tests and measures of group divergences. *Journal and Proceedings of the Asiatic Society of Bengal*, 26, 541–88.

Mahalanobis, P. C. (1936) On the generalized distance in statistics. *Proceedings of the National Institute of Sciences of India*, 12, 49–55.

Matusita, K. (1955) Decision rules, based on the distance, for problems of fit, two samples and estimation. *Annals of Mathematical Statistics*, 26, 631–40.

Millman, R. S. and Parker, G. D. (1991) *Geometry – a Metric Approach with Models*, 2nd edn. New York: Springer-Verlag.

Mitchell, A. F. S. (1988) Statistical manifolds of univariate elliptic distributions. *International Statistical Review*, 56, 1–16.

Mitchell, A. F. S. (1989) The information matrix, skewness tensor and α-connections for the general multivariate elliptic distribution. *Annals of the Institute of Statistical Mathematics*, 41, 289–304.

Mitchell, A. F. S. (1992) Estimative and predictive distances. *Test*, 1, 105–21.

Mitchell, A. F. S. and Krzanowski, W. J. (1985) The Mahalanobis distance and elliptic distributions. *Biometrika*, 72, 464–7.

Mood, A. M., Graybill, F. A. and Boes, D. C. (1974) *Introduction to the Theory of Statistics*, 3rd edn. Auckland: McGraw-Hill.

Murray, M. K. and Rice, J. W. (1993) *Differential Geometry and Statistics*. London: Chapman & Hall.

Oller, J. M. (1986) Information metric extreme value and logistic probability distributions. *Sankya A*, 49, 17–23.

Oller, J. M. (1989) Some geometrical aspects of data analysis and statistics. In Y. Dodge (ed.), *Statistical Data Analysis and Inference*. Amsterdam: North-Holland, pp. 41–58.

Oller, J. M. and Corcuera, J. M. (1993) *Intrinsic Analysis of the Statistical Estimation*. Barcelona: University of Barcelona.

Oller, J. M. and Cuadras, C. M. (1985) Rao's distance for negative multinomial distributions. *Sankhya A*, 47, 75–83.

Papaioannou, T. (1985) Measures of information. In S. Kotz, and N. L. Johnson (eds), *Encyclopedia of Statistical Sciences, volume V*. New York: Wiley, pp. 391–7.

Rao, C. R. (1945) Information and the accuracy attainable in the estimation of statistical parameters. *Bulletin of the Calcutta Mathematical Society*, 37, 81–91. Also in S. Kotz and N. L. Johnson (1992) *Breakthroughs in Statistics, volume 1*. New York: Springer-Verlag, pp. 235–47.

Rao, C. R. (1987) Differential metrics in probability spaces. In S. I. Amari, O. E. Barndorff-Nielsen, R. E. Kass, S. L. Lauritzen and C. R. Rao (eds), *Differential Geometry in Statistical Inference*. Hayward, CA: Institute of Mathematical Statistics, pp. 217–40.

Read, T. C. R. and Cressie, N. A. C. (1988) *Goodness-of-fit Statistics for Discrete Multivariate Data*. New York: Springer-Verlag.

Sato, Y., Sugawa, K. and Kawaguchi, M. (1979) The geometrical structure of the parameter space of the two-dimensional normal distribution. *Reports on Mathematical Physics*, 16, 111–19.

Skovgaard, L. T. (1984) A Riemannian geometry of the multivariate normal model. *Scandinavian Journal of Statistics*, 11, 211–23.

Spivak, M. (1970–5) *A Comprehensive Introduction to Differential Geometry, volumes 1–5*. Boston: Publish or Perish.

Vermeire, L. and Wauters, D. (1988) The g-LMMPUα test for the inverse

Gaussian family with a simple null hypothesis. Technical report, Catholic University of Leuven.

Villarroya, A. and Oller, J. M. (1991) *Statistical Tests for the Inverse Gaussian Distribution Based on Rao Distance*. Barcelona: University of Barcelona, Department of Statistics.

von Neumann, J. and Morgenstern, O. (1944) *Theory of Games and Economic Behaviour*, Princeton, NJ: Princeton University Press.

Yoshizawa, T. (1971a) A geometry of parameter space and its statistical interpretation. Memo TYH-2, Harvard University.

Yoshizawa, T. (1971b) A geometrical interpretation of location and scale parameters. Memo TYH-3, Harvard University.

A Brief Biography of C. R. Rao and a List of His Publications

Full Name: Calyampudi Radhakrishna Rao
Born: September 10, 1920, in Hadagali (Kamataka State), India

Academic Qualifications

		Degrees
1940	MA	Mathematics (Andhra University) with a first class and first rank.
1943	MA	Statistics (Calcutta University) with a first class, first rank, and a gold medal.
1948	PhD	Cambridge University on the basis of the thesis entitled "Statistical problems of biological classification."
1965	ScD	Cambridge University on the basis of published work in statistics.
		Honorary degrees
1967	DSc	Andhra University, Waltair, India
1970	DSc	Leningrad University, Lenigrad, USSR
1973	DLitt	Delhi University, Delhi, India
1976	DSc	Athens University, Athens, Greece
1977	DSc	Osmania University, Hyderabad, India
1979	DSc	The Ohio State University, Columbus, Ohio, USA

1982	Professor Honorario	Universidad Nacional de San Marcos, Lima, Peru
1983	DSc	University of Philippines, Manila, Philippines
1985	PhD	University of Tampere, Tampere, Finland
1989	DSc	Indian Statistical Institute, India
1989	DSc	University of Neuchatel, Neuchatel, Switzerland
1990	DSc	Colorado State University, Fort Collins, USA
1991	Doctoris	University of Poznan, Poznan, Poland
1991	DSc	University of Hyderabad, Hyderabad, India
1994	DSc	Slovak Academy of Sciences, Bratislava, Republic of Slovakia

Professional Employment

Indian Statistical Institute

1	Statistician	1944–8
2	Professor and Head of the Research and Training School (RTS)	1949–63
3	Director, RTS	1964–72
4	Secretary and Director	1972–6
5	Jawaharlal Nehru Professor	1976–84
6	National Professor (India)	1987–92

USA

7	University Professor, University of Pittsburgh	1979–88
8	Professor of Statistics, Holder of the Eberly Chair, Pennsylvania State University	1988–
9	Adjunct Professor, University of Pittsburgh	1988–

Fellowships of Academic Societies (by Election)

1951 *Member*, International Statistical Institute
1953 *Fellow*, Indian National Science Academy
1958 *Fellow*, Institute of Mathematical Statistics, USA
1965 *Fellow*, Andhra Pradesh Academy of Sciences, India
1967 *Fellow*, Royal Society (FRS), UK

1969	*Honorary Fellow*, Royal Statistical Society, UK
1972	*Fellow*, American Statistical Association, USA
	Fellow, International Econometric Society, USA
1974	*Fellow*, Indian Academy of Sciences
	Honorary Member, Indian Society of Human Genetics
	Honorary Fellow, King's College, Cambridge, UK (this life fellowship is limited to only eleven persons at any time)
1975	*Foreign Honorary Member*, American Academy of Arts and Science, USA
1983	*Honorary Member*, International Statistics Institute, The Netherlands (there are only eight such members out of a total world membership of 1400)
	Founder Fellow, The Third World Academy of Sciences, Trieste, Italy
1985	*Fellow*, The Indian Society for Medical Statistics
	Honorary Fellow, Calcutta Statistical Association
1986	*Honorary Life Member*, Biometric Society (only ten persons have been elected to this position since the society was founded in 1948)
1988	*Fellow*, The National Academy of Sciences, India
1990	*Honorary Fellow*, The Finnish Statistical Society

Presidentships of Academic Societies

1971–6	Indian Econometric Society
1973–5	International Biometric Society
1976–7	Institute of Mathematical Statistics, USA
1977–9	International Statistical Institute, The Netherlands
1982–4	Forum for Interdisciplinary Mathematics

List of Publications

Published books

Linear Statistical Inference and Its Applications

First edition	1965	John Wiley, New York
Second edition	1973	John Wiley, New York
Taiwan (English) edition	1976	Taiwan
Interscience (English) edition	1975	Wiley Eastern, India
Russian translation	1969	USSR Academy of Sciences, Moscow
German translation	1972	Deutcsher Verlag der Wissenschaften, Berlin

Japanese translation	1977	Tokyo Inc., Tokyo
Czech translation	1978	Academia Publishers, Prague
Polish translation	1982	Panstowowe Wydawnictwo Naukowe, Warsaw
Chinese translation	1987	Academia Sinica Press

Advanced Statistical Methods in Biometric Research

First edition	1952	John Wiley, New York
Reprint	1971	Haffner, New York
Reprint	1974	Haffner, New York

(with S. K. Mitra) *Generalized Inverse of Matrices and Its Applications*

First edition	1971	John Wiley, New York
Japanese translation	1973	Tokyo

(with A. Kagan and Yu. V. Linnik) *Characterization Problems of Mathematical Statistics*

Russian edition	1972	USSR Academy of Sciences, Moscow
English translation	1973	John Wiley, New York

Computers and the Future of Human Society
Andhra University, Waltair, and Statistical Publishing Society, Calcutta, 1970

(with R. K. Mukerjee and J. C. Trevor) *Ancient Inhabitants of Jebel Moya*
Cambridge University Press, 1955

(with P. C. Mahalanobis and D. N. Majumdar) *Anthropometric Survey of the United Provinces, 1941: a Statistical Study*
Asia Publishing House, 1950

(with D. N. Majumdar) *Race Elements of Bengal, a Quantitative Study*
Asia Publishing House, 1958

(with A. Matthai and S. K. Mitra) *Formulae and Tables for Statistical Work*

First edition	1966	Statistical Publishing Society, Calcutta
Second edition (with B. Ramamurti as additional author)	1975	Statistical Publishing Society, Calcutta

(with J. Kleffe) *Estimation of Variance Components and its Applications*
North-Holland, 1988

Statistics and Truth: Putting Chance to Work

First edition	1989	The Council of Scientific and Industrial Research, India

Reprint	1989	International Publishing House, USA
Second edition (in Japanese)	1993	Maruzen Co. Ltd, Tokyo
Second edition (in Spanish)	1994	Promociones y Publicaciones Universitarias, SA, Barcelona, Spain

Choquet–Deny Type Functional Equations with Applications to Stochastic models
John Wiley, 1994

Heavily cited books

Rao's book, *Linear Statistical Inference and Its Applications*, appears in the list of 78 "Heavily Cited Works in Mathematics (during the period 1961–1972), Part 1, Pure Mathematics," published in *Current Contents*, 47, November 1973.

Rao's book, *Linear Statistical Inference and Its Applications*, has been recently identified as one of the most cited items in its field, according to the data from the *Science Citation Index* and the *Social Science Citation Index*. A brief commentary on this work is published in *This Week Citation Classics* section of *Current Contents*, CC/Number 12, March 24, 1980.

Rao's book, *Advanced Statistical Methods in Biometric Research*, appears in the list of 72 "Heavily Cited Works in Mathematics (during the period, 1961–1972), Part 2, Applied Mathematics," published in *Current Contents*, 48, November 28, 1973.

Research papers

1944

a. (with R. C. Bose and S. Chowla). On the integral order mod p of quadratics $x^2 + ax + b$ with applications to the construction of minimum functions for $GF(p^2)$ and to some number theory results. *Bull. Cal. Math. Soc.* 15, 153–74.

1945

a. Familial correlations or the multivariate generalization of the intraclass correlation. *Current Science*, 4, 66.
b. Generalization of Markoff's theorem and tests of linear hypotheses. *Sankhyā* 7, 9–16.
c. Markoff's theorem with linear restrictions on parameters. *Sankhyā* 7, 16–19.
d. Information and accuracy attainable in the estimation of statistical parameters. *Bull. Cal. Math. Soc.* 37, 81–91.

e. Finite geometries and certain derived results in theory of numbers. *Proc. Nat. Inst. Sc.* 11, 136–49.
f. (with R. C. Bose and S. Chowla). On the roots of a well-known congruence. *Proc. Nat. Acad. Sc.* 14, 193.
g. (with R. C. Bose and S. Chowla). Minimum functions in Galois fields. *Proc. Nat. Acad. Sc.* 14, 191.

1946

a. Difference sets and combinatorial arrangements derivable from finite geometries. *Proc. Nat. Inst. Sc.* 12, 123–35.
b. On the linear combination of observations and the general theory of least squares. *Sankhyā* 7, 237–56.
c. Confounded factorial designs in quasi-latin squares. *Sankhyā* 7, 295–304.
d. Hypercubes of strength "d" leading to confounded designs in factorial experiments. *Bull. Cal. Math. Soc.* 38, 67–78.
e. On the mean conserving property. *Proc. Ind. Acad. Sc.* 23, 165–73.
f. Tests with discriminant functions in multivariate analysis. *Sankhyā* 7, 407–14.
g. On the most efficient designs in weighing. *Sankhyā* 7, 440.
h. Minimum variance and the estimation of several parameters. *Proc. Camb. Philos. Soc.* 43, 280–3.
i. (with S. J. Poti). On locally most powerful tests when the alternatives are one sided. *Sankhyā* 7, 441.

1947

a. The problem of classification and distance between two populations. *Nature* 159, 30.
b. Note on a problem of Ragnar Frisch. *Econometrika* 15, 245–9. A correction to note on a problem of Ragnar Frisch. *Econometrika* 17, 212.
c. General methods of analysis for incomplete block designs. *J. Am. Statist. Assoc.* 42, 541–61.
d. Factorial experiments derivable from combinatorial arrangements of arrays. *J. Roy. Statist. Soc.* 9, 128–40.
e. Large sample tests of statistical hypotheses concerning several parameters with applications to problems of estimation. *Proc. Camb. Philos. Soc.* 44, 50–7.

1948

a. A statistical criterion to determine the group to which an individual belongs. *Nature* 160, 835.
b. Tests of significance in multivariate analysis. *Biometrika* 35, 58–79.
c. The utilization of multiple measurements in problems of biological classification. *J. Roy. Statist. Soc.* 10, 159–203.

d. Sufficient statistics and minimum variance estimates. *Proc. Camb. Philos. Soc.* 45, 215–18.
e. (with D. C. Shaw). On a formula for the prediction of cranial capacity. *Biometrics* 4, 247–53.
f. (with K. R. Nair). Confounding in asymmetrical factorial experiments. *J. Roy. Statist. Soc.* 10, 109–31.

1949

a. On a class of arrangements. *Edin. Math. Proc.* 8, 119–25.
b. On some problems arising out of discrimination with multiple characters. *Sankhyā* 9, 343–64.
c. A note on unbiased and minimum variance estimates. *Cal. Statist. Bull.* 3, 36.
d. (with P. Slater). Multivariate analysis applied to differences between neurotic groups. *British J. Psychology, Statist. Sec.* 17–29.
e. (with P. C. Mahalanobis and D. N. Mazumdar). Anthropometric survey of the United Provinces, 1941, a statistical study. *Sankhyā* 9, 90–324.

1950

a. Methods of scoring linkage data giving the simultaneous segregation of three factors. *Heredity* 4, 37–59.
b. The theory of fractional replication in factorial experiments. *Sankhyā* 10, 84–6.
c. Statistical inference applied to classificatory problems. *Sankhyā* 10, 229–56.
d. A note on the distribution of $D^2_{p+q} - D^2_p$ and some computational aspects of D^2 statistic and discriminant function. *Sankhyā* 10, 257–68.
e. Sequential tests of null hypotheses. *Sankhyā* 10, 361–70.

1951

a. A theorem in least squares. *Sankhyā* 11, 9–12.
b. Statistical inference applied to classificatory problems. Part II. Problems of selecting individuals for various duties in a specified ratio. *Sankhyā* 11, 107–16.
c. A simplified approach to factorial experiments and the punched card technique in the construction and analysis of designs. *Bull. Inst. Inter. Statist.* XXXIII (2), 1–28.
d. An asymptotic expansion of the distribution of Wilk's criterion. *Bull. Inst. Inter. Statist.* XXXIII (2), 177–80.
e. The applicability of large sample tests fir moving average and auto regressive schemes to series of short length – an experimental study. Part 3: The discriminant function approach in the classification of time series. *Sankhyā* 11, 257–72.

f. Progress of statistics in India. In *Progress of Science in India (1939–1950)*, pp. 68–94. National Institute of Sciences, India.

1952

a. Some theorems on minimum variance estimation. *Sankhyā* 12, 27–42.
b. Minimum variance estimation in distributions admitting ancillary statistics. *Sankhyā* 12, 53–6.

1953

a. Discriminant function for genetic differentiation and selection. *Sankhyā* 12, 229–46.
b. On transformations useful in the distribution problems of least squares. *Sankhyā* 12, 339–46.

1954

a. A general theory of discrimination when the information about alternative population distributions is based on samples. *Ann. Math. Statist.* 25, 651–70.
b. On the use and interpretation of distance functions in statistics. *Bull. Inst. Inter. Statist.* 34, 90–100.
c. Estimation of relative potency from multiple response data. *Biometrics* 10, 208–20.

1955

a. Analysis of dispersion for multiply classified data with unequal numbers of cells. *Sankhyā* 15, 253–80.
b. Estimation and tests of significance in factor analysis. *Psychometrika* 20, 93–111.
c. Theory of the method of estimation by minimum chi-square. *Bull. Inst. Inter. Statist.* 35, 25–32.
d. (with G. Kallianpur). On Fisher's lower bound to asymptotic variance of a consistent estimate. *Sankhyā* 16, 331–42.

1956

a. On the recovery of interblock information in varietal trials. *Sankhyā* 17, 105–14.
b. A general class of quasi-factorial and related designs. *Sankhyā* 17, 165–74.
c. Analysis of dispersion with missing observations. *J. Roy. Statist. Soc. B* 18, 259–64.
d. (with I. M. Chakravarti). Some small sample tests of significance for a Poisson distribution. *Biometrics* 12, 264–82.

1957

a. Maximum likelihood estimation for multinomial distribution. *Sankhyā* 18, 139–48.

1958

a. Quantitative studies in sociology, need for increased use in India. In *Sociology, Social Research, and Social Problems in India*, pp. 53–74. Asia Publishing House.
b. Some statistical methods for comparison of growth curves. *Biometrics* 14, 1–17.
c. Maximum likelihood estimation for the multinomial distribution with an infinite number of cells. *Sankhyā* 20, 211–18.

1959

a. Some problems involving linear hypotheses in multivariate analysis. *Biometrika* 46, 49–58.
b. Expected values of mean squares in the analysis of incomplete block experiments and some comments based on them. *Sankhyā* 21, 327–36.
c. Sur une Characterization de la Distribution Normal Etablie d'apres une Propriete Optimum des Estimations Lineares. *Coll. Inter. du CNRS France* LXXXVII, 165.
d. (with I. M. Chakravarty). Tables for some small sample tests of significance for Poisson distributions and 2×3 contingency tables. *Sankhyā* 21, 315–26.

1960

a. Multivariate analysis: An indispensable statistical aid in applied research. *Sankhyā* 22, 317–38.
b. Experimental designs with restricted randomization. *Bull. Inst. Inter. Statist.* XXXVII, 397–404.

1961

a. A study of large sample test criteria through properties of efficient estimates. *Sankhyā A* 23, 25–40.
b. Asymptotic efficiency and limiting information. In *Proc. Fourth Berkeley Symposium on Mathematical Statistics and Probability*, University of California 1, 531–46.
c. A study of BIB designs with replications 11 to 16. *Sankhyā* 23, 117–27.
d. A combinatorial assignment problem. *Nature* 191, 100.
e. Generation of random permutations of a given number of elements using random sampling numbers. *Sankhyā A* 23, 305–7.
f. Combinatorial arrangements analogous to orthogonal arrays. *Sankhyā A* 23, 283–6.

g. Some observations on multivariate statistical methods in anthropological research. *Bull. Inst. Inter. Statist.* XXXVII (4), 99–109.

1962

a. Ronald Aylmer Fisher, FRS (an obituary). *Science and Culture* 29, 80–1.
b. Some observations on anthropometric surveys. In *Anthropology Today, Essays in Memory of D. N. Najumdar*, pp. 135–49. Asia Publishing House.
c. Use of discriminant and allied functions in multivariate analysis. *Sankhyā A* 24, 149–54.
d. Efficient estimates and optimum inference procedures in large samples (with discussion). *J. Roy. Statist. Soc. B* 24, 46–72.
e. Problems of selection with restriction. *J. Roy. Statist. Soc. B* 24, 401–5.
f. A note on generalized inverse of a matrix with applications to problems in mathematical statistics. *J. Roy. Statist. Soc. B* 24, 152–8.
g. Apparent anomalies and irregularities in maximum likelihood estimation (with discussion), *Sankhyā B* 24, 73–102.

1963

a. Criteria of estimation in large samples. *Sankhyā A* 25, 189–206.
b. (with V. S. Varadarajan). Discrimination of Gaussian processes. *Sankhyā A* 25, 303–30.

1964

a. Problems of selection involving programming techniques. In *Proceedings of the IBM Scientific Computing Symposium on Statistics*, 29–51.
b. The use and interpretation of principal component analysis in applied research. *Sankhyā A* 26, 329–58.
c. Sir Ronald Fisher – the architect of multivariate analysis. *Biometrics* 20, 286–300.
d. (with H. Rubin). On a characterization of the Poisson distribution. *Sankhyā A* 26, 295–8.

1965

a. Efficiency of an estimator and Fisher's lower-bound to asymptotic variance. *Bull. Inst. Inter. Statist.* XLI(1), 55–63.
b. The theory of least squares when the parameters are stochastic and its applications to the analysis of growth curves. *Biometrika* 52, 447–58.
c. On discrete distributions arising out of methods of ascertainment. *Sankhyā A* 27, 311–24.
d. Covariance adjustment and related problems in multivariate analysis. In *Multivariate Analysis, Vol. 1* (P. R. Krishnaiah, ed.), pp. 87–103. Academic Press, New York.

e. (with A. M. Kagan and Yu. V. Linnik). On a characterization of the normal law based on a property of the sample average. *Sankhyā A* 27, 405–6.

1966

a. Characterization of the distribution of random variables in linear structural relations. *Sankhyā A* 28, 251–60.
b. Generalized inverse for matrices and its applications in mathematical statistics. *Festschrift for J. Neyman. Research Papers in Statistics*, 263–99.
c. Discriminant function between composite hypotheses and related problems. *Biometrika* 53, 315–21.
d. Discrimination among groups and assigning new individuals. In *The Role of Methodology of Classification in Psychiatry and Psychopathology*, pp. 229–40. US Department of Health, Education and Welfare, Public Health Services.
e. On some characterizations of the normal law. *Sankhyā A* 29, 1–14.
f. (with M. N. Rao). Linked cross sectional study for determining norms and growth curves: A pilot survey on Indian school-going boys. *Sankhyā B* 28, 231–52. (Partly published under the title, Methods for determining norms and growth rates, a study amongst Indian school-going boys. *Gerentologia* 12, 200–16.)

1967

a. Calculus of generalized inverses of matrices: part I – general theory. *Sankhyā A* 29, 317–50.
b. Cyclical generation of linear subspaces in finite geometries. In *Combinatorial Mathematics and Its Applications*, chapter 28, pp. 515–35. University of North Carolina Monograph Series No. 4.
c. Least squares theory using an estimated dispersion matrix and its application to measurement of signals. In *Proc. Fifth Berkeley Symposium on Mathematical Statistics and Probability, Vol. 1*, pp. 355–72. University of California Press.
d. On vector variables with a linear structure and a characterization of the multivariate normal distribution. *Bull. Inst. Inter. Statist.* XLII (2), 1207–13.

1968

a. A note on a previous lemma in the theory of least squares and some further results. *Sankhyā A* 30, 259–66.
b. (with C. G. Khatri). Some characterizations of the gamma distribution. *Sankhyā A* 30, 157–66.
c. (with C. G. Khatri). Solutions to some functional equations and applications to characterization of probability distributions. *Sankhyā A* 30, 167–80.

d. (with B. Ramachandran). Some results on characteristic functions and characterizations of the normal and generalized stable laws. *Sankhyā A* 30, 125–40.
e. (with S. K. Mitra). Simultaneous reduction of a pair of quadratic forms. *Sankhyā A* 30, 313–22.
f. (with S. K. Mitra). Some results in estimation and tests of linear hypotheses under the Gauss-Markoff model. *Sankhyā A* 30, 281–90.

1969

a. A decomposition theorem for vector variables with a linear structure. *Ann. Math. Statist.* 40, 1845–9.
b. Some characterizations of the multivariate normal distribution. In *Multivariate Analysis II* (R. P. Krishnaiah, ed.), pp. 322–8. Academic Press, New York.
c. Recent advances in discriminatory analysis. *J. Ind. Soc. Agri. Statist.* XXI, 3–15.
d. A multidisciplinary approach for teaching statistics and probability. *Sankhyā B* 321–40.
e. (with S. K. Mitra). Conditions for optimality and validity of least squares theory. *Ann. Math. Statist.* 40, 1716–24.

1970

a. Estimation of heteroscedastic variances on a linear model. *J. Am. Statist. Assoc.* 65, 161–72.
b. Computers: a great revolution in scientific research. *Proc. Indian National Science Academy* 36, 123–39.
c. Inference on discriminant function coefficients. In *Essays in Probability and Statistics*, chapter 30 (R. C. Bose et al., eds), pp. 587–602. University of North Carolina and Statistical Publishing Society.
d. (with B. Ramachandran). Solutions of functional equations arising in some regression problems and a characterization of the Cauchy law. *Sankhyā A* 32, 1–30.

1971

a. Characterization of probability laws through linear functions. *Sankhyā A* 33, 265–70.
b. Some aspects of statistical inference in problems of sampling from finite populations. In *Foundations of Statistical Inference*, pp. 177–202. Holt, Rinehart and Winston of Canada.
c. Estimation of variance and covariance components – MINQUE Theory. *J. Multivariate Analysis* 1, 257–75.
d. Minimum variance quadratic unbiased estimation of variance components. *J. Multivariate Analysis* 1, 445–56.

e. Unified theory of linear estimation. *Sankhyā A* 33, 370–96. Correction. *Sankhyā A* 34, 477.
f. Data, analysis, and statistical thinking. In *Economic and Social Development, Essays in Honor of C. D. Deshmukh*, pp. 383–92. Vora and Co., Bombay.
g. (with J. K. Ghosh). A note on some translation-parameter families of densities for which the median is an m.l.e. *Sankhyā A* 33, 91–3.
h. (with S. K. Mitra). Further contributions to the theory of generalized inverse of matrices and its applications. *Sankhyā A* 33, 289–300.
i. (with S. K. Mitra). Generalized inverse of a matrix and applications. In *Sixth Berkeley Symposium on Mathematical Statistics and Probability, Vol. 1*, pp. 601–20. University of California Press.
j. Some comments on the logarithmic series distribution. In *Statistical Ecology, Vol. 1*, pp. 131–42. Pennsylvania State University Press.
k. Taxonomy in anthropology. In *Mathematics in Archaeological and Historical Sciences*, pp. 19–29. Edinburgh University Press.

1972

a. Recent trends of research work in multivariate analysis. *Biometrics* 28, 3–22.
b. Estimation of variance and covariance components in linear models. *J. Am. Statist. Assoc.* 67, 112–15.
c. A note on IPM method in the unified theory of linear estimation. *Sankhyā A* 34, 285–8.
d. Some recent results in linear estimation. *Sankhyā B* 34, 369–77.
e. (with P. Bhimasankaram and S. K. Mitra). Determination of a matrix by its subclasses of *g*-inverse. *Sankhyā A* 24, 5–8.
f. (with C. G. Khatri). Functional equations and characterization of probability laws through linear functions of random variables. *J. Multivariate Analysis* 2, 162–73.

1973

a. Unified theory of least squares. *Communications in Statistics* 1, 1–8.
b. Some combinatorial problems of arrays and applications to design of experiments. In *A Survey of Combinatorial Theory*, chapter 29, pp. 349–60. North-Holland.
c. Prasantha Chandra Mahalanobis. *Biographical Memoirs of the Fellows of the Royal Society* 19, 485–92.
d. Representation of best linear unbiased estimators in the Gauss–Markoff model with a singular dispersion matrix. *J. Multivariate Analysis* 3, 276–92.
e. (with S. K. Mitra). Theory and application of constrained inverse of matrices. *SIAM J. Appl. Math.* 24, 473–88.
f. (with A. Kagan and Yu. V. Linnik). Extension of Darmois–Skitovic

theorem to functions of random variables satisfying an addition theorem. *Communications in Statistics* 1, 471–4.

g. (with D. C. Rao and R. Chakraborty). The generalized Wright's model. In *Genetic Structure of Populations* (ed. Morton), pp. 55–9. University Press, Hawaii.

h. (with C. G. Khatri) Solution to some functional equations and their applications to characterization of probability distributions. *Contributions to Statistics and Agricultural Sciences* (presented to Dr. V. G. Panse), 147–60.

i. Mahalanobis era in statistics. Special supplement to *Sankhyā, Series A and B*, 35, 12–26.

1974

a. Functional equations and characterization of probability distributions. In *Proceedings of the International Congress of Mathematicians* (Vancouver) 2, 163–8.

b. Statistical analysis and prediction of growth. *Proc. 8th Int. Biom. Conference*, 15–21.

c. Projectors, generalized inverses and the BLUE's. *J. Roy. Statist. Soc.* 35, 442–8.

d. Teaching of statistics at the secondary level – an interdisciplinary approach. In *Statistics at the School Level*, pp. 121–40. Almquist and Wiksell Int., Amsterdam.

e. (with S. K. Mitra). Projections under semi-norms and generalized inverse of matrices. *Linear Algebra and Appl.* 9, 155–67.

1975

a. Simultaneous estimation of parameters in different linear models and applications to biometric problems. *Biometrics* 31, 545–54.

b. Growing responsibilities of government statisticians. In *Occasional Papers* No. 4. Asian Institute of Statistics, Tokyo.

c. Some thoughts on regression and prediction – part I (dedicated to Professor J. Neyman on his 80th birthday). *Sankhyā C* 37, 102–20.

d. Theory of estimation of parameters in the general Gauss-Markoff model. In *A Survey of Statistical Design and Linear Models* (ed. J. N. Srivastava), pp. 475–87. North Holland.

e. Inaugural Linnik Memorial Lecture – Some problems in the characterization of the multivariate normal distribution. In *Statistical Distributions in Scientific Work, Vol. 3* (G. P. Patil, ed.), pp. 1–13. D. Reidel Publishing Company.

f. (with M. L. Puri). Augmenting Shapiro–Wilk test for normality. In *Volume Dedicated to A. Linder*, pp. 129–39.

g. (with S. K. Mitra). Extension of a duality theorem concerning g-inverse of matrices. *Sankhyā A* 37, 439–45.

h. Some problems of sample surveys. *Adv. Appl. Prob.* 7, 50–61.

1976

a. Estimation of parameters in a linear model – Wald Lecture 1. *Ann. Statist.* 4, 1023–37, with a correction in Vol. 7, 696.
b. Characterization of prior distributions and solution to a compound decision problem. *Ann. Statist.* 4, 823–35.
c. On a unified theory of linear estimation in linear models – a review of recent results. In *Perspectives in Probability, Papers in Honor of M. S. Bartlett* (J. Gani, ed.), pp. 89–104. Academic Press, New York.
d. (with C. G. Khatri). Characterization of multivariate normality through independence of some statistics. *J. Multivariate Analysis* 3, 81–94.
e. Statistics in search of truth. Convocation speech, Athens University, Greece, pp. 257–66 (printed in Greek).

1977

a. A natural example of weighted distributions – a classroom exercise. *American Statistician* 31, 24–6.
b. Simultaneous estimation of parameters – a compound decision problem. In *Statistical Decision Theory and Related Topics* (S. S. Gupta and D. S. Moore, eds), pp. 327–50.
c. Cluster analysis applied to a study of race mixture in human populations, Michigan University Symposium, pp. 175–9.
d. Statistics for accelerating economic and social development. Anniversary address, 25th Anniversary of the Central Statistical Organization.
e. (with G. P. Patil). The weighted distributions: a survey of their applications. In *Applications of Statistics* (P. R. Krishnaiah, ed.), pp. 383–405. North-Holland.
f. Prediction of future observations with special reference to linear models. In *Multivariate Analysis IV* (P. R. Krishnaiah, ed.), pp. 193–208. North-Holland.

1978

a. Least squares theory for possibly singular models. *Canadian J. Statist.* 6, 19–23.
b. (with G. P. Patil). Weighted distributions and size biased sampling with applications to wildlife populations and human families. *Biometrics* 34, 179–89.
c. (with Nobuo Shinozaki). Precision of individual estimators in simultaneous estimation of parameters. *Biometrika* 65, 23.
d. A note on the unified theory of least squares. *Commun. Statist. Theor. Meth. A* 7, 409–11.
e. Choice of best linear estimators in the Gauss–Markoff model with a singular dispersion matrix. *Commun. Statist. Theor. Meth. A* 7, 1199–208.
f. P. C. Mahalanobis (biography). In *International Encyclopedia of Statistics, Vol. 1* (W. H. Kruskal and J. M. Tanur, eds), pp. 571–6. The Free Press.

1979

a. (with H. Yanai). General definition and decomposition of projectors and some applications to statistical problems. *J. Statist. Planning and Inference* 3, 1–17.
b. Estimation of parameters in the singular Gauss-Markoff model. *Commun. Statist. Theor. Meth. A* 8(14), 1353–8.
c. MINQUE theory and its relation to ML and MML estimation of variance components. *Sankhyā B* 41, 138–53.
d. Separation theorems for singular values of matrices and their applications in multivariate analysis. *J. Multivariate Analysis* 9, 362–77.
e. (with R. C. Srivastava). Some characterizations based on a multivariate splitting model. *Sankhyā A* 41, 124–8.

1980

a. Matrix approximations and reduction of dimensionality in multivariate statistical analysis. In *Multivariate Analysis V* (P. R. Krishnaiah, ed.), pp. 3–22. North-Holland.
b. (with R. C. Srivastava, Sheela Talwalker and Gerald A. Edgar). Characterization of probability distributions based on a generalized Rao-Rubin condition. *Sankhyā A* 42, 161–9.
c. Discussion on a paper by Joseph Berkson. *Ann. Statist.* 8, 482–5.
d. (with Jurgen Kleffe). Estimation of variance components. *Handbook of Statistics, Vol. 1* (P. R. Krishnaiah, ed.), pp. 1–40. North-Holland.

1981

a. A lemma on g-inverse of a matrix and computation of correlation coefficients in the singular case. *Commun. Statist. Theor. Meth.* A 10, 1–10.
b. (with C. G. Khatri). Some extensions of Kantorovich inequality and statistical applications. *J. Multivariate Analysis* 11(4), 498–505.
c. Some comments on the minimum mean square error as a criterion of estimation. In *Statistics and Related Topics* (M. Csorgo, D. A. Dawson, J. N. K. Rao and A. K. Md. E. Saleh, eds), pp. 123–43. North Holland.

1982

a. Analysis of diversity: a unified approach. In *Statistical Decision Theory and Related Topics, III, Vol. 2* (S. S. Gupta and J. O. Berger, eds), pp. 233–49. Academic Press, New York.
b. Diversity and dissimilarity coefficients: a unified approach. *Theoretical Population Biology* 21, 24–43.
c. (with C. G. Khatri). Some generalizations of Kantorovich inequality. *Sankhyā A* 44(1), 91–102.
d. (with Ka-Sing Lau). Integrated Cauchy functional equation and characterizations of the exponential law. *Sankhyā A* 44, 72–90.

e. Diversity: its measurement, decomposition, apportionment and analysis. *Sankhyā A* 44, 1–21.
f. (with Jacob Burbea). On the convexity of some divergence measures based on entropy functions. *IEEE Trans. Inf. Theory* IT-28(3), 489–95.
g. Optimum balance between statistical theory and applications in teaching. In *Proc. First International Conference on Teaching Statistics Vol. 2* (Grey, Holmes, Barnett and Constable, eds), pp. 34–49. University of Sheffield.
h. (with Jacob Burbea). On the convexity of higher order Jensen differences based on entropy functions. *IEEE Trans. Inf. Theory* IT-28(6), 961–3.
i. (with Jacob Burbea). Entropy differential metric, distance and divergence measures in probability spaces: a unified approach. *J. Multivariate Analysis* 12(4), 575–96.
j. Gini-Simpson index of diversity: a characterization, generalization, and applications. *Utilitas Mathematica* 21 B (the second of two special volumes issued on the occasion of the 80th birthday of Dr Frank Yates), 373–82.
k. Theory of statistics and its applications, a lecture delivered to the Statistical Association of Guangdong Province, Peoples Republic of China on July 10 (in Chinese), 1–6.

1983

a. Multivariate analysis: some reminiscences on its origin and development. *Sankhyā B* 45, 284–99.
b. Likelihood ratio tests for relationships between two covariance matrices. In *Studies in Econometrics, Time Series, and Multivariate Statistics*, pp. 529–44. Academic Press.
c. An extension of Deny's theorem and its application to characterizations of probability distributions. In *A Festschrift for Erich Lehmann*, pp. 348–66. Wadsworth Statistics/Probability Series.
d. (with P. R. Krishnaiah and T. Kariya). Inference on parameters of multivariate normal populations when some data is missing. *Developments in Statistics, Vol. 4* (P. R. Krishnaiah, ed.), pp. 137–84. Academic Press, New York.
e. Statistics, statisticians, and public policy making. *Sankhyā B* 45, 151–9.

1984

a. Prediction of future observations in polynomial growth curve models. In *Proceedings of the Indian Statistical Institute Golden Jubilee International Conference on Statistics: Applications and New Directions*, pp. 512–20.
b. Use of diversity and distance measures in the analysis of qualitative data. In *Multivariate Statistical Methods in Physical Anthropology* (G. N. van Vark and W. H. Howells, eds), pp. 49–67. Reidel Publishing Co.
c. Convexity properties of entropy functions and analysis of diversity. In *Inequalities in Statistics and Probability*, IMS Lecture Notes. Monograph Series, Vol. 5, pp. 68–77.

d. Inference from linear models with fixed effects: recent results and some problems. In *Statistics: an Appraisal*, Proceedings of the 50th Anniversary Conference (H. A. David and H. T. David, eds), pp. 345–69. The Iowa State University Press.
e. (with Ka-Sing Lau). Solution to the integrated Cauchy functional equation on the whole line. *Sankhyā* 46, 311–19.
f. (with Robert Boudreau). Diversity and cluster analyses of blood group data on some human populations. In *Human Population Genetics: the Pittsburgh Symposium* (Aravinda Chakravarti, ed.), pp. 331–62. Van Nostrand Reinhold Co., New York.
g. (with J. Muller and B. K. Sinha). Inference on parameters in a linear model: a review of recent results. In *Experimental Design, Statistical Models, and Genetic Studies* (K. Hinkelmann, ed.), pp. 277–96. Marcel Dekker, Inc.
h. (with Thomas Mathew and B. K. Sinha). Admissible linear estimation in singular linear models. *Commun. Statistics A* 13, 3033–46.
i. (with Jacob Burbea). Differential metrics in probability spaces. *Probability and Mathematical Statistics* 3, 241–58.
j. Optimization of functions of matrices with applications to statistical problems. In *W. G. Cochran's Impact on Statistics* (Poduri, S. R. S. Rao, eds), pp. 191–202. John Wiley, New York.
k. Invited discussion on "Present position and potential developments: some personal views, multivariate analysis" by R. Sibson, *J. Roy. Statist. Soc.* 147, 205–7.

1985

a. (with Haruo Yanai). Generalized inverse of linear transformations: a geometric approach. *Linear Algebra and Its Applications* 66, 87–98.
b. Matrix derivatives: applications in statistics. In *Encyclopedia of Statistical Sciences, Vol. 5* (Kotz and Johnson, eds), pp. 320–5. John Wiley, New York.
c. (with J. Kleffe). Mixed linear models. In *Encyclopedia of Statistical Sciences, Vol. 5* (Kotz and Johnson, eds), pp. 542–8. John Wiley, New York.
d. Tests for dimensionality and interactions of mean vectors under general and reducible covariance structures. *Journal of Multivariate Analysis* 16, 173–84.
e. (with Robert Boudreau). Prediction of future observations in a factor analytic type growth model. In *Multivariate Analysis VI* (P. R. Krishnaiah, ed.), pp. 449–66. Elsevier Science Publishers.
f. Weighted distributions arising out of methods of ascertainment: what population does a sample represent? In *A Celebration of Statistics*, The ISI Centenary Volume (Anthony C. Atkinson and Stephen E. Fienberg, eds), pp. 543–69. Springer-Verlag, New York.

g. A unified approach to inference from linear models. In *Proc. First International Tampere Seminar on Linear Statistical Models and Their Applications* (Tarmo Pukkila and Simo Puntanen, eds), pp. 9–36. University of Tampere, Finland.
h. (with Tapan K. Nayak). Cross entropy, dissimilarity measures and characterizations of quadratic entropy. *IEEE Transactions on Information Theory* IT-31 (5), 589–93.
i. (with Haruo Yanai). Generalized inverses of partitioned matrices useful in statistical applications. *Linear Algebra and Its Applications* 70, 105–13.
j. The inefficiency of least squares: extensions of Kantorovich inequality. *Linear Algebra and Its Applications* 70, 249–55.
k. Evolution of data collection: censuses, sample surveys and design of experiments. In *Proc. 45th Session of the Int. Statist. Inst. Amsterdam, Vol. 1*, pp. 6.2-1–16.

1986

a. (with Abdulhamid A. Alzaid and D. N. Shanbhag). An application of the Perron–Frobenius theorem to a damage model problem. *Sankhyā A* 48, 43–50.
b. (with Abdulhamid A. Alzaid and D. N. Shanbhag). Characterization of discrete probability distributions by partial independence. *Communications in Statistics, Theory and Methods* 15, 643–56.
c. (with C. G. Khatri and Y. N. Sun). Tables for obtaining confidence bounds for realized signal to noise ratio with an estimated discriminant function. *Communications in Statistics, Simulation and Computation* 15, 1–14.
d. (with G. P. Patil and M. V. Ratnaparkhi). On discrete weighted distributions and their use in model choice for observed data. *Communications in Statistics, Theory and Methods* 15, 907–18.
e. (with D. N. Shanbhag). Recent results on characterization of probability distributions: a unified approach through extensions of Deny's theorem. *Adv. Appl. Prob.* 18, 660–78.
f. Rao's axiomatization of diversity measures. In *Encyclopedia of Statistical Sciences, Vol. 7* (Kotz and Johnson, eds), pp. 614–17. John Wiley, New York.
g. (with J. F. Keating and Robert L. Mason). The Pitman nearness criterion and its determination. *Communications in Statistics, Theory and Methods* 15, 3173–91.

1987

a. (with Abdulhamid A. Alzaid and D. N. Shanbhag). An extension of Spitzer's integral representation theorem with an application. *Annals of Probability* 15, 1210–16.
b. (with Abdulhamid A. Alzaid and D. N. Shanbhag). Solution of the

integrated Cauchy functional equation on a half line using exchangeability. *Sankhyā A* 49, 189–94.

c. (with C. Veerendra Rao). Stationary values of the product of two Raleigh coefficients: homologous canonical variates. *Sankhyā B* 49, 113–25.
d. (with C. G. Khatri). Effects of the estimated noise covariance matrix in optimal signal detection. *IEEE Trans. Acoustics, Speech & Signal Processing* ASSP-35 (5), 671–9.
e. (with C. G. Khatri). Test for a specified signal when the noise covariance matrix is unknown. *J. Multivariate Analysis* 22, 177–88.
f. ANODIV: generalization of ANOVA through entropy and cross entropy functions. In *Probability Theory and Mathematical Statistics*, Proc. of the Fourth Vilnius Conference, Vol. 11 (Prohorov et al., eds), pp. 477–96.
g. Prediction of future observations in growth curve type models. *J. Statistical Science* 2, 434–71.
h. Differential metrics in probability spaces. In *Differential Geometry in Statistics, IMS Lecture Notes, Vol. 10* (S. S. Gupta, ed.), pp. 217–40.
i. Estimation in linear models with mixed effects: a unified theory. In *Proc. Second International Tampere Conference in Statistics* (Tarmo Pukkila and Simo Puntanen, eds), pp. 73–98. University of Tampere, Finland.
j. Strategies of data analysis. *Proc. 46th Session of the International Statistical Institute, Tokyo, Book 4*, pp. 279–96.

1988

a. Some recent results in signal detection. In *Statistical Decision Theory and Related Topics IV, Vol. 2* (S. S. Gupta and J. O. Berger, eds), pp. 319–32. Springer-Verlag, New York.
b. (with A. S. Hedayat and J. Stufken). Sampling plans excluding contiguous units. *J. Statistical Planning and Inference* 19, 159–70.
c. (with Abdulhamid A. Alzaid, Ka-Sing Lau and D. N. Shanbhag). Solution of Deny convolution equation restricted to a half line via a random walk approach. *J. Multivariate Analysis* 24, 309–29.
d. (with S. Hedayat and J. Stufken). Designs in survey sampling avoiding contiguous units. *Handbook of Statistics Vol. 6* (P. R. Krishnaiah and C. R. Rao, eds), pp. 575–83. Elsevier Science Publishers.
e. (with Tarmo M. Pukkila). Pattern recognition based on scale invariant discriminant functions. *Information Sciences* 45, 379–89.
f. (with Z. D. Bai and L. C. Zhao). Kernel estimators of density function of directional data. *J. Multivariate Analysis* 27, 24–39.
g. Applications of multivariate analysis in signal detection. In *Advances in Multivariate Statistical Analysis*, Proc. of the International Conference, Calcutta (S. Das Gupta and J. K. Ghosh, eds), pp. 299–320.
h. (with Jogesh Babu). Joint asymptotic distribution of marginal quantiles functions in samples from a multivariate population. *J. Multivariate Analysis* 27, 15–23.

i. (with G. P. Patil and M. V. Ratnaparki). Bivariate weighted distributions and related applications. In *Advances in Multivariate Statistical Analysis*, Proc. International Conference, Calcutta (S. Das Gupta and J. K. Ghosh eds), pp. 261–78.

j. (with G. P. Patil and M. Zelen). Weighted distributions. *Encyclopedia of Statistical Sciences, Vol. 9*, pp. 565–71.

k. Methodology based on the L_1-norm in statistical inference. *Sankhyā* 50, 289–313.

1989

a. (with Z. D. Bai, P.R. Krishnaiah, Y. N. Sun and L. C. Zhao). Reconstruction of the shape and size of objects from two orthogonal projections. *Math. Computer Modelling* 12, 267–75.

b. (with Y. Wu). A strongly consistent procedure for model selection in regression problem. *Biometrika* 76, 369–74.

c. (with C. G. Khatri and T. M. Pukkila). Testing intraclass correlation coefficients. *Communications in Statistics, Simulation and Computation* 18, 15–30.

d. (with D. N. Shanbhag). Further extensions of the Choquet–Deny and Deny theorems with applications in characterization theory. *Quarterly J. of Mathematics, Oxford* 40, 333–50.

e. A unified approach to estimation in linear models with fixed and mixed effects. In *Contributions to Probability and Statistics, Essays in Honor of Ingram Olkin* (Gleser, Perlman, Press and Sampson, eds), pp. 357–67. Springer-Verlag.

f. (with Z. D. Bai, R. P. Krishnaiah, P. S. Reddy, Y. N. Sun and L. C. Zhao). Reconstruction of the left ventricle from two orthogonal projections. *Computer Vision, Graphics and Image Processing* 47, 165–88.

g. A lemma on optimization of a matrix function and a review of the unified theory of linear estimation. In *Statistical Data Analysis and Inference* (Y. Dodge, ed.), pp. 397–418. Elsevier Science Publishers.

h. (with D. N. Shanbhag). Recent advances on the integrated Cauchy functional equation and related results in applied probability. In *Probability and Statistics and Mathematical Papers in Honor of Samuel Karlin* (T. W. Anderson, K. B. Athreya and D. L. Iglehart, eds), pp. 239–53. Academic Press.

i. (with Z. D. Bai and Mosuk Chow). An algorithm for efficient estimation of superimposed exponential signals. *Proc. Tencon'89*, Fourth IEEE Region 10 International Conference, pp. 342–7.

1990

a. (with A. A. Alzaid and D. N. Shanbhag). Elliptical symmetry and exchangeability with characterizations. *J. Multivariate Analysis* 33, 1–16.

b. (with J. Babu). Estimation of the reciprocal of the density quantile function at a point. *J. Multivariate Analysis* 33, 106–24.
c. (with Z. D. Bai). Spectral analytic methods for the estimation of number of signals and directions of arrival. *Proc. Indo-US Workshop Spectrum Analysis in One or Two Dimensions* (S. Prasad and R. Kashyap, eds), pp. 493–507. Oxford and IBH Publishing Co.
d. (with Z. D. Bai and B. Q. Miao). Estimation of direction of arrival of signals: asymptotic results. In *Advances in Spectrum Analysis and Array Processing, Vol. 11* (S. Haykins, ed.), pp. 327–47. Prentice Hall, New Jersey.
e. (with Z. D. Bai and Y. Q. Yin). Least absolute deviations analysis of variance, *Sankhyā* 52, 166–77.
f. (with Z. D. Bai, X. R. Chen and B. Q. Miao). Asymptotic theory of least distances estimate in multivariate linear models. *Statistics* 21, 503–19.

1991

a. (with S. Konishi and C. G. Khatri). Inference on multivariate measures of interclass and intra class correlations in familial data. *J. Roy. Statist. Soc. B* 53, 649–60.
b. (with D. N. Shanbhag). An elementary proof for an extended version of the Choquet–Deny theorem. *J. Multivariate Analysis* 38, 141–8.
c. (with M. B. Rao and G. J. Babu). Nonparametric estimation of survival functions under dependent competing risks. In *Nonparametric Functional Estimation and Related Topics* (G. Roussas, ed.), pp. 431–41. Kluwer Academic Publishers, Netherlands.
d. (with Z. D. Bai). Edgeworth expansion of a function of sample means. *Ann. Statist.* 19, 1295–315.
e. (with D. S. Tu). Inference on the occurrence/exposure rate with mixed censoring models. *Calcutta Statist. Assoc. Bulletin* (Harikinkar Nandi Memorial Volume) 40, 65–88.
f. (with R. F. Fountain and J. P. Keating). An example arising from Berkson's conjecture. *Commun. Statist. Theory Meth.* 20, 3457–72.
g. (with R. Chakraborty). Measurement of genetic variation for evolutionary studies. In *Handbook of Statistics, Vol. 8* (C. R. Rao and R. Chakraborty eds), pp. 271–316. Elsevier Science Publishers.
h. (with Z. D. Bai and Y. Wu). Recent contributions to robust estimation. In *Probability, Statistics and Design of Experiments* (R. C. Bose Symposium Volume, ed. R. R. Bahadur), pp. 33–50. Wiley Eastern.
i. (with A. Kagan). Constancy of regression of a polynomial of sample average on residuals characterizes normal distribution. In *Probability, Statistics and Design of Experiments* (R. C. Bose Symposium Volume, ed. R. R. Bahadur), pp. 419–24. Wiley Eastern.
j. (with C. G. Khatri). Multivariate linear model with latent variables: problems of estimation. *J. Comb. Inf. and Syst. Sci.* 16, 137–54.

k. (with Y. Fujikoshi). Selection of covariables in the growth curve model. *Biometrika* 78, 779–85.
l. (with Z. J. Liu). Multivariate analysis under M-estimation theory using a convex discrepancy function. *Biometric Letters* 28, 89–95.

1992

a. (with Z. D. Bai and Y. Wu). M-estimation of multivariate linear regression parameters under a convex discrepancy function. *Statistica Sinica* 2, 237–54.
b. (with Gutti Jogesh Babu and M. Bhaskara Rao). Nonparametric estimation of survival functions under dependent competing risks and comparison of relative risk ratios. *J. Am. Statist. Assoc.* 87, 84–9.
c. (with L. C. Zhao). On the consistency of M-estimate in a linear model obtained through an estimating equation. *Statistics and Probability Letters* 14, 79–84.
d. (with C. G. Khatri). Empirical hierarchical Bayes estimation. In *Bayesian Analysis in Statistics and Economics* (P. K. Goel and N. S. Iyengar, eds), pp. 147–61. Lecture Notes in Statistics No. 75, Springer-Verlag, New York.
e. R. A. Fisher: the founder of modern statistics. *Statistical Science* 7, 34–48.
f. (with J. K. Baksalary and A. Markiewicz). A study of the influence of the "natural" restrictions on estimation problems in the singular Gauss–Markoff model. *J. Statist. Plan. and Inference* 31, 334–52.
g. (with L. C. Zhao and X. R. Chen). A note on the consistency of M-estimates in linear models. In *Stochastic Processes: a Festschrift in Honour of Gopinath Kallainpur* (S. Cambanis, J. K. Ghosh, R. Karandikar and P. K. Sen, eds), pp. 359–67. Springer-Verlag.
h. (wth G. J. Babu). Expansions for statistics involving the mean absolute deviations. *Annals of Inst. Stat. Math.* 44, 387–403.
i. (with D. N. Shanbhag). Some observations on the integrated Cauchy functional equation. *Mathematishe Nachrichten* 157, 185–95.
j. Statistics as a last resort: an autobiographical account. In *Statistical Heritage of India* (Ghosh, Mitra and Parthasarathy, eds), pp. 151–213. Wiley Eastern.
k. (with Z. D. Bai). Edgeworth expansion for ratio of sample means and applications to survival analysis. *Sankhyā A* 54, 309–22.
l. (with L. C. Zhao). Approximation to the distributions of M-estimates in linear models by randomly weighted bootstrap. *Sankhyā* A 54, 323–33.
m. (with L. C. Zhao). Linear representation of M-estimates in linear models. *Canadian J. Statistics* 20, 359–68.
n. (with S. Konishi). Principal component analysis for multivariate familial data. *Biometrika* 79, 631–42.
o. Sample surveys and design of experiments: Need for interface between the two. *Sankhyā* 54, 357–66.

p. Linear transformations, projection operators and generalized inverses – a geometric approach. In *Contributions to Statistics* (N. Venugopal et al., eds), pp. 1–10. Wiley Eastern.

q. (with D. N. Shanbhag). Further observations on the integrated Cauchy functional equation. *J. Combinatorics, Information and System Sciences* 17, 67–78.

1993

a. (with Lu Zhang and L. C. Zhao). Multiple target angle tracking using sensor array outputs. *IEEE Transactions on Aerospace and Electronic Systems* 29, 268–71.

b. (with L. C. Zhao). Asymptotic behavior of maximum likelihood estimates of superimposed exponential signals. *IEEE, ASSP* 41, 1461–3.

c. (with M. S. Srivastava and Y. Wu). Some aspects of quality control methods. In *Quality through Engineering Design* (*Advances in Industrial Engineering* 16), pp. 21–32. Elsevier.

d. (with R. L. Fountain). Further investigations of Berkson's example. *Communications in Statistics, Theory and Methods* 23, 613–29.

e. Current trends of research in statistics: small sample asymptotics, resampling techniques and robustness. ARO Report 93–1. *Transactions of the Tenth Army Conference on Applied Mathematics and Computing*, pp. 195–220.

f. (with E. B. Fosam and D. N. Shanbhag). Comments on some papers involving the integrated Cauchy function equation. *Statistics and Probability Letters* 17, 299–302.

g. (with Z. D. Bai and L. C. Zhao). MANOVA type tests under M-theory for the standard multivariate linear model. *J. Statistical Planning and Inference* 36, 77–90.

h. Statistics must have a purpose: The Mahalanobis dictum. *Proc. ISI 49th Session*, Firenze, IN01.1, pp. 21–36.

i. (with G. J. Babu). Bootstrap methodology. In *Handbook of Statistics 9: Computational Statistics* (C. R. Rao, ed.), pp. 627–61. North-Holland.

j. (with C. R. Sastry and Bin Zhou). Some recent contributions to multitarget tracking. *Multivariate Analysis: Future Directions* (C. R. Rao, ed.), pp. 319–46. North-Holland.

k. (with Paula M. Caligiuri). Analysis of ordered categorical data through appropriate scaling. In *Handbook of Statistics 9, Computational Statistics* (C. R. Rao, ed.), pp. 521–34. North-Holland.

l. (with Bin Zhou). Closed form solution to the estimates of direction of arrival using data from an array of sensors. In *Handbook of Statistics 10: Signal Processing* (N. K. Bose and C. R. Rao, eds), pp. 741–54. North Holland.

m. (with D. S. Tu and Z. J. Liu). Strong representations for kernel estimates of conditional medians. In *Statistics and Probability: a Raghu Raj Bahadur Festschrift* (J. K. Ghosh, S. K. Mitra, K. R. Parthasarathy and B. L. S. Prakasa Rao, eds), pp. 381–94. Wiley Eastern Ltd.

n. (with Lu Zhang and L. C. Zhao). A new algorithm for multitarget angle tracking. *IEE Proceedings, Part F (England)* 140, 335–8.

o. J. B. S. Haldane: a polymath in the Indian context. J. B. S. Haldane centenary lecture. In *Human Population Genetics* (P. P. Majumdar, ed.), pp. 1–6. Plenum Press.

p. (with Paula M. Caligiuri). On scaling of ordinal categorical data. In *Multivariate Analysis: Future Directions 2* (C. M. Cuadras and C. R. Rao, eds), pp. 97–112. North-Holland.

q. (with L. C. Zhao). Asymptotic normality of LAD estimator in censored regression models. *Mathematical Methods of Statistics* 2, 228–39.

r. (with Z. D. Bai and Z. J. Liu). On the strong consistency of M-estimates in linear models under a general discrepancy function. In *Handbook of Statistics, Vol. 11, Econometrics* (G. S. Maddala, C. R. Rao and H. K. Vinod, eds), pp. 381–92. North-Holland.

s. (with L. C. Zhao and B. Zhou). A novel algorithm for 2-dimensional frequency estimation. *The 27th Asilomar Conference on Signals, Systems & Computers, Vol 1. of 2*, pp. 199–202.

t. (with W. Schaafsma, G. M. Steerneman and G. N. van Vark). Inference about the performance of Fisher's linear discriminant function with applications to signal detection. *Sankhyā B* 55, 27–39.

u. (with D. N. Shanbhag). A stability theorem for the integrated Cauchy functional equation. *Gujarat Statistical Review*, Professor Khatri Memorial Volume, 175–84.

1994

a. Some statistical problems in multitarget tracking. In *Statistical Decision Theory and Related Topics V* (S. S. Gupta and J. Berger, eds), pp. 513–22. Springer-Verlag.

b. (with Lu Zhang and L. C. Zhao). Multitarget angle tracking, an algorithm for data association. *IEEE Trans. Signal Processing* 42, 459–62.

c. (with Rahul Mukerjee). Tests based on score statistics: power properties and related results. *Mathermatical Methods of Statistics* 3, 46–61.

d. (with C. R. Sastry and B. Zhou). Tracking the direction of arrival of multiple moving targets. *IEEE Trans. Signal Processing* 42, 1133–44.

e. (with L. C. Zhao and Bin Zhou). Maximum likelihood estimation of two-dimensional superimposed exponential signals. *IEEE Trans. on Signal Processing* 42, 1795–802.

f. (with T. Sapatinas and D. N. Shanbhag). The integrated Cauchy functional equation: some comments on recent papers. *Advances in Applied Probability* 26.

Accepted for publication (in the press)

a. (with Z. J. Liu). Asymptotic distribution of statistics based on quadratic entropy and bootstrapping. *J. Statist. Planning and Inference.*
b. (with R. Boudreau). Graphical representation of blood group data on human populations. *Statistical Methods in Anthropometry* (G. N. van Vark, ed.).
c. (with L. C. Zhao). Berry-Esseen bound for finite population t-statistic. *Prob. and Stat. Letters.*
d. (with Rahul Mukerjee). On posterior credible sets based on score statistic. *Statistica Sinica.*
e. (with L. C. Zhao). A limiting distribution theorem for testing exponentiality based on sample entropy. *Le Cam Festschrift Volume.*
f. (with Rahul Mukerjee). Comparison of Bartlett-type adjustments for the efficient score statistics. *J. Statistical Planning and Inference.*
g. (with L. C. Zhao). Law of iterated logarithm for empirical cumulative quantile regression functions. *Statistica Sinica.*
h. The use of Hellinger distance in graphical displays of contingency table data. *5th Tartu Conference on Multivariate Statistics.*

Papers submitted to journals

a. (with Z. D. Bai and L. C. Zhao). Weak representation of regression estimate in multivariate linear models obtained by minimizing a convex loss function. *Sankhyā.*
b. (with Z. D. Bai and Y. H. Wu). A note on M-estimation of multivariate linear regression.
c. A review of canonical coordinates and an alternative to correspondence analysis. Tech. Rept. 94–05, *JASA.*
d. (with L. C. Zhao). Strassen's law of iterated logarithms for Lorenz curves. *JMA.*
e. (with L. C. Zhao). Convergence theorems for the cumulative quantile regression function. *Mathematical Methods of Statistics.*

Books edited by C. R. Rao

1965 *Essays on Econometrics and Planning:* P. C. Mahalanobis 70th birthday volume.
1965 *Contributions to Statistics:* P. C. Mahalanobis 70th birthday volume.
1970 (with R. C. Bose, I. M. Chakravarti, P. C. Mahalanobis and K. J. C. Smith). *Essays in Probability and Statistics* (S. N. Roy memorial volume). The University of North Carolina Press, Chapel Hill.
1988 (with P. R. Krishnaiah). *Handbook of Statistics, Vol. 6, Sampling.* North-Holland.
1988 (with P. R. Krishnaiah). *Handbook of Statistics, Vol. 7, Quality Control and Reliability.* North-Holland.

1989 (with M. M. Rao). *Multivariate Statistics and Probability: Essays in Memory of Parachuri Krishnaiah*. Academic Press.

1991 (with R. Chakraborty). *Handbook of Statistics, Vol. 8, Statistical Methods in Biological and Medical Sciences*. North-Holland.

1993 *Handbook of Statistics, Vol. 9, Computational Statistics*. North-Holland.

1993 (with N. K. Bose). *Handbook of Statistics, Vol. 10, Signal Processing and Its Applications*. North-Holland.

1993 (with G. S. Maddala and H. K. Vinod). *Handbook of Statistics, Vol. 11, Econometrics*. North-Holland.

1993 *Multivariate Analysis: Future Directions*. North-Holland.

1993 (with C. M. Cuadras). *Multivariate Analysis: Future Directions 2*. North-Holland.

1993 (with G. P. Patil). *Multivariate Environmental Statistics*. North-Holland.

1994 (with G. P. Patil). *Handbook of Statistics, Vol. 12, Environmental Statistics*. North-Holland.

Index

DATE DUE

GAYLORD			PRINTED IN U.S.A.